The Archaeology
of
IRELAND

The Archaeology

of

IRELAND

ROBERT MACALISTER

BRACKEN BOOKS
LONDON

I dedicate this book to the honoured memory of George Coffey,
Thomas Johnson Westropp, Edmund Clarence Richard Armstrong,
Walther Emanuel Friedrich Bremer and Henry Saxton Crawford
who rendered high service in the quest for hidden truth.

The Archaeology of Ireland

First published in 1928 by Methuen & Company Ltd, London.
Second, revised edition published in 1949 by
Methuen & Company Ltd, London.

This edition published in 1996 by Bracken Books,
an imprint of Random House UK Ltd,
Random House, 20 Vauxhall Bridge Road, London SW1V 2SA

ISBN 1 85170 536 8

Printed and bound in Guernsey by The Guernsey Press Co. Ltd

PREFACE

THE first edition of this book was published in 1928, and it has now for some time been out of print. Knowledge grows apace : in its special department of knowledge, the scientific studies of the later years, grievously distracted though they have been with tumults and commotions at home and abroad, have been not less fruitful than those of the century which went before.[1] Most of our old beliefs have had to be revalued, if not discarded ; many facts, not so much as imagined in 1928, have been discovered ; it was found, when the preparation of this new edition was taken in hand, that nothing short of complete re-writing would be sufficient.

As originally designed, the book was intended to contain chapters on local manifestations of Comparative Religion, and on Social Institutions at different stages of development. Even then, however, practical considerations forbade ; the Outer Court of the Science, the history of Material Culture, soon proved to contain substance more than sufficient to fill the contemplated volume. Within this limitation, an attempt was made to cover the whole field of Irish Archæology, including the aspects of Art as enlisted in the service of Christianity in its early centuries, and the religious and secular buildings of the Middle Ages.

But in recent years there have been wide extensions in our knowledge of these subjects also ; they can no longer be discussed to any advantage in the restricted space that could here be allotted to them. They deserve, indeed demand, individual treatment, in separate volumes. I have therefore decided to do to them also the lesser injustice of exclusion ; the pre-Christian and " Overlap " Archæology will now fully occupy the available room.

Notwithstanding all such drastic elimination of important sections of our theme, it would be ludicrous to attempt to squeeze the *whole*, even of what remains, into a book of this size. While preparing it I have been ever conscious of a centrifugal force, immanent in its every division, urging each in its turn to burst the confining barriers and to establish itself as an independent monograph, thus securing sufficient scope for self-expression. And truly, Irish Archæology is a subject already so vast that only by planning and producing a series of such monographs will fitting justice be rendered to it. But that must remain a dream to be realized in a future generation.

[1] For much of this advance in our knowledge a cordial expression of obligation is due to the mission of Harvard University, which, under the leadership of Dr. H. O' N. Hencken, spent the working seasons of five years in Ireland, prosecuting intensive researches in various departments of Anthropology and Archæology.

The " Old Stone " or *Palæolithic* Age leads us back into depths of time inconceivably remote.   The earliest personal relic of Stone-age Man, hitherto found in Europe, is the jawbone recovered from a sandbank at Mauer, near Heidelberg, to which some authorities assign a date about 382,000 B.C.   The earliest human relic, found in England, is the skull discovered at Pilt Down in Sussex, which has been dated to about 157,000 B.C.   Dates assigned even to late Palæolithic remains make use of numbers five figures in length. In Ireland, humanity can claim no such colossal antiquity.   Never once has any trace of the men of the Old Stone Age been found in the country : it was then either uninhabitable by reason of continuous ice-sheets, or inaccessible by reason of its early acquisition of the status of an island.   The oldest known human relics in the country are contemporary and comparable with the remains of Mesolithic Europe ; and the first draft of the relevant chapter in this book was headed " Mesolithic Ireland ".

But in Ireland all the systematic classifications of implements and weapons, upon which such terminologies must be based, break down.   There, the word " Mesolithic " includes in its scope about half a dozen cultures, mutually irreconcilable,[1] having only this one thing in common, that, so far as we can discern, their populations were ignorant even of the rudimentary food-cultivating processes which we can trace in Mesolithic communities elsewhere.   They were mere Beachcombers and nothing more, living on shallow-water fish, shore molluscs, edible seaweed, and birds trapped or brought down with stones.   And as for the Neolithic, it can hardly be said to have had a separate existence there at all, in view of the early adoption of copper as a material for tools and weapons. Montelius[2] taught us to divide the Bronze Age in Great Britain and Ireland into a succession of five periods ; but, however applicable this system may be to Great Britain, we shall find ourselves in endless confusion if we try to force Irish antiquities into its compartments.   Throughout the Irish Bronze Age, old types persist into contemporaneity with types that should have superseded them. When we reach its end, the same difficulty confronts us ; bronze-age survivals overlap inextricably with late iron-age innovations. In the face of these complications we are obliged boldly to discard the Danish scheme of Stone, Bronze, and Iron Ages, with their subdivisions, time-honoured and elsewhere still of fundamental importance though it be, and accepted as such in our first edition. Instead of it we must adopt, for Ireland, a scheme of chronological

---

[1] I do not overlook the fact (which will come before us later) that attempts have been made to unify these.   At the moment I need say no more than that I cannot see my way to subscribe to them.
[2] O. Montelius " The chronology of the British Bronze Age " : *Archæologia*, 61 part 1 [1908] : 97.

classification radically different, due primarily to Adolf Mahr and
E. E. Evans ;[1] based not upon implements or weapons, but upon
types of megalithic monuments, the most important prehistoric
remains in the country.   It may be set forth thus :—

Beachcombers corresponding generally to Mesolithic.
Protomegalithic   ,,   ,,   ,, Neolithic and Early Bronze Age.
Deuteromegalithic   ,,   ,,   ,, Middle Bronze Age.
Epimegalithic   ,,   ,,   ,, Late Bronze and Early Iron Age.

The full Iron Age follows, in Ireland no more amenable than its
predecessors to any neat evolutionary formulæ ; and leads gradually
into the long and obscure epoch of slow transition, from Paganism
to Christianity.   Even when we have left behind its almost impenetrable fogs, and emerge into the full light of Christianity and of
Christian literature, we are again disconcerted with analogous
difficulties ; when, for example, we seek to marshal the constructional
and ornamental details of Irish mediæval churches into a historical
sequence, based upon the ordered evolutionary progress of contemporary buildings in England or the Continent, we find that it
simply cannot be done !

    These are illustrations of a disturbing fact which meets us on
the threshold of our study, and never leaves us ; which cannot be
evaded ; and which complicates all our efforts to classify the monuments and other relics of Irish antiquity on any chronological principle,
conformable with the European background.   This fact, which has
only in recent years been fully realized, has received the name of the
" time-lag ".   It means, that in the race of Civilization Ireland was
heavily handicapped : the hot winds and ocean-streams of the
Atlantic having had an enervating effect upon human energy and
initiative.[2]   The insular remoteness of the country from the
European mainland (except from Spain by way of the stormy Bay
of Biscay, with its one-way current which facilitated invasion but
blocked *reciprocal* action), inevitably retarded the wheels of progress.
The consequence of such adverse influences was a survival, into
late centuries, of surprisingly primitive phases of culture.   For
example, we should hesitate, *a priori*, to assign a date so recent as
the tenth century A.D. to Dún Aengusa, the huge fortress which
presents the appearance of having crowned the Aran Islands in
Galway Bay from days of hoariest antiquity.   Yet the occupation
of the fort called Cahercommaun, which in plan displays a close
analogy thereto, is dated to that century by objects found in the course

---

    [1] For a scheme differing in detail, but worthy of careful attention, see T.
Walmisley and J. M. Mogey, " The Peoples of Northern Ireland " : *Ulster* III
2 [1939] : 89.
    [2] Any reader of S. F. Markham's *Climate and the Energy of Nations* (Oxford
1942), who will consider carefully the implications of the statistical tables which
it contains, will have no difficulty in appreciating and accepting this fact.

of its excavation.[1]   As we proceed, we shall find such devices as lake-dwellings and souterrain-refuges surviving in Ireland, long after they had been discarded elsewhere.

Science must ever be true to itself, and must give no quarter in its fight against illusions.   If it see reason to dismiss as mere fantasy the idea that Ireland, at any stage in its early history, was the centre of an indigenous " civilization " (using the word in the limited sense which it bears on the lips of the preachers of this doctrine), it must do so remorselessly.   It must declare uncompromisingly that a patriotism which closes the eyes to facts is a false patriotism, destined sooner or later to collapse in dust and ashes ; and that to pretend that such a civilization ever existed in ancient Ireland, is not to close, but to blind, the eyes to all the evidence available. On the other hand, it must not withhold the very substantial compensation that it can offer for the loss of this discarded myth—the importance of Ireland in that, thanks to the " time-lag ", it has rendered to Anthropology the unique, inestimable, indispensable service of carrying a primitive European *Precivilization* down into late historic times, and there holding it up for our observation and instruction.[2]

This myth of Early Irish civilization is rooted in ignorance of all that Science has to say regarding the origin and nature of civilization itself.   Civilization was a very rare phenomenon in the Ancient World, and came into existence only in exceptional circumstances. No isolated community could ever develop it : on the contrary, if a community, which had acquired certain of the resources of civilization, should happen to become isolated (whether by settlement upon a lonely island, or by the development of exclusive theories of " race-purity " or the like, with their attendant malpractices), it would sooner or later lose these acquisitions ; witness the Guanches of Madeira, who are reported as being ignorant of navigation, although they must of necessity have *voyaged* to their island home at some time in the past.[3]   *Imperialism* is essential for the planting and fostering of civilization, for it brings many different peoples within its scope, and almost forces them into contact, so that they can " pool "

---

[1] H. O'N. Hencken, *Cahercommaun, a Stone Fort in Co. Clare*, Dublin 1938. This is not to be interpreted as an implication that the Aran structure is actually so late : I hold no such theory.   But it indicates that the aspects of general culture, to which the Aran fortress was appropriate, persisted unprogressively, and survived incongruously, down to the date of the occupation of Cahercommaun.

[2] In this connexion should be read " An Interpretation of Irish Culture " (*Ulster* III 4 [1941] : 12); also E. E. Evans " Donegal Survivals " (*Antiquity* 13 [1939] : 207) and references there, and the same author's *Irish Heritage* (Dundalk 1912).   The already inexhaustible treasury of records of " the Past in the Present ", daily accumulating in the archives of the Irish Folklore Commission, is rapidly making Ireland in this respect one of the most important countries in the world.

[3] I venture to borrow this illustration from Lord Raglan, *How came Civilization?* (London 1939), where an exposition of some of the views here briefly summarized will be found.

whatever spiritual, intellectual, and material commodities they may individually possess ; and supplies, for a developing community, a needful training, such as is supplied by parental and educational discipline for a developing child. I am aware that this thesis has been challenged ; Professor MacNeill, for example, expressed a desire to see a book written to expose the *de-civilization* of the Hinterland of Europe by Roman Imperialism,[1] quoting a remark of Tacitus in corroboration. But whatever civilization Central and Northern Europe may have enjoyed before the arrival of the Romans was not a spontaneous growth. It had been derived by transmission up the Danube, from the older Imperialisms of the Ægean and Eastern Mediterranean Sea : and while Rome may have broken down much that was admirable, it substituted good roads, a coinage, a universal language—the three primary essentials for the birth, early tendance, and perpetuation of any civilization—and at least an approximation to Law and Order.[2] That it brought many evils in its train, among peoples as yet too undisciplined to distinguish good from evil, is lamentably true : but that was the fault of human nature, not of civilization. Civilization, as such, cannot be blamed if backward peoples of Africa and Polynesia know no better than to demand from it the fire-water and the explosives with which, as they have unfortunately learnt, it can supply them. As for Tacitus, he was merely anticipating Rousseau's academical glorification of an idealized but essentially unreal " noble savage ", in self-conscious antithesis to the blatant social and moral evils of his own immediate surroundings, at a time when the local civilization (like all other earthly institutions), was dying, to be reborn in a new shape ; and we need not attach any more importance to his sentiments than we now accord to those of his antitype.[3] Favourable conditions of *Climate* and *Fertility* are essential to civilization, for these in a measure lighten the otherwise overwhelming preoccupation of breadwinning, and admit the indispensable element of leisure into human life ; although, on the other hand, life must not be made too easy, or it will stagnate into the unprogressive *dolce far niente* existence of Pacific Islands, at least as these are rhapsodized in popular sentimental literature. *Work*, which involves the active co-operation of whole communities, is equally essential ; we cannot

[1] *Early Irish Laws and Institutions*, p. 18 and elsewhere. The last chapter of Jullian's *Histoire de la Gaule* (vol. vi, p. 528) might have satisfied this desire.

[2] For a well-balanced statement of the debt which European Civilization owes to Imperial Rome, see H. J. Rose, *Primitive Culture in Italy* (London 1926), especially the concluding chapters.

[3] The apparently spontaneous birth and lofty development of civilization in China, in very ancient times, might be quoted in disproof of this principle. But who can say what diversity underlies the apparent unity of that enormous country ? The evolution and ethnology of Humanity in Prehistoric China are all but utterly unknown ; the birth-throes and early growth of civilization there may have followed, and probably did follow, the same course as in the rest of the " civilized " world.

over-estimate the debt which civilization owes to the early necessity of extensive irrigation-works in Egypt, Babylonia, and the Indus Valley.[1] In fact, it was only in regions such as these, lying in the genial territories south of the Alpine-Himalayan mountain barrier, that civilization could ever have come into being at all.

Equally baseless with this legend of a primitive civilization in Ireland, and scientifically no less pernicious, is the childish fiction that Ireland was " the most ancient nation in Europe "; which betrays an astonishing ignorance of the history of the egocentric outlook called " Nationality ".   This is merely one of the succession of transient phases in human evolution, fated to disappear with the inevitable but unpredictable developments of wireless communication, aviation, and the control of the appalling force of intra-atomic energy, on which the Chief of the Primates has laid his un-disciplined hands just as the finishing touches are being given to these pages.   In Ancient Europe there were no " nations ", only more or less predatory " city-states " : even the tiny land of Greece contained several of these, furiously jealous of one another ; the empire of Rome, like its prototype the empire of Assyria, was little more than such a city-state, hypertrophied.   Not until the collapse of that unwieldy amalgam, and of its successor and imitator, the empire of Charlemagne, could a sense of national unity develop, in self-protection, among the several fragments which broke away from them ; after the overlying Imperialism had hammered them, in accordance with the principle laid down above, into an at least superficial civilization.   The people of Ireland had been forced into a kind of psychological unity by the mere fact that they were im-prisoned in an island : but all efforts at establishing a political unity made by ambitious kings came to nothing.   Even the pressure of the Viking invaders failed to compass it ; after a united effort had culminated in the victory of Clontarf, rival jealousies and bickerings broke forth again : and all that the native historians can give us, for the century-and-a-half between that event and the arrival of the Anglo-Normans (heralds of a new Imperialism), is a list of the empty names of ghost-kings, candidly described as " Kings with Opposition ".

The Archæology of Ireland is worthy of a better fate than to become a playground for the Politician, the Poetaster, the Dilettante, the Sentimentalist, the Road-contractor, the Seeker for phantom Gold, the mere Tourist, the destructive Yahoo.   The " picnic " aspect of its study, while admittedly possessing some educa-tional value, should not be over-emphasized ; at the Univer-sities it should not hold a subordinate position in an incongruous

[1] Emphasis is laid upon this fact throughout V. G. Childe's *New Light on the most Ancient East* (London 1934).

" Faculty of Celtic Studies ", but should be elevated, as befits its
dignity, into a Faculty of its own, or at least made a branch of a
Faculty of Anthropology, where it properly belongs—equipped with
a full teaching staff of lecturers in special departments. For it
requires familiarity with an extraordinary range of external sciences,
in addition to the endless ramifications of Comparative Anthropology : with Geology, Biology, Botany, Zoology, Chemistry ; with
the arts of Mensuration, Surveying, Draughtsmanship, Photography ;
with an already overwhelming and still ever-growing mass of
scientific literature, in all the major languages of Europe. The
absurdity that the student should become a master in the whole of
this varied field of learning is, of course, not suggested ; he must
expect, throughout his career, to depend on the help of specialists.
But he should be qualified to choose his consultants judiciously, to
know what questions he should ask them, and to understand their
answers ; and this calls for more knowledge than might be supposed,
at a first approach to the problems involved.

In short, the cardinal purpose of this book is to plead for a more
systematic, not to say a saner, study of Irish antiquities than in past
days, on the ground that they are the property of the World of Science,
and to that World are of immense importance. Ireland's place is
that of trustee ; and Ireland must be prepared at any time to render
an account of the trust.

R. A. S. M.

March, 1949.

CONTENTS

ABBREVIATIONS

MOST of the references in the following pages will be found to be self-explanatory ; but a few publications, frequently mentioned in the footnotes, are indicated by abbreviations, as follows :

Belfast.	Proceedings of the Belfast Natural History and Philosophical Society.
BNFC.	Proceedings, Belfast Naturalists' Field Club.
Cork.	Journal of the Cork Historical and Archæological Society.
Evans, *Stone.*	Sir John Evans, *Ancient Stone Implements of Great Britain.*
Galway.	Journal of the Galway Archæological and Historical Society.
INJ.	Irish Naturalists' Journal.
IPCT.	Ireland in Pre-Celtic Times, by the present author.
JRAI.	Journal of the Royal Anthropological Institute.
JRSAI.	Journal of the Royal Society of Antiquaries of Ireland (in all its transformations).
Kerry.	Kerry Archæological Magazine.
Louth.	Journal of the County Louth Archæological Society.
North Munster.	North Munster Antiquarian Journal (Thomond Archæological Society).
PPS.	Proceedings of the Prehistoric Society
PPS (East Anglia).	Proceedings of the Prehistoric Society of East Anglia.
RIA.	Royal Irish Academy.
PRIA.	Proceedings of the Royal Irish Academy.
PSA (Lond., Scot.).	Proceedings of the Society of Antiquaries of London, or of Scotland.
TRIA.	Transactions of the Royal Irish Academy.
Ulster I.	Ulster Journal of Archæology, first series.
Ulster II.	Ulster Journal of Archæology, second series.
Ulster III.	Ulster Journal of Archæology, third series.
Waterford.	Journal of the Waterford Archæological Society.
Wilde, *Catalogue.*	Catalogue of the Museum of the Royal Irish Academy's Collection, by Sir W. R. Wilde.

BOOK I

THE BEACHCOMBERS

CHAPTER I

BEFORE THE FIRST IMMIGRATIONS

IN rock-formation Ireland is closely related to the side of Great Britain which it faces, and it obviously forms part of the same Continental extension. That it has passed through many vicissitudes is proved by Geological and Palæontological evidence. It has been sunk in the depths of ocean ; it has been an archipelago of islands, the tops of submerged mountains ; it has been embedded in the heart of an unbroken Continental mass. Its climate has by turns been warm and cold, dry and moist ; it has been covered with wide areas of swamp, and of dense forest ; it has been buried under sheets of ice ; it has witnessed the fires and the lavas of active volcanoes. It has harboured not only wolves and boars, which survived down to recent times, but also bears, hyænas, and the gigantic deer miscalled " the Irish elk ". There is scarcely any limit to the variety of pictures which former conditions in the country offer for our contemplation ; although every successive phase, in its turn, presented the same deceptive appearance of permanent stability as that in which we find ourselves. Except in such purely local catastrophes as volcanic outbursts, these revolutions proceeded imperceptibly and silently ; assuredly they still continue on their course, under our unconscious eyes. But this antecedent, pre-human history we must take for granted ; we have a long programme before us, and must submit to our limitations of time and of space. The pre-human ages have an important place in our history ; for it was then that the land was fashioned, and fitted with the endowments that made it a suitable habitation for those destined to dwell in it. But here we must pass them by, and with them the highly controversial subject of Tertiary Man and his alleged handiworks ; we take as our starting-point the Pleistocene period, when human life first made an unchallenged appearance in Europe, and might conceivably have drifted over into Ireland.[1]

---

[1] It is reasonable to assume that any serious student of Prehistoric Archæology will have acquired some knowledge of the elements of Geology, including the principles of stratification, the characteristics and nomenclature of the Geological periods, and similar aspects of the science. For a fuller extension of the matters glanced at in this paragraph there are many standard works available : we may mention A. J. Jukes-Brown, *The Building of the British Isles* (third edn. 1911), and L. J. Wills, *The Physiographic Evolution of Britain* (London 1929). For Ireland in particular, see Cole and Hallissy, *Handbook of the Geology of Ireland* (London 1924), brought up to date by J. Kaye Charlesworth, " Recent Progress in Irish

Climate in Europe had been deteriorating gradually, down from the sub-tropical Eocene period : the Glacial Age had begun at the time when our history opens.   So far as the actual area of Ireland is concerned, the relation of land and water appears to have been roughly much the same as it is to-day.   Geologically, Ireland forms an extension, or, as Cole expresses it, an " outpost " of the Continental mass of Eurasia : but at the beginning of our history its insularity had already become established.[1]

Heavy snows had, however, begun to fall in Scotland, and also in the regions of Ireland included within the modern counties of Fermanagh, Leitrim, and Tyrone : these, accumulating upon the mountain-tops, became sources of ice-streams, which increased and spread until they covered the entire country.   The Scottish glaciers flowed south and westward, down the bed of the Irish Sea and over the adjacent lands, finding an exit in the Atlantic Ocean.   The Irish north-western glacial area supplemented that of Scotland : many (but not all) authorities consider that the consequent total submergence of Ireland, under a solid sheet of ice, must have rendered it incapable of supporting any form of life.   The ice, no doubt, could have afforded a bridge across the Irish Sea, theoretically enabling living creatures to enter the previously inaccessible island ; but there is no obvious reason why they should have done so, and if they had, there is no obvious way in which they could afterwards have continued to find means of subsistence.

An interglacial period followed this first and severer glaciation. Ireland was released from the incubus of the ice.   But it had never actually lost its insular status, so that unless it had somehow acquired and maintained human inhabitants while the ice-bridge made the land accessible, it could not have possessed any during this genial interlude : and, in fact, no trace of such inhabitants has ever been discovered, on any site within its borders.   We have no reason to credit the men of that remote epoch with skill in navigation ; or with the instincts of a modern explorer, who may set off on a long voyage of discovery across barren ice-fields, not knowing whither it will lead him.   When the Pliocene period came to an end, Britain was still a northern extension of France—using these modern

Geology " INJ 6 [1936-7] : 266 ; G. A. J. Cole, *Ireland the Outpost* (Oxford 1919). The five volumes on " Ireland " and " The Provinces of Ireland ", edited by George Fletcher (Cambridge 1922) give accounts (necessarily limited by the available space, but rich and informing withal) of the general and local Geology, Zoology and Botany of the country.   For geographical influences on human life see W. Fitzgerald, *The Historical Geography of Early Ireland* (London 1926), an admirable study for its time, well deserving of revision and amplification in the light of later knowledge.

[1] The importance of this severance is emphasized by Mr. C. Blake Whelan. See his paper, " The Palæolithic Question in Ireland " (*Sixteenth International Geological Congress*, Washington 1933, p. 1209) for a very full statement of the evidence bearing on the early animal and human colonization of the country, and on the geographical conditions that affected it.   An extensive bibliography is added.

geographical terms for convenience ; the English Channel was still dry land, and transit from one side to another was merely the matter of a long walk—even if interrupted by marshes and waters, which would have to be crossed somehow. But by the time when the ice came, the Irish Sea had already been opened, and was impassable from end to end. Nevertheless, there must have been at some earlier time a pre-glacial land-connexion, which was not finally severed until after the immigration, into Ireland, of a restricted but representative early Pleistocene fauna. In no other way could such large animals as the mammoth, the cave hyæna, the bear, and the giant deer have intruded. That they did so, their bones remain to testify. It is less clear how they could have continued to survive a subsequent complete glaciation of the country : to meet this difficulty, some geologists postulate a westward or southward extension of the land-surface, now submerged beneath the Atlantic Ocean,[1] but, at the time, above sea-level and free from ice, and thus available as an asylum. But even if we admit this risky hypothesis, there is absolutely no evidence that any *human* company followed these animals westward, to share their refuge.

After the genial interlude, glacial conditions were restored, but with less severity than before. The lines of the end moraines, which have been carefully mapped, show that the lands within the modern counties bordering on the south coast, or at least the southern portions of them, were unaffected by the glaciers.[2] Here, therefore, and here alone, might we hope to find relics of late Palæolithic Man : for even if men had somehow penetrated into the country in the interglacial time, and had established settlements anywhere to the north of this favoured strip of territory, their remains would have been ground out of existence by the returning glaciers. Hitherto, all search for such relics, either inside or outside the non-glaciated region specified, has been fruitless.

As genial conditions became re-established, a complicated series of land movements ran its course. Northern Europe had been weighted down by the enormous sheets of ice lying over it, in which unnumbered thousands of tons of water were frozen hard. As the ice melted, these liberated waters found their way to the sea in such quantities that they made an appreciable rise in the elevation of the ocean surface ; and the depressed Continental masses, delivered

---

[1] Cole and Hallissy, *op. cit.* p. 58 and references there.
[2] J. K. Charlesworth " The Glacial Retreat fron Central and Southern Ireland " (*Quarterly Journal*, Geol. Soc. 84 [1928] : 293) ; in the same writer's " The South Wales End Moraine " (*ibid.* 85 [1929] : 335) a correlation is established between the South Irish and South British phenomena. See also the following papers, by the same author, on the glaciation of specific regions—N. Mayo and W. Sligo (PRIA 38 B [1928] : 100) ; Iar-Connacht (*ibid.* 39 B [1929] : 95) ; North Sea (*ibid.* 40 B [1931] : 67) ; N.E. Ireland (*ibid.* 45 B [1939] : 255) ; and A. Farrington " The Glaciation of the Wicklow Mountains " (*ibid.* 42 B [1934] : 173).

of their incubus, sought to recover equilibrium in a form proper to
sections of a spheroidal world. Thus, both land and water began
to rise. Naturally, the land-rise was on the whole slower than the
water-rise, but in the long run the land prevailed ; wide areas,
submerged during the domination of the ice, were ultimately raised
to a high elevation above the sea-level. Here we must content
ourselves with a bare outline summary of these movements.

1. *A rise in the sea*, stabilized long enough to form a beach (A), still
traceable along the Scottish coast. At this time Scandinavia was a long
and comparatively narrow island, separated from the mainland by a strait
open at both ends. This has been named, for reference, the *Yoldia Sea*,
from the generic name of a bivalve mollusc, *Yoldia arctica*, which flourished
within it.

2. *A rise in the land*, carrying the beach (A) upward ; followed by a
further *rise in the sea*, stabilized at a level 50 feet below the new position of
beach (A), and forming a beach (B), likewise traceable around the Scottish
coast.

3. A further, and considerable, *rise in the land*, which now became
covered with forests. Mosses formed upon fallen tree-trunks, and these
decomposed into peat which still partly covers, and is therefore later than,
the two beaches. The Baltic basin was now elevated high enough to become
a land-locked, fresh-water lake—named the *Ancylus Lake*, from the name
of another bivalve, *Ancylus fluviatilis*, which succeeded the Yoldia in its
occupation.

Many of the shallow sea areas, as we know them, now became dry
land—such as the North Sea, the English Channel, and the eastern border
of the Bay of Biscay. Britain and Ireland were embedded within a Continental plateau, the western shore of which, coasting along the Bay of
Biscay, afforded a highway into Ireland for certain forms of life ; there,
after the reversal of these conditions, they remained, and still survive,
cut off irrevocably from their Iberian home and kindred.[1] At the same time
the Irish Sea was another enclosed lake, fed by the rivers of eastern Ireland
and western Britain, and drained by a great river flowing into the Atlantic,
along a bed destined to become submerged outside the present S.E. and S.
coasts of Ireland.[2]

4. *A rise of the sea*, submerging the lower peats accumulated during
stage (3), as well as any beach which may theoretically have been there
formed along with them. The level was stabilized long enough to form a
third beach (C), about 25 feet below the level of beach (B) ; and, unlike

---

[1] This comprises the " Lusitanian flora " of S.W. Ireland (certain species of
saxifrage, arbutus, butterwort, etc.), as well as such zoological immigrants as the
Pyrenean house-spider—the dominant species in Dublin—the natterjack toad,
the Kerry slug, etc.

[2] This lake and river barred the westward progress of many species of plants
and animals, domiciled and more or less common in Great Britain. Polecats,
weasels, moles, snakes, the common toad, and, among plants, the daffodil and the
mistletoe, have no hereditary rights in Ireland, and when found must be recognized
as recent intrusions. Lists of British species of plants and animals absent from
Ireland, and non-British species there present, will be found in the Cambridge
Geography of Ireland, pp. 142 ff. See further Charlesworth, at p. 359 of the article
quoted in the next footnote but one below, where other Irish species, of American
and Arctic provenance, are enumerated.

its predecessors, overlying, and therefore later than, the accumulations of the peat. The Baltic was re-opened at its southern end, thus becoming an inlet of brackish water, rather wider in area than its modern representative, though of similar configuration. It is now referred to as the *Litorina Sea*, from its prevailing mollusc (*Litorina litoralis*, the periwinkle).

5. A slight further *rise of the sea*, followed by a corresponding *rise of the land*, which now attained to its present elevation. From the approximate heights above sea-level at which the three beaches stand, they are known respectively as the 100-feet, 50-feet, and 25-feet beaches.[1]

The foregoing statements have been designedly set forth in the shortest and simplest possible terms. Such matters as the increased denudation produced by the increased rapidity of river-flow resulting from the land elevation, with consequent increased accumulation of silt in the sea-bed ; highly controversial subjects such as the hypothetical land-bridge passing from Scotland to Iceland, including in its course what are now the intervening islands ; the extent of the westward encroachment of the Continental shelf upon the present area of the Bay of Biscay ; and the alternation of land-*depressions* with the elevations above enumerated, are all important as details of Geological history, but have little relevance to an Archæological study, and may be passed over.[2]

The configuration of Ireland, as these processes have left it, is exceptional. Islands, whatever their geological origin may be, are the tops of submerged mountains or mountain-chains ; so that their highest points appear either as isolated peaks, rising in the middle of the insular area, or else as a line of heights, running axially like a backbone, straight or curved, along their greatest length. But Ireland is a plateau, surrounded with a coastal ring of loftier mountains. The centre of the island is a wide plain, more or less flat, once thickly forested, and now extensively covered with the consequent turbaries. For its size, it is well provided with rivers. The western shore has many deep inlets, which afford a varied choice of harbourage : the estuaries of the larger rivers invite the establishment of trading centres—though, paradoxically, the invitation was at

[1] The convenience of a uniform nomenclature outweighs the slightly pedantic objection to the third of these names, that the remains of the beach so denoted are not all at an elevation of 25 feet above sea-level ; especially as it has apparently been found impossible to agree on a satisfactory substitute.

[2] For further details, and for the observed facts upon which the above reconstruction of the sequence of events has been based, see the relevant chapters of W. B. Wright, *The Quaternary Ice Age* ; J. G. D. Clark, *The Mesolithic Settlement of Northern Europe* ; H. L. Movius, *The Irish Stone Age* (part i) ; or, indeed, any other modern work dealing with glacial and post-glacial Geology. See also Charlesworth, " Some Geological observations on the origin of the Irish fauna and flora " (PRIA 39 B [1930] : pp. 358 ff., esp. p. 366). The subjects at present before us are there discussed with greater fullness than would here be possible or appropriate. R. Ll. Praeger, " Recent views bearing on the problems of the Irish fauna and flora " (PRIA 41 B [1932] : 125), presents opposing views on some of the subjects here touched upon.

first accepted, not by native enterprise, but by hostile aliens ; for most of the large maritime towns, as Dublin, Waterford, Limerick, owe their ultimate origin to Viking marauders, who established them as bases for piratical raids. Frankish merchants are said to have sailed up the Shannon in A.D. 548 as far as Clonmacnois, which is close to the very centre of Ireland.[1] Four hundred years later, the same river bore Viking raiders, bent on plunder, to the same place.[2] In the south, the Blackwater, the Suir (with its important tributaries, the Barrow and the Nore), and the Slaney are navigable for small craft for some distance from their mouths. The Liffey, on the other hand, is barred by shallows which prevent navigation higher than Dublin : but the Old Norse name borne by the village of Leixlip (*lax-hlaup*), some ten miles upward from the estuary, shows that Scandinavians penetrated at least thus far, in quest of the leaping salmon. Further to the north is the Boyne, up which St. Patrick is said to have sailed on his mission as far as the site of the modern town of Trim.

Owing to the peculiar coast-wise position of the mountains, mearing-lines between adjacent territories depended but little upon mountain-chains. Rather have the rivers been ever the chief lines of demarcation. Besides these, however, there is another form of natural boundary which, in Ireland, was of some political importance. The retreating glaciers left behind them, among various evidences of their passage, a series of long ridges of gravel, crossing the Central Plain. So characteristic of the Irish landscape are these ridges, that their Gaelic name, *eiscir*, in the Anglicized form " esker ", has only just escaped being adopted into the scientific nomenclature of Geology. One such ridge, *Eiscir Riada*, stretches almost across the middle of the island from Dublin to Galway : in modern times, it has ruled lines of canal and of railway ; in ancient times it was (at least theoretically) the boundary between *Leth Cuinn*, the " Half of Conn [of the Hundred Battles] " and *Leth Moga*, the " Half of Mug-[Nuadat] "—in other words, the division said to have been made by the two kings named, between the kingdom of Tara in the north, and that of Cashel in the south.[3]

[1] *The Latin and Irish Lives of Ciaran*, ed. R. A. S. Macalister (London 1921), pp. 92, 154. On trade between Ireland and Gaul in general see G. Coffey, " Archæological evidence for the intercourse of Gaul with Ireland before the first century ", PRIA 28 [1910] : 96 ; H. Zimmer, " Ueber direkte Handelsver-bindungen West-galliens mit Irland in Altertum und frühen Mittelalter " (*Sitzungsberichte der Preuss. Akademie*, 1909-10). But see *English Historical Review* 28 : 1, where Zimmer's views are controverted by Prof. Haverfield, as, in another connexion, they are by Mahr (PPS 3 [1937] : 400).
[2] *Annals of Ulster*, A.D. 921.
[3] See references under the name *Eiscir Riada* in E. Hogan, *Onomasticon Goedelicum* (Dublin 1910). There is some dispute or ambiguity as to the exact process of esker-formation ; the term is being discarded by Science because it is insufficiently definitive (see Wills, *op. cit.* p. 219).

The rich, but rather heavy soil ; the equable and, in consequence, rather enervating climate (maintained all the year round at a temperature relatively high, considering the latitude of the country, by the warm Atlantic winds and currents) ; the excess of moisture in the atmosphere ; all these combine to render effective the decree of Nature, that Ireland must be primarily a pasture-land, in the strict sense of the word, and that attempts to make it agricultural, however they may succeed for a time, are foredoomed to ultimate failure.[1] As a land of cattle, it has ever been famous. The third-century gossip-monger Solinus, copying Pomponius Mela, in an often-quoted passage, tells us that "if the cattle of Ireland were not restricted in grazing, they would die from overeating "[2]—an indirect testimony to the reputation of the soil as a rich grazing land. At all times the chief wealth of the people of Ireland has consisted in their cattle, which appear throughout the ancient legal documents as among the principal commercial standards of value and exchange.

On the other hand, there are large tracts of barren country, especially in the west, where stretches of uncovered rock alternate with sloppy and economically unproductive bogland. There, successive strata of exiles, driven by *force majeure* from the better lands of the east, have accumulated throughout the ages. From the days when (as legend tells us) the mythical *Túatha Dé Danann* expelled the antecedent and equally mythical *Fir Bolg*, down to less than three centuries ago, " Hell or Connaught " have been the alternatives set before the dispossessed. There is nothing specifically " Irish " in this : *mutatis nominibus* it happens everywhere, when a greedy conqueror elbows his way into a land which he covets ; it has been happening in contemporary Europe as these lines were being written. For all their scenic grandeur, the inhospitable regions of the west present an economic contrast almost painful, when set beside the grassy verdure of the more fertile areas. Such a contrast, especially when contemplated through the eyes of a hungry refugee, could not but sow seeds of envy. Inequality in the distribution of the good gifts of Nature is most fruitful among the causes of strife ; and in such inequalities must surely lie the roots of much of the strife which fills the pages of Irish history, legendary and authentic.

Unusual also is the situation of Ireland among the countries of Europe. It is inaccessible except over marine channels almost

---

[1] I pretend to no knowledge or experience entitling me to pronounce on this matter : I merely repeat the opinion which men who possess such qualifications have expressed to me.

[2] P. Mela, *De situ orbis* III viii : Solinus, *Collectanea rerum memorabilium* xxii 2. In my ignorance of veterinary science I was inclined to smile at this story : but I have been assured by a friend, with experience of cattle, that these animals are actually apt to induce in themselves a morbid flatulence, which often has to be surgically treated, by grazing too greedily on the spring pasture after their winter privations.

everywhere too wide for the sight to carry across them at sea-level.[1] On one side there is no land anywhere near : none that was known to exist, till the discovery of America at the end of the Middle Ages— disregarding, as we surely must, the fantastic idea that fragments of an Atlantic Continent survived till sufficiently late in the human period to afford a basis for current traditions about *Ui-Breasail* and other mysterious islands on the western horizon. Immigrants cannot come, therefore, except from the south and east : and the (usually rough) sea-crossing would be so unattractive, especially to people with nothing better than cockleshell canoes, that no one is likely to have ventured upon it unless he were driven to it unavoidably; or to return, when once he had safely accomplished the transit and established himself on the other side. In consequence, we should expect to find a population consisting originally of fugitives or refugees driven from home, and subsequently driven yet further to the west by fresh but similar waves of later immigrants. This leads to the inference that the oldest strata of the population are to be looked for along the western shore—an inference justified by the observed facts.

Ireland, it is true, has back doors as well as its front door. The mountain rampart, which surrounds the island like the wall of a fortress, is not continuous. It has one important breach on the eastern side, between Dublin and Dundalk : the " front-door " opening, which has always invited invasion from Great Britain, and by way of which, especially in later years, most of the influences of general European culture have come, crossing the larger and more accessible island. But some of the long Kerry inlets, as well as Galway Bay, Clew Bay, and the inner end of Sligo Bay, are equally possible lines of approach ; through these, other influences have made their way from remote prehistoric times. Not to be forgotten in this connexion is the Shannon estuary, with the long and wide, gently-flowing water-way, which runs back from it far into the interior, broadening at intervals into extensive lakes : the small and more or less portable ships of early traders or invaders would hardly find the reefs which cut across the river between Killaloe and Limerick a serious obstacle to penetration. The Spaniard Orosius was well aware of the importance to Ireland of *Scenæ fluminis ostium*, though his reference to it has been misinterpreted by early Irish historians and by their modern commentators.[2] Through such doorways as these,

---

[1] But in clear weather the mountains of Wales are easily seen from the tops of mountains south of Dublin.

[2] Orosius *Adversus paganos* i 2. In the Latin of Orosius, as in modern Italian, *sc* denoted the sound by us written *sh* ; compare the Vulgate text of Judges xii 6, where *Scibboleth, Sibboleth* correspond to the Hebrew *Shibbōlĕth, Sibbōlĕth*. Thus, *Scena* is a sufficient rendering of *Sinna* (pron. *syinna*), the Genitive case of the Irish name of the Shannon; and it has been borrowed by Irish historiographers in the form *Inber Scene* ," Scene Estuary ". This has been identified by modern writers, not with the Shannon mouth, but (quite arbitrarily) with the Kenmare River or some other Munster inlet. See MacNeill, *Phases of Irish History*, p. 93.

cultural and other influences have been making their way from remote prehistoric times. Ocean currents flow across the Bay of Biscay, linking together the island and the Iberian peninsula : the Lusitanian flora is not the only gift which the latter has made to the former : technological connexions between *Hibernia* and *Iberia* will come before us more than once as we proceed, giving a semblance of significance to the accidental similarity of the names.

But search for a refuge is not the only motive for immigration. There are impulsive as well as expulsive reasons for colonization. Expulsive causes are those which make the original home temporarily or permanently uninhabitable—the pressure of an inrush of enemies, of adverse climatic conditions, or what not. Impulsive causes are those which make the new home attractive ; and undoubtedly the gold, of which Ireland was understood to possess great stores, was the chief attraction which the country offered to invaders or to settlers.

The allusion, in the preceding paragraph, to the very important subject of adverse climatic conditions, may be explained and expanded here. Climatic changes certainly occur, with a periodicity of which the causes are obscure, though fluctuations in the earth's orbit, alternately increasing and diminishing the distance of the earth from the sun, are among the most probable. Here we must be content to take the variations of climate as we find them ; our concern is with their consequences, not their causes. Even slight modifications, if established for a sufficient length of time, will have an astonishing effect on all forms of life in the regions where they intrude. The main course of the post-glacial fluctuations of climate in Northern Europe was as follows ; for convenience of reference, we set it forth in a catalogue form :—

PERIOD	CHARACTER
Boreal (*Lower Forestian*) . . .	Dry, at first cold, but becoming warmer.
Atlantic (*Lower Turbarian*) . . .	Moist and warm.
Sub-Boreal (*Upper Forestian*) . .	Dry and warm.
Sub-Atlantic (*Upper Turbarian*) . .	Moist and cold.

After which an approximation to the conditions at present prevailing became more or less established, though with no prospect of greater permanence then their predecessors possessed. Indeed, there is actual evidence of later minor fluctuations. Thus, Mr. C. E. I. Wright, on the basis of the distribution of peat in the Wicklow Mountains, has shown that there was a dry period, which came to an end about 850 B.C., and was succeeded by an intensely moist period, which lasted until about 350 B.C. The moisture then diminished, till about A.D. 350, when the present " neutral " climate succeeded. But even that has not become completely stable : it has had sufficient irregularity to influence human life and activity to a very considerable extent.[1]

These facts have been revealed by many lines of investigation; the most recent and most important of which have been followed out, on the initiative of the late G. Lagerheim, sometime Director of the Botanical Institute of the University of Stockholm, in the deposits of peat, covering large areas of Scandinavia and of other countries. Peat-accumulations are formed in a variety of ways, and out of a variety of specific materials; but in general, it may be said that they consist of decomposed mosses, which once grew upon the trunks of fallen forest-trees, or in the mud of disappearing lakes and swamps. Embedded in the peat are seeds, pollen, and other relics of such vegetable life as was flourishing in the neighbourhood, at the time of its deposition. Now, every change of climate is necessarily followed by modifications in vegetation; tropical plants, moisture-loving plants, plants to which excessive moisture is injurious, will disappear respectively from regions in which cold, dryness, or moisture increases beyond supportable limits. It follows, that by taking a sample of peat from a specified depth in a turbary, studying it microscopically, identifying the plants whose pollen it contains, and estimating their relative frequency, a basis will be established for determining the nature of the prevailing climate at the time when the mosses were growing, and the peats forming, at that particular level.

A long series of such observations has been made, and already it is possible to fit any archæological relic found in a peat-bog into its proper chronological pigeon-hole, by pollen-analysis of the peat in which we find it.[2] Moreover, as the conditions of climate which prevailed over the Scandinavian countries and the British Islands were, on the whole, similar, peats of identical pollen-content, with

---

[1] C. E. I. Wright, " Recent Changes of Climate in Ireland ", INJ 4 [1932] : 46. See also C. E. P. Brooks, *Climate through the Ages*.   C. E. Britton, *A Meteorological Chronology to A.D.* 1450 (Meteorological Office, 1937), is a most valuable compilation of all the meteorological observations to be found in early chronicles.   In connexion with the (still open) question of the minor limit of the period of peat-formation, see O. Davies, " Ancient field-systems and the date of formation of the Peat ", *Ulster* III 2 [1939] : 61.   Complete finality cannot be claimed for some of the above details, and the relations between Insular and Continental Climatology still await a more exact determination.   See, for example, Dr. Zeuner's note, incorporated in Dr. Wheeler's report on the Maiden Castle excavation (Society of Antiquaries of London, 1943), pp. 25 ff.   For fuller studies of the larger aspects of the subject, see Elsworth Huntington, *Mainsprings of Civilization* (New York 1945), and F. E. Zeuner, *Dating the Past* (London 1946).

[2] Reference may be made to J. G. D. Clark's *Mesolithic Settlement of Northern Europe*, already cited, where extensive bibliographies will be found.   For the application of these methods of research to Ireland see especially INJ 5 [1934] : 125 ff. ; for a history of the work done in the country down to the date of publication, see Mahr's monograph, PPS 3, esp. pp. 272-81.   A " Quaternary Research " committee has been formed under the auspices of the Royal Irish Academy, for the special purpose of establishing and furthering this new line of investigation in Ireland.   See also Movius, *Stone Age*, index, *s.v.* " pollen ".

no more than comparatively slight local variations, are to be found at the same chronological levels in both regions. Thus it becomes possible to solve problems in relative chronology with a completeness which, so recently as 1928, could not have been anticipated.

The Boreal Period was preceded by the *Glacial* Age, and by the subsequent successive ameliorations of its severity, respectively named the *Arctic* and the *Sub-arctic* climate-stages. The Yoldia Sea, and the formation of the 100-foot Raised Beach, were contemporary with the latter half of the second of these, which, both in Ireland and in Scotland, preceded the intrusion of Man. In the south of England, which was not directly affected by glaciation, the establishment of human colonies was made possible, as we have seen, by the land-bridge then crossing what is now the English Channel ; and the immigrants, or rather their descendants, could, and did, penetrate inland, stage by stage, concurrently with the retreat of the ice. The Ancylus Lake corresponded to the Boreal phase : the Litorina Sea to the Atlantic and the beginning of the Sub-Boreal. To this latter is assigned the 25-feet Raised Beach : the peat-formation which underlies it, and which overlies the two preceding beaches, being of the Boreal.

Researches of deep interest, and impressive ingenuity, carried out in the sedimentary deposits which record the successive aspects of the Baltic Sea, have even made it possible to assign approximate dates, numerically expressed in years B.C., to these land-movements. The rivers washed a perennial tribute of mud into the sea-basin. They were in flood during the summer, owing to the melting of the snows, and were much reduced in winter, owing to the freezing of the waters which fed them ; so that the siltings of the summers were larger, heavier, and formed of coarser material than were those of the winters. In consequence, the sea-bottom deposits lie in well-marked layers, technically called " varves " (Swedish *hvarf*), alternately coarse and fine—each of these couples representing the tribute of a single year. This is a world-wide phenomenon ; similar varves have been observed in North America as well as in Scandinavia.[1] Evidently in a moist year there will be a greater flow of water, and consequently a greater thickness of deposit, than in a dry year. By the simple process of counting the varves it has been found possible to determine the number of the years during which any group of deposits was accumulating : and, by ascertaining their relative thicknesses, to follow out concurrent changes of climate, and even to establish correlations between climatic fluctuations in the widely separated regions above indicated. Not to enter with too great fullness into matters hardly germane to our present subject, we may content ourselves here with the following tabular statement of results :

[1] Also in Ireland. See a diagram of varves in the Silent Valley (Down), PRIA 45 B [1939] : 271.

B.C. (approximately)

Glacial time, down to	10000
Baltic, an ice-dammed lake down to	8300
Yoldia Sea	8300–7800
Ancylus Lake	7800–5500
Litorina Sea	5500–2000

The different species of trees make their appearance, in the peat-deposits of Ireland, in the following order :—

Birch : Pre-Boreal	Elm : Atlantic
Willow : ,,	Oak : ,,
Pine : ,,	Alder : Sub-Boreal
Hazel : Boreal	Lime : ,,

The lime is only sporadically found : the beech and the hornbeam, the latest arrivals in English deposits, never reached Ireland at all in those early times.[1]

Not only are these and similar vitally important chronological results being acquired from this new study : a clue to the general interpretation of history has been put in our hands. Let an adverse fluctuation of climate take place ; let the crops and grazing land fail ; and the inhabitants of the region affected, however they may have been fixed to their homes, must forthwith become so many wandering Ishmaels, their hand against every man, every man's hand against theirs. For the only alternative will be starvation.

The numerous waves of migration among the Semitic peoples, the Trojan War, the Gaulish assaults on Delphi and on Rome, the building of the Great Wall of China, the fall of the Roman Empire before the Goths—all these and many more of the major events of history were, directly or indirectly, automatic *sequelæ* of climatic fluctuations ; some of them taking place in regions far distant from the theatre of the events themselves—notably in Turkistan, where such fluctuations are often of catastrophic amplitude. Some time ago, I drew a graph [2] representing in diagram form all that I could find about climatic fluctuations in the past, especially in Northern Europe : and I compared it with a similar curve of the fluctuations of culture, and the movements of peoples, so far as they affected Ireland. The way in which the two curves fitted into one another, as exactly as the adjacent edges of two pieces of a jigsaw puzzle, convinced me that a study of what might be called the " Historical Climatology " of any country is a necessary preliminary to the study

---

[1] G. Erdtman, " Studies in the Postarctic History of the Forests of N.W. Europe ", *Geologiska Föreningen i Stockholm* : *Forhändlingar* 50 [1929] : 123. *Idem*, " Traces of the History of the Forests of Ireland ", INJ 1 [1927] : 242. Chap. v of Grahame Clark's *Archæology and Society* can be read in this connexion with profit. See further K. Jessen's table of the course of development of post-glacial Ireland, published in PPS 3 : 276.

[2] Published in my book *Ancient Ireland*, p. 278. It teaches, better than many pages full of words, the impotence of Man before the iron laws of Nature.

of its History, or Historical Geography.   It is not the achievements
of this great man or that which mould the life of a nation.   These
are mere puppets in the hand of the vast impersonal Forces of the
Universe ; the bidding of those forces must they do, whether they
will or not.   It is not in the long rows of manuscripts left us by the
labours of monastic scribes and annalists that the *essential* history
of a country is written : these are mere records of automatic secondary consequences.   The essential history is enshrined in minute
grains of pollen, embedded in the mud of peat-bogs.

We have already spoken of the colonization of Ireland by early
Pleistocene fauna.   When Man first made his appearance, several
species of these, some of them dangerous, still infested the country.
The *mammoth* and the *hyæna* had probably disappeared ; their
bones have been found in certain caves,[1] but are nowhere associated
with the remains of the body or of the activities of Man.   The
reindeer persisted, but it was already becoming rare.   The *bear*,
the *boar* and the *wolf* were abundant : and the *giant deer*, perhaps,
still roamed abroad.

The last-mentioned animal seems to have been the first of the
prehistoric fauna to disappear after the arrival of Man.   Indeed,
there was for long a dispute as to whether it survived at all into the
human period.   From the evidence supplied by the peat-bog of
Ballybetagh (Dublin), where a very large number of antlers, skulls,
and other bones of the species have been found from time to time,
it was confidently assigned to interglacial times, earlier than any
known indication of human occupation in Ireland.[2]   Almost immediately afterwards, however, came an account of the discovery
of similar bones, associated with human remains, in Ballinamintra
Cave, near Cappagh (Waterford) : [3] a discovery which seemed to
be corroborated by a subsequent examination of the cave floor,
stratum by stratum.[4]   These facts, so far as they go, make it unnecessary to recall such vague indications as were set forth in earlier

---

[1] E. Brenan, " Notice of the discovery of extinct Elephant and other animal
remains, occurring in a fossil state under limestone, at Shandon, near Dungarvan,
County of Waterford ", *Natural History Review* 6 [1859] : 494.   R. J. Ussher,
" On the discovery of Hyæna, Mammoth and other extinct Mammals in a carboni-
ferous cavern, in Co. Cork ", PRIA 25 B [1904] : 1.   See also Blake Whelan,
" The Palæolithic Question in Ireland ", already cited.

[2] W. Williams, " On an attempt to elucidate the History of the *Cervus megaceros*,
commonly called the Irish Elk ", *Scientific Proceedings*, Royal Dublin Society,
New Series 2 [1878] : 105.

[3] R. J. Ussher and A. Leith Adams, " Notes on the discovery in Ireland of a
Bone Cave containing remains of the Irish Elk, apparently co-existent with Man ",
Ibid. [1879] : 235.

[4] A. Leith Adams, G. H. Kinahan, and R. J. Ussher, " Explorations in the
Bone Cave of Ballinamintra, near Cappagh, Co. Waterford ", *Transactions* of the
same Society, New Series 1 [1880] : 177.   See also PRIA 16 [1880] : 73 ; also
R. F. Scharff's paper on the subject in INJ 1 [1926] : 109.

literature. [1] But the co-existence of the giant deer and Man is not universally accepted even yet : certainly Mr. A. W. Stelfox appears to regard it as still open, [2] and the most recent examination of the Ballybetagh bog has confirmed its pre-human date. [3] Most likely the final disappearance of the animal was primarily due to increased forestation, consequent upon post-glacial climatic amelioration. Its great antlers would prevent it from penetrating the woodlands, so that its range would become more and more restricted.

The caves of Edenvale and Newhall (Clare) yielded numerous bones of the *bear*, some of which seem to have been submitted to a cooking process, as well as a bear's tooth, rudely cut across by human agency : [4] another bear-bone, worked into a pin, was found in one of the burial-carns of Carrowkeel (Sligo). [5] This shows that the bear persisted in Ireland at any rate down to the Bronze Age.

The ancient literature of Ireland makes frequent mention of the chase of the *boar*, and tusks and bones of this animal are among the commonest yields of excavations in ancient habitation-sites.

The *wolf* was the last dangerous wild beast to survive. It has sometimes been said that the last wolf was killed in the year 1710, [6] but a later date—1786—is given in a letter (not a contemporary record) published in *The Field* in 1885, [7] for what such testimony may be worth. A correspondent (Mr. R. Webb, M.A., Leeds) told me that he had heard in 1903 or 1904, from a man in Mallow, then aged about ninety, that his father remembered having seen a wolf running wild. That would bring the date down some twenty years later still.

The mineral wealth of Ireland is as capricious as friends and foes alike represent its other qualities to be. There is *copper* in plenty in various counties, but it is not everywhere easy to obtain. *Iron* also exists in several centres, sometimes in very rich ores. Galena,

---

[1] Such as E. Benn, " On the contemporary existence of Man and the *Cervus megacerus* of Ireland ", JRSAI 4 [1856] : 155 ; S. M. S. " Extinct Animals of Ireland ", *Gentleman's Magazine*, 1834 ii : 147, reprinted in *Gentleman's Magazine Library*, Archæology i 6.

[2] " The Problem of the Irish Elk ", INJ 5 [1934] : 74. Dr. Movius does not share these doubts : *Stone Age*, p. 114.

[3] Knud Jessen and A. Farrington, " The Bogs at Ballybetagh, near Dublin, with remarks on Late-Glacial Conditions in Ireland ", PRIA 44 B [1938] : 205.

[4] R. F. Scharff and others, " Explorations of the Caves of Co. Clare ", TRIA 33 B [1906] : 1, esp. pp. 18, 19, 44.

[5] PRIA 29 [1912] : 337.

[6] Apparently on the authority of Charles Smith, *Antient and Present State of the County of Kerry* (Dublin 1756), p. 173. See H. E. Forrest, " Prehistoric Mammals of Ireland ", running serially through INJ 1 [1926] : and W. R. Wilde, " Upon the unmanufactured Animal Remains belonging to the [Royal Irish] Academy ", PRIA 7 [1859] : 181. See also R. F. Scharff on the subject, *Irish Naturalist* 31 [1922] : 133, 33 [1924] : 94. According to this authority, the wolf-dog is probably a derivative of the wolf. A pleasantly written essay on "Wild Beasts in Ireland " will be found in R. Ll. Praeger's *A populous Solitude*, p. 175.

[7] Brought to notice by Miss N. Fisher (Mrs. McMillan) INJ 5 [1934] · 41.

which yields *silver* and *lead*, is likewise found, in quantities that repay
the labour of extraction and mineralogical treatment. In the Bronze
Age the alluvial deposits of certain of the rivers were rich in *gold*.
The fame of this was spread over Northern Europe, and had an
important influence upon the destinies of the country : even although no gold-mine seems ever to have been worked, and the
numerous attempts made in modern times to discover an exploitable
" vein " have, one and all, been unsuccessful. The large collection
of gold ornaments in the National Museum show that the gold of
the river-gravels was industriously collected : in fact, the bronze-
age goldsmiths seem to have exhausted the supply, and there is now
no apparent reason to expect that Ireland will ever again be a gold-
producing region.

In contrast to its former wealth in gold, Ireland's resources of
tin are insignificant ; the small quantities of this metal which have
been found in Co. Wicklow are of no practical importance. This was
a serious matter in the Bronze Age, as tin was then necessary for the
manufacture of the alloy upon which the metal-workers of that phase
of civilization depended. The country's natural deficiency in this
respect had to be remedied by oversea trade, most conveniently
with the inexhaustible mines of Cornwall.[1] Mr. T. Hallissy has
drawn up a list of six places in Ireland where the " tin-stone " is
to be found : [2] adding, however, that " as far as we know, the mineral
was never found in quantities sufficient for the extraction of the
metal, even on the most moderate scale ". Mr. O. Davies is more
optimistic : he suggests [3] that Ireland was not necessarily always
as sterile as it is now ; that it might have possessed stores of the
metal, which in time were worked out : and even hints at the possibility that " somewhere in Ireland " may have been the mysterious
Mictis, " six days sail ' inward ' from Britain ", named by Timæus
and his copyist Pliny as an important source of tin. This is no
doubt possible, but it is hard to see how such a conjecture could
ever be substantiated : and we must note that in a later publication [4]
the same scholar gives chemical analyses of the metallic substance
of certain socketed hatchet-heads from Northern Ireland, with

[1] A list of the mineral resources of Ireland, from the point of view of modern
commerce, will be found in Cole and Hallissy's *Geology*, cited above, chap. v.
See also G. A. J. Cole, " Memoir and Map of Localities of Minerals of Economic
Importance and Metalliferous Mines in Ireland ", *Memoirs, Geological Survey of
Ireland* (Dublin 1922). On gold in Ireland, see E. C. R. Armstrong, *Catalogue
of Irish Gold Ornaments in the Collection of the Royal Irish Academy* (Dublin 1920) :
T. Hallissy, " Gold Resources of the Irish Free State " (*XV International Geological
Congress*, S. Africa 1929, p. 203). This latter report contains an account of the
attempts made in recent times to discover an auriferous vein.

[2] In an appendix to Armstrong's paper on " Bronze Celts ", PRIA 33 [1917] :
524.

[3] In a richly documented essay on " The Ancient Tin Sources of Western
Europe," *Belfast* 1931-2, p. 41.

[4] *Belfast* 1934-5, p. 88.

such a marked deficiency of tin as to suggest that it was not easily available.

The following chronological summary may here be presented to the reader as a clue to the maze through which we are now, as best we can, to conduct him. The dates are approximations, but they cannot be very seriously in error.

c. 7800 B.C. End of the Glacial and Post-glacial Age. The Yoldia Sea (pp. 4, 12). No human inhabitants in Ireland yet.

c. 7800-2000 B.C. *Mesolithic.* Larne Raised Beach and cognate cultures in various communities of shore-dwelling immigrants. Toward the end of this stage, Turanian colonists from the Baltic (?) and Iberian colonists from Spain establish inland settlements with concomitant forest-clearances. Beginning of the Megalith Cult, and of the Copper Industry.

c. 2000-1600 B.C. *Protomegalithic.* Iberian domination. Erection of the earliest chambered tumuli (Carrowkeel, Dowth). Exploitation of gold and copper.

c. 1600-1200 B.C. *Deuteromegalithic.* Later chambered dolmens ; rock-scribings of the earlier groups ; active oversea trade ; high development of the Bronze Industry. Toward the end of this stage, climatic fluctuations produce great unrest in Europe ; fall of the Cretan Empire ; establishment of the Etruscans, Philistines, Hebrews, Dorians and Achæans in their several homes. Beginning of the Iron Industry in Southern Europe.

c. 1200-200 B.C. *Epimegalithic.* Irruption into Ireland of the Alpine " Beaker People ", who had entered Britain from the Rhineland some six centuries before. Cists and unsegmented passage-graves. New Grange built by these foreign settlers in imitation of Dowth. Gold still exploited, but oversea trade lost. Introduction of the Celtic Language and of Mediterranean sexual rites ; rock-scribings of the later groups ; socketed bronze implements ; tentative beginning of the Iron Industry. At the end, another period of adverse climatic fluctuations produces depressed economic conditions ; Gaulish invasions of Delphi and of Rome ; the Irish gold-alluvium now apparently exhausted. Further immigrations or infiltrations of (probably Teutonic) foreigners into Ireland, who, though numerically insignificant, produce profound changes in social order.

c. 200 B.C.-A.D. 500. *The Iron Age.* Immigrations of druids, gradually pressed out of the Continent by Roman domination, lay the foundations of law and literature. Ogham writing. Slow infiltration of Christianity, carried presumably by refugees from the pre-Constantinian persecutions in the Roman Empire, and from the disturbances in Europe due to the predatory wanderings of the Teutonic peoples. Fall of the Roman Empire of the West. Lake-dwellings in Ireland, a certain indication of internal unrest.

c. A.D. 500-700. *The Overlap* of Paganism and Christianity, brought to an end by the Scandinavian raids. Development of ecclesiastical monasteries and of an energetic missionary enterprise, to the advantage of the native arts, which made great progress under Church patronage ; though there is no conspicuous indication of a lofty standard of material civilization in the country as a whole.

CHAPTER II

THE EARLIEST IMMIGRANTS

AMONG food-gatherers we may expect a range of local cultural independence, wider then we find among the more co-operative and less individualistic food-cultivators. This sounds paradoxical, but is easily explained. The mode of life of food-gatherers has no room for new ideas, or for cultural progress. They are content to go on, decade after decade, picking up shell-fish and trapping birds, using tools and devices which their ancestors had contrived, each group in its own environment; and which, once contrived, are good enough for their descendants. A small community of food-gatherers might live on through many generations, without even so much as knowing of the existence of another such, settled, it may be, not more than forty or fifty miles away, but isolated by intervening stretches of forests, lakes, rocky headlands, or wide rivers; and using tools and devices differing from theirs in form and in technique. The earliest inhabitants of Ireland actually present a number of variant facets of culture, most easily explained by such differences of origin, and by individual segregation.

It would be unreasonable to seek for interglacial human bones or artifacts except in the unglaciated strip of land bordering on the south coast; to discuss here any claims to have done so, would be a waste of time, trouble, paper, and printer's ink.[1] Even inside the specified area, the quest has been in vain, except for one solitary and much controverted discovery—the skeleton known as " The Kilgreany Man ", which is not so certainly unworthy of credit as to justify us in ignoring it altogether.

The cave of Kilgreany is one of a number of natural water-courses penetrating the limestone west and north of the town of Dungarvan (Waterford); the site will be found on the Ordnance Survey 6-inch map, Waterford, sheet 36, not far to the south of the railway station of Cappagh. The present entrance was originally an internal opening between two chambers : in modern times, quarrying has cut the rock face back for some 15 or 20 feet, destroying the outer section of the cave.

A joint expedition of the University of Bristol Spelæological Society and the Royal Irish Academy, after surveying several caves in the neighbourhood, selected that of Kilgreany for a special

---

[1] It will suffice to refer to Movius's *Irish Stone Age*, pp. 105-14, which disposes of all of them. See also J. Kaye Charlesworth, " Palæolithic Man in Ireland ", INJ i [1927]: 298.

investigation, which was carried out in the early part of 1928.[1] In 1934 a further examination was made by the Harvard Mission, under the direction of Dr. H. L. Movius, with conclusions strongly adverse to those of the Bristol party.[2] To these, the director of the former expedition, Mr. Tratman, who had by that time become Professor Tratman of Singapore, made a reply,[3] afterwards countered by Movius ;[4] and there for the present the matter rests.

The cave divides itself naturally into three segments, which we may here call A, B, and C.[5] Segment A, which contained practically all of the archæological material, had apparently been the original outer chamber, exposed and left roofless—indeed, almost destroyed—by the quarrying above mentioned : it was impossible even to determine the position of the original adit. Segment B is reached through a narrow opening, the present entrance to the cave : here the Bristol plan stops. The Harvard plan continues through a second narrow opening to segment C : this has a separate entrance from the quarry-face, passing through a small subsidiary chamber containing a water-spring, which supplies the neighbouring cottages. From all three parts of the cave there open out minor cracks and fissures, most of them, however, too narrow for human penetration. The work of both parties was principally concentrated upon the outer segment, here lettered A : the Bristol party sank a trial trench in segment B also, but the results were not encouraging. In segment C, where the roof comes close to the level of the floor, nothing was found except a few stray animal bones ; and, indeed, little else could be expected.

The Bristol excavation uncovered three hearth-layers in segment A, which ought to have afforded an acceptable stratigraphical division of the accumulation. Above the uppermost hearth, the stratification (in descending order) comprised a thin layer of humus ; quarry debris ; and pre-quarry fallen roof-debris : under which was a stalagmite floor at one end of the pit. Beneath this floor was the first hearth, indicating an occupation level. A layer of stones and brown earth intervened between it and the second hearth (still counting downward) : and this hearth lay upon a second stalagmite floor, in which a third hearth was embedded. Underneath all was

---

[1] Report signed by E. K. Tratman, B.D.S., *Proceedings* of the University of Bristol Spelæological Society 3 [1929] : 109. See also A. W. Stelfox, " Kilgreany Cave, Co. Waterford ", INJ 3 [1930] : 118, and a brief summary by Professor Ó'Ríordáin, *Antiquity* 5 [1931] : 360.

[2] Hallam L. Movius, jr. " Kilgreany Cave, Co. Waterford ", JRSAI 65 [1935] : 254.

[3] E. K. Tratman, "Observations on Kilgreany Cave, Co. Waterford ", *ibid.* 67 [1937] : 120.

[4] H. L. Movius, *The Irish Stone Age*, pp. 114 ff.

[5] A slight difficulty is put in the way of the student by a discrepancy in the plans accompanying the two reports cited above. This disappears, or at least diminishes, when we realize that one or other of the draughtsmen has misplaced his north-point : Movius's *East* faces Tratman's *North*.

a bed of loose stones, which was tested down to a depth of 12 feet without coming to the bottom.

The Harvard party extended the Bristol opening inward and outward, and, in so doing, they appear to have destroyed all the connecting links between the stratifications of the two sets of soundings : they happened to hit upon a part of the cave-debris which was much more disarranged by subsequent water-action than the Bristol section, and whether that was the primary cause or not, they found it impossible to tie the two excavations conclusively together. In one place, they confirmed the Bristol stratification, but they interpreted it differently ; a final judgement, based on this cave alone, is now for ever impossible. At present, the case appears to stand as follows.

The level of the *uppermost* (Bristol) hearth contained iron-age objects ; a common form of iron knife, a socketed bronze dagger, a shale bracelet, bone spindle-whorls, and late bronze-age or early iron-age pottery, indicating an occupation that might belong, on a rough estimate, to about 100 B.C.-A.D. 100. There were also certain other intrusive objects, even more recent, of which we need not speak. The level of the *second* hearth contained flint implements, but no metal : and a human skeleton was there found which (by reason of priority of discovery, not of antiquity) was labelled " Kilgreany A ". The *third* or lowest hearth was embedded between two layers of stalagmite—tufaceous above and crystalline below. Within it, was the skeleton of " Kilgreany B ", the kernel of the controversy. The Bristol excavators contended that as these bones were embedded in stalagmite, which underlay an apparently Neolithic layer, they must be pre-Neolithic. The Harvard party rebutted this by reporting a presumably bronze-age amber bead,[1] embedded in the upper three centimetres of the tufaceous stalagmite, which also contained skull A (but not B) : and cinders of oak and ash wood in the hearth itself—trees not recorded as existing in Ireland in times corresponding to the Palæolithic or early Mesolithic Ages. The Bristol answer to the latter argument is to the effect that the total absence of these trees at the time had not yet been proved, and that, even if it were, in the admitted impossibility of linking the two excavations together, the Harvard excavators might have mistaken the hearth, taking the second for the third. The same ambiguity affects certain ox-bones, which were likewise found by the Harvard expedition in the stalagmite ; nothing of the sort was found by the Bristol party—a remarkable fact, emphasized in Mr. Stelfox's report.

What is to be said of the skull itself ? Here again there is an

[1] An amber bead was also found in the Ballinamintra bone-cave, in the same neighbourhood, but in association with evidently later intrusive material : see R. J. Ussher in *The Zoologist* 3 [1879] : 333.

embarrassing conflict of expert opinion. Appended to the Spelæo-logical Society's report will be found a study, by Professor E. Fawcett, of the osteological material, devoting especial attention to the physical relationship between skeletons A and B. A was apparently a female, in early middle age. It has never been claimed that this person lived at a remote period of antiquity, and Professor Fawcett does not appear to have recognized any racial difference between the two ; B, in his opinion, being a male of the same human type.[1] The latter, he says, " is a long skull of low height which, nevertheless, is one presenting everywhere quite modern features ". He adds, however, that " its pentagonal appearance from behind reminds one of the Cro-Magnon feature ",[2] which would bring us back to a date as old as anyone ever thought of assigning to it.

On the other hand, Dr. C. P. Martin, who devoted much at-tention to the Kilgreany remains,[3] reached a conclusion radically different. He acknowledges the care with which the members of the Bristol party carried out their work, defending them against some rather slighting criticisms expressed by their rivals. He does not agree that skull B is racially similar to skull A : and he emphasizes the importance of the bones of certain sub-arctic animals, indicative of a glacial or sub-glacial climate, found on the level of B and below that of A.[4] A is not an essentially primitive skull : [5] but with regard to B, Dr. Martin gives a list of several primitive features which it presents. The face is broad in proportion to the breadth of the hinder part of the cranium ; the height of the skull is small in pro-portion to its length and breadth ; and there are certain other peculiarities of minor importance. All these idiosyncrasies can admittedly be matched among modern Irish skulls, but only among specimens which are otherwise exceptional ; it is in the combination of them all in the one skull—short face, low vault, broad jaw-bone, peculiar wear of the teeth, as well as some unusual details in the bones of the nose—rather than in the occurrence of any specific item among them, that the justification for describing it as belonging to an early and primitive man is to be sought. The wear of the teeth—a matter to which, in other connexions, we shall have to return later—suggests a flesh rather than a grain diet. It should not be overlooked that there are three other recorded skulls, which, though not identical

[1] Movius quotes Sir A. Keith (*New Discoveries relating to the Antiquity of Man*, p. 431) as expressing the same opinion (*Irish Stone Age*, p. 116).
[2] Spelæological Society's *Report*, p. 133.
[3] *Prehistoric Man in Ireland* (London 1935), pp. 45 ff. Excellent photographs of the skull will be found there, on plate ii, facing p. 42.
[4] Such as the reindeer and the lemming. Other animals, now extinct (at least in Ireland), represented in the cave, were the boar, giant deer, bear, wolf, and (wild) cat ; a lynx bone had the interest of being the only relic of this animal as yet found in the country.
[5] Like everything else relating to the discovery, this has been controverted, but—so at least it seems to me—on insufficient grounds.

with the Kilgreany skull in every respect, resemble it sufficiently to admit of the working hypothesis of a racial kinship between them. These are from Ringabella (Cork) ; [1] Stoney Island, near Portumna (Galway) ; [2] and Clonfinloch,[3] near Strokestown (Roscommon)—the two latter are later than the Ancylus period, according to the evidence of pollen analysis.[4] In opposition to other authorities who have examined the skull, Dr. Martin considers that it belonged to a female ; to my (confessedly inexpert) eye, the appearance of the occipital region seems rather more favourable to the contrary hypothesis, and I understand that the late Professor A. F. Dixon of Dublin University was of the same opinion.

Scanty and contradictory though the materials for forming a judgement admittedly are, we are left with a very definite impression that the Kilgreany man, though not a child of the Palæolithic Age, had somehow contrived to enter Ireland early in what would elsewhere be called the Mesolithic. If so, he can hardly have come alone ; bones of his brethren must await discovery in other southern Irish caves. But down to the present time, the record of cave exploration in Ireland, while (within narrow limitations) fruitful in the department of Palæozoology, has been discouraging to the Anthropologist. Human bones have been found, but nowhere in abundance ; and, with the possible exception of this solitary individual, they have all obviously belonged to intruders, even late intruders, who happened to use the cave as a habitation or as a place of refuge. The Kilgreany man is as yet the " one swallow " which proverbially cannot make a summer ; until more of his kind and his contemporaries are unearthed, we must not erect over him a heavier burden of hypothesis than he can legitimately be called upon to bear. No artifacts older than " Windmill Hill " pottery were found in the cave : such authorities as Mr. J. G. D. Clark [5] and Dr. Mahr [6] have accepted the adverse results of the Harvard excavation. On the other hand, Mr. A. W. Stelfox, who as a skilled scientific observer is entitled to be heard, and who was associated with the Bristol party as a representative of the Royal Irish Academy, has assured me in conversation that he still supports the Bristol results, on account of the peculiarities of the skull itself, and the want of conformity between the stratifications as determined by the two groups of excavators.

We must therefore leave the question of the physical remains of Irish Mesolithic Man in this as yet crepuscular stage, and with but little hope that its semi-darkness will ever be *fully* enlightened ; and we pass on to the later phases of the pre-Neolithic culture in

---

[1] S. P. Ó'Ríordáin, "A prehistoric burial at Ringabella, Co. Cork", JRSAI 64 [1934] : 86. This skull is figured in Martin, *op. cit.* plate iii.
[2] On which see Professor Shea's report, *Galway* 15 [1931] : 73.
[3] A different place from the similarly named site of the stone illustrated, Plate I. [4] Martin, *op. cit.* p. 64. [5] PPS 2 [1936] : 241. [6] *Ibid.* 3 [1937] : 281.

Ireland, about which there is fortunately less room for uncertainty—though plenty for disputation.

Much of what we shall now have to say is based upon a study of flint implements, their typological forms and geographical distribution. For the history of the formation of flint itself, and of the chalk in which it is found, in Nature, embedded, as well as for the peculiar properties which gave it an outstanding importance in Prehistoric times, the reader must be referred to specialist treatises on Geology, Petrology, and General Archæology. Chalk, with its successive layers of flint, survives in Ireland in N.E. Antrim only ; but it is believed that other parts of the country once had a similar covering, now worn away. This is deduced from certain observed phenomena of river-erosion, into details of which it would here be irrelevant to enter ; and also from loose nodules of cretaceous flint, found frequently in various now chalk-less areas of the south of Ireland, and, especially, in the sea outside the western coast.[1] But in these regions the supply of flint, for industrial purposes, must have been uncertain at best—most of it, indeed, submerged, and thus unavailable : such " residual flints ", if so we may term them, do not seem to have been exploited to any great extent. It is, in fact, rare to find flint implements at all, in such parts of the country as do not retain flint in its natural chalk beds ; other stones, some of them very unsuitable for the purpose, were pressed into service as substitutes or makeshifts : and even if worked flints should occasionally be found, the absence of associated waste flakes and cores may be taken either as an indication that the implements were manufactured at the Antrim chalk-beds, and imported ready-made to the find-place ; or else as a testimony to the high value set upon flint, the possessor of a lump of it using his prize down to the last available splinter. Notable evidence of trade in *unworked* flint was unearthed on Lambay (Dublin), where a large hoard of flint flakes was found, though the island possesses no native flint.[2] They must have been imported—presumably from Antrim—for use as material in a local manufactory.

N.E. Antrim is thus the primary siliciferous area of Ireland ; there, a constant supply was assured, as nowhere else in the country. The great majority of the remains of flint-using settlements are concentrated in the northern counties ; but we should be on our guard against too easy theories of causation. The accident of distribution, whereby the available supplies of flint are practically confined to the northern counties, could not have been discovered until most of the remaining regions had been explored, and their resources at

[1] See G. A. J. Cole, " The Problem of the Liffey Valley " (PRIA 30 B [1912] : 8, especially p. 12) and references there. See also *Idem*, "The Passing of the Chalk ", *Louth* 5 [1921] : 23.

[2] See the report of the discoveries there made : PRIA 38 [1929] : 240 ; also *post*, pp. 245-6.

least empirically ascertained. Moreover, tools made of stones other than flint, especially the rude products of primitive beachcombers, are not always to be readily recognized : with such less tractable material, it is only too easy to make both positive and negative mistakes, in endeavouring to discriminate between rudimentary tools of human handicraft, and fragments broken by some natural process. The industrial relics of flint-users can be identified much more easily than those of people who had no access to any source of supply of this substance.

To explain the practical confinement of flint-working sites to the north-east, a more important consideration is the fact that there, Ireland most nearly approaches to Great Britain ; on the reasonable hypothesis that the earliest settlers came across from the larger island, we should naturally expect to find them established, at least at first, in places within sight thereof. The earliest immigrants fixed their habitations along the shores, where they lived upon sea-produce : only here and there—as along the course of the Bann—is there any evidence that they followed the guidance of the rivers for any distance into the interior of the country. The landward side of the beaches beside which they squatted, in the N.E. corner of the country, now stands as the 25-feet Raised Beach, in consequence of post-glacial land-elevation : it is therefore readily available for our examination. But in the regions which had not been cumbered with ice in the latest glaciation, balancing downward movements appear to have caused the corresponding southern beach-line to be submerged. As we follow the line of the 25-feet beach southward, it gradually slopes down to the level of the present sea-beach, upon which it impinges in the neighbourhood of Dublin on the eastern, of Sligo on the western side : further south it presumably descends below the surface of the sea, thus passing out of reach. It is therefore impossible to determine by direct observation whether the Antrim coast dwellers had contemporaries on the southern shores.

In 1928 almost the only known relics of the earliest settlers were the tools embedded in the 25-feet Raised Beach, especially in the neighbourhood of the town of Larne (Antrim). These had been noticed, so long ago as 1867, by George V. Du Noyer, in the course of his work in the service of the Geological Survey of Ireland ; and he had the insight to see that they represented an industry different from, and presumably older than, the ordinary flake-knife-and-scraper industries which till then had provided most of the Irish material accumulated by collectors. Du Noyer was followed by other investigators ; [1] but all their work was superseded by studies

---

[1] For a history of early researches on the site, see W. J. Knowles, " The Antiquity of Man in Ireland, being an account of the older series of Irish Flint Implements ", JRAI 44 [1914] : 83.

made, from the standpoint of Geology, by Dr. R. Ll. Praeger, of Archæology, by George Coffey.[1] A summary of their results was given in the first edition of this work ; but the problem has since been complicated by the results of the investigations of the Harvard expedition. These would withdraw the geological horizon of the gravels from the archæological horizon of the implements ; in other words, would point to a conclusion that the association of the implements with the Raised Beach is secondary only ;[2] that they had belonged to a group of earlier shore settlements, dispersed by marine action, and thus washed out from their original context and redeposited in the incongruous situation in which they were found. Possibly this interpretation of the evidence is corroborated by a mammoth tooth and an elephant bone, found at Larne, and a mammoth tooth in the Grainger collection found in similar gravels at Ballyrudder ; these, as Coffey says, must have been derived from some older formation. The most important of these beach sites is a strip of gravel, known, from its sickle-like shape, as " The Curran " (= Irish *corrán*, " sickle "), jutting into Larne Loch, and containing humanly-wrought implements to a total depth of 19 feet.

The following is a classification of the flint implements found on the Raised Beach sites : they are very fully illustrated in Coffey and Praeger, *op. cit.* ; a few typical specimens are shown in Fig. 1.

1. *Cores.* These are more or less globular or cylindrical in shape, measuring up to about 3 inches or a little more in maximum diameter. Although the Belfast Naturalists' Field Club, in their investigation of the site, happened to find but few of these objects, they are not uncommon. Coffey says of them that " they are generally coarse and defective, as if discarded after a few trial flakes. . . . The good pieces were probably worked out, and fine cores are very rare, but the characteristic core-form of those which can still be collected in large numbers is unmistakable, though they probably should be looked on as wasters for the most part, rather than serviceable cores."[3]

2. *Flakes.* The flakes found in the Larne site fall, speaking generally, into two classes. The first are rough, wedge-shaped splinters of flint ; a noticeably large number of them have the bulb of percussion at the narrower end. The second are much more delicate in form, and were evidently intended to serve as knives. The edges show signs of wear, but it is doubtful whether they have indications of intentional secondary chipping. The flakes of the first class often have some of the outer calcareous shell of the

---

[1] G. Coffey and R. Ll. Praeger, " The Antrim Raised Beach : a contribution to the Neolithic History of Ireland ", PRIA 25 [1904] : 143. See further W. Gray, " The antiquarian aspects of the Co. Antrim Raised Beach ", JRSAI 21 [1891] : 388 ; W. J. Knowles, reports published PRIA 16 [1883-5] : 209, 436, and in BNFC II ii [1886-7] : 539. On the fauna of the Raised Beach see Praeger's report, PRIA 20 [1896] : 30. For earlier work on the site, see " Report of a Committee of Investigation on the Gravels and associated Beds of the Curran at Larne ", BNFC ii 3 [1890] : 198. See also a previous report in *ibid.* ii 2 [1886-7] : 517.

[2] This observation is anticipated by W. J. Knowles, " Report on Flint Implements of the North-East of Ireland ", PRIA 17 [1889] : 188. (See strictures by W. Gray, BNFC ii 2 [1883-4] : 287). Coffey and Praeger, *op. cit.* p. 192.

[3] Coffey and Praeger, *op. cit.* p. 173.

parent nodule adhering to them, and Coffey considers that these are mere wastes, struck off and thrown away in the process of shaping another implement.

3. The so-called *Campignian Pick*. This is a cylindrical bar of flint, about 4 to 6 inches in length, covered with coarse surface chipping. It has no cutting edge ; only a blunt point at each end. Coffey (*op. cit.* p. 184) gives a list of Raised Beach sites in Ireland where examples of this characteristic tool have come to light. It has been found also in Great Britain, as for instance at Pencaer in Pembrokeshire ; but there it does not appear to be common. Collectors have been in the habit of calling this tool the " Larne Celt ", a name open to several obvious objections. It is found, no doubt, at Larne, but it is not a peculiar property of that site ; and " celt " is a spurious word, with no real specific meaning. The name " Campignian Pick " is not much better. It is derived from the name of Le Campigny, a hill near the town of Blangy-sur-Bresle (Seine Inférieure), France, and is as essentially unscientific as are all such territorial designations of aspects of culture ; in this case especially so, for there is room for grave doubt as to whether the relic-beds of Le Campigny actually belong to the culture to

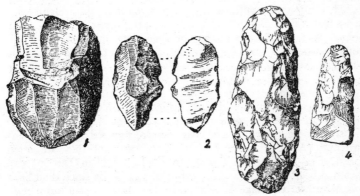

[*By permission of the Royal Irish Academy.*]

FIG. 1.—Types of Raised Beach (Larne) Implements.
(After Coffey : 1. Core ; 2. Flake ; 3. Core-axe ; 4. Flake-axe.)

which their site has given its name ! The term " core-axe ", used by Childe and others, seems to solve the problem of nomenclature more happily. Whatever we may call it, the phase of culture defined by these tools is one of those which usher in, for Europe, the New Stone Age. To it belong the settlements of Maglemose in the island of Seeland, those of Nöstvet in Norway, and the Ertebølle and other shell-heap relics of the Danish coast ; as well as the implements from the Raised Beach at Larne.

When Coffey described the Larne tools, the deposits of Le Campigny had only recently begun to attract attention ; and the close kinship of the Larne implements with those of the Danish shell-heaps had not yet been observed. He considered that the Larne flints were the remains of a fully developed Neolithic culture, comparable with the remains of a Neolithic culture—the polished hatchet-heads, in fact—to be found elsewhere in Europe. Their roughness he explained as due to incompleteness ; he considered the site to be not a dwelling place, but a factory, in which flint-workers had roughed out their flints—carrying them, presumably, to some inland site, there to apply the finishing touches. However, in the light of subsequent discoveries in Scandinavia and elsewhere, such an interpretation can no longer be maintained, and need not be further discussed. The Larne tools are not Neolithic, but belong to a phase of culture preceding the Neolithic of Northern Europe, and illustrated by objects from other Mesolithic sites.[1]

4. The *Tranchet* or " Kitchen-midden Axe " (Childe's " flake-axe "). This is a more or less flat, four-sided implement, wedge-shaped in outline, the longest side of the figure being the bevelled cutting edge. In the Danish shell-heaps the tranchet is associated with the core-axe, and it also appears in the 25-feet Raised Beach deposits. It occurs at Larne in relatively small numbers, but is more frequent at Portrush : it appears also in the Bann Valley deposits, of which we have still to speak.[2]

It must be noticed that none of the 25-feet beach sites in Ireland has yielded any pottery contemporary with their stone artifacts ; although pottery is associated with the analogous culture in Continental sites.[3]

The Campignian culture is thus contemporary in Ireland with the 25-feet Raised Beach, or, if we adopt the revised views already noticed, is prior thereto by an indeterminate space of time. In Scotland, where the same beach occurs, a different facies of Mesolithic culture is associated with it, named *Azilian*, after the Pyrenean cave known as " Le Mas d'Azil ". This culture is distinguished by flat harpoons, made of stag's horn, and by minute flint objects, generically called " pygmy flints ", which, though usually associated with Azilian deposits, were not reported from the " type " site.[4] The site where these objects were first recognized is at Fère-en-Tardenois (Aisne), in France ; on which account they are often spoken of as *Tardenoisian* flints. In 1928 no Azilian-Tardenoisian relics had been found in Ireland ; but this spell has since then been broken by Mr. C. Blake Whelan, who has discovered a number in a site at Castlereagh (Down) :[5] and others have been reported by Mr. J. Batty from the Bann Valley.[6] The makers of these objects had to utilize whatever local pebbles they could pick up around their dwelling-place : apparently they were ignorant of, or had no access to, the Antrim flint-beds, a fact which illustrates the remark made

[1] For a group of good typical specimens of these implements see *Archæologia* 63 [1912] : plate facing p. 128.
[2] W. J. Simpson, " On worked flints found on a raised beach at Portrush ", PRIA 17 [1887] : 76, to be read in connexion with Mr. Knowles's report at p. 177 of the same volume. See further W. J. Knowles, " Irish stone axes and chisels ", JRSAI 23 [1893] : 141.
[3] Simpson (*loc. cit.*) speaks of the discovery of small fragments of pottery at Portrush : but these appear to have come from a higher level.
[4] They may have been there notwithstanding : until subsequent discoveries elsewhere taught excavators to look out for them, these minute chips could easily have been overlooked.
[5] INJ 4 [1933] : 201.
[6] *Ulster* III 1 [1938] : 90. The author of this paper comments on the difficulty of fitting these objects into any of the recognized " pigeon-holes ".

above as to the *gradual* discovery of the resources and limitations of the country.

Although in 1928 the beginning of human life in Ireland seemed to be a fairly simple matter, a suggestion had already been given by Walther Bremer of the unexpected complications in which future research was to enshroud it. A particular aspect of Mesolithic culture had been recognized on the Continent, and had been named *Asturian*; it was first brought to scientific notice by Professor Obermaier of Madrid, on the basis of excavations conducted by Count de la Vega del Sella in certain caves and rock-shelters of Oviedo (Asturias).[1] Its distinguishing artifact is a special form of implement in flint or quartzite, with a base more or less flat, and a ridged back, produced by coarse flaking, which brings one end to a point, leaving the other as an unworked and rounded butt, suitable for gripping in the fingers. In Ireland, at least, the tool seems to have been made by shaping the nodule to a more or less round horizontal section, and then splitting it, thus producing two tools, each with a flattened side.

The Asturian industry, after its first identification, was found to extend over the whole Iberian peninsula and beyond it, eastward to Biarritz and northward to Brittany.[2] And a few examples of flint implements of this kind, from Island Magee (Antrim), were identified by Bremer in the Royal Irish Academy's collection, soon after his appointment to its Keepership; unfortunately, his untimely death prevented him from putting in permanent form the announcement of the discovery, which he made verbally at a meeting of the Academy.[3]

This was the point to which knowledge had attained by the year 1928. Soon afterwards, an intensive study of the problems of the early occupation of Ireland was inaugurated, partly by the Harvard Mission, partly by the energetic Archæologists of Northern Ireland, in whose province most of the relevant sites are to be found. The new facts which have thus been revealed have had an effect little short of revolutionary : and the end is not yet—not even so much as in sight. Every new year is adding its harvest of fresh results ; still so ambiguous in their implications, that we cannot reconcile the deductions set forth by different investigators, or even by one and the same investigator at different stages of his progress. We

[1] H. Obermaier, *El Hombre fósil* (Madrid 1916), p. 334. Conde de la Vega del Sella, *El Asturiense* (Madrid 1923) : Obermaier, " Asturias-Stufe ", in Ebert's *Reallexikon der Vorgeschichte* (Berlin 1924).

[2] A convenient summary of the successive discoveries, with references, will be found in C. Blake Whelan, "The Flint Industry of the Northern Irish (25-feet) Raised Beach ", JRAI 60 [1930] : 169.

[3] It is referred to in his paper, " Die Stellung Irlands in der Europäischen Vor- und Frühgeschichte " (*Festschrift* zur Feier des 75-jährige Bestehung des . . . Museums zu Mainz, 1927), p. 2. The draft of his communication to the Academy, posthumously published without the advantage of his final revision, will be found in PRIA 38 [1928] : 21.

may hope that at some future time all these perplexities will find their solution ; but at the present, no synthetic account of the fruit of recent work can claim finality as a sequential reconstruction of the course of events.

This local revolution in our knowledge of the Stone Age is only a limited, sectional aspect of a world-wide extension and revision of knowledge and beliefs, regarding the same stage of human culture. The results of the contributory researches have been summarized in a comprehensive work by Menghin, [1] which must form the starting-point for all future investigations.   The cloisons, with their French topographical nomenclature, into which the pioneer work of Gabriel de Mortillet had distributed the relics of the lithic cultures, have had their day of service ; they must before long yield place to some more adaptable system of classification, capable of embracing the many new forms, transitional, secondary, or supplementary, which have put in claims for recognition, but which will not fit comfortably into the established categories.   Fresh pigeon-holes have been constructed for their accommodation—" Larnian " in Ireland, " Cromerian ", " Cresswellian ", " Clactonian ", and so forth, in England, and similar complications in other countries ; but these cannot be more than temporary makeshifts.   In the end, the whole system is bound to collapse under the dead weight of its own cumbrousness—or, at the very least, to lose all the practical utility which it may have possessed in the days of its early simplicity.   Seriously, it is high time that someone with authority should call a halt in this endless creation of local industries, which often possess only the vaguest recognizable individuality : [2] and on principle, the use of place-names as labels is to be strongly deprecated.   We find what we suppose to be a new industry in Laputa, and call it " Laputan "—inevitably suggesting that Laputa is the centre in which it originated.   A few years later, an overwhelmingly more important site of the same industry is discovered in Brobdingnag : what are we to do then ?   To change the name will introduce confusion ; to retain it will show a lack of any sense of proportion, and will be more misleading than before.

It appears to be sometimes forgotten that the criticism and classification of flint tools, and the criticism and classification of metal implements, must necessarily follow different lines, on account of the larger scope for individual peculiarities inherent in the former. Given a mould, a whole village might produce bronze tools out of it, which would all conform to a stereotyped pattern.   Admittedly, there would be differences, induced by the unequal technical efficiency

[1] Oswald Menghin, *Weltgeschichte der Steinzeit*, Vienna 1931. See also V. G. Childe, " The Forest Cultures of Northern Europe ", JRAI 61 [1931] : 325.

[2] See H. Desmaisons, " Essai de nomenclature des noms attribués aux divers horizons préhistoriques " (*Bulletin* de la Soc. préhist. française, 36 [1939] : 416) where a list (not exhaustive) of 120 such names is given.

of the individual craftsmen : one of them might allow his metal to be filled with air-bubbles, another might combine the materials of his alloy in unsuitable proportions, another might permit the intrusion of injurious foreign impurities, another might be negligent in the final hammer-finish given to the metal after the casting, another (like the maker of a palstave in the possession of University College, Dublin) might carelessly allow one valve of his mould to slip out of place by about an eighth of an inch. But though all these faults detract more or less seriously from the appearance and efficiency of the tools affected, they do not prevent us from recognizing the type to which the whole group belongs : a generic mechanical mass-production overrides all such specific idiosyncrasies. This, however, is not the case in a collection of flint artifacts, each of which has been made individually, from start to finish, by an individual workman, with individual physical and mental limitations, trimming an individual lump of flint, following an individual process, with individual tools. Relics of Antiquity did not grow of themselves ; we owe each one of them to a man, our brother in his virtues and his failings, with an individual name, entity, and life-history. We know nothing whatever about him ; but we must be conscious of his presence in the background, when we seek to force the fruits of his industry into artificial schemes of classification.

Menghin has shown that the Mortillet system has really obscured the essential clue to the history : namely, that not one but three " cultures " make a progress through the Stone Age, from first to last, in parallel lines, and thus essentially independent of one another. These he calls *Klingenkultur, Faustkeilkultur, Knochenkultur*, names which we may render by " Flake Industry ", " Hand-axe Industry ", " Bone Industry ". The relation between these three, and the unconscious choice which secures for each respectively a domination in this environment or in that, depends ultimately, like every other human effort, upon local natural conditions. A region destitute of flint, or of stones which will serve as substitutes for flint, will force its inhabitants into the use of implements of bone (and presumably also of wood) as a substitute for those of stone. In an open land, with vegetation composed chiefly of an overgrowth of scrub, an industry will develop, making use of knives, choppers, and other flake-blade tools : in a forest-land, where the inhabitants are compelled to fell trees in order to clear spaces for occupation, and to obtain timber for houses, boats, and other constructions, an axe (and wedge) industry will come into being. We need not look further than the Mortillet classification for a proof of this. The Chellean and Acheulean phases of the Lower Palæolithic saw Europe under tropical conditions, with heavy forest-growths ; and in consequence, their typical implement was the *coup de poing* or hand-axe. The Mousterians of the Middle Palæolithic lived in a time of glaciation, when the forests had disappeared ; and they developed an industry based on flint flakes in various special forms. The people of the Upper Palæolithic, cave-dwellers and trappers, had at hand the accumulations of midden-debris bones, which littered their cave-floors ; and there they found plentiful material for easily made and effective tools.

The foregoing classification of industries is applied by Menghin to his *Protolithic* (= Palæolithic) and *Miolithic* (= Mesolithic) stages of development. For the later stages—*Protoneolithic* (= Neolithic) and *Mixoneolithic* (= Chalcolithic or transition to the metal culture)—he adopts other bases of classification, which do not concern us at the moment. Turning now to Ireland, where the Palæolithic is absent, we soon discover that the Beachcombers practised both varieties of stone culture ; and that even within the small area of Northern Ireland these fall easily and almost automatically into local independent groups.

I. THE HAND-AXE INDUSTRIES

We presuppose, in the above heading, a definition of the word " hand-axe " (" hand-pick " would on the whole be a more appropriate term) rather wider than its special application to the Lower Palæolithic *coup de poing*, so as to make it inclusive of the " Campignian " and " Asturian " picks and wedges. This enables us to take up, under the above heading, the further researches into the Asturian of Ireland, which we owe chiefly to the energy of Mr. Whelan. We have seen that Bremer had detected the presence of this phase of industry at Island Magee, on the basis of tools from that locality which had found their way to the National Museum. During his short life in Ireland, the effective part of which was still further diminished by grave illness, he had no opportunity of visiting the site itself. Mr. Whelan, who was at first inclined to be doubtful of Bremer's diagnosis of the Museum specimens,[1] examined the beach of Island Magee from end to end, and ultimately expressed his conversion thereto.[2] Moreover, specimens collected by Mr. Whelan helped to establish the faith of some of the Iberian archæologists, who had also been slow to accept Bremer's suggestions unreservedly.[3]

Discarding earlier theories which he had expressed in previous publications, Mr. Whelan assigns the Asturian relics in Ireland to the Litorina period, and defines Asturian as a boat-building industry —the picks being in his view boat-building tools. The Asturian

---

[1] *Man* 28 [1928] : no. 136.
[2] JRAI 60 [1930] : 178.
[3] Doubts are still expressed by Movius (JRSAI 67 [1937] : 196), and more strongly in later publications (PRIA 46 [1940] : 72, *Irish Stone Age*, pp. 205-6). See on the other side the letter of Pater E. Jalhay (misprinted Talhay) in *Man*, 34 [1934] : no. 40. Movius quotes Obermaier as disputing the Irish Asturian in a paper published in 1933, which I have not seen.

immigration is thus the result of maritime enterprise, not, as he had previously suggested, of a trek across now submerged Continental land-masses.[1]

But the Asturian culture is not necessarily confined to the sites examined by Mr. Whelan. The Bann Valley has yielded a fair number of Asturian picks, and we can now identify as Asturian some of those figured by Mr. Knowles in the paper in which he directed attention to the archæological importance of that water-course.[2] At a yet earlier date, [Sir] John Evans had found similar tools at Toome, the point of exit of the Bann from Loch Neagh, and had figured one of them in a publication of the London Society of Antiquaries.[3]

Of the other " hand-axe " culture, the Campignian, there is little to be said beyond what is contained in the monograph of Praeger and Coffey, apart from our more recently acquired conceptions of the date and affinities of this industry. In Ireland, as elsewhere, it seems to be altogether independent of the Asturian, and the presence of the two cultures in the country is indisputable evidence of the presence of two different populations. Whatever final decision may be attained as to the absolute dating of the Irish Asturian, and its connexion with the Spanish industry whose name it has borrowed, it appears to precede the Campignian stratigraphically. With regard to the Larne deposits, Mr. Whelan doubts whether they can be ascribed unreservedly to the Campignian at all : in his opinion, they belong to an auroral stage of this industry, the fully developed forms of which are represented by the yield of a site at Ballynagard on Rathlin Island. In addition to picks, scrapers, broad flake-blade choppers, and a tranchet or two (some in flint, others in other lithic material) this site yielded two sherds of pottery of Windmill Hill type.[4] With these he couples the diorite implements from certain Co. Antrim centres, which had been described by Knowles as early Neolithic factory sites.

II. THE FLAKE INDUSTRIES

Here also there are two, again to all appearance independent of one another—the Bann Industry, and the Antrim Coast Industry.

First in importance, as in date of discovery (though not in chronological sequence), is the Bann Industry. The river Bann rises in

---

[1] See PRIA 42 [1936] : 126 ; 44 [1938] : 116.

[2] W. J. Knowles, " Prehistoric Stone Implements from the River Bann and Lough Neagh ", PRIA 30 [1912] : 195. See especially his plate xvi, nos. 85-90. On the preceding plate will be found some implements with Campignian analogies.

[3] John Evans, " On some discoveries of Stone Implements in Lough Neagh, Ireland ", Archæologia 61 part 2 : 397 (Paper dated 1867). See there, plate xviii, no. 9.

[4] C. Blake Whelan, " Studies in the Significance of the Irish Stone Age : the Campignian Question ", PRIA 42 [1934] : 121, especially p. 129. (This paper contains a list of important sites classified according to their cultural horizons.) See also Belfast 1933-4, p. 107.

the Mourne Mountains (Down), and flows through that county to the border of Armagh, which it crosses about midway between Gilford and Portadown. Flowing north-westward, it eventually reaches Loch Neagh. The Lower Bann, which drains that·lake, forms the boundary between Armagh and Londonderry as far as the railway junction of Macfin, a little over four miles above Coleraine. After this point it enters the latter county, and reaches the sea to the west of Portstewart.

It is this lower part of the river which is of special archæological importance. Its wealth in fish may have been a determining factor in establishing, along its course, a number of settlements ; the remains of which, from Loch Neagh to the sea, have made its banks a famous hunting-ground for collectors. In 1859 [Sir] John Evans found a chipped implement in some gravel, carried to Antrim from the shore of Loch Neagh for a roadway in private grounds ; this led him, two years later, to explore the lake shore, when he found a considerable number and variety of implements. So impressed was he with the wealth of the site, that, in reporting his discovery to the Society of Antiquaries (in a paper cited above), he did not hesitate to rank it in importance with the caves of the Dordogne and the pile-dwellings of Switzerland, which, at the time when he wrote, had recently revealed their treasures to an astonished world. He was not alone among the early pioneers in selecting this site for exploration : in his paper he refers to objects from the lake and the river, found in drainage works and deposited in the R.I.A. Museum ; and to large numbers of flakes and other tools, collected by the indefatigable Robert Day of Cork.

This pioneer account, illustrated with one beautifully coloured plate of thirteen implements, was superseded by the elaborate monograph contributed by Knowles to the *Proceedings* of the Royal Irish Academy (also cited above), as the culmination of many studies, recorded in earlier papers from the same pen ; to which references will there be found, along with notices of the work of other students and collectors. It treats, however, in a manner too summary, an important description of the diatomaceous clay and its contents by [Dr.] J. Wilfred Jackson, based upon personal investigation, and on the late R. D. Darbishire's collections, now in Manchester Museum.[1]

Implements are to be found along the whole course of the river : but for the greater part they are concentrated at certain points, such as Mount Sandal (near Coleraine), Kilrea, and, especially, Toome Bar, the point at which the river issues from Loch Neagh. These happen to be places especially favourable for the capture of the salmon and the other fish in which the river abounds. Dredging

[1] J. Wilfred Jackson, " On the Diatomaceous Deposit of the Lower Bann Valley . . . and Prehistoric Implements found therein ", *Memoirs and Proceedings*, Manchester Lit. and Phil. Society, 53 (1908-9) : no. 10.

PLATE I

T. H. Mason

THE CLONFINLOCH STONE

and other deepening operations in the bed of the river itself, and the exploitation of brick-earth in its immediate neighbourhood, have speeded up the garnering of the harvest, with the result that all sorts and conditions of collectors have been attracted to the river— not invariably to the advantage of Science.

The types of implements, discriminated and richly illustrated [1] by Knowles in this monograph, are as follows :—

1. *Flakes*, the most characteristic group of the Bann implements. They fall into several subordinate classes. Some are broad, usually with a single ridge between two facets on the upper or outer surface, rounded at the base, above which the edges expand more or less symmetrically and then contract to a sharp point. The base, and occasionally one or both of the edges, may be trimmed by slight secondary chipping. Such flakes could be used for knives or javelin-heads. In others, however, a lack of symmetry which tilts the point to one side would seem to exclude the latter as a possible function. In a second type, which forms a predominant group in the Bann culture, the base is not rounded but shouldered, so that it presents a short

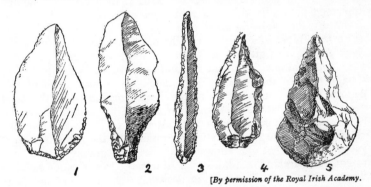

[By permission of the Royal Irish Academy.

FIG. 2.—Types of Bann Implements.
(After Knowles : 1. Flake ; 2. Tanged Flake ; 3. Chipped Flake ; 4. Borer ; 5. " Asturian " Pick.)

broad tang, presumably for fitting in a handle. Knowles figures a handle made of a root, found at Culbane on the Londonderry side of the river, a short distance north of Loch Beg : a flake, now in the National Museum, with a handle made of a wad of moss, has long been known as one of the most remarkable objects from this region (see p. 109 below).

2. *Borers.* These are narrow flakes, chipped as a rule on one or both edges along their whole length, and brought to a sharp point at one end. They would hardly have been suitable for any rough work involving the manipulation of wood, but might have served for making stitch-holes in leather.

3. *Chipped flakes*, in which the edge has received heavy secondary trimming.

[1] As against Evans's one plate with 13 implements, Knowles has seven plates with 123 implements.

4-6. In addition to the above, Knowles figures specimens of the characteristic *tranchets* and *picks* of the Raised Beach Culture, and a few pointed tools which appear to be Asturian in aspect. He further calls attention to certain types of implements in polished stone or slate, to which we shall return in the following chapter.

These early researches on the Bann had the then inevitable defect that little or no attention was paid to stratigraphy : a fault remedied by the work of Movius under the auspices of the Harvard Mission. By a systematic excavation at Newferry, a place about midway between Toome and Kilrea, the relevant stratigraphical and chronological facts were established.

This excavation [1] exposed a layer of diatomaceous clay, or " diatomite ", a freshwater deposit of considerable breadth, and ranging in thickness up to about 6 feet along the greater part of both banks of the Lower River. It is exploited for brick-earth and other commercial purposes, under the name " Bann Clay ". At the Newferry site it overlies a deposit of mixed ash, containing implements : under this is a thin layer of lacustrine silt, resting in its turn on a substratum of peat. Peat, in some places as much as 10 feet thick, also overlies the diatomite in various parts of the river course, though not at Newferry itself. On the basis of a palæobotanical analysis of the diatomite, Professor Knud Jessen, in an appendix to the paper quoted, dated the lowest layers of this deposit to the upper border of the Boreal maximum, with Hazel vegetation ; its later stages, and by inference the associated human relics, to the transition from Late Atlantic to Early Sub-Boreal.[2] He adds, however, " with strong emphasis ", the sometimes forgotten caution that our knowledge of the stratigraphy of the bogs of Northern Ireland is still insufficient to settle this question finally.[3] There is, in fact, a certain inconsistency in this finding. The epoch indicated would make the diatomaceous clay contemporary with the Larne Raised Beach ; but the evidence of the culture itself would suggest that it is later than any of the others which have occupied our attention in this chapter. The character of the artifacts would suggest that we are here well clear of the Intermediate Stage, and passing into what in other countries would be called a Neolithic civilization : a suggestion reinforced by the occurrence of a few sherds of pottery of the Windmill Hill type in some of the hearth-sites unearthed in the excavation—to say nothing of two

[1] Hallam L. Movius, Jr. " A Neolithic site on the River Bann ", PRIA 43 [1936] : 17. Further references to earlier literature will be found in this paper. See also his *Irish Stone Age*, pp. 239 ff.

[2] In his later paper, to which reference has already been made (" Early Post-Glacial site at Cushendun ", PRIA 46 [1940] : 1), Movius puts the Larne culture into the Atlantic, the Bann culture altogether into the Sub-Boreal.

[3] Ten catastrophic years have passed since this was written. Some improvement in our knowledge has been registered in the interval, but less than, in other conditions, would have been.

remarkable plaques of clay-slate, found in the diatomite, which are certainly analogous to the flat idol-figures familiar in Iberian Archæology.[1] The hearths mentioned were concentrated " islands " of ashes, consisting of charcoal, with spreading areas of ash-debris surrounding them, and were scattered over the not very wide area of the excavated site in considerable numbers. They did not appear to be associated with any habitation-site ; to the excavators they suggested temporary *al fresco* encampments, occupied, we may presume, during the summer months. Even although drainage operations have been carried out in modern times, the land is still liable to be flooded in winter.

Further indication of a comparatively late date is presented by the occurrence of polished stone hatchet-heads, found in association with these relics, and on the same Archæological level. Such objects would be at least unusual in true Mesolithic sites. The characteristic Bann flakes, with slightly touched-up bases—it is something of an exaggeration to call them tanged bases—are the most frequent tool : [2] they are thus indicated as being tools of a fishing industry, which was no doubt the chief occupation of the people who bequeathed the hearths to us.

Here and there groups of these flakes were found together, in a relative position which to the finders suggested *design :* as though they had been (let us say) blades of multiple fishing-spears from which the wooden shafts and binding thongs had decayed away. A comparison of these Bann flakes with tanged javelin-heads from Nörre-Lyngby has become current in the relevant literature, but we have only to glance at the contrast emphasized by such an illustration as that in Peake and Fleure's *Hunters and Artists*, p. 118, to see that the resemblance is superficial. The short stumpy tang of the Bann flakes has little in common with the business-like tang of the Danish implements : and to attempt to associate the two groups of artifacts in any way would involve us in chronological difficulties. It is worthy of passing notice that the complete absence of cores and hammerstones seems to indicate that these tools were not manufactured locally.[3]

In connexion with the Bann deposits, reference should be made to the " points " made of split bone, from 3 to 8 inches long, with a sharp point at one end and a blunted butt at the other. Mr. A. McL. May, who has described and figured them,[4] does not consider

---

[1] See C. F. C. Hawkes, " Engraved plaques of clay-slate from the Bann diatomite ", *Ulster* III 4 [1941] : 19, and references there.

[2] The line drawings in Knowles's paper, excellent though they are, should be supplemented by reference to the beautiful photographs, illustrating that of Jackson (*loc. cit. ante*).

[3] On the present state of knowledge regarding the geographical distribution of the Bann tanged flakes, see Dr. Raftery's paper, " The Bann Flake outside the Bann Valley ", JRSAI 74 [1944] : 155.

[4] " Some pointed bones [etc.] from the Lower River Bann," JRSAI 69 [1939] : 152.

that they are the points of fishing harpoons, presumably on account of the absence of barbs. He thinks that they were used in some construction of cords or nets to form a sort of fish-trap.

Other implements from the site include scrapers, flake knives, prickers, and borers, of typical Neolithic form, as well as arrow-heads, fabricators, and polished hatchet-heads of the ordinary type. Grindstones, whetstones, saddle-querns, and other later objects, have been found on the site ; but these come from the upper strata, not from the diatomaceous clay, and in the present connexion we may pass them over.

Besides the flake industry, as we have seen, the Bann has yielded evidence of the earlier penetration of bearers of the Asturian and the Campignian cultures inland along its course : presumably the com-munity which established the flourishing fishing station at Toome Bar, the outlet of Loch Neagh, followed this highway into the in-terior. As we have mentioned above, it has also produced the polished slate tools of which we must speak in the following chapter. These latter objects attracted the special attention of Dr. Jackson, who illustrates a selection of them in one of his photographic plates.

The " flake " element in the Larne industry is more prominent at Rough Island, at the northern end of Strangford Loch (Down).[1] This island is low-lying, and in the height of the Litorina period must have been completely submerged : the present high-water mark was then 18 feet below sea-level. When the land rose, toward the end of the period, the island was colonized by squatters who found sustenance in its abundant oysters and other shell-fish—some of them of species which haunt seas warmer than that of the locality under present conditions, and therefore indicating a climatic optimum. They had few needs—their extensive shell-midden, claimed to be the oldest post-glacial settlement-debris as yet discovered in Ireland, contained nothing artificial except charcoal (of oak, hazel and haw-thorn wood), and rude apologies for tools in the form of flakes and chips of flint. A later settlement, with Post-Mesolithic flints, overlay this early stratum.

When we turn to the industries of the Antrim coast we step back in time from the Bann sites. At Glenarm, about thirty-six miles north of Belfast, on the Antrim coast road, Movius excavated a Raised Beach section, to which Whelan had originally drawn attention,[2] lying over a glacial deposit of boulder clay.[3] The older deposit was pre-human, and contained no implements : but the

[1] H. L. Movius, " Report on a Stone Age excavation at Rough Island " (JRSAI 70 [1940] : 111). *Irish Stone Age*, p. 139 (and *s.v.* in index).
[2] In his paper, " Studies in the significance of the Irish Stone Age ", PRIA 42 [1934] : 121, especially p. 128.
[3] H. L. Movius, " A stone-age site at Glenarm, Co. Antrim ", JRSAI 67 [1937] : 181.

Raised Beach, and the soil above it, were rich in artifacts, and within it Movius distinguished two well-marked strata, as follows.

The lower group (Glenarm I) is essentially of the *blade-industry* : its tools are flake implements (chiefly knives and scrapers), coarsely fashioned, and as a rule showing no trace of retouching. Movius gives an elaborate and fully illustrated classification of these tools ; for this, reference must be made to his report, cited in the footnote. Some of them show evidence of heavy sea-rolling ; they had inferentially been swept up to the place where they were found, by storm-waves, from a lower level now submerged. Others, not necessarily of a later date, show no such indications—which means no more than that they happened to drop from their last owners' hands at spots further inland, beyond the reach of the sea. Although Glenarm I is roughly on the same geological level as the Larne industry, its types indicate a complete difference of environmental conditions in the life or the antecedents of the people to which it belonged : the axe-industry, as expressed by the Campignian pick, is absent, although a few specimens show a remote affinity with Asturian types. A cow's rib, with some marks of artificial treatment, was the only relic of an industry not of flint : it resembles the so-called " limpet-scoops " from the Oban caves.[1]

The upper group (Glenarm II) forms a stratum only about one-fifth of the thickness of the first, and contrasts with it impressively. Flake-axes (*tranchets*) are present, linking it to the Danish Mesolithic. In absolute chronology it seems to be contemporary with the British Neolithic : the land must have been still rising in Glenarm I, and become stabilized in Glenarm II—suggesting that Glenarm I is of the Litorina time (about 3000 B.C.) and Glenarm II of the later Sub-Boreal (*c.* 2500 B.C.). But the culture of Glenarm II is essentially Pre-Neolithic : the flake-axes, and the total absence of pottery are sufficient indications of that. The " time-lag " is already in operation.

In analysing the results of this excavation Dr. Movius reaches conclusions which appear to me to underline the remarks made already in this chapter, regarding the unsatisfactory nature of what may be called " topographical typology ". He tells us, that " Glenarm I appears to be a local specialization " of a " peripheral survival of the English Upper Palæolithic (Cresswellian) culture " which " presumably survived " in England until the 7th millennium B.C., and thereafter was kept alive in outlying places, such as Argyllshire. Is there not a danger that we may derive a false sense of chronological perspective, from the long æons of time so liberally doled out to the successive phases of the Palæolithic period—during which, generation

---

[1] The terminology is used here merely for convenience of reference : it is not intended to imply adherence to this theory of the use of such objects at either place.

after generation of unprogressive food-gatherers maintained a
stereotyped mode of life, until the subversive effects of slow climatic
changes had accumulated to an intensity sufficient to shake them out
of it ? A thousand years in the Old Stone Age was just as long as
a thousand years in our own—longer, indeed, when considered in
relation to the then shorter average duration of human life,[1] and the
more restricted scope for human interests and energies. The Mesolithic people were " speeded up " by their greater activities and by
their ever-increasing mutual intercourse : and, this being so, it is
surely not unreasonable to question if there is any real scientific
value in the proposition that a phase of culture in Ireland is a degeneration of a culture which, in England, had come to an end
4000 years earlier—an interval of time as long as that which separates
us from the supposed date of Moses, or even of Abraham. I have
read many books on the theory of the " diffusion of culture ", so
plausible that they have tempted me to ejaculate with king Agrippa
(as he is misrepresented by the Authorized Version) " Almost thou
persuadest me . . ." But even with a full acceptance of the theory
of the time-lag, I find it hard to believe that a man who lived at
Glenarm could never have chipped out a simple flint tool, to satisfy
his simple requirements, without incurring the risk of being prosecuted for infringing the patent of some contemporary of his
great[1]-great[2]-great[3]- . . . -great[117]-great[118]-grandfather, who lived at
Cresswell Crags !

  Mr. Whelan has reported his discovery, at Toome [2] (again upon
the Bann), of a settlement with flint artifacts showing affinities even
older than those which have been occupying our attention : it
is described by Movius as the only Early Post-glacial site in the
interior of the country.[3] Here was a community which manufactured
tools bearing an extraordinary, though admittedly degenerate,
resemblance to those of Aurignacian (early Upper Palæolithic)
cultures, including parrot-beak engravers and carinate scrapers.
Pollen analysis of the peat in which these relics were embedded
indicates a date on the transition from Boreal to Atlantic, when the
Alder was just beginning to establish itself. Whence and by what
route did these incongruous relics find their way to their resting-
place ? For the present, we must be content with docketing the
mere fact of a discovery, which adds one more knot to the terrible
tangle made of the beginnings of human occupation in Ireland by
the researches of the past dozen years.

  In the foregoing chapter, I have attempted to give a " bird's-eye
view " of this labyrinth—to vary the metaphor slightly—at the stage
to which its construction has thus far attained. Nothing more could

---

[1] On which see H. V. Vallois, " La durée de la vie chez l'homme fossile "
(*L'Anthropologie* 47 [1937] : 499, conveniently summarized in PPS 4 [1938] : 226).
  [2] INJ 4 [1933] : 149.   [3] *Irish Stone Age*, pp. 117-20.

be attempted in the few pages which can here be devoted to it. The reader who wishes to extend his knowledge is invited to follow up the footnote references, where he will find not only full statements of details which could here be presented in a brief abstract only, but also a wealth of illustrations without which it is impossible to distinguish between implements of various types.

An extensive amount of material for the study of pre-metal Ireland is now available : and Dr. Movius has heroically essayed the task of reducing it to an orderly sequence, at first in the elaborate report on his excavation at Cushendun, already cited, and later in his volume on the *Irish Stone Age*. With regard to the first-named, it would be impossible to summarize in these pages a paper so densely crowded with facts and with inferences : the reader must not only refer to, but sit down to and come to grips with it, if he wishes to understand and to appraise its full significance. Passing over the pre-human history of the site, its occupation layers are apparently three in number, which we here call I, II, III. Below I is a deposit of lagoon material in which some tools were found ; dropped accidentally into the water by fishermen, as Dr. Movius reasonably suggests. These tools are similar in type to those found in layer I, dated to the Early Atlantic (Early Litorina) period, and containing flint flake-blades. In layer II, Late Atlantic (Late Litorina), the implements tend towards the heavy tools of the classic Larne type ; and in layer III, Sub-Boreal (Modern Baltic), Dr. Movius recognizes a fully developed Neolithic. As has already been noticed, he repudiates the Asturian element which had been acknowledged by others, and he brings all these diverse forms together into one scheme, to which he gives the name *Larnian* (" Larnean " would be better), presented in successive evolutionary aspects—a scheme in which he finds a place for all the groups of implements discovered throughout Northern Ireland, from Toome Bar (which precedes Cushendun) to the Bann and to Glenarm II—which latter he equates to Cushendun III and dates as Neolithic.

We must " wait and see ". It is too early yet to accept *any* synthetic scheme, even as a working hypothesis, and Dr. Movius has himself given us grounds for hesitation. " Why ", he protests (p. 74), " with its very favourable environment and abundant flint supply, Ireland was not just as likely a place for the development of culture in Early Post-glacial times as elsewhere, it is difficult to understand. The region was fundamentally a refuge area." But the question, posed in the first sentence of this quotation, is answered by the second. A place " fundamentally a refuge area " is a place that essentially attracts refugees. Refugees, in Neolithic times, or earlier, cannot be imagined as sailing to their Promised Land in big flotillas : they must surely have come over in small independent groups, sometimes in mere isolated families (however the family

may have been organized), crossing over as they were compelled
by the postulated inconveniences (whatever these may have been)
of their old home, and as opportunity offered ; now here, now there ;
and establishing just that " conglomeration of intrusive elements from
widely separated geographical areas " which Dr. Movius (to me,
unaccountably) deprecates.   And moreover, we should remember—
what is often forgotten, but is not without importance—that refugees,
thus isolated, are likely to be afflicted with what we now call an
" inferiority complex ", retarding, perhaps for generations, all their
initiative and all their progress.   We should remember also, that a
systematic nomenclature, however Procrustean, does not necessarily
simplify a complicated subject.   To group collections of implements
into Larne I, Larne II, Larne III, does not make them any more
comprehensible than if we leave undisturbed the old and admittedly
haphazard labels Campignian, Asturian, Glenarm I and II, Bann,
Island Magee, and so forth—especially as some of the types in these
categories are apparently not found in Larne itself.   " Irish Flake- "
and " Irish Core-axe " Cultures is more like what is wanted—terms
sufficiently distinctive for definition, but committing us to nothing.

The foregoing paragraph was written before Dr. Movius's
monograph on the Irish Stone Age actually came into my hands.
After reading this monument of industry and erudition, I realized
that I had understood the ambiguous expression " a refuge area "
in a sense different from the author's intention.   I took it to mean
a kind of Noah's Ark, into which refugees from abroad had crowded,
to escape from some adversity incident to their life in their former
homeland :   I now gather that I should have understood it as sig-
nifying a stronghold from which its occupants refused to issue, to
avoid possible adversities outside ;   and into which foreign immigrants
did *not* penetrate, so that the ordered course of cultural evolution
progressed within its borders, unaffected by external influences.

But after consideration, I decided to let the paragraph stand as
I had written it.   The opinions there expressed are not seriously
modified by the changed definition.   This would assume the existence of an aboriginal indigenous population, of unknown but
presumably Palæolithic origin, within which this special " Larnian "
culture had automatically come into being.   But there is no real
evidence that there ever was such a population ;   and no reason to
expect that such evidence will ever be forthcoming.   Dr. Movius
appears to be aware of this difficulty, for (*Stone Age*, p. 120) he
admits that no trace of Pre-boreal sites has been found in the country,
and adds, almost regretfully, " such sites, if they exist, would have
an extremely important bearing on the origin of the Irish Mesolithic ".
But, so far as we know, they do *not* exist ;   science can take no account
of " might-have-beens " ;   and until some unexpected discovery

shall crystallize desire into reality, we must proceed on the assumption that the human species, and human industries, are Post-glacial importations into Ireland. The Toome site seems to be the earliest yet known ; and I am quite unable to see anything in common between its artifacts and those from " Early Larnian " sites at Cushendun and Rough Island (*op. cit.*, pp. 18, 25). I cannot interpret them otherwise than as representing two entirely different industries ; and if two could enter the country, there might be any number of such diverse immigrants.

The great wealth of the sites in artifacts—Dr. Movius does not hesitate to count Larne " among the richest secondary archæological localities in Europe " (*op. cit.*, p. 126)—is not necessarily a proof of extensive population ; rather does it indicate an intensive if not wasteful exploitation of lavish available wealth of raw material, by a long succession of unprogressive generations.

In a word, the revised sense given to the expression "refuge area " does not modify the difficulties involved in the assumption of an indigenous flint culture, overlying, and embracing, within its scope, all the heterogeneous aspects in which the flint industry of Ireland is manifested. In any case, a " civilization " is not likely to evolve in any isolated community, autonomous and self-centred, and debarred by a fairly wide sea-obstacle from external intercourse.

The earliest colonists found a home with a climate even moister than it is now. The land was covered, here with forests, there with forbidding swamps, swollen by the heavy rains and only partially drained by the large rivers ; elsewhere with barren stretches of rock. Nowhere was it by nature adapted for the cultivation of food-plants, even if the settlers had the desire or the skill to labour in that industry : there was no inducement to venture up the rivers, and so they left the interior to the undisturbed domination of formidable wild beasts which then haunted it. Except at Toome, no inland traces of the earliest colonists have been found : their remains are confined to the coast and to its immediate neighbourhood, where they display to us a consistent picture of primitive and unenterprising communities ; living chiefly on molluscs and fish, eked out with the flesh of such birds and animals as they were able to capture with their rudimentary traps or otherwise : and having little or no mutual relationship.

Food-gatherers are inevitably squeezed out after the arts of food-producing have by any means been established in the regions where they pass their unenterprising existence. Thereafter, they cannot compete with their more progressive neighbours in the battle of life ; sooner or later, they must either emigrate or perish. There were such backward peoples in Spain, on the coasts and islands of Great Britain, and in Denmark and Scandinavia. Ireland was in full view of some of the British sites : we need seek no further for the reasons underlying the first colonizations in Ireland, and for their heterogeneous origins and characteristics.

So far from becoming simpler, the history of the beginnings of human life and civilization the world over—not in Europe only, not in Ireland only—each year becomes more and more refractory against confinement in any all-embracing systematic scheme. The comprehensive phases of the Ice Age have been divided into sub-phases and under-sub-phases till we can scarcely see the wood for the trees. The simple stages of Palæolithic history, formulated by the early French authorities—Chellean, Acheulian, and the rest—have lost themselves in a similar wilderness of complications. And even the petty local Irish Mesolithic is diffusing rapidly into chaos—I will not say despairingly a hopeless chaos, but a chaos which, there is every reason to expect, will get very much worse before it begins to show any sign of getting better.[1]

[1] In connexion with the subject-matter of this chapter, a paper by A. W. Stelfox entitled " Geological and Prehistoric Traps " (INJ 7 [1936-7] : 317) should be read.

CHAPTER III

BALTIC AND IBERIAN IMMIGRANTS. THE LATER BEACHCOMBERS

WE have likened Ireland to a habitation with back as well as front doors ; and in the preceding chapter we have seen entrances on both sides opened, admitting immigrants diverse in culture, and also, as we cannot doubt, in race and in language—Campignians from the East, Asturians from the West, retaining these current, if more or less arbitrary, names for the sake of simplicity and convenience.

In the present chapter we are about to step upon rather thin ice. If this does not break under us, we shall see both doors once more opened, once more admitting a diversity of cultures ; the one from East and North, the other from West and South. The Apostolic mandate, *Test all things, hold fast that which is good*, is as valid in Archæology as in Theology ; and the reader must be warned at the outset that the matters which are now to occupy us are still under probation.

Dr. Adolf Mahr, when President of the Prehistoric Society, devoted a large part of his official address [1] to a preliminary account of certain remains of ancient culture, till then undescribed, for which, considering the nature of the sites in which its relics have been preserved, he proposed the name " Riverford Culture ".[2] This territory of Irish Archæology was unknown in 1928, and therefore no mention is made of it in our first edition ; even yet, all that we have to guide us is in the pioneer monograph quoted, and certain occasional criticisms thereanent, which are, however, little more than casual references.

The relevant discoveries have been made chiefly in the course of drainage operations, or in the freeing from obstructions of navigation channels, rendering it necessary to deepen former shallows adapted, in Antiquity, as fords across certain rivers. At such shallows fish are easy to capture, with cunningly devised trap-nets or otherwise ; and those who hold the fords also hold the trackways through the country, for the courses of these are automatically dictated by the positions of the fords. In fact, most ancient trackways even yet survive, on the routes which the fords established for all time, now developed into macadamized arterial roads, with bridges at the

---

[1] " New Aspects and Problems of Irish Prehistory ", PPS N.S. 3 [1937] : 261, especially pp. 283-331.

[2] The term (in the form " [lake and] river ford ", without the capital initial letters which give it a technical status) had been anticipated by Mr. Whelan : see PRIA 42 [1934] : 122.

old ford-sites.[1]   Settlements of fishing communities became established at the shallows, in forest-clearances on the river banks : and these settlements have provided the material upon which the theory of the " Riverford Culture " is based.

The typical objects are all of stone : metal tools have been found in some of the sites, but these are certainly later intrusions.   The stone used is not flint : associated flint tools have been found, it is true, in sites on the Bann, but this is an intelligible exception, as the Bann valley enjoys easy access to the Antrim flint-layers ; in the regions of the southern ford-sites, flint would be practically unobtainable.   So far as the facts hitherto collected permit of a judgement being formed, the stone favoured at each site is of the kind most easily available in the locality ; but, viewing the material as a whole, tools of schists or of slates are in a clear majority.

Weapons as well as tools are included in the collection.   These as a rule take the form of heavy clubs—to be used, not necessarily in human combat (though some of them would be quite effective for such a purpose), but for killing large fish.   Wooden clubs or mallets are used by modern anglers to administer the quietus to spent fish : and it is to the same end, in Dr. Mahr's belief, that the slate clubs were fashioned.

In fact, as he reminds us, heavy wooden bludgeons lie in the background of all such massive stone " pounders ".   Clubs, used either in hand-to-hand combat by striking, or from a distance by throwing, are among the most deadly of the engines available in primitive warfare, against both man and beast.   They must have been in far more nearly universal use, in ancient times, than the archæologist would suspect if he see with his bodily eye only ; for at least ninety-nine per cent. of the ancient specimens must long before now have perished utterly, by disintegration of the wood.

The sites of the Riverford Culture, accordingly, lie along the courses of the larger rivers—more particularly, the Bann, the Shannon, the Barrow, the Erne ; either at shallows on those rivers, or (and this especially) at the outlets of lakes from or through which the rivers flow.   River fish provided the staple diet of the settlers, just as the shore-dwellers lived chiefly upon the produce of the coastal sea-shallows : and, according to the fundamental hypothesis, the Riverford Folk travelled up the rivers in search of suitable habitation-sites, clearing them, when selected, of their forest-growths ; afterwards erecting weirs and traps, to capture the salmon in their annual migrations, at the narrows and the fords which determined the selection in every case.

The characteristic Riverford tools are :—

[1] In this connexion an interesting article on " The Winding Road ", by Mr. F. G. Roe (*Antiquity* 13 [1939] : 191), is worth reading.

1. *Clubs*, in the shape of slabs of slate, with triangular blades, from the apex of which a short handle projects. These objects may have served a variety of uses, besides the fish-killing function already indicated. Some of them, in which the side edges of the more or less triangular head have been sharpened, could have been used as choppers or cleavers : others, in which the base of the triangle is sharpened, might have served as log-splitting wedges. Such carpentry tools would be essential for a fishing industry of any elaboration, which would call for the construction of weirs and the like, as well as of canoes.

2. Similar clubs or *cleavers*, but with the blade rather more oval in outline than in the first type.

[*By permission, Prehistoric Society.*

FIG. 3.—Types of Riverford Implements.

(1. Club ; 2. Cleaver ; 3. Hatchet-head type ; 4. Macehead ; 5. Sinker ; 6. Small Cleaver.)

3. Tools of *hatchet-head* type, in that they are made of stone bars, are more or less oval (convex or flattened) in cross section, pointed at the butt end and brought to a screwdriver (double-bevel) edge at the point end : but differentiated from ordinary hatchet-heads by their enormous size, the length ranging from about 1 foot 3 inches to about 2 feet 4 inches. Naturally, the weight of such a tool would prevent its being mounted upon an ordinary hatchet-handle : the largest of the specimens recorded by Dr. Mahr (from Portglenone on the Antrim side of the Bann) weighs 24½ lb.

4. *Mace-heads*—oval or cylindrical blocks of hard stone, perforated for a handle.

5. *Fishing-sinkers*—more or less circular discs of shale, with a hole pierced through the middle.

6. Small cleavers, choppers, adzes, etc., of slate—often, to all appearance, mere adaptations of blade-like tools fashioned by nature—found in considerable numbers in the Shannon sites. Some of these show signs of having been shaped or trimmed by a sawing process.

With these stone objects, Dr. Mahr associates the bone points, mentioned above (p. 35), which, notwithstanding Mr. May's opinion there quoted, he considers to have been used as elements in the construction of fishing-spears with multiple points—three or four being mounted at the end of a wooden shaft in a diverging fan-wise disposition.   In fact, it will not escape notice that, in a sense, the Riverford Culture here takes the place of the Bone Industry, the third of Menghin's primary classes of Old Stone Age handicrafts. Mahr considers that the tanged flint flakes, of the Bann sites, were likewise heads of multiple fishing-spears.

The occasional appearance of metal objects in association with the Riverford Culture is easily explained.   The Riverford squatters could not have maintained a permanent monopoly of the fords ; wayfarers of every cultural category must have made use of them. Among these, any individual might stumble in the slippery mud of the river-bottom, relaxing his hold on some treasured object, and losing it, often irrecoverably.   Or he might find himself confronted by a hostile company, established for the special purpose of restraining transit across a river-boundary separating two neighbouring territories : an encounter from which it would be hard to escape without loss of goods, if at all.   Accidents such as these could have happened long after the Riverford settlement itself had passed into history, or at least had outgrown its specific cultural character.

Referring the reader to Dr. Mahr's paper for details, we may say here that he enumerates with more or less certainty thirty-six sites of this peculiar culture, distributed as follows :—

On the Bann	12
Elsewhere in the North . . .	6 [1]
In Connaught	4 [1]
On the Shannon	8
Elsewhere in the South . . .	6 [1]

For the ultimate origin of the Riverford Culture, Dr. Mahr looks to the uplands of Finland, where analogous relics are to be found.   He quotes the excavations at Skara Brae (Orkney) [2] and at Jarlshof (Shetland), [3] as yielding similar implements ; and on the basis of these correlations he traces a line of route from the Baltic Sea, passing through the northern and western Scottish islands, and ending, so far as the sea-voyage is concerned, at the Irish river estuaries.   He then shows us the immigrants making their way up the rivers, and finally establishing themselves at the inland ford-shallows, where we find them.

The evidence for this hypothesis has been marshalled with consummate skill ; but as yet it is scanty in tangible material ;

---

[1] Under some of these a few independent sites of minor importance are grouped together, thus increasing the actual number.

[2] See V. G. Childe, *Skara Brae* (London 1931).

[3] See Curle's reports, P.S.A. Scot. vols. 66-70.

the North Scottish analogies to me seem incomplete ; [1] and further evidence, from outside as well as from inside Ireland, is needed, to enable us to exclude what are still possible alternative explanations —for example, that these non-flint stone objects are merely the makeshifts of an indigenous population compelled to do the best they could with whatever materials came to hand, in the absence of any local flint-supply. More recently, Dr. Raftery has published slate implements from various inland counties,[2] in which he recognizes Baltic affinities and a certain typical individuality ; though he apparently dissociates himself from the leading chronological and cultural implications of the " Riverford " doctrine. But if these natural doubts should hereafter be resolved, in the light of future investigation, then a further line of research (at the moment rather more speculative, but not without promise of solid results in the future) would be opened up by geographical coincidences, to which Dr. Mahr calls attention, between his conclusions and those of Professor Eoin MacNeill. The latter scholar, basing his work entirely on historical and genealogical considerations, and without any reference to the evidence of Archæology, drew up a map setting forth the distribution in Ireland of communities identified with the *Cruithne*, the name given in Irish literature to the aboriginal people known more generally as the *Picts :* a people whose nature and origin present problems which are the nightmare of British ethnology.[3] The virtual identity of MacNeill's map of "Picts" and of Mahr's map of Riverford sites would be astonishing if the correspondences were a mere matter of accident : [4] and it might very well be established from a combination and extension of their independent researches, that the Picts of Ireland and of Scotland were a (probably Turanian) people of Baltic origin.

Further evidence, pointing in the same direction, may possibly be presented by the enigmatical inscriptions, found upon ornamental sculptured slabs in the Scottish Pictland. These are few in number, scanty in content, and admittedly beyond our best efforts at interpretation. It follows that they cannot be forced to bear a weight too great for their (and our) capacity. But two positive assertions can be made about them without the least hesitation : they are confined to a region which was occupied by Picts at the time to which the

---

[1] I had written " nebulous " here, but changed the adjective on discovering that Messrs. Davies and Evans had anticipated me by applying it to the whole " Riverford " theory : *Ulster* III 6 [1943] : 14.

[2] *Ulster* III 5 [1942] : 121.

[3] See especially E. MacNeill, " The Pretanic Background in Britain and Ireland ", JRSAI 63 [1933] : 1.

[4] The two maps are set side by side in Mahr, *op. cit.* p. 329. The only serious divergence is the absence of Riverford sites for the territory of the *Ciarraige* of North Kerry. This, however, might be due to the accident that hitherto no discoveries happen to have been made there : a negative is notoriously an unstable foundation upon which to build. But we are still badly in need of corroborative evidence to bear on both sides of the suggested identification.

art of their sculptures obliges us to date them,[1] and therefore they may reasonably be called Pictish ; and, whatever their language may be, it is certainly not Celtic—the pitiful futility of *all* the numerous attempts that have been made to interpret them on a Celtic basis is enough to demonstrate that.   A short time ago, once more working independently of the researches both of Mahr and of MacNeill, after examining personally every one of these mysterious inscriptions in order to secure accurate copies, I endeavoured to make a grammatical analysis of their contents so as to try to find if their words would hang together on any admissible linguistic basis, even though an actual translation might not be attainable.   The result was a surprise to myself—a Turanian system of construction revealed itself, not perhaps demonstrably (the material is too scanty for that), but at least persuasively, amid the encircling gloom.[2]   This minor study may possibly be found in the end to contribute its mite to the elucidation of the problems involved.

The Riverford people would fill the gap between the Beach-combers' of the preceding chapter and the Megalith-builders with whom we are presently to become acquainted.   That is, they would take the place of an early Neolithic people in Ireland : for the doubts expressed with ever-increasing emphasis by qualified writers, as to whether the word " Neolithic " should be used at all in connexion with Irish Archæology, are very far from unreasonable.   Owing to the exceptional stone technique of the Riverford people—the result of their voluntary or involuntary avoidance of flint—we can hardly call these people " Neolithic ", in any strict or narrow sense of the term : certainly they have little in common with the orthodox Neolithic of other regions.   In the Baltic regions, the " Arctic " slate culture exists, side by side with, but quite independently of, a flint culture of normal Neolithic character : [3]   Ireland in its own way presents the same phenomenon, although we may remind ourselves that the proximity of siliciferous deposits to the Bann valley makes a mingling of cultures there inevitable.   The reason for this differentiation would be the same in both regions : the slate-users were an intrusive folk, who had come from some region where flint was not, and who had carried with them a culture which their circumstances had compelled them to develop and to establish, following a different course, and making use of different materials.

---

[1] Professor MacNeill observed to me that in most if not all of these cases the inscription appears to be an intrusive addition to the ornamented stone, adapting it as a (second-hand) monument after the Pictish people had learnt to write : and the appearances certainly seem to justify the observation.

[2] See my essay, " The Inscriptions and Language of the Picts " in *Féilsgribhinn* (= " *Festschrift* ") *Eoin mhic Néill* (Dublin 1940), p. 184 ; and E. MacNeill, " The Language of the Picts ", *Yorkshire Celtic Studies* [1938-9] : 3.

[3] See Axel Bagge, " Om skifferspetsarna i svensk stenålder ", *Fornvännen* 18 [1923] : 9.   See also Ebert's *Reallexikon s.v.* " Schiefergerät " (and references there) ; also *s.v.* " Nordischer Kreis A " and plates 47-50 : and Montelius, " Minnen från Lapparnes stenålder i Sverige ", *Månadsblad*, 1874 : 97.

The early discovered, and easily collected, wealth of Ireland in gold started the inhabitants of the country, whatever their origin, upon the path of metallurgy ; an industry further extended as the rich endowment of copper at their service was gradually revealed. In such circumstances, a culture based exclusively upon stone would come to a premature end.

The northern-and-eastern front-door may thus ultimately prove to have admitted an energetic immigration, which left its mark permanently upon the culture of Ireland ; and bequeathed a very considerable share of its blood to the racial complex now inhabiting the country. Contemporary with these, the western [1] back-doors admitted certain isolated cultural phenomena, rather than a continuous culture-system. Through these portals we trace the effects of intercourse rather than of immigration, at the early date with which we are still concerned ; in the next stage of our study they assume a greater significance.

The old stories of our scholastic historians, who looked to Spain (when they were not looking to Scythia) as the land of their origin, may be dismissed without discussion. They are based, we now know, on misunderstandings of the history of Orosius, and on the superficial resemblance of the names " Iberia " and " Hibernia ". (Even less important are modern popular fancies that the folk of the West owe their dark complexions to the influx of Spanish blood carried by survivors of the shipwrecked Armada.) That there is a deep-rooted foundation of Mediterranean racial affinity in the Irish amalgam is commonly assumed, though the assumption has not escaped challenge in these sceptical days. [2] We must keep ourselves reminded that we are yet in the fact-gathering stage, and must wait in patience before we can begin to assimilate and interpret our accumulations.

For the moment, there are only two relics which call for attention in this connexion, and at this stage of our study ; the *Moytirra beakers* and the *Clonfinloch stone*. These are vauntcouriers of an invasion of Iberian culture (if not of Iberian race), which the following Megalithic Age witnessed in its full strength.

The pottery vessel known as the *beaker* apparently originated in Spain, about the time of transition between the Age of Stone and the Age of Metal. Its shape suggests that it was an attempt to copy a suspended bag or purse of leather : and it is generally accepted that the Iberian Peninsula was the primary centre of

---

[1] The Shannon and the Erne estuaries are admittedly in the West, but *ex hypothesi* the Riverford people must have approached those rivers from the North and East. The more or less figurative language in the text may therefore be allowed to stand.

[2] As will be seen on reference to Dr. G. M. Morant's paper, " The Craniology of Ireland ", JRAI 66 [1936] : 43 ff., especially p. 55.

distribution from which it spread over other parts of Europe.[1] Of the form of this vessel, and of its later development, the tulip-beaker, and of the movements of peoples associated therewith, we can more appropriately speak in a future chapter.

It is an important principle, which will come to our notice at intervals throughout our present study, that the lessons to be learnt from the distribution of pottery-types are different from those suggested by the distribution of stone or of metal. Stone and metal are more or less unbreakable. An object in these materials could conceivably pass uninjured from hand to hand, in a succession of barter-transactions, across the whole breadth of Eurasia from Finisterre to Corea. But the probability of a material so brittle as pottery surviving even a short journey, under ancient conditions of transport, is small indeed : so that when we find a *type of pottery* in some place in which it is exotic, we may reasonably infer the personal presence of exotic *potters*. A foreigner—let us say, a captured slave—undertaking to make a pot, would naturally do so in his or her traditional way. The beakers normally found in Great Britain are of the late tulip-beaker type, as we shall see in good time ; and so are the very few contemporary beakers which Ireland has yielded. But some fragments of bell-beakers, of Spanish type, were found long ago in one of the tumuli at Moytirra (Sligo), which place they (or their makers) had presumably reached by way of one of the western portals (see Fig. 28, p. 184). There seem to have been three such vessels ; but unfortunately the mound was dug, first, by the local tenant, one Pat Regan, who brought " the full of a good-sized hand-basket of human bones " to Lady L. Tennison, then " exploring " in the neighbourhood : and afterwards by a certain Bartly Foley, who found the potsherds.[2] In such circumstances it is hopeless to try to recover anything of value about the discovery, save in so far as the association of this essentially Iberian form of pottery with an apparently Megalithic monument is indicative of direct Iberian influence.

Of much greater importance is the Clonfinloch stone (Plate I), a slab lying on a slope near the farmstead of that name in the county of Offaly, a short distance from Clonmacnois. It was first described by Rev. James Graves,[3] who tells us that it was locally called " The Fairy Stone ", and that a mysterious horseman was alleged to ride

---

[1] See the elaborate and fully documented article " Glockenbecherkultur " in Ebert's *Reallexikon der Vorgeschichte*. See also C. F. C. Hawkes, *The Prehistoric Foundations of Europe* (London 1940), index, *s.v.* " Pottery, (Bell-)Beaker " : Ivor Herring, " The Beaker Folk " (*Ulster* III 1 [1938] : 135).

[2] See Wood-Martin, *The Rude Stone Monuments of Ireland* (Dublin 1888), p. 183. See also Bremer's observations, PRIA 38 [1926] : 27.

[3] James Graves, " On a boulder with presumed pagan carvings at Clonfinlough, King's Co.", JRSAI 8 [1865] : 354 ; M. C. Burkitt, " Notes on the art upon certain megalithic monuments in Ireland ", *Jahrbuch für prähistorische und ethnographische Kunst*, Leipzig 1926, p. 52.

round it from time to time. It measures 9 feet 9 inches in length by 8 feet 3 inches in breadth. Incised devices almost completely cover the flat upper surface, which is, as it were, divided into two compartments by an imaginary line. On one side of the line there are cup-marks, cruciform figures, and depressions in the shape of foot-prints ; on the other side, there are several repetitions of a figure resembling the Greek letter φ. Graves, writing in the early sixties of the last century, took this symbol for a representation of a penannular brooch, which, indeed, it resembles : it would be un-reasonable to chide one, who in his day laboured incessantly in the service of Irish Archæology, for being unaware of facts at the time not available ; and for his consequent inevitable failure—which the very title of his paper betrays—to appreciate the great significance of the monument. After Graves's publication, Archæologists lost sight of the stone altogether. But in the year 1920, M. l'Abbé Breuil, during a visit to me in Dublin, showed me some photographs of his most recent discoveries of Neolithic wall-paintings in Spanish caves. I suddenly remembered the lithograph of the Clonfinloch stone published by Graves, and, taking the volume down from my shelves, I placed it beside the photographs. My visitor at once agreed that there was an apparent identity of style and purpose between the Irish carvings and the Spanish paintings, and that the two were undoubtedly cognate. This was confirmed by a subsequent examination of the stone itself, which we made together. The Spanish analogies enable us to identify the φ-shaped characters as conventional figures of men, with the arms looped at the sides in the attitude called " a-kimbo ". The sculptor desired to represent a number of men on one side of the engraved stone surface, some of them, apparently, holding weapons. The cross-like figures may also represent men ; it might be thought that the φ convention, once established, would have been carried out consistently, but this is not borne out by the Spanish analogies, in which different forms of convention are often used simultaneously. It may also be that these figures are not all men : some of them have no heads, and the loops are not circular or oval, but D-shaped. Spanish analogies again suggest that the figures showing this peculiarity may be bow-and-arrow combinations. (See Plate I.)

But interpretation of a jumble of rudimentary figures like these must necessarily be a matter of mere conjecture. Our imagination, however, is not altogether unaided, for, in the Spanish homeland of the form of art which it exemplifies, there are groups, more realistic in character, clearly representing hunting, dancing, or fighting scenes—the usual activities, in fact, of primitive communities. What-ever specific interpretation we may choose to put upon the Clon-finloch sculpture, it is certainly the oldest contemporary record of any historical event in Northern Europe : for it is the sign-manual of an expedition which, for some now irrecoverable reason, must have made its way from Spain at a date in the course of the Stone-Bronze Overlap, entered the Shannon estuary, and sailed up the river to the very heart of Ireland, where the stone is lying.   The apparent weapons suggest that it was a military, probably a hostile expedition ; and the battle-scenes figured in the wall-painting of Alpera, or the lively combat of Morella la Vella,[1] may be Spanish prototypes of this ancient scene of strife.   Perhaps the men contemplating the sculptured field are victors in some encounter : before them is the battle-field, printed with the foot-marks of the flying foe, strewn with weapons cast away in their flight and with missile stones.   Or perhaps the engraving was executed before an expected engagement, the purpose being less to preserve a record for posterity than to secure the victory by magic : for recourse to magic to this in- tention is a commonplace among the materials of Ethnology.   It may even be that the local legend of the horseman may be a last lingering recollection of processions circling round the stone, as wizards sang their incantations.   Undoubtedly this sculpture was not made without some serious purpose : and whatever that purpose may have been—whether the crude guesses which we have here offered are approximately correct or are wildly off the mark—the stone is a monument of local (or even universal) history beyond all price.

After the Riverford people, who still belong to the dawn-period of the later Stone Age, we might have expected to find in Ireland a fully developed Neolithic culture.   But, as we have already indi- cated, this we fail to find.   Metal, in the form of copper tools, comes early into use : while, on the other hand, stone continues late—in fact, the prehistoric culture of Ireland, almost to the last, is an inextricable interlacement of stone-age and metal-age cultures, which often presents disconcerting anomalies.   The climatic " time- lag " preserves, in effective use, forms and expedients elsewhere obsolete ; while, at the same time, it blocks the introduction of innovations till long after they have become not only established but even antiquated in other regions.

The persistence of the beachcombing mode of life, from the early immigrants onwards through all the subsequent centuries— right on to our own day—is a notable illustration of the time-lag principle.   Ireland is girded round with a ring of shore-dwellers' sites of every possible date : collectors of cockles and periwinkles may be seen even yet, carrying on the chief industry of " Mesolithic Ireland " over sand flats, left bare at low tide.   Such sites tell us

---

[1] For Alpera see *L'Anthropologie* 23 [1912] : 529.   A representation of the Morella la Vella painting can be conveniently found in Schmidt's *Dawn of the Human Mind* (English translation 1936), facing p. 192.

of people living, like the earliest immigrants, on sea-produce ; but their midden heaps show that they kept cattle also. There is no indigenous breed of cattle, large or small, in Ireland : these animals must therefore have been imported on rafts or in canoes, for there was no practicable land-bridge at this time. The kine must have been ferried over as young calves ; no vessel then available could possibly have transported full-grown animals.[1] For the greater part, these later beachcombers appear to have belonged to the same immigrant stock as their inland contemporaries, having been compelled by poverty to sink to the archaic mode of life in which we find them : but mingled with them were representatives of earlier peoples, surviving from the times with which this and the preceding chapter are more especially concerned. In certain of the midden heaps, where the associated sea-shells indicate a climate rather warmer than at present, a few skulls have been found, long and narrow, but (unlike the Kilgreany skull) with high vaults ; though in some cases with the relative broadness of face which we see in that specimen.

Many artifacts, both in stone and bronze, as well as numerous sherds of pottery, have been unearthed in shore sites [2] : in fact, these valuable deposits have suffered severely from the depredations of collectors of the baser sort, who have found in them cheap and easy sources for filling their cabinets.[3] The most important shore site is Whitepark Bay, at Ballintoy (Antrim), which has yielded spoil to collectors unnumbered, but seems now to be a practically exhausted mine. Stratification layers have been dug over recklessly, and hut-sites torn in pieces—an army of destroying conquerors invading a peaceful village could not have wrought greater havoc.

The sites, especially in the north of Ireland—Whitepark Bay, Portstewart (Londonderry), Dundrum (Down), to mention only three of major importance—had been preserved, generally speaking, till the " collecting era ", by being covered by beds of sand, which accumulated over them during the intervening centuries. Through these sand-banks there run the occupation levels, indicated by one or more horizontal black layers ; the black colour being produced partly by carbon from the domestic fires, but principally by the decomposition of organic materials.

[1] I owe this suggestion to Mr. A. W. Stelfox.
[2] A list of shore sites, discovered down to the time of publication, will be found in JRSAI 44 [1914] : 183, but it needs revision (especially in the verification of references) and augmentation, even without any consideration of the results of the subsequent quarter-century of research. The rich series of flint implements of all kinds, illustrated by Dr. D'Evelyn, from Maghera (Donegal) must not be overlooked (JRSAI 63 [1933] : 88). It is surely needless to remark that the presence of metal in some of these sites makes it altogether injudicious to assign a Neolithic date and culture to others which, very likely by mere accident, possess no metal. Indeed, even *iron* slag has been found in settlements on the ferruginous sands at the mouth of the Bann.
[3] See the trenchant remarks of Mr. Knowles, JRSAI 17 [1885] : 104 ff.

At some sites, as at Ballintoy, there are caves, which might have afforded convenient habitations, permanent or seasonal—though the excavation of the Ballintoy caves has not encouraged us to identify, with any assurance, their inhabitants with the people who left the relics on the adjacent shore of Whitepark Bay.[1] When caves were not available, or (like most shore caves) were unserviceable by reason of tidal flooding, the squatters built them huts, circular on plan, constructed presumably either of intertwined flexible rods, after the manner of Zulu kraals, or (more probably) of logs, as in the habitations of the Navajos, bound together in a conical form—the outside of the structure being protected from weather, in either case, with earth-sods, or perhaps with hides.[2] The wooden framework was kept in position by being girded with a kerb of stones outside the feet of the uprights, which prevented them from spreading laterally. The wood having naturally perished, the ring of stones is all that remains of the dwelling : Knowles, in the paper last referred to, gives a plan of such a ring, which he found at Whitepark Bay, but which was utterly destroyed by some of those who came after him. It was circular, 27 feet in internal diameter : the ring was only one, or at most, two stones in thickness, and nowhere more than one stone in height, so that it would be absurd to take it as the base of a stone beehive hut. The village on Carrowkeel Mountain, which will come into view in a later chapter, is now represented by a group of similar stone rings ; most likely this was a normal mode of construction, especially for the poorer dwellings. Only by chance would a ring of comparatively small stones survive at all ; for after the wood of the house had rotted away, the stones would be at the mercy of any local Balbus who wanted to build a wall. And only by chance would the ring, even if it survived, be noticed by a modern visitor.

The black layer, as a whole, may be a few inches deep only : but the floors of the hut sites have thick beds of accumulation, indicating that they had been sunk as pits, beneath the outside level of occupation. The sand covering the occupation layer was in places found to be as much as 20 to 30 feet in thickness, when the exploitation of the sites began, in the seventies of the last century. Mr. Knowles has pointed out [3] that this accumulation could not be due to wind-action alone, as such would remove the sand at about the same rate as it would deposit it : he attributes it to the growth of grass over the well-fertilized occupation-layer, which captured and retained the sand falling upon it—thus forming another layer, fertilized in its turn by the decomposition of the grass, over which the process was repeated indefinitely. Coins and other later objects, dropped on an upper level of later formation, have sometimes worked

---

[1] The results of this work are summarized on a later page.
[2] In this connexion read J. G. D. Clark on " Mesolithic Houses ", PPS 5 [1939] : 98.
[3] Loc. cit., also PRIA 16 [1881] : 106.

their way down through the sand, and have been found in incongruous association with the early remains : but it should be emphasized that many of the shore sites in the country are themselves of a comparatively late date. Each one has to be appraised separately, without reference to the others. We need do no more than study collections of flint implements from different sites to convince ourselves of this : every possible variety of technique is illustrated ; and every possible kind of tool or weapon that can be made in this material is represented. In shore sites in the South and West, where flint is not available, the squatters had to make shift with more or less shapeless stone chips, often hardly recognizable as implements at all. On the East coast, in the sandhills sites, flint begins to thin out about Cranfield Point (Louth), though it is still found in minute flakes as far south as Dublin.[1] But within reach of the Antrim chalk, flint was accessible and was freely used.

Of all the implements yielded by the shore sites, *Scrapers* are by far the commonest : they are of a wide range of variety in shape, and show considerable differences in the skill with which they are made ; some of them are neatly formed, with delicate secondary chipping on the working edge ; others are merely roughed out. They served many purposes : with a scraper, its owner could clean the hides of animals, could smooth down wooden surfaces, could reduce to powder lumps of such substances as ochre : every day of his life he would find a fresh use for this tool.

Only a specialist treatise on flint implements could afford space for the enumeration and adequate illustration of the different varieties of scrapers which have been isolated and described by writers on the subject : a handbook, covering so wide a field as the present work, cannot enter into such minute details.[2] Scrapers are scrapers, whether they are ear-shaped, oyster-shaped, kite-shaped, or anything else. It is possible that each specific form was connected with its own specific aspect of industry : it is possible that an elaborate classification of the varieties of this implement will advance knowledge in the technological, chronological, and ethnological questions, the solution of which is the chief end of the study of flint implements. But these possibilities cannot yet be established as certainties.

Two forms of scrapers may, however, be accorded a special mention—the ridged scraper (often called, on account of its shape, " the slug ") ; and the notched scraper. The one has a flat base, and a rounded back, by which it could be held in using the tool as a smoothing " rubber ". The other has a hollow notch in its edge,

[1] PRIA 17 [1891] : 619 ; contrary evidence presented by R. Welch, JRSAI 36 [1906] : 85. Pottery, plentiful in the Antrim and Down shore sites, also appears to thin out further south, and most of the reports from the southern sites make no mention of it. Fanore (Clare) is an exception : PRIA 22 [1901] : 353. .
[2] A few references to such classifications are given in a later chapter.

which could be used for the purpose of smoothing down a rod of wood intended to serve as a javelin- or arrow-shaft.[1]

Tranchets, or " Flake-axes ", like those which we have already noticed in the earlier sites, persist in some of the later settlements, such as Whitepark Bay. There are also roughly chipped *Axes* and *Choppers*—the latter being described by Knowles as "spalls of flint not dressed to any particular shape, but having in some part a cutting edge, which one can easily see has been used for cutting or chopping ".[2] He proved by experiment that one of these tools was serviceable for cutting a branch from a tree. Only as rare exceptions are polished stone tools to be found in these shore-settlements.

Another specific form of tool, though classed by Mr. Knowles in the general heading of " knives ", may be called an *Oblique-edged Tranchet*. This resembles the tranchet in general form, but the edge, instead of being at right angles to the long axis of the tool, makes a more or less acute angle with it, so that whatever object is operated upon is struck not with an edge but with a point. If fitted chisel-wise into a handle, such a tool might have been used for cutting hides, or else for splitting bones or wooden rods.

Knives, like " scrapers ", is a general term which covers a large number of various-looking implements, whose use it would be impossible to discriminate specifically. They are blades of flint, having cutting edges, usually touched up with secondary chipping, sometimes to the extent of approximating them to the appearance of a saw. Here and elsewhere, variety of form may be significant of inequalities in the technical skill of individual makers, rather than of varieties in the destined use of the implements.

Javelin- and *Arrow-heads* are not common, except in the later settlement sites : a fuller description of their various types would therefore be more appropriate to a subsequent chapter (p. 110). We regard the large forms as points of *javelins* (intended to be cast from the hand) rather than of *spears* (retained in the grasp of the wielder) : because, if the spear had been invented in the Stone Age, that useful weapon would surely have been tipped with bronze much sooner than was actually the case. The absence of arrow-heads at Whitepark Bay was emphasized by Knowles ; but a triangular specimen was found by Blake Whelan in the oldest occupation layer.[3] This does not encourage us to admit the vast antiquity which some have claimed for the Whitepark site.

Awls, or *Borers*, chips of flint with a sharp point formed at the end, are not infrequent.

More heterogeneous are the *Flakes* and *Cores*, terms which must of necessity form general classificatory dump-heaps for objects

---

[1] It has also been explained as a two-toothed saw. Experiment has shown that it is possible to cut through a stick with such a tool : but on the whole the explanation in the text above seems more probable.

[2] *Op. cit.* p. 112.　　　　　　　　[3] INJ 4 [1932] : 95.

incapable of distribution under more specific headings. Flakes are the spoils from the operation of manufacture—the chips struck off from a flint in reducing it to a desired shape. They may also be failures, cast away by the maker. They were, however, not all waste material—sometimes the edge of a flake shows signs of use, as though

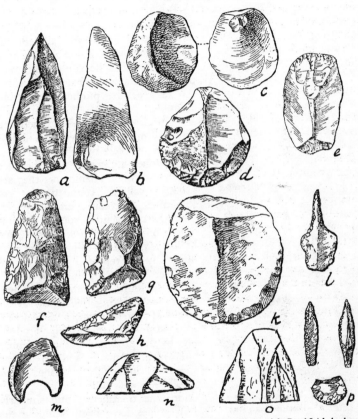

[*By permission of the Royal Irish Academy.*

FIG. 4.—Flint Implements from Shore Sites.

(After Knowles : *a, b, c,* Flakes ; *d, e,* Scrapers ; *f,* Flake axe ; *g, h,* oblique Flake-axe ; *k,* Chopper ; *l,* Awl ; *m,* Notched Scraper ; *n,* Ridged Scraper ; *o,* Core ; *p,* Pygmy Flints.)

it had been picked up and made to serve some passing need of the moment. Cores are what is left of the nodules after serviceable tools have been chipped off from them. These are rarely of large size : even in the flint region the makers were economical, and used as much of the raw material as was possible.

For the manufacture of flint tools two instruments were necessary, a Hammer and an Anvil.

The *Hammer* was any hard stone, of a size and shape to be grasped conveniently in the hand. Such stones, displaying the marks of abrasion resulting from their use (in pounding, striking, or crushing) are common in the shore sandhills and in other domestic sites.[1]

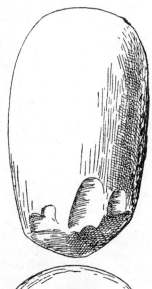

In the later settlements quartzite is the material most commonly used; but Knowles notes especially that in earlier sites, such as Larne, the only hammers which he could find were pointed flints, at least down to 1883, the date of the publication quoted below.[2]

The *Anvil* has been identified in a type of stone block, in which a hollow has been worked by repeated blows. Such stones are common in the sites which also contain hammers; they are usually oval and rounded, but are sometimes discoidal; and they display a circular cup-shaped or conical hollow on one or on both sides. This hollow is presumed to have been produced by the repeated impact of the hammer while chipping the flints: Knowles found specimens at Dundrum Bay showing the hollow at all stages of development, and he made successful experiments in producing, by the process suggested, similar hollows in stones picked up on the shore.[3] Some of the stones upon which he was thus operating split

[*By permission of the Royal Irish Academy.*
FIG. 5.—Hammer and Anvil.
After Knowles.

under the treatment; and similarly split stones have been found in the shore sites.

As might be expected, the hollow formed in this casual manner is often quite rough : but sometimes it is so smooth and symmetrical as to suggest lingering doubts as to whether the " anvil " explanation is complete. It may be that the hollow, started in the manner suggested, was afterwards worked up to serve some other purpose—

[1] For illustrations see PRIA 22 [1901] : 344, Fig. 14 ; 382, Figs. 115, 116.
[2] PRIA 16 : 210.
[3] PRIA 16 : 112 ; for illustrations see PRIA 22 [1901] : 382, Figs. 117-18 ; JRSAI 17 [1885], plate vii (facing p. 114).

such as that of a small mortar, for pulverizing ochre to make paint; of an oil or tallow lamp; or of a breast-pad, for holding firm the free end of a rotating drill.

After the first hollow had been sunk to a certain depth, a second hollow was begun—sometimes on the same side as the first,[1] but much more commonly on the opposite side. Seldom if ever are the opposing hollows in such a position, or of such a shape, as to afford an easy grasp to the thumb and fingers; this is enough to forbid us to call these objects " hammer-stones ".

The abundant literature relating to Whitepark Bay has been systematically and conveniently analysed by Rev. L. M. Hewson,[2] with long extracts from papers extending over fifty years of work. One of the most disconcerting revelations of this summary is the extraordinary amount of contradiction between observations, and the inferences drawn therefrom, as set forth by different observers. W. Gray [3] finds the ordinary flakes, scrapers, cores, hammer-stones, which all collectors report, and in addition beautifully worked arrow-heads, polished " celts ", large quantities of pottery, including several urns, and what he rather loosely describes as a stone circle, in which was a skeleton (no particulars given) lying on a stone pavement, considered (for no adequate reason apparent) as a secondary burial. Though " polished celts " are reported from Ballintoy and elsewhere on p. 127 of Gray's article quoted, they are indicated as absent in a table on a later page (142), where a summary down to the date of publication is given of finds at twenty-seven sites. Knowles, in the paper to which we have already referred, adds tranchets, expressly deducts arrow-heads, and includes choppers (including " an implement of chalk which was probably a chopper "—*not* a very probable material for such a tool !), bone needles and pins, and bones of animals—ox, deer, sheep or goat, hog, wolf or dog, human bones and human teeth, these greatly worn down as if from using gritty food. He concludes that the site is entirely Neolithic, and even covers pre-Neolithic remains : some flint material from this earlier layer having been retouched by later finders. But the state of the teeth, indicating a grain diet in contrast with the primitive flesh diet, is unfavourable to this extreme dating : and Buick [4] emphasized the finds of flint knives, of which he himself possessed over three hundred specimens, and which he regarded as based upon iron models, and therefore very late. The same late date is contended for, and apparently extended to the whole of the sandhill culture, by Hassé.[5] In 1889, Knowles [6] repeated his assurance that the sites were Neolithic, accounting for the bronze pins and

---

[1] See, for example, PRIA 17 [1889], plate xii (facing p. 186), Fig. 8.
[2] JRSAI 66 [1936] : 154. A previous communication by the same writer on sites in Londonderry will be found in JRSAI 65 : 231.
[3] JRSAI 15 [1879] : 109.   [4] JRSAI 18 [1887-8] : 241.
[5] JRSAI 21 [1890] : 130.   [6] PRIA 17 : 174, 184.

other later objects discovered by various collectors as intrusions, comparable in this respect with the coins of any date from Queen Elizabeth onward, which have also been found there ; and he maintained this opinion in 1901, in a report which contained more extensive particulars about the shore-dwellers' sites, and the finds made therein, than any previous publication.[1] Even the discovery of a bronze-caster's crucible and mould in the black layer did not shake his faith : bronze-age squatters, he argued, would leave a black layer just as much as their Neolithic predecessors. But this admission gives away the whole case. It shows that in Ireland the word "Neolithic" has no chronological significance ; that people in the Neolithic culture continued to exist contemporaneously with people of bronze-age, iron-age, and even Christian culture. The troublesome necessity of going oversea for tin added greatly, in Ireland, to the expensiveness of bronze, and kept the flint industry alive after experience had taught metal-users the inadequacy of unalloyed copper as a material for withstanding rough usage. A bronze brooch decorated with *millefiori*, belonging therefore to the Pagan-Christian "Overlap", found in a sandhill at Castleport (Donegal), is illustrated by Knowles in the same paper : in such a site, in this country, its connexion with flint implements and a beachcombing economy need not create any surprise : any more than an iron-age pin from the sandhills at Ballybunnion (Kerry).[2]

The occasional discovery of lumps of pumice in these early shore sites calls for at least the acknowledgement of a passing mention, though the source of the material and the use that was made of it are still matters of conjecture.[3]

Knowles and his friends discovered a skull at Whitepark Bay in 1897 ; in his report he describes it as a typical Neolithic skull, but such a description calls for rather closer definition. A series of measurements determined by A. C. Haddon is incorporated in the paper.[4] Though the observation should be registered for future reference, it means little more at present than this, that there was a racial as well as a cultural persistence : just such a survival as we should expect to find among beachcombers.

This paper adds to the earlier report, already summarized, a

[1] PRIA 22 : 331-89.
[2] Described and figured by Dr. Raftery, *Cork* 45 [1940] : 55.
[3] See *Ulster* III 5 : 11.
[4] PRIA 22 : 334. There are several misprints in the technical terms of this list of dimensions, which leaves a little discomfort as to possible misprints in the less easily checked numbers. For example, in the beginning, "The contour falls with the ovoides group of sergi"—Haddon's manuscript must surely have given to the name of the eminent Italian anthropologist the capital S which is most justly his due. Martin, however, accepts these dimensions, which he has presumably checked, as he is able to present a photograph of the skull ; and he tabulates them with those of other skulls ostensibly of the same period (*Prehistoric Man in Ireland*, pp. 57, 70 : the photograph will be found on plate iii). Though slightly shorter, the skull seems most closely comparable with "Kilgreany A".

number of types of flint implements which had not been identified at the time of Knowles's earlier investigations. Pygmy scrapers of Tardenoisian type are reported from Bundoran (Donegal); and small points or prickers are illustrated, though not localized. Neatly made knives, fashioned with pressure-chipping over the whole surface, as well as arrow-heads, some of them of admirable workmanship, were found in the sandhills, though arrow-heads at Ballintoy are rare, and are all of poor and imperfect manufacture. It is a familiar principle that arrows are tipped with obsolete materials—with stone in the Bronze Age, with bronze (in Southern Europe, wherever bronze was procurable) in the early Iron Age, with iron only after the abundance and cheapness of iron had been demonstrated—for it would have been wasteful to expend valuable material on a weapon which would be shot away once, and in the vast majority of cases never recovered. From this point of view, we sometimes are inclined to wonder over the excessive skill and care which must obviously have been expended on the manufacture of weapons with such an ephemeral term of service as flint arrow-heads: many of these are real works of art. The to us strange " timelessness " of uncivilized life could have no better illustration. Admittedly, an expert in the art can turn out such artifacts as these in an astonishingly short space of time: but how much time must have been expended in acquiring that expertness !

The pottery tell the same tale. The specimens figured by Knowles,[1] for example, which he calls " Neolithic ", range through all periods from Windmill Hill to Iron Age.

More systematic than any preceding research on the site was an investigation carried out in 1927 by Messrs. A. H. Davison, J. Orr, A. W. Stelfox, and J. A. Stendall. They were fortunate in finding one of the few fragments of the black layer left undisturbed by collectors, and cut a section through it, exposing a vertical face. Here they found four well-defined black strata, separated by layers of sand, and below them a fifth, less significant in size and content. The uppermost layer was 2 feet below the existing surface, and the others followed at depths of 2 feet 10 inches, 3 feet 10 inches, 5 feet 1 inch, and 6 feet 1 inch respectively, measuring to the upper surface of each. Apparently shells (limpet, periwinkle, whelk) were found *only* in the uppermost layer. The fifth layer was quite sterile, being marked by a thin bed of black material only, containing no relics so far as it was tested. Of the others, all four contained pig and ox bones, to which the first layer added the hare, and the third an animal which might have been a dog or a wolf. The excavators comment especially on the absence of the sheep, although Knowles mentions it among the animals from this site: they refer

[1] PRIA 19 [1895] : 650 ff.

to a paper by Mr. H. E. Forrest (*The Naturalist*, 1923, p. 135), where the existence of the sheep in Ireland in " Neolithic " times is denied.[1]   Besides charcoal, which permeated the whole of the layers, the only artifacts found were flakes of flint, pottery, and one rounded stone in the second layer which had apparently been used as a hammer.   The flints were mere flakes ; only in the two uppermost layers was there any trace of secondary chipping.   The pottery was all fragmentary : in the uppermost layer it bore no decoration ; in the second and third layers it was richly decorated, in what may be regarded as a middle bronze-age (Deuteromegalithic) style ; and it was much simpler, one form with a " stab-and-drag " ornament, the other with an impressed cord decoration.[2]

[1] The absence of sheep and goats from the *indigenous* fauna of Ireland has been put forward as an explanation of the unrestricted growth of forests through the country.   There were no animals to prey on the young shoots.   But Mr. McL. May announces the discovery of sheep bones in a cave at Port Braddon, at the western end of Whitepark Bay (INJ 5 [1934] : 56).

[2] The report of this excavation is published in INJ 1 [1927] : 280.

BOOK II

THE MEGALITHIC AGE

CHAPTER IV

MEGALITHS, THEIR CLASSIFICATION AND CHRONOLOGY

AT a date which may be provisionally assigned to about 2000 B.C., new forms of religious beliefs and practices began to extend over parts of Europe. These, to our long-belated generation, are most conspicuously expressed by constructions made of great, often gigantic, blocks of stone; but we cannot doubt that they included in their scope other elements, not so directly recorded by surviving evidence, but to be inferred from analogy with other cults, current elsewhere, at similar stages of civilization. A list of such elements would include *sacrifices* (of men, as well as of animal and vegetable produce); the *worship of gods*, in human or animal form; specific *rites to secure fertility* in crops, cattle-stalls, and the family; popular *assemblies* at critical seasons of the agricultural year, with dances, songs, processions, and other ritual acts, accompanied with a wild din of drums, pipes, and that universal noise-making instrument, the bull-roarer. Among these activities, and of primary importance, would be *rites for the care and cult of the dead*; with this department of the esoteric life, the stone structures mentioned were especially associated.

This aspect of religion in antiquity is comprehensively called " the Megalithic Cult ", a convenient term, in that it is appropriate,[1] begs no question, and commits us to no theory of its origin and the process of its diffusion. Whence the Megalithic Cult came to Europe; through what channels; how it expanded over a large part of the Continent; why it did not expand over the whole—these are questions the answers to which still elude us, in spite of many efforts to find them; and to discuss them here would occupy too much of our necessarily limited space. We must be content with a statement of the bare facts. The cult arrived in Europe some time about 2000 B.C.; and its relics are there found in areas, wide indeed, but definitely limited. A very few megalithic monuments exist in Italy—practically none, in Europe, further to the east; there are, however, many in the islands between Italy and Spain; while Spain itself has a great number, including some of the finest examples

---

[1] Perhaps it would be more exact to say " *approximately* appropriate " in view of the fact that there are many structures which must be taken into account in any study of the subject, but which cannot be said to be made of *great* stones.

in the whole Continent. France also is very rich in them, and so is Ireland.[1] Great Britain, though possessing specimens that can bear comparison with the best in other regions, is on the whole less rich numerically ; but this may be due to a more intensive process of destruction ; ancient monuments, for long ages protected by superstitious fears, have little chance of survival, after superstitions come to their inevitable end, if they should then stand in the way of ambitious agriculturists, or should have acquired an unmerited reputation for being treasuries of hidden gold ! Leaving the British Islands, and travelling eastward along the north coast of the Continent, we journey over Holland and Northern Germany, finding numerous megalithic monuments on our way ; and we finally enter Denmark and Scandinavia, where the range of megalith distribution, in Europe, comes to an end. They are practically unknown in Central Europe.

Ostensibly these monuments were erected for the reception of the bodies of the dead, and of offerings deposited with them by the survivors, to secure welfare in the other world for the departed spirits, and to buy their favour and protection for the donors. But they are not to be regarded as mere charnel-houses. They are, in fact, model houses for the dead, designed to represent real houses ; and thus to establish, by the processes of sympathetic magic, spiritual houses for them in the world of spirits. We have no direct means of gratifying our curiosity as to where, within or without this material world of ours, that world of spirits was supposed to be situated ; this question, like the others already mentioned, we must be content to leave on one side.

Architecturally, megalithic monuments display a wide range of variety, from the irreducible simplicity of a single pillar-stone, to the complexity of a chambered tumulus ; and we may presume that this variety is the index of a variety of dates, or of a variety of essential purposes. Here, as in all the other sections of this work, there has been much progressive research since the appearance of our now obsolete first edition. Here and elsewhere, the material has had to be re-written ; indeed, so many new facts have accumulated that it has been found impossible to include them all. We are obliged to live in hopes of returning to the subject at some future time, in a special study, at greater length, and in fuller detail.

[1] The richness of Ireland in megalithic monuments of all kinds is shown by the enumeration in W. Copeland Borlase's *Dolmens of Ireland* (published 1898). He catalogues 780 " dolmens ", in addition to 50 chambered tumuli and 68 megalithic monuments of uncertain character. These statistics were patiently compiled from the haphazard material at the author's disposal, in the absence of the authoritative official survey which we still await ; so that the figures cannot be completely trustworthy. If, however, we adopt them as an approximation to the truth, and compare them with the statistics from France—a country whose area is six or seven times that of Ireland—we should infer that, in the same proportion, France would contain between 4,680 and 5,460 dolmens ; the actual number is given as 4,458 (Déchelette, *Manuel d'archéologie*, i, 386).

PLATE 11

TWIN STANDING STONES, KNOCKROUR, CO. CORK

T. H. Mason

LEAC CON MIC RUIS, FACING EAST

Entrances to the eastern subsidiary chambers (one retaining its lintel) in the background. The western chamber, with its entrance (two jambs and a fallen lintel) in the foreground

The Megalithic Age, the time in which the Megalithic Cult flourished in Western and Northern Europe, has been divided into three stages, to which have been given the names already listed in our preface (p. ix)—Protomegalithic, Deuteromegalithic, Epimegalithic. The purpose of the present chapter is to explain these names, and to set forth the differences between the megalithic constructions by which they were distinguished. But first, we must say a few words about the general subject of the disposal of the bodies of the dead.

Many devices for this purpose have been followed in the world as a whole. *Exposure* on the open land, on platforms erected in trees, or in roofless towers, where beasts and birds of prey could obtain access to them and devour them : *mummification*, by the application of heat or of antiseptic substances : *submergence* in the sea : *cannibalism* : *cremation* : *inhumation*. In dealing with Irish Archæology, we need not take special note of any but the last two of these, though the others must not be allowed to drop into complete oblivion.

In what would elsewhere be called the Stone Age, inhumation was the normal procedure. This in Ireland corresponds to the *Pre-Megalithic* and *Protomegalithic* stages. With the Bronze Age, cremation begins to take its place, and in time all but ousts inhumation altogether. With the Iron Age, inhumation again becomes the normal way of dealing with the dead. The buried dead, in the first of these three stages, was laid in a grave, which might be a cave (natural or artificial) ; a trench-grave, like those in a modern cemetery ; or one or other of the types of megalithic structures presently to be described. It lay outstretched, on the back or, more commonly, on one side ; or else it was tightly crouched, with the knees drawn up under the chin. But often the bones are so

FIG. 6.—The Castle Saffron Burial-jar.

much disturbed that we must infer that the body had been dismembered before interment ; or else that it had been laid in a temporary grave to await the decay of the flesh-covering, after which the bones were dug up, to be deposited in the permanent grave— sometimes with an attempt at reconstructing their proper order, but frequently in a random pile. No evidence has yet been noticed, in Ireland, for the use of any kind of coffin ; but one case of jar-burial, familiar in Spain and elsewhere, was found at Castle Saffron, Cork, in 1737. This is, so far, unique in Ireland. The illustration of the jar is here reproduced from Smith's *History of Cork*,[1] which

[1] Published 1756 ; vol. ii, p. 403.

contains the only record of the discovery. The buried skeleton, however deposited, may be accompanied with *grave-goods*—offerings of garments, ornaments, weapons, tools, or food ; such things as were the primary needs of the now dead man during his lifetime, and were assumed to be his primary needs in the world to which he had passed. Offerings of food are, for us, represented by their receptacles, the so-called " food-vessels ", which are presumed to have contained them. The actual substance of the food, if fluid, has long ago dried up, evaporated, or been absorbed ; if solid, has long ago decayed away, except for a few chance animal bones ; so that as a rule the food-vessels are found containing at most a little earth ; often they are empty, often broken. I suspect that in most cases they were actually deposited empty ; that instead of material food-offerings, magical spells had been uttered over them, by functionaries skilled in such *arcana*, and that by the virtue of these spells it was expected that the empty pot—or rather its trans-ferred soul—would assume in the other world the form and the function of an ever-full cauldron, for the perpetual satisfaction of the owner of the tomb. This also explains their frequently broken condition : they had thus been " killed ", to set their spirits free.

The ashes of a cremated body were collected from the pyre and, like the unburnt bodies, deposited in a cave, a grave, or a built sepulchre. A large pottery urn was inverted over them, before the grave was closed in. Such urns are usually known as " cinerary urns " ; but although the placing of the ashes in an urn is not un-known, much more commonly the vessel is inverted as described. It is then to be explained,˙ not as a receptacle, but as a model house, a makeshift imitation of a " beehive " hut, such as the dead man had occupied during his lifetime : and, as before, it magically provided him with a similar hut in the next world.

It must be admitted that the actual number of undisturbed interments found in Protomegalithic monuments is very small indeed ; so that the time is not yet for dogmatic statements about the racial connexions of the Protomegalithic people. In the year 1935, Dr. C. P. Martin, then Assistant Professor of Anatomy in Dublin University, after diligent search, failed to find more than nine measurable skulls available for determining this question ; [1] and even those nine could not all be attributed to Protomegalithic individuals with complete assurance. It is now certain that we cannot always assume that bones found in a megalithic monument belong to the primary interment. That such monuments contained hidden stores of gold or other valuables has been a popular obsession throughout history ; when old tabus lost their inhibiting efficacy, or could be negatived by some counter-magic, the contents, bones and all, might be cleared out ; the valuables, if any, appropriated ;

[1] See his *Prehistoric Man in Ireland*, chap. viii.

and the empty graves could then be used again, and perhaps yet again, as cheap substitutes for a new and costly building.

However, the evidence, such as it is, indicates that the Protomegalithic population was predominantly dolichocephalic (with long narrow heads). The only skull in all the nine which had a cranial index over 80 was that of the woman found in the structure called *Labbacallee*, of which we shall hear more, presently ; she certainly belonged to a later stage, and does not at the moment concern us. Their stature was moderate, if not short ; a man no more than 5 feet 6 inches high would have appeared tall among them. Complexion, the third of the principal criteria used, by Ripley and others, for the racial discrimination of the peoples of Europe, can naturally not be determined directly when we have nothing but fleshless bones at our disposal ; but there is some indirect evidence to indicate that they were dark. For, in a later age, conquering immigrants reduced the then representatives of this race to serfdom ; and the literature, which under aristocratic patronage began to develop in the early centuries of Christianity, speaks almost invariably of these " lower orders " (as they had become) with disdain, as dark and crop-haired—cropped, or even shaven, heads being a badge of servitude, if we may trust a passage in O'Davoren's *Glossary* [1]— thereby indicating and emphasizing a contrast with the flowing golden locks which adorned their overbearing masters. Long, narrow heads ; comparatively short stature ; dark complexion ; these are the physical characters which we find in an Iberian population, and the few discoveries that have been made since the publication of the results of Dr. Martin's work do not disturb his conclusions.

The Protomegalithic grave-monuments fall into two classes ; horned carns and chambered tumuli. The former are almost entirely confined to the northern half of Ireland, the latter to the middle and south. In both varieties, the monument consists of a heap of ballast, covering a structure of large stone blocks, set upright in two parallel rows to define a passage, and supporting a succession of horizontal roofing slabs. In horned carns the passage widens at the outer end, to make a portico, but has no expansion at the inner end ; in chambered tumuli the passage at the inner end expands into the grave-chamber, but otherwise is of uniform breadth throughout. The outer aspect of the monuments is also contrasted ; the horned carns are on a long, more or less elliptical base, the tumuli on a circular base.

The portico of the horned carns (Fig. 7) is semicircular or hemi-elliptical in outline ; the entrance to the interior being a doorway, approximately about the middle of the curved wall which defines it. This curved wall gives to the monument the horned aspect from

[1] *Archiv für Celtische Lexicographie*, 2 : 235.

which its specific name is derived.   The roofing-stones are frequently supported on balanced corbels, resting on the tops of the side walling-stones of the passage ; thus securing a passage not inconveniently narrow, which can be roofed with slabs not too unwieldy.   The passage is divided into segments, up to four in number, by means of jamb-stones and (sometimes in addition) sill-stones ; projecting inwards from the walls, and upwards from the floor. Such segmentation is unknown in the passages of chambered tumuli.

It is one of the many striking illustrations of recent progress in the study of Irish Archæology that horned carns, now of such paramount importance, were practically unknown when our first edition was published.   The term will not be found anywhere in its pages : only three monuments of the group are so much as mentioned ; the degenerate example at Carrowkeel (Sligo) ; the now totally destroyed monument at Annaghclochmuilinn (Armagh) ;

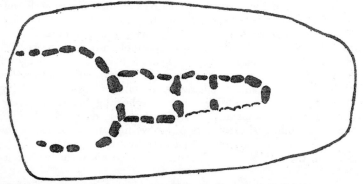

[By permission of the Belfast Nat. Hist. and Phil. Society.

FIG. 7.—Plan of Horned Carn.   Clady Halliday (Tyrone).

and the exceptional Deerpark monument (Sligo) which, although then familiar to students, was not recognized as a variant form of horned carn till later.   But now we know of a very large number— Mahr has published a catalogue of no less than ninety-six recorded examples,[1] though some few are admittedly doubtful.   Of these ninety-six, eighty-two are in [pre-partition] Ulster ; a fact which adequately expresses their geographical distribution.   Except for one, subsequently found, at Ballynamona (Waterford) [2] there is no specimen recorded from the province of Munster.

All the known horned carns have been previously rifled.[3]   We are therefore unable to reconstruct the burial ritual appropriate to these monuments, or to define with exactitude their archæological horizon. All that have been left to us are fragments of early forms of pottery

---

[1] PPS 3 [1937] : 426.   [2] By Mr. T. G. E. Powell ; JRSAI 68 [1938] : 260.
[3] A partial exception is at Ballyalton (Down), excavated by Messrs. Evans and Davies (Belfast 1933-34, p. 79).

(displaying affinity with the Windmill Hill types of British ceramics) ; chipped flints ; and burnt or broken human bones—showing that both cremation and inhumation were associated with structures of the kind. There is not sufficient material available to lead to a decisive conclusion as to whether this indicates an actual contemporaneity of the two rites, or a succession of interments, the later making use of a burial vault originally prepared for the earlier.

In plan, horned carns display close affinity to the *Tombe dei Giganti* of Sardinia, which show the curved portico, though not the characteristic segmentation.[1] Scotland has similar structures, especially in the northern counties (Sutherland and Caithness), but they do not contain Windmill Hill pottery. This, however, is found in a group of roofed passage graves, segmented, but without the horned portico ; containing pottery identical with that in the Irish monuments.[2]

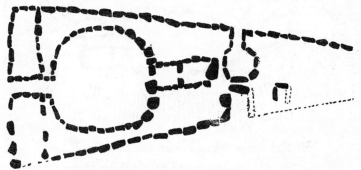

[By permission of the R.S.A.I.

FIG. 8.—Plan of Creevykeel.

There are three types among which horned carns can be classified. The simplest form has the portico at one end (Fig. 7), with the passage opening out of it, and running for some distance into the heap of stones—the rest of the heap, so far as can be determined without trenching it destructively, being devoid of any construction or deposit. The second type has a portico at both ends : the additional portico may be a dummy, with no passage behind it ; or it may have such a passage, in line with that of the first portico, but not continuous with it, transit from one to the other being prevented, either by a barrier slab, or by a block of sterile carn-material intervening between the two constructions. In the third type the plan of the second is, as it were, turned inside out ; the porticos are not back to back at the extremities of the carn, but face to face in the

---

[1] See Mr. Davies's account of these monuments *Ulster* III 2 [1939]: 158 ; see also *Man* 38 [1938] : no. 95.
[2] See V. G. Childe, *The Prehistory of Scotland*, chap. iii.

middle, forming an open and probably roofless court, with the burial passages radiating from it in opposite directions. As a variety of this last form we may mention the so-called lobster-claw type, in which one of the burial-passages is suppressed, and its entrance gives admission from outside to an oval court, not the mere semicircular portico of the first type. A splendid example of this form (Fig. 8) is at Creevykeel (Sligo) excavated with great skill by Dr. Hencken.[1]

In the same county, in the Deerpark, about three miles from the county town, is the best example of the first kind of the third type (Fig. 9). It goes by the name *Leac Con mic Ruis*, " the flag-stone of Cu son of Ros ", whoever he may have been. The long

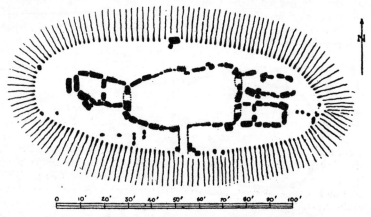

[By permission of Mr. W. J. Hemp and the Editors of " Antiquity ".

FIG. 9.—Plan of Leac Con Mic Ruis.

axis of the structures lies east and west. The central area is 50 feet long and about 25 feet broad. Trilithon doorways, 3 feet square, give access to the subsidiary passages. These are 20 to 22 feet long, 6 to 7 feet broad, and are each divided into two segments by projecting jambs (Plate IIb). They are now roofless, but we may assume that they were originally covered with slabs, and embedded in a carn. Excavations (as they have been euphemistically termed) made here from time to time, have revealed fragments of human and animal bones (none of them displaying any marks of fire), and a few chips of flint. Some of the bones are said to have been contained in small cists ; but no plan or detail of these is given in the paper recording these raids.[2] There are *two* parallel passages

[1] See his report, JRSAI 69 [1939] : 53.
[2] S. F. Milligan, " Recent archæological explorations in Co. Sligo ", *Belfast* 1886-7, p. 40. For a well illustrated description of this monument, see E. T. Hardman, " On a remarkable megalithic structure near Sligo ", JRSAI 15 [1879] : 57. This is, however, superseded by Mr. W. J. Hemp's careful survey in *Antiquity* 5 [1930] : 98.

opening out of the portico-curve on the eastern side of the central court, but only one on the western.

Many more details might be given, were we in command of unlimited space ; but fortunately we are now able to refer the reader to a full summary of the whole subject of the Horned Carns of Ulster,[1] to date, published by Messrs. E. E. Evans and O. Davies, who have done so much to call attention to their importance and to put their study in a sound scientific basis.

While the inhabitants of Northern Ireland were erecting their horned carns, those of the south were building chambered tumuli. These are mounds—sometimes of earth, but in the majority, including all those of importance, of stones ; hemispherical, or approximately conical, in form (the largest with a more or less flattened top), on a circular base, differing conspicuously from the oval base of a horned carn or its related structure, a long barrow ; with a chamber in the heart of the structure, formed of large slabs, accessible through an opening in the side of the mound, and along a passage leading from it inward, lined with vertical side-stones, and covered with horizontal roofing-slabs resting upon them. The chamber is not necessarily at the mathematical centre of the mound ; though we can point to no definite evidence, we can never completely suppress a natural suspicion that there may be other chambers lurking unknown and (without drastic demolition) undiscoverable in other parts of the mound. There is certainly plenty of room for them. The chamber is of a diversity of shapes, from square to roughly circular ; in the sides there are frequently (not always) recesses, made to receive the actual burials. Of these recesses there are usually three, making with the entrance passage a cruciform plan ; but there is no specific rule as to this, and the number actually ranges from one to five or six.

In geographical distribution these monuments lie chiefly on a belt lying through the middle of Ireland, excluding both the northern and the southern counties. In Sligo, the extensive series on the summit of Carrowkeel mountain is of primary importance, as it gave unusually favourable opportunities for excavation, which was carried out in 1911 by myself in partnership with Dr. R. Ll. Praeger and the late Mr. Edmund Armstrong, then Keeper of the Irish Antiquities in the National Museum.[2] These are heaps of stones about 20 feet in height and 70 to 100 feet in basal diameter. A pioneer piece of work like this must be subjected to revision as later discoveries bring new relevant facts to light, and this excavation and the deductions founded upon it are already antiquated by the fruits of over a quarter of a century of subsequent activity. We are now in a

---

[1] It will be found in *Ulster* III 6 [1943] : 7.
[2] See the full account of this work, PRIA 29 [1912] : 311.

position to assert that the interments and the other grave deposits unearthed did not belong radically to the tumuli, but were later intrusions, taking the place of the earlier deposits for which the mounds had been primarily erected ; this accounts for the haphazard way in which the remains were strewn about ; for the use of the later rite of cremation in place of the earlier inhumation ; and for the, on the whole, rather late objects found associated with the human remains. A full statement of the present position of the subject must, however, be reserved ; it is far too complex to be treated exhaustively within the covers of a general conspectus of Irish Archæology.

On the left (northern) bank of the river Boyne, about five miles upstream from Drogheda, is situated the most important group of monuments of this class. It includes three tumuli of great size, generally known under the names Dowth, New Grange, and Knowth ; and about eight smaller structures, as well as a number of standing stones and earthen enclosures, among the latter one of great size and importance. This enclosure is the first relic of antiquity which we encounter, as we approach the cemetery from Drogheda. It measures about 150 by 166 yards across, and, most likely, it originally enclosed the compound of the *Brug* or palace, which gives its name to the whole cemetery—*Brug na Boinne*, " the Palace of the Boyne " ; to all outward appearance the residence of the great man for whom the neighbouring tomb called in Irish documents " Dubhadh " (*anglice* " Dowth ") was erected. We have naturally no direct information as to who he may have been ; but both in literary tradition and in modern folk-lore there appears a mysterious being named *Oengus of the Brug*, constantly associated with this cemetery— not necessarily with New Grange alone—and it is no undue straining of probability to see here a lingering memory of the king who once ruled from this palace, and was buried in the neighbouring tumulus, his earthly divinity enhanced by the mystery of death ; still lording it over his ancient kingdom. Dowth (Fig. 10) appears as a heap of stones on a circular base, 280 feet in diameter, and originally about 47 feet high. Within this stone-heap there is a chamber (A) of the normal cruciform plan, length over all 40 feet, breadth along the axis of the side arms a little over 20 feet. There has, however, been subsequent interference with the mound in the neighbourhood of the entrance, which has shortened the length of the passage by about 18 feet. The entrance passage is segmented with sills, but not with jambs. The chamber is roofed with broad flat stones, supported by great upright slabs. At the inner end of the right-hand burial-cell there is a prolongation, entered by a gap left for the purpose in the wall of the cell, and containing two burial-cists. This produces a strong impression, in the spectator, of secrecy, as though the gap had been intended to be specially closed ; certainly it looks as though the

PLATE III

T. H. Mason

THE MOUNT BROWNE DOLMEN

DOLMEN OF UNUSUAL FORM, ARAN MÓR (GALWAY)

extension had been made to receive the remains of the Lord of Dowth and his wife or wives, the rest of the structure being prepared for his household of slaves and dependants : whom (in accordance with a custom almost universal at a certain stage of the development of civilization) we may presume to have been all slaughtered at the death of their lord, and thus sent to the world of spirits to serve him there, as they had served him in this life.

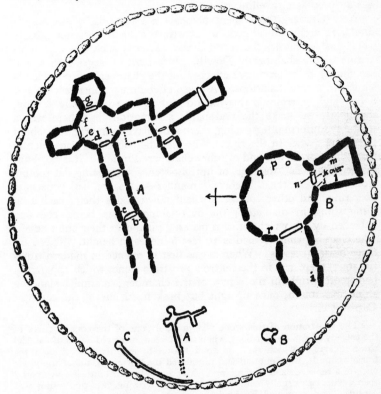

Fig. 10.—Sketch-plan of Dowth.

(In the bottom of the circle the internal constructions are set in their proper places, and to the scale of the drawing. In the middle are enlarged plans of the two principal constructions. The letters inside these plans indicate stones with scribings).

To the south of this passage, and independent of it, there is another structure (B) embedded within the carn, in plan bearing a striking resemblance to that of the Mycenæan tomb called the " Treasury of Atreus ". It consists of the same three parts—a *dromos*, or entrance-passage 11 feet 6 inches long, leading to a *tholos* or central court, circular on plan and about 15 feet in diameter, with a *taphos* or burial-cell, measuring about 9 feet by 7 feet, opening out of it. I am of opinion that this structure is an intrusion, not originally belonging to the scheme of the monument; but the reasons for this opinion, and the purpose which this addition may have been intended to serve, involve a long and complex argument, which must be held over for a more convenient season. The third structure (C) is a comparatively late souterrain, apparently made when the cave was adapted as a dwelling-place.

New Grange (the ancient name is not certainly preserved) is similar in architectural style to Dowth, though it does not possess (so far as we know) the secret grave which is such a conspicuous feature of the chamber of Dowth. It is built of larger stones, and has a much more grandiose effect; but the chambers are remarkably similar in their dimensions. A circle of standing stones, each about 8 feet high, surrounds this mound; of these, twelve only remain, though, if we make the reasonable assumption that there was a tolerably uniform interspacing, there must have been originally about thirty-five stones in the ring. The chamber differs in construction from those of Dowth and of other chambered tumuli: it is not built in the "dolmen" manner, of upright stones supporting flat roofing stones; but in the "beehive" manner—slabs are laid prostrate, in a ring, and other courses are laid down above them, each ring diminishing in diameter; the over-sailing stones being counterbalanced by the weight of carn material piled over their outer edges. The chamber thus formed is 19 feet 6 inches in height. There are three burial recesses. When it was first re-opened in modern times (in 1699) there was in the centre a prostrate stone, which apparently had stood upright in the centre of the chamber: a similar standing stone was found, once upright but broken, in one of the carns at Carrowkeel.

The prostration of this stone was probably one of the consequences of the tragedy of A.D. 861 (or 862), when (as we read in the old books of Annals) three "caves", which there is good reason to identify with these three burial mounds, were entered and plundered by Norsemen, under the guidance of a renegade son of the king of Meath. We read, with less sympathy than such cases usually call for, that in the following year this traitor was captured and punished by having his eyes put out. The emptied and desecrated New Grange must have been closed soon afterwards; the very site of the entrance was forgotten, till it was accidentally rediscovered in 1699. Then the whole surface of the floor was found to be covered with a litter of broken stones and bones—the raiders must have pulled up the paving in search for hidden treasure, even breaking one of the large slabs which covered the floors of the burial recesses: the pillar-stone would no doubt have been thrown down as being a probable mark of something desirable, underneath. Sixty years ago, when the Government took this and other monuments of antiquity into public Guardianship, the then Inspector of Ancient Monuments made it all tidy again, not by endeavouring to reconstitute the pavement, but by digging an oubliette in front of the entrance, and bundling all the debris unceremoniously into it. (See note on p. 103.)

The third of the great mounds, Knowth, has as yet been only superficially tested by an excavation, in which the chamber was not found. It would be premature to say anything about it at present.[1] Nor can we profitably speak here about the group of carns of the same type crowning the Lochcrew Hills and at present under examination in the competent hands of Dr. Joseph Raftery. His conclusions down to the date of writing have been revolutionary, and in what state the theory of the subject will be, when he has finished with it, it is impossible to foresee. He most kindly permits me to say that he has proved—in my opinion, beyond all possibility of question—that the Lochcrew Mounds, though built with old bronze-age material, and laid out to a bronze-age plan, are actually iron-age structures ; an impressive illustration of the action of the time-lag.

Many of the stones in all these monuments, except those of Carrowkeel, are decorated with symbolic or ornamental carving of bronze-age patterns—spirals, circles, zigzags, lozenges and other geometrical figures. Here, again, I cannot say all that I would ; but in some cases at least—notably in New Grange and the Lochcrew group—I am convinced that the ornamental stones are there at second-hand ; that they were originally grave-marks, and were collected by the mound-builders and appropriated to their own purposes, without any reference to the signification of the decoration.

The typical monument of the Deuteromegalithic stage is what is usually called a *Dolmen*. This name was artificially fashioned (out of Breton words, meaning " stone table ") in the early days of Archæological study, by pioneers influenced by two untenable theories : that rude stone monuments such as these are " Celtic " and, specifically, " Druidic " in their origin ; and that the Breton language, as spoken in modern France, is there a survival of the primæval Celtic speech of the Continent. It would be well if such words as " dolmen " and some other similar inventions could be discarded, along with the obsolete ideas which gave them birth.

These structures, however we may call them, are in the line of evolution from the earlier chambers which we have just been discussing. They differ from them by their comparative simplicity, as expressed by the smaller average size of the component stones, and by the absence of the side burial-recesses ; and especially, by the withholding of means of access to the central chamber. The chambered tumulus had an entrance to the burial chamber approached by a passage ; the " dolmen ", which was no doubt covered by a similar though smaller mound of stones or of earth—otherwise it would not have served the necessary purpose of concealment—had no such entrance. Once the mound was closed upon it, it was sealed

[1] See the preliminary report, PRIA 49 (1943), p. 131.

away for all time, and the superstitious fears centering upon it (even yet not forgotten, though now moribund) were most probably induced at the first by terrific tabus, laid upon it by the magicians who presided at the burial rites.

The Deuteromegalithic culture appears to be the result of an automatic evolutionary development from the Protomegalithic, stimulated by more or less peaceful trade-contacts with neighbouring oversea communities.   It is impossible to draw a hard-and-fast line between the two ;   old forms gradually go out, new forms gradually come in, with a consequent overlap which defies all efforts at chronological discrimination.   There is no ascertained physical differentiation between the peoples of the two phases, though here as before, we must frankly admit the poverty of the material available upon which to base a judgement.   But certainly there is no evidence of the immigration or invasion of alien peoples, such as we shall find in abundance when we cross the border into the Epimegalithic phase.   The Pharaonic regime which made Dowth possible could not continue, as advancing culture widened current ideas and developed individual aspirations.   Such an autocracy would inevitably break down into a broader oligarchy of individuals, whose despotism, though still real, would be much more restricted, both in intensity and in geographical extent.   The huge chambered tomb gives place to a smaller structure in the same style, or more frequently to the less elaborate though still individualistic and often impressive " dolmen ".   This change testifies to the diminution, by diffusion among a larger number of participants, of a power previously centred in single individuals, one in this region, another in that, unquestionably basing their prestige and their personal security upon a generally accepted theory of the divinity of kings. Holocausts of wives and of slaves accompanying the obsequies now belong to the past, though there are reasons for attributing a reintroduction of the practice to the barbarian Epimegalithic invaders who were to follow.

The apparent clearance of the early interments in the Carrowkeel mounds, followed by an adaptation of their receptacles as communal charnel-houses, points in the same direction.   The presumably Iberian immigrants who introduced the Megalithic Cult were by now completely fused with the Riverford Turanians—assuming the actuality of that colonization, and the ethnological affinities suggested for it ;   probably also with the relics of the still earlier " mixed multitude " of the Beachcomber sites.   This fusion had effectively broken down Protomegalithic exclusivism ;   had, indeed, to a large extent unified the culture of North and South.

Immigrant individuals from the brachycephalic Beaker Folk, who were rapidly mounting to ascendancy in the larger island, were beginning to obtain a footing in Ireland ;   the round-headed woman whose bones were found in Labbacallee, and the prominent position which she had apparently made for herself, was a portent of the "wrath to come". But as yet, she and her kindred had no more bearing on the local ethnology than a chance negro whom we may meet in a London street.

For present convenience, though under protest, we shall here continue to use the current term "dolmen" to designate the typical Deuteromegalithic stone monument. Generically, dolmens are structures consisting of groups of large vertical supporting stones upholding one or more horizontal cover-slabs. Specifically they are subject to a wide range of variation, depending on the number and disposition of both of the component elements. There may be only *one* supporting stone, as in the *taulas* of Minorca ; these have two attenuated analogues in Ireland, at Kenmare and at Killeacle, both in Co. Kerry. There may be only two supports, upholding a horizontal lintel, as in the trilithons at Stonehenge, and the entrances to the subsidiary chambers in the Deerpark monument, already described. These form component parts of a larger ensemble ; but there are three independent trilithons in Ireland—at Lochmoney (Antrim), at Knockalassa on the slope of Mount Callan, and at Drumanure, both in Co. Clare—though the second is uncertain, as there is reason to suspect that it has been reduced to the trilithon form by the removal of stones which had once given it a different character. At best, these are abnormal in Ireland ; but when we add a third support to the scheme we find ourselves in the presence of the typical and normal dolmen, of which there is a large number in the country.

Starting from this simple scheme, we can increase the number of supporting stones up to about eleven (as in dolmens at Howth and at Kiltiernan, both in Co. Dublin) ; we can also supplement the covering with more than one roofing-slab, if one be found insufficient. But the addition of a second cover more frequently produces a monument of a different type, the *allée couverte* or "covered passage-grave" ; a chamber in the form of a passage defined by two rows of side lining-stones supporting a succession of roofing slabs. As the dolmen seems to carry on the tradition of the burial chamber in the earlier tumuli, this carries on the tradition of the entrance passage, now (so to speak) fitted with an independent existence, and no longer merely ancillary to the burial chamber. These passage-graves are cognate with the horned carns, but they have no portico entrance, and are not segmented by side jambs.

When we contemplate these erections, involving the transport and fitting together of stones weighing many tons—up to 100 in one example at Mount Browne (Carlow, Plate IIIa), a weight which has been surpassed only by a stone in a dolmen in Spain, we naturally ask how this heavy work was carried through (Plate III, Fig. 1). We must recognize that it involves a high degree of social organization, which brought many individuals together in the interests of a common

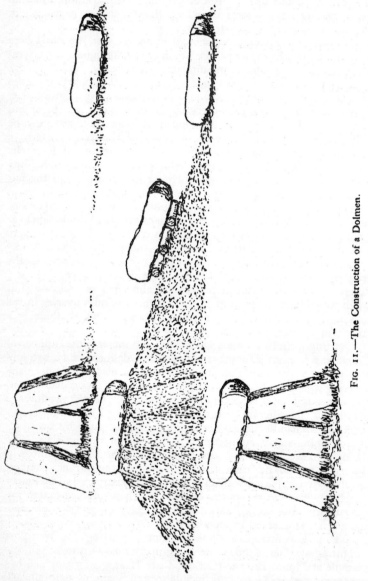

FIG. 11.—The Construction of a Dolmen.

purpose. The supporting stones were, we may presume, gradually raised to an upright position by means of levers, inch by inch, wedging-stones being thrust underneath them at every stage.   When it was ascertained that they were secure, and sufficiently close to hold up the cover slab and prevent it from falling between them, but at the same time sufficiently distant, each from the rest, to prevent the cover-stone from overbalancing—and for this purpose, there must have been a competent overseer, with technical knowledge of construction, and skill in making measurements—a sloping bank of earth was heaped up against the upright stones to their tops, and the cover-slab was then drawn up and set in its destined position with the aid of rollers ; see Fig. 11 which represents the successive stages of the process of erection.   The stone-work finished, the temporary earth bank was dug away, the burial deposits with the grave offerings laid down in their appointed place, and a permanent mound of stones or of earth was heaped over all.[1]

This last has sometimes been questioned.   Fergusson, in his pioneer work on Rude Stone Monuments, asks whether the mound-builders would have been willing to hide away for ever a fine structure of which they might justly have been proud.   It is doubtful if this question is psychologically justifiable ; the builders had a practical, not an æsthetic purpose in view, and this was to them of paramount importance.   If the monument had been left uncovered it would fail in its primary purpose, concealment and protection of the burial deposits ; it would fail in its secondary purpose of providing a magical house for the dead in the other world.   The fact that so many monuments of the kind now stand bare of all covering is easily explained as due to the operations of plunderers, who dug away the earth sufficiently to let them get at the deposited valuables ; subsequent rain-storms would wash it all away.   It has also been objected that in some cases the component stones are so far apart that if carn material, whether earth or stones, had been heaped over them it would run in under the cover-slab, thus frustrating any purpose that there might have been of keeping the space beneath it as an empty chamber.   But this could easily be countered by leaning planks up against the roofing slab all round, and leaving them to be buried in the carn material : they would bank it up, and when in the course of time they decayed, the earth would by then have compacted to a sufficient solidity to stand without collapsing.   This seems to be corroborated by the evidence of a dolmen on the Great Aran Island (Plate IIIb), where stone slabs take the place of the theoretical planks—which, on an island where timber must always have been scarce, might not have been available in sufficient numbers.

Returning for a moment to the passage-graves, we must note

---

[1] Reference should be made to P.S.A. Scot. 68 (1933-4) : 81 ff., where will be found a statement, and an ingenious solution, of the problems that must have faced those who erected these great stones, by Mr. H. Kilbride-Jones.

that in the south-west of the country there is a variety commonly called " wedge-shaped dolmens ", in which the side walls of the passage are not parallel, but are set at an angle each to the other, so that the space between them widens toward the outer end of the chamber.   A notable wedge-shaped dolmen, lying on the road from Glanworth to Fermoy (Cork), was excavated in 1934.[1]   It is known as " Labbacallee ", i.e. *Leaba na Caillighe*, " the old woman's bed "— a name of considerable interest, as we shall see, in view of the results of the excavation.   For a full description of the monument, and of the discoveries made therein, reference must be made to the report quoted ; only the main facts need here be referred to.   Excluding subsidiary extensions, the purpose of which will possibly become clearer as researches are prosecuted in other, cognate, sites, the structure is over 32 feet long and about 20 feet 6 inches broad at the western end, diminishing to 10 feet 6 inches at the eastern.   Inside, there were two chambers, a western (21 ft. 6 in. by 5 to 6 ft.) and an eastern (3 ft. by 4 ft.).   These were separated by a vertical slab, out of the upper corner of which an opening was broken ; analogous to the porthole occurring in similar partitions in British and French megaliths, though rare, if not unknown, in sepulchral structures in Ireland. No doorway entrance from the outside was originally provided for either chamber ; but there was a row of slabs on edge butting against the outer face of the slab which closed the " wedge " at its narrower end, and so placed that the cover-slab of the smaller chamber could be slipped on to them and back again, thus opening and closing the chamber at the top.   The principal interment in the tomb was that of a woman—a striking fact, whether the current name of the monument represent a genuine tradition, or be a mere accidental coincidence.   The bones of the skeleton, except the head, were piled up in the inner or smaller chamber ; what there is every reason to regard as the skull belonging to them was in the outer chamber. In racial type this subject corresponded in all respects with the brachycephalic invaders of the Epimegalithic phase : she must therefore have been an intruder, but withal an outstanding personality in her day ; the tomb provided for her reception was of great size, and built of massive stones : and, like the Deuteromegalithic tombs, was originally intended to be an individual sepulchre, not a communal vault, for no means of access had been provided, other than the sliding roof of the smaller chamber.   The now dilapidated extension of the structure to the east—for which see the excavators' plan, published with their report—may have been a " false portal ", as is there suggested ; it was certainly not a practicable entrance as originally built, though later spoliation made it less absolutely exclusive.   The body must have been buried temporarily, perhaps

---

[1] H. G. Leask and L. Price, " The Labbacallee Megalith, Co. Cork ", PRIA 43 [1936] : 77.

merely to await the completion of the sepulchre ; there is, however, probably much more in the fact than this, but we cannot here find space to discuss possible theoretical alternatives. The bones of the principal interment were afterwards taken up from their temporary depository and then laid, bare of the flesh, in the smaller chamber. The skull, however, as the seat of the nobler activities of the human personality—or, as we may venture to say boldly, of the soul— was ceremonially deposited apart in the larger chamber. This conception of the function of the skull is at least as old, in Europe, as the Azilian period. It supplies the motive for the practice of head-hunting, familiar in many parts of the world, and attributed by Poseidonius to the Celtic inhabitants of Europe in his time— a testimony fully corroborated by the evidence of Irish literature ; and also for the analogous custom of collecting brain-balls—the brains of conquered enemies, kneaded up with lime to preserve them. This practice, attributed especially to the Ultonian warriors, was essentially a collection of the souls of the conquered enemies, en-slaving them to the service of their conquerors in this world and the next. The less important bones were apparently carried, as in other cases, from the temporary grave in a bag of hide or of some textile substance, secured with a bone pin, which still remained : similar pins were found associated with the intrusive cremated deposits in the Carrowkeel tombs. In grave-goods, however, the tomb was very poor, apparently because the lady was not allowed to rest in peace. In and above the earth in which her bones were buried in the inner chamber was a quantity of cremated human bones, clearly belonging to a secondary use of the tomb ; and the outer chamber showed signs of having been adapted as a habitation, in the late Bronze or early Iron Age. These intruders had left unimportant fragments of pottery : and two other uncremated skeletons, those of a young man of about nineteen years and of a child of about five, were also in the outer chamber. The later intruders had pushed these bones to one side, and had dumped the woman's skull into the middle of the broken fragments of the man's skeleton.

In the general absence of datable grave-goods, thanks to the activities of generations of plunderers, we cannot always maintain the division here indicated between Protomegalithic and Deutero-megalithic monuments with an unyielding dogmatism. It cannot be that every man in the earlier period, though he may have felt entitled to possess a great sepulchral monument like Dowth, or even one of the smaller Carrowkeel mounds, was in a position to command its erection ; while on the other hand, there are certain monuments which we might call at first sight Protomegalithic but which, for one reason or another, must be brought down to the Deuteromegalithic Period. Every monument has to be considered on its own merits. And, especially in the Deuteromegalithic, we find it possible to sort out the monuments into types, easily distinguishable, and into less definite forms which we may call hybrid, transitional, or anomalous.   As an example, we may quote a common kind of dolmen in which the roofing stone is only partly upheld by the upright supports ; one side of it rests on the ground.   We have to decide, in each individual case, if this represents the original intention of the builders (possibly a mere shirking of the heavy labour of raising the stone completely) ; or if it be due to a subsequent accident— resulting from the removal of the support which had been afforded by the covering carn, in consequence of the operations of treasure-hunters, or else from a collapse due to the " fatigue " or fracture of the overweighted supporting stones.   Decision between these alternatives is often difficult : but it can frequently be helped by observing whether there are any upright stones not now supporting any part of the roofing stone, from which it could have slipped off—the Howth monument is a case in point.   The Mount Browne monument, already mentioned (p. 77), was originally a " table ", supported on six uprights, two of which have collapsed and allowed the huge cover-stone to fall into its present sloping position.

Such individualities of type, taken as a whole, surely mean something ; it may be historical, ethnological, social, magico-religious, or evolutionary ; but we are not yet in a position to say what that meaning may be.   To attain that consummation we need, first, a final agreement on typological classification ; and secondly, a series of maps displaying the geographical distribution of the several types ; and to this end, once again, a full and completed official Archæological Survey is the first essential, without which it is impossible to put the subject on a scientific basis.   Till that is accomplished, we shall be merely collecting odds and ends of disconnected facts with no very clear idea as to what they mean, and what may be their relation to one another, and to history in general. Mr. T. G. E. Powell has made a beginning, with a most promising attempt to reduce to order the diversity of the tomb-architecture of S.E. Ireland, and to determine its evolutionary sequence : [1] it is much to be hoped that he will be encouraged and enabled to continue his good work when, if ever, stability is restored to a world maddened with war and crazed with politics ; few if any could do it better.

At a time estimated at between 2500 and slightly after 2000 B.C., immigrants from different regions in East Central Europe, especially the Rhineland, began to enter Great Britain.   We are not to picture invading expeditions, which would require us to postulate impossibly great fleets of ships : the process was rather a gradual infiltration, extending over many years—perhaps over centuries—not without

[1] JRSAI 71 [1941] : 9.

analogy to the insidiousnesses with which we have become only too familiar in these times of ours.   There is no evidence that any of the component incidents of this movement was distinguished by excessive manpower, or by conspicuous violence ; but (perhaps for that very reason) it produced in the end a complete revolution, ethnic and cultural, over the larger part of Great Britain.   The new-comers established themselves firmly over what are now the southern and eastern littoral counties, from Hampshire westward to Kent, and thence northward as far as Elgin.   Inland from the coast their relics are less thickly concentrated ; but, even there, they are suffi-ciently extensive to testify to the secure hold which the intruders acquired and maintained, in a situation which automatically gave them the control of all oversea trade.

For want of a specific ethnological name, not open to objection on one ground or another, a makeshift label, " The Beaker Folk ", has been devised for them, derived from the type of pottery especially associated with their remains.[1]   The map of Great Britain is covered thickly with sites that have yielded beakers, especially the area east of a line drawn from Duncansby Head to a point a little west of the Isle of Wight.[2]   To the west of that line, they are still fairly numerous, but more sporadic : in many areas in that part of the country, the map mentioned in the footnote is almost or altogether blank.

In 1932, when this map was first published, only four beaker-sites had been recorded in Ireland.   The contrast between the two islands, as they are there shown, is most impressive : and it was then sufficient to justify us in saying that beakers were practically un-known in Ireland.   Indeed, they were even less plentiful than the map indicated.   One of the four sites was marked on the evidence of a vessel from a carn at Mount Stewart (Down), which had for a long time been lost to sight, and was recorded only in a poor drawing a century old : it has since been re-discovered, and has proved not to be a beaker at all.   A second site was Moytirra (Sligo), the beakers of which are of the Iberian bell-beaker form, and have therefore no direct bearing on the migrations of the Rhinelanders.   And a third represents collectively a number of fragments from sandhill sites, resembling beaker sherds, but too small to be conclusive.

Since 1938, a few more beaker-sites have been discovered ; but these are not sufficient to disturb the conclusion that the beaker cannot be called a normal Irish form of pottery.   If we were to base

[1] For a convenient summary of current knowledge regarding this people see Ivor Herring, " The Beaker Folk " (*Ulster* III 1 [1938] : 135).

[2] See [Sir] Cyril Fox, *The Personality of Britain* (3rd edition, 1938)—a work indispensable to all serious students of this subject.   A map of " beaker sites " will be found there at p. 11 : it is reproduced in the article quoted in the preceding footnote, on p. 136.   It has been brought up to date for the 1938 edition of *The Personality*, and there records *six* beaker-sites in Ireland.   The fourth edition of this work was published in 1943, but no change was made in the map.   The student will derive great profit from a perusal of the succinct and admirably clear *Prehistoric Britain*, by Mr. and Mrs. Christopher Hawkes.

ethnological deductions on the distribution of beakers in the country, we should be obliged to conclude that the Beaker Folk never had any relations therewith, commercial or other, beyond the compulsory or voluntary immigration of a few individuals. This was the underlying presupposition of the first edition of the present work. Even in a later work, *Ancient Ireland*, the absence of the Beaker Folk is assumed ; though the fact of a later bronze-age invasion is there recognized, and the solution of the problem, here adopted, is hinted at (*op. cit.* p. 54).

The excavation of a carn at Well Glass Spring, Largantea (Londonderry),[1] was the first in recent times to put beakers, in current phrase, upon the map of Ireland. The plan of the enclosed structure, which had been much injured by agricultural operations, consisted of two chambers, the one L-shaped, the other rectangular and fitting into the angle of the L. A façade about 14 feet long, formed of five upright stones in a virtually straight line, each 4 to 5 feet high,[2] had two door-openings, one for each chamber, flanking the central stone of the row. This structure seems to look back, architecturally, to the earlier, more complex graves, rather than forward to Epimegalithic simplicity : in fact, the excavator shows himself aware of the possibility that the contents were secondary, not belonging to the original appropriation of the monument. Corroborative evidence is presented by a mass of cremated human bones and Protomegalithic pottery (" Neolithic " types) found in the L-shaped chamber, and also at the back of the carn outside. This included bones of eight persons (six adults and two children) mixed up together : the irregular intensity of the firing indicated that they had been piled up in a heap and all cremated at once, suggesting that their bodies, or their bones, had been torn from their graves to get them out of the way, heaped up unceremoniously, and burnt. It is the sort of action that we should expect from the " Beaker " invaders ; and beakers, of late and degenerate form, were found with the secondary interments. These belonged to the unshouldered " B " class,[3] and were probably imported by immigrants from Scotland or N.W. England. One of these vessels was anomalous, both in profile and in decoration, the latter being laid out on a panel-scheme unusual in beakers.

The sudden appearance of brachycephalic skulls, among the human remains associated with the " beaker " civilization in Great Britain, is one of the cases where ethnological evidence completely justifies a historical postulate. No one would assert that the earlier inhabitants of that country had attained to the practically impossible (and biologically undesirable) ideal of " a pure race " ; but at least

---

[1] Reported by Mr. I. Herring, *Ulster* III 1 [1938] : 164.
[2] Scaling from the published plans and sections.
[3] More particularly defined below, p. 185.

their racial affinities do not seem to have had any brachycephalic admixture. But simultaneously with the beakers, round skulls, with no local antecedents, begin to appear. And that the owners of those round skulls were foreign immigrants, and were the carriers of the beaker culture, are the obvious, the only reasonable conclusions to be drawn from the fact.

The Beaker Folk had short round skulls, with the normal concomitant of short round faces. In stature they varied considerably, but on the whole they were taller than the aborigines : the latter might average about 5 feet 5 inches, the newcomers about 5 feet 9 inches, and might even rise to 6 feet. The limb-bones are more slender than those of the earlier people. Their teeth show much more intensive wear than those of their predecessors, indicating the use of gritty food—bread, made of flour unavoidably mixed with fine dust from the quern-stones—in increasing quantity, relatively to the meat and milk diet which had been the staple sustenance of their predecessors.

In the first edition (p. 52) we wrote : " The Beaker Folk never came with their arts to Ireland " : explaining thus the practical absence of beakers in the country. But we know better now ; the sentence quoted must be expunged, and another explanation of the undeniable fact of that absence must be sought and substituted. Martin [1] has emphasized the predominantly brachycephalic character of the skulls revealed, in such megalithic structures in Ireland as belong to the later stages of the Bronze Age, by the more carefully conducted excavations of recent years. Between later and earlier sites there is the same ethnological contrast in Ireland as there is in Great Britain ; and it must be due to the same cause— an immigration, producing a complete ethnological revolution in both countries. The Beaker Folk most certainly *did* come with their arts into Ireland, and they occupied it, spreading over its whole length and breadth. Why, then, did they leave practically no beakers behind them ? The answer is quite simple : they did not come to Ireland till they had all but ceased to make beakers—a form of vessel which even in Great Britain began to disappear at an early stage of their occupation.

But in Ireland, we have no slow and peaceful infiltration to deal with. The invasion of Ireland by the Beaker Folk, coming from their now firmly established bases across the narrow Irish Sea, may be likened to the ravages of a pestilence. They brought the flourishing Deuteromegalithic civilization to an abrupt end. This is not to say that it may not have been preceded and perhaps prepared for by a gradual process of infiltration : the woman of Labbacallee and the inmate of a cist at Loughry (Tyrone) [2] may have been among

[1] *Prehistoric Man in Ireland*, chap. ix.
[2] E. E. Evans, *Cist-burial at Loughry, Co. Tyrone, Ulster* III 4 [1941] : 145.

its forerunners. The latter was a broad-headed youth, apparently male, of about fifteen years, crouched inside a cist in a burial tumulus of *earth*—a usual form of grave in that region—accompanied by an early and very ornate food-vessel. There was some charcoal in the cist, possibly the remains of a purificatory fire, for the body itself was unburnt.

It is easy to assign a determining cause, and an ultimate purpose, for this raid. The Beaker Folk were essentially metallurgists—certainly in Great Britain the art of metal-working appears to begin with their immigration, although it began in Ireland independently of their influence. And that was the mainspring of the trouble. Ireland was rich in copper and in gold, and had advertised those riches by its lucrative trade. Its serious deficiency in tin was made up by drawing on the inexhaustible resources of Cornwall. But the tin-owners there were good business men, fully alive to the value of their monopoly. We know how they kept the secret of their sources of supply from the Mediterranean traders. If we may believe Diodorus of Sicily,[1] the tin was carried from the mines to a market at a distance, in the Island of Ictis—most probably the Isle of Wight [2] —and the negotiations with foreign purchasers were there transacted. It has been observed that pure tin is seldom found in hoards of the appliances and stock-in-trade of bronze casters—leading to the inference that the mine-owners kept the secrets and processes of alloying in their own hands.[3] Thus, any bronze object made or found in tin-less Ireland is a proof of contemporary trade and transport. And Ireland had the good fortune to possess gold enough to deck the native lords and ladies, and to leave a surplus sufficient to satisfy even the rapacious Cornish mine-owners.

There is, however, an alternative possibility, which was stated by the late Dr. Bremer in the following words :—[4]

The Beaker Folk—a people who obviously entered Great Britain from the Rhinelands—came to England, Wales, and the east coast of Scotland about 2500 B.C. This people never penetrated to Ireland ; one single beaker from Co. Down must have been imported from the opposite shore of Scotland, which is actually within sight of Ulster.[5] Now it is very striking how extraordinarily rare the slender beaker is in the mine regions of Cornwall. We can point to only three graves which have yielded beakers, and a fourth with a later handled variety.[6] This is a singularly small number, considering

---

[1] *Bibliotheca* v 22.
[2] See Clement Reid's exposition of this identification, *Archæologia* 59 ii [1905] : 281. [3] Evans, *Ancient Bronze Implements of Great Britain*, p. 425.
[4] *Die Stellung Irlands in der europäischen Vor- und Frühgeschichte*, p. 5. The quotation is here made from the English translation, published in Bremer's memory after his death, but unfortunately soon afterwards destroyed by an accidental fire at the publishers.
[5] It will be remembered that this was written in 1926.
[6] Bremer here refers to Sir Cyril Fox's earlier map in *Archæologia Cambrensis* 80 [1925] : 1, but the later map does not seriously disturb these statistics. On the early history of tin see further O. Davies, " The Ancient Tin Sources of Western Europe ", *Belfast* 1931-2 : 41.

the severe pressure which must have been brought to bear on the tin district during the Bronze Age. We are forced to conjecture that the Beaker Folk secured no more influence in Cornwall than in Ireland ; the bronze industry was thus able to develop in both these regions along its old lines without interruption, from the time of the first copper artifacts onward. . . . Ireland was not affected by this invasion and [it is probable that] Cornwall was not affected either—in other words, that the ancient Iberian population continued to be the transmitters of this development in the chief centres of industry.

Thus whoever held Cornwall—native aborigines, an Irish commercial or military colony, or both together in partnership—had succeeded in excluding the Beaker Folk : until the latter had gathered strength in men and a powerful fleet, sufficient to break the Iberian monopoly, to strike at the heart of the people who barred the way to the prizes which they withheld, and to secure for the immigrants a control of the Cornish tin—to say nothing of the Irish gold. The Beaker invasion of Ireland was almost a small-scale rehearsal of the world-shaking events of the times in which these words are being written ; and like them, was an episode in the unending struggle between the " haves " and the " have-nots ".

But there may have been a further determining cause. If we accept a suggestion made by Mr. O. G. S. Crawford,[1] England was itself invaded at about the same time [2] by adventurers from Switzerland or Armorica, who introduced a whole armoury of new implements—the leading types of Montelius's " Fifth Period ". Such a movement could easily take place as a repercussion of the unrest in South-Eastern Europe, which shrouds from our eyes the history of the transition-time from Bronze to Iron, and during which the great empires of the Ancient Orient fell in ruins, and the new city-states began to make their appearance on the stage : and it might not only stimulate a westward movement of the people already in Britain, but reinforce it.

Ireland never completely recovered from the disaster. The enterprise manifested, for us, by the construction of vast megalithic monuments, and doubtless in other departments of activity, now in the nature of things less conspicuous ; the promising beginnings of trade and of art ; all were killed. The destroyer, aided by the adverse climate of the Upper Turbarian phase, which was just now setting in, effectually prevented any hope of a renascence : for he exterminated the men, or at least reduced them to slavery. As for the women, they met the usual fate of women in warfare : " to every man a damsel or two," as the savage old Hebrew pæan expresses it.[3] And to assure us of this, there comes into view the

---

[1] " A prehistoric Invasion of England ", *Antiquaries' Journal* II [1922] : 27.

[2] Crawford fixes the date at about 900-700 B.C.   E. E. Evans, who accepts the thesis, would put the invasion to a century or two earlier ; this would synchronize it with the cultural and racial changes which testify to an invasion of Ireland. See *Man* 31 [1931] : 209.   [3] *Judges* 5 : 30.

impressive fact to which Martin has called attention, that nearly all of the dolichocephalic skulls found in Epimegalithic cist-tombs are those of women.[1]

Whatever may have been written in previous studies, the Beaker people *did* come to Ireland. Not only so—they exploited and enslaved it. They left no beakers behind ; they left the Gaelic language instead. For after, so to speak, " trying over all the moves ", I have been forced, however unwillingly, to the conclusion that the Beaker invasion is the only event in the country's history with which it is possible to associate this linguistic revolution ; it was the only catastrophe of ancient times, subversive enough to have effected such a complete change of language.

The stone monuments attributed to the Epimegalithic people are of two kinds ; cists, and the various types of non-constructional monuments which consist of standing stones, singly or in groups.

Cists are box-like receptacles composed of slabs, normally six in number—four side slabs, a floor- and a roof-slab. But the floor-slab is often, the roof-slab occasionally, omitted ; the sides may be composed not of one slab only, but of several, set edge to edge ; and the plan of the enclosed chamber, though usually, need not necessarily be, rectangular, but may be circular, or of a variety of more or less irregular shapes.

The body, unburnt, or (more commonly) cremated, is deposited inside the cist ; in the latter case a large urn is usually inverted over the ashes. The grave-goods are as a rule insignificant, in quantity or in apparent intrinsic value. Frequently the ashes under the urn-cover are accompanied by a pygmy urn or miniature food-vessel such as used to be called an " incense cup " : this absurd name should be discarded altogether, not even quoted. The purpose of these small vessels, like that of all other grave-deposits of the Megalithic age, was magical. They were in fact nothing but miniature food-vessels, made small because one of normal size would not fit, with the ashes, underneath the urn-cover ; and they served the same purpose, of securing unlimited and ever-renewed supplies of food for the dead in the other world.

Even the cist itself was often reduced to " its lowest terms " with an economy of trouble, though no doubt supplemented by means of magic. A good example, instructive in several ways, was found at Creggan (Antrim).[2] Here the urn was inverted over a flat stone, and another stone was laid upon its upturned base ; the side-stones of the cist were omitted. Upon the lower stone, under the urn, were the cremated remains of three persons—a woman of about thirty years, an infant only just born, and another

---

[1] *Prehistoric Man in Ireland*, p. 101.   [2] JRSAI 56 [1926] : 56.

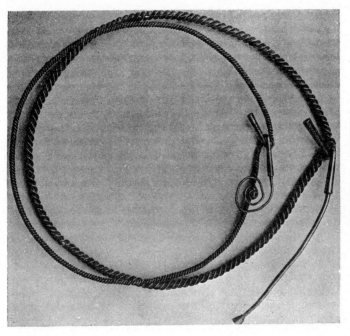

THE TARA TORQUES

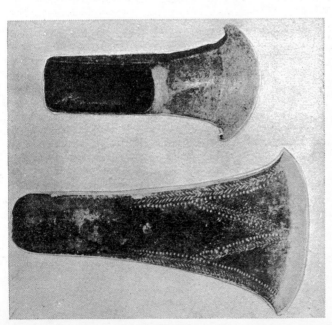

DECORATED HATCHET HEAD AND PALSTAVE
From the Reports of the Dublin National Museum:
by permission).

child of about seven years. That the woman had died in child-birth, with the infant, is obviously a reasonable conjecture, if it is nothing more ; but what was the elder child doing in that galley ? How did it come to die at a moment sufficiently close to the other deaths to earn for it a place in the same sepulchre ?

If this were an isolated case, the question could be brushed aside with perfect reason. Such melancholy coincidences do take place on occasion, within the experience of all of us. But in the Epi-megalithic Period they took place rather too frequently. I had noted several cases, in reading reports of excavations in sepulchres of this period, of the bones of a young child, not an infant, associated in an unquestionably simultaneous sepulture with those of an elder person ; not necessarily a woman, as we might reasonably expect. I had been asking myself if this could possibly be fortuitous ; when I learnt by a chance remark made to me by Dr. Jameson, Professor of Anatomy in Dublin University (to whose ready assistance in the solution of osteological problems Irish archæologists are under a heavy debt), that he had observed the same thing, and was asking the same question. Was the child in such cases sacrificed, that its young life might requicken the dead adult ? Or, possibly in the Creggan case, that it might give back to the dead infant the life of which it had been cheated, and secure for it a chance of re-birth ? There is no use in pretending that an affirmative answer to these questions is improbable : devices to secure the re-quickening of stillborn infants are familiar to all anthropologists. A cist ex-cavated at Halverston (Kildare) by Dr. Raftery showed exactly the same combination—a woman, a fœtus, and a child under a year old, in this case represented by three teeth only. In the same con-nexion we must recall the elaborate funeral of what was apparently a person of importance, reconstructed in a most masterly manner by Sir Cyril Fox, after his excavation of Pond Carn, Glamorgan.[1] Here, the first incident of the ritual was certainly the burning of the body of a child of about seven years, and the scattering of its ashes. We need not feel any surprise at finding such a custom in the back-ground of a society in which it was possible for a story to be told about a girl being fed on the flesh of other children, that she might grow up the sooner to marriageable age, and so earn her bride-price for her guardians as quickly as possible. Incidentally, the already enormous ethnological interest of this tale is enhanced four-fold when we read further, and learn that after the lady had been suc-cessfully settled in life, she used to lop off the little fingers of her own children, " to make them live longer ". This plunges us right into the heart of African Bushmen and sundry Melanesian societies, where similar mutilations for analogous purposes are practised as a matter of course.[2]

[1] *Archæologia* 87 [1937] : 142.   [2] Stokes and Windisch, *Irische Texte* 3 : 363.

Now read this account of a cist-burial found at Ballybrew (Wicklow).[1] Here was buried a man—not cremated this time—probably of early middle age, in the crouched attitude, but lying on his back (not on the side, as is more frequent in crouched burials), with the arms, not in the normal position (folded over the breast) but with the humeri along the sides and the forearms flexed upwards. To maintain such an attitude the body must have been tightly bound up, almost like a mummy, and so deposited. There was a food-vessel in a corner of the cist.

Some of the bones of a young child surrounded the adult skeleton ; the skull below the feet, a few of the long bones flanking the right-hand side ; a vertebra and a fragment of rib *in the food-vessel* ; and one of the clavicles close to the left shoulder. The discoverers expressed the opinion that the cist had originally belonged to the child, and that its bones had been scattered when its tomb was appropriated for the man. But such a usurpation would hardly account for the evidently purposeful disposition of the child's bones. At Cuillare (Mayo) a cist was found which contained a cremated interment ; a few bones from an earlier inhumation disturbed by the later burial had been collected and preserved, but *not* inside the cist ; they were laid upon the cover-stone, and another stone was laid over them, probably as an element in a propitiatory rite, to appease the outraged spirit of the former owner. This significant difference indicates that the Ballybrew deposit was something more than accident. We seem to have here another case of child-sacrifice, the child being killed, and some of its bones stripped of their flesh—*scarnitura* being expedited by boiling—and disposed around the corpse. In the particular case before us, there was a special reason why this should be done. Some time before his death, the man had broken one of his legs across the tibia and fibula, and the fractured bones had never joined ; he must have been badly handicapped ever after, in locomotion. The child had been " commandeered " to provide a sound pair of legs for him in the next world. If the body of the child was boiled, it was almost certainly ceremonially eaten ; and the deposition of a couple of its bones in the food-vessel shows that the dead shared in the communal feast, and was expected to absorb a profit from the victim's healthy personality. Analogies from Melanesia and elsewhere might be cited to prove that ideas of this kind are normal and natural at certain stages of cultural development ; and Epimegalithic Ireland, or for that matter Epimegalithic Europe, had not travelled very far beyond the Melanesians on the road to civilization.

I can here present only a small selection of the facts which I have collected on cist-burial in Ireland. They are full of suggestiveness, and illustrate, among other matters, the practice of *sati* (the

[1] PRIA 43 [1926] : 255.

immolation of wives and dependents at the funeral of their lord) ; double interment—a temporary disposal of the bodies to be transferred later to their final resting-place ; racial or social distinctions, illustrated by the various treatment of the bodies in adjacent and contemporary burials (as when *one* unburned skeleton is found in association with cremated remains in a single receptacle) ; and so forth. As yet we are only in a position to indicate that there are still many problems, even of preliminary classification, which have not yet begun to be solved. An apparently degenerate structure will yield grave-goods of the standard type, suggesting contemporaneity. The evolution of culture in Ireland has an anarchic quality which, by adding to its perplexities, certainly adds to its interest ; and every year the subject is becoming more and more unmanageable.

I must therefore reluctantly close the present account of the remains of burial monuments in Ireland during the Megalithic period, with a sense of inadequacy, tempered by the reflection that no private person or public body could hope to attain to any ideal of completeness ; and that, even already, no single volume could contain the fulfilment of any such ideal. We must now turn to the non-constructional monuments and say what little we may in the available space.

Standing stones are among the commonest remains of antiquity in Ireland. Though none of them can compete with some of the Brittany giants, they are often of a considerable height. About 20 feet above ground appears to be the extreme limit ; the average height may be about 8 to 12 feet ; and there are many not more than about 4 to 6 feet.

Unless some external evidence be available, it is impossible to date such monuments as these. Some of them may, indeed, have been erected in modern times, as scratching-posts for cattle. On the other hand, they occasionally rise over bronze-age graves, with which they are certainly contemporary. Between these two limits there are other examples, equally uncouth in external aspect, which bear Ogham inscriptions and even crosses cut upon them, and thus appear to fall within the Christian era. In a word, such a stone might have been set up at any moment of the world's history ; and unless those who performed the feat had left some indication of the purpose of their action, we could not tell *a priori* whether it was to be dated to 1900 B.C. or A.D. 1900. When it is associated with a grave containing datable deposits, these are almost if not quite invariably Epimegalithic in character.[1]

But it was in the Bronze Age that such exceptionally large stones

---

[1] It is not to be understood that " standing stones " are necessarily *confined* to this latest phase of the Megalithic cult : individual specimens may have been erected at any moment in its course. But *groups* of such stones, in circles, alignments, and so forth, are probably to be assigned, in general, to the Epimegalithic.

were habitually manipulated ; that was essentially the " Megalithic " period.   Later, building with small stones took its place—an operation in which the labour was equally heavy when reckoned in foot-pounds, but was spread over a longer time, and was therefore less concentrated.   A pillarstone of more than, say, 10 feet in height is most likely to belong to the Megalithic period : if it should bear Oghams, or crosses, or any other indication of a later date, we are justified in assuming that these had been imposed upon a monument already existing, adapted by later people for their own purpose— that of securing for themselves the spurious prestige of a monument, stately if second-hand.

Besides being grave-marks, standing stones could serve other purposes ; as landmarks, and as images or altars, the visible recipients of devotions addressed to an invisible being.   These uses can be deduced from passages in the Irish Law tracts.   Thus, in the glosses to the tract called *Bretha Comaithchesa* (" Judgements of Joint Tenancy ") we find a list of different kinds of landmarks, among which there is a reference to " Land which a ' Stone of Adoration ' marks out ".   The same expression, " Stone of Adoration " (*ailche adrada*) appears in another tract called *Fastad Cirt ocus Dligid* (" Confirmation of Right and Law "), where details are given about ancient practices of ordeal.[1]

Of the worship of stones, as representatives of deities, we have evidence down to a very late date.   The Church Councils of Gaul were compelled, century after century, to denounce the perpetuation of such heathen rites.   Indeed, even yet, they are not extinct,[2] as facts set forth in the books quoted in the footnote below clearly show.   Ecclesiastics were ultimately reduced to compromising with cults which were found impossible to extirpate.   By the expedient of cutting crosses upon the stones which were the objects, or at least the centres of cult, they hoped to exorcise the paganism out of them, and so to transfer their ancient sanctity to the service of the new Faith.   This is the explanation of the crosses so often found upon such rude monoliths.

Pairs of standing stones are common.   These may have been, what they often resemble more than anything else, nothing but the jamb-stones of the entrance-gate to an enclosure, sacred or secular.   They may mark the head and foot of a grave.   But sometimes they may represent a pair of divinities—either a Dioscuric twin-pair, or a male-and-female couple like the Gaulish Grannos

---

[1] *Ancient Laws of Ireland* (Rolls Series) iv 142, v 472.
[2] See Bertrand, La *religion des Gaulois*, pp. 400 ff., for full particulars of the relevant decrees of the Councils ; for modern survivals see Sébillot, *Le folk-lore de France*, vol. iv, and the same author's *Le Paganisme contemporain chez les peuples celto-latins* (Paris 1908) ; Z. Le Rouzic, *Carnac* (Vannes 1924) ; and S. Reinach's essay, *Les monuments de pierre brute dans le langage et les croyances populaires* (in *Cultes, Mythes, et Religions*, 3 : 364).

and Sirona. In this connexion, attention should be called to pairs of stones, one blunt-topped, the other sharp-topped, understood to indicate a female and a male respectively. A good example is to be seen at Knockrour (Cork), here illustrated (Plate IIa); Ogham scores, now defaced, have been cut upon one of them, but this is a later intrusion.

Groups of standing stones may be set in straight lines ("alignments") or rings (stone circles). Alignments are not very common in Ireland; there is nothing in the country that can bear comparison with the wonderful complexes of the kind to be seen in Brittany. Single lines, containing not more than three, four, or five stones are the limit. Circles are comparatively more numerous but they are fewer, and less impressive, than the average of those in Great Britain; Ireland can show nothing comparable with Stonehenge or Avebury, or even the smaller group known as "Long Meg and her Daughters" in the neighbourhood of Penrith.

Only a man of great wealth or influence could command the construction of such a mound as Dowth. But even great men may have honours, like in degree, though specifically very different; and here we must say some words about one of the most remarkable burial mounds ever opened in Ireland, very skilfully excavated at Drimnagh (Dublin)[1] by Mr. Kilbride-Jones.

There were here two mounds, A and B, of which A was *inside B* —an earlier burial, overlaid, absorbed and superseded by another of later date.[2]

The structure of mound A was of some complexity. A rather irregularly constructed cist was set on the ground-surface, within the middle of the area. This cist contained a pottery "hanging bowl" of a Spanish type, absolutely unique in Ireland (Fig. 12); and the skeleton of a man, apparently between thirty and forty years of age—dolichocephalic, and about 5 feet 5 inches in stature. The body lay on the right side, outstretched as far as the knees, but below that level forcibly flexed (and probably tied in that attitude) so that the heels were pressed close against the back. The cist was covered with a small carn of stones, with a number of other small stones making an interrupted fence around it; and in the adjacent area there was a remarkable complication of air-pits and air-passages which had apparently been filled with loosely-packed inflammable material. Over these preliminary deposits a mound of sods had been heaped up: and on the flat top of this mound, just over the now buried cist, there was laid down a number of small stones arranged

---

[1] Report in JRSAI 69 [1939] : 190.
[2] Though (so far) otherwise unknown in Ireland, such double mounds are recorded elsewhere; see, for example, the description of the tumulus on the Noordsche Veld near Zeijen (Drenthe, Holland), in A. E. van Giffen, *Die Bauart der Einzelgräber* (Leipzig, 1930), pp. 10 ff.

in what certainly appears to represent the form of a swastika, with other stones at intervals making a ring around this symbol.

The next stage in the operation was the erection of a conical framework of elder-wood, with a surface coating of similar sods on

FIG. 12.—Hanging Bowl, Drimnagh.

its outer surface—a " Navajo " hut, in fact, no doubt essentially similar to the hut which the occupant had inhabited during his lifetime : who knows whether it might not have been the same hut, taken down, transported, and re-erected ? And when all was finished, the whole was sent to the other world in the vapour of a mighty blaze. The air-holes below, packed with inflammable material to start the fire, and the burial hut above, between them made a fire which may have burnt for several weeks, and calcined the sod structure as if it had been built of peat. " A good deal of fore-thought ", says Mr. Kilbride-Jones, " had been given to the problem of " [the erection of the mound]. So much " care was necessary, owing to the fact that it had to be set on fire, and because it was desired that combustion should be complete throughout ". And he shows that the air-pits were not scattered about at haphazard, but were contrived to counteract the influence of the prevailing winds, which might have caused the burning to be less thorough in the sheltered side.

In spite of a superficial similarity of outline to a smaller bowl found in a chambered carn at Clachaig in the island of Arran (Scotland)—which has no suspension-holes, or lug handles,[1] and is rather differently decorated, with cord impressions—the bowl found in the cist was of a character so exceptional, so unprecedented in Ireland, that we should be obliged to assume the deceased to have been an exceptional man, even if the *ensemble* had not presented these remarkable ritual features. It is no far-fetched flight of imagination to suppose that he was a magician of some sort—king, diviner, wonder-worker, what you will—and that the bowl, like Joseph's silver cup, was the instrument of his sorceries. As such, it would be carefully safeguarded during his lifetime, and might have passed down to him from some earlier practitioner ; who might have brought it with him from Spain. All these con-jectures are set forth here in order to show that though we must date the bowl, on account of its type, to some time previous to 2000 B.C., it does not necessarily follow that the burial was of such extreme antiquity. Two fragments of Windmill Hill vessels were found on the top of the sod-mound—possibly belonging to vessels accidentally broken while serving the meals of the builders.

The grave of such a man, who had been buried in such a spec-tacular way, would make a long-lasting impression on the inhabitants : indeed, Mr. Kilbride-Jones records local traditions, extant even yet, which seem to reflect that impression. And other persons, perhaps in their day of some importance, would, by their friends, be thought worthy of being buried in this hallowed mound. Accordingly, two later burials, one dated to middle Bronze Age (Deuteromegalithic), the other to late Bronze Age (Epimegalithic) were intruded on the original potentate. The one was a cremation interment, dug into the sod-mound and near the base, with a decorated food-vessel ; the other was also a cremation interment, placed underneath a

---

[1] There are, however, lug handles on another vessel of different type from the same place.

cinerary urn of late type.   The urn had been inverted on the top of the burnt sod-mound, and a mound of about 100 feet in diameter had been heaped over it—this being the mound B.   The whole height of the composite mound was between 13 and 15 feet.   Even this did not complete the record of burials, for two inhumations had been made at a still later time, working through mound B and penetrating into mound A.   These were not simultaneous burials, though they had been made in the same grave ; the bones were hopelessly decayed, and there were no grave goods.

We have seen that burial mounds began as the graves of individual despots, comparable in their way with the Egyptian pyramids —few in number, and each the tomb of some great man, belonging to the end of the Stone and beginning of the Bronze Age.   We have now seen that as time goes on, three things might happen to these monuments :—

1. They might become centres around which cemeteries accumulated.
2. They might be intruded upon by later interments, which was never intended at the first.   Such interments might be deposited in secondary cists, sunk under the surface of the mound ; or they might be substituted for the primary interments, which had been unceremoniously cleared out.
3. They might be imitated, in the attenuated form of " dolmens " and similar simpler structures : all through the world's history the little man thinks himself qualified to ape the big man.

We may see this principle at work in such a site as Knockast (Westmeath).   Here we encounter a complete " democratization " of the aristocratic burial mound.   The tumulus of Knockast was erected on the surface of the ground, without even taking the trouble to clear the vegetation.   It measured 60 feet in basal diameter, 4 feet in height, and was formed of a core of stones carelessly thrown together, covered with dark soil.   There was not, and never had been, any primary interment : it was simply a collective grave-mound, in which the remains of 42 persons had been deposited— 3 unburned, 39 burnt.   Some of these were laid in little heaps, others in small cists, others pushed into hollows between stones, others in urns : later interments had disturbed older ones ; the pottery, though meagre, showed a surprising range of affinities : some round-bottomed vessels had a Neolithic aspect, while fragments of one incrusted vessel could hardly be older than the date to which the excavators assigned the whole complex, the seventh or sixth century B.C.   Once more we see the survival of obsolete forms, complicating the chronology.   One skeleton, of a racial type different from the rest, appeared to have been intruded in the Viking age, and thus to have introduced an incongruous silver ringed pin of that period, which had worked its way down to the bottom of the mound.   The two parietal bones of an infant were placed, one on the left arm, the other beneath the sternum, of this skeleton : the excavators do not seem to have considered how the second of these got there, although

PLATE V

ENCRUSTED URN, BURGAGE, CO. WICKLOW
(by permission).

SPEARHEAD
LOCH GUR

of are con
n

it seems an obvious question to ask.   Was the body opened and this infant " soul-box " placed within it to secure a re-birth of the owner of the skeleton ?   A wild guess, admittedly : but taking the facts as they are presented to us, how otherwise could the space beneath the sternum in a buried body have been accessible to an intrusive parietal bone, or to anything else ? [1]

We may close this chapter with the word or two which is all that will here be possible to say about the symbols carved on some of the component stones of rude stone monuments, as well as on rock-surfaces having no evident connexion with such monuments : a subject upon which the Irish material alone could even now supply material for a large book.   Such carvings, with which we may associate rock-paintings, are found scattered over the Continent of Europe, in a geographical distribution so exactly similar to that of the Megaliths, that it is impossible to doubt that they form an element in the same cult-complex.   We say nothing about the vastly more ancient sculptures, engravings, and paintings of Palæolithic caves, which are here irrelevant ; setting them aside, we find that wherever megaliths are to be found—in Spain, France, Ireland, Great Britain, Scandinavia—there we find rock-decorations ; and where they are absent, or practically so, as Italy, the Balkan Penin-sula, Central Europe, there bronze-age rock decorations are absent also.

The decorations—we intentionally use this non-committal term for them, without expressing any opinion as to whether they are symbolic, magical, historical, or merely ornamental—are of various types ; and certain types are prevalent in certain regions, others in other regions.   They may be realistic, representing easily recogniz-able figures of men, ships, chariots, weapons, birds, animals ; which, however, does not help us far on the road to their interpretation, as we have no direct means of discovering what ideas the artists associated with the various men, animals, or things which they depicted ; we ask in vain *why* they took the trouble to carve them. They may be sub-realistic, not at first presenting self-evident mean-ings, but, when set out in a series which displays the working of progressive deterioration, revealed as in essence identical with the realistic figures, degraded by having passed through the hands of incompetent copyists.   Or they may be mere geometrical abstrac-tions, saucer-marks, spirals, circles and other Euclidean figures, which (like x in the calculations of a mathematician) would convey an intelligible message only if the artist were at hand to tell us what meaning he had for the occasion put into them.   The Arunta of Central Australia draw startlingly similar patterns with pipe-clay,

[1] For a very full account of this remarkable deposit, with an ethnological analysis of all the bones see H. O'N. Hencken and H. L. Movius, " The Cemetery Cairn of Knockast " (PRIA 41 [1934] : 232).

on smoothed surfaces of earth, in preparation for their tribal ceremonies, part of which is the instruction of adolescent boys in the
tribal traditions—using these diagrams as something analogous to
explanatory blackboard diagrams, to assist comprehension and
memory.[1]   We cannot reconstruct the unrecorded details of nomadic history ; but we must admit the possibility of waves of migration, starting from some Asiatic centre, and gradually making their
way—some to the end of the world in the north-west, some, by way
of the Malay Peninsula, to the end of the world in the south-east :
severally carrying, from the original homeland, beliefs, customs,
art-conventions, to the remotest ends of the Continental land-mass.
When a seal comes to light at Mohenjo-Daro on the Indus, bearing
the figure of a divinity, seated on a stool in the *Yoga* attitude (i.e. with
legs bent double, and foot-soles pressed together), with three faces,
with horns upon his head, wearing elaborate torques and a belt,
and surrounded with horned and other animals ; [2] and when
sculptured figures come to light in the land of Gaul, displaying a
Gaulish divinity called by the Celtic name *Cernunnos*, with three
faces, horns, a conspicuous neck-torque, seated upon a stool in a
cross-legged attitude, and surrounded by horned animals,[3] who
can deny a direct relationship even between cults so widely sundered ?
One of these Gaulish figures, a bronze statuette from Autun, shows
the god circled, not with a belt, but with two snakes, having horned
rams' heads and fish-tails ; and one of the horned serpents in the
great frieze on the kerb of Knowth has also a fish's tail.[4] A ram-
headed serpent appears, again, on an altar from Beauvais,[5] and
on a grave-monument found in the neighbourhood of Mycenæ.[6]
And some Arunta representations of their mysterious traditional
serpent, the *Wollunqua*, though not, apparently, endowed with rams'
heads and with fish-tails, have more than a family resemblance to
the Knowth snakes.[7]   The bull-roarer was in use in Ancient Ireland,
as in the Eleusinian Mysteries, no less than among the living aborigines of Australia ; [8] the Australian boomerang was in use in
Mesolithic Denmark ; the Australian *churingas* have their analogies
in the painted pebbles of Le Mas d'Azil ; the Australian javelin-
propulsor has its analogies in late Palæolithic Europe, and among
the modern Eskimo.   The following sentences, from an account
of the inhabitants of New Guinea, might stand unaltered as an

---

[1] See *Ancient Ireland*, p. 48.
[2] Sir J. Marshall, *Mohenjo-Daro*, vol. i p. 52, plate xii fig 17.
[3] Courcelle-Seneuil's *Les dieux gauloises d'après les monuments figurés*, pp. 14-
100, provides a series of illustrations in which the permutations and combinations
of this *ensemble* of characters can be conveniently studied.
[4] PRIA 49 [1943] : 159 fig. 26.   [5] Courcelle-Seneuil, *op. cit.* p. 71.
[6] Frazer, *Pausanias*, vol. iii p. 187 and references there.
[7] Spencer and Gillen, *The Northern Tribes of Central Australia*, pp. 232-6.
[8] See my *Tara*, pp. 137-48 ; see also INJ 5 [1934] : 24, where the survival of
this magical instrument as a children's toy (under the suggestive name " thunder-
spade " or the like) is reported.

explanatory footnote to the (intrinsically almost incomprehensible) monetary complications of the Irish " Brehon Laws " :—

A slave is the standard of value throughout the western parts of New Guinea . . . so that when the price of any article is said to be so many slaves, it is intended to mean the value of a slave in blue and red calico or other articles of trade, all of which bear a fixed proportionate value. It is therefore, like the " pound sterling ", an imaginary standard of value.[1]

In fact, it is not too much to say that a study of the contemporary cultural ethnology of the South Sea Islands must now be regarded as a *necessary* preliminary to any serious study of the cultural ethnology of Ireland down to at least 1500 years ago. A student of Prehistoric Ireland may go to school under the instruction of a lowly Arunta of Central Australia, without the least sense of incongruity ; and he will assuredly come back from his teachers, enlightened with an illumination which he could never have drawn from any other source.

Coffey, whose work, *New Grange and other inscribed tumuli in Ireland*, remains the standard study of the Irish megaliths and their decoration, has treated these figures as ornamental, without any esoteric religious or historical idea behind them. To this simple theory there is a grave objection. The decoration of bronze-age objects in pottery or metal shows that the artists had an instinct for *rhythm* as an essential of ornament. The decoration of such objects consists of the repetition of motives of design with a patterned regularity. But the decoration of rocks and stones very rarely shows either rhythm or symmetry. The few exceptions (as in certain of the stones of the kerb of Knowth) only throws the fact into the greater relief.

In Scandinavia a conspicuous realism is to be observed in the rock-scribings. In the Iberian sculptures and paintings, realism merges into what we have called sub-realism ; the Clonfinloch stone (*ante*, p. 50) is a good example of Iberian sub-realism. In Great Britain and Ireland the rock-scribings are almost all geometrical abstractions. They are found upon rock-surfaces, or upon the component stones of megalithic monuments. It is probable, though naturally the effects of centuries of adverse weather conditions make proof impossible, that such decorations were also applied to stone surfaces with paint ; there is actually one example of painted ornament remaining, inside one of the Lochcrew carns.[2]

Most of the sculptures were made on the stone with a pocking-tool. The design was presumably first outlined with some easily-manipulated substance that would make a mark—paint, mud, chalk

[1] G. W. Earl, *The Native Races of the Indian Archipelago* (London 1853), p. 84.
[2] First observed by Breuil, and published in his stately monograph *Les peintures rupestres schématiques de la Péninsule Ibérique* (Lagny-sur-Marne 1933), vol. i p. 62.

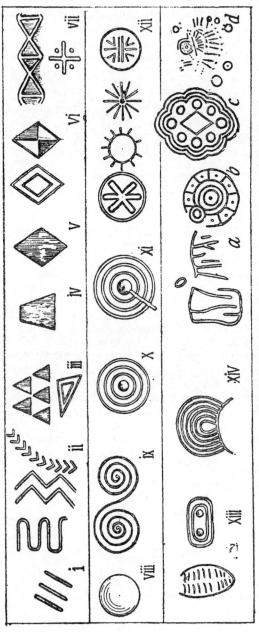

FIG. 13.—The Chief Elements in the British Province of Rock-scribings.

(if available), or what not—or lightly scratched on the stone surface, and then crushed out with a sharp-nosed stone hammer along the lines thus defined. Sometimes the artist contented himself with a single hammering, so that the design appears as a series of pocks so disconnected that they have to be joined up again with chalk in order to define the pattern intended ; sometimes the blows are close, so that the line is fully defined, but so light that it is hardly sunk below the surface ; sometimes the artist has been more diligent, and has made well-depressed grooves, still retaining the scars produced by the pocking-tool ; and sometimes these grooves have been rubbed smooth, so as to remove the roughness caused by the pocking. But an altogether different technique appears on occasion ; the lines are not pocked, but cut out with a metal chisel ; forming continuous lines, like knife-drawn gashes, with no trace of the pocking process. This introduces us to the all-important subject of the *super-position* of symbols, first observed at New Grange by Coffey, though its full significance was not realized till some of the stones of that and the associated monuments had passed under the practised eyes of Breuil.

In the Subsidiary Chamber of Dowth there is a stone (Fig. 14) [1] which has been adorned with simple geometrical patterns—squares with their diagonals, circles with radii, etc., *chisel-cut*. Among these there is a suggestion of a human face with conspicuous teeth and long hair. At some later time this stone was *pocked* smooth in patches, themselves apparently of a purposeful shape, which on the whole avoid interference with the elder devices. Later, *pocked* linear circles and spirals were added to the stone, one of them in the middle of one of the pocked areas. This indicates the work of successive groups of rock-scribers, separated by an appreciable though indefinable interval of time—the second manipulating the stone which his predecessor had left, but, while adding his own devices, refraining (doubtless for superstitious reasons) from tampering with the older figures. What is of even more momentous importance, it proves that the stone must have had a period of service in some other capacity before the mound-builders made use of it ; for such a manipulation is not likely to have taken place after the stone had been buried away in an underground burial-chamber, sealed up and inaccessible. And there cannot be the slightest doubt that it began its life in human service as a standing pillarstone. It has a pointed butt end, which for the lower half of its length is devoid of carving. Its present visible length is 7 feet. At a guess the total length may be 10 feet, the remaining 3 feet being concealed in the masonry of the chamber in which it is now set. The uninscribed butt end being buried in the ground, and supported with boulders wedged in around it, it may have stood free to a height of

---

[1] It is the stone lettered *l*, on the plan of Dowth, *ante*, p. 73.

7 to 8 feet, thus giving ample opportunity for the alterations and additions which its sculpture has undergone.

This is not the only other example ; a minute examination of all

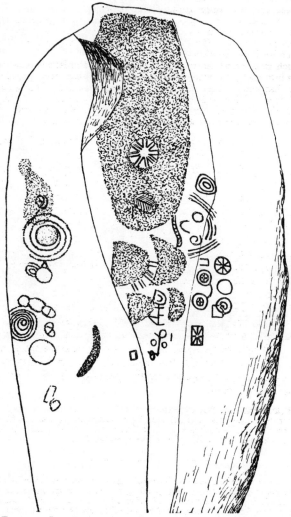

FIG. 14.—Inscribed Stone in the Subsidiary Chamber of Dowth.

the stones, one by one, will reveal others.   As I write, I can think of four other stones, in New Grange, on which I have made similar observations.   This suggests three inferences which are of primary importance in any discussion of the purpose, meaning and history of the symbols, and of their relation to the megalithic monuments in which we sometimes find them :—

1. Scribings are not essential to these monuments : they are wholly absent from the Carrowkeel series, for example.

2. *In the New Grange region,* chisel-cut markings are older than pocked markings ; when there is interference the former are superseded by the latter, never *vice versa.* (Breuil has made the same observation on a stone from Traprain Law, Edinburgh.) [1]

3. Such interference is more likely to have taken place before the stone was built into the place where we find it, in the heart of a burial mound. It follows that some at least of the inscribed stones in New Grange are there *at second-hand.* They had been used in some other capacity before being built into the structure where we find them, and their carvings *have no relation to the structure or to the purpose for which it was built.*

In fact, the majority of the carved stones which add so much to the interest of New Grange have really nothing to do with it ; they are merely there by accident, and tell of nothing more than the pillage, for building material, of an earlier monument or group of monuments. One of these stones has been fractured to make it fit the place where the mason desired to set it, mutilating the ornament ; and almost all of the stones in the entrance passage of the same monument have had the devices which they once bore chipped away, leaving nothing but a few insignificant traces. Whatever the reason may be, this is certainly a matter of deliberate policy.[2]

There is much more to be said about these carvings, their significance and their bearing upon the religion and culture of the megalith cult. My own notebooks are filled with material of which I would gladly make use ; but under the rigid limitations imposed by wartime and post-wartime conditions I must for the moment forbear. I have said enough, however, for the immediate purpose of defining and justifying the chronological subdivisions upon which the following chapters, describing the general culture of the Megalithic Age, are planned.

[1] PPS (East Anglia) 7 [1934] : 292.
[2] It is to be noticed that this refers to New Grange only : those in Dowth and Knowth are different in their purpose and their relation to the structure where we find them. But here we cannot pursue the quest further.

Postscript to p. 74.—Several indications suggest to me that there is actually a secret chamber in New Grange, corresponding to that in Dowth, and in an identical place—the right-hand burial recess. The floor of this cell is covered, not, as usual, with a mere slab, but with a huge boulder, certainly not less than a couple of tons in weight. It would not surprise me to learn that this had been found to close the opening of a shaft-grave of Mycenæan type.

CHAPTER V

THE PROTOMEGALITHIC CULTURE

I. SOCIAL CONDITIONS

THE Protomegalithic Culture coincided, in time, with the most favourable climatic conditions that Ireland ever enjoyed in the post-glacial epoch. It does not necessarily follow that there was high civilization, or even high prosperity. Nor can we assume that the country was at first thickly populated—this, indeed, is improbable ; for the favourable climate produced dense forest-growths, which not only occupied much land unprofitably, but also interposed barriers between the regional communities. Such barriers retard progress, for they prevent free intercourse between different population groups ; and we must bear in mind that when they are too suddenly broken down, as may happen at any time—even an extensive forest fire could have far-reaching consequences—they may make for hostile rather than friendly relations between peoples whom they have for so long kept separate.

The differentiation of the northern from the southern megaliths shows us these barriers " in working order ". On the other hand, the cultural contaminations which we may suspect, even in the scanty materials as yet available, are a sign of their gradual dis-appearance. But extensive research will still be necessary before we can present a complete study of this aspect of social history. Osteological evidence for or against racial differentiation between north and south, and a much more intensive investigation of the typology and geographical distribution of various classes of artifacts, are still among the many primary *desiderata*. For these we need unplundered Protomegalithic burials and habitation-sites from all parts of the country ; and the prospects of finding them, in satisfying numbers, are not very rosy.

The most important influence, making for a weakening of the barriers, was the concentration into one small area of the available supplies of flint. An at least rudimentary trade must have grown up, rooted in the desire to secure a sufficiency of this indispensable material ; and with it must have developed such transport devices as trackways, fords, perhaps simply-constructed bridges, and the conquest of beasts of burden. And the same epoch witnessed the discovery and partial exploitation of the mineral wealth of the country, an advance which could hardly have been made so rapidly if the supply of flint had been more evenly distributed. In some regions, such as North Sligo, chert was available in considerable quantities : but this is a poor substitute for flint, and evidence for its industrial use in the country has been rarely found. One of these exceptional cases was at Creevykeel, in the county named. Under the stimulus of such impoverishment, an early exploitation of metal is not surprising.

The one inexhaustible and universal industrial material was wood. We may be sure that woodwork (including basketwork) provided the greater part of the domestic utensils, and also the implements possible within its limitations : digging sticks and serviceable spears and daggers, as well as clubs, could be fashioned in hard wood ; and, with the help of sand and water, wooden drills and wooden saws could be made to cut and perforate blocks of stone. In fact, if we could recover the whole of the furniture of a dwelling of this period, we should be tempted to call its epoch " the Wood Age ", in preference to any of the other names with which it has been labelled. But wood decays and burns ; very little evidence of the industrial use of this potential material in the period at the moment under discussion has come down to us.

Assuredly the initial contrasts between North and South were gradually reduced, as fresh clearances opened out roads of intercourse and, especially, after the gold trade had begun to develop. In Ireland, as elsewhere, gold was at once a blessing and a curse. It was certainly the foundation upon which the overseas trade in metal artifacts was based, and was therefore the chief source of the country's wealth, and the chief stimulus to the foreign relationships which were essential to cultural progress. But it was a perennial attraction to invaders and plunderers ; we can trace its sinister influence, from this point of view, even after the actual supply of the metal had been exhausted.

In Egypt the Pyramids tell us of the unlimited power of individual despots. In Ireland the Protomegalithic tumuli tell the same tale— of populations kept in awe by omnipotent rulers, to all intents and purposes priest-kings if not god-kings. The traditions of such functionaries lasted long in the country, even after the inevitable blunting of their initial prestige ; some of these I have collected in a monograph on the remains and traditions of Tara, the chief royal residence in the country : [1] and while it would be premature to claim a finality for the views there expressed, or for any other, until that important site can be excavated with the most anxious care, I see no reason to modify them as knowledge stands at present. For the present, therefore, we may picture the population of the country at this time, divided into a number of communities, each governed by a divine despot, and practising the arts of food-cultivation in a complete if elementary form.

[1] Published by Scribner's of New York and London, 1931.

Bremer,[1] on the basis of a paper by Schuchhardt,[2] and with further references to a later paper by Loth,[3] enumerates the following as the elements of West European (Iberian) civilization in which Ireland had a share : megalithic tombs and their furniture, the cult of standing stones, horizontal zonal geometrical decoration of pottery and metal objects, lunulæ, torques, archers' bracers, conical buttons with V-shaped thread-holes, circular beehive houses, small stone beads (such as have been yielded by some of the southern chambered passage-tombs), and flat flint javelin heads with polished sides. He also mentions (without reference) callaïs : but I cannot recollect or find any report of the discovery of this rare material in Ireland. We may add to the list the Moytirra bell-beakers,[4] the Clonfinloch stone, and the Drimnagh burial, as well as the copper halberds.[5]

II. HOUSES

The Protomegalithic people do not appear to have made any advance worth mentioning on the house architecture of their Beachcombing predecessors. We must picture to ourselves a development of pre-existing tents, in the shape of cones of logs, meeting and secured somehow at the apex ; the whole consolidated with a basis of wattle-work, overlaid with sods, skins, dried mud, or some other simple form of roofing. As in the house at Whitepark Bay, a ring of stones kept the feet of the logs from slipping laterally outward. The wooden erection which capped the Drimnagh mound (*ante*, p. 94) was a model of just such a house.

Time would leave nothing of a construction of this kind except the ring of stones. A large series of such rings was observed and planned on a spur of Carrowkeel Mountain, during the excavation of the carns, and was identified as the remains of the village of the people who had erected the monuments.[6] These rings measured from 20 to 45 feet in diameter : each had an outer and an inner face of upright slabs, with a filling of small stones between ; the average thickness was about 3 feet, the height rarely more than 2 feet. There was no doorway—anyone entering the hut would be obliged to step over the stone ring. These thin and comparatively flimsy foundations

---

[1] PRIA 28 [1928] : 26.

[2] " Westeuropa als alter Kulturkreis ", *Akademie der Wissenschaften*, Berlin 1910.

[3] " Relations à l'époque énéolithique ", *Mémoires de la Société d'histoire et d'archéologie de Bretagne*, 1924, p. 152.

[4] Of which Bremer himself gives a description, *loc. cit.* p. 28.

[5] In this connexion reference should be made to the later study by P. Bosch-Gimpera, " Relations préhistoriques entre l'Irlande et l'Ouest de la péninsule Ibérique ", *Préhistoire* 2 [Paris 1939] : 195.

[6] PRIA 29 [1912] : 331. The identification is accepted by Childe, who remarks upon the resemblance of this village to that of Los Millares (Almeria) in Spain : *Prehistoric Communitie of the British Isles*, p. 78.

could hardly have supported a "beehive" dome ; and while we might speculate on the possibility of walls carried up vertically as cylinders, with flat lintels closing the top, the absence of doorways would be a fatal objection, even if there were any known precedent in the country for such a construction.   That they supported conical wooden constructions of the kind described above is the only reasonable interpretation.   For the same reasons—the weakness and narrowness of the stone ring, and the absence of a doorway—the wooden cone cannot have rested upon the ring itself ; it must have been based on the ground, within it, and there kept in place by the ring.

Most of this village site is a bare rock surface, in which there is nothing to excavate : there is no midden accumulation around the houses.   The anomaly is explicable by the nature of the site : Carrowkeel Mountain is fissured with deep valleys, having almost precipitous sides, running longitudinally through its mass.   The spur bearing the village-site is a narrow platform between two such precipices, and rubbish of every sort could be most easily got rid of by tipping it over one or other of the cliff-edges, where rain and winter streams would rapidly dispose of it.   In addition, there are several deep swallow-holes here and there in the mountain, which could also have been used as rubbish-pits.[1]

III. MODE OF LIFE

We have said that the beginning of the Megalithic cult more or less coincided in Ireland with the introduction of the art of food-cultivation.   This is true, but the statement must be qualified by an acknowledgement of the scantiness of our information, from the earliest Megalithic phases, on this important subject.   The discovery, identification, and excavation of habitation-sites of this period is in fact now even more necessary to Science than further research in burial sites.

Food cultivation was seriously handicapped at the beginning by the insular status of Ireland.   There was no native breed of wild cattle or sheep : these essential food-animals had to be imported, and herds had to be artificially established and maintained, as a preliminary to local domestication.   Cereals also had to be imported, as the agriculturist had no native plant out of which to develop his industry.

We are not likely ever to have sufficient material for a study of the full evolutionary development of food-cultivation in Ireland.

---

[1] Some remarks on Neolithic architecture in Dudley Buxton's *Primitive Labour* (London 1924) may be read in this connexion : but the experiences of many of us, in days still recent, with back-garden " air-raid shelters " which rapidly became permanent reservoirs of muddy rain-water, make us sceptical about " pit-dwellings " in these northern climates.   I do not think that any true " pit-dwellings " have been found in Ireland.

We may presume that it reached its climax in the Epimegalithic phase : we shall therefore postpone our survey of the whole subject to the chapter on Epimegalithic culture.

IV. STONE IMPLEMENTS

These may be divided broadly into two classes, chipped and polished.

Chipped Stone Implements

The following is a summary list of the types of post-Mesolithic tools and weapons of flint, usually found in Ireland : except in minor matters of detail they resemble those from other European countries. The Irish craftsmen attained to a high degree of skill in working flint : although they could not challenge comparison with the best of the Neolithic Egyptian or the Scandinavian flint-workers, their products are often excellent ; it is frequently possible to infer, from the results of their work, that they were inspired by nodules of a pleasing colour to put forth every endeavour to produce a real work of art.

I must content myself with referring the reader to publications in which he will find a plenitude of illustrations, without reproducing them here : not because I do not fully realize the importance, indeed the necessity, of illustrations, but because I have a vast field to cover, and must economize space.   The few illustrations for which room might be found would be of little value : the ideal way in which the list should be illustrated would be with an album of at least 200 photographs.   But that must be left to the volume on Irish flints, in the dreamland series of National monographs, spoken of in the Preface.

1. *Cores.*   These are merely the wastes, remaining after serviceable flakes had been struck off from the parent nodule.   They may be of any shape and size.[1]   While fairly common in the siliciferous regions, they are not found elsewhere in the country.   Where flint was not obtainable, the material was too valuable to waste, and a lump of it would be used down to the last particle.

By studying cores from which flake knives have been struck off, we can infer that an oval nodule of flint was taken, and broken in two with a sharp blow on the middle ; this produced a smooth plane of fracture at right angles to the long axis of the nodule.   The flakes were then detached with blows struck on this fracture-plane, near its circumference and working round it spirally until the core was reduced to a size too small to be of further service.[2]

2. *Flakes* are abundant in sites of almost any date down to the Iron Age. They display such a variety of shape, that it would be impossible here to reduce them intelligibly to any classificatory scheme without a large album of illustrative plates.   Knives, scrapers, borers, javelin-heads are all, ultimately, varieties of flakes ; and many flakes could be used for several purposes, according to the nature of the handles in which they were mounted.

[1] Illustrations in Wilde, *Catalogue*, p. 8 (copied in Wood-Martin, *Pagan Ireland*, p. 373).   See also PRIA 30 : plate xvi, Figs. 93-6.
[2] Knowles in PRIA 16 [1883] : 210.

Mention has already been made of the knife (Fig. 15) found in the river Bann, made of a long narrow flake with a wad of moss wrapped around the butt to serve as a handle.[1] Knowles figures other flakes from the same region fixed for the same purpose into the roots of plants.[2]

3. *Scrapers.* These are flakes, touched up with secondary chipping along one or both edges (or at the end), in order to make them suitable for the purpose, or rather the wide range of purposes, implied by the name bestowed upon them. They are found in many varieties, which have been minutely classified,[3] though (as we have said already) such classifications are of doubtful utility. At most, a division into "side-scrapers" and "end scrapers" is necessary, according to the position on the flake of the scraping edge; although a special name might be kept for a few eccentric forms, such as the "spoon-scraper" figured by Wilde.[4]

4. *Awls or Borers.* These are flakes which have been narrowed by chipping to a point at one end.[5]

5. *Hollow Scrapers.* Flakes with a semicircular hollow broken out of one edge.[6]

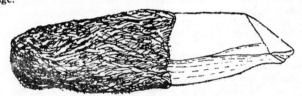

FIG. 15.—Flake Knife with Moss Handle.

6. *Saws.* Flake knives in which the cutting edge is more or less deeply toothed with secondary chipping.[7]

7. *Minute Flakes.* Knowles figures and describes a series of minute flakes found by him at Bundoran (Donegal).[8] These resemble the "pygmy flints"—minute scrapers or borers—characteristic of the Continental Azilian-Tardenoisian culture; but the associations in which they were found bear no other relationship to that aspect of industry. However, we are not obliged to confine pygmy flints to the Tardenoisian culture: they may have been used at any time, for such purposes as harpoon-barbs or saw-teeth.

8. *Choppers.* These also were first described by Mr. Knowles.[9] They

[1] For a similar object from S. Australia (though the handle is made differently) see W. Gray, " The Character and Distribution of the rudely worked flints of the North of Ireland " (JRSAI 15 [1879] : 118); this paper contains a large number of illustrations of various types of flake implements. See also the same writer's "Worked Flints", BNFC II : 3 : 548, 612; Wilde, *Catalogue*, p. 12; Wood-Martin, *op. cit.* pp. 375-6.
[2] In his paper, already cited, on "Prehistoric Stone Implements from the River Bann " (PRIA 30 : plate xiii). Reference to this paper may be taken as repeated under most of the following paragraphs in the present context.
[3] For examples of such classifications see G. R. Buick, " On Flint workshop sites at Glenhue, Co. Antrim ", JRSAI 16 [1883] : 120; W. J. Knowles, " Irish Flint Scrapers " (with many illustrations) JRSAI 28 [1898] : 367). See, for further illustrations, JRSAI 17 [1885] : plates ii, iii facing p. 111, and Knowles's papers on Irish Sandhills, PRIA vols. 16-22.
[4] *Catalogue*, p. 16.   [5] PRIA 30 : plate xiii, nos. 21-3.
[6] PRIA 22 [1901], plate facing p. 372, Figs. 79-86 : British Museum *Stone Age Guide*, p. 117.   [7] See JRSAI 24 [1894] : 341.
[8] PRIA 22 : 360 ff. See also *ante*, p. 61.
[9] JRAI 7 [1878] : 203; 9 [1880] : 324.

are " tools larger than scrapers, not of any well-defined shape, but all with a thick back and cutting edge, capable of being held in the hand and used for chopping ". He adds that " seen singly or found in a different situation one might not feel inclined to acknowledge the greater number of them to be implements at all, but when compared together they have a common character ". They first came to light at Whitepark Bay and Portstewart ; later, similar objects were found at Fisherstreet (Clare), and are described, rather loosely, as " celts ".[1]

The foregoing tools are all derived from the flake, and the only treatment which they have received is along the working edge. We shall now consider the tools which are *surface-chipped*, that is, formed and finished by means of minute pressure-flaking over the entire surface of the object. The workmanship of many of these tools is often of a very high order of merit.

9. *Knives.* Surface-chipped knives are usually oval in outline, and are about 3 to 6 inches in length. Sometimes they are of a semi-oval outline, with one edge straight and the other curved.[2]

The surface-chipped knife seems to be a refinement, ultimately derived from a crude flake knife. There is an intermediate form which has been described by Buick,[3] in which there is one sharp straight cutting edge, forming the longest side of a scalene triangle.

10. *Javelin-* and *Arrow-heads.* These are distinguished, each from the other, by size, the javelin-heads being of twice or three times the average length of the arrow-heads. There is a considerable variety of types. The heads are oval (leaf-shaped), lozenge-shaped, or triangular ; the edges may be straight, convex, or concave ; the *lozenge-shaped* heads may be equilateral ; or else may be as though formed of two triangles, base to base, the butt being a small triangle with a wide if not an obtuse angle at the apex, the point a long triangle with an acute angle. The *triangular* heads may have either a straight base, or else a concave base, thus forming rudimentary barbs at the basal angles. There may or may not be a tang accompanying a head of any shape ; sometimes no barbs flank the tang ; sometimes there is one barb (as in the Solutrean *pointe à cran*) ; sometimes two. As arrow-heads of different types are found grouped together indiscriminately, the varieties do not appear to have any chronological or other importance. It is clear, from the associations in which flint arrow-heads are sometimes found, that they continued in use down to a very late date.[4] They were mounted upon wooden shafts, split for receiving them ; the head and shaft were glued together with resin, and the joint was strengthened with a tight binding of gut or sinew. This has been inferred from actual examples found in peat-bogs, which still retained their shafts.[5] Although, like all other flint objects, most of the recorded javelin- and arrow-heads come from the North of

[1] In PRIA 22 : 355. See also JRSAI 17 [1885] : plate iii, facing p. 111 ; plate iv.
[2] See PRIA 22 : 373, bottom row.
[3] G. R. Buick, " On a particular kind of flint knife common in the county of Antrim, Ireland ", P.S.A. Scot. 22 [1887-8] : 51 ; *Idem*, " On the development of the knife, as shown by specimens common in the county Antrim ", JRSAI 18 [1887] : 241. Another specimen is figured in Wilde, *Catalogue*, p. 15.
[4] Thus, R. S. Charnock in PSA London II, ii 118 reports a polished green-stone " celt ", flint arrow-heads, a dug-out canoe, lead bullets, and a 10-inch mortar all found in engineering works near Toome, Loch Neagh !
[5] Knowles, JRSAI 17 [1885] : 126, describes and figures one from Kanestown (Antrim) : another from Ballykillan (Offaly), now in Cambridge, is figured in Wilde, *Catalogue*, p. 254.

Ireland,[1] Day publishes a barbed arrow-head of large size from Co. Cork.[2] A javelin-head (hardly a spear-head, though described as such) said to have been found near Oldcastle (Meath) is published by E. C. Rotherham : [3] but it does not look Irish, and is probably a recent importation—the writer quoted himself admits that he knows of nothing analogous from anywhere nearer than Behring Straits.

Arrow-heads are rare in the shore sites, though not unknown. They are, however, all to be assigned to *later* participants in the Beachcombing life (for whose existence there is ample evidence).

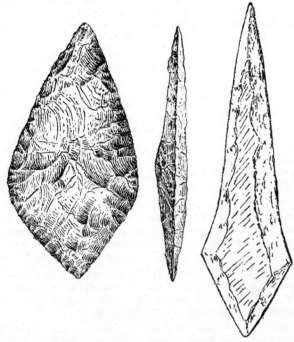

FIG. 16.—Lozenge-shaped Javelin-heads.

Lozenge-shaped javelin-heads of large size (Fig. 16) carefully formed by chipping round the edges, with the flat sides ground smooth, and with the basal angle a little less acute than the tip, are very characteristic of Ireland.[4] Specimens formerly in the Knowles collection (now in Belfast Museum) still display the stain of the resin with which they had been secured in their

---

[1] Buick (JRSAI 25 [1895] : 41) illustrates a large number of examples.   Facing JRSAI 18 [1887] : 89 will be found a plate of varieties (rather roughly drawn) from Sligo.   See also Wilde, *Catalogue*, pp. 19, 22 ; W. J. Knowles, " Irish Flint Arrow- and Spear-heads ", JRAI 33 : 44 ; R. L. May, " Javelin- and Arrow-heads from the Lower Bann Valley ", *Ulster* III 2 [1939] : 104 ; E. E. Evans, " Some recent finds of flint arrow-heads ", INJ 6 [1936] : 9 ; and for comparative purposes, R. A. Smith, " Flint Arrow-heads in Britain ", *Archæologia* 76 [1926] : 81.
[2] Cork II 13 : 197.   [3] JRSAI 26 [1896] : 171.
[4] Evans, *Stone*, p. 372 ; Wilde, *Catalogue*, p. 26.   British Museum, *Stone Age Guide* (3rd edn.), plates facing pp. 116, 117.   An oval specimen is figured by O Ríordáin, *Cork* 42 [1937] : 117.

shafts. This type of javelin-head has long been recognized as a link between Ireland and the Iberian Peninsula, where it is very familiar.

The use of arrows necessarily implies the use of a bow. This is not verified by the survival in Ireland of actual specimens, but it is confirmed by the existence of some specimens of *bracers*. These are rectangular discs of bone or, more commonly, of stone polished smooth, about 3 inches long and 1 inch broad, with one, two, or three perforations at each end. Cords passed through these holes secured the bracer to the left wrist of the archer as he held the bow, and protected it from the lash of the released bowstring.[1]

11. *Fabricators* are tools which may loosely be described as resembling miniature Campignian picks, but slender in proportion to the length, used to execute the fine pressure-flaking with which surface-chipped tools were made.[2] They are rare in Ireland : Blake Whelan figures an example from Rathlin Island.[3]

12. *Daggers*, leaf-shaped knife-blades with sharp point, chipped over the surface. They are familiar in England,[4] but typical specimens from Ireland are not recorded : approximations to the type are, however, not unknown.[5]

Daggers with the handle as well as the blade chipped out of flint, characteristic of Scandinavia, are among the finest products of the flint-chipper's art to be found in the world. There is one example of Irish provenance, but from an unknown locality, in the Royal Irish Academy's collection ;[6] another, from Scarriff (Clare) was in the Day collection.[7] These are more likely to be importations than native products.

The foregoing list makes no attempt at establishing a chronological sequence. This would, indeed, be unwise, if only because subjective impressions, personal and traditional, would inevitably override the very scanty objective evidence. My own instincts would cause me to remove all the artistic surface-chipped tools from the Protomegalithic phase and transfer them to the succeeding Deuteromegalithic ; and along with them the awls and hollow scrapers possibly, and (with greater assurance) the arrow- and javelin-heads. Arrow-heads have admittedly been found in the sandhills ; but we cannot assume that all the sandhill sites and relics are as old as some have supposed them to be.

For heavy operations, such as the breaking of rocks in mining operations, massive stone *mauls* were in use. These are egg-shaped blocks of a hard grit-stone, with a groove encircling the minor diametral plane (though sometimes nearer to one end of the major axis than the other) : on an average about 6 inches in length, but specimens are recorded weighing up to 40 lb. They were probably hafted in a way familiar in Australia and elsewhere (Fig. 17) : there, a flexible withe is bent in the groove, round the stone, and then bound tightly, its ends being carried out in a straight line from the stone

[1] A specimen is figured in Wilde, *Catalogue*, p. 89, but is there described as a " burnisher ".   [2] See PRIA 30 : plate xvi figs. 88, 91.
[3] INJ 3 [1930] : 18.   [4] Evans, *Stone*, pp. 349 ff.
[5] Wilde, *Catalogue*, p. 27 (there called " pick ") ; PRIA 27 : 108.
[6] Wilde, *Catalogue*, p. 14.
[7] R. Day, " Danish Spear-head ", JRSAI 25 [1895] : 176. But the object is certainly a dagger, not a spear-head.

to serve as a handle, strengthened if necessary with a wooden rod tied up between them, the binding being tightened by forcing smaller stones or wooden wedges within its embrace. Mallet-stones of this kind have been found in association with copper-mine workings at Killarney and elsewhere, thus indicating at least one of the uses to which they were put.[1] An interesting hammer-stone girdled with the remains of a *leather* binding, found at a depth of 7 feet in a bog at Aughentaine (Tyrone), is described by Mr. Davies.[2]

Other stones of this kind, of lesser size, which are sometimes to be found, might have been used in the same way, as lighter hammers ; or else as fishing-sinkers or as weights. Decision between a variety of possible uses for such simple objects as these is always difficult, usually impossible.[3] An individual specimen might, indeed, have served several purposes.

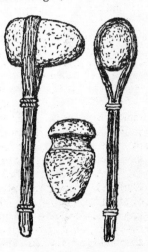

Though these and other tools of the kind are described in the present chapter, there is no implication thus expressed that they belong essentially to the cultural stage with which it deals. They may be of any stage, even one comparatively recent. The researches of Mr. Davies appear to give reason to suppose that some of the copper-mines are not so old as they have been supposed to be.[4]

Polished Stone Implements

Polished stone implements were first fashioned into shape by chipping, and then polished by rubbing upon another stone, which gave them their final form, and a smooth outer surface. This polish may be confined to the cutting edge ; but in most specimens, and in all those

Fig. 17.—Maul-stone and its Mount.

of good workmanship, it covers the whole surface of the tool. Any hard stone of homogeneous texture could be used as the material.

Some of the older French writers called the Neolithic period *l'âge de pierre polie* : but the associations in which polished stone implements are usually found leave us in no doubt that they belong to the overlap of stone and metal, and often to an even later date.[5]

[1] See Evans, *Stone* 233 ; Wilde, *Catalogue*, p. 85.   [2] INJ 7 : 112.
[3] See E. E. Evans, " Grooved Hammer Stones from County Antrim ", *Ulster* III 4 [1941] : 27.   [4] As hinted by E. E. Evans, *op. cit.* p. 29.
[5] One hatchet-head in polished stone is said to have been found at Ballyday (Wexford) associated with a socketed bronze hatchet-head (the latest form) : PRIA 34 [1918] : 90. But this is not very conclusive. They were embedded at a depth of six feet in a peat-bog ; and in a magma so soft, small but heavy objects might easily sink out of their proper strata.

Certainly the majority are later than the Protomegalithic phase ; and for the moment, the only tools in polished stone with which we need concern ourselves are *hatchet-heads* (Fig. 18). Such objects as these have, it is true, been found in lake-dwelling sites, and even in the earth of Norman mottes : but we can base no chronological conclusion on such facts, which mean no more than that the tools chanced to be contained in earth manipulated by the builders of the later structures. We must, however, acknowledge that polished stone implements provide a warning against too confidently trusting, for chronological guidance, to the " three-period " classification, based on the material of the implements alone.

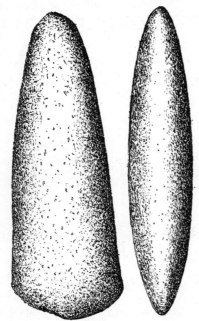

[*By permission of the Royal Irish Academy.*

FIG. 18.—Polished Stone Hatchet-head.

A polished stone hatchet-head is a wedge-shaped bar, usually of some basaltic or similar homogeneous stone, artificially fashioned to have a bevelled edge at the broader end and a more or less pointed tail at the other. In cross-section the body is a flat oval ; in vertical section it swells slightly towards the middle. This may be taken as a general description ; in detail there is a great variety of individual forms, as is inevitable in tools made of blocks of stone which are themselves fundamentally individual in form, and are shaped in individualistic operations. Some are triangular, with a pointed butt. Others are quadrangular in outline, the long sides being parallel or tapering to the butt end ; which may sometimes be ground to an edge, or (more usually) to a flat face of oval outline, as a rule at right angles to the central axis of the tool, but sometimes set obliquely to it. Again, the sides, while most frequently rounded (corresponding to the oval cross-section), are sometimes flattened, perhaps under the influence of the form of the corresponding metal tools, or as a result of the process of sawing ; and the edge, usually not broader than the natural end of the expanding "wedge", sometimes broadens rapidly, with projecting pointed horns at each end—again, apparently, under metal influence. Knowles has given us an elaborate classification of

these varieties, with numerous illustrations : [1] some of the forms
there figured might fairly be called freaks rather than types.

Armstrong endeavoured to discover evidences of chronological
development by studying associated forms in finds of groups of
these tools,[2] but without any important result.

The size of these tools varies as much as their shape. Knowles
gives statistics based upon his own immense collection.[3] About
a score (not more) of his specimens run up to between 12 and 18
inches in length ; those from 8 to 12 inches were rather more
numerous. The majority lie between 3 or 4 inches and 7 inches in
length, but exceptionally small examples, only about 1 inch in

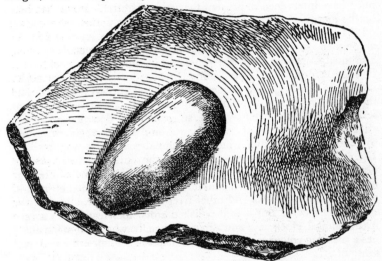

[By permission of the Royal Irish Academy.

FIG. 19.—Hatchet-head and Grinding-stone, Culbane.

length, are sometimes to be found, which, however, were probably
amulets rather than tools or weapons. An example, 14½ inches
long, has been described from Co. Monaghan.[4]

It is no doubt true that polished stone hatchet-heads provided
the models on which the first copper hatchet-heads were modelled.
But the stone prototype, difficult and tedious though its manufacture
might be, in comparison with its easily fused and moulded copper
rival, had too many advantages over it to be discarded altogether.
It was heavier than the copper hatchet-head, and therefore as a

[1] JRSAI 23 [1893] : 140. See also Wilde, *Catalogue*, pp. 41-5.
[2] PRIA 34 [1918] : 81. Reference may also be made in this connexion to
R. A. Smith, " Hoards of Neolithic Celts ", *Archæologia* 71 [1921] : 113.
[3] *Ulster* II 9 [1903] : 6.
[4] W. F. de Vismes Kane, " Account of two Antiquities presented to the
Academy ", PRIA 15 [1870] : 2.

smiting implement was more effective ; and its edge, such as it was, while it might get chipped, did not become useless by turning, as the edge of a soft copper tool must have been doing continually.

A polished stone hatchet-head was found in the bottom of a peat-bog at Ballyclosh (Antrim),[1] along with a flat plate of sandstone upon which it seemed to have been polished. The Royal Irish Academy possesses a similar grinding stone (Fig. 19), from the Knowles collection, along with six hatchet-heads that had just been finished, but had not yet received their final polish ; these were found all together at Culbane (Antrim), on the banks of the Bann. Some accident (perhaps, as Mr. Knowles suggests, a sudden flood) must have intervened to prevent the artificer from resuming his work on the morrow, after he had (as he supposed, temporarily) " knocked off " for the night.[2] From any large collection of Irish antiquities a complete series of stone hatchet-heads can be selected, showing a gradual transition from the roughed-out, unpolished block to the finished product. The polishing first appears upon the edge ; indeed, in the beginning, it seems to have been nothing more than the result of continual wear produced on the stone by use. Observation of this effect may have suggested the finishing-off of the edge, making it more effective by rubbing away irregularities and so reducing the friction which its original roughness would cause. Later, the process was extended over the entire surface. Often, however, even in a completely polished specimen, some of the preliminary chipping had been sunk too deeply to be altogether ground away, and thus hollows and other irregularities are produced in the smooth surface.[3] But a well-polished stone tool testifies to a very real technical efficiency, and often, especially when the stone itself has a pleasing colour or vein-pattern, displays evidence of a very real sense of art.

The process of manufacture, as above described, can be reconstructed from waste specimens, unfinished or spoiled, such as strew the ground wherever there has been the site of a manufactory. The most remarkable sites of the kind, in Ireland, are in the neighbourhood of Cushendall (Antrim), and have been described by Mr. Knowles.[4] Some of the specimens from the Bann seem to have been first *sawn* into shape [5] (doubtless by means of sand-and-water agitated with flat slabs of stone or with wooden laths) before receiving the final polish.

To avoid the unscientific ghost-word " celt ", we here speak of " hatchet-heads " and " axe-heads " ; making a distinction between

[1] JRSAI 23 [1893] : 157 (Knowles).
[2] PRIA 30 : 219, plate xix p. 126. See also *ibid.* 34 : 82.
[3] Examples are figured in *Ancient Ireland*, Fig. 1 (facing p. 26).
[4] " Stone-age factories near Cushendall ", *BNFC* II 5 [1905-6] : 421 ; JRSAI 36 [1906] : 383 ; JRAI 33 : 360. A representative series of specimens from these sites will be found in the National Museum, Dublin.
[5] PRIA 30 [1912] : 215.

those which are perforated with a hole for receiving a wooden haft ("axe-heads") and those not so perforated, and intended to be fitted into some kind of socket in the handle ("hatchet-heads"). But this distinction must be made with discretion. Thus, Fig. 20 represents a tool of the kind with a perforation too small to receive a handle of any efficiency. It must have been made for a securing-peg, passed through holes in the sides of the socket in the handle, and strengthened with tightly bound thongs. This tool therefore, notwithstanding the perforation, must be called a hatchet-head, not an axe- or adze-head. It was in the Killua collection, from which I acquired it : and is now in the possession of University College, Dublin.

Hatchet-heads wrought in highly ornamental stone, and brought to a fine polish, are sometimes found. These beautiful objects—

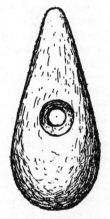

for they are such—could scarcely have been intended for the rough treatment inevitably in store for an ordinary stone tool : the surface would soon have been chipped and scratched, and the attractiveness of the colour and veining of the stone (which the artificer evidently appreciated and sought to enhance) would have been dulled if not destroyed. Rather must we suppose that they were ceremonial in intention. They may have been mounted in elaborately carved wooden handles, like the ceremonial adzes from Mangaia, to be seen in any well-equipped ethnological museum. It must be admitted, however, that we cannot always feel assured of the Irish provenance of such ornamental hatchets. Two specimens in jade are alleged to have been found, one in Co. Antrim, the other in Co. Down : [1] but these statements (intrinsically improbable)

FIG. 20.—Perforated Hatchet-head.

rested, apparently, on the testimony of the unlettered people from whom they were purchased ; Canon Greenwell and Sir John Evans agreed in assigning them both to New Zealand. They had probably "escaped", by unknown but easily conjectured means, from some private collection of curiosities.

On the other hand, there is good ground to expect that a systematic tabulation of the sites of discovery of recorded hatchet-heads, combined with a petrological analysis of the objects themselves, may lift a corner of the curtain shrouding bronze-age trade and commerce from our eyes. Note in this connexion, the two axes of stone from the Preselau Hills—the stone of which the famous intrusive blocks at Stonehenge are composed—of North Irish provenance, published by Mr. Alex. Keiller : [1] and implements found at Avebury, made of stones from Wales, and even from the Rhineland.

The ordinary hatchet-head was mounted in a wooden handle of about the same length as a modern axe-handle, by being passed into a hole cut through the end of the wooden bar ; which was thickened slightly, to give room for the hole, and to leave enough of the wood for strength. No doubt the head and the handle were reinforced with a strong binding of leather thongs, cords, or gut. Like the arrow-heads, hatchet-heads were sometimes smeared with resin, to make them adhere to their hafts ; a specimen showing traces of this treatment, from Co. Fermanagh, is now in the Belfast Museum. [2] A good example of a stone hatchet-head retaining its wooden handle, from Co. Monaghan, is in the Royal Irish Academy's collection. [3]

Some specimens display a cup-shaped depression in each of the broad faces, as though a beginning had been made to drill a hole right through the stone. The hole is seldom completed—Fig. 20, already commented upon, is one of the rare exceptions—most likely to avoid weakening the stone overmuch ; but possibly, as in the specimen quoted, the hollows were intended for securing-pins, one on each side. This explanation is at least more obviously acceptable than an alternative suggestion, that the hollows were religious or magical in purpose, analogous to the cup-marks cut in the surfaces of rocks. [4] Such hollows are rare in Irish specimens : indeed, they are not very common anywhere. Wakeman figures an anomalous example with hollows *on the narrow edges* in addition to those on the broad faces. [5] If these had any practical purpose, which is unlikely, it was presumably to make it possible to mount the tool as an adze, if so required.

Blocks of shale are sometimes found which bear a deceptive resemblance to stone hatchet-heads : I have a flat plate of shale found at Loch Gur which has a remarkable resemblance to a copper hatchet-head ; and another, which I picked up on Tara Hill, strangely like a flanged bronze tool of the same class. These are mere natural " sports " : but possibly objects of the kind were sometimes used as cheap imitation hatchet-heads for sepulchral use. [6]

Hones may here be mentioned among minor stone artifacts : they are a necessity to people whose tools are made of the

---

[1] *Antiquity* 10 [1936] : 220, plates v, vi ; *ibid.* 10 : 422.
[2] JRSAI 18 [1888] : 482 ; *Quarterly Notes, Belfast Museum* 23 : 4.
[3] Figured, Wilde, *Catalogue*, p. 46, and frequently reproduced. A handle also from Co. Monaghan, though the exact find-place is not recorded, is figured, JRSAI 44 [1914] : 171.
[4] This explanation is considered, and not wholly rejected, by Professor Capitan (*Revue de l'école d'anthropologie* 11 [1901] : 125) ; but on the whole he favours the explanation given in the text above.   [5] JRSAI 21 [1890] : 156.
[6] One such was found in a cist at Carnmoney (Antrim) : see PRIA 33 [1916] : 3. Others are figured by Wilde (*Catalogue*, pp. 33, 34) and (perhaps) among the illustrations of Knowles (PRIA 30, plates xviii, xix).

comparatively soft metals, copper and bronze, and so have to be continually re-sharpened. They appear very soon after metal comes into use, and as time goes on, become increasingly common : in the later stages of development, they are among the principal yields of excavation in any habitation-site. They generally take the form of small flat bars of some smooth homogeneous stone, rectangular in cross-section, and swelling slightly from the ends to the middle : up to about 4 inches in length—occasionally, though rarely, somewhat longer ; and are often perforated for suspension to the owner's person.

We may be certain that tools and weapons of wood—hammers, clubs, daggers, etc.—were in common use during the Stone and Bronze Ages : but we cannot point to any example of carpentry surviving from those early ages. We have, however, a few implements of horn : sawn-off antler-tines, which could have been used as picks, wedges, or perforators have been found in shore sites such as Whitepark Bay, as have also the butt-ends of stags' horns, perforated to make them serve as mallet-heads.[1]

V. POTTERY

A monograph on Irish pottery, comparable with Lord Abercromby's two great volumes on British pottery, with a *corpus*, as complete as it can be made, of photographic illustrations and diagrams, is one more of the many urgent primary needs of Irish Archæology. At present, the study, to be of profit, involves the collection of a vast store of photographs, supplemented with the harvest of a search through endless volumes and periodicals ; where illustrations of vessels will be found, executed with very various degrees of artistic competence and of scientific accuracy. These figures would have to be traced and mounted on cards (so that they may be shuffled about for purposes of comparison), with a tabulation of the circumstances (often imperfectly recorded) in which the vessels were found. A study pursued along such lines would make a very serious inroad upon a human lifetime ; and none of us has more than one lifetime at his disposal.

The history of Irish pottery begins in the shore settlements, especially those round Dundrum Bay, where a considerable number of sherds has been found. At this time its chief affinities are with the Neolithic ware of Great Britain, which we now know more thoroughly since Prof. Stuart Piggott's systematic study.[2] It falls

---

[1] A number of illustrations of horn objects will be found in JRSAI 17, plate facing p. 119. See also Wood-Martin's *Pagan Ireland*, p. 405.

[2] "The Neolithic Pottery of the British Islands ", *Archæological Journal* 88 [1932] : 67, and references there. Refer also to an important supplementary paper on " The Mutual Relations of the British Neolithic ", PPS E. Anglia 7 [1934] : 373.

into two well-defined and independent groups, to which have been given respectively the names *Windmill Hill* and *Peterborough* ware (otherwise " Neolithic A " and " Neolithic B "). To that paper we must refer the reader for details and illustrations ; contenting ourselves here with the following summary table of the differentiation between the two groups :—

WINDMILL HILL	PETERBOROUGH
Bowls round-bottomed (never flat) ; at least nine varieties, distinguished by minor differences of profile.	Bowls round-bottomed ; occasionally flat, but otherwise of one unvaried form.
Ware well cleaned, smooth on surface, neatly modelled, and well fired.	Ware full of large grits, thick, clumsy, and badly fired.
Lug (or even loop) handles sometimes provided.	No handles of any kind.
Restrained ornament, confined to neck and rim of vessel, and limited to vertical lines and grooves (straight, zig-zag, or herring-bone), scratched with a pointed stick or with the potter's finger-nail. Ornament often absent altogether.	Profuse ornament, usually in horizontal lines surrounding the vessel, and including curved as well as straight lines. Sometimes scratched as in type " A ", but also impressed with cords. Cockle-shells sometimes used as dies to produce uniform repetitions of an ornamental pattern.
In England, confined to upland sites, and to a minor date-limit of 1800 B.C.	In England, found in low-lying regions, and surviving to be (at least in part) the parent of bronze-age pottery.

We have already spoken a word of caution against dating Irish antiquities by analogies with England. Cultures took time, and possibly followed circuitous routes, in reaching and crossing the Irish Sea and getting naturalized upon the other side of it : the two countries must accordingly be considered separately, on their local chronological merits. Mahr goes so far as to deny absolutely the existence of Neolithic pottery in Ireland.[1] This is to a large extent a question of terminology. No doubt it is true that the more closely we scrutinize the obscure interval between the early Beach-combers and the fully-equipped megalith builders, the more evanescent does the Neolithic culture appear : and the plunderers who violated the megalithic monuments, north and south, have not made the study any easier. As an illustration chosen almost at random, we read that Davies found in a carn at Clontygora (Armagh) a large number of sherds, the details and affinities of which he sets forth with painstaking minuteness.[2] Adopting his terminology, they include fragments of pots described as " Neolithic ", " probably Neolithic ",

[1] PPS 3 : 332. [2] *Belfast* 1936-7, pp. 32 ff.

" resembling Neolithic A and not very closely parallel to Scottish types " ; and on the contrary sherds " apparently hybrid between Beacharra and Unstan ware " ; [1] bronze-age (cinerary urn) ; later bronze-age (cinerary urn, food-vessel with panel decoration) ; vessel with encrustation, broken away ; early iron-age ; " degenerate English Hallstatt, but possibly later ". Such a welter inside a single burial mound fills the student with despair. No principle, chronological or other, is operative. The mound seems to have served at different times as a place for burial, a dwelling, or a source of loot, in which each phase of its history has left its appropriate relics. The potsherds may have belonged to picnicking builders, to deposits of grave furniture, to deposits of domestic furniture, or to picnicking plunderers ; and this monument is not unique in presenting us with such complicated typological problems and ambiguities.

These anomalies apart, the general impression that we obtain from a study of the results of horned-carn investigation is, that such of the pottery as is attributable to the original intention of the monuments and not to any later adaptation, is analogous to the ware of Windmill Hill, as set forth in the above table.

In the background of the pottery used by the peoples of Northern Europe are basket-work receptacles and porringers scooped out of blocks of wood. Their existence is inferential only, not evidential, as no object in these perishable materials has survived from the " times of beginning ", with which we are concerned here. But much of the decoration of bronze-age pottery from Northern Europe is obviously based on a basket-work prototype, with its heavier withes (reproduced in the ribbings which diversify the surface) and its smaller twigs interlaced with them (represented by the criss-cross of minor decorative lines). Such a pot calls up before our eyes an early housewife wanting to fetch water, having nothing but a basket to carry it in. A girl in an old nursery tale was in a similar predicament, when her cruel stepmother sent her to fetch water in a sieve ; a friendly frog advised her to " stop with fog [= grass standing in water] and daub with clay ". Our housewife did the same. Nay, more, she put her basket of water on the domestic fire to heat its contents : the fire burnt away the wood and baked the clay, endowing her with the first approximation to an earthenware domestic vessel—and inaugurating a total revolution in human life, with improved facilities for storage of grain and liquids, for

---

[1] For the characteristic features, fully illustrated, of these varieties of Scottish Neolithic pottery, see Childe's *Prehistory of Scotland* (the index there, under both names)—a book which a student of the present work should read concurrently with it, to mark the very instructive resemblances and contrasts between the two countries. See also J. Graham Callander, " Scottish Neolithic Pottery ", P.S.A. Scot. 63 [1928-9] : 29. Some sherds of pottery from the Lochcrew tumuli are described by Childe as closely cognate with Unstan ware, JRSAI 65 [1935] : 320.

hygienic cooking, for obtaining hot water, and for all the other advantages which pottery added to the amenities of life.   Concen-

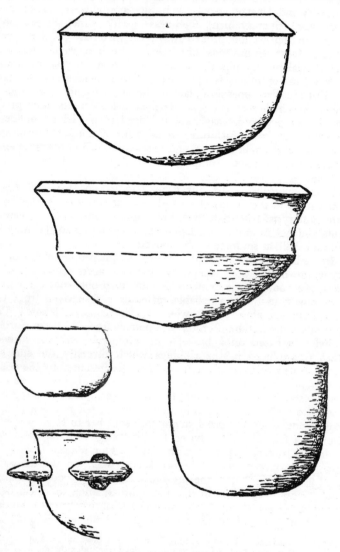

FIG. 21.—Profiles of Neolithic and Protomegalithic Pottery.

trated in this banal little parable is a series of countless trials and errors, extending over many long years.   But it enables us to realize something of the course which the evolution of pottery followed, and explains the basket-work decoration of North European pottery.[1]

The wooden porringer food-vessel has lasted in use from earliest down to modern times ; it is in the background of the first Irish pottery in which the Neolithic tradition is abandoned (Fig. 21). This is the cushion-shaped *food-vessel*, the most characteristically Irish form of early bronze-age pottery. It is shaped, in vertical section, like a pair of parentheses ( ), their lower ends united by a horizontal line to form the bottom of the vessel.[2]   A small saucer-shaped vessel from Aghanaglack (Fermanagh), decorated on the outside surface with impressions of stretched cords—horizontal round the rim, and alternately vertical and oblique below—is exceptional, both in shape and decoration, though not altogether unique.[3]

The hanging bowl found in the Drimnagh burial must here be recalled (*ante*, p. 94). Its base is of a flattened spheroidal shape, and the curve ends upwards in a prominent shoulder, above which there is a more or less flat top, with a circular mouth in the middle of it. There are four suspension-holes in the shoulder, dividing it into quarters ; and below, and just missing them, are lug handles. Ridges run downwards on the surface from these handles, and a lozenge of similar ridges enclosing their intersection gives a base on which the bowl can stand with stability. The vessel is richly ornamented with horizontal linear decoration : a vertical " ladder " which cuts abruptly across the horizontal lines in one of the quadrants looks like the vestigial relic of an antecedent symbolic device.[4]

The very remarkable ware from Tamnyrankin (Derry),[5] consonantly with that monument's character as a degenerate horned carn, will be more suitably noticed in the Deuteromegalithic section.

VI. MINING AND METALLURGY

Ireland is rich in manufactured objects of gold and of bronze, and also in the stone moulds in which the latter were cast into shape ;

[1] On this and other aspects of early pottery technique, see Rev. J. W. Hayes, " Prehistoric and aboriginal Pottery Manufacture ", JRAI 41 [1911] : 260 ; C. Schuchhardt, *Alteuropa*, pp. 44 ff., and, especially, the same author's " Das technische ornament in den Anfängen der Kunst ", *Prähistorische Zeitschrift* 1 [1909] : 37 ff. ; 2 [1910] : 145 ff. On the other hand, Nordenskjold stigmatizes the theory that pottery was derived from clay-smeared basket-work as " preposterous " (JRAI 59 [1929] : 287). The reader must decide for himself between these disagreeing doctors.

[2] Examples of vessels of this kind will be found illustrated in Abercromby, *Bronze Age Pottery* : plates 46, 47. The decoration of some of them strongly suggests an imitation of woodcarving : see for a later example, the food-vessel illustrated, *Ulster* III 5 [1942] : 96, from Ballynagarvy (Antrim).

[3] JRSAI 69 [1939] : 33-5.

[4] For a full, illustrated description with a discussion of the affinities of the pot, see Mr. Kilbride-Jones's account of the excavation, JRSAI 69 [1939] : 202 ff.

[5] JRSAI 71 [1941] : 31.

showing that a large proportion, at least, of the metal objects were locally manufactured.   There can be no question that in the early stages of metallurgy in Northern Europe, Ireland was a giver quite as much as a receiver.   Mr. O. G. S. Crawford has stressed the surprising importance of Ireland at that time, owing to its wealth of gold ; [1] an importance to which Sir Arthur Evans was one of the first to call attention.[2]   The collection of the Royal Irish Academy, now housed in the National Museum, Dublin, surpasses that of any other museum in Northern Europe in the number and aggregate weight of its gold ornaments ; and it may be taken as certain that at least an equal quantity—probably much more—found from time to time in agricultural or turbary operations, has been hustled post-haste to the melting-pot,[3] so as to evade the imaginary terrors of the Law of Treasure Trove.   Irish gold ornaments have been found scattered, far and wide, over the Continent ; [4] and it is a suggestive fact (made clear by distribution-maps accompanying Mr. Crawford's paper) that the places in England, where flat copper hatchets have been found, lie in lines of traffic radiating from Ireland, and directed towards Continental sites of discovery of Irish gold ornaments. Traders, carrying their precious merchandize, set out along these roads, equipped, for protection on their way, with the hatchets—which they sometimes lost, perhaps in an unsuccessful fight with bandits, who were so intent on making off with their more valuable loot that they omitted to appropriate the weapon.   Certainly Mr. Crawford has given us very good cause to agree that Ireland was one of the distribution centres from which the rest of Northern Europe acquired the first rudiments of metallurgy.

Of the sources for gold in Ireland enumerated in a monograph quoted above (p. 15), the best-known is the system of valleys radiating from the hill called Croghan Kinshela, in the border of

[1] " The distribution of early bronze-age settlements in Britain," *Geographical Journal*, 40 : 189.

[2] In his address on " The Eastern Question in Anthropology " (*British Association Report* 1896, pp. 912-13).

[3] See E. C. R. Armstrong, *Guide to the collection of Irish Antiquities : Catalogue of Irish Gold Ornaments in the Collection of the Royal Irish Academy* (Dublin 1920). In this official guide will be found a history of gold-working in Ireland—still useful, though perhaps ripe for revision—with descriptions and illustrations of every gold object in the collection down to the date of publication.

[4] I cannot, however, subscribe to the identification of two torque-like ornaments, found not long ago at Gaza in Palestine, as being of Irish origin.   I have examined these objects, and admit their astonishing similarity to the Irish objects with which they have been compared ; but considerations of chronology appear to me to stand in the way insuperably.   The stratum in which they were found at Gaza is dated nearly a thousand years earlier than any probable date that could be assigned to the Irish analogues.   If the coincidence means anything, it would indicate that the gold ornaments in our museums are not Irish at all, but belated importations (or imitations thereof).   I cannot see any other way out of the difficulty.   Compare the two very Irish-looking neck-torques (in *bronze*) from Dorset and Luristan respectively, figured side by side in *The Antiquaries' Journal* 17 [1937] : 198.

Cos. Wicklow and Wexford—especially those of certain tributary streams of the river now called " Ovoca ".[1] But it would be foolish to assume that there were no other river-beds in the country, perhaps even richer in alluvial gold. The bronze-age artificers took extravagant toll ; the Croghan Kinshela gold may have escaped notice altogether, till it was discovered by a local schoolmaster about 1775, who quietly collected it from time to time with some little profit to himself—and then, as I have heard it alleged, rashly divulged the secret to his wife, who spread it abroad, with the immediate result of a miniature " gold rush ", such as Klondyke witnessed on a larger scale in our times ; culminating in the discovery of sufficient treasure to attract the attention of the government. Official investigations began in 1795, but the search for the parent vein was fruitless ; and the works were destroyed in the troubles of 1798.[2] Literary tradition, for what it may be worth, vaguely indicates this region as the centre of the gold-trade in ancient times : for " the Roll of the Kings ", an appendix to the *Book of Invasions*, tells us that in " Eastern Life " (dissyllable) one Uchadan smelted gold in the days of King Tigernmas—to whom the Four Masters assign the date 3580 Anno Mundi (= 1619 B.C.).[3] Without knowing upon what foundation this statement rests, we cannot attach much importance to it ; the unsupported assertion of a mediæval pundit is no longer acceptable, even as evidence for the mere historicity of the persons mentioned, to say nothing of their remote antiquity and their reported actions ; and in any case, the Ovoca river-system named is at least eighteen miles from the region which in modern times has given its name to the river " Liffey ".[4]

That gold *mining* was ever carried out in Ireland, in the region named or anywhere else, is not indicated by any evidence, literary or archæological ; all the gold seems to have been here obtained by washings of alluvial gravels, as in Gaul (*teste* Diodorus Siculus, *Bibliotheca* v 27). Except for the nebulous Uchadan story, there is nothing to connect the Wicklow region in particular with the

---

[1] A modern (though probably justifiable) revival of a river-name recorded by Ptolemy, on (to us) unknown authority. His river must in any case have been somewhere in the neighbourhood.

[2] See Armstrong, *Gold Catalogue*, chap. i ; JRSAI 43 [1913] : 183. On the relation between prehistoric remains and the metalliferous regions in the county of Wicklow, see remarks by Mr. L. Price in PRIA 42 [1934] : 43 ff.

[3] E. O'Curry, *Manners and Customs of the Ancient Irish* (London 1873), references in the index under the heading " Gold " ; see also R. R. Brash, " The precious metals and ancient mining in Ireland ", JRSAI 11 : 509. Two papers by J. Windele on " Ancient Irish gold ", *Ulster* I, 9 : 28, 197 may be worth glancing through, with discretion. Other references in Armstrong, *op. cit.*

[4] Originally named *Ruirtheach* " (The) princely (river) " : the important tributary called " The King's River " (now practically extinguished by the hydro-electric reservoir) maintains the tradition of the old name. But it was also called *Aba Life ;* this means " The River of [the district called] Life ", but with ac hanging linguistic tradition came to be mistranslated " The River Liffey ", because the word *Life* does not happen to possess a special form for the genitive case.

prehistoric gold-trade ; and while admitting the untrustworthiness of negative testimony, which the turn of a spade may render impotent at any moment, it is at least worthy of passing notice that few if any finds of manufactured gold have been found in the region indicated. The actual sources of the gold in the bronze-age ornaments which we possess may have been so thoroughly exhausted that no tradition thereof reached the extant (early mediæval) literature ; and there is no surviving indication by which they could now be identified. To judge from the few analyses that have been made of Irish gold ornaments, the metal must have been much alloyed (by nature) with silver ; the admixture cannot have been artificial, as certain analysts have claimed, for there is no evidence for an independent silver metallurgy in the country till the Christian period.[1]

It is possible to find an explanation for the comparative scantiness of remains of early occupation, in the Croghan Kinshela region, as contrasted with other parts of the country : the inhabitants seem to have arrived there comparatively late in the Bronze Age, to judge from the relics that they have left behind. Apart from its endowment in metal, the region is economically inhospitable, and would not a priori attract permanent settlers. Conceivably the first discoverers might have held their peace, visiting the valleys sub rosa at intervals to collect fresh supplies of the river material ; and closely safeguarding their monopoly by elaborate secrecy, or perhaps by putting the whole region under some sort of tabu. But gold-hunger breaks through all tabus, religious, moral, or social ; the secret could not be kept indefinitely ; the richness and the wide distribution of Irish gold ornaments, even of the few leavings that we have been able to bring together, indicate no mere exploitation by selfish monopolists, but an almost universal assiduity.

Our conclusion must be that there is no evidence that the ancient gold came specifically from Co. Wicklow : and that the rapidity with which the Croghan Kinshela gravels were exhausted suggests that their deposits were comparatively poor.[2] Possibly similar insignificant discoveries of auriferous gravels had been made in some other of the tributary streams of the Liffey or Ovoca system, at a time sufficiently recent to affect the whole mediæval tradition.

To some extent this conclusion seems to be corroborated, if not confirmed, by an analysis of the localities mentioned in Armstrong's Gold Catalogue, already cited. This list enumerates 475 objects. Of the majority of these no locality is recorded, which is deplorable. I have made a rough estimate of the distribution of

[1] See Armstrong, Gold Catalogue, p. 6 and references there : and Maryon, in PRIA 44 : 222. Reference may also be made to G. Simoens, " The Gold and the Tin in the South-east of Ireland " (Dublin, Cahill & Co., 1921).

[2] Mr. Price records a conjectural estimate that 4,000 oz. may have been there collected, and refers us to the Journal of the Royal Geological Society of Ireland 16 [1892] : 147.

the remainder among the counties of Ireland, which will at least give a preliminary idea of the geography of Irish gold-finds. From Wicklow *not a single specimen is recorded in the catalogue.* Wexford, with nine, is more fortunate ; and Carlow has eight. But Kilkenny has only one, and Leix, like Wicklow, has none ; so that South Leinster does not show up so well as we might have expected, if Croghan Kinshela had been an important source in early times. At the other end of Ireland, Donegal leads off with fifteen sites. But somewhere in Eastern Limerick there was surely an important gold-field, to account for the great find of gold ornaments made near Newmarket-on-Fergus, Co. Clare, in 1854 [1] on the one hand, and the remarkable number of gold objects which have been recovered from the Bog of Cullen, in the border of Limerick and Tipperary, on the other ; [2] as well as such an exceptional object as the Glenin-sheen gorget (*post*, p. 195).

Of copper, the other important Irish metal, there were several possible sources of supply, in the regions now known as Counties Tipperary, Waterford, Kerry (Killarney), and Cork, and also in N.E. Ireland. In Waterford and Cork, and at Killarney, the metal was exploited by mining ; the workings are still to be seen, though they await adequate investigation. No ancient mines have been described and planned. No material, bearing upon their date, has been collected. Heavy stone mauls have been found at some of them ; but such tools might have been used, as being the most effective stone-breakers available, at any time before, and even for some time after, the discovery of explosives. In the Day collection there were some stone hammers from mine-workings near Killarney, described by their possessor in a brief note, [3] in which he mentions that " one of the Killarney guides " had sent him a hamper of thirty or forty, which he distributed among his friends. From the description given of the one specimen which he retained, it seems to have been of the grooved variety.

Close to Bunmahon (Waterford), the copper of which is still exploited, there are many traces of ancient workings. " One almost insulated promontory is perforated like a rabbit-burrow, and is known as the Danes' Island. . . . In the abandoned workings antique tools have been found, stone hammers and chisels, and wooden shovels." [4] At Derrycarhoon, near Schull (Cork), six copper-mine shafts were found, which are (too briefly) described by Thomas

---

[1] See *post*, p. 190.

[2] A careful summary of the evidence as to this site, with a complete list of all recorded finds, will be found in J. N. A. Wallace, "The Golden Bog of Cullen ", *North Munster* 1 [1938] : 89.

[3] JRSAI 16 [1884] : 281. See also *ibid.* 15 [1879] : 63 ; S. C. Hall, *Ireland* 1 : 240. Julius Andrée (*Bergbau in der Vorzeit*, Leipzig 1922, p. 42) quotes a privately expressed opinion of Armstrong, that the essential connexion of these mauls with copper-mining is not absolutely certain.

[4] R. Kane, *The Industrial Resources of Ireland* (Dublin 1844) : 179.

Swanton of Cranley.[1] Besides the usual stone mauls, a ladder was found in one of these mines, 18 feet in length, consisting of a board of black oak with thirteen steps cut in its edge (after the manner of saw-teeth) ; [2] this mine was sufficiently old for a natural growth of peat, 2 feet thick, to have accumulated over part of the spoil-heap at its mouth.   It also contained an object to which it is difficult (impossible rather) to assign a specific use ; it was lying, along with some of the mauls, at the bottom of one of the shafts, covered with what appeared to be the debris from another shaft, opened after the abandonment of the first ; and may be thus described.   A tube of yew wood, taper-ing in external diameter from $2\frac{1}{4}$ to $1\frac{1}{2}$ inches, "elbowed" with a sharp bend—the longer (and broader) branch being 17 inches, the shorter 13 inches in length.   A slot nearly $\frac{1}{2}$ inch wide was cut in the concave side, and what we may call a movable " mouthpiece " was provided, in the shape of two cylinders with their axes in line, the narrower cylinder being an exact fit in the broader end of the tube.   Without a knowledge of the purpose of this object it would be futile to conjecture its age, and whether its connexion with the mine was intrinsic or accidental.[3]

As Ireland does not appear ever to have been one of the few places where copper is to be found in a native form, the earliest artificers were obliged to smelt it out of its ore ; and though we have no direct evidence, we may reasonably presume that this was done in the usual way—by sending a blast from a bellows (however this apparatus may have been contrived) through alternate layers of the ore (crushed to powder with hammers), and glowing charcoal, in a pit furnace.   The copper which remained after the dross had thus been separated was broken up into lumps of convenient size, and when required was remelted in a crucible and poured into the mould. The crucibles that have actually been found, all come from lake-dwellings and other later sites, so that we have as yet no tangible evidence of the processes of fusing, and transferring to the mould, in the Megalithic Age : they are made of coarse pottery, of small capacity—never more than 50 cubic centimetres—with a pointed base, and a mouth, sometimes round or oval, but frequently triangular, to facilitate pouring.   Analysis has shown that they were sometimes used, not only for melting, but also for the preliminary smelting.[4]

In contrast to the country's wealth in gold and copper, there is what we may fairly call an emphatic poverty in tin ; without which

[1] *Ulster* I 9 : 212 ; reprinted IPCT p. 123.
[2] Identical ladders from an ancient Mexican mine are illustrated in Kraemer's *Weltall und Menschheit I* : 11, after an imperfectly specified French source.
[3] It is figured with a brief notice in *Proc. Soc. Antiq. Lond.* II v [1871], p. 223. A fuller and more satisfactory description, though without illustration, is in PRIA 4 [1847] : 64.
[4] See R. J. Moss, " A chemical examination of the Crucibles in the " [R.I.A. Collection] ; PRIA 37 [1927] : 175.

PLATE VI

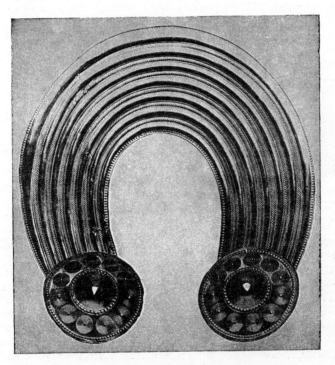

GORGET FROM GLENINSHEEN, CO. CLARE

metal there could be no true native " Bronze Age ". This prolonged the period during which pure copper, as opposed to bronze, was used as the chief industrial material. In fact, a " copper culture " developed in Ireland, better defined than in most other regions, which found expression in copper flat hatchet-heads, daggers and halberds, gold lunulæ, and Ceramic " porringer " food-vessels. These are the essential types of the Protomegalithic culture. We may add that Mr. Herbert Maryon's study of the technical processes followed by the ancient artificers in gold and copper [1] supersedes everything that had previously been written on the subject.

VII. COPPER TOOLS AND WEAPONS

The copper *hatchet-head* (Fig. 22b) is a translation into copper of the corresponding tool in polished stone, which we have already described. But to reproduce exactly the shape of the stone prototype in metal would have been both inconvenient and wasteful. With its convex sides, it would have used up too much of the costly material ; and it would have had to be hammered into shape, not cast, for its manufacture would require a double mould, such as was not in use in the beginning of the Metal Age.[2] The earliest metal hatchet-heads were cast in single moulds ; depressions of the required shape, cut in the flat upper surface of a stone block.[3] This could not produce tools shaped on both sides : for such a purpose a mould consisting of two pieces, with a channel for pouring the molten metal into the hollow intercepted between them, would be essential ; but it would be undesirable, for it has been shown by experiment that a pure copper object made in a closed mould is apt to be so full of airholes as to be useless. Moreover, a flat blade would not only be more economical of the metal, but would actually be more efficient.

Accordingly, the earliest metal tools found in Ireland are *flat* hatchet-heads, of practically pure copper, rather small in size, and wedge-shaped in outline, with a slightly rounded cutting edge. But when the manufacturer proceeded to fix the blade, thus produced, into a haft, and to apply it to practical use, he met with a difficulty. If he inserted it into a slot cut in a wooden handle, as he had been accustomed to do with the stone hatchet-heads, the striking of the blade would drive the metal backward into the handle, however tightly it might be bound with thongs ; the wedge-like pressure of the expanding blade might even split the haft. Some other method of mounting became necessary ; and it was found, by taking a section

---

[1] PRIA 44 [1938] : 181. With it should be read his description of metal-workers' tools, *Antiquaries' Journal* 18 [1938] : 243.

[2] Wilde (*Catalogue*, pp. 395-6) figures an Etruscan tool of metal shaped like a convex stone axe-head, as well as an Irish mould for casting similar objects ; but these are to be regarded as reversions rather than as steps in a forward evolution.

[3] Figured, Wilde, *Catalogue*, p. 392.

of the branch of a tree, having at its upper end the stump of a subsidiary branch—after the manner of the Greek letter Γ, but with the
horizontal [1] limb short in proportion to the length of the vertical.
This would be of extra strength at the junction of the side-branch,
owing to the presence of cross-grains in the wood.   Having trimmed

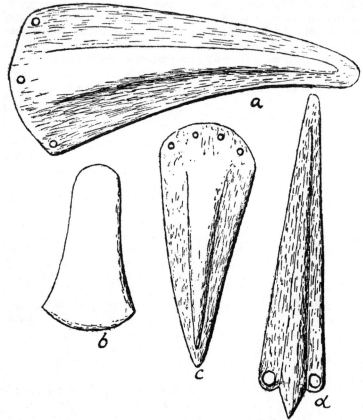

FIG. 22.—Types of Protomegalithic Copper or Bronze Artifacts.

his haft to the required size and strength, the artificer made a split
in the projecting stump, parallel with the haft for a hatchet mounting,
at right angles to it for an adze-mounting.   The blade was then
inserted into the setting thus provided, and was secured in position
with tightly bound thongs.   Thus was inaugurated the flat-hatchet
stage of the evolution of the implement.

[1] The word " horizontal " is not to be interpreted with mathematical precision.   As would be natural, the side branch was set at an angle to the main stem
slightly less than a right angle.

The earliest essays in the manufacture of such tools are naturally rough. The shape is irregular, and the casting bad, with many air-holes in the texture of the metal ; a very early copper-founder's hoard found in a cave, perhaps a primitive dwelling, at Carrick-shedogue (Wexford) contained some examples of these primitive forms, along with cakes of copper in the form of flat discs, collected from the smelting-furnace, but for some reason never utilized.[1] A similar hoard was found later on, in 1938, near Enniskerry (Wicklow), in a sandpit.[2] But, even during the course of the epoch of pure copper, an improvement in these respects can be traced, as Coffey has shown ;[3] the later copper hatchet-heads are shapely and well made, with curved sides, beyond which the edge projects. The flat type persisted into the true Bronze Age, for flat axe-heads made of the alloy are not infrequent. Armstrong figures a remarkable example overlaid with gold.[4]

The triangular dagger (Fig. 22 c) was the first *weapon* to be made in copper, though it is not certain that it was introduced at so early a date as the flat hatchet-head ; the two are, however, in contemporary use. It is derived from the dagger-blade of flint, already described, and consists of a rather broad, short, triangular blade, with a rounded butt in which there are rivet-holes, usually three in number, for securing it to the handle. The latter was of wood, bone, horn, and sometimes, in later times, of bronze. The triangular dagger is in universal use over Europe : Montelius assigns it to his First Period ; but it probably does not date from the very beginning of the First Period, nor is its use confined thereto. Until the discovery of bronze, the pure copper dagger cannot have been a very satisfactory weapon ; the delicate edge of the blade would have to be frequently sharpened, giving to the edges, originally straight, a hollow or concave shape. Specimens have been found in which the sides have actually been ground away, leaving little beyond the axial rib of the blade. This rib appears on both sides of the blade, showing that the daggers were cast in double moulds.

A copper dagger of a form quite unprecedented in Ireland formed part of a hoard of scrap-metal found at Killaha East, near Kenmare (Kerry). The whole group, containing flat hatchet-heads with slight flanges and fragments of a halberd, appears to belong to this chrono-logical section, though it might not be admitted to Montelius's First Period (Fig. 22 d). The total length of this dagger is 11½ inches : it has a triangular blade with a straight base and with a slight axial ridge on each side. From the middle of the base there projects a short triangular tang, and two holes, presumably for rivets,

---

[1] Described by Bremer in JRSAI 56 [1926] : 88. He dates the hoard to 2500 B.C. which is perhaps a little on the early side.
[2] JRSAI 68 [1938] : 305.
[3] G. Coffey, " Irish copper celts ", JRAI 31 : 265. For further illustrations see Wilde, *Catalogue*, p. 363.   [4] JRSAI 52 : 135.

occupy the basal angles of the triangle.   It is this combination of a tang with rivet-holes which gives the weapon its very unusual form.[1]

Halberds (Fig. 22 *a*) have all the interest of mystery, for they present more problems than might be suspected on a superficial glance at a museum case containing them.   They consist of dagger-like blades, mounted upon wooden or metal shafts to which they are riveted, the axes of the blades being set at right angles to those of the handles, or approximately so.   Of Irish specimens there are six types:—

1. A short round-tipped blade with a projecting tail containing four rivet-holes.
2. A more triangular and proportionally larger blade, with a similar tail.
3. A similar blade, but with three rivet-holes.
4. A similar blade, with no tail : instead, a triangular butt having three rivet holes.
5. A blade curved laterally like a scythe-blade : similar to the last in the butt and rivet-holes.
6. A short triangular blade, with a rounded butt containing four or more rivet-holes.

In all of these except the first, the blade is strengthened with a rib running down the two sides axially.[2]

Halberds are found in three regions, especially—Ireland, Southern Spain, and Germany : sporadic examples, found elsewhere, may be regarded as "wanderers" from one or other of these centres of distribution.   They are also represented in considerable numbers among the rock-scribings of the valleys around Monte Bego in the Italian Maritime Alps.   The Irish and Spanish halberds are generally similar, though the first three of the six types enumerated above are peculiar to Northern Ireland, and the curved form (type 5) has been found only in Ireland and Scotland.   But the German halberds are very different : the blades are long, straight-edged, and sharply pointed, and the handles, like the blades, are of *bronze*—copper with a considerable admixture of tin : whereas the Irish halberds are often [3] of more or less pure copper, and never had a metal handle.

The halberd is one of the earliest devices for hand-to-hand fighting which will keep the enemy at a distance.   Two combatants armed with daggers are at close quarters, and, other things being equal, it is largely a matter of chance as to who gets the fatal stroke in first.   If one of the combatants has his dagger at more than arm's

---

[1] The hoard is figured and briefly described by Capt. O'Connell, JRSAI 69 [1939] : 116.

[2] This classification is due to Ó Ríordáin (*Archæologia* 86 [1936] : 195) ; reference may be made to his study for details as to a few exceptional individual specimens, which do not conform thereto.   For other studies of this type of weapon see Coffey (PRIA 27 : 94), Wilde (*Catalogue*, pp. 451, 489 ff.), and the British Museum *Bronze-Age Guide*, p. 28.

[3] Not always : a *bronze* halberd from Highlake, Roscommon, is figured in the Report of the National Museum, Dublin, for 1933-4 ; and another from Breaghwy (pronounced Breaffy) is described and figured by Mitchell, O'Leary, and Raftery, Mayo, PRIA 46 [1941] : 287 ff.   Another from Breaghwy (Mayo, pronounced Breaffy) as described.

length, he has at least a certain advantage. The device appears to have been adopted even before the general use of metals ; flint weapons have been found in Antrim which have all the appearance of having been halberd-blades, the stone prototype of the simpler metal forms of the weapon. On the other hand, it is sometimes difficult to distinguish between the smaller specimens of halberd-blades and copper daggers.

The scythe-curved blade Professor Ó Ríordáin believes to have been mounted with the concavity upward, not downward, so that the cutting edge is on the convex, not the concave side. A little imaginative visualizing of such weapons in practical use will compel the admission that the theory is reasonable enough, though we should like to see it confirmed by such evidence as a contemporary rock-scribing could afford.

But there are many halberds which cannot have been intended for practical military use. These heavy blades, set possibly on a long and unmanageable handle,[1] would be too clumsy for use in the stress of battle ; while on the other hand, some of the lighter blades would be too fragile, and would snap, or would tear away from their rivets. The German halberds are especially unpractical as war-weapons ; they are heavy, and the excess of tin in their composition would make the handles liable to fracture. For such weapons as these, it is difficult to imagine any use other than ceremonial.

On the basis of a hoard of objects found at Birr (Offaly), where a copper halberd was found in association with three hatchet-heads of copper and a damaged triangular dagger, the halberd has been assigned to the First Bronze Period ; but the hatchet-heads were slightly flanged and (so far as minute distinctions between these periods are valid at all for Ireland) would be assigned typologically to the Second Period of Montelius. (Compare the Killaha find above mentioned.) The difficulty of procuring tin in Ireland introduces an element of complication into such neat classifications : with few exceptions the large halberd-blades characteristic of Ireland are made of copper, simply because bronze would be too extravagant ; the exceptions are exceptional in type as well, and almost certainly are foreign importations.

Much has compared Irish copper halberds with those from Spain on the one hand and those from Germany on the other : [2] concluding that the last are more highly developed, and clearly later in date, than the other two ; inasmuch as they are made of bronze, with bronze handles, and cast in one piece with the blade. Montelius,

[1] The length of some of the handles represented in the Monte Bego sculptures is merely ridiculous. It should be noted that Mr. M. C. Burkitt does not regard these sculptures as being of the extreme antiquity that has been assigned to them, and has made the attractive suggestion that the supposed halberds are really hoes. See *Antiquity* 3 [1929] : 155 ff.

[2] *Die Kupferzeit in Europa* (Jena 1893) pp. 127 ff.

however, has dated them to the beginning of the Age of Bronze in Germany. The Spanish halberds are regarded by Much as being older than those of Ireland : because they are (1) simpler in design— never having subsidiary ribs associated with the central midrib ; and (2) nearer in general shape to the parent dagger from which they are derived, inasmuch as they never show the scythe-like curve of the Irish specimens. Moreover (3), the uniformity of the type in Spain is regarded as evidence of greater antiquity ; the diversity found in Ireland being an indication that evolution has had time to develop the weapon in various directions. Though the book quoted is now to some extent antiquated, this argument seems to be sound, and it corroborates the dating here adopted, to an early but not the earliest stage of the Metal Age. The Birr hoard affords evidence of date and association which may be conclusive, but is not necessarily exclusive.

Halberds with metal handles are unknown in Ireland ; but there is one link with the German type in an Irish example, which has copper washers, of a hollow conical shape, interposed between the heads of the rivets and the blade.[1] As a rule, the rivets are of a simple dumb-bell pattern ; but they are well made, and their neatness indicates the attainment of a considerable skill in metallurgy. The necks of the rivets are remarkably short, showing that the handle at the point of junction must have been thinner than we should have expected it to be. But if it were made of a stout oaken staff, pared down at the point of junction but with a good backing behind it, and well bound with thongs, it would probably have been strong enough to resist all ordinary strains.

VIII.　GOLD ORNAMENTS

In the monograph quoted on a preceding page, Mr. Maryon has told us what we may learn from an analysis of the domestic establishments of metal-workers, especially those that have been found at Ty Mawr (Anglesey), and at Jarlshof (Shetland). At such sites, we find a circular hut, with a fireplace in the middle of the floor, and a melting-furnace in the thickness of the wall : beside the latter, the casting pit (for keeping the mould steady during the operation of casting). We find flat stones and heavy pounders (the anvils and hammers for crushing the ore before smelting) : and we observe aumbries recessed in the wall, to store the craftsman's tools. Of these, Mr. Maryon has compiled the following inventory, from a study of the objects manufactured by their means : broad stone anvils and heavy stone mallets (for beating ingots of copper into flat sheet-metal, to make shields and cauldrons) ; lighter hammers, for beating metal out over a mould (in making *repoussé* work) ; softer

---

[1] Illustrated by Coffey, PRIA 27 [1908] plate iii Fig. 20.

hammers made of the butt-end of a stag's horn, perforated for receiving a wooden handle (used in making bowls); small bronze
anvils (for the delicate work of a goldsmith) of an **L**-shape, one end
pointed for thrusting into the wooden working bench, the other
member flattened on what would be the top when the object was thus
set in position, to form the " table " upon which the artificer worked;[1]
tracers (pointed instruments for outlining ornament upon the metal
surface); drills made of sharpened bone; and other appliances for
special purposes, for full details of which we must refer to the
original paper. The function of a book like this is less to instruct
than to indicate to the reader where he can obtain instruction;
no mere abstract would do proper justice to Mr. Maryon's work,
or to its important subject.

It may not be without significance that the sites quoted above
are on *islands*, and are therefore comparatively obscure and difficult
of access. The artificers were no doubt habitually itinerant, and
travelled with their pedlar's packs from patron to patron—finding
hospitality with each in turn, here repairing, there manufacturing
to order, elsewhere hawking about and disposing of goods fashioned
in their workshops; and, as occasion offered, buying up scrap metal
for future use. Even such a nomad would need a *pied à terre*, in
which he could leave his stores and his supplies under the guardianship of trusted members of his family or of his guild (using both these
rather too specific words in the most general possible sense) while
he was abroad on his business tours, and to which he could return
for rest, and for replenishment of his stock. For such a purpose,
there could be no more suitable place than a remote island, where
he might hope to keep, private and secure, not only his portable
chattels, but also his trade secrets.

Evidence for such a gypsy life is offered to us from much later
times, by the inscriptions sometimes added to works of art made for
ecclesiastical use. These present us with three regular formulæ :—

> *Oroit do* NN. *do rigne in* . . .
>   "   *las ndernad in* . . .
>   "   *ica ndernad in* . . .

meaning " A prayer for NN., who made . . . ; under whose auspices
was made . . . ; at whose house was made . . . ; the " object,
whatever it might be. In the first, the person named was the
artificer himself; in the second, the patron—king, bishop, abbot, or
some other—who gave him his commission; in the third, the host
who entertained him while the work was in progress. All three
formulæ are included among the inscriptions on the famous twelfth-
century reliquary popularly known as the " Cross of Cong ".

[1] See specimens from Thomastown (Kilkenny) published by Professor
Ó Ríordáin (*Cork* 44 [1939] : 62).

The only type of ornament in gold which has been attributed with any confidence to the Protomegalithic period is the *lunula*. This, as the name implies, is in the form of a thin crescentic disc : the tips of the crescent, in all perfect examples, terminate in small plates, more or less oval, and more or less at right angles to the plane of the crescent. The surface of the disc is ornamented with delicately traced [1] linear patterns—lozenges, zigzags, triangles, etc., with or without contrasted shading : curvilinear forms are not used. This decoration is almost entirely confined to the horns ; on the broad central part there is hardly anything but a little shaded or stippled bordering, running along the edges. A study of the specimens in the Dublin Museum, and of the illustrations available in the proceedings of societies, does not seem to me to bear out the statement that the decoration was as a rule, " not exactly alike on the two terminals " ; to me they seem to correspond as nearly as could be, without the use of tracing-paper or other means of mechanical reproduction, differences being merely such accidents as discrepancies in the number of repetitions of a triangle, or some other elemental motive in the design. Letting that trifle pass, we may hear Mr. Maryon's authoritative exposition of the simple technical process of making a lunula ; nothing more elaborate than the careful hammering out of a gold bar, thinned towards the ends, was necessary to give it the shape required. The ornament was blocked out on the surface with a brush or with a pointed tool, and then made permanent by tracing—the gold disc being laid upon an anvil of stone, wood, or lead ; or perhaps on a pitch-bed, as suggested by Mr. C. J. Praetorius. [2]

But when we have disposed of this technical question, we are faced inevitably by further problems. How were lunulæ worn ? To what date are they to be assigned ? What are their affinities ?

Three answers have been given to the first of these questions. (1) That they were worn crossing the head in an upright position, after the manner of the conventional nimbus which decorates the representations of saints. In the discussion quoted in the preceding footnote, Mr. E. T. Leeds lent his weighty authority to a support of this theory (with the modification that he would put the crescent *behind* the head rather than over it). But it is open to the criticism that they are too delicate to be worn in such an exposed position without some solid backing, for whose existence there is no evidence— for unlike the so-called " sun-discs ", to be mentioned later, lunulæ have no thread-holes for fixing them to any support of the kind ;

---

[1] In the paper quoted above Mr. Maryon is careful to emphasize the difference between *tracing*, in which grooves are impressed (as by knife-cuts), but no metal is removed from the surface of the object ; and *engraving*, in which metal is excised. The later process did not come into use till the introduction of tools of iron.

[2] In a discussion upon Mr. R. A. Smith's paper, quoted below.

and, in such a position, they would exclude the possibility of any other head-covering, whatever the weather. (2) The now prevalent view, that they were worn as a neck-and-breast decoration, after the manner of a child's bib—the plates at the ends of the horns being buttons or toggles, for catching in a looped cord (separate, or attached to the back of a garment), or in button-holes, thus securing the ornament in its place. The chief difficulty in this explanation is that it assumes the decoration to be distributed in what would be a surprising way—not over the broad part of the crescent, where it would be conspicuous, but on the horns, where it would be less visible on the person of the wearer—probably, indeed, concealed altogether by his long and tousled hair. (3) Mr. Maryon makes a third suggestion, that the ornament was a neck-and-back decoration, otherwise worn as in the previous theory; the securing loops or button-holes being in *front* of the wearer's garment. This would bring the ornamental horns into prominence, over the owner's collar-bones, the plain surface at the back being visible, if at all, merely as a scintillation through his hair. Mr. Maryon adds that " experiment shows that the weight of the garment would tend to pull the terminal buttons into a position parallel with the front of the chest, and would then impart a very beautiful curve to the edge of the ornament ".

When a lunula was not in use, it was carefully protected from injury (to which its thinness would have rendered it liable) by being kept between two flat plates of oak, of a size and shape adapted to the outline of the ornament : a specimen of such a case was found in a bog at Newtown, Crossdoney (Cavan), and is now in the Royal Irish Academy's Collection.[1] This again raises the question of the delicacy of these objects : how were they prevented from being crushed ? With constant use, they would surely become crumpled beyond recovery, before very long. The most probable answer is that they were not meant for constant use ; only for wear on very special occasions, upon which the owner could not have indulged in active movement. They were ceremonial, rather than merely ornamental.

In fact, the late Reginald Smith proposed to regard these objects as belonging to cult rather than to culture : as being " moon-discs ", used presumably in some magico-religious ceremonies, not mere ornaments ; and he suggested that the engraved horns are differentiated from the plain middle portions, because they represent the " crumpled horns ", as contrasted with the smooth frontal portion, of a " moon-bull ".[2] Armstrong seems inclined to adopt this

---

[1] Figured in Coffey, *The Bronze Age in Ireland*, p. 51. A similar receptacle, but of much later date, hollowed out of a wooden block, containing four gold " cupped " rings, was found in a bog near Ardfert (Kerry) : see Raftery's report in *Cork* 45 [1940] : 56.

[2] R. A. Smith, " Irish gold crescents " (*Antiquaries' Journal* 1 [1921] : 131).

hypothesis ;[1] but carried out in its full detail it seems needlessly speculative.   It does not account for the terminal plates characteristic of the lunulæ, which have no counterpart on the horns of a bull, or on terra-cotta horns found in Swiss lake-dwellings and compared by Smith to the Irish lunulæ.   These objects bear a resemblance to the Irish gold ornaments—they can hardly fail to do so, for, after all, one crescent is much like another !   The crescent moon is an obvious model for a maker of gold ornaments to follow ; especially as its yellow sheen would inevitably suggest the material in which he worked.   We can adopt *this* hypothesis without necessarily expressing faith in any cult-use of the ornament, apart from the amulet value of any object in lunar-crescentic form.   (We have to remember that *all* ancient personal ornaments were primarily amulets, and that their merely decorative use was a secondary development.)

Coffey, and independently of him Mr. O. G. S. Crawford, have prepared distribution-maps of lunulæ in Ireland and elsewhere,[2] and have indicated the inferences regarding Irish trade to be drawn from them.   A paper in JRSAI 27 : 53 contains a list of lunulæ, with some illustrations, which may possibly be useful for reference ; but the main thesis of the paper, that these early bronze-age objects were made from Roman gold coins melted down, is merely one of the curiosities of archæological literature.

Leaving the first question thus open, with, for the moment, a slight inclination (open to reconsideration) towards Maryon's theory —partly because it accounts for the distribution of the applied decoration over the surface of the ornament, and partly because it would bring the lunulæ into accord with the later " gorgets " ; we now must proceed to the question of their date.   It is customary to assign these objects to the earliest phase of the Bronze Age, pre- ceding all other Irish gold ornaments.   This is based upon two grounds, which may be grouped as inferential and evidential.   The inferential arguments in favour of the early date rest, first, upon the linear ornament with which the objects are decorated, which most closely resembles the decoration of the earliest form of *bronze* hatchet-heads,[3] and therefore is presumably contemporary therewith ; and secondly, upon the wide area of distribution over which lunulæ are found, in Ireland, Britain, and especially on the Continent— suggesting that they belong to the " golden age " of Irish trade, before the exhaustion of the auriferous gravels, and the permanent

[1] JRSAI 52 [1922] : 140.
[2] George Coffey, " The distribution of the gold lunulæ in Ireland and North- eastern Europe ", PRIA 27 [1909] : 251 ; reprinted with little more than verbal alterations in the same author's *The Bronze Age in Ireland* (Dublin 1913), chap. iv. See also Coffey, " Two unpublished lunulæ and other objects ", PRIA 30 : 449. Crawford's map will be found in *The Geographical Journal* 40 : 195.   See also Armstrong's *Gold Catalogue*, already cited, and S. Reinach, " Les croissants d'or irlandais " (*Revue celtique* 21 [1900] : 75, 166).
[3] A study of which will be found in INJ 6 : 61.

set-back in Irish civilization consequent partly on the disastrous invasion of the Beaker people, and partly on the climatic deterioration which set in about the same time. But corroborative evidence, such as would be based upon a find of lunulæ associated with datable objects, is still pitifully scanty : indeed practically nothing to the point has been found since the Harlyn (Cornwall) find of 1864. This included two lunulæ—one with a surface perfectly plain all over, even in the horns, except for a little beading and zigzag ornament along the edges ; the other with a rich decoration of zigzags, lozenges, and varied shading in the horns, and an edge-ornament of rather greater elaboration than usual. With this was a flat bronze (possibly copper) hatchet-head, quite plain, without flanges or stop-ridge ; and another object, which the labourer (who had found it and thrown it away) obscurely reported to be " like a bit of a buckle ". These were buried in " made " earth, at a depth of 6 feet from the surface. No evidence of interment was observed.[1] Mr. Crawford visited the place in 1917, to seek for traditional recollections of the discovery, and obtained from the son of the proprietor of the site at the time the additional information that the digging was made to repair a pond ; that other things, in Mr. Crawford's words, " vaguely described as battle-axes " had been found and thrown away ; that all these objects had been found in a square stone cist—which makes no appearance in the publication of 1865 ; and that the labourer thought the lunulæ were brass, and came into the farm, after he had made the discovery, wearing them round the calves of his legs.[2] No slur is implied on any of the persons concerned by making the obvious remark that fifty-two years intervened between the dates of these communications, and that, in dealing with traditional memory extending over so long an interval, allowance has to be made for the intrinsic defect in human psychology which makes it possible for children to enjoy the entertaining game of " Russian Scandal ". We can only live in hope that at some time in the future more lunulæ will be found in association with datable objects, by some person better qualified to deal with them than the Cornish labourer of eighty years ago ; if we wish to establish the current theory of their date which, however probable, still rests upon the flimsiest of direct evidence.

Our third question, what are their affinities, presents two aspects for brief discussion. The first arises from R. A. Smith's " moon-disc " theory, which is closely cognate with the " sun-disc " theory

[1] Edward Smirke, " Notice of two golden ornaments found near Padstow ", *Archæological Journal* 22 [1865] : 275.

[2] O. G. S. Crawford, " The Ancient Settlements at Harlyn Bay ", *Antiquaries' Journal* 1 [1921] : 283. Mr. Robert Day, speaking out of a long experience of personal dealings with antiquity finders, says : " It is remarkable that when gold ornaments are found by the peasantry they are invariably supposed to be brass, while on the contrary those of bronze are mistaken for gold ". *Cork* 13 [1907] : 119. Mr. Crawford in the paper quoted comments on the same curious fact.

of circular gold discs, maintained by the same authority, and strongly supported by the evidence of the famous sun-chariot from Trundholm Moor. Here, however, we are again faced with a chronological difficulty. We might have expected " sun-discs " and " moon-discs " to have been more or less contemporary in time, representing, as they appear to do, identical expressions of an astronomical trend

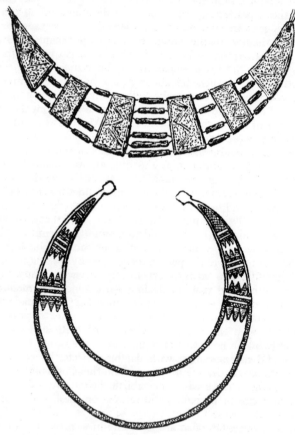

FIG. 23.—Diagram comparing a Jet Necklace and a Gold Lunula.

in religion or art. But the ornament of both classes of objects shows that to whatever absolute date the lunulæ are to be assigned, that of the " sun-discs " is quite different : this we can say with assurance.

The second arises from an ingenious suggestion made by the late James Craw of Edinburgh, that lunulæ are imitations of multiple jet necklaces (Fig. 23). Two or more strings of jet beads, held in position by transverse spacing-plates, would hang on the breast in a form strongly reminiscent of a lunula, narrowing to the triangular cap at the end, which would lie at and behind the shoulder. The geographical distribution of lunulæ and of jet necklaces are notably complementary, as a map illustrating Mr. Craw's paper indicates : [1] the necklaces being chiefly frequent in Eastern Scotland, the lunulæ in Great Britain and in Ireland. Acceptance of the theory involves the further acceptance of (1) a Scottish rather than an Irish origin for this type of gold ornament, its extensive Irish development being due to the abundant supply of gold available in Ireland ; (2) possibly a slightly later date for the lunulæ than had been assumed ; [2] (3) the neck-and-breast theory, as opposed to the neck-and-back theory. As Craw notes in his paper, the suggestion was, so to speak, adumbrated, but afterwards tacitly dropped, by Coffey : since its publication it has been accepted by Childe, [3] and also by Clark. It has likewise been accepted by Mahr. [4] The argument which most strongly weighs with these authorities may be stated thus. Craw drew up a classification of lunulæ, based on the varieties of their decorative detail. [5] Of these, one (which he regards as the parent form, the others being developments or degenerations) shows ornament exactly reproducing the shape and decoration of the jet necklaces—including the stippled ornament on the flat rectangular spacing-plates. This variety is found in the majority of the lunulæ from Scotland, and in a very small minority of those from Ireland— once more indicating a Scottish origin for the type, and an Irish localization of its later developments. On chronological grounds, I was doubtful of this theory when I wrote *Ancient Ireland* (p. 31) : though, since then, it has been borne in upon me with increasing force that hard-and-fast chronology cannot be pressed to extreme limits in dealing with Irish antiquities. Moreover, the decorated hatchet-heads with which the lunulæ are there compared are *flanged bronze* flat hatchets, a type which is more probably to be assigned to the early Deuteromegalithic. This would bring the date of the lunulæ down to that period also, and would afford a basis for a subdivision of the Deuteromegalithic period ([1] flanged hatchets : [2] palstaves) which might have some chronological utility. True, Hawkes would reverse the evolution. For him, multiple jet necklaces are a makeshift equivalent for multiple necklaces in amber, of Danish and, beyond that, Oriental origin ; [6] whereas the form

---

[1] J. Hewat Craw, " On a jet necklace from a cist at Poltalloch, Argyll " (P.S.A. Scot. 63 [1928-9] : 154).

[2] Mr. Clark (*Man*, 32 [1932] no. 46) regards the theory as confirmatory of the early date. But if the lunulæ are descended from the jet necklace, they should be slightly later.

[3] *Prehistory of Scotland*, p. 195.   [4] PPS 3 : 374.

[5] For this classification, which requires for its exposition a full series of illustrations, such as the author quoted provides, see his paper, cited above, pp. 175 ff.

[6] *The Prehistoric Foundations of Europe*, pp. 323-4.

assumed by the Scottish necklaces is dictated by the influence of the Irish lunulæ, themselves of Iberian origin.   But the apparently skeuomorphic panels which cut transversely across the crescentic decoration, and which certainly look like the spacing-plates of the necklaces, seem to me to add some weight to Craw's side of the balance ; the derivation of an ornament, talismanic or not, from a utilitarian feature, is more likely than a contrary course of development.[1]

[1] Mr. L. S. Gogan has expressed an opposition to Craw's theory in a paper to which reference may be made for the miscellaneous facts relating to the discovery and associations of lunulæ there collected : *Cork* 39 [1934] : 1.

CHAPTER VI

THE DEUTEROMEGALITHIC CULTURE

I. SOCIAL CONDITIONS

THE expression "Ireland's Golden Age" is a pleasant hyperbole, often applied by popular writers to the time about the eighth and ninth centuries A.D. It would be much more appropriate to the phase on the study of which we are now entering ; when, in climatic conditions still favourable, a culturally united people was making rapid progress in technology (especially in metallurgy) and was enjoying a large control over the markets of Northern Europe.

In fact, the distinction between the Proto- and the Deuteromegalithic phases is essentially cultural, not ethnological. The transition from the first to the second is manifested in the complete supersession of the Neolithic tradition in pottery by new types, and of pure copper [1] by bronze ; in the addition of new devices to the resources of the artificer and the warrior ; and in the extension and development of the art of the goldsmith. We may presume that there were similar advances in the arts of wood-working, of embroidery, of leather work, as well as in those of the special crafts of food-cultivation ; but of these the disintegration of organic materials deprives us of tangible proof. The commercial exploitation of the country's store of gold developed foreign intercourse ; and it is to such intercourse, rather than to racial changes due to extensive immigrations, that the cultural developments in this period are to be attributed.

II. HOUSES

An advance in the standard of domestic comfort, concurrent with these marks of progress, may be safely presumed. The extended use of the constructional device of *corbelling* increased the area which could be protected by a stone roof, or by any probable form of lintel construction in wood. Nevertheless, the "beehive" stone hut, which the corbel construction made possible, could hardly be said to be a great advance over the "Navajo" log hut of the Protomegalithic people. Until some kind of framed timber structure was devised, there could be little improvement in the capacity of houses : a large establishment would consist of a multiplicity of small and simple huts, rather than one all-embracing complex.

[1] By which is of course to be understood copper as pure as the early metal-workers could obtain it, without the *artificial* addition of any other substance. On the difficulty of obtaining pure copper by primitive methods of smelting, see Prof. W. Gowland, "The Metals in Antiquity", JRAI 42 [1912] : 242.

The preservation of any form of wooden structure, in sufficient measure to provide information of value, is not to be expected. The Drumkelin house, to which we must refer more fully later, in our general chapter on " Defences and Dwellings ", itself may or may not be as old as the Deuteromegalithic phase : but we have indirect evidence for the existence of just such houses, at a time probably late in the Deuteromegalithic, in the remains of a causeway crossing the Bog of Allen in Co. Westmeath, exposed by peat-cutters in 1932, and examined and reported upon by myself shortly afterwards.[1]

It had apparently been laid down on the surface of the Lower Turbarian peat, hardened and dried during the Upper Forestian period, which came to an end with the Deuteromegalithic phase. The rains of the Upper Turbarian were beginning to soften the ground again : and the causeway must have been laid down over what had become a sloppy part of some old trackway, to mitigate what may at the time have appeared to be a mere passing inconvenience. It still continued in use through the Epimegalithic ; this was indicated by a loopless socketed bronze spear-head, found lying *on the surface* of the causeway, presumably dropped by a wayfarer and lost in the mud that had already accumulated.

The *Packwerk* method of construction had been adopted. Oaken beams were laid down on the surface of the ground, across the line of the causeway ; others were laid upon these, parallel with the line of the causeway ; then a third layer across ; a fourth along ; and a fifth across. This description, however, gives a misleading impression of regularity : the beams were actually laid down so much at haphazard that it required close study to deduce this or any other arrangement from their disposition. Upon the fifth layer a vast number of birchen rods was laid down side by side, along the line of the causeway, with a regularity contrasting notably with the casual sub-structure ; and secured in position with pegs driven at intervals into the ground. These pegs were cut off flush with the level of the birch rods ; but, unless they were also covered with sods forming the actual *trottoir*, they would have hurt the feet of the probably ill-shod wayfarers.

There was a suggestion of haste in the irregularity of the sub-structure, as though the road had been made under the pressure of some urgent military or other necessity—it may be, of the Beaker invasion itself ; and the makeshift nature of the materials accorded with this view of the case. What we have called " beams " in the foregoing description were actually flat planks, crudely hewn into shape with axes ; about a foot, or a little more, in breadth, and in length ranging from a couple of feet up to about twelve. Most of them had a hole roughly " axed " through, at one or both ends.

[1] JRSAI 62 [1932] : 137.

No use whatever was made of these holes ; [1] a few of them contained a peg or a stone, but this was merely to fill them. It follows that all or most of the material was there at second-hand ; that, in fact, a number—a considerable number—of framed timber structures like the Drumkelin house had been demolished to provide it : for the Drumkelin house was composed of similar planks.

Was the causeway constructed under some military urgency, over-riding all other convenience, and demanding even the demolition of houses of harmless citizens—a projection back into the second millennium B.C., of conditions under our own eyes in this second millennium A.D. ? Or was it a work of public service, carried out by some equivalent of a modern contractor, who made use of material which had accumulated in his yard in the ordinary course of his business ? Both explanations are possible ; the former is the more likely, in view of the evidence of haste. The question, however, is merely academic, and of little importance ; the real significance of the causeway lies in the proof which it affords of the existence of a large number of framed timber structures at the time when it was made, and probably for some considerable time before.[2] An otherwise pointless story in the *Life of Colmán mac Luacháin* shows us certain monks making a great causeway across a bog by cutting down a wood : [3] evidently something like what is called a " corduroy road " is indicated.

III. MODE OF LIFE

As was noted in Chapter V, we pass over this important subject for the present.

IV. STONE IMPLEMENTS

In Chapter V we have spoken sufficiently of implements in *chipped* stone, and have indicated the groups of these which it would appear reasonable to assign to the Deuteromegalithic phase.

The *polishing* of stone reached its highest perfection in this phase ; its products display both technical excellence and typological variety. It is evident that the advance in metallurgy reacted on the art of the lapidary ; the two industries competed successfully. The metal-worker had an advantage in the greater tractability of his material, but in Ireland he was hampered by the difficulty of obtaining tin ; and a stone axe was on the whole more effective than any tool which he could produce in copper.

---

[1] A very similar causeway, though without the *Packwerk* substructure, was described by Lord Walter FitzGerald as crossing Monavullagh Bog (Kildare). There also, planks with apparently meaningless holes at each end were used (JRSAI 28 [1898] : 417).
[2] History repeated itself much later, in the Ballinderry lake-dwelling no. 1, which was partly constructed out of similar second-hand material : see PRIA 47 [1942] : 3 2. [3] *Betha Colmáin*, ed. K. Meyer, R.I.A. (*Todd Lecture Series*, 17 : 26).

An important technical innovation assignable to this phase is the *perforation* of stone tools, for the reception of a wooden haft. This was accomplished by means of a rotary drill, set in motion with a bow, and agitating a handful of watered sand ; the attrition of the sand, on the substance of the stone under treatment, gradually wore out the hole.　We are often told that the artificer turned the stone over, after he had pierced the hole about half-way through, and began again on the other side, the two depressions meeting in the middle ; this appears to be indicated by the shape of the section of the hole, which in such cases is like that of a dice-box.　But the exactness with which the central axis of the hole runs straight through the stone, with no sideslip in the middle of its course, suggests rather that a narrow perforation was first drilled in one operation right through, and was then widened to the required diameter from both ends.

On the other hand, the hole was sometimes left unfinished— most commonly because the stone fractured under the drilling process ; but sometimes, it may be, because the artificer wearied of his work, or perhaps for some other reason, equally simple, but now irrecoverable.　In such cases an unsevered cylinder of stone often rises from the middle of the floor of the hollow ; an indication of the use of a drill in the form of a hollow tube—the leg-bone of a bird, or perhaps a rod of elder-wood cleared of its pith.　The soft-ness of this wood, though no doubt it would necessitate continued replacement of the drill as it wore down, would not be altogether a disadvantage ; the sand would sink into its substance, and would give the drill, while it lasted, the efficiency of a rotating rasp.

Maces are the simplest tools with perforated stone heads : they are globular lumps of stone, of spherical, ovoid, or flattened spheroid shape—the second of these perforated through the longer axis, the third through the shorter.[1]　Of more advanced technique are :—

Hammers (with one or two striking butts, but no sharp edge or point) ;
Single axes (with one cutting edge at one end, and a heel, not fashioned into a striking butt, at the other) ;
Hammer-axes (with a cutting edge at one end, and a striking butt at the other) ;
Double axes (with a cutting edge at both ends, parallel with the line of the handle) ;
Adzes or *Hoes* (with the cutting edge transverse to the line of the handle) ;
Axe-Adzes (with two cutting edges in planes mutually at right angles) ;
Axe-Picks (with a cutting edge at one end, and a sharpened conical point at the other).

The foregoing descriptions speak for themselves, and need not here be illustrated or otherwise developed.　The double hammer is usually in the form of a polished stone cylinder, the perforation running through at right angles to the long axis; the striking-butts

[1] A fine spheroid mace-head found near Clonmel (Tipperary) is figured in *Waterford* 11 [1908] : 97, and again *ibid.* 18 [1915] : 118.

are slightly convex.[1]   Miniature specimens of this form, little more
than perforated pebbles, may be explained as metal-workers' hammers
or mallets ;   two such were found at Fethard (Wexford), associated
with a mould for casting bronze socketed hatchet-heads ;   this
association would suggest for them a date in the Epimegalithic phase,
thus illustrating the late survival of stone tools.[2]

Wilde figures a number of varieties of the hammer-axe group.[3]
Hammer-adzes also are not unknown, but they are rare.   Here,
admittedly, the perforation was sometimes worked from both ends ;
I had a specimen from the Bann (now in the possession of University
College, Dublin) in which the perforation was suspended after it
had sunk about ½ inch into the top and the bottom, and was never
resumed.[4]

To the *double-axe* class belong some of the most highly finished
tools in stone which we possess ;   it is evident that much care had been
lavished upon their preparation and polishing.   But some of them,
if they be really axes, must be regarded as intended for ceremonial
use :   the edges are too blunt to be effective, and the shaft-hole is
absurdly small in the bore—the handle would sometimes have to be
as thin as an ordinary lead pencil to penetrate it at all, so that it
would obviously be incapable of offering an efficient " grip ", or
of resisting the shocks of any practical work.   This remarkable
fact has been observed, not infrequently, in Ireland and elsewhere.
An endeavour has been made to explain it on the hypothesis that the
tool, when finished, was, so to speak, " threaded " on a young twig
of a living tree, and left there until the twig had grown into the shape
of the perforation, thickening out above and below, thus fixing the
head immovably.   The twig would then be cut from the tree, to
become the handle of the tool.[5]   There is, however, no direct evidence
for any such practice in Ireland ;   and I am half-inclined to think
that Frazer has for once hit the nail on the head when he identifies
a typical specimen from Rathvilly,[6] which he describes and figures,
as the " champion's hand stone " of sundry poetical rhapsodies,
quoted and hopelessly misinterpreted by O'Curry.[7]   A long cord,
its end passed through the narrow haft-hole and secured with a
knot, could be wound upon the wasp-waist of the stone as thread is

[1] See for a good specimen, from Portora (Fermanagh), *Ulster* II 2 [1896] : 47.
[2] JRSAI 19 [1889] : 289, 293.
[3] *Catalogue*, pp. 79, 80.   But for a full study of the different types, reference
must be made to R. A. Smith, " The Perforated Axe-hammers of Britain "
(*Archæologia* 75 [1925] : 77).
[4] Another good example is figured, *Ulster* I 3 [1855] : 234.
[5] Sir John Evans (*Stone*, pp. 155, 218) refers us to a similar though not absolutely identical practice current among certain American aborigines.   (But do
the makers or owners of such tools lay heavy spells or tabus upon them to save
themselves the trouble of unceasing vigilance against thieves ?)
[6] PRIA 17 [1889] : 215.   The object is now in the R.I.A. Collection.   The
specimen figured on p. 148 is from the Bann Knowles Collection (PRIA 30: plate
xix Fig. 215).   [7] *Manners and Customs* 2 : 275 ff.

wound upon a spool ; the free end of the cord being held fast, the stone might then be hurled at the destined victim. The uncoiling of the cord would give it a rapid spin ; if the cord should strike the victim's neck, the stone would whirl round in a spiral after the manner of a South American *bolas*, and enfold him inextricably. A stone in this form, thus manipulated, might be described in the words of the literary effusions above mentioned, as " an adder of nine coils " or as " a honeysuckle around a tree "—and indeed it is not easy to see how the most extravagant of poets could apply similes like these to what is elsewhere described as a " fiery hard stone ", unless he had the tradition of such a stratagem to inspire him. The stone would thus, like the *cateia* of classical literature, be an axe-head adapted to serve as a missile.

It is most likely that the perforation of such tools began with the much easier perforation of hammers made of horn. The filiation of a perforated stone-axe to a perforated axe of horn is very persuasively suggested by a comparison published by Mr. Hawkes in *The Antiquaries' Journal* 17 [1937] : plate xxvii (p. 72).

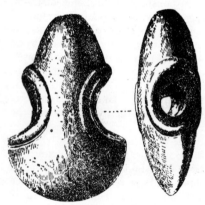

[*By permission of the Royal Irish Academy.*

FIG. 24.—Bolas-stone.

V.   POTTERY

In the Deuteromegalithic culture the Neolithic pottery tradition finally disappears. The round-bottomed bowl gives place to the flat-bottomed vase-shaped *food-vessel*, which may be described in the following general terms : a flat circular base, above which the vessel expands upward, in the form of an inverted cone, to a shoulder; where there is usually an abrupt change of curvature. The profile then contracts, perhaps with one or more ridges at and above the shoulder ; and then expands to the circular lip of the vessel : the diameter of the top of the vase being always greater than that of the base. But underlying the unity of type which may be thus formulated, there is a wide range of diversity in detail, conceivably of racial, historical, or geographical importance. This vase-shaped food-vessel does not supersede the porringer food-vessel : indeed the latter persists in use long enough to overlap with the Epimegalithic beakers. No ancient pottery from Ireland presents any evidence of the use of the potter's wheel.

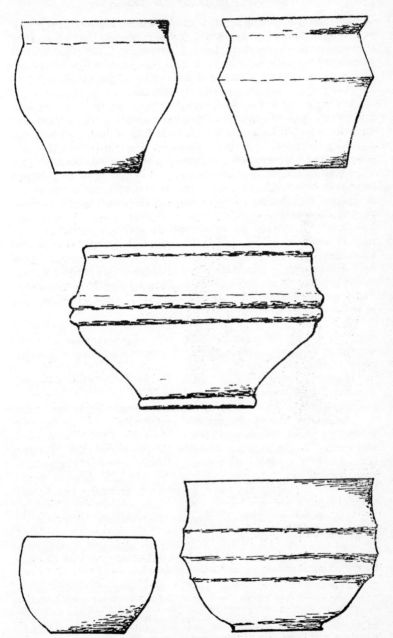

FIG. 25.—Types of Deuteromegalithic Pottery.

Obviously, a classification of the varieties of vase-shaped food-vessels is a matter for a specialist monograph on pottery; an Irish supplement to the work of Lord Abercromby. We must content ourselves here with indicating some of the deviations to be noticed within the framework sketched in the preceding paragraph.

Base : flat (normally), or slightly concave.

Lower part of body : an inverted cone, rising from the ground-line (normally), or from a small disc-like projecting base a fraction of an inch deep. In Ireland, a lateral thickening of this base (as though imitating the effect of a ring-support for a round-bottomed vessel) is rare ; and it never takes the form of a thin-walled ring such as is to be seen in a modern china tea-cup.[1] The profile of the inverted cone may be straight or convex (rarely concave) ; it is sometimes diversified with horizontal ribs encircling the vessel, and sometimes very slightly waved.

Shoulder : marked by an abrupt change of curvature, which may be emphasized by a rib. The rib is frequently double, the subsidiary rib being above or below the main shoulder-rib. In the hollow between the ribs there are sometimes (but infrequently) lug handles, usually three in number : still less frequently, loop-handles. Elaborate vessels may increase the number of these subsidiary ribs to as many as six or eight.

Neck above shoulder : usually concave, the profile roughly resembling a pair of parenthesis-brackets addorsed, thus) (; but sometimes straight in profile, contracting upwards from the shoulder-rib as the frustum of a cone, *not* inverted.

Mouth : always circular (never spouted) with lip projecting more or less horizontally outward or inward, its upper surface horizontal or bevelled inward ; but sometimes a plain unexpanding rim.

Ornament : always abstract and geometrical ; no attempt ever made to portray animal or vegetable forms.[2] Always rhythmical, and carried continuously round the vessel—" metopic " patterns (i.e., panels alternating with plain surfaces or with other panels) rare, though not unknown. Vertical ribbing is sometimes found, but is very unusual ; the main lines of the ornament run, almost invariably, in a horizontal direction.

This ornament is applied with various apparatus, such as :—

The potter's finger or finger-nail.

A stick or pointed bone, with which circular dots can be impressed by prodding the soft wet surface of the as yet unbaked ware ; or lines, produced by the action technically called " stab-and-drag ".

---

[1] That is, in Deuteromegalithic pottery. But it sometimes appears in Epimegalithic vessels, as in a pygmy vessel found beneath a cinerary urn at Greenhills (Dublin), the site of an important late megalithic cemetery (PRIA 21 [1899] : 338).

[2] A sherd found near Macroom (Cork) illustrated JRSAI 42 [1912] : 171 as there shown appears to have a branching tree-like device upon it, but later examination shows that it has been misinterpreted. The device is a damaged geometrical Epimegalithic " encrustation ".

A cord, stretched and pressed against the soft clay.

A " whipped cord ", i.e., wrapped spirally round a flexible rod.

A comb, producing a series of points or short parallel strokes.

A seal of some kind ; such as a close knot in a cord, the point of a knife, a bird's bone, the circular end of a hollow bone or of an elder-wood tube, the edge of a scallop or cockle-shell, or indeed any other instrument with which an ornamental motive can be repeated without difficulty as often as may be required.

It takes such forms as these :—

Linear patterns—lines, herring-bones, zigzags, basket-zigzags (as in this diagram)—

Geometrical figures—circles, elongated hexagons, lozenges bordered with single or double lines, and often discriminated from the background against which they are set by a diversity of shading.

Cord-patterns of various degrees of complexity, spreading either as a continuous network over the decorated surface, or else scattered over it in the shape of a *semée* of " maggots ", made by bending a rod of whipped cord into the shape of a sugar-tongs, and impressing the pottery with its convex end.

No colour decoration has ever been observed on Irish pottery ; irregular firing sometimes produces a diversity of colour, but there is no reason to believe that this is anything but fortuitous.

The above list is perhaps sufficient for our present purpose, though it is far from exhaustive. But even the few varieties which it enumerates could be grouped in about 90,000 combinations, so that an enthusiast can take up the study of Irish pottery in the happy assurance that he will never get to the end of it.

Though much more intensive study of the subject will be necessary before coming to a decision, it does not seem likely that it will be found possible to establish a provincial distribution of types of ornament over the comparatively small area of Ireland, analogous to those which Lord Abercromby has defined in Great Britain.[1] The question has still to be submitted to the test of distribution-maps ; but so far as can be judged, from the available material, different forms of profile and decoration are scattered indiscriminately through the country.[2]

The larger vessels, called cinerary urns, though they cannot be said to be unknown in Deuteromegalithic deposits, are more appropriate to the following Epimegalithic ; consideration of these

---

[1] Besides his monograph, see his paper, " The Ornament of the Beaker Class of Pottery ", PSA Scot. 39 [1904-5] : 326, supplemented by Dr. Margaret Mitchell's communication on the same subject, *ibid.* 68 [1933-4] : 132.

[2] Note (to mention but one illustration) the very varied series of food-vessels from a single district, figured and described in Messrs. Price and Walsh's survey of the antiquities of Lower Talbotstown (Wicklow) ; JRSAI 63 [1933] : 46.

may therefore be postponed to the chapter devoted thereto, as well as of the " pygmy urns " so frequently associated with them.

The pottery from the carn at Tamnyrankin [1] (Derry) may, however, be mentioned here, if only because there does not seem to be any other place for it. The vessels which call for special notice are (1) a hemispherical bowl on a disc base ; a food-vessel, if ever there was one, though not conforming to any ordinary type of such vessels, ornamented with horizontal lines of whipped-cord impressions and other simple ornament, superposed to which are panels of vertical ridges. Two of these panels, diametrically opposite, consist merely of five ridges, intercepting cord-suspension holes, but not interrupting the main scheme of the ornament : but two [2] others, joined by horizontal ridges at the top, enclose spaces which are at least partly treated with different ornamentation, and give a very strong impression of being influenced by the " doors " of house-urns, such as are familiar (in very different types) in Italy and also in Scandinavia. (2) Fragments of a round-bottomed bowl, decorated over its whole surface, so far as its imperfect condition permits us to judge, with the familiar " maggot " pattern. (3) A round-bottomed spheroidal bowl with a zigzag line made with cord-impressions surrounding its greatest diameter horizontally, and with lines of horizontal cord-impressions filling the space above up to the rim : below the zigzag the surface is blank.

V. METALLURGY

The absence of tin in Ireland made a " copper age " endure there for a much longer time than in other European regions, some of which hardly seem to have had a " copper age " at all. It was the opening to Ireland of the Cornish tin that enabled the country to establish on a firm basis the commercial pre-eminence which its gold had purchased, and so to make the advance in civilization which distinguished the comparatively brief Deuteromegalithic period. Nothing could compensate for the handicap affecting those who depended on soft copper in contention against those who had hard bronze at their disposal. Bronze, the alloy of copper and tin (normally nine parts of copper to one part of tin, though this, the most effective alloy, is not always attained) [3] is not only harder than pure copper, but it fuses at a lower temperature, so that it is more easily worked.

[1] JRSAI 71 [1941] : 31 ff.
[2] Presumably so, but only one is extant: the opposite side of the bowl was broken away and not recovered.
[3] Or even aimed at. Gowland, in a monograph quoted a few pages back, tells us that the proportion of tin to copper is regulated, especially in the later phases of the Bronze Age, by the purposes which the object made of the alloy was intended to serve (JRAI 42 : 243 ff.).

Where, when, and how this truly epoch-making discovery was made, are questions to which at most nothing but a vague guess-work answer can be returned ; and which are in any case irrelevant to our present study.   It was presumably in some stanniferous region ; so far as Ireland is concerned, it was at the end of the Protomegalithic period ; but as to " how " we can say no more than that the first discovery must have been the consequence of some now irrecoverable accident which brought the two metals together.   It is no solution of the problem to remind us that natural bronze might come into existence automatically in some locality which nature had endowed with the two component metals ; for that would imply the possession by the early bronze-users of a knowledge of the processes of chemical or spectroscopic analysis, to discriminate between the alloy and the pure metal.[1]

The introduction of bronze made possible the use of closed or double-valve moulds, with a consequent improvement in the whole aspect of the products of the artificer's industry.   Nevertheless, we must admit that it was not till the advent of the culturally barbarous but metallurgically expert Epimegalithic invaders that a rich variety of bronze tools and gold ornaments was produced ; the Deuteromegalithic artificers had high technical skill but limited constructional enterprise, so that all their products can be grouped into a small number of typical forms.

BRONZE IMPLEMENTS

Hatchet-heads

The first developments of the hatchet-head, after its primitive flat form, belong to this period.   However tightly the flat Protomegalithic hatchet-head might be secured to its haft, as already described (p. 129) it would inevitably slip sideways ; the thongs would never be so inelastic as to resist the heavy strain produced by even a normal use of the hatchet, and if they were, they would snap across.   At best they would stretch and loosen with continuous use ; sooner or later, they would relax their hold, and would let the blade drop out of its handle.   And although the wedge-like action of the blade was less perilous to the integrity of the haft than in the earlier method of hafting (with a hole or slot cut through the handle), still it was there, and might at any time cause a split that would render the haft useless.

A simple device mitigated this defect.   About the time when bronze replaced copper, raised flanges, running along the edges of the blade on each face, were introduced.   These caught on the

[1] Rickard's *Man and Metals*, chap. iii, contains suggestive hints toward a history of the evolution of the bronze industry.

sides of the slot into which the blade was inserted, thus preventing the sideways movement. In like manner, a stop-ridge, crossing each face of the blade, prevented it from penetrating too far into the wood. Thus the *flat flanged hatchet-head* was evolved.[1]

The addition of ornament to the surfaces of flanged hatchet-heads is in itself an indication of an upward step in civilization, stimulated by that intercourse with other communities which was the mainspring of the Deuteromegalithic progress. Artistry was now a goal, equally with efficiency. The tool was hardened by being hammered smooth, after withdrawal from the mould ; and the artificer did not content himself with mere mechanical hammering. Care was taken to give the implement a graceful and symmetrical outline. In hammering up the flanges, the outside edges were decorated with a screw or cord pattern, or else with a row of pyramidal knobs—evidences of a high degree of manual dexterity, considering the rudimentary nature of the tools at the craftsman's service. Especially characteristic of Irish tools of the kind is a decoration of the surface-areas on the blade not covered by the wooden haft ; upon these we may see traced or punched patterns in herring-bone, zigzag, or other simple rectilinear patterns (curves are seldom used).[2] In a few exceptional cases (such as one figured by Armstrong [3]) the decoration must have been hidden by the wooden haft ; but as a rule, the concealed tail is, at most, roughened with random tool-marks to prevent it from slipping. The ornamentation is clearly akin to, and therefore presumably contemporary with, that of the gold lunulæ.

It is exceptional to find a decorated tool of the kind without the flanges. One such from Stoneyford (Antrim) has been published, with punched ornament but no flanges.[4] A very few are illustrated in the paper by Megaw and Miss Hardy referred to in the preceding footnote : among them a pair of identical blades from Glencar (Sligo), may be mentioned on account of their unusual character ; they must have been cast in one and the same *double* mould, which for flat hatchets must be almost unique ; and they display ornament *in relief*, on both sides.

The flanges and the stop-ridge were at first of slight projection above the surface of the blade. But before long they began to in-crease in size. As the Deuteromegalithic phase advanced they coalesced to form, on each side of the blade, the margin of a pocket-like hollow, designed to receive the lips of the slot in the haft. The

---

[1] Illustrations in Wilde, *Catalogue*, pp. 364, 365, 390-1.
[2] See B. R. S. Megaw and Miss E. M. Hardy, " British Decorated Axes and their Diffusion during the Earlier Part of the Bronze Age " ; a very full and richly illustrated article with distribution-maps and bibliography. PPS N.S. 4 [1938] : 272. Add a fine decorated palstave found in the River Suck near Ballinasloe, figured JRSAI 71 [1941] : 111.
[3] *Galway* 10 : 70.   [4] JRSAI 13 : 513.

stop-ridge, now rising high, was bracketed out from the plane of the blade ; the bracket often assumes a form resembling a mediæval heater-shaped shield, cast on the blade.   Here, as in the Glencar hatchet-heads quoted above, we find for the first time *cast* ornament appearing on these implements, superseding the traced or punched patterns.   The blade of this new kind of hatchet-head is as a rule smaller than that of its flat or flanged predecessor (Plate IV, Fig. 1). It is generally known by the name *palstave* (corrupted from Ice-landic).[1]   A loop is usually cast on one side of the palstave to receive a cord, by which the head could be securely bound to the handle : this loop persists throughout the subsequent developments.   Some-times, but in Ireland rarely, there is a loop on each side of the tool : either to make it possible to mount it as a chisel, or else to admit of the blade being reversed in its handle (as might be necessary if one end of the edge became worn with use).[2]   (See Plate IVa.)

The palstaves did not share in the exuberant ornament of the flat-flanged hatchets : with the evolution of the latter the decoration disappeared.   A palstave from West Carbery (Cork), composed of 96 per cent. copper and only 3 per cent. of tin, illustrates the still inevitable scarcity of the latter metal.[3]

Mr. Davies figures a palstave[4] from Killycurragh (Tyrone) with no side loop, and with the tail curled at the end into a hook, or, as he calls it, a cross-flange.   He considers that this is intended to secure the cleft stick handle more firmly ; but it is difficult to make a mental reconstruction of the mechanics that would be involved. To me it seems more probable that the curl is due to hammering, the tool having been misused, unmounted, as a chisel.

Daggers

Like the hatchet, the dagger was now made of bronze, in a double mould.   The blade is at first of the same triangular shape, with rounded butt, and pierced like its copper predecessor with rivet-holes—usually three, but sometimes two, or four—for securing the handle.   This, as a few surviving specimens teach us, was made of

---

[1] From either *pállstafr*, the staff or handle of a *páll* (a digging-spud) ; or *pálstafr*, a kind of missile mentioned in some of the sagas (see *Kongsskuggsio*, ed. Halfdan Einersen (1768), p. 386 and footnote there).   In either case the name is an obvious misnomer : see the discussion of its origin by Mr. Kendrick in *Antiquity* 5 [1931] : 322.   Illustrations in Wilde, *Catalogue*, pp. 373-82 : on the last of these a palstave with two side loops is represented.

[2] On double-looped palstaves see H. St. G. Gray in *Antiquaries' Journal* 17 [1937] : 63, with a distribution-map and summary of finds.   Some remarkable palstaves, from Portugal and from Ireland, shaped on one side only, as though formed in a single-valve mould, are described by Miss L. Chitty, PPS N.S. 2 [1936] : 236.

[3] Described by Rev. P. Power, *Cork* 32 [1927] : 33.

[4] JRSAI 70 [1940] : 205.

bronze, wood, or horn.[1] The blade is rather longer, in proportion to its breadth, than in the copper daggers, and its surface is no longer smooth, but is diversified with ribs or ridges, symmetrically disposed in relation to the central rib, and filling the space between it and the edges of the blade. These ribs served a practical purpose, other than mere ornament. The blade was strengthened ; and friction was diminished, so that a dagger with such guiding ridges would more easily penetrate the flesh of the victim, and would be more readily withdrawn, than one with perfectly smooth sides. Later, however, but still within the period, the blade of the dagger became narrower, and the butt became a more or less rectangular or trapezoidal plate, with rivet-holes along its upper edge.

A *wooden* dagger found in a bog at Ballykilmurry (Wicklow),[2] though in the hand of a strong and determined man it could inflict a very nasty wound, was more probably made to serve as a form upon which to model clay moulds for bronze castings. For a complete account of the method followed in casting from such a wooden model, reference may be made to Mr. Maryon's monograph,[3] where a bronze sword in Belfast Museum is quoted, the surface of which reproduces the grain of the wooden model on which it was fashioned. A bone dagger, found in the bed of the Boyne near Clonard (Kildare), is also figured by Wilde (*Catalogue*, p. 258).

Rapiers

Still within the period, the Deuteromegalithic dagger developed, by an exaggeration of its size, into the rapier, or thrusting sword, which scarcely differs from its prototype except in length and comparative slenderness. The blade of a dagger is about 6 inches, that of a rapier about 15 inches, in length. Some of these rapiers are admirable as works of art : we may refer in especial to one found in Upper Loch Erne, and now in the Royal Irish Academy's collection, presented by Mr. Thomas Plunkett, as a memorial of the former keeper, Mr. Coffey. It is skilfully made and gracefully decorated, with raised ribbing. Another exceptional specimen, now in the same collection, was found at Lissane (Derry) ; it is distinguished

---

[1] See illustrations and descriptions of Irish daggers retaining their handles, JRSAI 4 : 286, 12 : 195, 14 : 186, 27 : 423 ; Wilde, *Catalogue*, pp. 458, 462-6 ; *Reliquary and Illustrated Archæologist* iii, plate facing p. 193. A dagger with part of a gold band, which apparently had surrounded the handle, was found, with a polished stone hatchet-head, in a carn on Toppid Mountain (Fermanagh) : see report by Plunkett and Coffey, PRIA 20 : 651.

[2] PRIA 4 : 440 ; Wilde, *Catalogue*, p. 452. A keg of bog butter was associated with it, perhaps by mere accident.

[3] PRIA 44 [1938] : 215. What is described as " a wooden sword " was found when the Drumkelin house was being dug out of the bog in which it was found— but was broken in pieces to satisfy the curiosity of inquisitive visitors.

by its length (2 feet 6¼ inches), and its slenderness : it is only ⅜ inch broad in the middle of the blade.[1]

Spears

Certain sharp-pointed stone-age weapons of flint or of bone have been described as " spear-heads " ; but " javelins " or " assegais " would be a preferable term for them for a reason already stated (p. 56).

The spear-head begins, in Great Britain, with a weapon known empirically as " the Arreton Down Dagger ", after the name of a place in the Isle of Wight where a number of typical specimens have been discovered. This is a triangular blade with a straight base out of the middle of which there projects a long tang for thrusting into the end of a wooden handle : a rivet-hole through the end of the tang enables the point to be fixed securely. But as this arrangement involves a combination of vertical and horizontal perforations which might cause the wood to split, especially if it were lengthened into a spear-shaft, a more or less cylindrical ferrule of bronze was slipped over its end to guard against such an accident.

An evolutionary process began shortly afterwards, producing the incorporation of the originally separate ferrule with the blade, and the consequent suppression of the tang ; thus developing that most important weapon the *socketed spear-head*, on which the bronze-age metallurgists exercised their highest technical and artistic skill.[2] It has the distinction of being the first metal artifact devised with a socket for receiving the handle.

In the earliest form of this weapon the socket was made quite short, and was perforated through the sides for a securing pin to be thrust through the shaft—a continuation of the " Arreton Down " rivet, although that went through from front to back. The socket was formed, at first, with a cone of compact clay fashioned in the mould, and then pared down to admit of a space into which the molten metal could be poured, to form the wall of the socket : a pin driven through the cone, and resting on grooves cut for it in the edges of the stone mould, kept it in position during the process of casting. This pin would automatically produce the rivet-holes, which were now in the seam between the two halves of the mould.

---

[1] For illustrations see Coffey, *Bronze Age in Ireland*, p. 59 : *idem*, " An Account of rapiers and early swords of the Bronze Age ", PRIA 30 [1912] 88 : Wilde, *Catalogue*, p. 442 : Evans, *Bronze Implements*, p. 252. For other specimens see Wilde, p. 448.

[2] This course of development was traced, with a wealth of illustrative examples, by Canon Greenwell and Mr. Parker Brewis, in a paper on " The Origin, Evolution and Classification of the Bronze Spearhead in Great Britain and Ireland " (*Archæologia* 61 ii [1909] : 439). It has been accepted by Coffey (*Bronze Age in Ireland*, p. 31) and, with some modifications in detail, by E. E. Evans, in a paper presently to be more fully referred to. True, it is dismissed by Mahr (PPS 3 : 370) with a few words of contempt—but contempt is neither evidence nor argument.

But the rivet-hole soon disappeared ; we must infer that clay had given place to wood. The wooden cone, wedged in position at the butt-end of the mould, would be less friable and altogether more trustworthy than a clay core : it could be made larger, and brought to a sharper point ; and although it must have been charred away by the molten metal which wrapped it round, it would endure long enough to form a socket extending through the blade, hollowing the mid-rib almost to the extreme tip. With a clay core this would scarcely have been possible. Instead of the rivet-holes, thus no longer produced, two loops were cast upon the side of the socket, apparently for cords to secure the head to the wooden shaft. As the stone moulds in our hands permit us to see, these loops were fashioned in a semi-circular form,[1] and in the final finish of the tool were hammered down with great care, reducing the opening to a narrow slot, and giving the outer surface a very neatly formed lozenge or oval shape. In a specimen figured in *Cork* 5 [1899] : 200, this surface is further enriched with traced or incised saltires.

It is natural to suppose, as indicated above, that these loops were meant for receiving cords, with which the head was tied firmly to the shaft ; but it is a little difficult to reconstruct the process, as cord and spear-shaft have alike disappeared by the disintegration of their substance. Was a groove cut round the spear-shaft ? To make such a device effective against the slipping of the cord, the groove would have to be of a depth dangerous to the integrity of the shaft in the violent stress of warfare. As an evasion of this difficulty, it has been suggested that the stumps of two branchlets, one on each side of the rod, were left untrimmed, trending obliquely downward in the manner of the barbs of an arrow-head ; and that the string was looped between these and the stem of the shaft. This is, however, open to the objection that, on such a hypothesis, the handle-end of the spear-shaft would have been the distal end of the branch— the end remote from the parent trunk, before the shaft was cut from the tree ; which seems unlikely. As a possibly preferable alternative we might conjecture that a metal (or wooden) pin was thrust through the shaft, some distance below the end of the socket, and that the cord was reeved around this.

But were these loops intended for fastening cords at all ? In some they seem so narrow in bore that no effective securing-cord could be pressed through them : in some, indeed, as has been indicated by Greenwell and Brewis, the loops are represented vestigially, by unperforated knobs (*op. cit.* p. 470). A possibility has occurred to me, that the real purpose of the loops was to increase the effective *mana* of the weapon, by fastening some magical fetish to it ; and a mould published by Coffey makes this suggestion not unreasonable. The mould in question formed part of a hoard,

---

[1] See, for instance, the moulds published by Coffey, PRIA 30 [1912] : 83 ff.

found near Omagh (Tyrone), some time about 1882,[1] relics from the property of an armourer who had specialized in spear-heads. The most interesting fact about this collection is its variety. We must refer the reader to the monograph of Greenwell and Brewis for the subordinate classification of spear-heads. Let it suffice here to say that different types, leaf-shaped, rapier-shaped, barbed, are there catalogued, and it may be possible that these varieties are of chronological importance ; but our Tyrone craftsman had moulds for several of these different varieties, once more illustrating a practical defiance of all neat theoretical chronology. Most remarkable in this collection was a mould, and a half of another (discarded and re-used for other purposes by the original owner) for casting ferrules, of the primitive Arreton Down type—although no such *ferrules* have actually been discovered in Ireland, and (so far as I know) no such *moulds* have ever been found in Britain. And in both these moulds there are loops provided, though it does not seem obvious why they should be necessary in this form of the weapon. The unattached ferrule, which would not be subjected to such a strain as might wrench off a socket attached to the effective blade, could surely be trusted to retain its hold on the shaft without a fastening of the kind. And in fact there does not seem to be any other evidence for the use of the loop on these ferrules : in the actual specimens extant the loops do not appear till the ferrules begin to lose their individuality, i.e., till they cease to be "simulated" ferrules, and become plain sockets.

In some—supposed, but not with complete certainty, to be the earliest forms—the loops are close to the lower end of the socket : but in the fully developed form they are about midway between this and the bottom edges of the wings of the blade. E. E. Evans has warned us not to think of a gradual upward creep of the loops ; there are, generally speaking, only three positions for them—at the bottom, at the middle, and at the top of the socket. An exceptional example of unrecorded provenance (Wilde, *Catalogue*, p. 496, Fig. 363) has one of the loops a short distance below the wings, and the other approximately midway between its fellow and the bottom of the socket ; this seems to be a mere individualistic freak, meaning no more than such freaks, ancient or modern, usually do. In all other examples the loops are exactly opposite one another. It is especially worthy of notice that in the Tyrone moulds the loops are *not* at the bottom of the socket, as we should naturally have expected on the postulated chronological theory.

In the later development of the spear-head, the loop loses whatever functional purpose it may ever have had in connexion with the securing of the head to the socket. These later forms are taken by Greenwell and Brewis to be evolutionary developments from those

---

[1] George Coffey in JRSAI 37 [1907] : 181, especially p. 185 ; see also *Archæologia, loc. cit.* plate 81.

which we have been considering hitherto : but E. E. Evans, in a paper which may be called a corrective supplement to theirs,[1] has shown clearly that this is not the case ; they are due to hybridization with an entirely different form, introduced later from abroad. It is one more addition to the growing evidence for the Epimegalithic revolution, and is therefore to be described in the chapter devoted thereto.

Of minor bronze objects, such as chisels, it will perhaps be most convenient to postpone the consideration to Chapter VII, where their history can be considered as an undivided whole.

The principle of division of labour, which becomes essential as specialized techniques increase in complexity, is illustrated by a hoard found at Ballyliffin (Donegal).[2] This was a collection of stone moulds for the manufacture of bronze implements—not the implements themselves, of which no trace was forthcoming. Some of the moulds were unfinished ; we must here have to do with the stock-in-trade of a man whose business it was to make moulds for sale to artificers in bronze.

Gold Ornaments

As the lunula may be provisionally regarded as the characteristic ornament of the Protomegalithic or earliest Deuteromegalithic phase, so the screw-twisted *torque* may be considered as belonging essentially to the full Deuteromegalithic.

In its simplest form, a torque is a bar of gold, all but the ends beaten out into a flat ribbon. The ribbon, after having had its edges neatly trimmed, was bound between two flexible supports—such as willow-rods—and with them was twisted into a screw form, which retained its " set " after the rods were withdrawn. The drawn-out ends, of which the points had previously been blunted by working them into knob-shaped terminals, were bent into hooks, and the " screw " was curved into a circular hoop—the hooks catching into one another, and the knobbed ends serving to keep them secure.

The sizes and shapes of the majority of torques show, as we should have expected, that they were intended for neck ornaments : but some are too small for such a purpose, and must have been meant for armlets, or possibly anklets ; others, smaller still, were presumably thumb- or finger-rings (though the twisting edge might have made them inconvenient for such a purpose), or, more probably, ear-rings. On the other hand, there are a few, too large for any such use : if worn at all on a human body, they must have been girdles. Conspicuous among these are two, found on Tara Hill in 1810,[3] and

---

[1] " The Bronze Spearhead in Great Britain and Ireland ", *Archæologia* 83 [1933] : 187.
[2] JRSAI 57 [1927] : 64.
[3] This is the date usually given : it may actually have been a little earlier.

PLATE VII

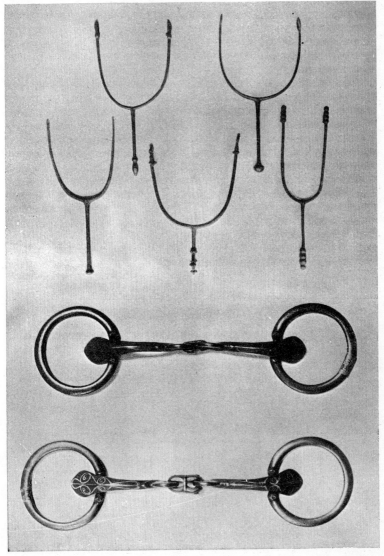

T. H. Mason

LA TÈNE HORSE-TRAPPINGS

now in the collection of the Royal Irish Academy [1] (Plate IV, Fig. 2). They were found by diggers for top-dressing, on the north side of the structure called *Ráith na Senad*, in the immediate neighbourhood of the mediæval church which stands on the hill ; in accordance with the usual principle determining the choice of church sites, it may be presumed that they were buried close to the site of an especially sacred pre-Christian sanctuary, which the Christian church superseded. These costly objects, which if pulled out in a straight line, would each be about 5 feet in length (Plate IVb), may have been votive gifts, proffered as adornments, not of a mere human being, but of a wooden or stone image, iconic or aniconic, representing some supernatural entity. The larger of the two weighs (according to Armstrong, *loc. cit.*) 27 oz. 7 dwt. 15 grs. ; the smaller, 12 oz. 7 dwt. 12 gr. Only two other specimens in the collection come anywhere near to these weights—one, broken, which must have weighed something over 11 oz. when complete, from Mullingar : and another, also broken, now weighing 12½ oz., from Gorey (Wexford). The twist is almost invariably right-handed : alternating right-and-left twists, such as are sometimes seen in torques from Scandinavia, are unknown in Ireland.

The goldsmiths did not rest satisfied with this simple form of ornament, but tried to make more elaborate torques with more than two concurrent screw-edges. Theoretically, this could be done by taking two ribbon-laminæ of gold, folding one or both of them longitudinally in V-wise, and soldering them together along the outer surface of the fold thus ⍦, giving three edges, or thus ⍦, giving four edges : or else soldering one broad ribbon between two narrow ribbons thus –|–, again giving four edges. Torques constructed by such processes are actually recorded from Oriental and Eastern-Mediterranean sources ; Mr. Maryon quotes from his personal knowledge four-bladed ear-rings from Enkomi (Cyprus), now in the British Museum, made by soldering together two V-shaped ribbons, angle to angle.

But the handiworks of the Deuteromegalithic Irish craftsmen show no evidence, as yet found by either chemical or spectroscopic analysis, that their makers had any acquaintance with, still less a practice in, the art of soldering ; that is, of using an alloy of low melting point—in the case of gold objects, an alloy of gold and copper—to form a kind of invisible cement between two metal surfaces. This technique was introduced to Ireland by the Epimegalithic metalworkers. The rods which Deuteromegalithic goldsmiths twisted into

---

[1] *Dublin Penny Journal*, 10 November 1832, p. 157 ; Wilde, *Catalogue*, p. 71 ; Coffey, *Bronze Age in Ireland*, plate vii ; Armstrong, *Gold Catalogue*, p. 59 and references there.

torques were shaped by hammering them out of solid bars before the actual twist was applied.

Sometimes the process was reversed : the bar, which might have been fashioned with a square or triangular section, was twisted, a process which would automatically produce a hollowing of the sides between the edges of the bar ; the hollow was then accentuated by hammering, making the edges appear as the borders of thin laminæ of gold, three or four in number as the case might be, projecting laterally from a central core, and intertwined into a screw.

This confirms the conclusion already indicated, on chronological grounds, that the Gaza torques cannot claim to be of Irish origin : for they are constructed with solder. Rather do the Irish torques appear to be laboriously fashioned imitations of Oriental models of the kind. But though we must put out of court such distant specimens, there is a sufficient number of Irish torques recorded from Wales, Jersey, and various places on the Continent, to show that the Irish gold-trade was still flourishing, torques taking the place previously held by lunulæ.

In the foregoing paragraphs we have assumed that the Irish torques are all of gold. The assumption is fairly safe, as there is as yet only the most shadowy evidence for the exploitation and industrial use of native silver in Ireland at any time before the age of the Víkings. Any earlier silver objects, of alleged Irish provenance, must lie under suspicion of being either importations or forgeries—most probably the latter. A silver torque, said to have been found at Rathcormac (Cork) beneath a stone in a field " with five others of a similar make " (but whether of a similar material or not, we are not informed), was exhibited by its then owner, Mr. R. Westropp, at a meeting of the R.S.A.I. in April 1883.[1] Very shortly afterwards, it must have passed into the collection of Mr. Day, for he described it at a meeting of the same Society in October of the same year,[2] illustrating it in a coloured plate, along with five ribbon-torques of gold—a selection from a hoard of fourteen such objects, found secreted between two flagstones in a field vaguely described as being " near Inishowen in Donegal ". This silver torque, however, is said to have come from Rathcormac, so that it was presumably either identical with Westropp's, or else was one of the five others in the background, of which we are not permitted to know anything further.

The drawing represents a twisted ribbon of the ordinary kind, decorated with groups of nested chevrons, having their axial lines along the central axis of the ribbon. It does not command confidence ; evidently the artist first drew the twisted metal, and then accommodated the groups of chevrons to the spaces *as they appear in his drawing*. Now as the chevrons must have been executed

---

[1] *Journal* 16 [1883-4] : 52.   [2] *Idem*, p. 182.

before the ribbon was twisted—to make them afterwards would have
been impracticable—they would not have disposed themselves so
conveniently.   The drawing thus stands self-condemned as a labour-
saving " fake ".   There is a " necklet " from Rathcormac in the
Farnham Museum (Dorset) : Professor Ó Ríordáin, who has seen it,
says that if the drawing here commented upon is intended to represent that specimen, it is quite wrong.[1]   We may, therefore, wipe out
the silver torque from Rathcormac from the Irish record.   If the
reader wishes for further confirmation of the poverty of pre-Christian
Ireland in manufactured silver, he has only to turn to the relevant
section of Wilde's *Catalogue*.[2]   As we have already seen, analyses
have shown that there is an appreciable amount of silver contained
in the gold from which Irish ornaments were manufactured : [3]
but apparently the metal-workers of Ireland never learnt the technique of extracting it until the Overlap period was dawning.

In this connexion some reference may fitly be made to the singular
gold hoard associated with the name of Strangford Loch, and to its still
more singular history.   I first heard of this discovery in 1911, from Professor
Sir William Ridgeway of Cambridge, who had heard of it from Canon
Greenwell of Durham.   I gathered that it had been made in a burial mound,
associated with what I afterwards heard was a cremated interment.   I
also heard that two dealers were competing for it (the reader will understand
that this is all mere hearsay evidence, and legally inadmissible)—and that
the successful candidate offered the hoard to the British Museum.   Sir
Hercules Read, then director of the relevant department of the Museum,
courteously communicated with the National Museum of Dublin ; and to
make a long story short, the latter museum acquired the find, with the generous
help of the Lord Iveagh of the day.

Meanwhile, vague rumours were being put about that the objects were
forgeries : and a second hoard soon afterwards came into the hands of the
same successful dealer, from whom Canon Greenwell acquired it.   By
him it was submitted to the judgement of the Royal Irish Academy.   I saw
it myself, and had no hesitation in saying that all its contents were such
obvious—such *pitiful* forgeries, that they seemed to offer an excellent
argument for the genuineness of the first lot ; for if these represented the
best that the forger could do, those represented a standard far beyond his
capacity.   So the second lot were returned to Canon Greenwell, who melted
them down—though it is surely prudent to keep suspected forgeries till a
future when the principles of discrimination shall be more fully established.

Mr. George Coffey, then Keeper of Irish Antiquities, but at an advanced
stage of his last very painful illness, had expressed scepticism about the
first lot ; and when the Museum acquired them, Col. Plunkett, then the
Director, asked me to accompany Mr. Armstrong, Mr. Coffey's assistant
and deputy, to London, there to submit them to the judgement of acknowledged authorities.   We saw Sir Arthur Evans, who, after a microscopic
examination, expressed the view that they were " all right ".   We then

---

[1] PRIA 42 [1935] : 181.
[2] This part of Wilde's work, for long left unpublished, was revised and brought
up to date by Armstrong and published, PRIA 32 [1915] : 287.
[3] TRIA 22 : 313 ;   PRIA 19 : 733.   See also PRIA 44 : 222.   On the general
subject of silver in antiquity, see Gowland's essay, *Archæologia* 69 [1918] : 121.

went to the British Museum to see Sir Hercules Read. Here Mr. Armstrong asked me to remain outside while he went in alone—I never understood why, but assumed that he wished to take the opportunity of consulting him on some confidential matters of Museum administration. When he came out he told me, *quite definitely*, that Sir Hercules had corroborated the favourable judgement of Sir Arthur Evans. He must have misunderstood him badly, however, for Sir Hercules afterwards expressed indignation with me for having quoted him in accordance with Armstrong's report of the interview, in a paper which I subsequently presented to the Royal Irish Academy ; [1] he said he had never expressed any faith in the genuineness of the objects. (But on the other hand, in his original letter, reporting the find to Dublin—which I was permitted to see—he never hinted at the slightest doubt thereof, though he might have been expected to do so, if he had felt any uncertainty about them.)

The disappointed candidate was in the background. The successful vendor having now been discredited by the second hoard, I understand that his rival came forward to say that he had himself manufactured the first hoard also. It may be so : some people seem to have believed him. I am not lawyer enough to know whether it comes within the legal definition of an " Accessory after the Fact " to accept such a statement and to repeat it, or otherwise to act upon it, without first giving the police an opportunity of testing it ; certainly I should hesitate to do so. Nor could I understand how the second dealer came to have a finger in the pie at all, if the statement were made as alleged, and expressed a truth. Once more we have to face hearsay evidence, and must make the best we can of it.

The collection included a couple of pins, a miniature gold model of a circular bronze shield, and a number of very neat little gold models of flanged hatchet-heads decorated with impressed spirals, such as might have been worn as amulets.[2] The attempts at similar hatchet-heads in the second lot were crude, all but shapeless, futilities, and they were associated with silver torques, which might be called almost impossible in Ireland. And that is all that there is to say on the subject.

[1] *Proceedings* 32 [1914] : 176, where will be found descriptions and illustrations of the objects, and an account of the find so far as it was possible to piece it together at the time. A few details are included in the above summary which came to my knowledge afterwards. Everyone concerned except myself is now dead, so that further light, if we are ever to have it, must come from some unexpected source. *Veritas praeualebit ;* for the present we can but hope that this conventional misquotation will ultimately find its justification, for *Veritas* has had many hard knocks throughout the discreditable episode. A chemical analysis of the gold objects might settle the question, if they were still available.

[2] See Armstrong's account of a small *gilt* hatchet-head in the RIA collection, with other illustrative Continental examples which he quotes (JRSAI 52 [1922] : 135). Among these are certain miniature gold axes (or rather axe-adzes, as defined above, p. 146) from Spain, some of which had passed into the Greenwell collection, apparently through the mediation of one of the persons who figure prominently in the Strangford Loch episode : they were reported in a paper presented to the Society of Antiquaries of London by Mr. R. A. Smith, Sir H. Read's assistant and successor at the British Museum (*Proceedings* 31 [1919] : 161). These coincidences add an element of disquietude which can neither be suppressed nor ignored.

CHAPTER VII

THE EPIMEGALITHIC CULTURE

I. SOCIAL CONDITIONS AND MODE OF LIFE

THE history of dwellings in this and the other later periods of pre-historic Ireland can best be discussed as a subject apart : to which, therefore, Chapter IX is devoted.

For information upon food and dress we are dependent on Archæology, with, as indispensable auxiliary sciences, Palæontology, Zoology, and Botany. Literary and linguistic evidence have no direct bearing on the remote times with which we are at the moment concerned. It throws valuable light on crops and cattle, methods and expedients, of the " Overlap " and " Early Christian " societies, possibly incorporating traditions from yet earlier ages : but this latter we cannot prove, and have no right to assume. Folklore admittedly preserves historic truth, often with surprising accuracy : but we cannot accept its evidence on such matters as those at present before us, unless there be some independent corroborative evidence of a material nature available, which by its very definiteness would render the folk-tradition superfluous. Popular traditions of the burial of gold have on occasion been verified by excavation ; but there are traditions of the same kind, even more numerous, which have not been so verified, and we must not emphasize the testimony of the former group to the neglect of the latter. On less concrete subjects, such as " Social Organization ", our information is in-ferential only, and at best of the scantiest.

This section indeed, might equally well be headed " Food and Dress " ; including " drink " under the former term, and " personal adornment " under the latter. Articles of food and clothing have usually an animal or a vegetable source, and are either gifts of wild nature or artificial cultures derived therefrom. The only important food substances with a mineral (non-organic) origin are salt and water ; and mineral substances enter the subject of dress only in the form of ornaments of metal or decorative stones, or at most of garment-fasteners.

A. FOOD

(i) *Vegetable Substances*

The contribution of Professor James Wilson to the Royal Irish Academy's *Clare Island Survey*, published so long ago as 1911, is still the best study of early agriculture in Ireland.[1]   In this brochure of 46 pages, most of the evidence, archæological and literary, known down to the date of publication, is brought together : and three decades have added little or nothing to our knowledge.   The earliest writer summoned to the witness-box is Pytheas : but the extant fragments of his work give us no direct information about agriculture in Ireland.   Strabo,[2] while indulging in his habitual diatribes against him, admits that he apparently " reasoned correctly " that people near the Arctic circle would feed upon millet ($\kappa\acute{\epsilon}\gamma\chi\rho\sigma$), and [wild] herbs, fruits, and roots ; would drink decoctions of corn and honey when these were available (there is a slight inconsistency here, for if millet were their only cereal food-plant, corn would *not* be available) ; and kept almost no domestic animals.   Of Ireland itself, all that Strabo has to tell—" perhaps ", as he candidly admits, " without very competent authority "—is that the inhabitants " were more savage than the Britons, fed upon human flesh, were great gluttons, and considered it honourable to devour their deceased fathers ".   Strabo's honesty is attested by his caution : but if he had had the knowledge of Ethnology which we possess, he would have seen that the last statement (coupled with charges of incest which we need not here enlarge upon), although it evidently engendered his doubt, is not only credible, but inherently probable. The honorific eating of aged parents, whether naturally deceased or killed for the purpose, is reported from almost all over the world— among Scythians and Slavs in ancient Europe and Western Asia, among contemporary peoples in Australia, Sumatra, India, and aboriginal America.   The purpose is to release the soul from the bondage of a weakening body, and to endow the parent with a new lease of life in the personality of the living and active offspring : a custom in which we can see nothing more than a pathetic expression of · filial altruism, altogether honourable to the people who practise it and to the country where it is practised.[3]   But this is a digression from the matter at the moment under consideration.

To Professor Wilson's article, a linguistic note, giving the names of cereals mentioned in Early Irish texts, was contributed by Professor Marstrander.   Omitting a few of uncertain meaning, these are *cruithnecht, tuirenn, dag, ruadán*—all denoting various kinds (?) of wheat ; *corce,* " oats " ; *eorna,* " barley " ; *secal,* " rye ".   Of these, *corce* is common to Irish and Welsh, and therefore presumably antedates the separation of these two linguistic groups ; *cruithnecht,*

---

[1] *A Biological Survey of Clare Island.* PRIA 31 [1911]. Section 5, *Agriculture.*

[2] *Geography* IV v 5.

[3] Cannibalism is not the mere crude horror pictured in uninstructed popular literature : it is a most complicated subject, of fascinating interest, with manifold roots and ramifications.   The reader desirous of enlarging his ideas about it can profitably begin the study with the article devoted to it in Hastings' *Encyclopædia of Religion and Ethics.*

tuirenn, eorna, cannot be proved to be mere loan-words, for they do not appear in any known language from which they could have been borrowed. Though this is not conclusive, it gives us good cause to believe that they, and the plants to which they were applied, were known in Ireland as long as the Gaelic language—which means, as far back as the Epimegalithic invasion : and were perhaps inherited by that language from one of its unknown predecessors in the country. It is difficult to avoid connecting the word *cruithnecht* with *Cruithne*, the Gaelic name for what we may broadly call the pre-Epimegalithic aborigines ; and it is equally difficult to believe that the Deutero-megalithic people, who had made cultural advances in so many directions, did not possess at least a rudimentary acquaintance with cereals and their cultivation. There is no evidence that Ireland had received any of these plants, in the wild state, from the hand of Nature ; they must have been imported in an artificially developed form : and the most probable method of their importation is obvious. Ridgeway and all other modern writers on the Archæology of Economics have taught us the use, from the earliest times,[1] of grains of cereal plants as standards of weight. Thus, the metal-trade would automatically bring cereals to the notice of the native merchant travellers, and a trade in this commodity, when its importance was realized, would follow as a matter of course.

In the face of centuries of decomposition, and of the haphazard methods of all but our most recent excavators, the preservation of tangible relics of cereals, and of other vegetable foods, is not to be expected. The wheat (*Triticum vulgare*) found under a carn at Baltinglass (Wicklow) [2] still remains the only actual specimen of ancient grain yet discovered in the country ; but there are also in existence a few food-vessels retaining the impress of grains upon their inner surfaces, as though they had been filled therewith while the clay was still soft, owing to careless firing.[3] From later times " burnt corn " is mentioned by Wood-Martin,[4] as among the yield of a lake-dwelling site at Monalty (Monaghan), but without referring us to any authority : in any case, lake-dwelling evidence is outside of our present quest.[5] Hazel-nuts and their shells have been found, not only at Baltinglass, but at other sites as well (see Wood-Martin,

---

[1] W. Ridgeway, *The Origin of Metallic Currency and Weight Standards* (Cambridge 1892) chap. viii.
[2] Excavated by Dr. P. T. Walsh : see the report, PRIA 46 [1941] : 221.
[3] I owe this information to Dr. Raftery.
[4] *Lake Dwellings*, p. 196, footnote.
[5] V. Hehn's *Kulturpflanzen und Haustiere* (Berlin 1902) should be studied as an introduction to the general subject of this section. We may add to this, for plants, A. de Candolle, *Origine des plantes cultivées* (Paris 1912) and, for animals, C. Keller, *Die Abstammung der ältesten Haustiere* (Zurich 1902). See also a most valuable paper by Mr. E. C. Curwen, on " Prehistoric Agriculture in Britain " (*Antiquity* 1 [1927] : 261). It is fully illustrated, and richly provided with bibliographical references.

op. cit. index), and there is frequent testimony to their use as a staple diet in the literature. Cherry-stones and other evidence of the use of fruit have been found in the same sites. But on the whole it is the apparatus of the cultivator, rather than his cultures, that we must hope for, in dealing with materials so transitory. The agriculturist must :—

1. fence his fields,	6. winnow it,
2. break up his soil,	7. store it in his barn,
3. sow his seed,	8. grind it when required for use,
4. harrow it,	9. knead it,
5. reap it when ripe,	10. bake it ;

and all of these ten processes require instruments of one kind or another. Our available material is here fragmentary as yet ; the chief value of a summary account of it will be to show how many gaps have still to be filled. Such gaps, indeed, are inevitable, as most of the instruments were made of wood, and other materials equally perishable, so that their survival cannot be counted upon.

(1) *Fencing.* Practically the only evidence as yet presented by Ireland, to balance the wonderful revelations of air-photography in England,[1] is the group of fences detected by Ó Ríordáin at Cush (Limerick) [2] associated with the elaborate early iron-age settlement which he there excavated : and possibly certain enclosures in Connaught described by Knox.[3] These at least give us to understand that in the bronze-iron transition, fields were divided by fences of dry-stone walls as they are to-day—though the complicated varieties of field-fences described in the law tract called *Bretha Comaithchesa* [4] are doubtless a later development : and they suggest hesitation before we passively accept any ancient literary statements to the contrary, such as those quoted by Joyce.[5]

(2) *Breaking up the soil.* Spades,[6] cattle-yokes,[7] and forks,[8] all of wood, have been found in peat-bogs ; and although later than our present period, are probably of types traditional from an equal antiquity. For bronze-age ploughs there is no direct evidence, so far as I know, though we may reasonably assume that instruments resembling those depicted in rock-scribings in Scandinavia and Ventimiglia were familiar in Ireland. Nor am I aware that any certain example of the plough-produced terraces called *lynchets* have been identified in the country : when visiting regions unfamiliar to

[1] On which see (for example) Crawford and Keiller, *Wessex from the Air* (Oxford 1928).   [2] PRIA 45 [1940] : 145.
[3] References in Ó Ríordáin, *loc. cit.*
[4] *Ancient Laws of Ireland*, vol. iv p. 72 ff.
[5] *A Social History of Ancient Ireland* 1 : 186.
[6] Wilde, *Catalogue*, p. 206.
[7] Wilde, *Catalogue*, p. 243, Wood-Martin, p. 79.
[8] Wilde, *Catalogue*, p. 206.

me, I have usually kept a look-out for them, but never with success.[1]
Objects identified as plough-socks and plough-coulters of iron have
been found in lake-dwellings ; [2] but so far as the associated finds
permit of a judgement being formed, these are all later than the
period now under consideration.

(3) *Sowing* and (4) *Harrowing* can hardly be said to be illustrated
by Archæological evidence.

(5) *Reaping*.   In this operation we encounter the sickle, of which
there is something to be said at greater length.   Bronze sickles are
of small size in comparison with those in modern use : the blade
measures in length from about $3\frac{1}{2}$ to 5 inches.   Frazer [3] compiled
a list of those recorded down to 1892 in Ireland, from which he was
able to indicate a scheme of classification.   They are all provided with
a socket for fitting them to a wooden handle ; usually a rivet-hole
is perforated through the side of the socket.   In the first class, the
socket is open at each end, and is not longer than the butt of the
blade, which springs from it sideways ; in the second, the blade
likewise springs sideways from the socket, but the latter is prolonged
downward, and is closed at the top ; in the third, the blade rises
from the closed top of the socket.   The blade is usually curved,
though there is a considerable range in the degree of curvature in
all three classes.   The concave side of the blade has a sharp edge,
the convex side being blunt like the back of a knife.   In the more
ornate examples the blade is strengthened with ribbing, following
the curve of the axis of the blade.   The tip may be blunt, or else
it may have a sharp point.

No bronze sickle without a socket is reported as having been
found in Ireland ; on the other hand, no mould for casting a socketed
sickle has, as yet, made its appearance in the country.   A double
mould for casting an *unsocketed* sickle formed one of a group of
moulds discovered in the neighbourhood of Ballymoney (Antrim),[4]
now in the Royal Irish Academy's collection.   The hoard contained
a number of moulds for casting looped socketed spear-heads, and
is therefore to be assigned to the Deuteromegalithic phase.

[1] But it is possible that a faint tradition of the construction of artificial hill-
side terraces (such as may be seen in the vineyards of Southern Italy) may be latent
in the story that the " Fir Bolg," before they came to Ireland, had been under
servitude in Greece, in which they were compelled to carry earth in bags (hence,
it is empirically alleged, their name, " men of bags ") and lay it on rugged mountain-
sides so as to turn them into flowering plains.

[2] See Wood-Martin, *op. cit.* index under these headings.

[3] W. Frazer, " On ' sickles ' (so-called) of bronze found in Ireland ", PRIA
17 : 381.   We need not trouble ourselves here with the doubts which the author
expresses as to the purpose of these objects, or with his guesses at alternative
theories.   For further illustrations see Wilde, *Catalogue*, p. 527.   See also Sir
Cyril Fox's account of the Llyn Fawr hoard, Glamorganshire (*Antiquaries' Journal*
19 [1939] : 369, especially pp. 371, 383 ff.) ; and the same writer's *Socketed
Bronze Sickles of the British Isles*, PPS 5 [1939] : 222.

[4] PRIA 30 [1912] : 83.

How then, is the anomalous conjunction of socketed sickles and unsocketed sickle-moulds to be explained ?

We must bear in mind that the Epimegalithic invasion coincided with a severe adverse climatic fluctuation : that the genial Upper Forestian phase had given place to the wet and depressing Upper Turbarian. The energy and impetus which had carried the Epimegalithic people on to conquest, and to an exploitation of the country's metallurgical resources (culminating in such notable works as the Gleninsheen gorget), worked itself out, and was succeeded by a decline into incompetence.

The unsocketed sickles were not satisfactory, but they were the only tool of the kind available at the beginning of the Epimegalithic phase. When socketed sickles were evolved, the people heard of them, and imported them freely ; probably turning their old unsocketed sickles and other obsolete things to scrap-metal to pay for them. But they now lacked the skill and the initiative to make them for themselves. The tide had turned from export to import ; foreign hucksters flooded the country with socketed sickles, and these won favour because (unlike most goods thus distributed) they were better than the implements which they superseded.

In subsequent periods, tanged *iron* sickles quickly superseded those of bronze, in accordance with the principle that the transition from bronze to iron first took place in agricultural tools.[1]

(6) *Winnowing* and (7) *Storing* are again outside the range of Archæological illumination ; but on (8) *Grinding*, there is fairly full information available. Grain-rubbers are found in three varieties —pestle-and-mortar combinations, saddle-querns, and rotary querns, introduced in this chronological order.[2]

In the first, the mortar is a block of stone with a bowl-shaped depression in the upper surface, and the pestle is a stone bar of any size convenient to use for the attrition of the contents of the mortar, whatever these may be. Such hollowed stones are to be found in almost every ancient site. They are locally known as " bullaun " stones (properly *bollán*, " a small bowl ") ; and among many possible uses for them—which range from stoups for holding holy water to basins for feeding poultry—" mortars " are certainly to be counted. The same may be said of the larger of the basin-shaped hollows often to be seen in rock-surfaces.

The saddle-quern, a device of universal use over Europe and Western Asia, was the only form of grain-rubber known before the Iron Age. It is a more or less rectangular slab of some rough

---

[1] See this fact demonstrated at length by Andrew Lang in *Homer and his Age* (London 1906) chap. ix, and again in *The World of Homer* (London 1910) chap. x. A typical specimen of a tanged iron sickle is figured in Wood-Martin, *Lake-dwellings*, p. 176.
[2] On this subject generally, see R. Bennett and J. Elton, *A History of Corn Milling*, vol. i (London 1898) *passim*.

granitic stone, with the upper surface curved like a segment of a hollow cylinder (the "saddle"); upon which another stone (the "upper millstone" of the English Bible, a prosaic periphrasis for the Hebrew *rekeb*, "rider") could be rubbed backward and forward over the grain spread upon the "saddle". This riding-stone has a flat base; and a rounded back, of a size and shape apt for a firm hand-grasp. To the rotary quern we shall return at the appropriate place; it belongs to a stage later than that with which we are at present concerned.

Gritty powder from the stone surface of any of these forms of grain-rubber mingles inevitably with the flour, and, as we have said, causes extensive wear in the teeth of the bread-eaters. This attrition begins to be noticeable in Deuteromegalithic skulls, and in the later phases increases progressively.

(9) *Kneading* may have been effected in flat wooden, more or less rectangular, trays, such as that figured by Wilde.[1] A stone hut which I saw many years ago at Ballynaveenooragh, Co. Kerry, had

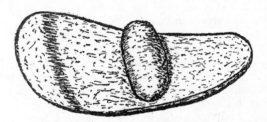

FIG. 26.—A Saddle Quern.

within it what may have been a baking oven—a circular cupboard-like structure with a small rectangular opening in the side—but except for that doubtful specimen I am not aware of any tangible Archæological evidence on the subject of (10) *Baking*.

No real progress could have been made with agriculture till a clearance of the forests had been effected: and that this was fully understood is shown by the interesting fact that practically the only point in which the legendary history of the country, as enshrined in the *Book of Invasions*, touches actual history, is the attribution to the more important kings of a clearance from the plains of the forests which cumbered them. Most of the *Roll of the Kings*, the appendix to that compilation, is expressed in an almost stereotyped formula : "Y, *having* [like the Priest of Aricia] *slain his predecessor* X, *and having thus assumed the functions of a king* [and consequently of an incarnate agricultural deity], *began to reign. He fought such-and-such battles. He cleared such-and-such plains. He reigned so many years,*

---

[1] *Catalogue*, p. 209.

till slain by Z [who succeeded him]." These clearances not only released for agriculture or for pasture the lands which had been thus uselessly occupied : they also helped to reduce the numbers of wild beasts which haunted the woodlands, a constant menace to human and to domestic-animal life.

(ii) *Animal Substances*

(1) The Chase

Food-cultivation never completely superseded food-gathering. The excitement of the chase ; the search for unexpected wealth in wild fruits, and the hunting down of a fugitive animal, had attractions which the monotonous labour of the fields and cattle-stalls could not offer. Nuts and wild fruit were eaten as freely as ever, even after agricultural processes had been established : marine molluscs and fishes have left their shells and bones in maritime middens (I have no record of the discovery of shells of terrestrial molluscs, such as snails, in inland sites), and bones of deer and boar mingle with those of the ordinary domestic animals. Boar tusks, most likely collected and preserved as amulets, are among the commonest yields of lake-dwelling sites.[1] The weapons of the hunter differed little, if at all, from those of the warrior—sling-balls, bolas-stones, javelins, and throwing sticks (at close quarters, clubs) formed the staple of his armoury. We may take it for granted that the hunting-dog, bred from the wolf, for which Ireland was already famous in the days of St. Patrick, had been established at least as early as the Epimegalithic Period. Nets of cordage have a small chance of survival : but the wooden valve-trap may already have been invented—although the recorded specimens seem to be of a later date, on which account we postpone the description of it to a later chapter. Some time ago, I saw near Aunascaul (Kerry) two artificial mounds, on the plan of a large **V** with a narrow opening at the angle. Limitations of time at the moment did not permit me to measure or to plan it ; I merely record here, with no great enthusiasm, an idea which crossed my mind, for what it may be worth— that these enigmatical mounds might have been the remains of a corral, for trapping herds of deer or other wild animals. Wood-Martin gives us a section of a pitfall, six feet deep and five feet in diameter, lined with birchen posts, which he tells was found in a

[1] Boar relics are not necessarily from the *wild* boar, though that animal was a stock quarry in the chase, was familiar to the inhabitants, and, if we may judge from the numerous stories of monstrous boars that have been handed down to us, was much dreaded. On the use of boar-tusks as amulets, see Ridgeway, " The Origin of the Turkish Crescent," JRAI 38 [1908] : 241.

turbary near Blessington (Wicklow), beneath a subsequent accumulation of two yards' depth of peat.[1]

From time to time, discoveries have been made of open-air hearths, with no evidence of permanent domestic occupation near by, usually in the neighbourhood of running water. These are pits, containing ashes, heating-stones, flint flakes, scraps of pottery, slight midden deposits, and, occasionally, relics of wooden vessels and the like. To Irish speakers, they are known as *fulachta fiad*, " cooking-places of the wild ", and are explained as places where hunters, on the chase, halted to refresh themselves. Both name and explanation probably express a true interpretation ; [2] the tradition is at least as old as Keating,[3] who calls these deposits *fulachta fian*, " cooking places of the ' militia ' " (as we may translate for want of a better term) who were in the hire of the Irish kings. These warriors, we are told, were billeted on the inhabitants of the country during the winter half of the year, but depended on the chase for their sustenance during the summer half. We read that they hunted and killed in the morning : sending their servitors to a hill having timber and moorland, where they were to dig two pits into the stiff yellow subsoil, and, having kindled two large fires, to cast many *eimhir-*[4] stones upon them. Some of the flesh of the " kill " was to be roasted on spits before the fire ; the rest, bound with straw ropes in dry bundles, was to be piled up in the larger pit, and the stones when red-hot were to be heaped over it till it was boiled. The second pit was to be a bathing-pool.

(2) Domestic Animals

All the known evidence of Palæontology is against the existence in Ireland of aboriginal wild cattle, sheep, or goats, from which it would have been possible to develop the domestic herds. An extravagant poem, printed with translation by O'Curry,[5] giving a list of wild animals, is of some lexicographical value ; but is not acceptable evidence for the existence of the wild cattle, which it includes in its enumeration.[6]

Dr. R. F. Scharff,[7] on the basis of an earlier study by Wilde,[8]

---

[1] *Traces of the Ancient Faiths of Ireland*, 1 : 69. In the reprehensible manner of that book, no reference is vouchsafed to the authority for this discovery, and I have failed to trace it.

[2] For examples from various parts of the country, see JRSAI 3 [1854] : 59 ; 17 [1886] : 390 ; INJ 2 [1928] : 94 ; *Cork* 42 [1937] : 57 ; 43 [1938] : 56.

[3] See his *History*, Irish Texts Society edition 2 : 328-9.

[4] Apparently some stone that would resist the action of fire, unlike *ael*, " limestone ", with which the term is usually contrasted. [5] PRIA 7 : 184.

[6] The wild goats in Co. Sligo are not naturally so ; they are descendants of animals which have escaped from domestication.

[7] " On the origin of the Irish Cattle ", *Irish Naturalist* 32 [1923] : 65. See also J. W. Jackson, " Discovery of remains of the Celtic Shorthorn Ox at Whitepark Bay, Co. Antrim ", INJ 7 [1936-7] : 189 ; C. Brymer Jones, " Notes on some skulls of cattle from " (certain lake-dwellings), *ibid.* 189. [8] PRIA 7 [1858] : 64.

distinguished four early breeds of cattle in the country, namely :—
1. *The old Irish cow* (small stature, long back, moderate-sized wide-spreading horns, red or black colour) ; 2. *The Kerry* (red, brindled, or black, small head, short horns turned upward) ; 3. *The Irish Long-horn* (wide-spreading horns, in some slightly curved, in others curved so much as actually to cross ; red or brindled with thick hide, and of considerable size) ; 4. The *hornless*, or *maoilín* (dun, black, or white). Of these, nos. 2 and 4 still survive in the country. Scharff quotes Professor J. Wilson as disagreeing with the statement that the Kerry breed is ever black, and as deriving the hornless breed from Scandinavia. A discussion of all such opposing views is in the exclusive domain of a zoological specialist, and the present writer cannot presume to trespass thereon : for further details reference must be made to the article quoted, and the numerous references which it supplies.

Elsewhere, in other volumes of the same journal, Dr. Scharff has dealt, as thoroughly as the available materials permit, with the remaining species of domestic animals. The modern *Pig* has within recent years superseded an earlier breed,[1] taller, more active, but less amenable to the artificial fattening which gives the animal its chief commercial value. This latter, on account of its long snout, comparatively long legs, and un-pig-like activity, is known to old writers on agricultural economics as "the Greyhound Pig". But we can get behind the greyhound pig to the animal spoken of with disdain by Giraldus Cambrensis as unshapely, cowardly, and degenerate—evidently contrasting it with the imposing (wild) boar then still extant in Great Britain. Here, Dr. Scharff warns us against falling into the mistake of Giraldus in identifying these "degenerate" animals with the genuine boar. Bones from crannog and other sites more or less contemporary with Giraldus present us with an animal, indistinguishable from the *Sus palustris* of Swiss lake-dwellings, the "Torfschwein" of German-writing authorities who have investigated those sites, and have systematized their fauna. This must be an artificial importation from the Continent—a breed semi-domesticated, and apt to run wild occasionally, as the specimens seen by Giraldus had done. Behind these again is the genuine "wild boar", a breed known in Ireland, so far, only by the scantiest record of specimens, though, as we have seen, conspicuous in tradition.

The general conclusions indicated by Dr. Scharff are these. The genuine wild boar, how imported cannot yet be determined, existed, but is known by a few bones only, found in cave and turbary deposits. *Sus palustris* was a later, but still fairly early, importation ; and it is possible that the greyhound pig is a cross between this breed and its feral predecessor.

---

[1] "On the Irish Pig", *Irish Naturalist* 26 [1917] : 173, and references there.

Of the *Sheep*, again, there is not much that can be said. We have already seen that its existence among the earliest human remains has been both denied and affirmed (*ante*, p. 62). A very small breed of sheep is found in some cave sites, comparable with the Soay sheep of Scotland. Some of them—Dr. Scharff does not regard these as a separate breed—have four horns : the wool was probably short. Later, a larger breed was introduced, with longer wool ; but how far the modern sheep of the country represents them genealogically is a question not certainly to be answered. Most likely all the modern breeds of sheep are recent importations, the old breeds having either disappeared or been bred out.[1]

Of the *Goat* there is even less knowledge available, and in view of the notorious difficulty of distinguishing sheep and goat bones it would not be profitable to say anything here about this animal. Of the *Dog*,[2] Scharff enumerates five native breeds, none of them, however, except the Wolfhound and possibly the Irish Terrier and the Irish Spaniel, reaching back into prehistoric times. The Wolfhound was apparently started by hybridization of the Irish wolf (the only species of the *Canidæ* native to Ireland) with some large kind of hunting-dog brought in by early (perhaps not the earliest) settlers.[3] A terrier-like dog was found in the Lagore lake-dwelling, and was, if not identified with, at least declared to resemble closely the *Canis palustris* of the Swiss lake-dwellings : as well as bones of other dogs very similar to *Canis intermedius*, apparently a sort of spaniel.[4]

On the *Horse* in Ireland it may be sufficient to refer here to Ridgeway's *Origin and Influence of the Thoroughbred Horse* (references in index, *s.vv.* " Ireland " and " Irish ". That the *Ass* as a beast of burden was a quite recent importation into Ireland has been maintained by Dr. J. P. Mahaffy ;[5] but the matter seems to be worth a less superficial investigation than he appears to have bestowed upon it. Ass-bones were identified from the lake-dwelling of Ballydooloch (Fermanagh) on the high authority of Professor Owen.[6]

The animals killed for food would have to be cooked, and that would need fire. How was that fire produced ? Sparks, collected

---

[1] " Some notes on the Irish Sheep ", *Irish Naturalist* 31 [1922] : 73.

[2] " On the breeds of dogs peculiar to Ireland and their origin ", *Irish Naturalist* 33 [1924] : 77.

[3] An inverted urn with (apparently) a pygmy urn inside it, and covering fragmentary human *and dog* bones is reported from Palmerstown (Dublin) in PRIA 10 [1868] : 336. But unfortunately the description of the find is based on the testimony of labourers who, under the usual buried-treasure obsession, smashed the urn and scattered its contents as soon as they uncovered it. They were later induced to collect the debris, but the evidence that the dog bones were actually inside the urn cannot be called watertight.

[4] Reference may be made to O. F. Gandert, " Forschungen zur Geschichte des Haushundes " (*Mannusbibliothek* no. 46, Leipzig 1930), which contains an extensive bibliography.

[5] PRIA 33 [1917] : 530.　　　　　　　　[6] JRSAI 11 [1870] : 362.

on something dry to serve as tinder, struck with flint upon ——— ?
We have no information from Ireland to fill up the blank for us,
like the well-known flint-and-iron-pyrites combination from a
Yorkshire barrow now in the British Museum.[1]   The objects
called "tracked stones"—hard stones of about the size and shape
of a flattened tennis-ball, with a straight groove across one or both
sides (a frequent discovery in habitation sites) have been supposed
to be in some way connected with fire-making, but it is not easy to
see how : the "track" is too short, and the stone as a rule too smooth,
to be used for any efficient frictional fire-making device.   It is,
indeed, difficult to find a satisfactory use for these objects : they have
been called "whetstones" ; but surely to rub a knife or a spearhead
in such a "track" in the only possible way, would be more apt to
take off whatever edge it had already.   Fire-raising must in any case
have been difficult : in the absence of evidence to the contrary, we
are probably to assume that the primitive fire-stick was the instrument
used.   There are references to the borrowing of fire in the ancient
Welsh Laws, with safeguards against lending it unless the owner of
the fire knew what his client proposed to do with it ; [2] evidently, the
simplest way of lighting the domestic hearth was to take a brand from
an obliging neighbour whose hearth was in working order.[3]

The earlier method of cooking used was doubtless roasting with
spits or boiling by means of hot stones—a pit being dug, the victim
laid in it, and the stones piled around it.[4]   Water-boiling could hardly
have been introduced till fireproof receptacles large enough to hold
the meat had been invented or acquired—such as the cauldrons
described later in this chapter.

But like everything else touched upon in this book, the subject
of food and its preparation, adequately treated, would require the
elbow-room of an entire volume ; and it would call for an author
equipped with special knowledge in various directions, which the
present writer does not possess.   Here we can but glance at it, and
pass on.

---

[1] British Museum *Stone Age Guide*, p. 107.

[2] The laws of Hywel Dda are of course too late to be applicable to the stage
at which we have arrived : still, it may be worth noting that among the nine ac-
cessories to an act of arson are reckoned the man who carried the fuel, who struck
the fire (obviously with a flint), who procured the tinder, and who fanned the spark
into a flame (Venedotian code II 3, Dimetian II 2 Gwentian II 2).

[3] We may compare the Andamanese, who "have no method of their own of
making fire.   Formerly " [before becoming acquainted with the white man's
matches] " they had no knowledge of any method by which fire could be produced.
Fires were and still are carefully kept alive in the village, and are carefully carried
when travelling " (A. R. Brown, *The Andaman Islanders*, p. 472).   This is a modern
picture of the primitive Italian village life, where the girls and boys, afterwards
sublimated respectively into the *Vestal Virgins* and the *Flamines*, tended the
ever-burning domestic fire under the protection of the hearth goddess Vesta.

[4] For an account of modern experiments to determine the expedition and the
efficacy of hot-stone cooking, see Miss N. F. Layard in PPS [East Anglia] 3 [1922] :
483 ff.

B. CLOTHING

Here again, as in the case of perishable vegetable foods, the record is almost a blank. At first, no doubt, the hides of animals provided the principal material for clothes ; " leather cloaks ", are heard of in the historical or quasi-historical literature. Of the early cultivation of flax in Ireland, there appears to be no material evidence : [1] but the hoard discovered at Cromaghs, Armoy (Antrim) in 1904 gave us welcome information on the subject of textiles of animal origin. It consisted of a group of late bronze-age or early iron-age objects—a socketed hatchet-head, a gouge of peculiar profile (the cutting edge being set at such an angle to the axis that the tool did not need to be held almost horizontal, in manipulating it, as was usually the case), a " sunflower " pin, and a double-winged razor, with a protecting case (a strip of leather folded over the blade and possibly secured with a cord, now lost). These objects were wrapped inside a woven cloak of goat's hair with, apparently, a leather belt fastening ; but of the latter, nothing can be said, as what was left of it was not preserved, and was reported only by hearsay. [2] With this cloak was associated—but here again the statement of the peat-diggers who uncovered the hoard is too vague to permit of a complete reconstruction of the relationship—a most ingenious fringe of tassel-work woven out of horse-hair. It testifies to high technical skill, developed by diligent pursuit of an art of which we can never hope to have many examples surviving for our instruction. The gouge and sunflower pin date the find to the Epimegalithic period or later.

The only direct information available on the subject of clothing is all too late for our present purpose. We have numerous literary references and descriptions : we have a wealth of material for study in the scenes depicted on the sculptured crosses : we have a few bodies of unfortunates who have been drowned in bog-holes, preserved with their garments by the antiseptic peat, and revealed by turf-cutters in after ages. In these we see both sexes clad in a *lene*, a tight-fitting linen garment worn next to the person, and a *brat* or cloak thrown over it. To the back of the *brat* was secured a *cochall* or hood, which could be thrown over the head against inclement weather : otherwise the only protection for the head appears to have been the natural hair, which was allowed to grow thick and bushy or flowing. On active work the *lene* could be girt up, to give play to the legs ; or a garment resembling a kilt might be substituted. On the feet were leather shoes, in appearance not unlike Indian mocassins ; the Aran Islanders' *broga úr-leathair*, " shoes of

---

[1] Literary references to " linen " cannot be pressed into evidence for the equipment of the Megalithic Age.
[2] See the report on the discovery by G. Coffey, PRIA 26 [1906] : 119.

fresh leather ", known to tourists (only) as " pampooties ", are modern representatives of the ancient shoes, though these cannot compete with them in the cleverness of their stitching, or in the variety of the incised ornament with which they are decorated. Some of the figures on the sculptured crosses, especially those representing persons engaged in active military or agricultural operations, are shown to us attired in what might now be called " shorts ", or in the *bracæ* which provoked the disdain of Classical Mediterranean refinement : these garments also appear among the attire of the bog-finds. But all of them are post-Megalithic : we cannot assume that they were survivals of the fashions of the Megalithic Age. They *may* be such : but considering the changes that in the course of centuries took place in types of objects which we can see and handle, it is more than probable that there were corresponding changes in the fashion of objects which have passed beyond our reach.[1]

Personal Adornment

Personal adornment takes many forms. Of some of these, we must take the existence for granted, for we can hardly hope to find any surviving evidence of mutilations (ear-, nose-, and lip-piercing, scarification, and the like) ; of paint or tatu (suggested by the occasional discovery, in domestic and tomb sites, of lumps of ochre, and by certain marks, which cannot represent natural features, intruded upon what appear to be attempts to represent human faces, in rock-sculptures and elsewhere) ; and of applied decorations made of perishable materials (textiles, flowers, garlands, feathers, etc.). We must accept the limitations which the course of Nature thus forces upon us, and confine ourselves to a consideration of ornaments of a more permanent character, made of stone, metal, shell, bone, or fossilized vegetable material such as amber or jet. At a later stage, ornaments made of siliceous materials, enamel and glass, will come into view, but not yet. In general, we may say that ornaments in such materials take the form of pendants or of dress-fasteners, though there are minor groups—finger- or toe-rings, necklets, bracelets or anklets, ear-rings, and hair-braids. These latter, however, being chiefly made of gold or of bronze, can best be considered in the sections devoted to artifacts in those materials.

While we may treat pendants as " ornaments ", it should be remembered that ornament is not their primary purpose. All such

[1] See H. P. McClintock, *Irish Dress* (Dundalk 1944) : and for older authorities entering into detail for which no room could here be found, Wilde, *Catalogue*, pp. 278-331 ; O'Curry, *Manners and Customs* 1 : 378 ff. ; 3 : 87 ff. ; Joyce, *Social History* 2 : 179 ff. On the subject as part of a larger whole see Hjalmar Falk, *Altwestnordische Kleiderkunde* (Kristiania 1919), G. Girke " Die Tracht der Germanen in der vor- und frühgeschichlichen Zeit " (*Mannusbibliothek* nos. 23, 24, Leipzig 1922), M. von Kimakowicz-Winnicki, " Spinn- und Webewerkzeuge ", (*idem* no. 27, Würzburg 1910), W. von Stoker, " Spinnen und Weben bei der Germanen " (*idem* no. 59, Leipzig 1938).

decorations began in magic, having been worn as amulets to avert some evil or to secure some good. A fossil shell, or a shining, highly coloured, or oddly shaped stone, in the eyes of a primitive man who chances to pick it up, is "big medicine"—to use for convenience the jargon put into his mouth by those who write about him; whether justifiably or not, at least it expresses the conception which he forms of it. It is charged with unknown powers for good or for ill, and his possession of it puts those powers at his service.

A good illustration of the magical use of stones is presented by the smooth oval pebbles of quartz, or, failing quartz, of limestone or some other white stone, so frequently found in tomb-deposits (as at Carrowkeel). These stones are hardly to be taken as personal decorations; in fact, there is no evident way in which they could be used as such, for they are not perforated for suspension. But their smooth white surface, their oval shape, are irresistibly suggestive of *eggs*; and this appearance would make them suitable carriers of magical spells destined to secure re-birth, the boon in one form or another most ardently longed-for by humanity in general. Pendant conical amulets, also of white stone, resembling in shape the pieces used in the game of "halma", perforated for suspension, are such a constant yield of excavation in the chambered tumuli (Carrowkeel, Lochcrew, and several other sites) that it is most likely that they are associated with similar ideas.[1]

Apart from these pendants, we have not much evidence for the use of ornamental stones in Ireland, because such stones were not available. There is nothing in Ireland to compare with the extensive use of garnets for inlays in decorative objects of metal, with which Scandinavian art presents us. The turquoises on the very late arm-shrine of St. Laichtín of Donaghmore are practically unique: amber, enamel, and crystal are the only materials which we usually find in ornamental inlays, down to the end of pre-Norman Christianity.

Bead necklaces are the principal form assumed by pendant decorations in the Megalithic period. These may be single or multiple—multiple strings being protected from entanglement by spacing-plates crossing the group at intervals (as in the jet necklace illustrated above, Fig. 23, p. 140; compare the group of jet beads in Fig. 27). How the necklaces were secured does not appear; perhaps the string on which the beads were mounted was merely knotted at the back of the neck.

The "beads" might be shells, as in a necklace found in a tumulus opened in 1838 at Knockmaree in Phœnix Park, Dublin. The mound was about 15 feet in height and 120 feet in diameter. The principal cist (which has been re-erected in the Zoological Gardens of Dublin)

[1] A collection of illustrations will be found in a monograph upon these objects by Mr. L. S. Gogan (*Cork* 35 [1930] : 90).

was about 4 feet in length and 2 feet in depth, and consisted of a flat stone supported by others. It contained the unburnt remains of three persons, along with a bone object—a rod about 2½ inches in length, with a hemispherical knob at each end, probably some sort of dress-fastener—and a necklace of shells of *Nerita litoralis*, strung ingeniously on a cord made, it is said, of seaweed. Urns of Deuteromegalithic type (though probably of Epimegalithic date), containing ashes, were found in subsidiary cists inside the margin of the tumulus.

Stones, usually (though not always) chosen for their pleasing colour or quartz-like reflective properties, were sometimes adapted, by perforation, to make beads.[1] Beads of enamelled faïence, such as were used from an early date in Egypt and other Mediterranean countries, and beads of glass, do not certainly appear in Ireland till the Overlap period : certainly, none are recorded from Megalithic monuments. The principal material for beads from our present period are amber and lignite (or jet). A fragment of coral, found with a crouched burial in a cist near Claremorris (Mayo) may be mentioned on account of the rarity of such a find in Ireland.[2]

Amber, the fossilized resin of *Pinus succinifer*, comes from the southern coast of the Baltic Sea ; other less important localities will be found enumerated in the article on this material in *Encyclopædia Britannica*, or any comparable work of reference. That its primary appeal, in antiquity, lay in its supposed magical properties—the electro-magnetic qualities which have made its Greek name epony-mous of the mysterious force of " electricity " ; and the insects often embedded within it, with no obvious indication of how they got there—are a commonplace which need not be stressed. In Ireland, according to Professor Ó Ríordáin,[3] amber does not appear till late bronze-age deposits. This is corroborated by most of the recorded finds ; as, for instance, a few beads found at Mount Rivers (Cork) associated with gold gapped rings and socketed hatchet-heads,[4] and a fine series, also associated with gapped rings, from Banagher (Offaly).[5] (But the amber found in the caves at Kilgreany and Ballinamintra [*ante*, p. 19] should not be forgotten). The largest Irish collection of amber beads on record was a group of about 300, found in a bog near Whitegates, on the border between Cos. Meath and Cavan. These were of various shapes, globular, discoidal, and cylindrical :[6] they can scarcely have all belonged to one ornament, but we shall have to discover a number of necklaces

[1] On beads generally the reader may be referred to the monographs by H. C. Beck, *Archæologia* 77 [1926]: 1 ; 85 [1935]: 203. See also some illustrated notes by the same writer on ten beads of various forms from Antrim, now in Salisbury Museum (JRSAI 64 [1934] : 268). [2] *Galway* 16 [1934-5] : 57.
[3] PRIA 42 : 164-5. [4] PRIA 30 : 86 ; *Cork* 36 [1931] : 71.
[5] Armstrong in PSA Lond., II 30 : 237 ff.
[6] E. C. Rotherham, in *Reliquary and Illustrated Archæologist* 3 [1897] : 49.

in position, and carefully re-thread them immediately, before our restorations can be anything but conjectural. Grouped beads are usually graduated in size—as indeed we should expect them to be, so that the largest should hang at the lowest point of the catenary, and the others diminish upward to the top : see, for example, a series of nineteen, found in Skeagh Bog, Kilbride (Cavan).[1] As a rule, amber beads found in Ireland are spheroidal, flattened on the sides, where each bead comes in contact with its neighbour on the chain : the flattened surfaces are not always parallel, but are set at an angle to one another, after the manner of the sides of a voussoir of an arch, and for an analogous reason. One bead, found with a number of others of more normal type at Sheastown (Kilkenny), and now in Salisbury Museum, is of a triangular barrel form, apparently unique.[2] Mr. H. C. Beck, reporting on these specimens, expresses the opinion that they are of an Eastern Mediterranean type ; but Armstrong [PRIA 30 : 87] considers that all the amber found in Ireland comes from the Baltic.

Jet, a black variety of the fossil coniferous wood called *Lignite*, of which the richest source accessible to Ireland is the coast at Whitby in Yorkshire, was (probably) also regarded as a magical material, though the evidence to this effect is perhaps less definite. The earliest examples are shaped into beads or buttons, of which there is a greater variety than in amber : they may be conical (with a Λ-shaped thread-hole rising from the flat base), cylindrical, spherical, spheroidal, or in disc form—the last-named usually rectangular or semicircular discs, the spacing plates or the connecting end-toggles of groups of strings of beads.[3] A number of large ellipsoidal beads was found in Moyne Bog, Cullahill (Leix) in 1848 ; in each the string-hole runs along the major axis, and a raised collar surrounds the aperture at both ends.[4] There is said to have been eighteen or twenty beads in the series when it was found ; but only ten were obtained by the R.S.A.I., in whose collection they now are. The largest weighed 3½ oz., and the others were graduated in size, like the amber beads already spoken of.

Bracelets of jet, or (to be more accurate) of dark brown lignite, are not uncommon in lake-dwelling and other late sites. They are circular in form, plano-convex in section, and (unlike the beads, which are often decorated with engraved or stippled ornament) are always quite plain. As it would be impossible by any means to enlarge the opening, and as this is rarely wide enough to slip over an adult hand of normal size, we must suppose that they were assumed while the wearers were still children, or at least immature,

---

[1] JRSAI 54 [1924] : 173. [2] JRSAI 64 [1934] : 268.
[3] See the diagram, Fig. 27, p. 182. (The grouped beads in this figure are from Cumber (Londonderry) : one of the Cullahill beads is also shown below.)
[4] JRSAI 1 : 32, 2 : 283 ; PRIA 22 : 285.

and never again removed. One of these is shown in Fig. 27 as well as one of the conical buttons.

Pins are the simplest of all dress-fasteners, and the simplest forms of pins are skewers of wood or of bone. Nothing remains to tell us

FIG. 27.—Jet and Lignite Ornaments.

of wooden pins, but pins of bone are fairly common, with a wide range of elaboration, starting from a section of the leg-bone of a bird, or one of the narrower long bones (a fibula or an ulna) of a quadruped, cut off obliquely to its long axis, thus giving it the necessary sharp point to penetrate into the substance of the garment : the epiphysis of the surviving joint being retained, to give the pin its necessary head. This may be kept in its natural form, or may be worked into a knob, which can be decorated further in a variety of ways.

Some important principles are involved in the criticism of a bone pin-head found in a cremation-cist at Currandrum, about seven miles from Tuam (Galway).[1] The ashes, much comminuted, were merely heaped, unprotected, on the floor of the cist ; with them was an empty food vessel of a rather late type, a couple of flint flakes, and the pin-head. This is cylindrical, and segmented with grooves, horizontal when the axis of the object is held upright : the type is rare, if not unique, in Ireland, but is familiar in Spain— at a time, however, by about a thousand years earlier than any date to which we could assign this cist. That being so, can we see in the resemblance any more than a chance coincidence ? Can we withhold from the Galway artificer the credit of an independent invention of this most rudimentary of ornamental patterns ?

Pins of bronze hardly come into our present period : the most important is the *sunflower pin*, which most probably appears with the beginning of iron, see Fig. 32, p. 214. Still less are we here concerned with bronze brooches, a later derivative of pins, designed to prevent those simple and not very trustworthy fasteners from slipping out of the garments which they are intended to secure.

POTTERY

The *beaker* is almost the heraldic symbol of the people who introduced the Epimegalithic culture to Ireland ; although we gather that it was obsolete, or at least obsolescent, among themselves, before they arrived. We may define a beaker in general terms as a vase with flat base, above which the body first expands, then contracts, then expands again to the mouth, so that the profile resembles a long narrow **S**. But under this generic description there is included a number of specific types, all of different *immediate* origin, though probably derivations from a common primal prototype. Two standard types are recognized among British beakers ; in the one (type A), there is an abrupt angle between the globular body and the expanding neck ; in the other (type B), often called the " tulip-beaker ", such angles are smoothed down, so that the vessel is truly of the **S**-shape just mentioned. In a third form, sometimes spoken of as type C, but more properly to be regarded as a by-form or development (not necessarily a degeneration) of type A, the proportion between the body and the neck is different, the neck being relatively shorter. These varieties are of fundamental importance in the

[1] Lily F. Chitty, " Notes on Iberian affinities of a bone object found in Co. Galway ". *Galway* 16 [1935] : 125.

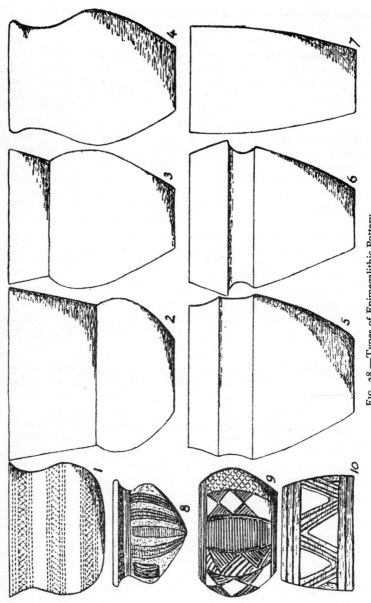

Fig. 28.—Types of Epimegalithic Pottery.

archæology of Great Britain, for they have supplied the clue for a differentiation of the groups of immigrants who there introduced the Beaker culture.[1]

The outlines in Fig. 28, nos. 2, 3, 4, show these types sufficiently for our present purpose (in the order A, C, B) : no. 1 is a restoration of one of the squat Moytirra "bell-beakers", inserted for contrast with the tall, slender, and often highly decorated "tulip-beakers" which are at present before us. In England the types are geographically segregated, indicating a corresponding segregation of the communities to which they respectively belong : it is a proof of the late importation of beakers into Ireland, that at Largantea (see *ante*, p. 84, and the description there quoted), the types are grouped together and display mutual contamination and artistic degeneration.

The vase-foodvessel, and its miniature representative the pygmy urn (Fig. 28, 8-10), continue in use during the Epimegalithic phase : the last of these, from Killucan (Tyrone), is an example of a not infrequent type, based upon an openwork basketry model. As we should expect, from the historical background and the less favourable climate, the pottery of this phase shows a notable deterioration, in technique, profile, and ornament, in comparison with that of its predecessor.

But the cinerary urn (Fig. 28, 5-7) increases in numerical proportion, and before long becomes the dominant form. This had already appeared in the Deuteromegalithic period, but it does not, so to speak, come to its own till the almost universal practice of cremation in the Epimegalithic. As the name implies, these vessels are receptacles, or rather (as we have seen, p. 66) *covers*, for the ashes of a cremated human body ; and their frequency increases with the expansion of this method of the disposal of the dead.

Again speaking in general terms, cinerary urns look like overgrown food-vessels : but there are certain types of a very different profile. Chief among them is the double conical form, in which the thickened rim surrounding the mouth of the vessel is of the shape of the frustum of a steeply-sided cone, the base of which projects all round the body of the vessel as a kind of inverted offset. This could have been, and very likely was, used for catching a cord to secure a cloth covering the mouth of the vessel—as a cord lies in a groove under the mouth of a jampot, for a similar purpose. Such a cover would obviously be necessary when the urn, filled with its bones, was inverted within the burial-place.

[1] See Kendrick and Hawkes, *Archæology in England and Wales*, 1914-1931, chap. viii, and references there, especially J. G. D. Clark's article in *Antiquity* 5 [1931] : 415. For a much wider view of the position of Beakers and their associated culture than would be appropriate to the present context, see H. J. Fleure and H. J. E. Peake, " Megaliths and Beakers " (JRAI 60 [1930] : 47) and Childe's comments, *Man* 1930 no. 142.

As compared with food-vessels, the decoration of cinerary urns is on the whole scanty, and is usually confined to the upper portion of the outside surface.   It shows a wide range of degrees of technical skill, from childish helplessness to the assured touch of a practised hand.   A striking exception to this poverty of decoration is presented by an unusually fine vase-shaped urn, from Tallaght (Dublin) [1] in which the sides are richly decorated with zones of zigzag ornament.

The most important innovation in Epimegalithic pottery is the decorative device known as *Encrustation*.   This consists in pressing strips, rings, or lumps of clay, separately modelled, into the still soft, unfired surface of a vessel ; working an incised rope- or rosette-pattern upon their surface ; smoothing down the joints between the insertions and the background ; and then firing the vessel.   Sometimes clay is chosen of a colour or texture differing from that of the vessel itself ; the encrustation on the surface of the pot thus stands up in a relief, enhanced by colour-contrast, and may be very effective. It is confined to cinerary urns, especially to those which in form resemble large food-vessels.

Attention was first directed to Encrustation by Lord Abercromby, [2] and the theory of the subject was set on a firm basis by Sir Cyril Fox, [3] in a paper which contained a list of forty-eight specimens then known—nineteen of them certainly, and possibly one other, of Irish provenance.   The technique, so far as the British Islands are concerned, seems to have begun in the North of England, passing thence to Ireland, and thence, possibly, to Wales.

In what are the simplest and probably the oldest examples, the encrustation is a mere zigzag surrounding the neck of the vessel ; but not long after their time, the decoration extended over the whole surface.   Usually, though not invariably, incised ornament is added, about and between the encrustations : almost extravagantly exuberant examples, from Tyrone and Down, are figured by Abercromby (vol. 2, plate ciii).   When Fox wrote, one example was known in Cork, two in the southern Midlands, and two in and around Sligo : the rest were confined to a line running from north to south, parallel with the east coast, and linking up with two specimens in Galloway. This confirms a probability, apparent on the rest of the pottery evidence, that the beaker invasion crossed into Ireland by the narrow strait between the modern ports of Stranraer and Larne.

Since these pioneer studies further discoveries have been made. A very elaborate example found at Kilwatermoy (Waterford) [4] can challenge comparison with the richest of the vessels in Abercromby's collection, though the encrustation is applied with strange irregularity. This was one of two encrusted vessels found in a cist ; each of them

[1] Figured PRIA 18 [1892] : 400.   [2] *Bronze Age Pottery* 2 : 53.
[3] *The Antiquaries' Journal* 7 [1927] : 115.   [4] JRSAI 61 [1931] : 57.

was inverted over a pile of ashes and bone fragments on a flagstone, and fixed in position in the cist with a packing of stone spalls.

One of the finest encrusted urns yet discovered in the country comes from a cist at Clonshannon (Wicklow). The cist was one of three, of a circular or hexagonal, not the usual rectangular, plan, set close together in a line. Outside the cist which here interests us were fragments of another urn, which have been conjecturally explained as relics of an earlier burial on the same site, accidentally discovered by the later cist-builders and by them thrown aside. In another cist of the same group was a vessel of a profile unique in Ireland, but cognate with some early iron-age Central European types : this was inverted over a beautiful pygmy urn, adorned with zigzags *in cavo rilievo* and other patterns. There were no deposits in these cists, to which the excavators assign a date of about 700 B.C., other than the urns and the cremated bones : it is to be noticed that the food-vessel has now disappeared, though its pygmy representative persists. In any case, the vessel just alluded to shows that novelties are still to be expected in Irish pottery. For a full analysis of the pottery from this find, reference should be made to the report of Messrs. Mahr and Price.[1] Another richly decorated urn from Kilbarry (Cork)—broken by the finder and recovered in fragments only—is recorded by Rev. P. Power.[2] Further examples have been found in the Greenhills (Dublin) cemetery,[3] and at Burgage, Co. Wicklow, here illustrated (Plate V).

A very valuable varied and representative series of pottery from a cist at Kilskeery (Tyrone) is reported by Messrs. E. E. Evans and T. G. F. Paterson.[4] The cist was discovered in levelling operations, without any scientific supervision ; it was destroyed and the contents scattered, though the police had intervened and rescued what they could. The intensely cremated remains of two people, a man and a woman of middle age, were identified, and fine specimens of pottery were thus preserved, in whole or in part.

Of the latter, the most important was an urn, about 1 foot 3 inches high ; flat base, inverted conical body, with slight shouldering under the rim, and decorated in its upper half with a series of lozenges and wavy lines in what the paper quoted calls pseudo-encrustation— that is surface-modelling in imitation of true encrustation (which would imply the application of separate strips of clay, sometimes of a different kind, to the surface of the vessel). Below, a series of nested **V** forms, incised, surrounds the body of the vessel. This urn was inverted over the bones which it protected, and beneath it was an exceptionally beautiful pygmy vessel of a flat-bottomed, globular form, decorated with vertical incised lines dividing the body of the vessel into 12 panels, filled with a variety of geometrical patterns—zigzags

[1] JRSAI 62 [1932] : 75. [2] JRSAI 63 [1933] : 221.
[3] PRIA 21 [1899] : 338 especially pp. 341 ff. [4] *Ulster* III 2 [1939] : 65.

vertical and horizontal, shaded triangles, criss-cross patterns, and so forth (Fig. 28, no. 9). The authors of the paper call special attention to one panel which, unlike all the other patterns, is nowhere repeated, having a series of horizontal strokes terminated with small pits " as though in imitation of a band of woven cloth which had been pulled together and secured ". Possibly this carries on the house-urn tradition of a door : looking at the development of the ornament in a continuous strip, illustrating the paper quoted, it is possible to read into it a door set in a circular fence. Two of the other vessels were food-vessels of a rather debased type, conforming with the late date suggested for the deposit. The fifth was a fragment only, deepening our suspicion that such worthless sherds were burdened, before burial, with magic spells, compelling them to appear before their ghostly owners as treasures of great price.

It was stated by one of the workmen who demolished the cist that one of the cover stones rested partly on the upturned base of the urn, not on a side-slab. The statement can only be docketed for future reference if necessary.

GOLD ORNAMENTS

In the Epimegalithic phase the commonest type of gold ornament is what may be provisionally called the *gapped ring*. This is a bar of gold, usually thickest in the middle and narrowing towards the ends, there, however, terminated with some kind of expansion ; and bent into a curve—not necessary circular—open for perhaps a little less than one-third of its circumference. In the first edition and elsewhere we have called these objects " cupped bracelets ", a name open to two objections : the expansions are not always " cups ", and there are many specimens which could not possibly have been worn as bracelets on any human wrist.[1]

Within the above definition there is room for variation, presumably to be taken as indicating correspondingly varied uses. Thus, they differ notably *inter se* in size and weight, from tiny loops no bigger than finger-rings, with expansions not larger than an ordinary pearl shirt-button, up to the giant from Castlekelly (Roscommon), in the Royal Irish Academy collection, which is 11 inches across and weighs over 16 oz. The bow may be slightly crescentic, thickening

---

[1] Whatever name we may choose to bestow upon these objects, none could be less scientific than *Eidring*, which we find in some German works, and which suggests an identity with the sacred ring that lay on the altar in Scandinavian temples. The name of this object was not *Eiðahringr* (though it is sometimes called " oath-ring " in English) but *Stallahringr*, " altar-ring " ; (though an oath taken upon it—its special purpose—was called *Baug-eiðr*, " armlet oath "). From *Kjalnesingasaga* we learn that it was of silver ; it was " without a join " (*i.e. not* " gapped ") according to *Eyrbyggjasaga :* and *Landnámabók* tells us that it had to be worn upon the arm of the *Góði* or priest who administered the oath. Nothing in the shape of a ring could be imagined less in accordance with these essential conditions than the Irish gapped rings.

in the middle and thinning toward the terminals, like the bow of a "leech" fibula; it may also be of a uniform thickness throughout; it may be either solid or tubular, the joint in the latter case being lapped and soldered, always on the concave surface of the bow. The expansions may be mere discs, large or small, or they may be cones—either solid masses, or else hollow ("cupped"). They may be cast in one piece with the bow, or fastened to it with soldering. The bases of these cones may lie in a plane at right angles to the sagitta of the ring, so that the object will stand upright in equilibrium on a table; or they may be at an angle with one another, so that such a setting would be impossible. The smaller bracelet-like rings were hammered in one piece, from an ingot.

It is unusual to find any traced ornament on the surface of these objects. One specimen of unknown provenance, thus decorated, is in the Library of Trinity College, Dublin:[1] another was found at Parkanore[2] (Tipperary), but was melted down and no record was preserved of it other than that it was large and highly decorated.

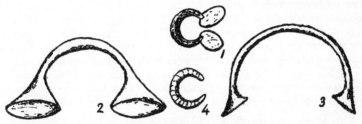

FIG. 29.—Gapped Rings.

On the basis of these variations, Armstrong has defined five types, as under :—

1. Bow crescent-shaped : expansions in the form of discs, set at an angle one to the other, attached to the bow at the edge next this angle (grotesquely suggesting the open bill of a duck). In a few specimens, a small loop on the outer surface of one of the discs. Bow usually decorated with longitudinal traced lines (Fig. 29 : 1).

2. Bow crescent-shaped; expansions cupped or hollow cones. The bases of these cones in a plane, so that the object will stand upright on a table (the outline of the cone being necessarily a scalene triangle) (Fig. 29 : 2).

3. Bow bracelet-like, of more or less uniform thickness. Expansions hollow cones, but set at an angle to one another, so that the object will not stand upright.

4. Similar to the last, but the conical expansions solid (Fig. 29 : 3).

5. Similar to the first type, but without the disc-shaped expansions : the objects being crescentic rings about 1 inch or less in diameter. Both types 1 and 5 are often decorated with traced lines, but in type 1 these are always in the line of the curve, in type 5 they are always transverse to it—dividing the ornament into sections like the segments of a maggot (Fig. 29 : 4).

[1] Wilde, *Catalogue*, p. 60.
[2] *Páirc an óir*, "The field of the gold". JRSAI 5 [1859] : 351, 445.

It is difficult to imagine any reasonable use for the larger and heavier specimens, like that from Castlekelly mentioned above ; their weight would make them inconvenient in any disposition.   But those of the normal moderate size could serve very suitably as morses or clasps for securing a garment, the " cups " being pressed through button-holes or cord loops, one on each side of the neck-opening. Sometimes, however, the expansions are hardly large enough to hold securely in such a situation, unless the neck-opening were so tight that the clasp would almost choke the wearer !

Objects of this class formed the bulk of the " Clare find " of 1854 : [1] a hoard of gold ornaments, weighing collectively at least 175 oz. [2] (and thus the largest assemblage of gold objects as yet found in Northern Europe) uncovered by labourers engaged in laying the line of the West Clare railway.   Among its contents were many gapped rings of the simplest kind : some gorgets ; a large closed ring with a smaller ring suspended to it ; one (or more) of the conical side-slotted objects described below ; and a " crown " of ten to twelve points from 4 to 5 inches high.   All but a very few of these objects were sold for their gold and were melted down ; casts of 150 of them were preserved.   They had been concealed in a pile of stones, not far from the great fortified settlement of Moghane,[3] and it has been conjectured that they were the loot acquired in an ancient raid thereon, hidden (as the thieves had vainly hoped) temporarily : but (as the event proved) permanently so far as they were concerned, presumably because in one way or another their sin found them out.

A deposit very similar in content must have been laid in the tomb of Salbuide, son of a king of Leinster.   When St. Patrick and his pupil and companion Benignus were traversing Ireland under the guidance of Cailte, they came to this man's burial-mound, and were told that he had there been buried with his retinue of thirty hounds, thirty servants, and thirty warriors, and fifty plates of silver—incidentally testifying to a tradition of the slaughter of a household of dependants, such as we have postulated in the case of Dowth.   We read, with some surprise (but the old Irish story-teller must

[1] See E. C. R. Armstrong's monograph (JRSAI 47 [1917] : 21) which, with its complete set of illustrations of the known objects, supersedes all previous literature on the subject.   See also the same writer's *Gold Catalogue*, p. 14.   Four objects of the same kind, the sole survivors of thirty or forty others, are said to have been found in the same county " in an earthen pot " by the author of an anonymous and obviously irresponsible paper (*Ulster* I 4 [1859] : 149).   Armstrong is probably correct in his conjecture that these formed part of the same find.

[2] This is in round numbers the sum of the weights of the recorded objects. Nothing is known of the weights of the many objects that were lost.

[3] Moghane Fort was first described adequately by T. J. Westropp, PRIA 27 [1909] : 218-25.   Its maximum cross-dimensions are 1,512 by 1,118 feet ; it consists of a triple rampart of stone, with a number of smaller circular enclosures contained within the two outer walls.   The innermost enclosure measures 363 by 386 feet.   The outer wall has a circuit of about 4,400 feet ; outside it there is a trench, part of which is quarried in the rock.   It is, in short, one of the most important prehistoric fortifications in Europe ; and if (as is reasonable) we may associate the great hoard of gold found in its neighbourhood directly with it, its date can be fixed with unusual precision to about 500 B.C.

bear the responsibility) [1] that the Saints promptly caused the tomb to be opened, and appropriated the treasures, which proved to consist of rings and bracelets to the depth of a spear-shaft. However, Patrick, at the suggestion of Benignus, at least gave the dead owner a *quid pro quo*, by withdrawing him and his company from Hell and sending them to Heaven.

It has been suggested by Sir W. Betham and others that these objects were a medium of currency, or perhaps that trade gold was shaped into this form for distribution. Such an explanation would give an adequate explanation of the larger and more cumbrous specimens. According to the *Life of St. Findian* in the Book of Lismore, [2] a " golden ring " was paid on occasion as the ransom for a captive. Stokes, commenting on this passage, quotes in illustration a paper by d'Arbois de Jubainville entitled *Bijoux et argenterie employés comme prix d'achat*. [3] In that case, however, we ought to find the weights of these objects fitting into some definite metrological scheme ; and, so far as I have been able to determine, the long series of weights which are given in Armstrong's *Gold Catalogue* would not do so, unless we assume a margin of error so large as to make the metrology of the objects useless : on similar grounds, the theory is severely criticized by Wilde. [4] But possibly different parts of the country used different standards. [5]

Objects of precisely similar form have been in use as currency in West Africa from at latest the sixteenth century. They are there known as *manillas*, a word of suggestively Iberian aspect : it would, however, be rash to attach too much importance to this accident. Such African specimens as I have myself seen are of bronze : but Windele [6] speaks of manillas of gold, and to a more limited extent of iron. He records that " English speculators " took advantage of this, and sent out to Africa cargoes of iron manillas, made in Birmingham, for trade purposes : a ship thus laden, sailing from Liverpool to the Bonny River, was wrecked at Ballycotton in 1836, and many specimens of its load found their way to the hands of local antiquaries, who were much impressed by their resemblance to the Irish rings. He adds that " Mr. Cuffe of the Bullion Office, Bank of England ", had told him that he had melted down large

---

[1] *Acallam na Senorach*, ed. Stokes (*Irische Texte* ser. IV), at p. 30.
[2] Ed. Whitley Stokes, at line 2622.   [3] *Revue archéologique* 1888.
[4] (*Gold*) *Catalogue*, p. 64.
[5] I find that Sir Flinders Petrie, with his larger experience in this very specialized branch of study, was more fortunate than I ; he succeeded in identifying six ancient weight-standards among the gold objects in the Dublin Museum—two Egyptian of different periods, Babylonian, Phœnician, Syrian, and Æginetan. See his *Ancient Weights and Measures* (London 1926), pp. 46, 47. A rather different conclusion is reached in Ridgeway's *Origin of Metallic Standards*, appendix C, where the author discusses " Keltic and Scandinavian Weight Standards ", and there reaches the conclusion that Phocæan standards, mediated by Massilia, are traceable throughout the whole series.
[6] JRSAI 1 : 329. Some further references bearing on this comparison will be found in *Cork* 46 [1941] : 132.

quantities of gold manillas " quite of the size and shape of the Irish, but a little closer at the opening ".

Is all this any more than a very singular coincidence ?   There are historians of civilization who would have us believe that coincidences and such accidents never happen.   The answer of course is that they do, within the experience of every one of us.   I cannot see how we are to bridge the chronological gap between the Irish rings and the African manillas, but that may be because I do not know enough about the history of native African commerce and its origin.   But whatever may be the true solution of this queer problem, we must be careful to guard ourselves against any fallacious circular reasoning in the formula—

The African rings are money.
Therefore the Irish rings are money.
Therefore the African rings are linked to the Irish rings by some un-explained affiliation.

It should be noticed that objects of this type in copper or bronze, identical in form with those in gold, are to be found in Ireland no less than in Africa.   But they are not common—Armstrong, writing in 1922, of one specimen, tells us that there were then only twelve examples in the National Museum.   Some of these were found in associated hoards, which unanimously spoke of a late date—at earliest from the very end of the Bronze Age, but more probably from some time when the Iron Age was well under way.   One such hoard, from Mount Rivers (Cork) included two gold specimens and one of copper, and with them two socketed bronze hatchet-heads and eleven amber beads.   Another, from Brockagh (Westmeath) included a number of bronze rings, of a class frequent in Ireland, and vaguely described as " dress-fasteners " or the like.   Although these objects are almost certainly of the Iron Age, as they have come before us we may as well say here what little there is to say about them. They are rings of bronze, and seem to fall into the following classes :—

1. Simple rings, about an inch or a little less in diameter.   The section of the metal hoop more or less circular, and always solid.

2. A pair of similar rings, fastened together side by side immovably, after the manner of a pair of spectacles.   The two rings may be in direct contact, or may be connected by a short flat plate of bronze.

3. Larger rings, about 3 inches in diameter ; sometimes the hoop of these larger rings is hollow.

4. Similar rings, with a small ring, $\frac{1}{2}$ inch or less in diameter, threaded loose upon the hoop.

5. Rings of the smaller size, with two transverse perforations running through the hoop opposite to each other, thus admitting a pin which can lie in the diameter of the ring : the perforation usually strengthened with a lip forming a conical flange at each side of the outer circumference.   An oft-quoted example from Trillick (Tyrone) shows us two such rings (but without the flanges) threaded on a long flat-headed pin.[1]

[1] JRSAI 10 : 164.   See a large series of illustrations of these rings, with a description by Armstrong, PRIA 36 [1922] : 144 ff.   Evans, Bronze, p. 398.

PLATE VIII

T. H. Mason

EXTERIOR OF A CLOCHÁN ON ARAN ISLAND, CO. GALWAY

All the associations of such rings are very late—socketed gouges and hatchet-heads, and in one case, from Kinnagoe (Armagh) a gold bulla which, whatever may be its exact date and purpose, belongs to what is certainly a very late type.[1]

For a full description of the elaborate and varied processes followed in making gapped rings of gold, here only outlined, reference must be made once more to Mr. Maryon's monograph.[2] We notice especially that the process of soldering has now been introduced : for all their barbarity, the Epimegalithic invaders were skilled metallurgists. Taking out the lunulæ and the torques, most of the gold objects which are the glory of the National Museum are of their handiwork.

The smaller gapped rings (type 5 above), which used to be called " ring-money ", are most likely intended to secure and to decorate braided locks of hair.   They were fashioned, round a cylindrical rod serving as a modelling-core, by means of a hammer or a swage (a hammer with a specially shaped striking edge) ; and they are sometimes decorated with a gold wire, inlaid in a spiral groove winding round the body of the ring (anticipating the decoration of the torques in the Broighter hoard).   They are not all of gold—some are of copper, bronze, or lead, covered with gilding.   The latter have been explained as ancient forgeries ; but Mr. Maryon demurs to this explanation, on the ground that " a forger would have hidden the joint more efficiently ".   But were all forgers efficient ?   And were all their customers wide-awake ?   On Coquet Island, Northumbria, a skeleton was found in the middle of the last century, having a *leaden* ring on one of its fingers, inscribed in Runic letters THIS IS SIUILFIR[N] (silvern)—with the sign of the Cross prefixed, as though in confirmation of the misspelt misstatement !   Faint traces suggested that the ring had been coated with silver.[3]

Another, and a rarer, form of hair-ring is represented by some specimens in the National Museum (eleven are recorded, without provenance except two, doubtfully said to come from Limerick). This is formed of two hollow conical discs, the bases apposited and secured by a lapped band running round the rim : a hollow tube runs axially through the object from apex to apex, and what we have called above a " side-slot " in the ring cuts through from the edge in to this tube.   Maryon speaks in the highest terms of the technical efficiency displayed by the makers of these objects.[4]

A small ring from Rathfarnham [5] (Dublin) and another of unknown provenance in the Dublin Museum [6] are probably *finger-*

[1] PRIA 36 [1922] : 148.
[2] See JRSAI 1 : 322 ; and several others noticed in Armstrong's *Gold Catalogue.*
[3] Stephens, *Old Northern Runic Monuments* 1 : 480, where in illustration a letter is quoted, describing how simple modern folk are imposed upon by cheapjacks with just such blatantly spurious jewellery.
[4] *Op. cit.* p. 203 ; Armstrong, *Gold Catalogue*, p. 38, where they are doubtfully called " hair-rings ".   [5] JRSAI 4 : 391.   [6] *Gold Catalogue*, no. 457.

rings. They are cylindrical, gapped in the side (presumably to allow of their adjustment to fingers of different diameter) and are grooved on the inside and outside surfaces so as to resemble a succession of tiny rings side by side. Their weights are given as 6 and 9 dwts. respectively.

Incidental reference was made above to a *bulla.* The word properly belongs to an amulet of gold roughly in the shape of two apposited watch-glasses, worn by boys in Rome and discarded when they assumed the *toga uirilis.* The practice was apparently borrowed from the Etruscans ; and doubtless its primary purpose was to protect the youthful wearer from the Evil Eye.

A few objects have been found in Ireland sufficiently like to the Etrusco-Roman prototype to justify the transference to them of its name. They are more or less heart-shaped lumps of lead, measuring about an inch each way, with bulging sides, and covered with a plate of gold folded over : how the plate is secured is not quite clear : the edges were apparently flanged, and beaten into the yielding substance of the lead ; as, on one or two of the extant specimens, an ornamental framing of fine twisted gold wire is beaten into the external surface of the gold covering itself. The ornamentation is traced on the surface : in one comparatively large example from the Bog of Allen, in the National Museum,[1] the chief element in the design is apparently a phallus, so that the prophylactic nature of the object is all the more probable. An example from Co. Cavan described by Armstrong has " a small stone " inside the gold ; another, alleged to have been found on the shore of the river Bann, in association with the inscribed handle of a late Christian bell-shrine—an association surely altogether fortuitous—is said to have contained " earthy matter "—clay, in fact—in which were "small irregular-shaped particles, probably altered blood-globules ".[2] All things considered, an explanation quoted by Armstrong that this is " earth which has been suffused with the blood of a martyred saint " is less likely than others that could be suggested.

Gorgets are the most impressive of the Epimegalithic gold handi-works—neck-ornaments, of the same general shape as lunulæ, and conceivably a development of the lunula idea. But even if so, the development has gone so far, both in technique and in design, that the two classes of objects must be considered independently.

Gorgets are of the crescentic shape of lunulæ, but much broader ; and they have not the decorative restraint of their prototypes. The surface is broken with prominent *repoussé* ribs, running in the same sense as the outer edges of the crescent. Between them is finer

[1] Armstrong, *Gold Catalogue,* Fig. 448.
[2] See Maryon, *op. cit.* p. 211 ; Armstrong, *Gold Catalogue* 43 ; and a further article, with drawings of all the specimens in the National Collection, JRSAI 52 [1922] : 133.

ornament, also *repoussé*, of knobs disposed in imitation of cord-work or braid-work. The ends are plain and cut off square, but concealed by circular discs, one on each. These discs are double, formed of a back piece and a front piece, secured together by lapping their edges : the former is attached to the body of the gorget ; the latter usually bears the *repoussé* decoration which enriches this part of the ornament. It was doubtless recognized that there would be too great a strain on these discs, which bore the responsibility of securing the ornament round the neck of its owner, to make soldering a trustworthy method of attachment in this particular case ; the disc was therefore secured with a stitching of gold wire, sometimes executed with great neatness, or else by passing the end of the crescent through slits in its back piece of the disc and folding it over to prevent it from slipping out. The decoration of the discs usually consists of groups of concentric circles.

These discs must have not only helped to secure the gorget, but also must have formed the most prominent element in its decorative effect. It is almost inevitable that the gorget was a neck-and-back ornament, with the discs standing up conspicuous under the ears, presenting a striking effect not otherwise obtainable. The famous Spanish statuette called *La Dame d'Elche* [1] gives us an idea of what they would look like, although her ear-discs are secured in a different way. The whole decoration of the gorgets is thoroughly Germanic in type, and accords well with the traditions and associations of the Beaker invaders.

The finest gorget as yet discovered in Ireland (Plate VI) was found a few years ago in a rock-crevice at Gleninsheen, near Ballyvaughan (Clare). It must have been forcibly pushed in by some one anxious to hide it, and suffered distortion in consequence ; apart from that easily remediable injury it is perfect, and shows the characteristic decoration of its type in the highest perfection.

Discs of gold, circular in shape, usually about 2-5 inches in diameter, are a product of Ireland, if we can rely upon the available statistics. [2] They are beaten out, flat, but not thin, trimmed to a circular shape, and pierced with thread-holes. The ornament is *repoussé* (sometimes with traced enrichment), pressed from the back so as to stand out slightly in relief, in the manner of a bracteate ; and consists usually of a circular bordering of concentric circles or of a zigzag, with a cruciform pattern in the centre. This wheel-like pattern is commonly explained as a piece of solar symbolism, the objects being described as " sun-discs ". Such an explanation is not necessary : it is not likely that they had a religious intention at all, or that they had any purpose more recondite than the decoration

---

[1] *Archæologia* 60, part 1 [1906] : 83.
[2] Mahr tells us (PPS 3 : 371) that about thirty-three specimens are recorded of which more than twenty are of Irish provenance.

of garments : they are frequently found in pairs, which does not favour the " sun-disc " theory. The story of the discovery of two specimens at Ballyshannon (Donegal), reported in Harris's edition of Ware's *Antiquities*, and in Gibson's edition of Camden,[1] is well known, and if we may believe it, is conclusive as to the purpose of the objects. A certain bishop of Derry, having heard an Irish harper sing a song, desired to have it interpreted ; it was to the effect that in a certain specified place " a man of gigantic stature was buried, with plates of pure gold upon his head and back, and with rings on his fingers so large that an ordinary man could creep through them ". This of course stimulated two bystanders to dig in the place indicated : they found the two plates, but nothing more. How the plates were actually disposed on the body was not regarded as being of any interest, and so was not recorded : we are left to assume the probability that they were sewn in front of the wearer's outer garment, one on each side.

The story is not impossible. A few similar traditions of the contents of grave mounds have survived to our day, which when tested by excavation have proved to be at least based upon fact. There seems to have been some such tradition underlying the story of the discovery of the golden horse-peytrel found at Bryn yr Ellyllon, near Mold, Flintshire, and now in the British Museum.[2] At Tingstäde in Gotland, Sweden, there was a tumulus outside the church, in which popular tradition told that a man had been buried in the skin of a bear, and gave a picturesque ætiological myth to account for this unusual proceeding. On examination, the grave was found, by the evidence of its goods, to be wellnigh 2,000 years old, and, whatever might be the truth of the myth, there was no room for any doubt about the bear-skin.[3]

The stitch-holes in these golden discs are usually in the centre, which would leave the edge unprotected, and free to fray out ; we may presume that it was covered with a framing-ring of harder material sewn over it. This would probably be coloured differently from the body of the garment, and would thus greatly enhance the effect.

It is inevitable that the " sun-disc " from Trundholm Moor, Denmark, should be quoted in connexion with these objects.[4] This,

[1] Conveniently reprinted in the *Dublin Penny Journal* 1 [1833] : 244, with a reproduction of Gibson's illustration. See also *Ulster* I 4 : 164. They were similar to, though not identical with, the pair illustrated in Armstrong's *Gold Catalogue*, plate xix Figs. 429, 430, from Ballina (Mayo).

[2] *British Museum Bronze-Age Guide*, second edition, p. 94.

[3] Harald Hansson, " En grav och en tradition " (*Fornvännen* 18 [1923] : 225).

[4] For the sun-disc theory and for numerous illustrations see R. A. Smith in PSA Lond., series II vol. 20 [1903] : 6 ; *British Museum Bronze-Age Guide*, p. 110. See also R. Day, " Gold plates and discs found near Cloyne, County Cork ", JRSAI 29 [1899] : 314 ; Petrie, " Irish antiquities ", *Dublin Penny Journal* as quoted above ; R. MacAdam in *Ulster*, I 4 [1856] : 164 ; R. Ousley in TRIA 6 : 31. On the Lattoon disc see Armstrong, *Gold Catalogue*, p. 47 ; *Man*, vol. 20 no. 45.

apparently a votive offering, is a bronze model of a wheeled chariot drawn by a horse, bearing an upright circular disc of bronze with traces of gilding.   No doubt, *this* disc represents the sun, on its daily course : it is decorated with a rich spiral pattern.   But the central stitch-holes on the Irish specimens forbid us to press the

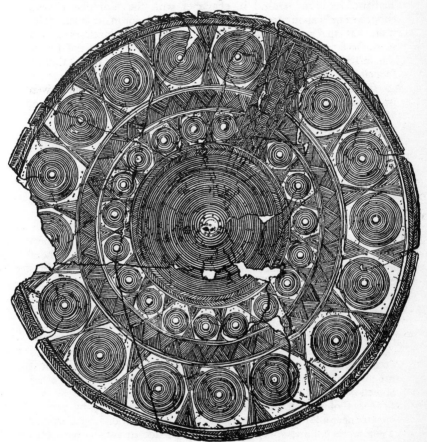

[*By permission of the Royal Anthropological Institute.*

FIG. 30.—The Lattoon Disc.

analogy too closely : there is, however, one disc, from Lattoon (Cavan) which seems comparable with the Danish specimen.   It is larger than the other Irish discs—nearly 5 inches in diameter—and it bears a rich decoration, composed chiefly of groups of concentric circles—strangely interrupted by a radial bar of shaded zigzag patterns.   The disc was found in association with a number of

gapped rings, and is therefore to be referred to the Epimegalithic.[1]
Mr. Maryon suggests that it might have been secured to a bronze
disc by means of a copper wire running round its circumference,
hammered into a groove provided for the purpose on the surface of
the bronze. There is one *bronze* disc of Irish provenance in the
British Museum identical in character with the Trundholm disc,
though of only about $\frac{1}{3}$ its diameter and very inferior in ornamentation.
This has the same marginal loops as the Trundholm disc, and
possibly formed part of a similar object. But it does not follow
that all the Irish discs illustrated in Smith's paper (PSA London,
loc. cit.) had the same purpose.

Gold *boxes* are of late date, and may be soldered ; but this is
uncertain. A cylinder is formed of a strip of gold ribbon, overlapping.
If the joint be secured with solder, the solder has been carefully
prevented from escaping visibly beyond the joint. The bronze
edge of the cylinder is turned outward and the bottom disc is lapped
on to it and folded up close, to make a roll moulding. The surface
is then decorated with traced lines and compass-drawn circles. These
objects show much technical excellence.

Bands of gold, some plain, some with slight ornament, and one,
from Lambay, with a *repoussé* decoration apparently of the Iron
Age, are recorded : some are in the National Museum and are
figured and described in Armstrong's *Gold Catalogue*. The most
remarkable, however, seems to have disappeared : it may have been
an ornamental hair-fillet ; but the available description and illustration [2] are difficult to understand and are otherwise inadequate. We
gather that it was formed of nine twisted cords of gold wire laid side
by side, and secured, by obscure means, to each other along their
lengths, and, at each end, to a plaited ring of the same material and
technical construction. The whole was $20\frac{1}{2}$ inches in length, and
came from Duhallow (Cork). Most of the plain bands and ribbons
do not seem to be strong enough to stand the strain of any independent
use ; they were probably secondary decorations applied to other
objects.

A set of golden *balls* was found in or about 1834 by potato-
diggers near a " fort " on the west bank of the Shannon near Carrick.[3]
They were hollow, spheroidal in shape, made in two halves, fitted
together so that the edges overlapped, and were soldered.[4]

---

[1] In contrast with a " garment disc " from Mere Donn, Wiltshire, which was
found in association with a copper dagger. A similar interruption of the design
has been noticed in the hanging bowl from Drimnagh (p. 94), possibly illustrations
of the superstition against completed rings, of which we shall hear again in connexion with bronze shields.

[2] By J. Windele ; *Ulster* I 9 [1861] : 28 ff.

[3] Carrick-on-Shannon is in Leitrim, but the find-place was actually in Roscommon.

[4] Mr. Maryon (PRIA 44 : 193) quotes Armstrong as saying that they were
directly joined together without solder, and proceeds to refute him. But reference
to Armstrong's *Gold Catalogue* at the place indicated (pp. 8, 9) shows that he does

For the large variety of minor gold objects—beads, ear-rings, bands, pins, etc.—considerations of space compel us to refer the reader to Armstrong's very fully illustrated *Catalogue*.

BRONZE OBJECTS

The development, and introduction to Ireland, of the device of fitting the blades of metal tools with sockets for securing them to their handles, must be laid to the credit of the Epimegalithic immigrants. In fact, socketed tools are their most important contribution to the culture of the country, anticipated only in the socketed spear-heads.

We left the *Hatchet-head*, in the last phase, in the form of the palstave. In an intermediate stage, not represented in Ireland at all, a further development took place, in which the sides of the characteristic " pockets " in the tail of the palstave became increased in size, so that they could be hammered down upon the side-branch of the wooden handle ; thus making them clasp it with a tightness sufficient to make the stop-ridge unnecessary. This produced the *winged* hatchet-head : a blade with two wings rising on each side from the ends of the tail, curving toward, but not meeting one another, in the manner of this typographical combination (——) ; where the " dash " represents the end of the tail, and the parentheses the curve of the wings. This phase of the evolution is familiar in England, but it never reached Ireland. Its entry there was fore-stalled by the Beaker Invasion.[1]

At last the wings met, overlapped, and coalesced : the tail of the blade, now a useless encumbrance, disappeared ; it was no longer necessary to weaken the handle by splitting its side branch ; the tool had been fitted with a socket, into which it could be thrust. The side loop of the palstave was retained for its function of receiving a securing thong ; the bronze hatchet-head had now attained its final form. Palstaves are sometimes provided with two loops, one

not make so categorical a statement ; he says that " according to Wilde, solder was used but *it is possible that* [my italics] the parts were directly fused together " ; though on p. 37 of the same work, where he returns to these objects, he says defin-itely that the half-spheres " overlap for about 1/16th of an inch, and are then soldered. Each ball [the writer continues] is pierced with openings for the in-sertion of a string, the edge of the aperture being everted, as if to prevent the sharp edge of the metal cutting the string." The original number of these balls is variously given as 11 or 13 : 9 of them are known to have been preserved in the National Museum and elsewhere (see PRIA 30 : 450 and references there). They were probably meant for the decoration of the horse of some person of wealth : what look like similar balls are represented, strung on the reins of horses on the well-known Hallstatt Scabbard.

[1] See Armstrong's paper on the " Distribution of Bronze Celts in Ireland ", PSA Lond. II 27 [1915] : 253, where the relative frequency of the different types, with distribution-maps, is set forth. This pioneer paper is here quoted in full recognition of the fact that it is now out of date, as is inevitable in a paper by a merely human author who cannot anticipate subsequent discoveries : it has sometimes been referred to in terms which seem to imply that such an inability calls for censure ! In any case, the absence of winged hatchet-heads still remains an undisturbed fact.

on each side ; socketed hatchet-heads with two loops are not unknown, but they are very rare.[1]

On the outer surfaces of the sides of the socket, ornament is
usually cast in relief which frequently takes the form of two **C** curves
back to back, thus)(. From the days of Sir John Evans onward,
these curves have been explained as vestigial survivals of the edges of
the wings of the winged hatchet-head, and as a clear proof of the
evolution here recapitulated. Like everything else in these days, this
theory has been severely criticised ; [2] and it must be admitted that
origins of the manifestations of human culture are not always to be
determined on an evolutionary basis with the assurance with which
we apply the same principle to the phenomena of the visible Universe,
inorganic and organic. A writer with limited comprehension may
well fear to tread the region of modern physico-philosophical subtleties as to the relation of Mind and Matter ; but while physical
evolution proceeds, to outward seeming, automatically, cultural
evolution does sometimes appear to depend on the caprice of accident,
or on human volition. Two people meet somewhere by a seeming
hazard, and casually exchange ideas on some matter of current
interest—a man has over-eaten, and has had a vivid dream in
consequence—an intelligent child asks his father a chance question
—and a movement may be set on its course which will completely
revolutionize this or that aspect of human life. And it is quite
possible, when we are dealing with such mentally and physically
mobile beings as men, for cultural development to follow more
lines than one ; and to end in a conflation in which the two streams
become indistinguishable. The winged hatchet could, and in spite
of criticism did, develop into the socketed tool, and could bear the
C curves as a memorial of the process (otherwise how are we to
account for the curves ?). But somewhere or other, a man may have
broken his palstave, and (being a person of resource) may have
improvised an attachment out of a hollow marrow-bone ; an
emergency measure which suggested a most valuable improvement
in the implement, by-passing the slow evolutionary process. So
that in the end, the disputants may drop their chunks of Old Red
Sandstone : it is quite likely that they are both right.

With one doubtful exception,[3] none of the numerous recorded
specimens of socketed hatchet-heads found in Ireland show the **C**
curves. This suggests to me that the importation took place comparatively late in the evolution of the tool, and that the **C** curves had

---

[1] A mould for casting such an object, from Fethard (Tipperary) is published
by Frazer, JRSAI 19 [1889] : 289.

[2] As for instance by Mahr, in PPS 3 : 374. The fault is doubtless in myself
that I cannot see the relevance of the article in the German periodical *Mannus*
to which he there calls attention, though I have read it several times. Götze,
in Ebert's *Reallexikon*, accepts the evolution, though with reservations analogous
to those here expressed.

[3] Figured in Evans, *Bronze Implements*, p. 132, Fig. 156.

PLATE IX

CRYPTICAL OGHAM FROM BALLYHANK,
CO. CORK

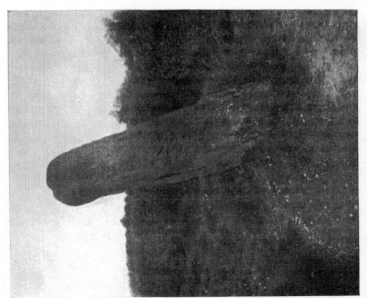

PSEUDO-OGHAM AT HAWKINSTOWN, CO. MEATH

already been abandoned when it was introduced; but it is also possible, assuming a complex history involving two or more parallel lines of development, that the Irish specimens are derived in some other way; this view of the case is favoured by the absence from Ireland of the winged hatchets.

An elbowed wooden bar, the shorter branch of which was fixed into the socket of the metal head, was the normal handle of such tools. A variant, probably a makeshift form, was found at Oldtown Kilcashel (Roscommon) and is reported at second-hand from the description of the finder by Professor Ó Ríordáin [1]—the wood having disintegrated almost immediately after the removal of the object from the bog. Here there was a straight handle, with a hole in it through which a short length of wood was thrust, to provide a spindle on which the hatchet-head was mounted. There was a second hole in the longer shaft, the purpose of which was not clearly indicated. Associated with the object was a fragment of the side of a wooden bowl with a loop handle, affording definite evidence of the use of such objects in the latter part of the Bronze Age.

The ideal monograph of the future must not only complete Armstrong's distribution-maps by bringing them up-to-date; it must also subdivide them. For under the heading of "socketed hatchet-heads" several different types are included, differing in the horizontal section of the socket (circular, oval, square): in the proportions of the length and breadth of the tool; in the shape and length of the cutting edge; and, to some extent, in the ornamentation. The most casual glance over a large collection will be sufficient to convince the reader of this. Indeed, a large collection is not necessary: I am not myself, and never was, a collector; but I have kept at hand a few type specimens to be used for the purpose of class demonstrations, and even among the half-dozen or so socketed hatchet-heads included in these there are differences which suggest questions that cannot easily be answered.

It is, however, in the manufacture of weapons rather than of tools that the Epimegalithic people excelled, as we should expect from such predatory warriors. The spear-head and the "slashing sword" carried them to easy victory over aborigines equipped with daggers, rapiers, javelins, and sling-balls.

In Chapter VII we trace the evolution of the socketed *Spearhead.* We do not speak of the great variety in outline and ornamental treatment, as well as in size, which that weapon displays: the papers of Coffey, of Greenwell and Brewis, and of Evans, there cited, contain many illustrations of the several subordinate types, for details of which we cannot here find space.[2] We have left the securingloops at the top of the shaft: in the latest specimens in which these

---

[1] *Galway* 18 [1939] : 41.
[2] See also Wilde, *Catalogue,* pp. 496-502 ; Coffey in JRSAI 41 [1911] : 20.

loops are effective they are rectangular in shape, and a continuation
of the moulded ribs which flanked the socket, and strengthened and
decorated the blade. We now see the loops enter the blade, becoming ornamental apertures—enhancing their beauty, but, except
for a certain lightening of their weight, not improving their practical
utility in any way.[1] When this happened, the loops ceased to be
functional, and there was a reversion to the peg-fastening, for which
once more, as in the beginning, holes were provided, in the seam of
the casting. This, as E. E. Evans has shown, is due not to local
evolution (which would mean an unnatural reversion) but to the
influence of foreign communities which had never adopted the loop-
fastening : in other words, the Epimegalithic invaders. They were
not inferior in skill to their predecessors : they took as great a pride
in the excellence of their handiworks as the Deuteromegalithic
artificers could have done. They produced spearheads of great
size and consummate artistry, sometimes decorated with applied
ornament—as is illustrated by a beautiful spear-head from Loch
Gur (Limerick), which is enriched with inlaid strips and bands
of gold (Plate Vb). The outlines of their blades have always
what may be called a " sweeter " curve than those of the Deuteromegalithic spears. As we have already indicated, the " rivets "
must have been mere pins, which could be easily withdrawn ; no
specimens have been found retaining the rivets in position, as would
no doubt have been the case if the spear-heads had been secured
with immovable rivets. A small spear-head of this kind was found,
embedded in a human skull, at Greenvale (Kilkenny).[2]
There is another variety of perforated spear-head, in which the
blade is flat and broad, and the apertures in the wings are very
small slits, protected by slight raised flanges along the outer edge.
A specimen, found in Loch Erne, is figured by Mr. Day.[3] Part of
the shaft still remained in the socket of this weapon. It was split
at the end : Mr. Day supposed that this was to admit a wedge already
placed in the inner end of the socket which would force the split
end open and make it grip tightly on the inside of the socket. The
weapon is, in fact, a strange hybrid ; a combination of an ordinary
socketed spear-head and a quite exotic type illustrated by a specimen
from Amorgos.[4] This is a flat, more or less triangular, blade with
a short tang, which fits into a slit at the end of a shaft. A binding
round the base of the slit, where it contains the tang, and another
near the outer end of the slit and passing through the apertures in the
blade, keep the latter firmly in position. In the Irish specimen the
slits are merely vestigial, and quite functionless.
The phenomena of diffusion (which are stated adequately in

[1] See for illustrations Coffey's paper," Ornamental bronze spear-heads with
apertures in the blade ", PRIA 30 [1913] : 445.   [2] JRSAI 1 [1849] : 30.
[3] Cork II [1901] : 122.   [4] British Museum Bronze Age Guide, p. 163.

Evans's paper, but which in a special monograph would have to be set forth with a laborious minuteness that would require the joint labours of a syndicate of scholars) point unanimously to the conclusion that the invaders, having at last possessed themselves of the Irish copper and gold, and of the Cornish tin, also captured the Continental trade which had been established by the Deuteromegalithic people. The " Germanic " characters (the word is used here in a territorial, not in a racial sense), which such later Irish gold products as the Comerford bowl and the Gleninsheen gorget, present, in common with typical German objects as those from Messingwerk, do not necessarily mean—as they have hitherto been supposed to mean—that the flow of trade was reversed : that in the early phases of the Bronze Age the natives of Ireland were exporters who sent native goods to the Continent, and that in the latest phase the same people were importers, who depended for such commodities as we have been considering upon foreign sources of supply. The true explanation is that the country itself fell into the hands of immigrant foreigners, who used the local resources in their own way, with their own technique, and for their own profit. The native energy and initiative was finally destroyed with the Epimegalithic invasion : it passed from the natives to their conquerors.

The story of the evolution of the *Sword*, and its subversive influence in mid-bronze-age Europe, must be read in the pages where Peake has given us an exhaustive study of the subject.[1] We must here content ourselves with a much briefer abstract. The bronze-age sword has a sharp point, above which it widens, then narrows again, and then widens slightly to the haft. The curves are always very graceful ; next to spear-heads, swords are among the products of the Bronze Age which best show the artistic skill of the craftsmen. The use of the sword as a cutting weapon imposed a side strain upon the handle, which made the riveted rapier-mounting no longer sufficient : the rivets would tear through the thin tongue of metal at the butt of the blade, if a vehement blow were given. Accordingly, a handle was cast in one piece with the blade, in the form of a tongue of metal, shaped so as to give a convenient grasp to the hand, and ending in a triangular or fish-tail expansion. It was provided with two or more rivet-holes, whereby hafting-plates could be secured to the sides, thus giving the necessary thickness to the handle. It is seldom that the hafting-plates remain : they were usually of wood, bone, or other perishable materials. A sword from a bog at Muckno (Monaghan) has partly preserved its hafting-plates, which have been identified as being made from bones of a whale ;[2] another from Mullylagan (Armagh) had plates supposed to be of deerhorn.[3]

[1] Harold Peake, *The Bronze Age and the Celtic World* : London 1922. See also W. P. Brewis, " The Bronze Sword in Great Britain " (*Archæologia* 72 [1922-3] : 253) and E. E. Evans, " The Sword-bearers " (*Antiquity* 4 [1930] : 157).
[2] JRSAI 9 [1867] : 24.   [3] *Ibid.* 12 [1873] : 257.

In the later swords of this type—Montelius divides the two kinds between his " fourth " and " fifth " periods—there is a small triangular notch, the *ricasso*, cut out of each edge, immediately beneath the handle.   The necessity for this has been found in the shrinkage of the wooden scabbard, which left the upper end of the blade exposed and apt to hurt the hand of the owner.   Two groups of swords published by Armstrong [1] illustrate the contrast.   In the one, a set of three from Latteragh (Tipperary) there are no notches : in the other there are two, both notched, and associated with socketed loopless spear-heads.   But two swords, *without* the *ricassi*, associated with similar spear-heads, are figured on the following page from Youghal (Cork)—one more warning against the mechanical application of chronological principles to Irish antiquities. [2]

Swords, when not in use, were kept in *scabbards*, which must have been, as a rule, of wood or of leather, as the bronze mountings of such objects survive, but not the scabbards themselves.   Fragments of a bronze scabbard are recorded as having been found, with other pieces of scrap bronze, in a hoard collected for remelting by some artificer working in what is now Co. Roscommon. [3]   The wood and leather scabbards were tipped at their lower end with a bronze *chape*.   What appear to be the earlier specimens of this group of objects are simply formed, following generally the outline of the tip of the sword, and sometimes terminating below in a knob.   Later forms are of larger size, and they have bars projecting horizontally from the sides, which gives the object, roughly speaking, the shape of an inverted T.   These bars are not mere ornaments ; they served the useful purpose of giving a purchase to the foot of the owner, if for any reason the sword was jammed in the scabbard and difficult to draw. [4]

The *Dagger* now has a leaf-shaped blade, like a miniature sword, and like other tools and weapons is provided with a socket, having rivet-holes for securing it to a handle.   The socket is not circular, but a rather flat oval in cross-section, and the rivet-holes, as in the spear-heads, are in the seam produced by the meeting of the two halves of the mould.   A group of weapons found near Arklow (Wicklow)—such a dagger, a spear-head with the loops incorporated as openings in the blade, and two socketed hatchet-heads—gives useful chronological information. [5]

Chisels may be tanged or socketed, the former being the commoner. In some (as in a modern chisel) there is a round flat shield which acts

[1] PRIA 36 : 143.
[2] The groups of spear-heads in these two hoards differ notably in the proportion of the size of the blade to that of the stem : this may possibly be of chronological importance.
[3] JRSAI 11 [1870] : 120, 15 [1880] : 265-6.   A similar hoard, from Boa Island, Loch Erne, is recorded in the latter volume, p. 259.
[4] See Wilde, *Catalogue*, p. 461, Fig. 338.   [5] JRSAI 70 [1940] : 94.

as a stop, to prevent the metal blade from sinking too far into the wooden or horn handle ; or the neck of the blade thickens around the base of the tang and so maintains the relative position of the two parts of the tool ; [1] while in others, trunnions project from the sides of the tools to serve the same purpose : the body of the tool being flat, straight sided, and carried for some distance below the trunnions, where it suddenly expands into a crescentic blade with projecting horns.   The socketed chisel resembles the socketed hatchet-head, but the blade is narrower than the diameter of the socket, and the tool is longer in proportion to its breadth.   In contrast with chisels, *Gouges*, which are commoner in Ireland than in Great Britain, are all but invariably socketed—there is only one tanged gouge in the National Museum, resembling the tanged chisel with a circular stop.   *Chisels*, or punches resembling them, must have been in existence as far back as the time of flanged hatchet-heads, as tools of the kind must have been used for ornamenting them ; but it is clear from this striking contrast that bronze gouges cannot have been invented, or at least become general, till socket-joints had been introduced and become almost universal. [2]

Throughout the Bronze Age *Shields* must have been made of wood, wicker, or leather—materials sufficiently hard to resist the comparatively feeble weapons which they had to oppose, and at the same time lighter than metal would have been.   But these materials are perishable, so that shields are of very rare occurrence.   There are a few bronze shields remaining, which may be of the end of the Bronze Age or beginning of the Iron Age.   These are in the style of the fine shield from Aberystwyth, now in the British Museum, [3] which is a thin circular plate of metal with an umbo in the centre, surrounded with *repoussé* concentric rings, each pair of them enclosing a ring of hemispherical knobs.   A handle crossing the inside hollow of the umbo is riveted to the inner surface, and two other rivets, which remain in the body of the disc, secured the shoulder-strap.   There is a good example, though less artistic, of this type (from Loch Gur, Limerick) in the Royal Irish Academy's collection (PRIA 15 [1872] : 155 [4] ;   JRSAI 12 [1872] : 118) ; and a smaller specimen, said, though with some doubt, to have been found, with a large spear-head, in an earthen fort near Athenry (Galway), is also in the British Museum.

The round bronze shield of Northern Europe has been very

[1] Dr. Raftery prefers to consider such a tool as a knife, probably for leather-cutting, rather than a chisel : see *Ulster* III 5 [1942] : 128.

[2] In a short but very valuable paper, complete with distribution-map, on " The Bronze Socketed Gouge in Ireland " (JRSAI 74 [1944] : 160) Mr. Eoin MacWhite makes the attractive suggestion that these tools are derived from cut bone scoops.

[3] British Museum *Bronze-Age Guide* 2nd edition (1920) ; frontispiece.

[4] It may be well to note that another shield of the same type, figured later in the same volume (p. 277), is of British, not Irish provenance.

thoroughly studied, typologically and historically, by Ernst Sprock-hoff.[1] He names the type, which we have just described, after a specimen found at Yetholm (Roxburghshire), the " Yetholm type " ; and from the distribution of the known specimens he infers that it was essentially British—though a representation of a similar shield in a rock-carving at Bohuslån in Sweden carries its influence across the North Sea.

We need say nothing here of most of the other shield-types described and illustrated in the monograph quoted ; they are not represented in Irish finds, with one notable exception. This is what Sprockhoff calls the " Herzsprung type ", and describes as the most interesting of them all. Its distinguishing character is a notch in the umbo, with or without corresponding notches, or at least interruptions, in the surrounding circles.

Three Irish examples of this type are on record—from Annadale [2] (Leitrim), Clonbrin (Longford), and Cloonlara (Mayo) respectively.

The Annadale shield is of alder-wood. It was found in a bog, and, when first uncovered, measured 2 feet $2\frac{1}{2}$ inches in length, 1 foot 9 inches in breadth ; but as the wood dried it became distorted and shrunken. In the centre is a hemispherical boss, surrounded by seven raised ribs, the outermost single, the other six grouped in pairs. The curve of the five outer rings is not continuous ; it is interrupted in them all, at one of the long sides, by a shallow U-shaped indentation.

The Clonbrin shield is a thick disc of leather, 1 foot $8\frac{1}{2}$ inches by 1 foot $7\frac{1}{2}$ inches in diameter. There is a central hemispherical umbo, laced to the shield with leather thongs. This served to pro-tect the owner's hand as it grasped a leather handle, likewise laced to the shield, and lying in the diameter of the boss. Surrounding the boss are three raised concentric oval ribs, which follow the curve of the margin of the shield, and intercept between them small raised knobs grouped in threes. As in the Annadale shield, these ribs are not continuous curves : the innermost is open at one side, and the others are interrupted by abrupt V-shaped deflections, which fit into one another and into the opening in the innermost ring.[3]

The Cloonlara shield,[4] like that from Annadale, is of alder-wood but is more nearly circular than the other two. Four rings *in cavo rilievo* surround the umbo, and are deflected slightly inward, as in the Annadale shield, at one end of the shorter diameter ; and there is

---

[1] In his monograph, " Zur Handelsgeschichte der germanischen Bronzezeit " (*Vorgeschichtliche Forschungen* no. 7, Berlin 1930), pp. 1-43.
[2] Not " Annandale " as miswritten in our first edition.
[3] E. C. R. Armstrong, " Prehistoric leather shield found at Clonbrin, Co. Longford " (PRIA 27 [1909] : 256 ; the Annadale shield is also figured in this paper. For the latter see also Wilde, PRIA 8 [1864] : 487. See also JRSAI 54 [1924] : 122).
[4] PPS 3 [1937] : 383, plate 25.

a corresponding notch in the edge of the shield.   In the accompanying diagram these three shields are drawn, for purposes of comparison, to a uniform size and a uniform circular shape.   They are, actually, a little longer than they are broad ; on which account Armstrong described them as of the Iron Age.   But the difference is very slight —not enough to justify us in dissociating them chronologically from the bronze shields enumerated in Sprockhoff's monograph, which are

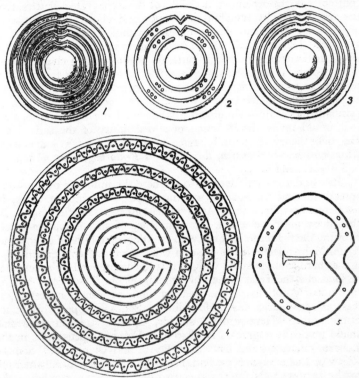

FIG. 31.—Diagram of the Decoration of " Herzsprung " Shields mentioned in the Text.
(1. Annadale ;   2. Clonbrin ;   3. Cloonlara ;   4. Dali, Cyprus ;   5. Rock-carving, Estremadura, Portugal.)

dated to the late Bronze Age by objects found in connexion with them.

Sprockhoff gives a list of seven shields of his " Herzsprung " type known to himself—one each from Bohemia and Denmark, one, exceptionally ornate, from Sweden, two from the type station of Herzsprung in Northern Germany, and two from Ireland—the Cloonlara shield had not yet been published when he wrote.   He also notices two representations, one upon a figured situla from Certosa in Italy, and one forming part of a group of rock-scribings in Estremadura, Portugal.   He emphasizes the fact that the Irish examples are in perishable materials, so that they are not likely to have been importations ; indeed, he goes so far as to say that the type may well be of Irish origin.

Armstrong quotes two conjectural interpretations of the discontinuity in the ornament of shields of this type ; Déchelette's, that the ring with its upturned breach [1] is a vestigial relic of a representation of the solar bark, and thus connected with solar symbolism ; and Undset's, that the notch was made to imitate some celebrated shield, which had suffered injury in battle. [2]   Surely such a hypothesis is a psychological improbability ; a shield which had so far failed in its *mana* as to permit itself to suffer any such injury would hardly be an acceptable model for copying ; on the ordinary principles of sympathetic magic a simulated injury would not be " apotropaic " —it would invite the infliction of a real injury of the same kind. On this theory, I entirely agree with Sprockhoff's judgement : *Man wird zugeben müssen, dass Undsets Erklärung heute nicht mehr zufriedenstellend ist.*

It would appear preferable to see here the influence of the widespread superstition against wearing knots, or complete rings, in garments or otherwise. [3]   An explanation even simpler would be that these gaps are a faded reminiscence of an observation-notch, allowing the fighter to look out with as little risk to himself as possible. True, Mahr rejects this suggestion with scorn, as " amateurish " [4]— it is as hard to understand why, as it is to comprehend his acceptance of Undset's theory as " the only intelligent one ".   Undset himself involuntarily puts us on the track of finding another suggestion, at least as sensible as any.   He claims a South European origin for Sprockhoff's " Herzsprung " shields, on the strength of a fine shield found in fragments in 1850 near Dali in Cyprus, now in the Louvre, described and figured by Perrot and Chipiez. [5]   When we follow up this reference, we find that the authors quoted call attention to the abrupt angle interrupting two of the rings surrounding the umbo, and that they suggest that these are less for ornament than for an indication (which the owner of the shield might require at a moment's notice) of the position and direction of the handle.   A diagram of this shield is here added to those of the Irish shields for

---

[1] Coffey pointed out that the breach is not at the side of the shield but in the top, the position of the handle showing that in defence-position the shield was held with the long axis horizontal (PRIA 27 [1909] : 262).

[2] JRSAI 54 [1924] : 122 and references there ;   especially *Zeitschrift für Ethnologie* 23 [1891] : 241.

[3] On which see Frazer, *Taboo and the Perils of the Soul*, p. 293.   This may have some bearing on the radial ornament which cuts across the decoration of the Lattoon disc, *ante*, p. 197.   [4] PPS 3 [1937] : 38.

[5] Perrot and Chipiez, *Histoire de l'art dans l'Antiquité* iii 860 f.

comparative purposes, as also of the Estremadura rock-scribing. The latter has a very conspicuous notch on the edge : the (supposedly vestigial) notches on the other shields have left the outer edge, but the Cloonlara shield retains a rudimentary notch in the actual rim. In view of Sprockhoff's suggestion, that these notched shields may be of Irish origin (he rejects Undset's Cypriote theory as completely as he rejects his other suggestion), it is not amiss to recall that the golden model shield in the much-disputed Strangford Loch hoard had a very notable notch in the edge.

Three bronze *Arrow-heads* of various form are figured by Wilde : [1] but they are probably of much later date than the Megalithic period. Bronze was still too valuable to waste on missiles so liable to loss : the probability is almost overwhelming that these objects are of the Iron Age (in the most unrestricted sense of the term, which would include the centuries after the break-up of the Roman Empire and the establishment of Christianity).

The objects called *Razors* are delicate blades of bronze, mounted on a stem. They may be either single or double-edged—the latter being the more frequent. They are usually of small size : it is hard to believe that they were very effective for the purpose suggested by their name : but the Cromaghs find (*ante*, p. 177) shows that their owners were as careful of the edges as any owner of a modern steel razor could be : a strip of leather bent over the blade made a case to protect the edge. A hole drilled through the upper part of the stem was probably for suspension to a wall.

WOOD, BONE, AND HORN

To speak about these materials in general ; our information about objects fashioned out of them, doubtless in common use, is strictly limited by their perishable nature. Horn is a little more enduring than wood, and a few implements in this material are still left to us, coming, however, more especially, from the preservative peat in which the later lake-dwellings are embedded. Whitepark Bay and similar shore sites have yielded tines of antlers, apparently used as picks or perforators : butt-ends of stag's horns were perforated and mounted on wooden handles to serve as mallets. As Mr. Maryon has reminded us, the softness of horn would make it an appropriate material for hammers to be used in delicate metallurgical work.[2]

[1] *Catalogue*, p. 503.
[2] PRIA 44 : 183. For specimens of horn and bone objects see JRSAI 17 [1885], plate facing pp. 119 ; Wood-Martin, *Pagan Ireland*, pp. 104 ff. ; Wilde, *Catalogue*, pp. 247 ff.

BOOK III

AFTER THE MEGALITHIC AGE

CHAPTER VIII

THE INFILTRATION OF IRON

IN Europe generally, we can discern broad outlines of the history of the introduction of Iron, and of its consequences for the civilization of the Continent ; although fog hides from us many details of its early stages. Of the couple of centuries before, and the same span of time after, the year 1000 B.C., the complex history is still, and must for long remain, obscure. A fresh pulsation of climate in Central Asia may be reasonably postulated, and, indeed, is indicated by the influence which it exercised upon the populations of the European Continent. Just as a much later pulsation of the same kind sent the Teutonic tribes helter-skelter over the decaying remnants of the Roman Empire, to bring its pride to naught, so, about the beginning of the last millennium B.C., the tribes known in Egyptian documents as " the Peoples of the Sea " were launched upon their several Odysseys, culminating in the settlement of the Etruscans in Italy and of the Philistines on the coast of Palestine ; the Achæans and the Dorians were driven into Greece ; the Trojan war—whatever may be the historical basis of that saga—was waged ; and the empires of Mesopotamia, of the Hittites, of Crete, of Egypt, passed as effective actors from the stage, giving place to the new-born city-states of Greece and Rome. In a word, the curtain rose for the first act of the drama of the modern world. The two foundation-stones of our present Civilization, Iron and Alphabetic Writing, were well and truly laid. But no historian chronicled these complicated events for us in any satisfying form : we must painfully fill out the picture-puzzle for ourselves, piece by piece, as each comes to hand.

Iron and Alphabetic Writing—we have not yet acquired perfect knowledge of the means by which Europe became endowed with these two great gifts ; [1] we know only that they came to her in a time of bitter strife and confusion, of slaughter, plunder, and the wreck of empires. But when she regained her feet she pursued a steady course of progress, until the predacity of Rome once more forced her life into other channels.

The history of the Iron Age in Europe is divided by Archæologists into two volumes, entitled respectively, " Hallstatt " and " La

---

[1] Alphabetic writing appears already among the marvels of Ras esh-Shamra (North Syria) at least as early as the middle of the second millennium B.C.

Tène ". These (altogether unsatisfactory) labels are borrowed from the names of two places, one of them a small town in the Austrian Alps, the other the site of a military settlement, of about the third century B.C., on the lake of Neuchâtel in Switzerland. They have been chosen for the merely accidental reason that in those places representative handiworks of the two divisions indicated were first discovered ; and they are open to the objection, which affects all such territorial designations, that they suggest the identification of a chance place of provenance with the place of ultimate origin. But to discuss far-reaching questions of nomenclature, and to formulate or suggest any alternative scheme, would not be appropriate in the limited field of our present study.

The Hallstatt period is regarded as extending from the first appearance of the use of iron in Europe—say from about 1100 B.C.— to about 500 B.C. Its culture was essentially South European : its remains are concentrated in Austria, Italy, Spain, and the Balkan Peninsula, and their types display numerous local or provincial variations, which have no special bearing on our present study.[1] In its earliest stages, it is little more than a later phase of the culture of the Bronze Age, distinguished chiefly by the gradual supersession of bronze by iron ; though other elements, such as changes in burial ritual, attract our attention as we study its relics more closely. As for Europe north of the Alps, the introductory chapters of the Hallstatt history scarcely touch it at all : the populations there dwelling were still bronze-users, and seem to have had little or no conception of the revolution taking place on the other side of the mountain barrier.

Still, the barrier was not impassable ; here and there what, for the convenience of the moment, we may call " Hallstattism " seeped through. Travellers and traders could carry with them rumours of novelties ; could sometimes corroborate their tales with confirmatory object-lessons, in the shape of swords, embroideries, or ornaments. Even in the Bronze Age, Spanish tin and Baltic amber were in demand among the Mediterranean grandees, whose own countries did not yield those commodities in any satisfying measure : to remedy their deficiencies, trading caravans had already established commerce-routes and market-centres—where news, as well as merchandise, could be exchanged. Bronze swords and bracelets of Hallstatt type have been found in Ireland ; pottery of Hallstatt type has been found in Wiltshire ; and, in Ireland, on a lacustrine site at Knockalappa (Clare), and in a cave at Ballintoy (Antrim)—to these we shall return later, reminding ourselves in the meanwhile of the principle that exotic pottery indicates an immigration of exotic potters, rather than

[1] The reader will find a very full and richly illustrated account of them in M. Hoernes' " Die Hallstattperiode " (*Archiv für Anthropologie* 31 [1905] : 233).

an importation of their handiworks.   For the present, these discoveries are isolated ; though—as in the analogous case of the Beaker
Folk—they may presage unexpected developments in the future
which will stultify the confident assurance of sixteen years ago, that
the Hallstatt culture was foreign to Ireland, and that the few objects
which it has intruded on the country, as enumerated by Armstrong
in a paper more particularly referred to below, have no real bearing
on the history of the local civilization.

The La Tène culture (which is considered to have come into
being about 500 B.C., and to have continued until about A.D. 100,
when the absorption of most of Europe into the Roman Empire had
reached its climax) grafted on to the uninspired monotony of Hallstatt
art a freshness born of impulses radiating from the Near East, from
Athens, and from Etruria.   Pleasing and fanciful decorative patterns,
half floral, half geometrical, came into being, always perfectly recognizable though, like their Hallstatt predecessors, with some local
variations.

When, how, to what extent, in what guise, did this later phase of
the Iron Age come to Ireland ?   On these questions there is at
present a fog almost as heavy as that which shrouds the origin of
Iron in Europe itself.   I cannot see any reasonable answer alternative
to that which I have put forward elsewhere.   It came partly by
infiltration ; partly by direct transference, in the hands of a *small*
band of foreign invaders or groups of invaders.[1]   These must have
been people of Northern (Teutonic or Scandinavian) blood : the
tall stature and the yellow hair, as well as the long narrow skulls which
characterize the few individuals whose remains have been exhumed
and examined, or whose personal descriptions are recorded in the
early literature, testify to that.[2]   They must have been chiefly, if
not exclusively, *men :* settling in the country, they took to themselves
wives of the native women, so that, while bequeathing their racial
characteristics to their descendants, they did not disturb the linguistic
conditions which the Beaker invaders had established.   In this respect,
the new invasion differed essentially from the Beaker Immigration :
though the Beaker men helped themselves freely to the native aboriginal women, they introduced a sufficient number of wives of their
own kin to bring up children speaking the imported language, and

[1] The preliminary results of the Ethnological survey of Northern Ireland
(under the auspices of Queen's University, Belfast) are in remarkable accord with
this conclusion.   See J. M. Mogey, " The People of Northern Ireland ", *Belfast*
(1938-9), p. 14, especially p. 17.

[2] Although the evidence appears to be more ambiguous than we should like,
the results of a very thorough scientific examination of the great collection of
bones unearthed at Gallen Priory (Offaly) is not adverse to this view of the
case.   See W. W. Howells, " The Early Christian Irish : the skeletons at Gallen
Priory " (PRIA 46 [1941] : 103 ff., especially p. 215).   But the collection shows
nothing so clearly as the inextricable ethnological mixture of the population at the
time of these interments.

so to establish it in the country. To these immigrants we can reasonably ascribe the introduction of the *gouge* and the *sunflower pin* (Fig. 32) which now appear in Ireland suddenly without any antecedents, and to which Mahr and others assign a Scandinavian origin.[1] It is highly probable that more than one type of bronze artifact, automatically classified as of the Bronze Age by reason of its metal, will ultimately have to be relegated to the Iron Age. This, however, hardly matters : for in Ireland the bronze-iron overlap is of such long duration, and the process of transition is so gradual, that the present chapter is as much a postlude to the Epimegalithic as a prelude to the Iron Age.

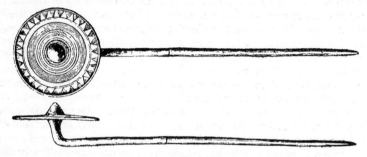

FIG. 32.—A "Sunflower" Pin.

THE HALLSTATT CULTURE IN IRELAND

The first serious attempt at collecting the material available for a study of the Iron Age in Ireland was made by E. C. R. Armstrong, who had contemplated the publication of a book on the subject, to continue his predecessor Coffey's work on the Bronze Age. He died, however, before he could give a final revision to his notes on the La Tène relics, though these were set up in proof during his lifetime ;[2] and he left the Hallstatt section of his work in an incomplete manuscript form.[3] A year before, he had published a brief " Note on the Hallstatt Period in Ireland ";[4] and for the present, while

---

[1] PPS 3 : 381. " A Scandinavian origin " is here to be understood as indicating the source from which these objects reached Ireland : no opinion is expressed as to the *ultimate* origin and previous history of the types. The sunflower pin is not uncommon in Ireland ; another specimen is figured in *Galway* 12 [1922-3] : 44. On the other hand, the Hallstatt " swans'-neck " pin is here rare ; there is a specimen recorded in Galway 11 [1920-1] : 76. As an instructive " group ", illustrating the sentence following in the text above, reference should be made to a hoard of implements found at Bansha (Tipperary) consisting of a gouge, two chisels, a hatchet-head, and a sickle, all socketed (*Waterford* 10 [1907] : 11, where a good photograph will be found).

[2] " The La Tène Period in Ireland " : JRSAI 53 [1923] : 1.

[3] " The Early Iron Age or Hallstatt Period in Ireland " : JRSAI 54[1924] : 1, 109.   [4] *The Antiquaries' Journal* 2 [1922] : 204.

we await a fuller monograph which, I understand, is ready,[1] and which will certainly introduce revolutionary ideas into our knowledge of the subject, we must be content with Armstrong's essays as the chief foundation for a study of Irish Hallstatt relics.

Armstrong's first list of Hallstatt objects (published in *The Antiquaries' Journal*) was as follows : About twenty-four bronze swords : one iron sword : seven winged scabbard-chapes : [2] seven bucket-shaped cauldrons : between fifteen and twenty riveted vessels of bronze, and one of iron : a fragment of a gold cup : a band, and some ribbons, of gold : two flesh-hooks : two shields.[3] As doubtful he mentions nine horse-bit cheek-pieces, and two iron spear-heads ; still more doubtful, two bracelets and four brooches. He also enumerates the following classes of Hallstatt objects of which Ireland had (at the time) yielded no specimen—razors, cordoned buckets, horseshoe-handled swords, swan-neck pins, and a variety of bracelets, brooches, and pendants, such as the cemetery at Hallstatt itself contained ; as well as glazed and coloured pottery. It is evident that the objects in the above list of "finds" are of just such types as would be most likely to pass from one country to another by the agency of traders or of travellers. We may take it as a basis, expanding it with the aid of Armstrong's later (posthumous) publication, and with reference to a few subsequent discoveries.

Bronze Swords. The Hallstatt bronze sword resembles super-ficially the leaf-shaped swords of the end of the Bronze Age, but is distinguished from them by the absence of a sharp mid-rib—a gentle convexity takes its place ; and by the end of the tongue to which the hafting plates are attached, which in the Bronze Age is either triangular or fashioned like a fish-tail, but in the Hallstatt sword is in the form of a half hexagon or of a **Y** (Fig. 33 *a*). In the extant examples, the hafting plates, which were of wood or of bone, have perished. The rivets which secured them remain in some cases : a number of these have cup-shaped heads, intended, it is supposed, to receive an ornamental knob of enamel.[4]

[1] By Dr. J. Raftery. There are foretastes of it in his essay " Zur Zeitbestim-mung der irischen Eisenzeit " (*Marburger Studien* 1938) : in paragraphs con-tributed to Mahr's essay, already quoted (PPS 3 : 409) : in " A Suggested Chrono-logy for the Irish Iron Age " (*Féilsgríbinn Eoin Mhic Néill*, p. 272) : and in a paper on " A Decorated Bronze Disc from the River Bann " (*Ulster* III 3 [1940] : 27). These reveal the new orientation in which the whole subject will be studied, and to them we refer the reader. Obviously the ordinary conventions of scientific etiquette forbid us to forestall the completed study to which we are looking forward, by presenting even an abstract of these preliminary contributions : we must restrict ourselves to these references, which no serious student will neglect.

[2] This term is used here in preference to the less accurate " sword-chapes ", used by Armstrong himself.

[3] These are the Annadale and Clonbrin shields, which have been discussed already (*ante*, p. 206).

[4] None of the Irish examples preserve this enamel, but Armstrong quotes information which he received from Mr. Parker Brewis regarding an example in Paris (JRSAI 54 : 119).

Certain swords appear to be of an intermediate form, combining the convex blade with the fish-tail tang. Two such swords, found,

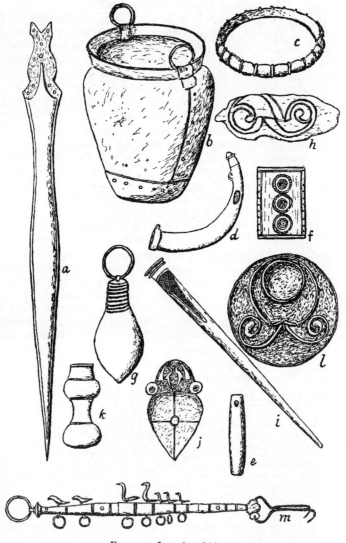

Fig. 33.—Iron-Age Objects.

in association with riveted socketed spear-heads, at Knockadoo (Sligo), and three from Latteragh (Tipperary) were described and

PLATE X

THE MONATAGGART STONE

THE MONUMENT OF THE POET LUGUTTOS

figured by Armstrong.[1] Swords with handles having ∪-shaped
" horns ", so frequent in the Hallstatt civilization of Southern
Europe, are still, as in Armstrong's time, unknown in the country.

It was suggested (in the first edition) that four or five bronze swords
" leaf-shaped, and measuring 12 to 18 inches in length, found when deepening the river Nore at Shanagoonagh Bridge, in association with a conical
iron helmet ",[2] by reason of that association, might have been Hallstatt
blades. But a river-ford may contain an accumulation of relics of many
ages, so that the association has no demonstrable significance : the objects
themselves are apparently lost, and their comparative shortness is unfavourable to the suggestion, which may without loss be withdrawn.

The Iron Sword. This object, first identified and described by
Coffey,[3] still remains without a companion. It was dredged out of
the Shannon above Athlone (Westmeath) in 1847, and is in the
R.I.A. collection. It is a mere fragment, 18½ inches in length,
so badly corroded that close inspection is needed to determine its
character. Only the stump of the tang, with one rivet hole, remains,
along with a very small portion of the edge. The chief discriminating
feature is a ridge—not a *rib*—running axially along the blade.

Scabbard-chapes. These are the metal " shoes " or "ferrules ",
stitched or riveted on to the lower ends of wooden or leather sword-
scabbards, to preserve them, and the tip of the enclosed sword, from
injury. They are of two kinds, distinguished by the absence or
presence of knobbed horns projecting laterally from the upper
angles—the former type assigned by Montelius to his fourth, the
second to his fifth period of the Bronze Age. Both types are found
in Ireland, but as a whole, objects of this class are here not very
common.

Cauldrons are made of plates of bronze, riveted together ; and
are in two forms—bucket-shaped (Fig. 33 *b*) ; or globular—a rather
flattened spheroid. The one iron cauldron in the list, from Drumlane
(Cavan), is of this globular form, but owing to its more intractable
material its workmanship is naturally less neat than in the bronze
vessels.[4] Two handles are provided for these vessels in the shape
of free rings, secured by loops attached to the rim : the handles in
the Drumlane cauldron are fashioned with a rope-like twist, and are
no doubt an imitation of loops of rope.

The bucket form appears to be of North Italian origin, but it
penetrated to the remotest regions of Europe, and is found in Denmark
as well as in Ireland. There is some evidence that vessels of this
kind were used on occasion as media for commercial barter : a

[1] PRIA 36 [1922] : 142. See further, *Antiquaries' Journal* 18 [1938] : 185.
[2] JRSAI 1 [1849] : 30.   [3] PRIA 26 [1906] : 42.
[4] Figured JRSAI 54 [1924] : 113. See also *idem* 17 [1885] : 149. On the
subject generally, see Mr. E. T. Leeds' monograph, based on a specimen from
Oxfordshire (*Archæologia* 80 [1930] : 1), and Sir C. Fox's account of a cauldron
from Llyn Fawr (Glamorgan), *Antiquaries' Journal* 19 [1939] : 372 ff.

legend of St. Patrick turns on his having been betrayed by a treacherous host for the bribe of a bronze cauldron : and later in the same document we read of a cauldron, bestowed on the saint as an act of homage.[1] They were highly valued, as is shown by the care with which accidental injuries were patched by riveting metal discs to cover them.[2] Armstrong, in the paper quoted, figures several vessels of the globular type, and many others are recorded : their use cannot have been confined to the Hallstatt period, and probably extended over a wide range of time. As illustrating the technical skill displayed in their manufacture, special mention should be made of one specimen from Urlingford (Kilkenny), made of plates so thin that although it is estimated to hold about twenty gallons, its weight is only six pounds ;[3] and another from Cloonascaragh Bog, near Tuam (Galway), in which the usual everted lip is strengthened with a ring of alder-wood round which the metal has been turned.[4] This, indeed, was probably the usual practice : the peat happens to have preserved the wood in this particular case. The rivets were brought into prominence with conical heads, and were symmetrically disposed —far beyond mere constructional necessity—to produce an ornamental effect. An admirable example from Co. Tyrone, now in the National Museum, illustrates this.[5]

Certain large wooden vessels, apparently made in imitation of these bronze cauldrons, have been described by Mahr—notably a specimen from Altartate (Monaghan) with a debased La Tène ornament engraved on its outer surface.[6]

Joyce[7] has quoted examples of the attribution of magical virtues to such cauldrons—as that they will cook just enough food for the assembled company and no more, and that the man who strikes a flesh-fork into the meat will fish out just that joint which is appropriate to his station in life.[8] At least, these stories illustrate (a) the use of cauldrons as cooking-pots, and (b) the use of boiled as opposed to roasted meat. He likewise quotes references in the Law Tracts to cauldrons that were of a size large enough to hold the carcases of several sheep or hogs, or even of a cow and a hog together. No cauldron known is of such a capacity, even assuming that the animals were dissected into their component joints. This, however, is not

---

[1] Lives of Saints from the Book of Lismore, ed. Whitley Stokes, lines 194 ff., 556 ff.

[2] See PRIA 22 [1900] : 285 for an illustration of a specimen correctly described as " much mended ".

[3] JRSAI 3 [1854] : 131.   [4] Galway 11 [1920-1] : 72.

[5] Illustrated Ancient Ireland, p. 84. Reference may be made to other examples from Cavan (JRSAI 17 [1885] : 148), Antrim (ib. 13 [1874] : 20), Armagh (ib. 27 [1897] : 437), Down (Ulster I 5 [1857] : 82), Longford (JRSAI 29 [1899] : 256). See also Ulster II 14 [1908] : 21, where some peculiar vessels are figured.

[6] PRIA 42 [1934] : 11 ; Ancient Ireland, p. 86.

[7] A Social History of Ancient Ireland 2 : 125.

[8] On the apportionment of joints among guests according to rank, see my Tara, pp. 62 ff.

surprising, for the only way in which so large a vessel could be preserved would be by burying it : if it remained above ground and became superannuated by ordinary "wear and tear", it would inevitably be melted down for its metal.

The Whigsborough hoard, the most remarkable collection of bronze objects as yet found in Ireland, described below (p. 221), was deposited in a vessel of the globular kind.

Gold Objects. Two *gold vessels* of Hallstatt type have been found in Ireland. One of these, discovered in 1692 on the Devil's-bit Mountain (Tipperary), was for long preserved by the Comerford family and, turned upside-down, was supposed to be an "old Irish crown". It was taken to France in the eighteenth century, and has never been heard of since ; probably it has long ago found its way to the crucible, the fate to which all ancient gold ornaments are liable.[1] Wilde, in a footnote, almost timidly pointed out analogies with Scandinavian objects which tended to suggest that the object was not a crown but a bowl ; and all modern writers have adopted this interpretation.[2] Kossinna, and, following him, Armstrong, considered that it was of Germanic, not native Irish, workmanship, on the ground of its stylistic analogy, in form and in decoration, with certain objects that formed part of the gold hoard found at Messingwerk. In this he was so far justified, that on the theory here expounded it was made by a Germanic craftsman established in Ireland with this new immigration—like the Gleninsheen gorget —not a foreign object imported from abroad. Of the other gold vessel only the bottom survives, which is now in the Royal Irish Academy's collection.[3] Its provenance is unknown ; like the Comerford bowl, it has all the appearance of being of North Germanic type, and can hardly be considered as being an "aboriginal" native product.

The *gold bands* mentioned in Armstrong's list, which are also of unknown provenance, have nothing distinctive about them, and may be of almost any date. They are three in number ; one of them is decorated with small *repoussé* dots along the margin. More important is a broader band, found on Lambay (Dublin), and

---

[1] See, for the only available record of the appearance of this object, the illustration in Wilde's *Catalogue of Gold Objects*, p. 8, copied from Dermot O'Connor's translation of Keating's *History of Ireland* (1723). A rather different representation has been frequently reproduced, and has indeed become traditional ; a good print of it will be found in G. Kossinna, " Der germanische Goldreichtum in der Bronzezeit ", *Mannusbibliothek* no. 12 (1913], p. 50. Bremer (*Die Stellung Irlands*, p. 10) very reasonably considers that it is too uncertain to be of any scientific value.

[2] If we except the artists of *Punch*, who, during the Repeal agitation, were wont to adorn their caricatures of Daniel O'Connell with a parody of this " crown ", anachronistically decorated with shamrocks.

[3] Wilde and Kossinna, *opp. cit.* ; Armstrong, *Gold Catalogue*, p. 40. Also illustrated JRSAI 54 : 116.

attributed to the Hallstatt civilization by Armstrong.[1] In this identification he was influenced by an analogy which he traced between its *repoussé* decoration, and that of the gold and bronze belts found in the cemetery of Hallstatt.[2] But the analogy is not close, and there is every probability that the object is to be assigned to a later period. Bremer pointed out to me that the decoration bears a much greater resemblance to that of the well-known La Tène shield from Witham, now in the British Museum ; and this comparison has been made yet more reasonable by the subsequent discovery of important La Tène objects on the same island.

" Flesh-hooks " (so-called). Certain objects have been described as flesh-hooks ; but I question this identification. The most noteworthy of these was found in Dunaverney Bog, near Ballymoney (Antrim) and is now in the British Museum (Fig. 33 *m*).[3] To me, it appears to be more probably a steelyard.[4] It is a tube of bronze, with a pivoted double hook at one end and a fixed ring at the other : the total length of the object is 1 foot $11\frac{1}{4}$ inches. Two small perforations run through the rod from side to side, about one-third of the length from each end ; into either of these a pin could be inserted, upon which to balance the rod. When opened, the rod was found to contain what looked like fragments of a spring. Seven suspension-rings hang from the under surface of the rod, between the terminal ring and the remoter pivot-hole. These rings are attached to pins, which run vertically through the rod, and terminate upward in figures of birds. There are, first, three small swan figures ; then two larger swan figures, with a family resemblance to the swans which decorate various metal objects from Hallstatt— numerous illustrations will be found in the plates of Von Sacken's monograph, quoted above ; and then come two other birds, not unlike thrushes. Movable weights could be suspended from the rings in using the object as a steelyard, and the birds by their relative size or position might afford an expression of weight quantitatively interpretable : but I cannot see of what possible use the rings and birds could be, if the object were merely a flesh-hook. The other specimen, found at Largy (Tyrone) is similar, but it lacks the suspension-rings and the birds.[5]

---

[1] Armstrong, *Gold Catalogue*, p. 42 ; JRSAI 54 : 123. (Incidentally we may note that the Norse name, now locally spelt " Lambay ", means " Lamb Island ", so that the expression " Lambay Island ", which we see so frequently, is a pleonasm).

[2] Von Sacken, *Das Grabfeld von Hallstatt* (Vienna 1868), plates ix-xi.

[3] British Museum *Bronze Age Guide*, second edition, p. 104. See also *Dublin Penny Journal*, 6 April 1833, p. 324 ; JRSAI 3 [1854] : 64, 65.

[4] After this interpretation of the object had occurred to me, I suggested it to Mr. Armstrong, and he quoted it as mine. But I afterwards found that I had been anticipated so long ago as 1833, by a writer signing himself T.A. (*Dublin Penny Journal*, 22 June 1833, p. 416).

[5] It should be noted that a small bronze figure of a bird, found near Christ-church Cathedral (Dublin), has no relevance to these objects. It is clearly the bow of a zoomorphic brooch, with a vague similarity to certain Hallstatt types. (See JRSAI 21 [1891] : 483).

In connexion with these supposed "flesh-hooks"—and admittedly that such appliances, whatever their form, were in use in association with the cooking-cauldrons is *a priori* probable, and seems to be indicated by the traditions quoted above from Joyce—passing reference should be made to a *harpago*, certainly Etruscan in origin, described by a Mr. George Stephenson.[1] He tells us that he bought it in the year 1845, from a travelling pedlar, who had obtained it from a woman, said to have found it in a streamlet near Saintfield (Down). The history of this object is thus ill authenticated; Armstrong, after investigating the available evidence, could not satisfy himself that it was genuinely an *ancient* importation into the country. It cannot be anything more than what is sometimes picturesquely called a "wanderer"—an object of foreign provenance, having no bearing upon local anthropology, and possessing only the special interest of being the sole record of an irrecoverable train of historical but dateless events, which transferred it from its distant homeland to its resting-place—here, specifically, the bed of an Irish streamlet. Perhaps it was carried home as a curiosity by an eighteenth-century scion of some wealthy house, who had completed his education with the then orthodox "grand tour". It is now in the Royal Irish Academy's collection.

Bracelets. Armstrong elsewhere described two bracelets from Antrim: they are of bronze, and show the bead-like treatment characteristic of bracelets and pins from Hallstatt (Fig. 33 *c*).[2] Bremer figured and described a "manchette" bracelet acquired by the Royal Irish Academy at the sale of the Knowles collection.[3] It is said to have come from Castledawson (Londonderry), but doubtless was ultimately a foreign importation, probably from Central Europe, not a native product. The same may be said of a heavy bronze bracelet of a similar type from Passage West (Cork), decorated on its convex outer surface with punched groups of concentric circles and dotted lines.[4]

The Whigsborough Hoard

This deposit was found in a site close to Loch Cowra, north of Birr (Offaly) some time about the year 1825. There are obscurities about the circumstances of the find, for the peasants, from whom the chief objects were obtained, pledged purchasers to secrecy during their lifetime; so that only vague notices of individual specimens, published in the *Dublin Penny Journal*, were at first allowed to get into print.[5]

The first account of any value was presented to the Royal Irish Academy in November 1848[6] by Rev. Dr. Robinson, who says that the find was made sixteen years before (which would be 1832) in the townland called Doorosheath, near Whigsborough: a small triangular area of land, indicated near the middle of sheet 30 of the 6-inch Ordnance map of Offaly. But in December 1849, T. L. Cooke, of Birr, announced that " having a desire to

---

[1] *Ulster* I 4 [1856] : 96.   [2] JRSAI 41 [1911] : 58 ; 54 [1924] : 124.
[3] JRSAI 56 [1926] : 58.   [4] *Cork* 33 [1928] : 39.
[5] " B " and P[etrie], " Ancient Irish bells, or crotals ", *Dublin Penny Journal*, 18 May 1833, p. 376 ; P[etrie], " Ancient Irish trumpets ", *ibid.*, 27 July 1833, p. 27.
[6] PRIA 4 [1848] : 237.

preserve the antiquities of the country " he did not rest until he " became possessed of several of the articles found ".[1] He there reveals himself as the author of the note signed " B " in the *Dublin Penny Journal*, quoted in a preceding footnote ; in which the discovery is said to have been made " a few years " before ; though he admits in his second paper that he cannot find any memorandum to fix the exact time. He uses this discrepancy of date to weaken the authority of Robinson's informant, and adds that so far from any pledge of secrecy being involved, he was frequently in touch with the persons concerned in the transaction, one of whom, then deceased, he names, but not the others, who were still living when he wrote. He contradicts Robinson's informant who told him that they were found on Dowris-heath (so he spells it), and says that the " site was on part of the extensive townland of Dowris ". But in all Ireland there is no " townland of Dowris " indicated on the Ordnance map. There are several called " Dooros ", and one called " Dooross " ; but except Robinson's " Dooros-heath " (thus spelt, with the hyphen inserted) none of these is in Offaly ;[2] so that we may fairly accuse Mr. Cooke here of picking holes with a blunt bodkin— a favourite amusement of Irish critics. Coming to details, he tells us that the find was made by men trenching potatoes on that part of Whigsborough known as Derreens, between Whigsborough paddock and " Lough Cowr ". This would be to the *north-west* of Whigsborough ; but the name Derreens does not appear on the Ordnance map. Dooros-heath is *south-west* of Whigsborough. The spelling " Dowris " seems to have been an invention of Cooke's,[3] and though it has unfortunately obtained some currency in Archæological literature, it is best forgotten ; it would be better to call the find the " Doorosheath " or, perhaps, to keep the balance true between rival authorities, the " Whigsborough " find, in the lamentable want of definite information.

The hoard contained more than 200 items, which were dispersed among several collectors. A few of them came into the possession of the Royal Irish Academy. Lord Rosse obtained others, which are enumerated in Robinson's paper : and Cooke acquired a large number, of which he prints an unsatisfactory list. He admits having given away some of the specimens to casual friends, and as these pieces are no longer traceable, a statistical reconstruction of the hoard is now impossible.[4] What remained in his hands passed afterwards

---

[1] PRIA 4 [1849] : 423.

[2] The name, however spelt, is an Anglicized form of *dubh-ros*, " black copse ".

[3] Cooke (admitting his claim to be the " B " of the *Penny Journal*) has, unconsciously, handed to us a test by which to appraise his own scholastic attainments. In connexion with the " rattles " in the collection, he quotes some nonsense from Ledwich about " crotals " and " crotalins " being " bardic instruments ". The latter, from Ledwich's description, are obviously latchet brooches, a form of dress-fastening belonging to a period later than the time-limits to which this book is confined ; the former are mediæval or modern harness-bells. For " crotal ", Ledwich cites a Latin passage from " Joh. Sarisber "—clearly John of Salisbury, in a quotation borrowed unintelligently from somewhere else at second-hand (the omission of the full stop of abbreviation demonstrates that) ; and Cooke, in an act of faith worthy of a better cause, accepts the mythical Mr. Sarisber without a qualm.

[4] H. S. Crawford has done his best to supply this, JRSAI 54 [1924] : 14 ; and Armstrong (PRIA 36 [1922] : 134) has collected, in a richly illustrated paper, all the information about the find available. See also British Museum *Bronze Age Guide*, plate ii.

to the British Museum (so much for his desire to " preserve the antiquities of the country " !).   There were no iron objects in the collection ; but there were four cauldrons or buckets, of Hallstatt type, and as some of the objects were of the latest bronze-age types, we may safely date the hoard to the bronze-iron transition.   It was doubtless the stock-in-hand of an individual craftsman, as we may infer from a peculiarity in the composition of the alloy of which all the objects are made—the presence of lead in a notable proportion. Analysis [1] of one of the trumpets in the collection yielded the following results :—

Copper	.	79·34 per cent.
Tin	.	10·87 ,, ,,
Lead	.	9·11 ,, ,,
Impurities	.	·68 ,, ,,
		100·00

Disregarding the impurities, the metal thus shows a rough proportion of 89 parts of copper *plus* lead to 11 parts of tin.   This is not far from the orthodox proportion for gun-metal bronze, as used in the best implements (9 parts copper to 1 part tin), so that the manufacturer, by this adulteration, has saved on his copper rather than on his tin—although it is in the latter material we should have expected him to be economical.   The bronze of the hoard has a peculiar golden lustre, it is supposed owing to this peculiarity of its composition ; and it has received on that account the special name " Dowris bronze ".

The hoard, as reconstructed by Crawford, contained the following 219 objects :—

Rattles [2]	.	48	Socketed knives	.	4
Spear-heads	.	44	Cauldrons	.	4
Hatchet-heads [1]	.	43	Punches	.	3
Trumpets	.	24	Chapes	.	3
Gouges	.	7	Spear-butts	.	3
Fragments	.	7	Buttons	.	3
Sandstone rubbers	.	6	Bronze cakes	.	2
Swords	.	5	Dagger	.	1
Razors	.	5	Hammer-head	.	1
Knives	.	4	Halberd	.	1

and we may give a few words of description of some of these to supplement Armstrong's list of Hallstatt objects.   (It is a pity that we are not allowed to know more about an ostensibly similar find of " several specimens of bronze articles, such as celts, rings, and a gouge " . . . and also a portion of an instrument [not more specifically defined] " apparently of an alloy resembling speculum metal " found in an earthenware urn at Kilmuckridge (Wexford).

[1] See PRIA 4 : 463 ff.
[2] By Crawford called " crotals " and " axe-heads " respectively.

There were no associated bones, so that this also may have been a manufacturer's hoard.) [1]

Rattles.   It has become a convention to apply the name " crotals " to these, certainly the most remarkable, as they were the most numerous, objects in the hoard (Fig. 33 *g*).   *Crothals* would be more nearly accurate : an Irish word (with an English plural suffix) derived from the Latin *crotalum*, "a rattle, castanet ".   There is nothing to justify the assumption that the Whigsborough coppersmith knew enough Latin to have affixed such a label, or anything like it, to this department of his handiworks : and as we have the English word " rattle " at our service, and not elsewhere needed in Irish Archæology, there is no valid reason for pre-judging the meaning of a misspelt Irish loan-word in order to add one more item to the already too extensive vocabulary of spurious technical terminology.

These rattles are hollow balls of the peculiar " Dowris " metal : and their like has never been found anywhere, except in this hoard. They are pear-shaped, but cut off flat at the upper end, where there is a movable suspension-ring playing in a loop ; beneath this, the surface is decorated, usually with a horizontal ribbing.   One specimen in the group is more globular than the rest, and is not thus adorned. There is no other enrichment on the surface of these objects, which are completely closed except for a longitudinal slot cut through the wall of some of them.   There is something hard and loose inside, which causes the instrument, when shaken, to emit a faint tinkling sound ; Cooke opened one of those in his possession, and found it to contain a small piece of metal.   These objects are too large, and use up too much valuable bronze, to be mere toys ; they are too carefully made, and emit too feeble a sound, to be cattle-bells (I doubt if the normal motions of wandering cattle would make them sound at all) ; and they must surely have been made to serve some special purpose *collectively*, for if they had been intended to be used individually we might have expected to find them in single specimens, widely distributed.   That this is not the case suggests that the whole series was intended to form one indivisible group : I can offer no explanation better than the guess put forth in the first edition,[2] that they were meant to be hung upon a wooden frame in some tonal sequence, to form a sort of *Glockenspiel*, sounded by being sharply tapped with a rod or rods.[3]   This would assume a musical relationship between the sounds which they severally emit ; but it is now impossible to prove its existence, as the collection has been broken up and dispersed.   Even were it not so, it would be difficult to justify the assumption, unless means were discoverable for tuning

[1] PRIA 4 [1850] : 369.
[2] But anticipated by Armstrong, *loc. cit.* p. 141.
[3] Not *shaken*—the rattle, as such, is too feeble for any effective musical purpose. Indeed, it is not obvious why the rattling nodule is introduced at all.

PLATE XI

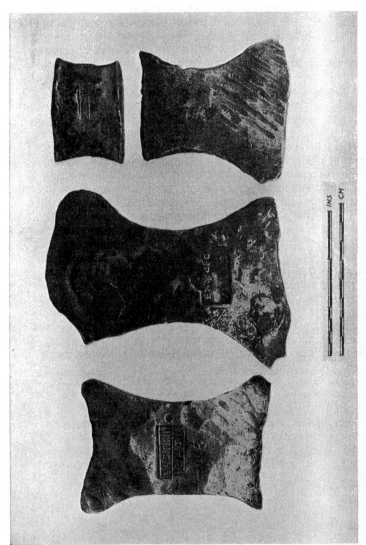

SILVER INGOTS FROM FOYNES

each " rattle " to fit it for its destined place in the scale ; and I admit my inability to see how this could have been done, unless the slot cut in the side of some of them had such a purpose in view.

Spear-heads. The Whigsborough spear-heads have plain leaf-shaped blades, and were secured to their shafts with rivets, holes for which are provided through the socketed stem. Only one of them appears to have possessed side loops ; not one has ornamental openings in the blade.[1] The *hatchet-heads* are all socketed, and show some variety of detail in their shape—in length of body, outline of socket-mouth, width and degree of expansion of cutting-edge, and so forth ; but not sufficient to establish any individual typology within the group.

Trumpets. These call for longer notice (Fig. 33 *d*). Polybius (II 29) and Poseidonius (as quoted by Diodorus Siculus V 30) both tell us of the din made in battles by the Gallic war-trumpets : and the statue of the *Dying Gaul* in the Capitoline Museum shows a trumpet, closely resembling the Whigsborough specimens, lying beside the stricken warrior. Such trumpets have nowhere been found so frequently as in Ireland ; and it is reasonable to conclude (as some claim for the gold lunulæ, of which the same is true) that they were an Irish invention, and that from Ireland they spread to the Continent.[2] Their prototype was clearly a cow's horn ; which likewise served, in later times, as a model for one type of drinking vessel. The horn, when used for either purpose, was protected from splitting with a metal collar encircling the open end, and secured in position by rivets ; representations of which remain, as otiose ornaments, on some of the bronze trumpets. The embouchure of the trumpet is either a round opening at the narrow end ; or (more frequently) an oval opening, adapted to the shape of the pouted lips, near the narrow end, in the concave side of the tube. In this form, care is taken to make the edge of the opening blunt and smooth (so as to avoid injuring the mouth of the trumpeter), and the narrow end is stopped ; the decorative treatment of the end being suggestive of a plug with moulded ornament turned upon it, probably copying an actual wooden plug which stopped the end of the ancestral cow-horn. This, incidentally, points to the use of some kind of turning-lathe by the carpenters who supplied the plug.

Most of the extant trumpets were moulded by the *cire perdue* process. A clay model was made of the interior of the trumpet, and was then covered with a layer of wax. Metal pins were driven at intervals through the wax into the clay core ; an outer covering of clay was spread over the wax surface, and the whole was subjected

---

[1] At least among the specimens figured by Armstrong. There is one represented on the plate, referred to above, in the British Museum *Guide*.

[2] See R. Day, " Irish Bronze War Trumpets ", JRSAI 13 [1875] : 422, where several grouped finds are enumerated.

to heat. This melted out the wax, and baked and thus hardened the clay : the pins kept the clay core and the outer covering in their proper relative positions after the wax had flowed away. Molten bronze was then poured into the space which the wax had occupied, and automatically assumed the exact form that had been given to the wax. When the bronze had cooled and hardened, the clay moulds, inside and out, were broken and the supporting pins were filed down flush with the surface of the metal. The supporting pins, embedded in the metal of the trumpet, have a smaller proportion of tin in their composition than the body of the trumpet itself ; indicating a knowledge of the fact that the larger the proportion of tin in the alloy, the lower is the temperature necessary for melting it : had the pins been quantitatively of the same composition as the bronze of the trumpet, they would have been melted by contact with the hot molten bronze. These facts, determined first for a series of trumpets found in Pomerania,[1] were confirmed by Armstrong by an examination of Irish specimens.

In other places besides Whigsborough, trumpets have been found in groups, especially in Ireland : as a rule, only single specimens have been found in Continental sites. Most likely, as at Whigsborough, these groups are the stock-in-trade of a manufacturer ; it is on the whole less probable that they are the store of some establishment, religious, military, or what not, that maintained a corps of trumpeters.[2]

Other types of trumpets may be mentioned here, though some of them are perhaps later in date. They are sometimes made in two sections, fitting into one another, like clarinets and other modern instruments, which are jointed for convenience of tuning or of carriage.[3] A greater length of tube, giving a deeper fundamental note, is thus obtained.

Another technique of manufacture is illustrated by a specimen in the Royal Irish Academy's collection ; in which the tube is not cast in a piece, but is formed of a sheet of metal bent round a core, like the wooden mandrill upon which organ-builders model their pipes. In the specimen referred to, when the tube had been fashioned,

---

[1] H. Schmidt, " Die Luren von Daberkow " : *Prähistorische Zeitschrift* 7 : 94. For illustrations of Irish trumpets see *Dublin Penny Journal*, 27 July 1833, p. 27 ; Robert MacAdam, " Ancient Irish Trumpets " (*Ulster* I 8 [1860] : 99) ; *Reliquary and Illustrated Archæologist* 5 : 116. For a very thorough study of ancient bronze trumpets see Angul Hammerich, " Studier over bronzelurerne i Nationalmuset i Kjøbenhavn ", in the Norse *Aarbøger* 8 [1893] : 141.

[2] A list of such groups is given by Armstrong in PRIA 36 : 141. See also Day (as quoted above) ; Bigger, *Ulster* II 8 [1902] : 11. These lists, however, are now superseded by the exhaustive classified catalogue, with distribution-map, published by Mr. Eoin MacWhite (" Irish Bronze Age Trumpets ", JRSAI 75 [1945] : 85). I may personally feel a little hesitant about the judiciousness of the qualification " Bronze Age ", but that does not in the slightest degree detract from the high value of Mr. MacWhite's admirable and comprehensive study of these most interesting objects.   [3] See a specimen figured PRIA 28 [1910] : 105.

a strip of metal with a row of rivets, points upward, must have been laid on top of the mandrill (itself lying prostrate on the workman's bench). Rivet-holes in the two edges of the trumpet tube must then have been pressed down upon the upturned points of the rivets, and the points hammered down. This is a masterpiece of delicate manipulation.[1]

A tapering tube of willow-wood 6 feet 4 inches long, bound with a ribbon of bronze winding from end to end, was found toward the end of the eighteenth century at Bekan (Mayo) and now is also in the Royal Irish Academy's collection.[2] It may have been a trumpet : this is not certain, but no other satisfactory suggestion has been put forward.

The Ballintoy Caves

Between Ballintoy and Whitepark Bay, on the north coast of Antrim, there is a series of caves in the chalk, in which excavations have been made from time to time, without any especially important results. But in 1933, under the direction of Dr. Wilfred Jackson of Manchester, two caves known as Park Cave and Potter's Cave (the former a local tradition, the latter an artificial name, devised by the excavators themselves for distinction) were carefully cleared. From the reports [3] the following summary has been drawn up :—

At Park Cave : Stratification—

> Surface soil
> Layer of blown sand
> Occupation layer
> Beach pebbles.

The occupation layer, which was of the usual dark colour due to the admixture of ash-dust and decomposed organic matter, contained bones (ox, sheep, pig, and horse) some of them showing marks of manipulation (splitting, sharpening, and wear from polishing) : shells (limpet and peri-winkle) : flints (including a knife, 3½ inches in length) : pottery of the coarse type generally associated with the souterrains, most of it here unattached broken sherds, though the fragments of a cooking pot found in one place could be pieced together. Some of these fragments were outside the cave mouth as it is at present : a shelter-wall seems to have been built partly across this mouth, and there was a natural concentration of the finds in the part of the cave protected thereby. The blown sand and the occupation layer (which had an average depth of about 12 inches) petered out before reaching the inner end of the cave (which is 30 feet in depth from front to back) ; the lowest layer, of beach pebbles, was raised-beach material preceding the cave occupation : it contained a number of flint flakes, some of them showing evidences of workmanship.

The entrance to the Potter's Cave was found to be blocked with an impenetrable breccia of stone and chalk ; the excavation was therefore

---

[1] Described in detail by Sir D. J. Norreys, JRSAI 14 [1877] : 277.
[2] Viscount Dillon and R. Ouseley, " Description of an ancient Irish instrument ", TRIA 4 : 33.
[3] INJ 4 [1933] : 230.

confined to an area outside the actual entrance, but it was well rewarded. Four occupation layers were uncovered, the first a few inches,[1] the fourth about 6 feet, below the present surface. Connected with the topmost of these was found what was reasonably explained as a potter's kiln—a construction consisting of two rows of slabs on edge, 8 feet long, 4 feet broad, partly roofed with chalk slabs, and containing much burnt earth, charcoal, and sherds of pottery. In connexion with the third layer there was a hearth-site, marked out by a ring of stones.[2] Below the fourth occupation-layer were found four additional charcoal layers, descending to 11 feet 3 inches beneath the surface.

The finds made here were substantially similar to those in the Park Cave, but far more rich and important. In the four underlying charcoal layers there were bones of horse, ox, and pig, limpet and other shells, and flint flakes. These all were probably of the Bronze Age, though no metal was actually found. The overlying occupation layers showed a fairly uniform culture extending through them all, though there were signs of an improvement in the manufacture and ornamentation of the pottery in the

Fig. 34.—Types of Early Iron-age Pottery from Ballintoy and Knockahollet (Antrim).

topmost level. The lowest showed ox and pig bones, to which the upper layers added the sheep and (later) the horse. Metal seems to have been absent, except for an iron rivet, which had secured an ornamental plate to a double-toothed comb of the crannog type, found in the second (first important) layer, counting from the top. Pottery was absent in the fourth and scarce in the third layer, but abundant in the two upper layers, that in the topmost being decorated with finger-impressions *on the edges* (not on the sides) and impressed points and scratches. The vessels seem to have been roughly modelled, in coarse ware, with cylindrical walls and flat bases, and, by comparison with pottery of apparently identical type found by

[1] There is a possibility of a misunderstanding in the report on this further work (INJ 5 [1934] : 104), to which attention is called here in no critical spirit, but to try to help the reader over a difficulty which gave a few moments' pause to the present writer. Doubtless it will be smoothed over in the final monograph on this important work, to which we look forward, and which obviously we must not try to anticipate. This upper layer is called OX by the excavators : on p. 104 it is said to have been found " on the removal of some 9 inches of surface soil " : on p. 106, in a trench alongside the first, it was encountered " after the removal of some 4 feet of broken chalk rubble banked against the cliff ". Clearly this rubble was piled up *over* the surface below which the first measurement was taken.

[2] Illustrations of these structures will be found in connexion with the report cited in the preceding footnote, plate 6, facing page 107. See also a section and plan in INJ 6 : 34, 41.

Prof. Gordon Childe in Scottish sites, it has been assigned to the Hallstatt stage of culture [1] (Fig. 34)

Flint knives, bone needles, a tool-handle made of a stag's antler, filled up the measure of the finds hitherto reported, except for one outstanding discovery in the third layer. This was a clay figurine, of which the upper half only had been preserved. What remains is about 4 inches high. The head and neck are in the shape of a cylinder of uniform diameter, with rounded top, the mouth being represented by a horizontal slit, the eyes, apparently also the ears, by the marks of more or less circular prods. In the forehead, above and between the eyes, there is a wider hole, apparently inexplicable except as a steam-vent, to prevent the clay from being cracked by internal pressure when fired. The arms are broken off, and not enough of them remains to suggest a restoration : between them are the breasts, conspicuous and pendent. The figure has close analogies with Neolithic or bronze-age statuettes, which have been found in such Danubian sites as Butmir or Vinĉa.[2] The Ballintoy figure is a belated and artistically degenerate member of the family, but its cultural affinity can hardly be doubted.[3] Its importance has made it seem desirable to give as full a description of its archæological setting as the available space would permit.

Another Ballintoy Cave, called "The Chimney Cave",[4] was found to have four occupation-layers within, one without. Outside the cave the only discovery calling for notice is an iron pot with a wire handle, in shape resembling a paint-pot. Inside the cave the finds in the upper layers corroborated but did not greatly supplement those in the other two caves : the lower layers appear from the nature of the few potsherds found in them to have belonged to the culture of the bronze-age squatters of Whitepark Bay. At the bottom was raised-beach material with flint flakes.

THE LA TÈNE CULTURE IN IRELAND

The Hallstatt culture cannot as yet be said to have ever been more than a late exotic influence in Ireland ; in essence, a mere appendage to the late bronze-age culture. The La Tène culture is, locally, but little better ; in Ireland we find evidences of nothing more important than a back-wash, a mere preface to the subsequent art-developments fostered by ecclesiastical patronage. We can never hope to obtain a satisfactory picture of the course of cultural development in Ireland in the early days of the Iron culture, on account of the scantiness of the material available for study. For an analogous reason we cannot follow as we should wish the early development of Art under Irish Christianity. As there are years at the beginning of the life of every

[1] Miss M. Gaffikin, " Preliminary report on Pottery from Ballintoy Caves, Co. Antrim ", INJ 5 [1934] : 109, with numerous illustrations. Apparently comparable ware comes from a domestic site at Knockahollet (Antrim) : see an account by H. C. Lawlor at p. 171 of the same volume.

[2] See Childe, *The Danube in Prehistory*, numerous references to "figurines" in index : M. M. Vassits, " Die Hauptergebnisse der prähistorischen Ausgrabung in Vinĉa, 1908 " (*Prähistorische Zeitschrift* 2 [1910], especially p. 27 plate 9) ; Radimsky and Hoernes, *Die Neolithische Station von Butmir* (Vienna 1895-8), Part I, plates 2, 3 ; Part II, plates 2, 3, 4. See also Hoernes, *Urgeschichte der Bildenden Kunst in Europa* (ed. Menghin) pp. 284 ff.

[3] For illustrations see *The Antiquaries' Journal* [1934] : 180 ; JRSAI 64 [1934] : 139 ; *Ancient Ireland*, p. 80.

[4] INJ 6 [1935] : 31. For the latest work in these caves see INJ 7 [1936-7] : 107.

individual which he has completely forgotten, so there is a beginning
of the art of that phase, as practised in Ireland, which can be restored by conjecture only. They belong to years which have left
no outstanding monuments, and a singular dearth of artifacts, at
least so far as the published material goes.

This may appear at first sight surprising. On the lawn in front
of Turoe House, near Loughrea (Galway), there stands a block of
granite, oval in horizontal section, with rounded top; it was carried
to its present position early in the nineteenth century from a small
and insignificant earthen enclosure called " Feerwore ".[1] Sculptured
upon it is one of the finest examples of La Tène decorative art in the
world. A little below the middle of the stone is a horizontal belt
of a simple rectilinear ornament, which illustrates by its irregular
setting-out the lack of sympathy with straight lines and designs
founded thereon, characteristic of La Tène artists. This band is
the only weakness in the whole monument. Above it, the surface
of the stone bears an intricate pattern of foliage and geometrical
devices. The studied lack of mechanical symmetry, while maintaining a well-proportioned balance—one of the chief charms of
La Tène work—is nowhere carried out better than in this monument.

A portable object (such as a gold ornament) might have been
made anywhere, and carried into the country; it would then have
only an accidental connexion with the local culture, and could not
reasonably be used as a basis for a claim to a share in the aspect of
Art of which it is an example. But a heavy block of granite, weighing
a ton or more, could hardly have been imported—certainly not in
the La Tène period, when the people of Europe no longer felt the
divine " urge " to transport and manipulate large blocks of stone.
When we find such a work of art as this in Ireland, we must of
necessity assume that it was executed in Ireland, and therefore that
an artist capable of executing it was temporarily or permanently
resident in the country.

Then why does it stand alone? We cannot believe that so
accomplished a craftsman exhausted his resources and his energies,
like Mac Enge, the armourer, of whom we shall hear presently, in

[1] The discovery of the stone is reported by Miss M. Redington, *Galway* 2
[1902] : 18. For a plan of this enclosure, with an indication of the original position
of the stone, see *Galway* 9 : 190. The site was excavated in 1938 under the superintendence of Dr. Raftery, with, on the whole, disappointing results, as he himself
admits (see the very full report, JRSAI 74 [1944] : 23). Still, they were not without suggestiveness. The finds were merely the leavings of a domestic household ;
but a floor of yellow clay had been spread before the enclosure was made, and
renewed when it was enlarged, possibly to provide a ritually purified foundation.
There were interments of two women under or beside the sites of the domestic
buildings, possibly foundation sacrifices. Assuming the stone to have been a
centre of cult, the permanent establishment of a religious functionary to conduct
the rites of that cult and to safeguard the stone from desecration might fairly be
postulated. Dr. Raftery dates the stone to about 300 B.C., and the dwelling to
about 100 B.C.-A.D. 100 ; the discrepancy does not raise a serious difficulty, as the
dwelling might have been added at a late date in the history of the cult.

adorning this one stone.   We cannot believe that he had no rivals
and no imitators.   There are, in fact, two inferior stones of the
same class, one at Castle Strange (Roscommon) the other at Killycluggan (Cavan), evidently of later date : but had the Turoe stone
no contemporary counterparts ?

It must have had : but it is hard to believe that any of them remain
above ground.   They would surely have been discovered long before
this.   Then what has become of them ?

We shall see on a later page that iconoclasm has deprived us of
many monuments once inscribed in the Ogham character.   This was
an alphabet specifically associated with druidry, and when after a
long struggle—to outward appearance uneventful, but none the less
real—Christianity was gaining the upper hand over paganism, many
monuments with this pagan taint upon them were destroyed.   And
so for stones of the Turoe type.   The standing stones of the Megalithic periods—these were no longer of any special account : if they
had had any pagan or otherwise objectionable emblems painted upon
them (as we may reasonably assume to have sometimes been the
case) these would have been already defaced by rains, frosts, and
other atmospheric agencies : and by cutting a cross upon them, the
demons of paganism could be rendered powerless.   But the Oghams
had come down out of a recent and still vividly remembered paganism,
and they had to face the hostility of converts in their first enthusiasm.
Even more was this the case of stones of the Turoe type : these also
speak of a paganism, and moreover a variety of nature-paganism
repugnant to Christian ethics ; though from the standpoint of
Anthropology it is an important field of investigation, for it has had
endless influence on human life and beliefs, in Ireland as everywhere
else ; and we must be prepared to find relics of it anywhere over its
world-wide domination.   Through the decoration of the Turoe
stone we can see clearly the outlines and surface anatomy of an un-
disguised phallus.

The Castle Strange stone, mentioned above, is smaller than
the Turoe stone, and its ornament, though of the same kind, is
inferior in both design and execution.   The stone is of a flattened
globular shape, and the enrichment is merely outlined : in the Turoe
stone variety is gained by sinking the background of the pattern.
I am still inclined to regard the Castle Strange carving as late and
degenerate in comparison with the Turoe monument ; but I would
no longer venture to suggest a distribution of this and the other La
Tène monuments of Ireland among the three periods which modern
criticism has reduced to a system in the Continental and British
areas.   The technical treatment of the Turoe ornament is evidently
suggested by a metal object prepared for decoration in champlevé
enamel, which in any case would hardly be older by more than a
century than the Roman occupation of Britain.

The Killycluggan stone has suffered seriously from iconoclasm in modern times. It appears to have stood above the surface of the ground, and to have had originally the same shape as the Turoe stone ; but it was smashed down to ground level, apparently to get it out of the way, and nothing remains of it but the plain base, which had been buried, and the bottom of the ornament remaining along the fractured edge. The leading feature of the surviving ornament is a number of regular close-coiled spirals ; we seem to be looking forward to the formal geometry of the earliest art in Christian service, as illustrated by the Athlone book-cover or the Reask stone cross, rather than back to the flowing curves of the La Tène optimum.[1] We are certainly entering the transitional period in which we find ourselves with the Mullaghmast stone.[2] This latter relic has all but completely shed the special features of La Tène art, and has assumed the more formal construction of the decorations of the Christian period. The spirals of anthemion-petals still remain, but that is all : the stone cannot claim to be specifically a monument of the full La Tène period.

O'Curry [3] quotes from the MS. classed H 3 17 in the Library of Trinity College, Dublin, a story to the effect that the Ultonians had a law that their warriors should each have silver shields made for them, and that the decorations chased upon each shield should be different from those of all the rest. There is some mistake here about the material of the shields ; the day for an extensive use of silver in Ireland was not yet. It is, however, fully in accordance with what we know from other sources, that each warrior should have a different device upon his shield.[4] Cu-Chulainn, hearing of this edict, ordered a shield with a peculiar device for himself ; but Mac Enge, the armourer, confessed that he had already exhausted his powers of invention upon the patterns of the shields of the other Ultonian braves,[5] and was consequently unable to invent a new pattern. Cu-Chulainn threatened to kill the unfortunate artist— in spite of his being under the protection of the Ultonian king, Conchobur—unless he should succeed in carrying out the order.

---

[1] For illustrations of these monuments see G. Coffey, " Some monuments of the La Tène period recently discovered in Ireland " (PRIA 24 : 257) ; see also JRSAI 53 [1923], plate facing p. 30 ; Coffey, " The carved boulder at Castle Strange ", JRSAI 37 : 346 ; R. A. S. Macalister, " On a stone with La Tène decorations recently discovered in Co. Cavan ", JRSAI 52 [1922] : 113 (Killycluggan).

[2] Coffey in PRIA 24 : 257 as above cited ; *Ancient Ireland*, p. 180.

[3] *Manners and Customs of the Ancient Irish* ii 329. The importance of the story was first indicated by Sir W. Ridgeway, in his paper on " The Date of the first Shaping of the Cuchulain Saga " (*Proceedings* British Academy, vol. ii).

[4] Compare Diodorus Siculus, *Bibliotheca* v 30.

[5] Does this at first sight incomprehensible precedence accorded to the other warriors enshrine a hint that the great Cu-Chulainn was, after all, a foreigner and an interloper ? Evidence to the same effect could be collected from the relevant literature.

While the artist was sitting disconsolate in his hut, a stranger made his appearance, and asked the cause of his trouble. " Good cause have I ", answered the armourer, " for I am to be slain unless I can make a shield for Cu-Chulainn ". " Clear the floor of thy workshop ", said the stranger, "and let it be sprinkled with ash, to the depth of a man's foot ". This was done. Then the stranger produced a " fork ", the name of which was *luath-rindi*, " ash-graver ". One prong of the fork he placed in the ash, and with the other he described the device to be graven on the shield. Then he departed, and the armourer saw him no more ; but he had left behind a pattern such as the armourer, unaided, would have been unable to invent, and thus made it possible for him to satisfy the exacting Cu-Chulainn.

The story belongs to an extensive group of folk-tales which profess to account for the existence of works of art transcending, to outward seeming, mere human capabilities. Possibly it was told originally of some remarkable shield, supposed to have belonged to Cu-Chulainn : such a shield as the splendid example from Battersea, now in the British Museum. Giraldus Cambrensis records an analogous tradition of the origin of the now lost *Gospels of Kildare*, with its wondrous illuminations ; a local legend tells us how a demon gave to the architect the design for Cologne Cathedral in exchange for the artist's soul, and, when outwitted (as he usually is, in stories of this type), vented his wrath by pronouncing the doom that the artist's name should remain for ever unknown, and that he should never see the work completed.[1]

But, however interesting the folk-lore aspect of the tale may be, its essential importance lies elsewhere. It affords us a welcome glimpse into a La Tène artist's studio. Where no cheap paper and india-rubber were available, a bed of fine sand or of ash would be the most economical tablet for the use of a designer, a geometrician, or any other, whose work involved the making and effacing of diagrams, figures, or sketches. The mysterious designer drew out his patterns with a " fork "—which is, being interpreted, a pair of compasses. It is well known as one of the most remarkable features of La Tène designs that free use is made in them of circular curves, drawn in this mechanical way.

Ash was not the only material used for this purpose. In both the pagan and the Christian sections of the Celtic period in Ireland, bones were used for such artistic experiments ; the Royal Irish Academy's collection contains some remarkable specimens. A large number of flat slips of bone, resembling blades of paper-cutters, were found in mid-nineteenth century excavations in one of the carns on the Lochcrew Hills. They have been supposed to be for use as tablets upon which to trace decorative designs (Fig. 33 *h*) : but it may be found that this current theory will have to be revised

[1] F. J. Kieser, *Die Sagen des Rheinlandes* (Mainz, n.d.), p. 257.

as a result of the researches recently inaugurated.[1]   The designs are various, but are all essentially of La Tène type, and many of them consist of compass-drawn curves in various combinations.[2]   With them we may perhaps compare a series of " neatly polished rect-angular laminæ of ivory, or at least resembling ivory "—the alterna-tive is a well-advised piece of caution, though walrus or narwhal ivory is quite possible—found in a fort at Ballymooney near Mullinavat (Kilkenny).   These objects were not inscribed, though some of them had round holes in the middle ; some were oblong, about 1 inch by 2, and some square.[3]   They are no longer forth-coming, but most likely were not so much tablets for designs as inlaying slips for decorating wooden objects.[4]   Such objects, in bone, are a common yield of lake-dwelling sites.[5]

The designs which the armourer was expected to produce were evidently not the infinite variety of birds and beasts, or parts thereof, which formed so large a part of the heraldry of the Middle Ages : they were abstract patterns, permutations and combinations of a limited number of quasi-geometrical motives.   An artist of small capacity would quickly come to an end of his inventive resources : the troubles of the unhappy Mac Enge doubtless afflicted many others of the less expert journeymen of his age.   In the light of this story of the designing of Cu-Chulainn's shield, coupled with the evidence of native workmanship which the Turoe stone affords, we may now turn to a consideration of the scanty La Tène relics which are avail-able, in an enhanced confidence that at least most of them are genuinely native products.

Gold.   When we consider the richness of bronze-age Ireland in gold and the extravagant wealth involved in the descriptions of

---

[1] In any case they could have been used in this way only by more or less incompetent hacks of the Mac Enge type.   As Dr. Raftery has shrewdly pointed out (JRSAI 74 : 44) the impossibility of projecting the ornament of the Turoe stone upon a two-dimensional surface for purposes of illustration shows that the artist of that great work cannot have made a preliminary plan on any sort of cartoon. If he prepared any such, he must have executed it in paint, upon the stone itself.

[2] Conwell, *Tomb of Ollamh Fodhla*, pp. 54 ff.   See also H. S. Crawford, " The engraved bone objects found at Lough Crew ", JRSAI 55 [1925] : 15, with a full bibliography.   They are also illustrated in *Archæologia* 47 ii [1883] : plate facing p. 478.   A large number of these engraved bones, by some not clearly explained accident, disappeared from view and were given up for lost.   By un-merited good fortune, they came to light again, a few weeks before these words were being written, and are now safe in the National Museum : their promised publica-tion will be a welcome addition to our knowledge of the methods of these artists. Meanwhile, Crawford's paper, referred to above, is indispensable.   From the materials there collected it is evident that many of the bone slips were prepared for their own sake, as combs, inlays, etc., not as mere " trial-pieces ".

[3] JRSAI 1 : 385-6.

[4] With the Lochcrew tablets may be compared the fragments of stone found in what appears to have been an art school in the Monastery of Nendrum.   See H. C. Lawlor, *The Monastery of St. Mochaoi at Nendrum*, p. 144.

[5] See Wood-Martin, *Lake-dwellings*, plate xxx, also Figs. on p. 139.   See also the example in Fig. 43 *f*.

dress and equipment in ancient Irish literature, some of which, at least in its embryonic form, comes down to us out of the heart of the La Tène culture, we are inclined to a feeling of surprise that there is so little La Tène gold surviving in the country.   But it is not so surprising after all.   The bronze-age gold had mostly been withdrawn from circulation, so to speak—buried in tomb-deposits or in secret hiding-places, or else lost in bogholes ; and the supplies in the alluvial gravels had for the greater part been exhausted.   What remained above ground, and was extracted from tombs by plunderers, might be melted and remodelled more than once, according to the taste and fancy of successive owners ; especially if, as suggested above, the La Tène art became unpopular by reason of its pagan associations. Ultimately most of it, having passed into monastic hands, by the gift of penitents or of devotees, would once more be re-fashioned, into vessels, instruments, or ornaments intended for Church use ; and the gold in monastic hands received the particular attention of the Scandinavian pirates.   Some of the Scandinavian museums contain gold ornaments of Irish provenance, representing types now completely unknown in Ireland.[1]   What the Scandinavians left no doubt ultimately went to enrich those who gleaned material profit from the dissolution of the monasteries in the sixteenth century.

The Broighter Hoard

A hoard of gold objects brought to knowledge toward the close of the nineteenth century at Broighter, near Limavady (Derry) must first be described.   It contains the following items, all now in the National Museum :—

1. A model of a boat.
2. Its oars, mast and other fittings.
3. Two torques.
4. A bowl.
5. Two plaited wire chains.
6. A collar.

(1) The boat is made of a single sheet of gold, much alloyed with silver ; the plate has been slit and rejoined at the bow and the stern.   Inside, nine thwarts or rowers' benches (the first of them, counting from the bow of the boat, now missing) are riveted at their ends to the sides of the boat.   The central thwart is wider than the others, and has a hole in the middle into which to step the mast. The rowers of two oars are provided for in each bench, for there are rowlocks (represented by twists of gold wire passing through pin-holes in the gunwale of the boat) at *both* ends of each bench.   On the starboard side of the stern of the boat (which, like the bow, is pointed) there is a similar loop, provided for the steering-oar.   The boat measures $7\frac{1}{2}$ inches by 3 inches, and weighs 3 oz. 5 dwt.

(2) The fittings of the boat, which weigh collectively 6 dwt., consist of the following pieces :—

[1] See, for example, *Christian Art in Ancient Ireland*, vol. i, plates 29-32, 34.

(a) Oars, of which there must have been eighteen : of these three are lost.

(b) The steering-oar, distinguished from the rowing-oars by its short handle and long broad blade.

(c) The mast (at first explained as a boat-hook, because by some accident it had been bent at the top). A plain rod of gold wire, resembling a knitting-needle in size and shape.

(d) The yard of the mast, a bar of gold broadened in the middle with a perforation to allow it to slip over the mast.

(e) Booms, three in number, forked at one end to play upon the mast.

(f) A punting-pole.

(g) A grappling-iron or anchor, with four flukes twisted spirally.

When the model was complete, the ropes and sails were presumably represented by threads, and by pieces of linen cut to the appropriate shape, as in a well-finished toy model. The rigging was certainly more elaborate than the simple lug-sail which supplements the oars of a modern *curach*.

(3) The torques, one of which is broken. These are looped bars of pure gold, with a groove running round each in the manner of a female screw, the thread being rounded in section : inside the groove a gold wire is inlaid. The technique of manufacture is thus entirely different from that followed in the making of torques in the Bronze Age. The weight of the perfect specimen is 3 oz. 7 dwt. 9 gr.

(4) The bowl is a hemispherical vessel beaten out of a plate of the same kind of gold as the boat : it weighs 4 dwt. 12 gr. There are four double perforations at equal distances around its circumference, each pair with a small ring of wire looped into it. Two of these loops retain a larger ring dependent from them. It is difficult to imagine a use for this object : we may say that it resembles the scale of a balance, but in view of its material it would be a counsel of despair to adopt that explanation.

(5) The chains are flexible plaits of fine gold wire, of the kind known as " Trichinopoly work ". They are of a gold of different colour from that of which the bowl and the boat are made, and their workmanship belongs to a different school of art. Chains of this kind have been found in Alexandria, in surroundings and associations which would date them to the first century B.C.—a little older than the probable date of the collar still to be described. They are provided at the ends with securing-catches, in the form of hinges with sliding rivets.

(6) The collar is a hollow tube of gold, 1 inch in diameter. Some baser material, presumably wood, used at first as a modelling-core, must have been retained in the hollow to serve as a backing,[1] thus stiffening the tube, and preventing it from becoming indented. This, however, has decayed away, and has disappeared. The collar is made in two halves, each half ending at one termination in an

---

[1] Compare the wooden rings which support the turned-over edge of cauldrons.

expanding disc.   From the centre of the disc in the one half there
rises a **T**-shaped bar, resembling a miniature stop-cock ; in the other
disc there is a slot into which the head of the **T** fits, and locks when
the collar is on the neck of the wearer.   The ends of the collar
opposite the locking discs are now mutilated, so that it is impossible
to say how they were finished and secured ; the ornament was
perhaps torn with violence from the neck of the man who wore it
last.   Possibly there was a sliding cylindrical band passing over the
ends of the two halves of the collar ; though the *repoussé* ornament,
which is carried to the edge of the fracture, does not seem consonant with this.   To remove the collar, the now mutilated end
would have to be released in whatever manner was appropriate to
its fastening, and then one half would have to be turned through a
quarter-circle, so as to release the fastening of the other end.

The *repoussé* ornamentation of the two halves of the collar is
identical in pattern, and was most likely beaten out over a mould of
bone or of bronze.   It is founded upon the interlocking of two
S-curves, enriched with devices half-floral, half-geometrical, in a
very characteristic La Tène style.   On the other hand, the hatching
of the background, with traced compass-drawn curves, is unique
among extant La Tène ornaments.   It is hardly an exaggeration to
say that this is the finest ornament in gold that the entire La Tène
period of Europe has bequeathed to us.

The above description of the Broighter find is transferred with a few
verbal modifications from the pages of our first edition.   But it is necessary
to append a paragraph or two, containing an abstract of the perplexing
circumstances in which the discovery was made.
    The story, current and (till recently) accepted without any question,
was to the effect that the objects were found by two ploughmen in the em-
ployment of Mr. J. L. Gibson, farmer, of Broighter, a maritime townland
a short distance from Limavady.   The plough " struck something hard "
at the bottom of the furrow : one of the ploughmen, James Morrow by
name, went back to ascertain what the obstruction may have been, and discovered the gold objects.   Armstrong [1] expands this slightly : he tells us
that the objects were " all lying together in a space about 9 inches square ;
one of the objects, the boat, was injured by the plough ".   The chains
" were inside the collar, [2] the oars were inside the boat, the boat was crumpled
up ".   The ploughmen took the objects to their employer, from whom they
passed into the possession of a Belfast jeweller, [3] who sold them to the late
Robert Day of Cork.   Mr. Day was a saddler of that city, with large business
connexions throughout the country ; and he used these to promote the
interests of his great collection of Irish antiquities.   He had already had
relations with Mr. Gibson ; Sir Arthur Evans describes the latter as a

[1] *Gold Catalogue*, p. 26.
[2] Which might mean either inside the circular loop, or inside the gold tube
which enclosed it.
[3] *Gold Catalogue*, p. 27.   The intermediation of the Belfast jeweller is not mentioned in this otherwise full account of the story, nor yet in Sir Arthur Evans's paper
quoted in the following footnote.   It appears in what purports to be an abstract
of the official report of the subsequent law case, printed in *Waterford* 5 [1899] : 120.

personal acquaintance of Mr. Day's, " a shrewd hard-headed Presbyterian upon whose word Mr. Day could thoroughly rely, and who was most precise about the facts ".

Mr. Day purchased the find, and put the damaged specimens into the hands of Messrs Johnson, goldsmiths, of Dublin, for repair. These repairs had been effected by 21 January 1897, when the objects were exhibited at a meeting of the Society of Antiquaries of London, with a description by Sir Arthur Evans, afterwards published, with a very full series of illustrations, in *Archæologia*.[1] Within the week following the meeting, the *Athenæum* presented its readers with a brief report, which for the first time made the discovery generally known. The Council of the Royal Irish Academy, to which body the duty of administering the Law of Treasure Trove in Ireland has been delegated, immediately entered a claim for the find, as Treasure Trove. For some personal reason, it appears, Mr. Day was unwilling that the find should pass into the custody of the Academy ; accordingly, he carried the objects to London, and sold them for £600[2] to the Trustees of the British Museum, who exercise similar privileges in England. After their acquisition they were conspicuously displayed in the Gold Room of that Museum, where I myself saw them for the first time, a few months after the above date.

The custody of the objects thereafter formed the subject of questions in Parliament, of a Royal Commission to determine the standing of the various Museums concerned, and finally of a legal case, cited as *The Attorney General* versus *The Trustees of the British Museum*, June 1903. A wide range of subjects was taken into account in the course of the proceedings : the nature of Treasure Trove ; the geological evidence for land-oscillations in the region of the discovery ;[3] the evidence for votive offerings—for it was claimed that the hoard was an offering to a sea-god, cast into the sea (and therefore not intended to be recovered by the last owner, and in consequence not Treasure Trove, as legally defined).[4] After a four days' judicial investigation it was determined that the objects were Treasure Trove, and therefore Crown Property : and King Edward VII, exercising his prerogative of disposal, ordered their return to Ireland and their delivery to the custody of the Royal Irish Academy. They have been in the Academy's collection, now housed in the National Museum in Dublin, ever since.

It is important to review the story with special reference to the hands through which the objects passed : Mr. Gibson, described by all those who knew him as a shrewd and trustworthy man ; Mr. Day, a collector of long standing, well accustomed to all the wiles of commercial traffic in antiquities ; Sir Arthur Evans, by heredity and by personal attainment one of the greatest Archæologists who ever lived, and at the time an experienced Museum Administrator ; the Trustees and officials of the British Museum, who are not in the habit of spending £600 on " pigs in pokes " ; and the lawyers, some of them of the highest eminence in their profession, who took part in

---

[1] " On a votive deposit of gold objects found on the North-west coast of Ireland ", *Archæologia* 55 ii [1897] : 391. See further an analysis of the ornament on the collar in E. T. Leeds, *Celtic Ornament in the British Islands down to A.D. 700* (Oxford 1933). (This work should be carefully read in connexion with any serious study of the subject-matter of the present chapter).

[2] *Gold Catalogue*, p. 26.

[3] The study by Praeger and Coffey of the Antrim Raised Beach, to which we have had occasion to refer in an earlier chapter, was a by-product of this trial. Dr. Praeger gave expert Geological evidence before the legal tribunal, and he includes an account of the enquiry in his autobiographical *The way that I went*, at p. 63.

[4] The model ship suggested a thankoffering for escape from shipwreck : compare the many model ships stored for a similar intention in such a shrine as that of *Notre-Dame de la Garde* at Marseilles.

the case. If anything could be described as a solid water-tight body of attested facts, it would surely be the foregoing narrative.

But now, some thirty-eight years after the completion of the case—forty-five years after the first discovery—another story is being put about, which for the moment has been crystallized into the following sentences :—

> The Broighter " hoard " must be struck off the list almost completely as a discovery illustrating La Tène Art in Ireland. This is not the place to enter into a full statement of facts which have come to light quite recently, and which, moreover, the writer is not at liberty to divulge, as far as names and circumstances of discovery are concerned. The facts which are now stated must be taken at face value, and the responsibility for setting them out rests entirely with the present writer [Dr. Mahr]. It can be taken for granted, however, that the Broighter find is an exploded myth. The objects were found together, it is true, but they constituted a nineteenth-century " hoard ", not a votive offering or a hoard of the first century A.D.[1]

That is all very well, but Science cannot tolerate such vague reticences about a story, whatever it may be, antiquated now by a generation and a half. The rumours that have come my own way, filling in these bare outlines, for what they may be worth, are to the effect that the objects were the property of a local collector, gathered at various times and in various parts of the world ; that his home was raided by burglars ; and that the thieves, for some reason, wrapped their loot in the cover of an old umbrella and buried it where the ploughmen happened to find it. The umbrella story is accepted by Mlle. Henry ;[2] but until convincing answers are given to the questions which arise automatically, I shall find a very serious difficulty in following her lead. Who was this mysterious collector in the background ? Why did he not come forward to claim his property when the newspapers were full of the case ? Or if he was dead, why did not his representatives do so ? Surely a collection of gold antiquities valued at £600 was worth a little effort ! Did he report his loss to the police ? If he did, why did not the police put two and two together when the case was before the courts ? If he did not, how did he escape prosecution for compounding a felony ? Why did the thieves hide easily recognizable loot in a place so insecure ? How did they come to possess and to use so improbable a receptacle as the cover of an old umbrella ? Why was nothing ever heard of this old umbrella in all the investigations made, between the first discovery and the final deposition of the objects in the Dublin Museum ? Here are nine questions which the story suggests at first sight. There may be satisfactory answers to all of them ; and in the sacred name of Science, which overrides all personal and national considerations, it is nothing short of a duty to press for those answers.

It must be conceded frankly that the hoard is a very strange one ; this has been obvious from the first. Sir Arthur Evans[3] was quite awake to the possibility of its being a modern assemblage. " The great variety in character of the objects ", he says, " might suggest the conclusion either that it contained relics of different periods, or that the treasure itself had been collected from more than one source by its original modern possessor " : but he adds " with regard to the last possibility, Mr. Robert Day had made most careful investigations and has completely satisfied himself as to the *bona fide* character of the find ". He then asks, accepting the find as genuine, " is it possible that the hoard itself contained objects of different periods ? " He admits that it is clearly divided into three groups, each formed of gold of a different alloy—the boat and the bowl of pale gold (much alloyed with

---

[1] *Christian Art in Ancient Ireland* ii [1941] : 11.
[2] *Irish Art* (1940), p. 13.   [3] *Op. cit.* p. 405.

silver) ; the chains, made of gold of a somewhat dull hue ; the collar and the torques of bright pure metal. The collar is unquestionably La Tène, and Evans himself had no doubt of its being an ancient Irish fabric, referring it, on grounds of style, to the first century A.D. The chains might conceivably have been made in Britain, but, as already indicated, they most closely correspond with Alexandrian objects of a slightly earlier time—late Ptolemaic or early Roman. The boat and the bowl are less easy to assign to their appropriate time and place, but there is nothing against their being more or less contemporary with the other objects.[1]

After the foregoing paragraphs had been set up in type, a copy of the official report of the case, as tried in the High Court of Justice before Mr. Justice Farwell (11-20 June, 1903) came into my hands. A study of the evidence, there printed *verbatim*, dispels many errors in the narrative as set forth above. We learn that when the case came to trial Mr. Gibson and his head ploughman, James Morrow, were both dead. The second ploughman, Thomas Nicholl, gave the only evidence as to the finding of the gold. Morrow was ploughing down to a depth of about 6-8 inches, in stiff soil—evidently not disturbed by any recent digging, so that the burying burglars fade from the scene : Nicholl was following with a deeper plough, at a depth of about 14½ inches. The first plough passed above the gold objects, and so missed them ; the second cut through them, breaking and carrying away a fragment of gold. This caught Nicholl's attention ; and when he had reached the end of his furrow he turned back to investigate, and then found the whole hoard. Morrow apparently knew nothing of the find ; Nicholl alone saw and collected it. To the direct question " Did you find any trace of wood or cloth or anything of that kind ? " he replied with a direct negative. The old umbrella therefore also fades away. We may rescue it by an arbitrary guess that some such jetsam might have been lying close by, on the field or the adjacent shore, and that Nicholl picked it up and used it as a convenient wrapping, for safe carriage of the collection ; but if so he did not think it worth mentioning. He carried the objects home to his wife, who washed them ; and then he surrendered them to Mr. Gibson, who gave him a reward. Morrow remained out of the picture altogether. We must make allowances in interpreting this evidence ; the deponent seems to have found a difficulty in expressing himself intelligibly. The question on which we paused a moment ago—the exact meaning of " inside the collar "—was raised, but he failed to convey a clear answer to the questioners. He admitted that he could not understand a map. And his visual memory was unequal to perceiving any difference between the crushed and distorted objects which he had found, and the same objects exhibited to him seven years later, after they had undergone expert restoration. He makes it clear that the field was not being ploughed for the first time ; and that just in the place where the find was made there had been a hedge, the removal of which had left the site of the deposit free ; which explains why the find had not been made before, and thus further

---

[1] Dr. Praeger, who gave evidence in the lawsuit as an expert geologist, and was in close touch with the whole matter from the beginning, has contributed a further note on his recollections of the case to JRSAI (72 [1942] : 29). This quite independent testimony may be referred to in corroboration of the opinions here expressed. Moreover, I read the foregoing paragraphs to a kinswoman of my own, a member of a family prominent in Limavady at the time of the discovery. I found that she had a very clear recollection of the excitement produced by the find and the subsequent events, and of the endless tattle to which they naturally gave rise. But no whisper of the plundered collector, the burglary, or the umbrella had ever reached her, though it is hard to imagine how such melodramatic details could have escaped the local quidnuncs.

weakens the evidence for its having been a *recent* deposit. The "Belfast jeweller" also disappears ; Mr. Day dealt direct with Mr. Gibson, and then carried the objects, "crushed like balls of paper", to Messrs. Johnson. These found the task of restoration to tax all their skill and technical re- sources. They had no idea of what the boat actually was, until they had gradually smoothed out all the folds and creases, one after another.

The only other important La Tène gold object recorded from Ireland, is a collar found at Clonmacnois. It is a hollow tube of gold bent into a ring ; at one end there is a cylindrical expansion with conical ends, covered with punch-marks and with characteristic La Tène ornament in relief : the other end of the tube fits into a socket at the free end of the expansion, where it can be secured with a movable pin. The joint of the collar, when closed, thus presents an appearance as of two conical terminals, one on each end of the ring, pressed base to base. At the opposite side of the ring there is an expansion, the form and decoration of which seems to have been suggested by a well-known type of glass bead.[1]

This form of fastening—the thrusting of one end of a loop into the hollow end of the other—is foreign to the Bronze Age, and it helps us to date an otherwise enigmatical bronze bracelet from Co. Galway, described and figured by Frazer.[2] In this specimen, the greater part of the loop is of uniform thickness, and is decorated with three rows of small hemispherical knobs. One end is drawn out into a thin prolongation, slightly bent sideways at its extremity : this is thrust into a hollow at the other end, and hooks into a hole drilled through the wall of the hollow. Another bracelet of this kind from Co. Louth, described as copper (but more probably bronze),[3] had a screw-like twist engraved upon it (thus resembling the Broighter torques). In this case, the pointed end, thrust into the hollow end, must have been kept in position with a rivet-pin, for which a perforation was provided.

The pellet decoration on the Galway bracelet mentioned above is not a usual form of bronze-age ornament, and may possibly be taken as another indication of a later period. It reappears on a gold collar from Co. Waterford.[4] This is a loop with open ends, bent into hooks which catch into each other to secure the ornament : the side of the loop opposite the opening is hammered flat for some length, and the flat surface is decorated with two rows of pellets. A finger-ring from Co. Cork, and a collar from Co. Limerick, both of gold, show a similar pellet decoration.[5]

Swords. The La Tène sword has a long, straight blade, with sharp edges for cutting ; but with a blunt point, not adapted for thrusting—unlike the shorter leaf-shaped swords of the Bronze

Age and the Hallstatt period, which could be used on occasion as rapiers. The best Irish examples of La Tène swords come from Lisnacrogher [1] (Antrim). Every scholar must feel, when this place is mentioned, that a periodical Act of Humiliation should be performed in the Shrine of Irish Archæology—if only it were not a waste of time to do so, analogous to the proverbial folly of crying over spilt milk. Let it suffice to say that Lisnacrogher was the site of a lake dwelling which had the misfortune to lie close at hand to the dwelling of a collector of whom it was said, among other virtues recorded in an obituary notice, that " he made it a rule never to leave his house without carrying back something to enrich his collection ". The lake-dwelling of Lisnacrogher was for such a man a gold-mine, and he spent much of his spare time in looting it (to use the only adequate expression). A rival collector, Mr. Knowles, has written, " I paid little attention to this crannog during his lifetime, except when he took me there himself : as he called it ' his crannog ' and was very jealous of anyone interfering with it ". He himself does not seem ever to have recorded what he found, still less the circumstances or associations in which he found them. The stratification of the site must have been of the first importance, for the objects recovered from it belong to very different periods. It is not too much to say that the plundering of Lisnacrogher wiped out all hope of establishing a systematic history of the civilization of Ireland during the last century B.C. and the first two or three centuries A.D., unless some other site of equal importance should unexpectedly (and undeservedly) come to light, and should be explored by an excavation party, properly equipped with scientific knowledge and a sense of scientific responsibility, as well as with material resources. There are some unsatisfying articles by Wakeman on the contents of the site ; these have been abstracted by Wood-Martin. [2]

Some swords, of the kind described above, were found, contained in scabbards of bronze, decorated with rich scroll-work of very characteristic La Tène style. [3] The bell-shape of the guard at the junction of the hilt and the blade, in these swords, would lead us to attribute them to the second La Tène period (c. 300-100 B.C.) if we could feel any security in transferring Continental Chronology and Evolutionary Typology to Ireland, without much precaution. A similar sword, from Loch Gur, was found by Dr. Raftery in the National Museum, where it had lain forgotten since its acquisition in 1852. The blade was in a very broken condition : a (possibly

---

[1] This is the spelling of the Ordnance Map.

[2] JRSAI 16 [1884] : 375, 19 [1889] : 96, 21 [1891] : 542. Wood-Martin, *Lake dwellings of Ireland*, numerous references in index, especially pp. 173 ff. See also Canon Greenwell in PSA Lond. II iv : 256.

[3] See Wood-Martin, *op. cit.* ; JRSAI 53 [1925] : 5-9 ; *British Museum Iron Age Guide*, 2nd ed., p. 160.

makeshift) handle, adapted from the metatarsal bone of a sheep, had been slipped over the tang.[1] There was also the upper end of a bronze scabbard, with two figures of birds mounted upon it,[2] recalling the birds in the Dunaverney steelyard. Other objects from this lamentable curiosity-shop were iron sickles, richly decorated objects of bronze, and some fragments of gold. The top beam of a frame of a harp with perforations for the spindles of thirteen strings, alleged to have come from Lisnacrogher, was purchased by Mr. Knowles after local petty jealousies had been dissolved by death.

A sword with a hilt in the form of a human figure was dredged up in the harbour of Ballyshannon (Donegal). The blade is about 15 inches in length : the hilt has a human head, with short projections representing the limbs. This type of sword-handle is well known in France, not so certainly in England : [3] the Ballyshannon specimen may have been lost by some wandering Gaul. It is now in the National Museum.[4] The Iberian bronze statuette of a woman, said to have been found at Sligo and now in the National Museum, is a similar " wanderer ".[5]

Spears and Javelins. A bronze spear-head from Boho (Fermanagh) with La Tène decoration,[6] an iron spear-head from Corofin (Clare) with a decorative bronze inlay deftly inserted into an opening in each wing of the blade,[7] and a spear-head found near Limerick, encircled with inlaid threads of gold surrounding the socket, may be mentioned here. All these are in the National Museum.

Spear-butts. These are ferrules of bronze in the form of a strip of metal bent into a gently tapering cone, about 1 foot 5 inches in length (Fig. 33 *i*). The upper diameter of the cone is about $\frac{3}{4}$ inch, the lower diameter about $\frac{1}{4}$ inch ; the upper end broadens into a ring which brings the total diameter there up to about an inch. Slight La Tène ornament decorates the side.[8] Another variety resembles in shape an ordinary modern door-handle ; it may be up to 3 inches in length [9] (Fig. 33 *k*).

A cone of bronze, with a square tang projecting from its base, was found near Tara Hill.[10] It is identical in form with the iron end-pieces, intended for capping the butts of spear-shafts, found at La Tène itself.[11]

---

[1] See description and illustrations in JRSAI 69 [1939] : 170. This is worth recalling in connexion with the speculations on the origin of sockets, *ante*, p. 200.
[2] JRSAI 27 [1897] : 114.
[3] The *British Museum Iron Age Guide*, 2nd ed., p. 59 figures a specimen said to be from Yorkshire, but with some uncertainty as to its provenance.
[4] JRSAI 55 [1925] : 137.
[5] Published by Dr. P. Jacobsthal, JRSAI 68 [1938] : 51.
[6] PRIA 24 : 263.   [7] PRIA 28 [1910] : 102.
[8] JRSAI 53 : 21. Wilde, *Catalogue*, p. 504.
[9] JRSAI 53 : 20.   [10] PRIA 15 : 25.
[11] See Vouga, *La Tène* (Leipzig 1923), plate xiv, Figs. 15-20.

Horse-trappings. (1) Bridle-bits appear in several varieties. The mouthpiece may be made with two links (Plate VII, No. 6), or with three (Plate VII, No. 7) : as a rule, the middle link of the latter form is attenuated to a mere figure-of-eight double loop, contrasting notably with the British examples figured by Mr. Ward Perkins.[1] But a fine specimen from Killeevan (Monaghan) has the central link of full size ; the end rings in this example are decorated, the one with a wall-of-Troy pattern, the other with running spirals set off by a champlevé background filled with red enamel.[2]

(2) Plume-standards (Plate VII, Nos. 1-5) are sometimes found associated with these objects : they are in the shape of a capital **Y**, but with the angle rounded. A pivot hole runs from side to side through the extremities of the branching members, and the stem ends with an ornamental knob. They seem to have been placed over the neck of the horse, and secured to the ends of the bit, thus keeping the latter in place. The knob should be pointed upward, to serve as a stand to which a plume could be secured (they are inverted in Plate VII). Sir C. H. Read suggested this explanation of these enigmatical objects,[3] but he was forestalled by Wilde.[4]

(3) Terrets are loops of bronze, sometimes bearing La Tène decoration, attached to the horse-collar, for receiving the reins and preventing them from drooping to the ground or becoming entangled.[5]

Brooches. The ordinary La Tène brooch, with the bow continued beyond the catch and then turned back to touch the outside of the curve, is practically unknown in Ireland.[6] In fact, considering the importance of the fibula in La Tène art generally, the rarity of iron-age (pre-Christian) fibulæ in Ireland is remarkable : and the few decorated examples that have been found are altogether divergent from orthodox La Tène standards. One peculiarly Irish form may perhaps be identified with the *delg nduillech* or " leaf-brooch " of early Irish literature ; in this the fibula is of the ordinary safety-pin construction, but the back of the bow is flattened and worked into a realistic likeness of a long, willow-like leaf.[7]

Ardakillen (Roscommon) is the site of a lake-dwelling where, among other objects, a unique brooch was found, now in the Royal Irish Academy's collection : indeed, were it not that the evidence for its authenticity is fairly good, it might be regarded as an ingenious forgery. It is of bronze ; the ornamental back consists of a rectangular plate of metal, bent up into a semi-cylinder in the

---

[1] J. B. Ward Perkins, " Iron Age Metal Horses' Bits of the British Isles ", PPS n.s. 5 [1939] : 173.

[2] JRSAI 4 [1857] : 423. See also Wilde, *Catalogue*, pp. 604-5 for other specimens.

[3] *Archæologia* 66 [1915] : 349 ; *British Museum Iron Age Guide*, 2nd ed., p. 162.

[4] *Catalogue*, p. 609. [5] PSA Lond. 20 [1904] : 56.

[6] An ornate example from Clogher (Tyrone) is illustrated in the *British Museum Iron Age Guide*, 2nd ed., p. 160.

[7] Wilde, *Catalogue*, p. 568 ; Ridgeway, *Date of the Cu-Chulain saga*, p. 24.

middle.   The flat parts, at each side of the cylinder, have a simple
but beautiful pattern in relief upon them, clearly of La Tène type.
The curve of the cylinder, however, is decorated with a granulated
ornament, in shape a simple interlacing plait, much more closely
akin to the art of the Christian period.   In any case, the object must
be of a very late date, the La Tène pattern being of the nature of a
revival rather than a survival.[1]

Another very beautiful brooch, of unknown provenance, comes
from the same place.   Here the back is triangular, and is made into
an open-work pattern, the members of which are of the characteristic
leaf-shapes that form primary motives of La Tène decoration.[2]

Pins. A bronze pin found near Ballybunnion (Kerry) and described by Raftery,[3] is of importance as bringing the date of sus-
pended-ring pins back from early Christianity into the late Iron
Age.[4]   The disc-shaped ring has the well-known La Tène characteristic of avoiding concentric circles : the outer and inner margins
are circular, but struck from different centres.   A simple ornament
of spirals and curved lines adorns the surface, surrounding a cup-
shaped depression which may or may not have contained a setting
of some ornamental material.   Dr. Raftery attributes it to a date of
about A.D. 300, and more than hints that other pins in the National
Collection, heretofore regarded as objects of " Christian Art ", may
have to be referred back to about the same comparatively early date.

Discs. Under this name we may speak here of a class of objects,
so far as is yet known, peculiar to Ireland.   They are circular discs
of bronze, about 8 or 10 inches in diameter, with a circular saucer-
shaped depression a little off the centre of one of the sides, once more
illustrating the La Tène decorative motive of nests of *non-concentric*
circles (Fig 33*l*).   The rest of the surface of the disc, around and
above the depression, is decorated with the characteristic scroll-
development of the anthemion petal.   Sometimes, though not
always, there is a small perforation, rectangular in shape, in the
bottom of the depression.[5]

On account of the presence of other discs, of a different type,
reference may here be made to the remarkable find of objects made
upon Lambay in the year 1927, in the course of harbour improvements.   Lord Revelstoke, proprietor of the island, kindly deposited
the objects for special study in the National Museum, and they were

---

[1] For an illustration (which has often been reproduced) see Wilde, *Catalogue*,
p. 569.
[2] Wilde, *Catalogue*, p. 567 ; JRSAI 53 : 13, where some other brooches similar
to this are illustrated.
[3] *Cork* 45 [1940] : 55.
[4] A conclusion confirmed by Mr. Kilbride-Jones (" The Evolution of Penannular
Brooches with Zoomorphic Terminals ", PRIA 43 [1937] : 379).   Refer, however,
also to Dr. Raftery's criticisms, JRSAI 71 [1941] : 56 ff.
[5] See JRSAI 53 [1923] : plate facing p. 1 ; *British Museum Iron Age Guide*,
p. 149.

reported upon by myself to the Royal Irish Academy.[1] They represented two different occupations—a late stone- or early bronze-age habitation-site : and a late La Tène cemetery. The objects having been found at intervals in the course of engineering works, and not published at the time, there could be no question of a formal excavation.

The first series contained a large quantity of flint flakes, which must have been imported, as there is no native bed of flint on the island. Such a wasteful accumulation of unworked or only slightly worked fragments is unusual in a non-siliciferous region. Lozenge-shaped Iberian javelin heads were included in the series, as well as an unusual proportion of polished adze (not hatchet) heads.

[By permission of the Royal Irish Academy.

FIG. 35.—La Tène Objects from Lambay.

The objects in the second series (Fig. 35) display Romanizing influence to an unwonted degree. A circular mirror with projecting handle, of iron—quite unmistakable, though much corroded and broken, and so far unique in Ireland, was the most remarkable of them (Fig. 35 (1)).[2] An anomalous form of bronze shield-umbo,

[1] *Proceedings* 38 [1929] : 240.
[2] On such mirrors see G. C. Dunning, " An engraved bronze Mirror from Nijmegen, Holland " (with statistics and a distribution-map) : *Archæological Journal* 85 [1930] : 69.

and the blade of an iron sword, with a quillon perforated at both ends (found in the same grave), were also noteworthy. There were also an armlet with eight movable beads of bronze playing on one side of it (Fig. 35 (2)), a flat disc between each pair of beads ; fastened in the way already described, a spike on one side of the opening fitting into a socket on the other : three mounts from a sword-scabbard, with open-work La Tène (or rather sub-La Tène) decoration, unlike anything found elsewhere in Ireland, though analogies have been found in the Roman camp at Newstead (Fig. 35 (3, 4)); safety-pin fibulæ of Roman provincial type (Fig. 35 (5, 6)), one of which (no. 6) was a " dummy " counterpart of one of the others—the pin, which ought to lie loose in the catch, being actually of one piece with it, so that the brooch could not be worn at all in any normal way ; [1] and a number of fragments of discs with *repoussé* ornament. With great trouble these were pieced together, so far as was possible, by the expert staff of the Ashmolean Museum at Oxford, under the superintendence of Mr. E. T. Leeds, and were revealed as fragments of a circular disc (Fig. 35 (7)), 7 inches in diameter, with a *repoussé* ornament consisting of a triangular arrangement ot three **S**-curves, with an additional **S**-curve making a triskele at each angle—the free end of the additional **S** coiling spirally round a pellet : in the centre an equilateral triangle of pellets enclosing a rosette.[2] Other fragments, apparently of similar discs, but too badly broken for certainty, were also in the hoard.

Some ten years later, another disc, very similar, but a little smaller, was dredged up at Lochan Island in the Bann. Though differing in detail, the ornament was designed on the same lines ; and whatever its purpose may have been, it was presumably similar to that served by the Lambay disc. It has been carefully described, though without reference to the Lambay analogue, by Dr. Raftery ; [3] he dates it to about A.D. 300. Another disc, with generally similar (though perhaps slightly later) ornament, was found at Killeevan (Monaghan).[4]

Castanets. The objects thus named are oval spoon-like objects, flat at one end, with a depression at the other (Fig. 33 *j*). The flat end is decorated with simple ornament of La·Tène type, traced upon the surface : these objects are generally found in pairs, and

[1] It was presumably intended to be sewn into the texture of the garment on one side of the opening, with the end of a securing tape lapped and stitched round its bow : the other end of the tape being fastened by the movable brooch, and released when it was required to loosen the fastening or to draw it tighter. Its two-fold function was to hold the fastening tape, and to balance ornamentally its partner in office.

[2] Minutes of Proceedings, RIA, 23 May 1932, pp. 19, 20. See also E. T. Leeds, *Celtic Ornament*, p. 59, where a very interesting comparison is suggested with a well-known rock-scribing at Ilkley, Yorkshire.

[3] *Antiquaries' Journal* 20 [1940] : 280 ; *Ulster* III 3 [1940] : 26.

[4] JRSAI 4 [1857] : plate facing p. 423.

one of each pair is commonly perforated. They are usually called *spoons* : but Dr. Bremer pointed out to me their identity in shape with the castanets of dancers, in which the flat projections are gripped between the fingers, the " bowls of the spoons " projecting out from the back of the hand ; the convex outside surfaces of the depressions, thus held back to back, being rattled by striking them against one another with a rapid shaking or waving of the hand or the fingers. It must be admitted that this explanation leaves the perforation unaccounted for : but it is in any case difficult to see what practical purpose this perforation could have served on *any* theory of their use ; why is it in only one of the pair, and why is it not always in the same place ? (It is sometimes on the edge, sometimes in the middle, of the depression.) [1]

Armlets. Heavy coiled armlets of bronze, with rather coarse ornament in relief upon them, are Scottish rather than Irish : numerous specimens have been obtained from the Culbin Sands and elsewhere in Scotland. One specimen, probably an importation, was found near Newry (Down). [2]

Helmet Spikes. Two hollow conical spikes of bronze, with concave discs attached to their sides, tastefully decorated with La Tène curves and with studs of red enamel, are in the Royal Irish Academy's collection. They have been enthusiastically described by Kemble [3] and (rather fantastically) made the basis of a restoration as a spiked crown. [4] The well-known horned forehead-piece of a helmet from Kirkcudbright, with *repoussé* La Tène decoration upon it, [5] may perhaps afford a clue to the signification of these ornaments. University College, Cork, possesses a set of three similar spikes, larger, but more simply decorated. [6]

Knives. Small tanged blades with a convex cutting edge, meeting a slightly wavy back in a sharp point, are among the most characteristic objects from La Tène sites in Ireland and elsewhere ; they are found in all sites belonging to that period. [7]

We cannot find space here for more than an acknowledgement of the existence of other objects of ordinary domestic use, a full discussion of which would require the elbow-room of a syndicated

---

[1] See A. Way in *Archæological Journal* 26 : 52 ; another paper, by Canon Rock, at p. 35 of the same journal, may be neglected. See also Armstrong (JRSAI 53 : 26 and references there) and Evans, *Bronze Implements*, p. 406, with further references. A pair (not of Irish provenance) is illustrated in the *British Museum Iron Age Guide*, 2nd ed., p. 149. For a descriptive inventory of these objects, see PSA Scot. 58 [1924] : 145 ff.   [2] JRSAI 53 : 18.   [3] *Horæ Ferales*, p. 79.

[4] Probably influenced by the fancy portrait of " Brian Boru ", prefixed as a frontispiece to O'Connor's translation of Keating's History of Ireland. *Archæologia* 47 part ii [1883] : 473, where the objects are very fully described and illustrated.

[5] Anderson, *Scotland in Pagan Times (Iron Age)*, p. 113.

[6] PRIA 28 [1910] : 104 ; JRSAI 53 : plate facing p. 22. M. Murphy in *Ivernian* 3 : 110.

[7] See, for example, PRIA 39, plate 19, Figs. 7, 10, 11 (Togherstown, Co. Westmeath).

encyclopædia. Such are iron tanged sickles, iron horsebits (rare, even after iron had superseded bronze in general use), nails, horse-shoes, fishing-spears with multiple points (not infrequent in crannog sites), etc., etc.

Enamel and Glass

Enamel was not much used in the decoration of La Tène objects in Ireland, and the few examples recorded are unimportant. The Royal Irish Academy possesses a large lump of red enamel, evidently part of a metal-worker's equipment, said (doubtfully) to have been found on Tara Hill. It seems to have been intended for cutting up to make buttons or studs, riveted to the surface to be decorated—an early La Tène technique, abandoned on the Continent after the first La Tène period.[1]

The use of glass as a material for beads conceivably (not probably) goes back in Ireland to the Bronze Age : but lamentably little is known about Irish glass beads, as most of the known examples have been purchased by collectors from itinerant pedlars, so that their history, ancient and modern, is utterly unknown.

Greenish glass beads, formed of two conjoined spheres, not perforated—the so-called " dumb-bell " beads—have been found in the Lochcrew tumuli. Two fragments of perforated glass beads, also of a greenish colour, were found in a small iron-age burial mound excavated at Grannagh (Galway).[2]

Of the later beads, as all the known examples have been detached from their archæological contexts, and even bead-groups have been broken up for commercial purposes—and, what is worse, arbitrarily strung together in modern chains—they have to be considered on their own merits, without any reference to the historical value which they might have possessed.[3] Knowles has indicated a scheme of classification based upon their material, shape, and ornament. But as we have already said of other groups of objects, classification for its own sake is useless : it is only of value when facts of chronology, history, or ethnology can be deduced from it. For these we must wait until properly authenticated finds of Irish beads are made in sufficient numbers ;[4] with these as basis, a study of the whole

[1] The object is described by V. Ball and M. Stokes, TRIA 30 : 277, and Armstrong, JRSAI 41 [1911] : 6, 53 [1923] : 16. It cannot have been intended for *melting* into inlay-cloisons, as we might *a priori* suppose : experiment has shown that when melted it loses its rich colour.

[2] PRIA 33 [1917] : 509.

[3] A fine series is illustrated by W. J. Knowles, JRSAI 15 [1881] : 522 ; see further R. Day, JRSAI 10 [1869] : 335 ; Rev. L. Hassé, JRSAI 21 [1891] : 359 (with numerous references) ; Wilde, *Catalogue*, pp. 163-5.

[4] It is not clear what we are to make of a " glass-factory " at Melitia (Wicklow), described by Rev. J. F. M. ffrench (JRSAI 17 [1886] : 420). Whatever it may be, it appears to be of rather later date than the period with which we are at present concerned.

subject can be begun.[1]   We have no assurance that the more highly
decorated beads, with polychrome ornamentation, are of Irish origin
at all : certain beads found at Dunworley (Cork) seem to be comparatively recent Oriental importations.[2]

Meanwhile, we may content ourselves with noting that beads in
stone and in glass are found which may reasonably be assigned to
the Iron Age ; some at least seem to be as late as the Víking period,
as appears from evidence presented by Mr. Armstrong.[3]   Those in
amber, jet, and certain beads and conical pendants in limestone we
may assign to the Bronze Age.[4]   The stone beads are usually made
of material which will take a high decorative polish ; they are either
regular spheres or circular discs, or else are irregular pebbles, not
shaped to any definite form.   Mr. Knowles remarks that the perforation, in the last-mentioned form, is usually of the sectional shape
of a dice-box, showing that it has been drilled from both sides of the
pebble.   The glass beads, which are of various colours, are usually
flat discs or spheroids, and are decorated in various ways.   In some
of them heavy rope-like ridges of glass run over the surface, either
straight or else twisted into various devices.   These ropes often
differ in colour from the body of the bead, and from each other when
there are several ropes on one bead.   Other beads are decorated
with knobs of varied colour.   In others, again, the bead is itself an
intricate twist of strands of glass of different colours.   It is hardly
too much to say that there are scarcely two absolutely alike : only
these broad outlines of description can be attempted here.[5]

Iron

By now the reader will be complaining that we are committing
the proverbial solecism of playing Hamlet with Hamlet left out.
We have been speaking of the art and civilization of the Iron Age,
and have as yet said nothing of its eponymous industry.   We would
remind him of the wording of the caption of this chapter, which
has been carefully devised to anticipate such a criticism.   Iron
is still subordinate to bronze ; not only because the products of the
iron industry are few and fragmentary, by reason of the liability
of the metal to destruction by oxidation, but also because bronze
continues in full use throughout all the centuries with which the
chapter is concerned.   It was not till after La Tène had been established—so far as it ever was established—or even had passed its

---

[1] Mr. Alexander Nesbitt contributes a creditable attempt at discussing the
date of these objects to JRSAI 15 : 592.   See also a note by Mr. G. M. Atkinson,
JRSAI 16 [1883] : 69.

[2] JRSAI 5 [1858] : 59 ; PSA Lond. II 2 [1862] : 47.

[3] " Two Irish finds of glass beads of the Víking period ", *Man* 21, No. 40.

[4] See examples in Wilde, *Catalogue*, p. 95 ; PRIA 29 : plate xxiv.

[5] Reference may be made further to a short note by Armstrong in JRSAI
53 : 17 ; Wilde, *Catalogue*, pp. 94, 122.

apology for a zenith, that the use of iron in Ireland became common. Iron slag is a universal "yield" of sites of the late crannog and contemporary dry-land settlements ; evidently each family smelted its own metal and fashioned its own implements, either personally, or, more probably (having regard to the mystical nature of the smith's craft), through the agency of itinerant smiths. The iron seems to have been smelted out of peat-bog material : the manufactured tools were the most commonplace implements—axes, goads, fishing-spears, knives, horseshoes, pots, clippers, chains, pins, nails : this bare list must suffice, for the only way in which it could be amplified would be by a large number of illustrations.[1]

Pottery

The pottery of the La Tène periód in Ireland, so far as we know, differs little from the rude pottery of the preceding Bronze Age. There is nothing that we can set beside the vessels from Aylesford (Kent) except possibly those from Drumnakilly (Tyrone) to which we compared them in our first edition (p. 111). The total absence of pottery from the soil excavated on the Hill of Uisneach and con-temporary sites is a most remarkable fact, in view of the evidence which was there afforded of extensive feasts : wooden dishes and drinking vessels, such as were still in use in the nineteenth century, must then have been the only utensils employed. On the other hand, pottery is a regular "yield" of crannog or lake-dwelling excavations ; and though the vessels are usually broken and little turns up but fragmentary sherds, it is possible to restore some of these, and to learn, first, that there are two different types of ware, the one coarse and the other rather finer ; secondly, that both types are totally different from the wares of the Bronze Age, in texture, profile, and ornament ; and thirdly, that the vessels can be grouped into several kinds of utensils, though most of them are one-handled jugs with a narrow neck, or else two-handled pots with a wide mouth and a flat bottom. The differentiation of the two classes of ware was first noticed by Dr. Bremer, though his early death, which was a calamity disastrous for Irish archæology in general, prevented him from completing and recording his observations in this department of the subject. The ornamentation of these vessels consists either of combinations of incised lines, or else of impressions made with the teeth of a small comb-like instrument.[2]

The highest attainment of the iron-age potters in Ireland is a vessel with a conical cover from Danesfort (Kilkenny),[3] ornamented

---

[1] Reference may be made to a paper by Wakeman, " On the antiquity of Iron as used in . . . [artifacts] found in Ireland ", JRSAI 28 [1898] : 237.

[2] Examples of lake-dwelling pottery are figured in Wood-Martin, *Lake Dwellings of Ireland*, pp. 91 ff.

[3] Described by Rev. J. Graves in JRSAI 6 : 168.

with a finely-traced linear decoration.   The pattern does not suggest
to the mind the special characters of La Tène ornament ; the vessel
may be even later than that period.   In shape, it seems to be an
imitation of a metal original.   A somewhat similar pot (now known
only from an apparently idealized drawing by Windele [1] on which
it would be rash to rely too heavily), is said to have been found in a
chambered carn called " Carn Thierna " at Knockan na Corrin
(Cork).

Burials

There is not much that we can say as yet about burials : no
great iron-age cemetery has been excavated.   Some interments which
have been assigned to the Bronze Age will probably have to be brought
down to the latter period ; such, for example, is a cremated burial
of a woman, in an earthen mound without any stone structure, and
with no deposits except a (possibly accidental) thin calcined plate of
unworked flint, from Aghnascrebagh (Tyrone). [2]

But even graves lined with stone slabs are not necessarily prehistoric.   Dr. Raftery has claimed these for the Iron Age : [3] and
others of even later date have been found associated with Christian
sites.   One of these, on Church Island (Kerry) has been described
by Mr. P. J. Lynch. [4]   It lies east and west, and is lined with slate
slabs, one at the west end, two in the north side, one in the south
side ; the east end is left open.   The cist is divided into two compartments by a cross slab.   There are two cylindrical corner-pieces
of stone, with a sector cut longitudinally out of each.   These were
apparently intended to receive and support the ends of the slabs ;
some error must have been made in the actual construction, however,
for they stand inside, not outside, the corners of the cist in which
they had been placed.

Equally late are the stone-lined graves at Ballymacus (Cork),
described by John Windele with an amazing wealth of irrelevant
sciolism ; [5] and one at Belladooan, Mayo : [6] and I have myself been
associated with the excavation of similar tombs within the precincts
of Iona Cathedral, and undoubtedly belonging to an earlier Christian
establishment on the site.   The interment at Dromiskin (Louth),
which included a small stone box with sliding lid, containing a yew-
wood box with a similar lid, containing in its turn a fragment of a
bronze pin, belonged to this type, and probably was eighth or ninth

---

[1] Reproduced in Borlase's *Dolmens* 1 : 12 and in *Cork* 34 [1929] : 57.
[2] Described by E. E. Evans, *Ulster* III 1 [1938] : 189.
[3] J. Raftery, " Long stone cists of the early Iron Age ", PRIA 46 [1941] : 299.
[4] JRSAI 30 [1900] : 155.   Other slab-lined Christian graves are described,
Louth 8 : 100.
[5] JRSAI 2 [1853] : 230.   [6] JRSAI 62 [1932] : 191.

century.[1] Although the " finds " were scanty, a group of burials at Carbury (Kildare) examined by Mr. G. F. Wilmot may be mentioned, as illustrating the occasional survival of cremation.[2]

The Knockast "multiple tumulus" described (ante, p. 96) under "Epimegalithic monuments" might, more reasonably perhaps, be included here : and certainly there can be no doubt about a group of interments at Pollacorragune, Tuam (Galway), excavated and described by Mr. F. T. Riley.[3] There were here four skeletons, three male, one female, stretched at length, in a line N.W.-S.E. and all lying on the back. No cist or other stone structure enclosed them : they had merely been laid in shallow trench-graves. Small corroded fragments of iron were associated with the interments, and offer conclusive evidence of their date : such a direct identification of an iron-age grave is rare, and makes the human remains, carefully described by Professor Shea, of special value.[4] Like other skulls from iron-age sites, to which Professor Shea makes reference, they seem to indicate the country re-assuming its dolichocephalic normality after the brachycephalic inroads. Another mound, close by, was rather older, and just preceded (as this mound followed) the transition to iron. It contained a cremated burial, covered with an inverted urn, in which was also a decorated bronze razor of unusual pattern. A local tradition of an upright burial was heard, but was not substantiated by the excavation.

Few of the early descriptions of " finds " are more unsatisfactory than the following ; especially so, on account of its apparent relation to a quasi-historical tradition. It is related of Loiguire, the last pagan king of Ireland, that when he died he was buried at Tara in an upright position, facing Leinster, in fighting array, " for he was ever an enemy of the men of Leinster ".[5] This burial is said to have taken place within the circular earthen ring called the Fort of Loiguire, on the summit of the Hill of Tara near its southern end. Whether that be so or not, a similar upright burial is alleged to have been found at a place called " Croghan Erin ", in the neighbourhood of the royal site. In a tumulus in shape the frustum of a cone, about 60 feet in diameter at the base and 12 feet high, there was found, by trenching, a stone chamber consisting of a horizontal slab (size not specified) supported at a height of 7 feet above ground-level, by an upright flag-stone at the back, and large rounded stones at the sides. Within this chamber was a skeleton, held in an upright position by a packing of earth—the skull immediately beneath the

---

[1] JRSAI 7 [1862-3], 199, 341 ; PRIA 22 [1900] : 286-7. Some curious speculations, regarding this admittedly very curious discovery, are referred to in our first edition, p. 206, but are too ludicrous to be given a further lease of life.
[2] JRSAI 68 [1938] : 130.   [3] Galway 17 [1936] : 44.
[4] Galway, loc. cit. p. 55. But a little more care should have been exercised in proof-reading : some of the technical terms have been badly mauled by the printer.   [5] See my Tara, p. 15 and references there.

roofing-slab, the feet raised slightly above ground-level. A bronze sword-blade and an iron spear-head were found with the skeleton ; so we are told in the beginning of the note which contains the only available description of this important find, though in the end this is watered down to " in the vicinity the spear-heads (*sic*) were taken up ".

In a pit in the ground beneath the base of the tumulus, filled with a different soil, was a small bowl-shaped vessel, highly decorated. With it was a thin piece of either brass [bronze ?] or copper about 18 inches long and 3 inches wide, which was figured or carved round its edges—and lost or stolen irrecoverably, immediately after its discovery.[1]

If we are still perplexed by the comparative poverty of the La Tène relics in Ireland, we should remember that just before the La Tène civilization reached its height, the country was escaping from the enervating damp of the Upper Turbarian climate-phase. This excessive moisture had poisoned the atmosphere between about 850 and 350 B.C., and was enough to account for any depth of decline in human culture and energy. No longer are great blocks of stone manipulated to form grandiose tombs : no longer is there an active trade. The gold is all gone from the rivers : the land is held in subjection by its racially Teutonic, linguistically Celtic tyrants. Wealthy individuals could still manage to secure individual works of art : but this fact only throws into relief the pitiable poverty and helplessness revealed to the excavator of sites belonging to the period in question.

[1] PRIA 4 [1849] : 388 ; supplemented from Wilde, *Catalogue*, p. 194.

CHAPTER IX

DEFENCES AND DWELLINGS

Earthen " Forts "

SCATTERED over most of the sheets of the six-inch Ordnance map of Ireland are the conventional marks which indicate defensive fortifications in the shape of ramparts of stone or of earth. The number still existing is enormous ; the number that has disappeared before the plough is probably no less, and is increasing annually.

We need not emphasize the necessity for such defences : that necessity was universal ; it is so still, and will remain so until the elimination of the burglar. The historical or romantic literature of Ireland treats internecine " hostings " between rival communities, raids by wandering marauders, and individual acts of jealousy or of revenge, as mere matters of course ; and the swoop of the brachy-cephalic invaders which inaugurated the Epimegalithic period, as well as the Scandinavian *razzias* which ended the age of Pagan-Christian syncretism, superposed foreign aggression upon internal unrest. And to human hostility was added the ubiquitous menace of the wolf.

Defences may be natural or artificial : included in the former are lines of mountain or of river, esker-ridges, and precipices ; in the latter, a great variety of structures of different materials and of very different grades of efficacy—walls of stone, earth, or wood (the last including wattle-work and thorn entanglements).

Under the general heading "dwelling-places" we include, at the one extremity, fortification-sites, either for continuous occupation or for refuge in the stress of war : and at the other, humble cattle-pens, for the protection of flocks and herds from human and feral marauders—or to supply the necessary accommodation for the traditional practice of " booleying " (*buailteachas*), *i.e.* the seasonal transference of cattle to fresh pastures, for a change of food and to allow the ordinary grazing-grounds to grow again.[1]

There are other structures, which, although in their present condition and aspect indistinguishable from these domestic estab-lishments, were certainly burial sanctuaries, as is proved by the existence of burial deposits within them. In fact, we cannot always draw a hard-and-fast distinction between domestic defences and the protecting ramparts of such burial-enclosures. On the one hand, we must frankly recognize the possibility of the burial being that of

---

[1] See several articles (in Irish) on this ancient custom in *Béaloideas* 13 [1943]: 130 ff.

a victim of the universal commonplace, a preliminary human sacrifice, offered for averting ill-luck at the time of the first establishment of the dwelling, or to ensure for its protection a permanent ghostly guardian : the story of the immolation of Oran at the establishment of Colum Cille's monastic settlement on Iona, absurd though it may seem in its context, just because of its absurdity could never have been told at all, except in a society where such foundation-sacrifices were familiar, at least in tradition.[1] On the other hand, the burial may be that of the chief lord of the house, interred after his death within his abode—again a common practice, as any ethnologist could tell us.

But we are not altogether without discriminating criteria. Chief of these is the presence or absence of traces of occupation : ashes of domestic fires, midden refuse, stones for grain-rubbing, and the like. Habitation-sites soon become littered with midden-waste and similar odds and ends of household economy. This (to our prejudices) inconvenient accumulation was to the ancient occupants a matter of iudifference : the excavator in almost any habitation-site can collect animal bones sufficient to fill many sacks. The absence of such relics is therefore a practically conclusive indication that the site was something different. For example, the virtual absence of midden-refuse from the elaborate structure at Togherstown (Westmeath),[2] coupled with its very peculiar plan—in both respects contrasting with the great hilltop fort above it—is for me a *proof* against its having had a primary residential or military purpose. Midden-rubbish *may* occur in a dwelling-enclosure containing a grave, for it could not have been *completely* dug up and removed when the site was adapted for burial. It follows that when midden-refuse is absent, we may assume that the grave is the primary element in the site ; when it is present, the grave is secondary, the site having been originally a habitation. If there is no midden-refuse, but at the same time no trace of burial, we may reasonably infer that we have to do either with a cattle-pen or with a sanctuary : preferring the former alternative as a working hypothesis, but reserving final decision till discriminating evidence becomes locally available, by excavation or otherwise. (We learn from the analogy of the Todas that the two alternatives are not of necessity mutually exclusive.)

This variety of use, and the all-dominant " time-lag " which has retarded progress over many centuries, together explain the enormous accumulation of such structures remaining in the country. But notwithstanding the mass of material thus ready to our hands, which is sufficient to afford scope for research-work occupying a considerable number of lifetimes, very little is certainly known about these remains.

Around us, in any part of the country, lie the raw materials of a great monograph on the subject of this chapter ; but many expensive

---

[1] See for further evidence V. Gordon Childe, *Skara Brae*, pp. 142, 153.
[2] PRIA 39 [1931] : 54 (Abstract in *Ancient Ireland*, pp. 107 ff.).

PLATE XII

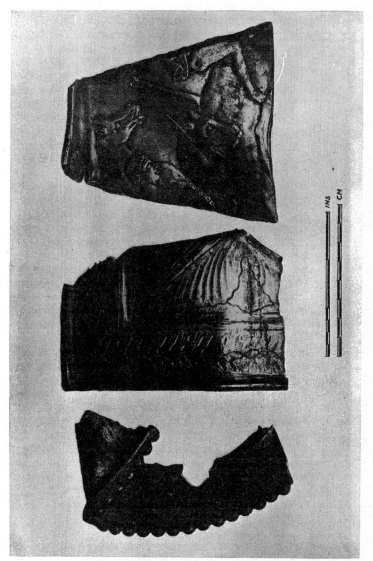

SILVER FRAGMENTS FROM FOYNES

excavations, under properly qualified superintendence, will have to be carried out before its destined authors can put pen to paper. A field for investigations of an importance, not merely National, but European, if not Universal, is dangled before our eyes ; but is kept out of our reach by financial exigencies and other hindrances, and it is only too likely to be withdrawn from us for ever by the extension of tillage. No completely satisfactory scheme of classification can as yet be drawn up, to help us to group these structures into types : still less can we say anything about the distribution of such types over the country. Nor are we in possession of adequate chronological criteria ; there is, in fact, no established evidential test for determining with security the age of any particular structure of the kind. Some of them may conceivably be of the Bronze Age or even earlier, though a less remote date is preferably to be assumed unless we have tangible evidence to the contrary ; others are certainly later, by several centuries, than the arrival of Christianity. Only the spade can settle questions of date ; and the investigation necessary to obtain the verdict is always costly, and not always conclusive. Though to the eye they may conform, more or less, to a uniform type, we may take it as certain that they are very various, both in purpose and in date.

We must lay special emphasis upon the illusory nature of their apparent identity of pattern. Two circular enclosures of earth, between which there is no perceptible difference as we visit them in the middle of the twentieth century, may have presented very different aspects in the tenth or the fifth century. We have, as it were, nothing but the bones left ; and just as there may be a difficulty in distinguishing between the bones of two dogs, approximately equal in size but different in breed, though no one could mistake the identity of the living animals, so our two " ring-forts " might have presented criteria which would have dated them and identified their use, and at the same time demonstrated at sight their diversity in both respects, if we could have visited them when they were " in working order ". Thus, in the present state of knowledge, we are under the unfortunate necessity of renouncing any attempt to distribute the material among our chronological or cultural subdivisions, and must treat " Defences and Dwellings " as one general subject, extending, with no external mark of evolutionary development, through the whole history.

The fullest summary of the subject as yet at our disposal is a careful and, for its time, very thorough study by T. J. Westropp,[1]

---

[1] " The ancient forts of Ireland, being a contribution towards our knowledge of their types, affinities, and structural features." TRIA 31 [1901] : 579. For the same writer's many other contributions to the same subject, including surveys of defensive structures in various special regions, we must here content ourselves with referring the reader to the published indexes of the PRIA and of the JRSAI, where most of the results of his monumental labours is enshrined.

based on many years of personal *surface* exploration; this must form the starting point of all subsequent investigation, for which the spade will be indispensable. By a painstaking analysis of the six-inch Ordnance maps, Westropp found that 28,759 "forts" were recorded as still existing in the country, an average of a little less than one to every two townlands : the largest number (2930) being in Co. Cork, the smallest (58) in Dublin. These latter statistics are easily explained : Cork is the largest county ; Dublin, one of the smallest, has suffered, archæologically, from the spreading of a great city and its suburbs over much of its area, with consequent economic and social influences over the surrounding countryside. More instructive are the comparisons which he gives of the acreage of each county with the number of forts extant within it. According to this, Limerick leads off, with one fort to every 317 acres ; Sligo, with one fort to every 327 acres, is not far behind : while at the other end of the list, the rocky and sparsely-populated county of Donegal has only one fort to every 5550 acres. The complete figures will be found in the monograph cited (pp. 587-8), and they were repro-duced in our first edition (p. 176); but it has not been thought necessary to repeat them here, for there are important factors which diminish their scientific value. First of these is the comparative modernness of the county division of Ireland, upon which the table is based. This was begun in the reign of King John, and was not finished till 1611, when the lands of the O'Byrnes and the O'Tooles were shired, under the new name of Co. Wicklow ; [1] and it hardly seems logical to take it as the basis of a study of the geographical distribution of structures, most of which are certainly older, some of them considerably older, than those limits of date. Secondly, the numbers are not those of the forts : they are merely those of forts which happened to attract the attention of (archæologically un-instructed) surveyors, which is a very different thing ; and of course no account is taken of destroyed, not to say forgotten, monuments, which have a right to enumeration in such statistics. Thirdly, such a table is undiscriminating : it includes in a single category buildings erected for a variety of heterogeneous purposes, and in many different centuries.

Even for structures which are certainly defensive or residential, the name "fort" or "ring-fort", while convenient and generally understood, is too definite in its apparent meaning. It must be interpreted in the most generalized sense, so as to include, not only the military stronghold which it suggests, but a defence not more

---

[1] C. Litton Falkiner, "The Counties of Ireland", PRIA 24 : 169. The other divisions of the country are much earlier : the "townland" or homestead ; the "barony" or *túath* territory (originally *tricha cét*, the group of homesteads which could collectively supply "thirty hundreds" of fighting men) ; and the provincial grouping of these territories into a pentarchy, now reduced to the four "provinces". On this subject see Professor James Hogan, *The Tricha Cét* (PRIA 38 [1929] : 148).

important than a railing surrounding an apple-yard. This being premised, we may retain it ; for all attempts to disturb current nomenclature, at the present stage, would be premature, and would lead only to ultimate confusion. The native names, *dún, cathair, caiseal, ráith, lios,* and the like, have the fatal disadvantage from which all vernacular terms suffer—they disregard the important fact that the Archæology of any country is not the exclusive concern of that country ; it is a branch of a universal science, and should speak, so far as possible, a universal language. Moreover, they are not any more specific in their meaning than the English word or words used in current speech : less so, indeed, for the native word most frequently used, *ráith* (*anglice* " rath ") includes within its scope, as defined by current popular use, even such unrelated structures as earthen burial-mounds.[1]

We shall accordingly retain the word " fort " for the buildings with which this chapter deals : admitting that the word is rather too " grandiose " for a true denotation of the many insignificant structures that must be brought within its range : and that almost every one, even of these, presents us with problems of their use, and of their chronological and ethnological setting, which for the time being are unsolved.

Defined thus broadly, the ancient forts of Ireland are enclosures, usually but not invariably circular on plan, surrounded with one or more ramparts. We shall take them as we find them, without prying into the unknown underground mysteries that excavation may reveal, or the forgotten mysteries now beyond our reach—the erections of wood, thatch, textiles, and other perishable materials, which we may reasonably presume to have once been associated with them, but which are now gone for ever.

The choice of material for the ramparts—earth or stone, and often, most likely, wood—seems to have depended primarily on the nature of the surrounding region. When the surface is stony, as in the Aran Islands or parts of Co. Clare, stone is the obvious material to use ; in rich alluvial soils, it would hardly be possible to use anything but earth. Earth is the commonest material, though it may be mixed with stones ; sometimes, indeed, an apparently earthen rampart will be found to have a stone wall as a core. The stone walls are always built of loose rubble, and no form of mortar is ever used. (Mortar seems to have been unknown in Ireland till the seventh-century ecclesiastical missionaries were introduced to it on the Continent, and brought the knowledge home with them.)

The outline of the enclosure, as a rule, is so truly circular, that it must have been laid out by means of a cord, attached to a central

---

[1] On the various names of forts in general, and of individual examples in particular, see the discussion in Westropp, *op. cit.* pp. 588 ff.

peg, and used as a travelling radius. The size of the protected area varies greatly, from a few yards in diameter up to an acre or more in extent.

In many, indeed in the majority, of these enclosures there is now no external sign of any building remaining within the area. Only excavation could determine whether any such buildings had existed : and even excavation cannot do so, if they were of wood, with their supporting-posts set in horizontal sleepers, or not sunk deep enough in the earth to penetrate to the subsoil. But we may reasonably assume that a small enclosure, having no visible or discoverable evidence of buildings within its area, was a night-pen to guard cattle from wolves. In fact, the "forts", in general, were much more probably protections against these creatures than against human enemies : the obvious strategic shortcomings of many of them, to which we shall return later, favour this view of the question. Inside an earthen enclosure, reinforced with a fence of thorny brushwood on the top of the vallum, and guarded by watchmen, cattle were probably as safe from this menace as care could make them. An earthen fort excavated by myself at Lackan, near Blessington (Wicklow), illustrates this aspect of the case. It was carefully laid out, and defended with a fosse and a single vallum : but absolutely nothing was found within it, though the whole surface was dug over down to the virgin soil. There were occasional pockets of ashes, apparently the relics of small cooking fires ; but there was no midden debris, so that there cannot have been any continuous occupation. A series of shallow post-holes, in a curve concentric with the enclosure, showed that a flimsy shed had been constructed at one side, inside and backing against the vallum, and serving merely as a penthouse protection against rain. At the last moment an iron object, resembling a small spear-head, was found (now deposited in the National Museum, Dublin). This was to all appearance the head of a cattle-goad, and confirmed the interpretation suggested for the whole structure.

The fortification, in the simplest of these structures, normally consists of two elements—a rampart, with a fosse or ditch running alongside of it ; the latter produced automatically, in the first instance, by the digging out of the clay to form the rampart, but remaining to serve as a valuable addition to the defence. When the ditch appears to be absent, the very first operation of the excavator should be to make quite sure that the ditch is not there after all, choked up with a later accumulation of midden debris or otherwise. Outside the vallum of the Feerwore fort (*ante*, p. 230) there was a ditch, but it was not visible until the excavation revealed it.

I venture to suggest at this point a classification-formula which would express, in a way at once terse and graphic, the lay-out of the Irish forts. The ordinary type is that specified above, in which a ditch or *fosse* runs outside the rampart or *vallum*. The two together form a unit of defence, and by using the initials L[evel], F[osse], V[allum], the whole fort can be exactly described by the formula L–[F V]–L, in which the first L denotes the level of the ground outside the structure, the second the level of the space enclosed. This can be adapted to suit all varieties, as we shall show when we describe them.

Occasionally, the fosse is *inside* the vallum, L–[V F]–L. Assuming that the fort *is* a fort, to be defended against human marauders, I can offer no explanation for an arrangement so obviously inconvenient : but if in such cases the fosse was meant as a wolf-trap, to hold up for a moment a predatory wolf which had contrived to get past the vallum, and to give time for the cattle-guardians to despatch him, it would be more intelligible. The obstruction could be rendered more efficient with a sunk fence of brushwood or of stakes.[1]

As a rule, the fosse, as it exists to-day, has become partly filled up with earth, washed in by the rains of centuries, and the vallum has been correspondingly reduced in height by the same agency. A section has to be cut in order to determine the original profile of the fosse : and the vertical difference between this and the present section, added to the present height of the mound, will give a fair approximate idea of the original height of the latter. We may suppose that the efficacy of the mound, as a defence, was enhanced with palisading, or with a thicket of thorn-trees : and the thorn-trees, which now frequently grow within these enclosures, may possibly be a sort of hereditary evidence for the use of such a device. Some means would have to be taken to prevent this additional protection from interfering with the duties of that essential functionary, the watchman.[2]

An entrance-gap is usually left in the vallum, giving admission to the enclosure. This we may presume to have been filled with a wooden framing containing a strong door. In fact, in some excavations conducted on modern scientific principles, post-holes and other evidence for a more or less elaborate wooden door-framing have been discovered : see, for instance, the description of Ó Ríordáin's excavation of Garranes (Cork).[3] We may often see an L-shaped foundation just inside one of the jambs of the entrance-gap ; all that is left of a door-keeper's lean-to " sentry-box ". Access to the doorway was sometimes provided by interrupting the excavation of the fosse for, say, three or four feet, thus breaking the circle and leaving a causeway across it. When there was no such causeway, the fosse being continuous, it must have been crossed by means of wooden planks, which could be raised in military emergencies.

[1] For parallels, see C. Hawkes, " Hill-forts " : *Antiquity* 5 [1931] : 60, especially p. 66. The whole of this article should be studied in connexion with the present chapter.　　　　　　　　　　[2] But see Hawkes, *op. cit.* p. 72, on this point.
[3] PRIA 47 [1942] : 77, especially pp. 82 ff.

Often, however, there is no gap in the vallum—at least a gap is no longer traceable. In some cases this is apparent rather than real : the rains of centuries have been fretting the earthen walls and levelling them ; modern agriculturists have been pillaging them for the valuable top-dressing which they yield ; and in a dilapidated, grass-grown vallum, intentional gaps are often indistinguishable from accidental gaps. A vallum which may originally have been eight or ten feet in height, with its associated fosse of corresponding depth, may be reduced by such means to little more than a ring of wavelets on the surface of the ground. Sometimes we are faced by the difficulty, ever present in determining the plan of house-foundations, that the sills of door-openings may have been raised to anything up to a foot or so above the level of the surrounding floor, to hinder a too free intrusion of rainwater, and also, possibly, to restrain young children from wandering at will. If the wall has been degraded down to a foot above the foundation, as is often the case, nothing remains to show where the doorway may have been.

Nevertheless, when all such accidental cases are excluded, there remains a considerable number of forts in which the vallum is sufficiently intact to enable us to say that it never had an entrance-gap ; and the fosse is sufficiently open to show us that it was never interrupted by a causeway. We must conclude either that no practical use was ever made of the enclosure—that it was a sacred place apart, tabu because of the presence of an important grave, or for some other reason now indeterminable; or else that those who used the enclosure submitted themselves to the trouble of climbing the walls (thus in a short time trampling, involuntarily and automatically, a pathway which would give access to friend and to foe indifferently), as a preferable alternative to the provision of an entrance-gap, convenient—but vulnerable, and needing to be guarded night and day.

Were the fossæ filled with water, like the moat around a mediæval castle ? Water will lie in them, at least in pools, after heavy rains, for a length of time varying with the porosity of the soil and the current intensity of sun-heat. But there is no recognizable evidence that the defenders deliberately allowed water to accumulate within them, or that they took steps to carry water into them by cutting conduits from neighbouring springs or rivers. On the contrary, one of the ditches excavated on Uisneach Hill had a drainage-channel running *out* of it, as though to *prevent* the accumulation of water.[1]

While the normal plan of the forts is circular—hence the conventional name " ring-forts "—there are other varieties, oval, semi-circular (" **D**-shaped "), or quadrangular. It is probable, though not as yet universally certain, that quadrangular forts are late, indeed,

[1] PRIA 38 : 89.

mediæval in origin.[1] The fact (observed by Westropp) [2] that the majority of the quadrangular forts are in S. Leinster, especially Counties Kilkenny and Wexford—*i.e.* within the English Pale—is confirmatory, though not necessarily conclusive.

The next basis of variety lies in the relative levels inside and out. The enclosed space is usually on the same level as the surrounding surface outside the fort : it is indeed a section of that surface, cut off by the excavations with which the defence was constructed. But sometimes it is at a higher or a lower level. The latter is rare, and would be avoided for obvious reasons of strategy and convenience—the defenders would be completely at the mercy of a successful assault, and the drainage of surface water would be impossible. The former, though abnormal, is not infrequent. In some of these cases, the difference is produced by the introduction of soil-material into the fort, spread over the original surface—either at the beginning of the occupation, or subsequently, to form a new occupation floor : indeed, the mere accumulation of midden debris may raise the floor-level considerably. In others, the raised level is due to the fortification of a small natural hillock, the summit of which is surrounded by the enclosing vallum.

Difference of plan may be expressed by adding to our classification-formula a word which will express it—in the form $L - [F V] - L$ (oval), or (quadrangular), as the case may be : circular plans being assumed in the absence of such specification. Difference of level may be expressed by $L - [F V] - L^{+}$ or $L - [F V] - L^{(-)}$ according as the inner level is *above* or *below* the level of the surrounding country.[3]

The simple plan which we have been considering hitherto is complicated, in many individual cases, by a multiplication (*a*) of the defences, (*b*) of the enclosures.

(*a*) The defenders may add to the single vallum a second or even a third, outside and concentric with it, each with its associated fosse : formulæ $(L - [F V] - [F V] - L)$ or $(L - [F V] - [FV] - [F V] - L)$. In these cases an intruder from outside must pass the fosse-vallum combination twice or thrice before he reaches the central enclosure. As a rule, the [F V] groups follow one another immediately ; but sometimes there is an interval between the vallum and the next fosse inside. This would be expressed by the formula $L - [F V] - L - [F V] - L$. More than three rings is extremely rare : I doubt, indeed, if any ordinary fortification shows such elaborate protection. Some triple-ringed forts—I have noticed them especially in Co. Galway, but they are not necessarily confined thereto —have a specious appearance of having four ramparts when viewed

<hr/>

[1] Thus Mr. B. St. J. O'Neil reasonably compares a quadrangular fort at Ballyraine, near Arklow (Wicklow) to a fourteenth-century moated house-site (JRSAI 71 [1941] : 26). [2] *Op. cit.* p. 583.
[3] In all these formulæ the members of the complex are expressed in the order in which we meet with them as we pass from the outside to the central enclosure.

from a distance : the reason being, that a slightly sunken causeway runs round the top of the central rampart, presumably for the accommodation of a patrolling watchman, the deceptive appearance being produced by the low protection parapets on each side of it. On the Hill of Ward, Athboy (Meath), the ancient sanctuary and assembly-site of *Tlachtga*, there is a small enclosure surrounded by *four* concentric earthen ramparts ; but this is altogether exceptional.[1] Westropp quotes from the story called *Siabur-charpat Con-Culainn*,[2] a reference to a place called *Dún Scéith* protected by *seven* ramparts : but in the first place the passage quoted occurs in a most fantastic poem, describing contests with all manner of monsters, and its statements can hardly be accepted as evidence ; and in the second place, Dún Scéith, if it ever was anywhere at all, was certainly not in Ireland. It may have been in the Island of Skye, as understood by Crowe (the editor of the text quoted) and Hogan's *Onomasticon*. It has been suggested [3] that the multiplication of defensive ramparts is a direct consequence of the invention or introduction of the sling, which increased the range of hostile artillery.

When there is more than one rampart surrounding the enclosure, there is usually an entrance gap in each of them. Sometimes these entrances, with their associated causeways, are in line : but sometimes this is not the case, the entrance in the inner rampart being, perhaps, one quarter of the way round the circle from the entrance in the outer rampart. This would have the obvious advantage that an intruder, having forced the first entrance, would be obliged to turn his flank to the defenders while making his way along the ditch to the second : an advantage perhaps sufficient to balance the inconvenience which it must have caused to those who visited the establishment on legitimate business.

(*b*) As to a multiplication of enclosures, within one structure, that also is a well-established principle : I say " within one structure ", for we may have two independent forts not more than a stone's-throw apart, which never had any organic mutual connexion. The cases here envisaged are those in which we have two enclosures conjoined, in a figure-of-eight, with their outer defences impinging or interpenetrating ; or at least so close to one another that they cannot but have formed one establishment : or else two (or more) enclosures, each with its own defences, side by side but not in contact, and all contained within an outer rampart surrounding the whole area which they occupy : formula L — [F V] — L — {([F V] — L)

---

[1] I am inclined to believe that this is not a fortification at all, but a huge model of a cup-and-ring symbol. The central space appears to be too small to justify such elaborate defences ; while on a site which was the centre of periodical " assemblies ", some such expression of a religious mystery would be appropriate.

[2] " The Ghostly Chariot of Cu Chulainn ", published JRSAI 11 [1870-1] : 371. The special reference is to pp. 384-7.

[3] By Dr. Mortimer Wheeler : see *Antiquity* 13 [1939] pp. 58 ff., esp. pp. 62 ff.

+ ([F V] — L)}. A good example of this is to be seen in *Ráith na Ríogh*, " The Fort of the Kings ", on Tara Hill ; but there are many others.

We have said that there is often no surface evidence of the existence of subsidiary buildings within the enclosure. Excavation in modern times has sometimes revealed post-holes, the only available relics of vanished wooden houses ; and, especially in the stonier regions of the west, foundations of (unmortared) stone houses are not infrequently to be seen or similarly discovered. Sometimes, but rarely, we may come across an entrance which it is not an exaggeration to call " megalithic " : there is one near the village of Cowrooch on the greater Isle of Aran ; another, near Rinvyle (Galway) is illustrated by Kinahan.[1] These may possibly be adaptations of pre-existing megalithic structures. " Stone columns in the doors of royal *raths* " are referred to in an admittedly imaginative passage in the tale *Mesca Ulad*.[2] As the forts now remain, practically the only structurally interesting details are the souterrains, of which we shall speak presently.

In three places—at Tara, at Uisnech, and at Loch Gur—recent excavation has revealed a circular ditch *inside* the enclosure, apparently quite independent of the fortifications, completely filled up, showing no external sign of its existence until the spade discloses it ; and, so far as we can judge from appearance, perfectly useless. It seems to have been dug and then filled up again with its own material—the Tara ditch was partly quarried in rock. At the last moment before our present publication, comes to hand Dr. Bersu's report on his fruitful excavation at Lissue (Antrim), which greatly strengthens his theory and opens a new and surprising chapter in Irish Archæology (*Ulster*, III, 10 [1948] : 30 ; see also *Illustrated London News*, 10 Jan. 1948, p. 52). Dr. Bersu found at this site also such a hidden ditch as is described above ; he explains it simply as that of an earlier structure on the same site. Further discoveries may enlarge and clarify our ideas on this as yet obscure novelty : and we must await further discoveries to settle a revolutionary question raised by Dr. Bersu as a consequence of investigations carried out by him in the Isle of Man—a question too important to be passed over in discourteous silence, but still admittedly *sub judice*— Were these round walls fortification ramparts, or were they the foundations of large cylindrical houses, once covered with a roof which extended over the whole enclosure ?[3]

We have envisaged the possibility that certain of these enclosures were sacred places which, for some reason no longer assignable, were under a tabu. This is a fact to which outstanding importance

---

[1] JRSAI 10 [1868-9] : 282.   [2] Ed. Hennessy, pp. 20-1.
[3] Gerhard Bersu, *Celtic Homesteads in the Isle of Man*. Journal of the Manx Museum, v. 72.

must be accorded in any discussion of the problems of the forts and their purpose ; if only because of its persistence through all the subsequent centuries, and down even to our own time.   No relics of Irish antiquity have been the centre of intensive superstitious fear to such an extent as these prosaic and apparently commonplace enclosures.   Every book and magazine-article, popular and scientific, which touches upon Irish folklore, has something to say of the forts and of the terrors which they inspire.   They are haunted by fairies and by even more grotesque supernatural beings ; music and other unexplained sounds are frequently heard to issue from them ; grave penalties are exacted from the man foolhardy enough to injure them in any way, to cut trees and (especially) thorn-bushes within them, or on occasion, merely to enter them.   The culprits have died, become paralyzed, been stricken with a variety of maladies, had bad luck in their worldly affairs ; and, contrariwise, the incidence of such untoward events has been explained as a penalty for a presumed sacrilege of the kind on the part of the victim or of one of his kindred —for the suffering in such cases is frequently vicarious, affecting not the guilty person himself so much as some member or members of his family, or else his farm stock.   These superstitions have hitherto been potent in protecting the old " forts " from the plough ; and it is hard to see how they could have come into being at all, if the forts had never been anything but the farmsteads and cattle-pens which they appear to be.   The puzzle is solved immediately if we suppose that a few of them, for a variety of reasons, were tabu from the first ; and that the legitimate terrors, inspired by such (probably exceptional) cases, gradually extended their scope, as the traditions became blurred in specific detail, till they threw the mantle of their protection over commonplace secular structures, resembling them in external form, but entitled to no essential share in their sanctity. In this connexion, however, it should not be forgotten that even the most summary reading " between the lines " of the ancient Irish law-tracts will show us that an aura of tabu enfolded members of the upper ranks of society in the country, their property and their dwellings, certainly down to the beginning of Christianity and probably much later, with an intensity comparable to that recorded of the chiefs of Maori New Zealand.   The dwelling of a man of rank was not a place which a commoner could approach without due precaution.   Thus, even a mere habitation-site might possess a sanctity not less than that which protected the more specifically " sacred " sites from violation.[1]

Whether the rank of the owner of the dwelling had an influence in determining the elaboration of his defences is a question that cannot be answered ; though that this should be so is not unlikely.

[1] It is worth passing notice that there appears to be no such superstition centring in Lake-dwellings (see JRSAI 17 : 149).

The law-tract called *Crith Gablach*,[1] which deals with the privileges and the disabilities of the various castes of ancient Irish society, high and low, tells us how the size, and to some extent the plan, of a man's house was determined by his rank in life. But it is as yet impossible to establish any correlation between the assertions of this and other documents, and the remains of antiquity in the fields, because these deal with different matters. Nothing is left for us to contemplate but the protecting ramparts : at the time when this literature was produced, the houses and their out-buildings were naturally the centre of interest in any steading. These, being of wood, have disappeared : nothing can possibly remain of them except the groups of holes in the ground which received the supporting posts : and until a very much larger number have been excavated out and planned, we can say practically nothing about the dwelling-houses within the enclosures.

Besides the outer ramparts, there are sometimes, in the larger forts, internal divisions formed of earthen or stone walls ; sometimes such a wall may divide the enclosure into two areas, to explain which we should have to possess some information regarding the social conventions of the occupants of the steading. In some (few) cases radial lines divide the enclosure—this is notably the case at Togherstown, where the space between the outer and the inner rampart is so divided : [2] but we have seen already that whatever this structure may have been, its primary purpose was probably not residential.

We have made a casual reference to the strategic short-comings of these structures. This must now be emphasized, as having a bearing on the purposes which they served. Not infrequently they are placed upon sites easily commanded from higher ground, even at a time when projectile weapons of offence were confined, at best, to arrows or to sling-balls. A small body of raiders, established on such a commanding ground, could, with little danger to themselves, pick off most of, if not all, the inhabitants of a fort beneath them, though the defensive ramparts might have been much more efficient than they would be now, after centuries of detrition. An even more serious drawback from the military point of view is the absence of a steady water-supply. I have only once seen a spring of water inside a fort-enclosure : it lay in a field in Co. Carlow, where I happened to visit it casually in the course of an afternoon walk. If the occupants had no means of storing water, it is obvious that long sieges were never expected or provided against. This is intelligible : most raids would be of the nature of " cattle-drives " : plunderers swooped down on the cattle, the chief if not

---

[1] *Ancient Laws of Ireland* (Rolls series) iv, 298 ff. More recently published in the series of " Mediæval and Modern Irish " Texts, under the editorship of Professor D. A. Binchy, with a vocabulary and valuable notes (Dublin, Stationery Office, 1941). [2] PRIA 39 : 58 ff.

the only wealth of their victims, and drove them away. Only a minority of the houses would contain anything else to tempt their cupidity : the chief advantage of the fortification-walls would be to delay the operations of the attackers, thus giving the defenders time to muster all their resources. Westropp has commented on the absence of water-supplies, and explains it as a sanitary precaution. If there had been a spring or other water-source within the enclosure, and if cattle were sheltered within the same walls at night, the water would quickly be trampled over, and rendered unusable.[1]

Even so late as 1928 the only attempt at a *serious* report on any excavation in one of these enclosures was that presented, by Mr. J. G. A. Prim, to the Kilkenny Archæological Society, on what may be charitably called the excavation of a fort at Dunbell (Kilkenny), so long ago as 1852.[2]

There was here an enclosure contained within a double vallum and, close by, three similar but smaller structures. Prim contents himself with describing the main structure as having been " constructed on so large a scale, and possessing its rampart and double fosse in such excellent preservation, as to be a prominent and most remarkable object in the landscape for miles round " : but no drawing, plan, or measurement of the fort itself seem to have been preserved. The work was not a scientific investigation, even by the rudimentary standards of 1852 ; it was undertaken for agricultural, not for archæological purposes, and it was not superintended continuously : the fort was being levelled by the farmer for top-dressing and surface clearance, and the antiquaries merely visited the place from time to time, to purchase from the labourers such relics as had accumulated since their previous advent. The farmer had destroyed one of the three smaller forts long before : another had been trenched in 1842 : the excavation described was that of the third and last of the smaller forts, which was already all but obliterated when the report was presented to the Society. Later, the great fort itself was attacked, apparently without yielding any important archæological harvest : but Prim's final communication, recording this subsequent work, fails to specify clearly which objects came from the one fort and which from the other.[3]

Enormous quantities of bones were found in the course of this work, as is usual in all excavations on residential sites in the country. Incidentally, a sidelight is cast upon the economic conditions and conventions of the time, by the fact that the labourers contracted themselves to the farmer for no wages other than the bones, which they collected and sold for manure on such terms as to realize from two to three shillings a day. These bones belonged to red and fallow deer, ox (*Bos longifrons*), horse, swine, and, it is said, domestic fowl : most of them were found in the inner fosse, which was apparently the recognized midden-dump of the establishment ; but they were also distributed through the central area of the fort in layers down to a depth of 2 feet from the surface. There is no record of the discovery of human bones. If the labourers had to work for this meagre pay for their employer, they seem to have made what is called " a good thing " out of the

[1] What is believed to have been a water-conduit leading into a stone fort in Co. Cavan is more particularly referred to on a later page. Hencken, speaking of a spring well in the analogous fortress called Chun Castle (Cornwall) comments on its rarity (*Archæology of Cornwall and Scilly*, p. 126).

[2] J. G. A. Prim, "Notes on the excavation of a rath at Dunbell, county of Kilkenny", JRSAI 2 [1852] : 119. See also summary descriptions of further objects from the same site in JRSAI 15 [1879] : 181.

[3] See JRSAI 3 [1954-5] : 133, 397.

antiquaries, who soon found themselves confronted with the difficulties inevitable in such cases—concealment of finds if the offered rewards were considered inadequate, and " salting ", not to say actual forgery, if they were satisfactory. The objects collected in this casual way, or such of them as have been preserved, are now housed, with the rest of the collections of the Royal Society of Antiquaries, in the Dublin National Museum. They are all late, being similar to those found in lake-dwellings of the seventh and eighth centuries A.D. ; they include querns, hones, sling-balls, horse-shoes, spindle-whorls, buttons, beads, and amulets in stone. Discs of stone bearing rude linear ornamentation scratched upon them are (to say the least) of doubtful authenticity. In bone and horn there were pins, beads, combs, and knife-handles ; in bronze there were pins and simple ring-fibulæ, with one or two other odds and ends. Two among the latter were most curious, but were lost to sight in Kilkenny and never reached the Museum : for us they exist only in the unsatisfying statement that the one was a small box, " about the substance [sic] of a half-crown ", consisting of two parts hinged together ; and the other was a long narrow strip of bronze showing some trace " of an illegible mediæval inscription, the letters being apparently in the Roman character ". In iron there was a small cow-bell, which we need not assume with the finders to have been " used for religious purposes " by the inhabitants ; there were also pins, fibulæ, knife-blades, shears, an axe, a cattle-goad, a chisel, some horse-shoes, and a reaping-hook. Other " finds " included fragments of baked and glazed pottery and of leather shoes, as well as some other early modern objects (such as a halfpenny of William and Mary). An underground passage was found in the rampart of the smaller fort, at the entrance to which were two stones with Ogham inscriptions, thus confirming the late date of the occupation to which the antiquities uniformly bore testimony. At a subsequent date a pin with attached ring, and the clasp of a book-cover, came to light. The pin seems to have been exceptional in that the ring was not one single piece, but had been formed in a number of segments, jointed together. The book-clasp bore simple key and interlacing patterns, certainly of the Christian period, but without any specially distinctive character.[1] Besides the souterrain, the only recorded " structures "—if we may thus extend the signification of the word—were small pits, 2 feet deep, 1 foot 6 inches across, full of ashes. These were reasonably explained as cooking-pits, though the presence of iron slag in some of them suggests that they may alternatively have been used for smelting-furnaces. They were not lined with stone.

Souterrains

Reference has been made to " souterrains ". To these we must now direct our attention, and say what we can of them in as much space as can be reasonably devoted to an almost inexhaustible subject. Blanchet's work, *Les souterrains-refuges de la France* (Paris 1923), contains over 300 octavo pages. A book could be written on Irish souterrains, even on those that are known as yet—even on the comparatively limited number that I have myself explored—that would challenge comparison with the French work, in bulk as well as in varied interest ; and what is *not* known as yet, we cannot imagine. There are probably dozens in every county, still buried out of sight, with no surface indication of their existence.

[1] These objects are illustrated JRSAI 6 [1861] : 307-8.

A souterrain is a passage, a chamber, or a combination of passages and chambers constructed underground. In some cases, but not very many, it is tunnelled out of stiff underlying boulder-clay which can be trusted to stand by itself without any stone lining : in still fewer cases it is wholly or partially quarried in rock, as in a complicated labyrinth at Ballintemple (Londonderry).[1] But in the great majority the souterrain was built by a process which can be easily reconstructed. Deep trenches were dug, of a predetermined size and plan. The sides of these trenches were lined with drystone walling up to a height of, it might be, some six feet above the bottom, and a foot or two below the surface of the ground. If there were a sufficient number of long stones available, these might be used as a lining : the famous cave at Drumlohan (Waterford), lined and roofed with pillar-stones, ten of which bear Ogham inscriptions, is an example. But as a rule, the long stones—often pillaged, like these, from a neighbouring graveyard—were reserved for the lintels, being laid down to cross the passages, resting upon the drystone facing aforesaid. These lintels were rarely close-set : long stones of the required size and shape were not everywhere so common as to dispense with the necessity of economy. Rather were they laid at short intervals, the intervening spaces being closed with smaller boulders or flagstones laid over them, crossing them at right angles from lintel to lintel. When the construction was complete, the trench was filled up above this roofing to the level of the ground.[2]

Admission to the souterrain is usually provided by an opening in the roof : a block of stone being sometimes left beneath it, in order to serve as a step. But sometimes there is a doorway in an internal construction of the enclosure, with a rudely constructed flight of steps, or a sloping ramp, leading downward to the underground chamber. The entrance hole is sometimes in the middle, sometimes at the edge of the enclosure (at the side of the inner rampart) : more rarely it is between the ramparts. Sometimes there are two or more souterrains within one enclosure, each with an independent entrance, and not connected with one another : sometimes there is such a connexion, so that it is possible to enter the underground structure by one doorway and to leave it by the other. The depth of the roofing stones beneath the surface of the ground is never very great ; the presence of a buried souterrain may occasionally be revealed by differences in the vegetation growing within the enclosure, plants with deep tap-roots being unable to establish themselves above the roofing-stones, though they may grow freely over the rest of the area.

[1] Planned and described by A. McL. May and D. C. Cooper. *Ulster* III 2 [1939] : 82.
[2] Occasionally, but very rarely, the covering stones are above the natural level of the ground, and concealed with an artificial earth-work. An example of this at Sallagh (Down) has been described by Davies (*Belfast* 1 : 27 ff.).

When a chamber within a souterrain is too wide to be roofed with lintel-stones of any manageable length, there may sometimes be a supporting pile of masonry in the middle ; [1] but much more commonly a corbelled vault, after the manner of a beehive hut, is used to cover it. A similar method of construction is followed in the passage, when the width is too great for any long stones locally available—balanced corbel-stones, projecting in the manner of cantilevers, reducing the width to be spanned to manageable dimensions.

In plan, souterrains present great variety : in fact, it is hardly too much to say that no two souterrains, more elaborate than mere single chambers, are constructed to an identical architectural design. The simplest form is a single small chamber, more or less oval on plan, measuring say 6 to 8 feet in length and 3 or 4 feet in breadth—but, though simple, and never very large, even these can show a considerable range of variation in proportion and shape. Greater complexities may take such forms as these :—

(1) A *passage* leading to a small chamber : a common type of plan. Sometimes the apparent disproportion between the size of the passage and the chamber to which it leads is to the superficial eye so ludicrous that some very important purpose of secrecy or mystery must be postulated to account for it. Take, as a single example, a souterrain at Dunbin (Louth). [2] We enter at the south end of a passage about 3 feet, or a little more, in width and height, and proceed along it in a northerly direction for 12 feet. Here it seems at first sight to come to an end : but we find there, on arrival, a hole in the floor, down which we drop 2 or 3 feet ; thus entering another passage running in the same direction for another 12 feet. At the end of this, our experience is repeated—we drop once more into a third passage at a lower level, this time directed westward for 15 feet, and thereafter turning once more northward for another 7½ feet. Once again, a hole in the floor admits to a continuation, no less than 48 feet long, finally ending in a beehive chamber 8½ feet in diameter. Ventilating shafts have been provided—narrow stone-lined tube-like ducts, passing through the earth to the outer air—so that a person could be confined in the chamber, with all the trap-doors closed, and yet not be suffocated : such ventilators are not infrequent in these underground structures. Thus we have to traverse an awkwardly constricted tunnel, 94 feet 6 inches long, with three traps in its course, before we can attain to this insignificant chamber. But although we in our ignorance may call it " insignificant ", surely it must have had great importance in the eyes of those who built and made use of it, whatever that use may have been.

(2) A succession of small chambers, up to about five or six

---

[1] As in an example at Dundalk, *Louth* 8 [1933] : 95.
[2] Plan and Section in *Louth* 7 [1932] : 498.

in number, each of them opening out of the one before.   A greater number of such chambers is exceptional : a row of " seven or eight " is recorded in a souterrain at Scart (Kilkenny) : [1] and there are nine in another at Cloghane (Kerry).[2]

(3) A passage as in type (1), but with side branches consisting (a) of chambers, (b) of passages leading to chambers, or (c) of passages leading to roof-openings affording an exit, either within or without the enclosure.

(4) A passage, with or without traps and blinds to baffle pursuers, leading to an exit outside the enclosure.

The passages may be straight, bent at right or other angles, or curved.   In some cases there are two storeys of passages, one running beneath the other ; but this is very unusual.[3]   It is not always to be supposed that a fortification with elaborate earthworks has an elaborate souterrain.   Exploration has not advanced sufficiently far to justify us in asserting categorically that the exact contrary is the case ;   but certainly my own observations seem to point in that direction.   Forts with three fine ramparts often have no souterrain at all, or merely a small chamber ; [4] while others, with but one rampart, may have a souterrain almost labyrinthine.   This is not necessarily so surprising as it might at first sight appear to be ;   the lord of a fortress with elaborate ramparts might feel himself much more secure, and therefore requiring fewer of these special precautions, than the occupant of a dwelling surrounded with a single vallum. But to speculate on the reasons for such varieties of plan—they may be practical, chronological, or geographical [5]—would be premature, until we have the fuller knowledge which can be attained only by a comprehensive survey.

With regard to the purpose of these structures, the single chambers were most probably underground store-chambers.   It is an obvious objection that they must have been too damp ; precautions would have to be taken, when the site was in use, to prevent the penetration of rain and silt.   *At present*, the exploration of a souterrain is difficult and disagreeable ;   mud, earth, and stones have accumulated ever

---

[1] JRSAI 1 [1851] : 386 (the vague statement of the number of chambers belongs to this notice).   [2] PRIA 19 [1893] : 105.

[3] An apparent example is described by Rev. W. Falkiner, " Notes upon a rath souterrain at Gurteen, Gainstown, Co. Westmeath ", PRIA 21 [1898] : 211, but it must be remarked that the description, even with the help of the accompanying drawings, is not easy to follow.

[4] Of course, a thorough excavation would, in all cases, be necessary to make it absolutely certain that no souterrain exists ; but there is a sufficient number in which the souterrain is open and accessible for at least a preliminary generalization. Even then, however, there may be unknown *additional* souterrains within the enclosure.

[5] Within the limits of present knowledge, there seems to be a certain capriciousness in the geographical distribution of these structures, which is as enigmatical as everything else about them.   This is well brought out as an incident in an admirable survey by Mr. E. Watson of the " Prehistoric sites in S. Antrim " (*Ulster* III 3 [1940] : 142).

since the fort was abandoned, to say nothing of dead and rotting sheep and other unpleasant things, which are often cast into them, to get them out of the way. Usually an explorer is obliged to wriggle prone rather than to crawl, over fallen stones (too often porcupined with unavoidable sharp points, always painful and in such a situation not without danger) embedded in a slush of sticky mud, where there may once have been a passage six or seven feet high. Not always, however : at Tullyglass (Cork) there is a souterrain with two rectangular chambers united by a passage 3 feet 8 inches in length, and never more than 1 foot 8 inches high by 1 foot 6 inches wide. It is hard to imagine a constant *peaceful* use for such a rat-hole. This souterrain is entered by a lintelled doorway in the side of one of the chambers, approached by a sunk passage which was apparently hollowed in the earth, but never stone-lined.[1] On the whole, such sunken chambers are at best hardly fit for habitation, even under the very modest conditions of comfort and sanitation which all these ancient dwelling-places indicate ; but the general absence of any traces of interment, coupled with the signs of human occupation remaining in the fort as a whole, is adverse to an otherwise possible alternative suggestion, that the souterrains were sepulchral *hypogæa.*

Souterrain passages leading to an exit outside the fort were most probably provided to serve as sally-ports, through which the defenders could escape with their lives if they failed to hold their ground against an assailant.

Sometimes it has appeared to me a possibility that these underground excavations might have served as cisterns. Mr. Raymond Firth [2] gives us a description of Maori hill-forts in New Zealand which in many details appear to present remarkable analogies with the Irish structures at present under our consideration. He says (p. 77) : " practically all the cultivations of the people lay outside the fort, so that to be able to resist a siege stocks of provisions had to be kept inside the enclosure. Vegetable foods were stored in pits underground, and flesh foods were dried and preserved in store-houses or on tall stages. But the weak point was usually lack of water. As a rule, the hill-fort had no spring within it, and anyone venturing out to get water was cut off by the besiegers. In some forts attempts seem to have been made to keep an artificial supply " in gourds, in underground pits, or in bottle-shaped subterranean chambers. As in like manner the Irish forts were unprovided with a natural supply of water, it may be that some of the smaller and simpler souterrains were reservoirs. Even long and elaborate passages might be useful for this purpose, on account of the convenience of being able to tap them from different parts of the enclosure and of its contained buildings. If the masonry joints were caulked with stiff clay, well tamped, they might hold water for a considerable time : in fact, water frequently stands in them now, after heavy rains—dirty, and unusable even to people untroubled by the terror of microbes, but that is because the souterrain has itself become dirty after centuries of neglect ; if it were cleared out at intervals and kept in repair, it might serve the purpose suggested not inadequately.

[1] *Cork* 40 [1938] : 50.   [2] *Antiquity* 1 [1927] : 66 ff.

The extensive souterrain discovered at Togherstown (Westmeath)[1] showed polishing on the stones, as though they had been rubbed by the passage of sheep. Similar polishing was noticed by Mr. A. W. Lindsay in a souterrain at Dunalis near Coleraine (Londonderry) : [2] it has also been recorded in several of the French souterrains : [3] and in all cases the explorers have explained them in the way suggested. But the farmer at Togherstown was of opinion that this explanation was inadmissible, as sheep are so easily smothered that to crowd them into such a narrow passage would imperil their existence ; and his practical experience—he told us that he had himself lost sheep by their being too closely crowded in a railway truck—coupled with a very considerable personal endowment of intelligence, adds weight to his opinion.

Possibly the same objection might not apply to goats, which animals are more particularly specified by Mr. Lindsay, in the paper quoted.[4] In the Togherstown souterrain, a little past the place where the stones were rubbed, the floor of the passage dropped suddenly to a lower level, and it may have continued as a water-store—especially as there were two pits at the further end which looked like sumps.

Other souterrains, again as in the analogous Maori structures, may possibly have been used for the temporary reception of siege stores ; though it is difficult to see how they could have been maintained, sufficiently free from damp to keep them fit for such a purpose, except for a very short time. Even when the passages and chambers are of a reasonable size, the entrance portals, and (still more) the internal doorways, are often extravagantly inconvenient— low and narrow, impossible to traverse (even when not cumbered by later accumulation of silt, etc.) except on all fours, and sometimes with a disconcerting drop on one side or the other. Such entrances may possibly have been designed for resistance from within—the last refuge of a body of conquered defenders. Only one person could intrude at a time, and he would be easily dealt with while struggling through the hole. In this connexion, we can assign another use to the ventilating shafts ; they might have been intended, not merely to renew the air inside the chambers, but also to serve as a precaution against the terrible danger of being smoked out. In the year 1063, according to the *Annals of Loch Cé* and of the *Four Masters*, something of the kind actually happened at the Cave of Aille in Ceara, Co. Mayo, where 160 persons were smothered by bandits and treasures in their custody carried off. In a souterrain on Dromvalley

[1] PRIA 39 : 74.   [2] *Belfast* 1934-5, p. 65.
[3] A. Blanchet, *Souterrains-refuges*, p. 39.   This writer quotes Xenophon as a witness for keeping domestic animals in underground houses in Eastern Armenia.
[4] Mr. Stelfox suggested, in a letter to me, that pigs rather than sheep or goats might have caused the polishing—or even men, habitually squatting on the floor and leaning against the wall.

townland near Aunascaul (Kerry), to which Capt. O'Connell, R.N., conducted me some time ago, a side branch led from the main passage to a small chamber, entered by a rectangular porthole cut through a wide slab which otherwise closed the end of the passage. Behind it was the movable slab with which the defenders could close the porthole from the inside, and a number of other stones which could be piled against it and would make a forced entrance to the chamber from without practically impossible. Portholes are not uncommon in megalithic monuments (though rarely found, if ever, in Ireland), but I have never seen one elsewhere in a souterrain.

The most interesting souterrains are those containing puzzle-passages. In these, the straight way leads to a *cul de sac*, while the road to safety is a branch passage, hard to find, opening out of the side, the floor, or the roof of the main passage.[1]

Souterrains with hidden chambers are analogous to those with puzzle-passages. An entrance-hole leads to a small chamber, which at first sight appears to be all that there is. But the chamber is floored with flagstones, and concealed underneath one of these is a hole which opens in the roof of a second chamber underneath.[2] Here the most treasured possessions of the defenders could be stored, with a reasonable hope that the spoilers would fail to find them. We may, perhaps, see in these primitive " burglar-proof safes " tangible relics of the terrors induced by the Víking raids. It should not, however, be forgotten that the condition in which the Norse raiders left New Grange in the year 861 shows that they were quite awake to the possibility of treasure being hidden under paving-stones. (See *ante* p. 74.)

Sometimes souterrains are found in the open fields, without any earthen enclosure. In such cases it is natural to suppose that the ramparts have been ploughed away. But this is not absolutely certain : it might indeed have been no more than common prudence to construct the hidden refuge *at a distance* from the dwelling, where it might escape the attention of raiders. A remarkable example of such an isolated souterrain exists at Curraghcrowly near Ballineen (Cork), and has been described by the late Admiral Boyle Somerville.[3] It consists of a succession of low chambers, quarried with some care

---

[1] The Dunbin souterrain is an example : another is described, rather obscurely, in JRSAI 16 [1883] : 11 ; others by C. H. Foot at Doon (Offaly), JRSAI 6 [1860-1] : 222, and by E. C. Rotherham near Oldcastle (Meath), PRIA 19 [1893] : 305 ; JRSAI 27 [1897] : 427. There is a well-known example at Parkmore (Clare), described JRSAI 1 : 295, of which a rather idealized section is given in Wood-Martin, *Pagan Ireland*, p. 208.

[2] This type seems to be especially common in Co. Galway : good examples in the neighbourhood of Tuam are described, with excellent photographs, by Dr. T. B. Costello (*Galway* 2 : 109, 3 : 1) and others in the same county and elsewhere by H. T. Knox (*ibid.* 9 : 178, 10 : 1). See also *ibid.* 19 : 178.

[3] *Cork* 35 [1930] : 1 ; *Antiquaries' Journal* 10 [1930] : 246. Another rock-cut souterrain, at Curraghely about 15 miles away, but in the same county, has been planned and described by Brash, PRIA 10 [1867] : 72, and plate 10.

in the rock, entered from the southern end, and united by awkward creep-passages and small doorway openings. What appears to have been a long drain runs out from it northward. There are at least four ventilation shafts : but anything more miserable and unhealthy even as a temporary habitation it would be difficult to imagine.

The above paragraphs may appear to prejudge the problem of the date of these structures. They have been transferred, with trifling verbal modifications and some additions, from our first edition, where, for what at the time of the publication seemed to be good reasons, the souterrains were all brought down to a late (post-Scandinavian) date. For if the question " When were the souterrains built ? " had then been asked of any serious archæologist, the answer would almost certainly have been, unhesitatingly, " In quite recent times : say round about A.D. 800-900." That is a time when (as is hinted above) we might actually have expected such refuges to have been necessary, in view of the raids of the Northmen : and I have no doubt that a large number of these structures were, in fact, prepared to meet that emergency. There are two external testimonies which bear this out. Although not much excavation has been carried out in any of these structures, and still less has been productive, a few in N.E. Ireland have yielded specimens of rude pottery, late in aspect, along with fragments of iron and chips of flint, all combining to indicate a very late occupation.[1] Again, as we have seen, some of the lintels are rough pillar-stones, originally tomb-memorials, inscribed upon their edges in Ogham. In the stress of the emergency, the builders even pillaged neighbouring cemeteries in search of lintels : the fact that they did so is presumptive evidence that the emergency was pressing. Obviously a souterrain containing such material cannot be older than the fifth to the seventh centuries, the dates which may be provisionally assigned to the period of Ogham writing : and as it is reasonable to allow the lapse of a sufficient time to kill off all relatives of the owners of the memorials (who would presumably have protected tombs in which they were personally interested) we must add something to those dates, again carrying the " souterrain age " down to about the time of the Scandinavian raids—a time of disorganization when (as we have all experienced in our own days) military exigencies call for expedients which override traditional values.

In this connexion, it is interesting to recall that when I was associated with a company, privileged to uncover and to rescue for science no less than six Ogham inscriptions which had been buried

[1] H. C. Lawlor, " Some investigations on the souterrain " (PRIA 35 [1919] : 214). *Idem*, " Some notes on the investigation of dwelling-places of prehistoric man in N.E. Ireland " (*Belfast* 1915-16 : 31, 1917-19 : 77). See also M. Hobson, " Some Ulster Souterrains " (JRAI 39 : 220) ; H. W. Gillman, " The problem of the souterrains " (*Cork*, vols. 2, 3). Ferguson's paper, " On some Evidence touching the Age of Rath-caves " (PRIA 15 [1872] : 129), though inevitably antiquated, should not be overlooked.

in a souterrain at Knockshanwee (Cork), and there lost to sight and memory, an old woman came up and, taking me aside, pointed to a neighbouring field with these words : " There was once a graveyard there, and the fairies came in the middle of the night and took all the stones away ". It was difficult not to connect this modern folk-story with the ancient act of sacrilege ; it was tempting to fancy that this was the tale which the fort-builders told their credulous neighbours long ago, in order to cover their tracks.

Two Ogham stones *with crosses upon them*, and therefore presumably associated with Christianity,[1] have been found in Co. Kerry souterrains, at Whitefield and Coolmagort respectively ; and in another souterrain in the same county, at Aghacarrible, in addition to three Ogham stones, there is a small, certainly Christian monument, uninscribed, but bearing two crosses.[2] These three souterrains must therefore have been constructed after Christianity had begun to make headway in the country. On the other hand, the presence of a souterrain beneath the church of Dunbullog (Cork),[3] and another close to the cathedral of Killala (Mayo),[4] may illustrate the reconsecration of originally pagan sites to Christian uses.

Moreover, we have literary evidence, from both the Irish and the Scandinavian side, for the raiding of " caves ". The history called " The Wars of the Gaedil with the Gaill " describes a raid by the Scandinavian leader Barait and " the son of Amlaib [Olaf] " on the people of Leinster and Munster, " where they did not leave an underground cave unexplored " ; the editor of the document, Dr. Todd, conjectured that the " caves " were burial-caves with grave-goods ; but the comparatively small number of these in the country makes it much more probable that *souterrains* are intended, stored, as the circumstances of the times would make it natural, with the domestic valuables, whatever these might have been.[5] The Scandinavian evidence is provided by *Landnámabók* (I iii 3) where we read :—

Leif plundered in Ireland, where he found a great earth-house (*iarð-hús*). He went in, and it was dark, till light came from a weapon which a man held there. Leif killed the man, and took the sword, and much other treasure ; after that he was called " Sword-Leif ".[6]

But this still leaves the problem of the origin of the souterrains unsolved. Did they suddenly spring into existence just at the time specified ? Did they immediately come into universal use over the country ? Did they develop, in so short a time, so great a variety of plan ? If not, what lies behind these ninth-century souterrains ? The answer seems to be suggested by the excavation carried

---

[1] Not necessarily, and, in fact, not probably, Christian monuments, but tampered with by Christians before their adaptation as building-stones, as is more particularly explained on a later page.
[2] Roughly illustrated in *Kerry* 1 : 14.   [3] JRSAI 1 : 843.
[4] JRSAI 28 [1898] : 291-2.   [5] *Op. cit*. pp. lxxiv, 24.
[6] Vigfusson and Powell, *Origines Islandicæ* i 20.

out by Professor Ó Ríordáin at Cush, Co. Limerick,[1] and (as often happens when answers to difficult questions are at last discovered) it has proved to be almost absurdly simple. *Souterrains* lie behind the ninth-century structures ![2]

This site has been known for its elaborate earth-works ever since that great field-worker, T. J. Westropp, called attention to it. It was reserved for Professor Ó Ríordáin to test its nature by excavation ; and even if his conclusions did not corroborate those of Westropp, even if Westropp's identification of the site with the *Temair Erann* of mediæval Irish literature has been countered by Professor O'Rahilly with a blunt denial that such a place ever existed, the credit due to him for his recognition of its importance is in no wise diminished.

It proved to be a bronze-age habitation-site : the first of the kind to be explored in the country. There were seven ring-forts in the complex, each of them containing a souterrain : and as a later bronze-age interment lay directly above one of these underground structures, the latter must have been earlier in date. Inside the enclosures were post-holes, the surviving records of wooden houses, rectangular on plan : and old field-enclosures surrounding the complex showed that it was inhabited by a farming community. The domestic relics indicated an occupation lasting through the late Bronze Age into the Iron Age. Even if some, perhaps the majority, of the known souterrains be of the ninth century or thereabouts, we now realize that there are others unknown, unsuspected, unexplored, which carry the tradition back to the Bronze Age. When we crawl through a souterrain, our vision is no longer bounded by the Scandinavians and the ninth century. We look back to the bronze-age dwellers in Cush and their contemporaries, and then, taking a wider vision, our eyes cross the seas, and we contemplate the long chain of *souterrains-refuges* which burrow into the soil of France, whose antiquity had hitherto forbidden us to mention them in connexion with the Irish structures. So we reach the Mediterranean, once more explore the underground mazes of Malta and, turning eastward, find ourselves wandering through vast labyrinths cut in the soft rock of Southern Palestine, the work of long forgotten people who had to make for themselves shelters against their brother men.

But here we must pause. We must remind ourselves and our

---

[1] S. P. Ó Ríordáin, " Excavations at Cush, Co. Limerick ", PRIA 45 [1940] : 83 ff., especially p. 178. See the references there for the other writers named, to which add T. F. O'Rahilly, " Dun Cermna ", *Cork* 44 [1939] : 16.

[2] But we must not overlook the possibility suggested by Messrs. Mullin and Davies as a corollary to their excavation of a bronze-age carn containing three roughly circular cists which had been cleared out and inhabited in the Iron Age : that souterrains were suggested by such appropriations ; the later squatters endeavoured to copy the constructional technique of their tomb-building predecessors (*Ulster* III [1938] : 102). Once again we see illustrated the possibility of a problem having two solutions.

readers that we are dealing with a subject which *even now* would provide ample material for an extensive monograph ; and which after a course of excavations hardly begun as yet will be overwhelming. Such a work must necessarily fall into the province of a State-aided Archæological Commission, parallel with the Historical MSS. Commission which during the few years of its existence has done so much admirable work ; and its labours would be a national memorial no less honourable to the country than the long series of volumes which the Manuscripts Commission named has already published. There are doubtless many interesting items of detail (like the Dromvalley port-hole mentioned above) awaiting discovery among souterrains that lie open ; what may be hidden among the scores of souterrains not yet opened (or even discovered), we cannot attempt to guess.

Stone Forts

The greatest of the earthen fortifications are surpassed in magnificence by the *Stone Forts*, the most remarkable prehistoric monuments in Ireland. These, in contrast to the fortified residences of individuals, may be fairly described as " Community Fortifications ". They have generally been assigned to the Bronze Age ; but on the whole a more moderate estimate of their antiquity is preferable, though the question cannot be considered as closed. No datable objects have ever been found in essential association with the majority of these monuments.[1]

The following are the chief monuments of this class remaining in Ireland :—

Grianán (" *Sun-palace* ") *of Ailech*, near Londonderry. A circular area, 77 feet 6 inches in diameter, surrounded by a stone wall with one entrance. The wall is 15 feet thick, and is built in stages on the inner face (a characteristic common to all or most of these structures, stairs being provided to facilitate mounting them. Their obvious purpose is to provide a stance for the defenders). Openings on the inner face of the wall give admission to two passages running inside it for part of its course. An enigmatical building, presumably a house of some kind, stands in the middle of the enclosure. Outside the stone wall there are three much abraded earthen walls. It is estimated that the stone wall encloses an area of a quarter of an acre, and the outermost earthen wall about 5½ acres.[2] There is literary evidence that the structure was still in occupation in the year A.D 939.[3]

---

[1] INJ 5 [1934] : 78.

[2] Most of the descriptions of this structure depend ultimately on the memoir contained in " Ordnance Survey of Co. Londonderry, parish of Templemore " (Dublin 1834) ; of all the series of monographs in connexion with the Ordnance Survey, planned by the Director, Sir Thomas Larcom, the only one which attained to print. See also W. Bernard, " Exploration and Restoration of the ruin of the Grianan of Ailech " (PRIA 15 [1875] : 415). Other descriptions will be found in JRSAI 32 [1902] : 302, 45 [1915] : 205.

[3] MacNeill, *Phases of Irish History*, p. 266.

A very similar structure, a little larger in diameter but with slightly thinner walls, at *Moneygashel* (Cavan). This shows the remarkable peculiarity of a water-conduit, apparently intended to bring a supply into the fortress, and so to avoid the trouble and risk of going out to fetch it.[1]

A group of forts on the Aran Islands (Galway). Much has been written about these buildings ; all the cream of the earlier literature is gathered in two papers by Mr. Westropp, to which the reader must be referred for full details.[2] These include the following :—

Dún Aengusa, on the edge of a cliff rising sheer from the surface of deep sea to a height of about 300 feet. All the enclosing walls may be described (though loosely by a rigidly geometrical standard) as horse-shoe shaped or semicircular, the ends of the curves abutting on the edge of the precipice. The innermost enclosure is 130 feet across at the edge of the cliff, and is bounded by a stone wall 12-14 feet thick. Outside is another wall, showing signs of having been altered at some time to conform to a change in plan, enclosing a space measuring 470 feet in diameter along the edge of the cliff. Outside that again, there is a belt of closely set fragments of broken stone, apparently designed to prevent the fort being taken by means of a rush : two or three others of the Irish stone forts display this device.[3] Outside all there is another wall, of irregular plan, enclosing an area measuring 1300 feet along the edge of the cliff.

It is natural to assume that the fort was at first completely enclosed, and that its present exposed openness to the precipice, and the deep sea far below—a permanent danger to children, cattle, and even to sound and sane adults on a dark night—is due to marine encroachment, which has fretted away the cliff under the now missing half of the encircling ring walls. This view is expressed by everyone who has described the structure, and it finds a place in the first edition of this work, p. 171. But I have since been assured by expert geological opinion that at least it needs reconsideration. The underlying rocks are hard, and the strata in which they lie are horizontal. Had they been vertical, or even tilted, they might have fallen into the sea in successive masses. The great height of the cliff at this point, and the even straightness of the line of the cliff face, forbids us to assume that the waves had excavated a cave which has collapsed (making a great cleft such as is actually to be seen at a little distance from the fort, to the south-west). The conclusion indicated seems to be that, while it is not *impossible* that one-half of the site of the fort has been washed away in accordance with the common belief, even the force of the Atlantic waves could hardly have effected this except through a waste of years connoting an inconceivable antiquity for the structure. In the fort—inland, and therefore not liable to marine erosion—called Cahercommaun (Clare), which we have already mentioned (p. ix) and to which we shall return, we have a precedent for a **D**-shaped enclosure of which a precipice has always formed the straight side. In fact, the present evidence makes it more probable that Dún Aengusa was **D**-shaped from the first. A protecting parapet built along the existing edge of the cliff might have been demolished by marine erosion in a comparatively short time : it might have been destroyed by a conquering intruder in order to render the fortress so unsafe

---

[1] (Mrs.) P. Richardson, " The Cashels of Moneygashel, County Cavan ", *Ulster* III 1 [1938] : 19.
[2] PRIA 28 [1910] : 1, 174.
[3] Such as *Dubh Cathair* on the same island, and *Ballykinvarga* (Clare), a complex fort also described by Westropp (JRSAI 27 [1897] : 122, 30 [1900] : 398).

as to be useless : it might even have been destroyed piecemeal in the Middle Ages or later, before the structure attracted scientific attention, by mischievous boys finding amusement in throwing the stones into the sea ; unfortunately, the present-day boy population of the island derives pleasure from similar practices. In spite of indefensible operations, euphemistically called restoration, carried out in the latter years of the nineteenth century,[1] the situation and architecture of this building make it one of the most striking prehistoric monuments in Europe.

Dún Eoghanachta (Onaght)—A circular enclosure about 90 feet in diameter, surrounded with a wall of large stones, at present 16 feet in height and about 14 feet in thickness. There are the foundations of three small stone chambers within the enclosure.

Dún Eochaill (Ochil)—An enclosure 75 to 90 feet in diameter, surrounded with a wall of the usual kind, 20 feet in thickness ; and an outer wall enclosing a space of about 200 feet by 250. Though lacking in the grandeur of situation which distinguishes Dún Aengusa, this is another most impressive structure.

But *Dún Conchobhair* (Connor), on Inismaan (the middle island of the same group), is yet more splendid. It is an oval, 227 feet by 115, surrounded with a wall 18 feet 7 inches thick, and 20 feet high. There is an outer wall, which, however, does not completely surround the inner enclosure as in the other forts : it turns in to touch the citadel wall at each end.[2]

Granted that stones are the commonest objects of the bare, rocky Aran Islands, and that ample material for the building of these gigantic constructions twenty times over is there available for the picking up, the question still remains, why did any company think it worth their while to build them in such a desolate place ? And the only reasonable answer which presents itself is, that the essential germ of the story transmitted to us by the mediæval scholastic historians is true, whatever we may think of its specific details : they were the last shelter of expelled refugees, fleeing from some rapacious conqueror. Driven, step by step, back to the western coast and to the islands beyond, they here made their final stand, by no mere conventional metaphor but in grim, literal reality, " between the devil and the deep sea ". Nothing but massacre, or drowning in the Atlantic deeps, awaited them outside their island fortresses : in desperation they heaped them up these vast walls, to shield them from the fury of the tempest that had burst upon their country and their kindred. The subtle point that the doorways of the enclosures are all turned so as to command a view of the nearest landing-places is an indication of the life of unceasing vigilance which the homeless unfortunates had to lead in these, their bleak cities of refuge.

Returning to the mainland, we note that there was a similar fort near Cong (Galway), internal diameter 150 feet, thickness of walls

---

[1] There are good photographs showing this and the other monuments of the island as they appeared before they were subjected to such treatment, in the Earl of Dunraven's *Notes on Irish Architecture* (London 1875) vol. i.

[2] Description and plan in JRSAI 25 [1895] : 267.

24 feet, height of walls about 10 feet, which was entirely cleared away in the first half of the nineteenth century to provide building material. Apparently, the only existing record of this fine structure is a brief notice in Petrie's manuscript account of Irish Fortifications, now preserved in the Royal Irish Academy's Library. Among others of the same design (more or less circular spaces, enclosed by thick stone walls), we may mention Staigue, near Waterville (Kerry),[1] and Cathair Geal, near Caherciveen.[2] Another fort, in the same neighbourhood, called Leacanabuile, brings the occupation of such structures down to a date evidently posterior to the limit which we have set for our present study. Its plan, and the evidence for reconstruction which it presents, are worthy of notice.[3]

Knockdrum, near Castletownsend (Cork). A ring-wall of stone 10 feet thick, enclosing an area 75 feet in diameter : one entrance passage, with a janitor's cell recessed in the side towards the right hand of an entering visitor. In or near the centre of the enclosed area was what appeared to be the foundation of a house, about 17 feet square, with an entrance doorway facing the entrance-passage in the surrounding wall. The proprietor cleared this foundation some time ago, revealing a pavement covering it all ; but it is needless to say that the place was visited on a subsequent night by unknown yahoos, who tore the pavement up, either for mere mischief or to search for buried treasure. In the corner, at the left-hand end of the wall facing the entering visitor, there is a low lintelled opening, admitting to a descending passage ; this leads to a chamber sunk through the stiff boulder-clay covering the rock, partly quarried in the rock itself ; and roofed with flat stones in the usual way. Nowhere is this chamber more than 3 feet high. On the left-hand side a hole in the rock admits to a second, and another thence to a third, of similar exiguous dimensions. A built fireplace, with a chimney, had been constructed in the third chamber, and traces of cooking operations were revealed. This also was destroyed by yahoos, and the destruction was repeated when the damage was repaired. Outside the structure was a stone bearing two crosses, and, incongruously, a slab with cup and circle devices. Whether the association is more than accidental it is difficult to say.

It is to be noted that almost all the large stone forts are in the western side of the island : which, so far as it goes, confirms the "refugee" theory of their origin. The only considerable example in the east is *Ráith Gall*, near Tullow (Carlow), which was first brought to notice by Dr. G. H. Orpen.[4] This is a circular area, enclosed by four concentric stone ramparts : the inner space measures about 150 feet, the outermost enclosure about 1000 feet in diameter.

These notes must suffice : it is impossible here so much as to enumerate the greater stone forts of Ireland. Although those

---

[1] On which see Dunraven, *op. cit.* 1, p. 24 : TRIA 14 : 17 ; JRSAI 27 : 316, and literature there noted.

[2] See Dunraven, *op. cit.* 1, p. 22.

[3] See the report of the excavation there by S. P. Ó Ríordáin and J. B. Foy, *Cork* 46 [1941] : 85.

[4] "Rathgall, Co. Wicklow", JRSAI 41 [1911] : 138. "Rathgall, Co. Wicklow, Dun Galion and the 'Dunum' of Ptolemy", PRIA 32 [1913] : 41.

mentioned above are among the most important, there are many others that are scarcely inferior to them in interest. The series of stone buildings of all kinds in the south-west of the Dingle peninsula must not be passed over without some allusion ; but for details regarding these the author may be permitted to refer the reader to his special monograph on these structures.[1] There are other similar groups of structures in the same barony, notably a remarkable series on the townland of Ballynavenooragh, which apparently has so far escaped scientific notice.

Mr. Westropp, in the monograph to which several allusions have already been made, summed up such general conclusions as were attainable with the knowledge then at his disposal. He rightly emphasized the importance of comparative study ; and by a large series of references and sketches, to which we can here do no more than call attention, he showed that over a great area of Europe, there are structures, generically and specifically identical with those of Ireland : and that we cannot advance the study of the Irish forts without taking these into account. Some of the Irish forts show evidence of alteration and of rebuilding : but on the whole the architectural style, if we may use a term so dignified, remains unchanged throughout a history which Westropp believed to have lasted " from a time long antecedent to the introduction of Christianity down to (probably) the fourteenth century ". The doctrine of the " time-lag " had not been established as the leading principle in Irish archæological criticism in Westropp's day, but here he has anticipated it by a flash of insight. In the strictly military sense, Westropp continues, very few of the forts are defensive—he is referring to the strategical shortcomings to which we have already alluded. The masonry is, on the whole, poor, and it may be added that no evidence has yet been found in Irish walls of the use of en-closed wooden framing, such as Cæsar describes in the Gaulish fortifications, and such as has been found in certain Scottish defence-walls. Mr. H. S. Crawford has expanded these strictures on the masonry with specific charges.[2] The walls were built on the surface of the ground, without any foundation-trench : thus the weight squeezed out the underlying clay (a process intensified by running rainwater) depriving the heavy wall of any secure basis. Moreover, only the two faces of the wall were built with care : the space between was filled with broken chips and boulders thrown in anyhow— very frequently with sharp points and edges turned downward. These act as wedges, working downward with the weakening of the foundation, and with expansions and contractions due to fluctuations of temperature : and in time they force the two faces of the wall apart. The only tool used in dressing the masonry of which Westropp could find any evidence was the hammer : chisel-dressing seems to

[1] Published in TRIA 31 : 209 ff.   [2] JRSAI 55 [1925] : 67.

have been unknown, or at least unpractised. Leaving out the wooden framework, just mentioned, Westropp sees evidence of the occasional use of wood in gateways too wide to be spanned with a stone lintel, and in wall-recesses and terraces with no means of access provided in the masonry, and too high to be reached without ladders.

In connexion with Dún Aengusa we have twice mentioned *Cahercommaun* (pp. ix, 279), excavated in 1934 by Dr. H. O'N. Hencken of the Harvard Mission. This fortress is situated about 4½ miles north of Corofin in North Clare.[1] It is on the brink of a precipice ; the outer walls, as at Dún Aengusa, are semicircular only, the precipice forming the diameter which cuts them off. Of these walls there are three, the innermost enclosing an irregular oval of a little over 100 feet in maximum diameter. It is about 20 feet thick : the two outer walls are much thinner. The maximum diameter, across the whole structure, from outer face to outer face of the outer wall, is about 360 feet. Except that the precipice is here inland, the resemblance to the plan of Dún Aengusa is very suggestive ; and as marine erosion cannot here be invoked to explain the plan, it underlines the doubts regarding Dún Aengusa that have been expressed above.

The two spaces enclosed by the outer walls appear to have been cattle enclosures, the residential part being inside the innermost wall. The area was covered with hut-sites, eight in number, and with a number of open-air hearths. The huts, like all the rest of the building, were built of dry stone, not mortared in any way : in none of them was there more than one small chamber. From this evidence there is absolutely no escape. This fortress, estimated to be the fifth largest of the more than 2000 fortified structures in the county, testifies to a standard of living not higher than that of a Zulu kraal.

Absolutely no pottery was discovered ; we are obliged to conclude that the art of the potter was in abeyance at the time when the place was in occupation : an important corroboration of observations to the same effect made at other sites of contemporary date. A simple but well executed silver brooch, with a ring (ornamented with animal figures) suspended from the head of the pin, was the most interesting and artistic object found. It bore traces of partial gilding, and may be dated to some time in the first half of the ninth century A.D. With this date, so far as we can judge, the other objects found are in accordance : and as there is no rebutting evidence, we must assume this as the date of the occupation of the dwelling. These other objects consist of such odds and ends as small bronze pins, rings, and studs for decorating leather : iron brooches, pins, knives, nails, buckles, shears, sickles, billhooks, and other tools : bone pins, and beads and bracelets of glass, lignite, and other simple decorative materials. Bronze was scanty in comparison with iron : but polished stone hatchet-heads still survive in use, as well as a few flint scrapers ; thereby confirming the suspicion which has long been held, that such stone implements were not confined to the Stone or even to the Bronze Age, but that (in this country at least) they persisted in use down to well after the beginning of Christianity.

The presence of lumps of iron slag indicates that the lord of the fortress, whoever he may have been, smelted his own iron, or at least caused it to be smelted on his premises : this was apparently the usual practice. Iron is scarcely an æsthetic material, and except some iron pins of the simplest kind with loops in their heads, there were no iron ornaments at Cahercommaun. A few bronze pins, one of them with a decoration of red and yellow enamel, were found ; these, with the silver brooch and the beads, were

---

[1] See the plan in Hencken's report of his excavation (reference above, p. x).

the only objects which revealed any artistic instinct. " Despite the late date of the fort ", says Dr. Hencken in his report of the excavation, " numerous types of objects represent survivals traceable to the Roman period, the pre-Roman Iron Age, and even to earlier times. Once again we see conspicuous evidence of the ' time-lag '." These are Dr. Hencken's words, not mine. By the ninth century A.D. the tale of the Fir Bolg chieftains who found in Dún Aengusa a refuge from their oppressors was fully established among the scholastic historians. This means that *that* structure was then already so old that its true story was forgotten ; that Dún Aengusa must already have been an ancient monument when Cahercommaun was erected, on a similar plan.

There were not many weapons or other objects found in the excavation to suggest warfare—the finds indicating peaceful, if primitive, agricultural and pastoral pursuits : though the possibilities of assault were present in the minds of the fort-builders. They had constructed an underground passage which led to an opening in the face of the cliff : if the occupants were hard pressed in a siege they could pass through this, and, scrambling unseen down the precipice, could at least make off with their lives.

Large numbers of animal bones were recovered from the site—over 9000 pounds of them were collected. These represented the ordinary domestic animals, as well as deer, hare, rabbit, fox, dog, and cat. Evidently they were midden refuse, most of the larger bones having been hacked and broken. The atmosphere cannot have been of the most agreeable, these bones having been left to lie where they were thrown away : no attempt was ever made to cleanse the fort, but at intervals a new floor of earth was strewn over the garbage. It is interesting to notice that some fragments of bones of the raven were found : these birds must have visited the site from time to time, and, while pursuing their own profit, served the useful and most necessary function of scavengers.

Even more suggestive was the fact that there were similarly hacked and broken *human* bones, mingled indiscriminately with these hacked and broken bones of food animals. The excavators of Cahercommaun have been reticent as to the inferences to be drawn from this disconcerting fact ; but the fact is there, and will have to be grappled with sooner or later. Hacked and broken human bones, mingled in a midden-heap with hacked and broken food-animal bones, *may* have some explanation other than the obvious one. But if subsequent investigation in similar sites forces us to draw the obvious conclusion,[1] the squeamish may reflect, for their comfort, that there is an excellent, not to say a wholly praiseworthy, reason for eating a conquered enemy : the desire of acquiring some enviable quality which he notoriously possesses—skill in this craft or that, valour, wisdom, or what not. But we need not invoke such subtleties in view of the crude fact that our books of Annals tell us that in the year A.D. 699 a severe famine drove the people to seek relief in cannibalism. Conceivably these bones may witness to the truth of the tragic tale.

Other indications of a late date for the use, if not the construction, of some of these drystone fortresses are not lacking. Thus, two

[1] And in fact analogous discoveries *have* been made, in the midden debris of the Romano-British community which occupied the great cave of Wookey Hole, Somerset. See the reports of its excavation by H. E. Balch and R. D. R. Troup in *Archæologia* 62 ii [1911], especially p. 584 ; 64 [1913], especially p. 345 ; where we read " Smashed tibiæ (and other bones) were embedded in the undisturbed wood-ashes of the fires from wall to wall of the cave, lying side by side with the bones of deer, goat, pig, and cow : all of which had been broken in a similar way ". See further, Grahame Clark, *Archæology and Society*, p. 185.

miles north of Croom (Limerick) is Killonahan fort, a structure 162 feet in diameter and surrounded with a wall 14 feet thick and in places 8 feet high. In this wall a cannon-ball was found ; someone must have thought it worth his while to bombard it after the invention or evolution of ordnance.[1]

Promontory Forts

A special kind of fortification is the *headland* or *promontory fort*. Here a headland is selected, jutting into the sea and connected with the mainland by a sufficiently narrow isthmus. A trench is cut through the isthmus, the material dug out being piled up as a vallum alongside. This forms the only essential defence, though it may be reinforced by additional structures in individual cases ; the sea, and the precipitous sides of the promontory rising from it, " do the rest ". All Ireland is girdled with a ring of such strongholds. Of these, one of the most interesting is the fort called Dún Beag,[2] in the Dingle peninsula series above alluded to. This is a thick wall cutting off a triangular headland, with guard-houses formed in the body of the rampart, and ingenious devices for blocking the entrance against unwelcome intruders. Outside the stone wall there are four earthen walls ; and a souterrain runs underneath. There was one stone house erected on the headland thus protected : it seems to have been nothing more than a large " beehive " hut. It is possible in this and similar cases that the stone wall was erected as an after-thought, after the flimsy earthen ramparts had proved inadequate in an emergency. The wall itself has been strengthened : originally its thickness was from 8 to 11 feet, but additions on the landward face increased this thickness, at least at the entrance, to 22 feet.

A yet more important promontory fort is one called in all the books " Dubh-Chathair ", the " Black Fort " on the Great Island of Aran.[3] It has suffered severely from inroads of the sea, and from injudicious restoration ; at present it consists of a huge wall, over 200 feet in length, cutting off a tongue of land with high precipices on each side, and protected on the landward side by an *abattis* of broken stones, like that which we have seen in front of Dún Aengusa.[4]

A promontory fort well worth mentioning, if only for its picturesqueness, is *Dún Briste*, " the broken fort ", in North Mayo. Here the encroachment of the sea has cut the once fortified headland

[1] E. J. Bennett in JRSAI 64 [1934] : 140-1.

[2] Macalister, *op. cit.* p. 220 ; P. J. Lynch, " Notes on Dunbeg Fort ", JRSAI 28 [1898] : 325 ; T. J. Westropp in JRSAI 40 [1910] : 267.

[3] I suspect that this name has been taken down incorrectly, and has now been foisted by tourists upon the local speech, like the ungrammatical perversion " Dun Ang-gus ".

[4] See Westropp's full description in PRIA 28 : 179. See also JRSAI 44 : 333.

away from the coast-line altogether, so that what is left of the fort now stands, completely inaccessible, on the summit of a precipitous and now isolated mass of rock about 150 feet in height.[1]

There is a remarkable *inland* promontory fort, though this may seem to the reader to be a contradiction in terms. It is known as *Cathair Conroí*, and is situated near the eastern end of the Dingle peninsula : giving its name to a mountain on the summit of which it stands. The top of this mountain is a flat space, triangular in shape, and measuring about a couple of acres in extent. Two sides of the triangle are precipitous, but the third is easy of access from the *col* connecting the mountain summit with the next beside it. Across the base of the triangle, and connecting the two precipices, a slightly curved wall has been built, with a single gateway in its course : this wall was about 350 feet in length, 15 feet 6 inches in breadth, and something over 10 feet in height, but is now much ruined.[2] Some excavations were carried out within the enclosed area, but without result.[3]

Military Forts

The so-called " forts ", therefore, from the huge Aran Island structures down to the most insignificant ring-wall of earth, are at best protected dwellings of single families or of larger but still limited communities, and have no function as the permanent or temporary headquarters of a specifically *military* body. Naturally, we should not expect to find any such establishments before the introduction of a standing army, an innovation that literary tradition assigns to king Cormac mac Airt in the third century A.D. There are, however, a few structures—a very few—to be seen in Ireland which may not unreasonably be considered as " forts " in this more accurate restricted sense of the word. The assault of *tuath* upon *tuath*, of province upon province, was an event only too familiar, as the most superficial perusal of the collections of Annals will make clear : and a garrisoned outpost guarding the pass which led from one territory to another would be a precaution dictated by common sense. Especially was the Northern Province obliged to take precautions against the ambitions of the Connaught dynasty, which was seeking to establish a suzerainty over the whole country.

Conspicuous among these territorial fortifications is the " Dane's Cast " (Armagh and Down) ; and the series of detached earthworks known collectively as " The Black Pig's Dyke ", which run discontinuously across Ireland from Bundoran (Donegal) to the head

---

[1] See a photograph and description by T. J. Westropp in JRSAI 42 : 104.
[2] P. J. Lynch, " Caherconree, Co. Kerry ", JRSAI 29 : 5.
[3] R. A. S. Macalister, E. C. R. Armstrong, and Rev. H. Browne, " Cathair Conroí and neighbouring structures ", JRSAI 41 [1911] : 46.

of Carlingford Loch, delimiting the southern boundary of the
Ulidian Territory.[1] Of the latter, which is now much levelled by
agricultural operations, we may say that it consists of a chain of
earthen mounds, roughly about 30 feet thick at the base and 20
feet high, running between two trenches each about 10 feet deep.
They were strengthened with oaken beams buried within them, and
serving to tie the materials together. The idea of carrying such a
series of defensive earthworks across the island may have been
suggested by the example of the Roman Walls in North Britain :
in spite of its discontinuity, it has been plausibly explained as a
defensive work of the Ultonian kings, designed to check the aggressive
policy of king Cormac mac Airt in Tara, and his successors, between
the third and fifth centuries A.D. As in " Offa's Dyke ", the gaps in
the wall may have been filled by patches of forestland.

The entrenchment known as the Dorsey (doirse, i.e. " doors "),
which commands the main road leading southward from the Ulidian
capital, Emain Macha, must be regarded as another monument of
such precautions. It is an enclosure, about ten miles N.W. of
Dundalk, of an irregular oval shape, a little over a mile in length in
a line lying N.N.E. to S.S.W., and about a fifth of a mile across.
It is surrounded by a single earthen rampart, which in certain vulnerable places is doubled ; a fosse was outside it, and in some parts
at least there is a second fosse within it. This description is written
in the present tense ; but in fact agricultural " improvements "
have played havoc with this ancient stronghold, and for much of its
length the rampart cannot be traced without difficulty, if at all.

The ramparts were not mere earthen mounds. There are considerable
traces still remaining, and more extensive traces are recorded as having
been found from time to time in the past, to show that this structure also
was strengthened with wooden piles. Streams and marshlands (the latter
now reduced by drainage, but at one time probably more or less impassable)
intersect the area, and seem to have been pressed into service as auxiliary
defences. Notwithstanding its exceptional size, the fortress makes hardly
any appearance in Irish native literature—one more illustration of the
essential cleavage between the Archæology and the traditional but more or
less artificial History embedded in the literature : the only important reference that has been found to it being in the Annals of Loch Cé, where under
the year 1224 we read how Doirse Emhna, the " Doors of Emain (Macha) ",
was one of certain places fortified by Aed ua Néill, king in Aileach, against
the " Foreigners ". Leaden bullets and a cannon ball are recorded as
having been found within it, and testify to even later military operations on
the site. Apart from these, the recorded discoveries have been singularly
few : a bronze horsebit, found in a bog near, but not necessarily within the
limits of, the enclosure, and now in the National Museum, is the most
important or, perhaps we may fairly say, the least unimportant. It is late

---

[1] See H. W. Lett, " The Great Wall of Ulidia ", Ulster II 3 [1897] : 23, 65 ;
W. F. de V. Kane, " The Black Pig's Dyke, the ancient boundary fortification of
Ula[i]dh ", PRIA 27 [1909] : 301, 33 : 539. See also important criticisms by
Professor MacNeill in Galway 16 [1934-5] : 111.

PLATE XIII

IV   III   II   I

THE WHITE ISLAND SCULPTURES

La Tène in character, but less ornamented than usual, and a modern repair has not improved it. " Sword-blades and skeans " (knives), presumably of iron, are specified as having been dug up within the area, in a letter dated 1707 in the Molyneux collection of MSS. in Trinity College Library : but this tells us nothing. A wooden " mallet ", perhaps a pile-driver, is recorded in a later document dated 1838, which also notes that the upper parts of the piles in the wall show traces of fire. Apart from these stray finds, wood ashes, querns, and old tobacco-pipes complete the record. A bronze-age socketed spear-head, found at ¾ of a mile to the N.E. of the fort, and figured by Mr. Tempest in the paper quoted in the footnote below, seems to be too old to be associated with this essentially late, almost mediæval structure ; the same may also be said of the horsebit. Whether or not the Dorsey is actually part of the " Black Pig " group of defences—a question about which there is room for two opinions—it is constructionally akin to them : and the filial connexion apparent between such long earthworks and the Roman Walls in the North of Roman Britain discourages us from assigning them to an earlier date.[1] We must, however, guard ourselves against founding too much on a comparison between these rudimentary walls on the one hand, and defences erected *and maintained*, with all the military resources of a mighty Empire, on the other. The Roman walls are a local aspect of the whole scheme of protection around Imperial Rome and its dominions : the Irish walls are little more than obstacles in the way of local raiders.

Another frontier fortress is that of Drumsna (Leitrim). It has not been excavated, but a good surface plan and description, with indications of the historical character of the site, have been published by Mr. De Vismes Kane. To this we may refer the reader.[2]

Vitrified Forts

These are stone structures in which the building material has been fused and so consolidated in a solid mass by a powerful fire. They are especially characteristic of Scotland,[3] but the record for Ireland is negligible. One specimen is recorded, at Shantemon (Cavan), but as the local gentry carried away most of its material for the purpose of making rockeries, not much of it is left.[4] Mr. Davies refers me to another at Banagher (Derry) but it is equally unimportant : at present, it is recorded only in the Ordnance Survey Letters, folios 3 and 4. He suggests that in both structures the vitrifaction may have been due to fires, intentional or accidental, against but not in the core of the walls. And modern scientific

[1] On the Dorsey see a description by Rev. H. W. Lett (JRSAI 28 [1898] : 1) and especially a very thorough survey by Mr. H. G. Tempest (*Louth* 7 [1930] : 87), in which all the earlier literature is summarized. See also the description by Dr. D. A. Chart, in *Antiquity* 4 [1930] : 453 ff. accompanying the reproduction of an admirable air-photograph by the Ulster R.A.F. See also the report of the excavation there by Mr. O. Davies, *Ulster* III 3 [1940] : 31.

[2] PRIA 32 [1915] : 324. There is some reason to hope that a further investigation will be undertaken here when peace and sanity return to the world.

[3] See Childe's *Prehistory of Scotland*, index *s.v.* " vitrified forts."

[4] Cæsar Otway, " Observations on some remains in the county of Cavan, supposed to be those of a vitrified fort ", TRIA 13 : 123.

opinion is coming to the conclusion that the vitrification is always the result of a destructive conflagration, which brought the occupation of the structure to an end.[1]

Houses

We now turn from the defences to the dwellings. Dwellings may be caves, natural or artificial : shelters of non-permanent materials—tents of hides or of textiles, shacks of wattle-work or of wood, and other structures, also of wood, of more pretentious character : and buildings of what we may call relatively permanent materials, as earth, stones, or brick.

Caves we may leave out from our present consideration ; cave-dwelling was never a common characteristic feature of Irish life. Brick and earth may likewise be passed over—there is no evidence of the early use of sun- or fire-baked clay for building, and the weather has not left to us any earth-built houses, other than the dwellings of the dead, called tumuli. The often-quoted passage in Tírechán's " Collections concerning St. Patrick ", *Ecce Patricius perrexit ad agrum qui dicitur Foirrgea filiorum Amolngid . . . et fecit ibi aeclessiam terrenam de humo quadratam, quia non prope erat silua*,[2] shows us that (sods of) earth, rather than stone, were used in the fifth century, when wood was, for any reason, not available : and the story describing how the saint told the presbyter Ailbe of his discovery of an underground stone table, laden with four glass chalices, adding a warning against " breaking the edges of the excavation ", suggests an earth-house, or tunnelled souterrain, which had been found and adapted for their ceremonies by some pre-Patrician Christian community. (We need not take seriously the statement that the cups were of *glass*.) As we have seen above, there are souterrains excavated in stiff clay, without any stone lining, still in existence. But these cases are at best exceptional, and do not call for special attention here. We may concentrate our attention upon houses of stone and of wood.

Stone Houses

Owing to the absence of any form of cement, other than mud, we cannot expect to find remains of stone houses of any pretensions, nor do we look for them in our literary sources, except in those that have been worked over at a date too late to make them trustworthy. In special circumstances and for special purposes, stone was used in building ; and grandiose tomb-structures, and souterrains, which

---

[1] See V. G. Childe, *Scotland before the Scots* (London 1946) index *s.v.* " Vitrified Forts ".

[2] *Tripartite Life of St. Patrick*, ed. Stokes, vol. ii, p. 327.

could be built of great blocks of stone without the use of mortar, survive in plenty. But the only domestic buildings in this material are " beehive " huts (Plate VIII). A more particular description may appropriately be given here. On the ground is laid a circular or oval stone foundation. Upon it is laid a course of a similar outline, but a slightly shorter diameter ; a third course, again reduced in diameter, laid upon that : and the process is continued till the space in the middle is reduced to a size which can be stopped with a single slab of moderate dimensions. Additional stones, laid down over the outer edge of the courses, serve as counterpoises, and prevent them from overbalancing and falling in upon the floor of the structure ; these even-up the outer surface into the regular " beehive " shape, which has given this type of hut its popular name. It is likely that the outer surface was covered with sods of earth, as a protection against driving rain-storms, and to secure additional warmth. Indeed, one of the beehive huts belonging to the monastic group on the Greater Skellig (Kerry) has stones projecting from the outer surface, apparently to key-in such a covering : this also displays a further concession to comfort (unusual, though we might have expected it to have been universal)—a venthole to permit the escape of smoke from the domestic fire. In most cases the smoke, if blocked from penetration through the loosely-set walls by a covering of sods, must have escaped through the extremely narrow doorway, which is sometimes so small that it has to be entered on all fours, as is the case in the Aran house above referred to : in the Skellig house the smoke might have suffocated the inmates if such a precaution had not been taken.

Like so many others of the typical antiquities of Ireland, individual specimens of beehive huts cannot be dated. The unprogressive time-lag is here supreme. Nothing datable to a remote antiquity has ever been found within any of them ; but they have occasionally yielded odds and ends of Christian date : and in one or two cases building-stones marked with crosses have been found forming part of their structure, or else crosses are formed with five or more stones distinguished by shape or colour, and built into the masonry above the lintel.[1] Their association with the early monasteries, especially those on the Western Islands—Skellig, High Island, Inismurray, and the rest—also fixes them in the age of early Christianity : indeed we may bring the tradition of the style down to a later date still, for in parts of the Dingle peninsula, where ancient models survive in plenty, they are imitated down to this day for farm outhouses.[2]

---

[1] There is an example of this in a hut on the Magharee Islands, to the north of the Dingle peninsula (Kerry).

[2] And not for outhouses only. See Mitchell, *The Past in the Present*, pp. 58 ff., for evidence from Scotland.

The most elaborate stone dwelling-house yet discovered in the country is that unearthed in the Royal Irish Academy's excavation on the Hill of Uisneach (Westmeath) ; see the plan in *Ancient Ireland*, p. 105. Its resemblance to the huts of Chysauster [1] in Cornwall will not escape notice.

The masonry, if we can dignify it by such a name, is of the crudest drystone construction. There is much clay associated with the stone, but this can hardly be taken as any kind of clay mortaring : it has most likely been blown or washed later into the interstices by rain, after the building was ruined. But the thicker walls were made of mud from the first, and merely faced with a stone revetment. Before excavation, the house looked like nothing more than an earthen ring about 44 feet in diameter ; there were practically no indications of the comparatively elaborate internal plan. After excavation, when finally exposed, it was seen to be divided into a number of compartments, contained within a wall of earth, revetted with stone facings, the whole being about 10 feet thick. The main entrance faced east ; it was a passage (*a*) 4 feet wide at the outer end, 3 feet at the inner, where there was a raised sill. It was continued 2 feet 8 inches beyond the outer face of the wall by a porch. Post-holes indicated the place where the door was hung. The passage floor was covered with a pavement of flat stones, in character resembling a modern gardener's " crazy pavement ". A narrow room (*b*) 6 feet 6 inches by 3 feet 6 inches to the left of the entrance at the inner end was probably a guard chamber : passing this, the passage led into two chambers (*c, d*) approximately 13 feet by 9 feet, which evidently formed the chief living-rooms of the house. A post-hole in the floor of one of these chambers must have contained the foot of the pillar which supported a conical roof. At the side, lintelled doorways led into rapidly downward sloping passages which ended in smaller chambers (*e, f, g*) at a lower level.

Such was the plan of what was evidently an important house of about the second century A.D., and it probably represents the domestic architecture of that period fairly well.[2] It afforded a striking illustration of the importance of a systematic and scientific excavation of the ring forts.

This accords tolerably with the literary evidence, presented us by Cæsar and other classical writers, as to the houses in Northern Europe at the time. They were generally, it appears, of a beehive shape, and were sunk in the ground so as to make them inconspicuous, while allowing a sufficiency of head room.

---

[1] See Hencken, *The Archæology of Cornwall and Scilly*, *s.v.* index, especially p. 134 (Fig. 38). See also *Archæologia* 83 [1933] : 237.

[2] See the report of the excavation for a detailed description with photographic illustrations (PRIA 39 : 54).

Wooden Houses

But there can be no question that down to, and for long after, the introduction of Christianity wood was the normal building material; not only in Ireland, but also in all Northern Europe. Though Tirawley in North Mayo, the territory specified in the passage from Tírechán quoted above, is close to the sea, it is a little surprising that there was no wood to be had there; throughout most of the country, wood must have been available in an almost embarrassing abundance. On the other hand, until some knowledge had been gained of the process of manufacture of mortar, and its manipulation and use, stone construction could never have been in more than a rudimentary state of development. Even after such knowledge had been acquired, wood was not superseded by the rival material. This is well illustrated by the large monastic establishments such as Glendaloch, Clonmacnois, Kilmacduagh and the rest. There we see collections of *church* buildings of various dates from the earliest beginning of church architecture in stone down to well after the Anglo-Norman invasion; but little or nothing remains of the *domestic* buildings, which must have been associated with the churches when the establishment was occupied as a centre of activity. The churches were built of stone so soon as the art of building in stone was acquired, in order to guard their irreplaceable treasures against the risk of fire : there was no such necessity in dealing with the monastic dwellings. And the frequency with which monasteries are recorded, in the annalistic literature, as having been burnt and yet in full activity only a short time afterwards, leads to the same inference.[1]

But wood is perishable, and yields without resistance to destruction by fire and decay. In a country with the damp climate and the turbulent history of Ireland, the survival of any wooden structure would be surprising. Indeed, the only chance of such a survival would be, for the building to have early become submerged in a growth of peat, with its preservative antiseptic properties : and to have been discovered and dug out by peat-cutters who had a fitting regard for the requirements of Science ! This ideal has never been attained except in one case, that of the house discovered, in June 1833, at Drumkelin (Donegal).

It has often been described : this is inevitable, as it has as yet no rival to supplant it. But it can hardly have been a typical dwelling of any period : anything less conformable to ordinary common-sense convenience—we need say nothing of comfort—it would be

---

[1] Between the eighth and the eleventh century Clonmacnois was burnt (not reckoning mere raids and plunderings) no less than fifteen times : see the annalistic tables set forth in my *Clonmacnois Memorial Slabs* (Dublin 1909), pp. 112 ff.

difficult to imagine.[1]   It was surrounded with an enclosure of stakes, in which the gate-opening could be identified.   The floor rested upon a layer of branches covered with fine sea-sand.   The building was 12 feet long and 9 feet high, constructed of rough logs and planks of oak.   The top of the roof was 4 feet below the then surface of the peat, but as many layers had been cut away before the discovery, it is empirically estimated that it had been sunk 16 feet deep in the bog.

Two horizontal sleepers, made from the trunk of a large tree split in two, had been laid down, flat surface downwards, parallel with one another. Mortice-holes had been cut or rather crushed into them, with stone hatchets, and in the two end-holes in each sleeper the four large corner-posts had been set.   The walls were made of planks resting on edge, each one on the plank below, and kept in position by smaller uprights on each side of the wall, fitting into intermediate mortice-holes in the sleepers.   Horizontal beams, with corresponding perforations, on the top of the house, received the upper ends of these uprights and kept them in position.   Half-way up the corner-posts there was a hole, through which a beam of wood, one on each side, was passed, to serve as the support of an intermediate floor of planks : a similar " floor " formed the roof of the house.   A polished stone hatchet-head was found within the building, and some of the woodwork displayed marks corresponding to it.

This intermediate floor divided the house into two storeys, each of them not more than 4 feet high.   It follows that the structure could not possibly have been a house in which ordinary domestic vocations were carried on ; its only conceivable purpose would be that of a nest of sleeping-bunks, resembling the berths of a ship's stateroom.   Moreover, one side of the house was entirely open, and did not appear ever to have been closed with a wall.   From this open side a paved causeway of beach shingle, spread over a substructure of logs and hazel-branches, led to a hearth-site, marked by a flat stone, covered with much charred wood and ashes : a great quantity of hazel-nut shells was found here and elsewhere on the site.   The " finds " made in the house appear to have been scanty, though they might conceivably have been richer if the site had been recovered and searched by a modern scientific excavating party—a flint arrow-head, part of a wooden sword, and a fragment of a leather shoe.   Pottery was altogether absent.

Whatever may be the exact date of the building itself, it preserves traditions of constructional methods of the Megalithic age ; for as we have seen (p. 145), the fact that very similar beams, to all appearance the *disjecta membra* of very similar buildings, were used in the construction of the Westmeath bog road there described.   There is reason to believe that the Drumkelin structure was only one of a group, forming collectively a small village.

A similar framed house was found in Timahoe (Leix) ; but only a vague description of it is on record.[2]   It is interesting to note, that on the floor of this dwelling there was found an oaken beam, with a wedge inserted into one end, and a mallet, made of a single piece of wood—a section of the branch of an oak-tree forming the head, and a subsidiary branch springing from it acting as the handle.

[1] It was first described by W. Mudge in *Archæologia* 26 [1836] : 361.
[2] JRSAI 2 [1852] : 207.

The construction appears, therefore, to have been incomplete when it was abandoned.

Some further information may be gleaned from the sagas which have survived in Irish Literature, and from the legal documents, set in the light which comparative ethnology can throw upon them. Elaborate houses, like that of Bricriu, or the palace of Cruachu, are described, sometimes with a wealth of extravagant detail—often anachronistic, as when Bricriu's house is fitted with glass windows.[1] Naturally, we must neglect such embellishments, as we should do in criticizing a modern folk-tale in which some hero of antiquity is represented as smoking a pipe or sending a telegram. But we need not apply the axe too ruthlessly. A Maori chieftain may live in a wooden hut skilfully constructed and adorned with artistic carvings : the Öseberg queen's yacht was built and decorated with equal skill :[2] and we need not deny the possibility of a comparable degree of barbaric magnificence to the dwelling of an Irish chieftain. We may accept, with no more than the minor reservations demanded by errors of chronological judgement, the testimony of the romance-writers as being in essence correct : otherwise their descriptions would have been mere idle dreams, such as would not have entered the head of a story-teller without some external stimulus. It must still remain an unsettled question whether such a stimulus came from something actually seen *in Ireland* ; or from a folk-memory of experiences in an earlier and happier home from which the refugee colonists had been driven forth into the wilderness of a remote island : or whether it was merely based upon vague rumours of the Classical glories of the distant Mediterranean.

One fact which greatly enhances the credit of the romance-writers is the honesty with which they admit without expurgation details of what we should describe as squalor. They are taken as a mere matter of course. In my book *Ancient Ireland* I gave a brief analysis of the Bricriu story (pp. 156-8), and referred to the unpleasant incident of the lord of the house falling into the courtyard surrounding this new building, built on a gradiose scale as a palace in which to entertain the greatest of the land, and getting so bespattered with filth that he could not be recognized except by his voice. An indignant reviewer quoted the Irish text (*isind otruch for lar ind lis etir na conaib*), and drew the inference that Bricriu fell into a dirty dog-kennel (" among the dogs where the dirt was "). We need not pause to labour the criticism that Bricriu, considering the rank of his expected guests, should not have allowed his kennels to get so dirty ; for the passage means the exact converse—he fell " into the dirt *on the middle of the enclosure*, amid the dogs ". The dogs,

[1] *Bricriu's Feast*, Irish Texts Society ii, p. 4.
[2] See the splendid official publication *Ösebergfundet* (Kristiania (Oslo) 1917 and subsequent years).

of which my critic thus rashly reminded me, so far from mitigating the unpleasantness, add to it. This house, though its building had only just been completed, was already surrounded with uncleanness, and the dogs were not confined in kennels but, after the disagreeable habit of their kind, were prowling about and sniffing at it luxuriously. If the story-teller admit details like these, we may fairly assume that in essence his description is correct, even though he may illegitimately import glass and other later refinements.

The circular plan appropriate to beehive houses in drystone is unsuitable to framed wooden structures ; and the frequently quoted testimony of Bede, who speaks of a church being built at Lindisfarne *more Scottorum non de lapide, sed de robore secto*,[1] is testimony to the Irish use of framed timber structures in the middle of the seventh century A.D. and for an indefinable time before it. Though framed timber structures of any sort more elaborate than the Drumkelin house have disappeared, we can restore them in imagination with the help of the earliest stone churches, in which the wooden external features are translated into the new material, just as, long before, stone hatchet-heads were reproduced by the earliest coppersmiths.

These churches are of a rectangular form, at first without any nave-chancel subdivision.[2] The two gable ends are flanked by pilasters running up the corners, representing the stout wooden corner-posts which bore the principal weight of the roof. Lying on the top of these corner-posts, and well secured to them by mortice-and-tenon joints, were the two wall-plates, running along the tops of the long sides of the structure—their ends projecting a foot or so beyond the face of the gable, so as to counteract the inevitable weakness resulting from the mortice-hole, and thus to prevent the tenon from tearing its way out if subjected to any chance longitudinal stress. These projections are represented in the stone churches, by otiose corner-brackets, which project from the corresponding parts of the faces of many of the stone churches. Above the wall-plates, at each end, there rose the roof-principals, steeply pitched, halved into one another where they met, and forming a saltire-crossing at the top : into the lower [3] angles of these crossings the

---

[1] *Hist. Eccl.* iii 25. See further evidence collected in Reeves' *Adamnan* and Petrie's *Round Towers*.

[2] Like mortar, this complexity of plan was probably introduced into Ireland by returning missionaries from the Continent. There it had most likely been imposed upon the South European Basilican church by the northern Teutonic peoples, under the influence of the *lang-hús* and *af-hús* subdivisions of their pre-Christian sanctuaries. Shetelig and Falk (*Scandinavian Archæology*, English trans., p. 422) make the influence run in the opposite direction, the temples being derived from the churches. In that case, however, we should not have had so many pre-Scandinavian churches in which there is no nave-chancel subdivision.

[3] Not, as might be supposed at first, the *upper* angles ; this would have confronted the builders with constructional impossibilities when they came to lay down the roof-rafters. I have to thank Mr. H. G. Leask for confirming my qualms about this.

ridge-beam was firmly secured. Such was the framework of the building : the spaces between these primary timbers might be filled in various ways—the walls with wattle-work or with clinkered planks, the roof with rafters, supporting boards covered with wooden shingles.

A building thus constructed would necessarily be *narrow*. The roof-pitch would have to be steep, to diminish lateral thrust so far as possible ; the builders apparently never thought of counteracting it with buttresses or props. If more floor-space were required, it had to be obtained by substituting, for the solid side-walls, two rows of pillars supporting the wall-plates, and building the side-walls themselves parallel with, and at a distance of some feet out from them : in other words, by erecting a structure resembling a rectangular church with side aisles, but without transept or chancel. And that this was the normal plan of all important houses the literary evidence, so far as it goes, confirms. The " nave " formed the living-room : the bays of the aisles were partitioned into sleeping-chambers (*immdai*) ; the first bay, or two bays, at the door end of the building were not so partitioned, but formed a hall running across the house, which could be used as a kitchen (*ircha*) ; [1] the length of the house was approximately double its breadth, and the size of the house varied with the rank of its occupant : it was valued according to the number of its pillars. The door was low, as we may judge from the penalties attached to carrying a child " pick-a-back " into a house (by reason of the danger of bumping its head on the lintel) ; [2] the roof was thatched. [3] The plan thus indicated is followed in *Tech Midchuarta*, the Banquet Assembly-hall of Tara, as it is represented in the *Book of Leinster* (checked by the evidence of the remains to be seen on the spot) : [4] except that the rule of proportion between length and breadth is not there maintained, and there are *double aisles* on each side of the " nave ". The row of subsidiary apartments was here entered not from the interior, but, by independent doorways in each, from the exterior of the building. I may add also that I have examined all the passages in the laws of Hywel Dda and in the other ancient Welsh laws referring to houses, and, though it would involve a digression too lengthy to enter here into the details, have satisfied myself that such a plan as this lies consistently in their background.

A loft could be formed in the high gabled roof by inserting a

---

[1] See *Crith Gablach* (" Ancient Laws " iv 298 ff.) *passim*.

[2] *Ancient Laws* i 174, 178. But it is possible that the reason for this prohibition lies deeper than the superficial explanation here suggested. We may recall a Bantu belief, that " if a father picks up one of his children and places it on his back or shoulders, the father becomes *thahu* " (i.e. under a curse analogous to that which follows the violation of a tabu) and the child will die : if he carries the child in front of him there is no evil result " (C. W. Hobley, *Bantu Beliefs and Magic*, p. 118).

[3] Penalties for injuring thatch, *Laws* i 166, etc.

[4] See my *Tara*, pp. 60 ff.

plank ceiling over the "nave". At the reference just quoted, I have shown reason to believe that such a ceiling covered at least one-half of the Banquet-Hall at Tara. This may well have suggested the double roof, which is a striking constructional detail in some of the early churches.

Considerations of space make it impossible to do more than indicate the above conclusions, which have been skilfully and convincingly set forth, with the arguments in support of them, by Mr. I. A. Richmond. For fuller details, with interesting Scandinavian analogies, reference must be made to his paper.[1]

These considerations emphasize the necessity, in all future excavations, for a meticulous hunt for, and recording of, post-holes. Wood rots and burns, and leaves nothing for the spade to unearth : metal ornaments, which might have been applied in decoration (as is suggested by some of the ancient romances, etc., which we possess), are made of a material intrinsically valuable, and are liable to be looted so soon as the householder becomes incapable of defending it : so that of most houses we can expect little to survive but the post-holes, into which the supporting beams of the house were thrust. These, when they penetrate into the drift subsoil, become recognizable by the differently coloured humus which has filled the cavity, as a result of the decay of the wooden stump : and in all modern scientific excavations in Ireland these post-holes have been noted and mapped. The nucleus of a collection of observations has thus been made ; but this is as yet too scanty to permit us to generalize. As the work proceeds it will doubtless yield important, as yet unknown, scientific truth in coming years. The evidence of post-holes is not always clear ; sometimes, owing to complete or partial rebuilding on a site, the post-holes of successive structures are intermingled in a maze, through which it is almost if not quite impossible to find a clue. Even here, however, the difficulties which baffle critical students of one excavation may be resolved later on by the revelations of another.

One of the items of our imaginary series of monographs will certainly be a critical study of buildings and furniture, as revealed by excavation, by pictorial sources, such as the sculptured figures on the stone crosses, by the evidence of native and foreign literature, critically studied and compared, and by the modern survivals which come within the universal embrace of "Folklore", and considered

---

[1] "The Irish Analogies for the Romano-British Barn-Dwelling", *Journal of Roman Studies* 22 [1932] : 96. I must thank my friend Prof. M. V. Duignan for calling my attention to this most valuable study, which I might otherwise have missed. Many important further references will be found within it. See also Iorwerth C. Peate, *The Welsh House* (Liverpool 1944), especially chap. vi in this connexion, but the whole book should be read carefully. Reference for parallel structures in another *milieu* may be made to W. Schulz-Minden, " Der Germanisches Haus im vorgeschichtliches Zeit " (Mannusbibliothek no. 11, Leipzig 1913).

in the light which comparative ethnology can throw upon them. It will assuredly fill several volumes, when all the available materials have been discovered, marshalled, and expounded.

Lake-Dwellings

In various parts of Europe, from the Stone Age downward, dwellings have been erected over the surfaces of lakes.[1]   The purpose was, it is needless to say, defence : a water-obstacle being interposed between the defenders and their enemies, human or animal.

Lake-dwellings are of two kinds—pile structures and artificial islands.   In the *former*, wooden piles are driven through the shallow water of a lake into the subsoil, and support a platform upon which the houses of the occupants are erected.   This form of construction was followed in stone- and bronze-age Switzerland, and it may yet be seen in practice in New Guinea and elsewhere.   In the *latter*, earth and stones are heaped up on the bottom of the lake, forming a mound which rises above the surface of the water.   Of course, if a lake contained a natural island use would be made of it ; the artificial-island device is resorted to where nature had failed.   It is this latter kind which was favoured in Ireland, as it is in Mala in the Solomon Islands.[2]

The process followed in building such an island dwelling, in Ireland, appears to have been as follows.   A circle of stakes was driven into the lake-bottom, and so far as possible secured with wickerwork : this made a hedge to prevent the escape of the accumulated material by diffusion through the water.   If no shallows ever appeared in the lake, a raft of tree-trunks, or else of wickerwork and brushwood, was set afloat in the area thus delimited, and boatloads of earth and stones were ferried over from the mainland and heaped up on it.   In time, a weight of such material had been piled up, sufficient to sink the raft to the bottom of the lake, where it made a footing which prevented the accumulation from sinking into the soft underlying sand or peat.[3]

But that the footing was *always* a floating raft is assumed too absolutely in our first edition.   Hencken has shown that in

---

[1] For the general subject of European lake-dwellings the reader may be referred to Munro's *Lake-dwellings of Europe* (with a very full bibliography) or to the second part of the same author's *Palæolithic Man and Terramara Settlements in Europe*, as well as Keller's standard work on *The Lake-dwellings of Switzerland*. For Irish remains Wood-Martin's compilation *The Lake-dwellings of Ireland* (Dublin and London 1886) and Munro's *Ancient Scottish Lake-dwellings* (Edinburgh 1882) are still useful, though naturally not up to date.   Wood-Martin's work gives full references to other writings down to the date of its publication.   See also R. Munro, " The structural features of lake-dwellings " (JRSAI 24 [1896] : 105, 209).

[2] See W. G. Ivens, " The Island Builders of the Pacific " (London 1930).

[3] For admirable photographs of the wicker-work basis of such an island see various plates in Gray and Bulleid, *The Glastonbury Lake Village*, vol. i (Glastonbury 1911).

Ballinderry (lake-dwelling no. 1) it was laid down upon the surface of the underlying lake-deposit and there pegged down,[1] doubtless at a time when the waters were for some temporary climatic reason exceptionally low. The radiating beams which we see in such a footing as that at Cloneygonnell (Cavan)[2] must likewise have been thus deposited. On the other hand, we have the remarkable precedent of the Maglemose settlement to authorize us to admit the possibility of a raft being constructed, not merely as a footing but as itself a habitation,[3] in the same way. When the wickerwork binding of the encircling stakes goes down to the bottom of the construction, as for instance at Lochrea (Galway),[4] we cannot suppose that the site was seriously submerged while the island was a-building.

When the island had thus been constructed, a palisade, or sometimes a drystone revetment, was set up around it ; the necessary houses and other enclosures were built upon it ; and the dwelling was complete. In Ireland, this class of habitation is usually known by the name *crannóg*, a diminutive of the word *crann*, " a tree ".[5]

The island might be surrounded by deep water, in which case the only means of access was by rowing in a boat or canoe, or by swimming. When the water was sufficiently shallow, a gangway was sometimes provided, connecting the island with the mainland ; this passage is now usually represented by the stumps of the piles which supported it. In most cases it is not likely that the gangway offered more than a passage that could be waded, being always covered with water.[6] Sometimes the causeway was paved with stone slabs,[7] and extended beyond the shore of the lake, carrying a road through any soft bogland that might surround it.

Antiquities of earlier date sometimes chanced to be in the earth that was ferried over to make the island, and these come to light when the island is excavated. Such an accident is apt to disconcert an unwary excavator. The best example of such incongruities was presented by the motte of Greenmount (Louth)—a Norman structure, the substance of which contained a strip of bronze with a Scandinavian

---

[1] PRIA 43 [1936] : 109.
[2] PRIA 8 [1863] : 274 ; Wood-Martin, *Lake-dwellings*, p. 198.
[3] G. F. L. Sarauw, " Maglemose ", *Prähist. Zeitschrift* 3 [1911] : 52, especially p. 82.   [4] PRIA 8 : 418.
[5] G. H. Kinahan, " On the exploration of crannogs ", JRSAI 11 : 459.
[6] Wood-Martin (*Lake-dwellings*, p. 44) says that the passage was not invariably straight, but that it sometimes ran in a zig-zag course, to baffle unwelcome strangers —those who had the right of access to the island knowing by long practice the way along these submerged gangways, while a visitor who had no legitimate business there would miss his footing at the bend and would step unexpectedly into deep water. But he quotes no authority, and no illustrative examples ; I have never been able to discover any corroborative evidence. A story to this effect was told at Loch Enagh (Londonderry), but when tested was found to be mere baseless folklore : the alleged winding causeway was nothing but a glacial ridge of natural formation. See O Davies in *Ulster* III 4 [1941] : 88, and compare the so-called " Serpent Mound " at Loch Nell near Oban, which has given rise to much speculation, but is of similar origin.
[7] As at Loch Tarmin : Wood-Martin, pp. 165, 166.

inscription in very late Runes, a flanged bronze hatchet-head, and a miscellaneous assortment of midden debris, all scooped up with the material of which the mound had been constructed.

If Nature had provided a convenient lake-island that could be fortified with a stockade or with a stone wall, so much the better. Examples of such fortified islands have been found in Loch Skannive (Galway) [1] and Loch Cullen (Mayo). [2] Or its area could be artificially extended by ordinary crannog construction outside the natural boundary, as at Loch Enagh. [3] We may presume that it was by such artificially fortified or extended natural islands that the practice of constructing entirely artificial islands was first suggested.

The important lake-dwelling at Lagore, near Dunshaughlin (Meath), was the first in Ireland to attract scientific attention (1839). A local pedlar from the latter place was in the habit of bringing to Petrie antiquities for sale, which, he said, he had procured in a peat-bog near the village. Petrie and Wilde determined to visit the spot ; and in a drained lake they found an artificial mound entirely overgrown with peat, which the turf-cutters had partially removed. On making further enquiries they learned that the site had been well known as a source of supply for bones, of which already about 150 cartloads had been dug out and sent to Scotland for manure. Petrie and Wilde made arrangements to publish the discoveries, the former describing the antiquities and the latter the bones. But owing, it is understood, to some quarrel, the publication never appeared : nothing was put on record except an abstract of Wilde's part of the work, though the antiquities acquired by Petrie passed into the collection of the Royal Irish Academy. [4] Subsequently Wakeman had a chance of seeing further excavations on the site, and wrote a brief account of them. But these communications, and the paragraph based upon them in the first edition of the present work, have in recent years been put altogether out of date by the elaborate excavation of the Harvard Mission, the publication of which is still awaited.

The following table, adapted from a map constructed by Wood-

---

[1] JRSAI 27 : 373.   [2] JRSAI 29 : 32.

[3] Reference in footnote ([6]) above. This island was first settled by a neolithic fishing community, which used ware of " Peterborough " type. Special attention should be called in this connexion to Mr. Davies's " Contributions to the study of Crannogs in South Ulster ", *Ulster* III 5 [1942] : 14.

[4] The matter is passed over in complete silence in Stokes's *Life of Petrie*. I looked into the recently published biography of Wilde (T. G. Wilson, *Victorian Doctor*, London 1942) for possible side-lights upon it, but found nothing but the statement in the text above, quoted (p. 79) from the first edition of the present work. This, of course, is mere hearsay, not evidence, and should not be taken as authoritative, however intrinsically probable the story may be. I cannot now recollect from whom I heard of the alleged quarrel ; most likely it was a museum tradition imparted to me by Mr. Armstrong in one of the countless conversations that I had with him during our long and close association. For Wilde's contributions, see PRIA 1 [1840] : 420, 7 : 192, 211 ; for Wakeman's, JRSAI 15 : 325.

Martin, will give some idea of the number and the distribution of these structures in Ireland. It is not complete, for a few unknown to Wood-Martin have come to light since the appearance of his work. Thus, Clare has certainly more examples than one.[1] Co. Cork is credited with no examples, but Rev. Professor Power has described the site of one inside Cork city : [2] and Mr. J. P. Conlon, of University College, Cork, has kindly called my attention to another in the lake of Inchigeelagh.[3] Sir Thomas Esmond has described a crannog site in Wexford.[4] The general proportion of the distribution is, however, of more importance than the actual numbers, and this is but little influenced by recent discoveries.

Fermanagh	.	39	Donegal	.	6	Louth	.	3	Carlow	.	o
Leitrim	.	24	Tyrone	.	6	Meath	.	3	Cork	.	o
Cavan	.	21	Down	.	5	Tipperary	.	3	Dublin	.	o
Antrim	.	20	Westmeath	.	5	Offaly	.	2	Kerry	.	o
Galway	.	19	Limerick	.	4	Longford	.	2	Kildare	.	o
Monaghan	.	19	Leix	.	4	Clare	.	1	Kilkenny	.	o
Roscommon		14	Armagh	.	3	Mayo	.	1	Wexford	.	o
Sligo	.	13	Derry	.	3	Waterford	.	1	Wicklow	.	o

Total . 221

It is possible to exaggerate the importance of the numbers in such a list as this : on which account I have transferred it as it stands from the first edition, without taking the trouble to bring it up to date. They depend upon *casual* factors, quite as much as upon *causal* ethnological conditions : and their bearing upon these latter would give them their only value or significance. What we call *casual* factors are the number of available and suitable lakes, and the number of diligent and competent observers. Fermanagh and Antrim have been very thoroughly explored, the former by the enthusiastic Wakeman, the latter by a number of competitive collectors ; while, on the other hand, some counties may be bare in record for want of workers, or for want of sufficiently shallow lakes and lake-bottoms. Here, as in the case of the forts, the use of *counties* as geographical units is open to criticism.

To correct a misapprehension, a passing mention should be made to a lake-dwelling found many years ago under the sea at Ardmore (Waterford). This was not really a " marine crannog " as some have supposed, like the dwellings of the Cauci described by Pliny.[5] It was a lacustrine structure ; an inroad of the sea has here absorbed an ancient inland lake, on which the dwelling had originally been built.[6]

[1] JRSAI 31 : 433, 35 : 391.   [2] JRSAI 50 [1920] : 179.   [3] *Cork* 2 : 78.
[4] " Notes on crannog and other finds in North Co. Wexford ", JRSAI 29 : 404. A few other publications of crannog sites found since Wood-Martin's book appeared in 1886 may be noted : in Mayo, JRSAI 1899 : 32 ; near Clones (Monaghan), *ibid.* 1900, pp. 204, 253 : Inchiquin (Clare), *ibid.* 1901 : 349.
[5] *Natural History* xvi *ad. init.*
[6] See a letter on the subject by Mr. R. J. Ussher in JRSAI 15 : 154, and a later account, by the same writer, *ibid.* 33 : 387. Also *Waterford* 1 [1894-5] : 198.

Like the Lisnacrogher site, of which we have already spoken sufficiently, and which was potentially by far the most important lake-dwelling site in Ireland, the outstanding site at Ardakillen (Roscommon),[1] already mentioned (p. 243), was ransacked by private collectors before it was properly examined, so that several objects, some of them apparently of great interest, were dispersed and lost. Happily, the remarkable bronze brooch (spoken of at the above reference) was rescued for the Royal Irish Academy,[2] as well as some other objects.   The most suggestive find was made in a large dug-out canoe close by : a neck-shackle of iron, with 20 feet of iron chain attached to it, associated with which was the skull of a young man, displaying the marks of no less than twenty sword-cuts.   None of these was sufficient individually to cause immediate death ;   they indicate that the unfortunate victim had been chained up by his enemies or judicial executioners, savagely hacked, and then set afloat, dead or alive.[3]   The story of how king Niall of the Nine Hostages chained his enemy Eochaid king of Leinster to the holed stone called *Cloch an Phull*, still to be seen in the neighbourhood of Tullow (Carlow), with the intention of having him shot to death by archers, is recalled by this gruesome discovery.[4]

Another Antrim crannog, that of Moylarg, had a better fate ; its excavation was well described by Dr. Buick,[5] and its chief contents ultimately found their way to the National collection.

The Irish lake-dwellings are the richest source of supply of late portable objects of domestic use that has been tapped in the country. One room in the National Museum is devoted to, and filled with, crannog material, which belongs almost if not quite exclusively to late Iron or early Overlap times.   In fact, there are records of the occupation of some of these artificial islands so late as the end of the sixteenth century.[6]   A general survey of the " finds " in such sites is therefore more appropriate to our concluding chapter.

But we cannot assign the practice of island-dwelling or even of island-construction to a time so uncompromisingly late as appeared to be justifiable in 1928.   Since then some disturbing facts have come to light, obliging us to admit an earlier beginning for the practice in the country, as in the similar case of the souterrains. But again, as there, we can still continue to believe that the majority

[1] Wood-Martin, p. 236.

[2] Wilde, Catalogue, p. 569, Wood-Martin, p. 117.

[3] PRIA 5 [1851] : 213.   Two identical shackles, with identical chains attached to them, were found at Söllested, north-east of Assens in the island of Fyen ; see the description and illustration by King Frederick VII of Denmark, *Antiquarisk Tidsskrift*, 1862, p. 16.

[4] Keating's *History* (Irish Texts Society edition) 2 : 406. A similar neck-shackle, designed for the restraint of a gang of at least four captives, was included in the important find recently made in Anglesey (see Sir Cyril Fox, *A find of the early Iron Age from Llyn Cerrig Bach, Anglesey* (National Museum of Wales, 1945)).

[5] JRSAI 23 : 27, 24 : 315.   [6] See, for example, PRIA 7 [1859] : 163.

of the monuments, and the greatest intensity of the practices which called them into being, lie in the late period to which they have been ascribed. The facts as they are at present understood are as follows.[1]

The most important of the known lake-dwellings, some of which (such as Ballinderry No. 1 and Lagore) have been excavated with unprecedented care, are as late as the eighth century A.D., which excludes their contents, important though they be, from the scope of the present work : reluctantly we must pass over such outstanding discoveries as the Víking Sword, the solitaire board, and the unique bronze hanging lamp, found in the former site. The evidence from other sites examined on previous occasions, which have yielded objects consonant in character with the yield from these two typical sites, is in full agreement with this result. On the other hand, Island McHugh, and the island in Loch Enagh, have yielded flints and pottery of Peterborough type, which on any normal chronological basis would indicate a pre-Megalithic occupation. These, it should be noticed, are *natural* islands, though the second of them shows that the occupants endeavoured to increase the area available by artificial constructions with timber and earth.[2]

After this there is at present a hiatus, followed by two artificial lake-dwellings which antedate, by perhaps a couple of centuries—not more—the time-limits previously set to this form of habitation. Whether we speak of them as late bronze-age or early iron-age is a mere question of terminology, depending on an always difficult question : at what stage are we to regard *infiltration* as having established *occupation?* One of the two sites is in a lake called Rossroe Loch, by Knocknalappa (Clare) ; the second is one of two sites in that part of Ballinderry Loch which lies in the County of Offaly. The first has been dated to between 500 and 300 B.C., the second to " between the fourth and the first " of the pre-Christian centuries. These dates accord with the evidence, such as it is, from Lisnacrogher ; we may therefore assign the beginning of lake-dwelling in Ireland (apart from the few vague Neolithic adumbrations) to about, or a little after, 500 B.C.

The Knocknalappa site, first noticed by Mr. J. W. N. Wallace of Limerick, has been examined and reported upon by Dr. Raftery.[3] It presents certain enigmatical features, chief among which is the fact that in Dr. Raftery's opinion it was never occupied as a dwelling-place at all. He believes it to have been prepared as a refuge by dwellers on the mainland round the lake, but never used as such, the expected necessity never having arisen. On a natural ridge or mound of marl an oval enclosure (120 by 60 feet) had been marked

---

[1] Pile-dwellings as old as the Stone Age have been found in Sweden : see for example O. Frödin, " En svensk pålbyggnad från Stenåldern ", *Fornvännen* 5 [1910] : 29.   [2] See *Ulster* I 4 [1941] : 88.   [3] *North Munster* 3 [1942] : 53.

out with stakes or piles in three irregular rings, and heaped up with successive strata of brushwood, peat, midden material and marl. The midden material was not, apparently, accumulation from an occupation on the spot, but had been ferried over to the island to serve as filling. The only construction—apart from what seems to have been a rudimentary boat-jetty—was a platform of nine timbers in contact side by side, with an area of just under 6 feet by 2 feet 9 inches. This does not seem very intelligible : Dr. Raftery does not consider that it was a habitation floor, an opinion with which we must agree. A few objects found in the covering marl agree with the contents of the midden material, and show that the whole construction belongs to one period.

That period, as Dr. Raftery indicates, is fixed by the pottery. A flat-based, shouldered jug, of which one good specimen was found (in fragments) and sherds of others, collectively represented a type of domestic (as opposed to funerary) ware different from the ordinary bronze-age pottery of Ireland, but analogous with that found in the Hallstatt settlement of All Cannings Cross, Wiltshire.[1] In fact, Knocknalappa yielded a large bronze sword of Hallstatt type, as well as amber and bronze beads, fragments of a lignite bracelet, and two saddle-querns. This is an identification of capital importance, for, taken in connexion with the evidence of the Ballintoy caves, it confirms the conclusion that " the infiltration of iron " began early enough to carry some elements of the Hallstatt culture into Ireland ; which had formerly been imagined to be free from it, except for casual " wanderers ". The evidence is still very fragmentary, but it is growing : and several other minor, but remarkable, coincidences between the Knocknalappa finds and those of All Cannings Cross are noticed by Dr. Raftery—all the more remarkable when we take into consideration the scanty " yield " with which Knocknalappa rewarded its excavators. Just as we said on an earlier page that the absence of bronze does not prove that a hoard belongs to the Stone Age, so we must here observe that the absence of iron does not prove that a hoard belongs to the Bronze Age ; and some of the groups of objects that have been described as late Epimegalithic may be properly attributed to a local phase of the Hallstatt culture—which it now appears was spread more widely over Europe than had hitherto been supposed.

The Ballinderry crannog—called No. 2, to distinguish it from another site in the same lake, which, though much later, has earned numerical precedence by priority of discovery and by its superior wealth and importance—is the lower level of a lake-dwelling, overlaid in the seventh or eighth century A.D., by a later and quite independent settlement with which we have in this place nothing to do. It has

---

[1] M. E. Cunnington, *The Early Iron Age inhabited site at All Cannings Cross Farm, Wiltshire :* Devizes 1923, plates 29, 30.

been excavated and reported upon by Dr. Hencken.[1] The burial of three skulls under the site points to a foundation sacrifice : their faces had apparently been sliced off—possibly in a quest for one of the ingredients of brainballs. The manner of construction seems to have followed the same lines as at Knocknalappa—enclosing an area with rings of stakes or posts, covering the space with brushwood, and then laying down a bed of stones. Below the brushwood, and therefore presumably a little earlier, was a number of cylindrical pits lined with wickerwork—too narrow to be explained as " pit-dwellings ", even if this term be not a misnomer in all circumstances ; they were possibly, as Dr. Hencken suggests, grain-stores, though it might be thought that they were likely to be too damp even for that purpose. On the summit was a remarkable and at present unique building, consisting of eight more or less parallel rows of sleepers of wood, end to end, butting against a similar row at right angles across one of the ends : post-holes, as for the palisading of wattled walls, were cut in these sleepers. The whole structure was about 37 feet square, and the palisades would have divided its area into seven parallel " stalls " about 5 feet in width.

The pottery showed flat-based vessels, very similar (if perhaps not identical) in general outline to the vessels from Knocknalappa, and without doubt belonging to the same culture. Other coincidences with the Knocknalappa site are lignite rings, " sunflower " pins, and beads of amber as well as fragments of saddle-querns. Dr. Hencken comments on the scarcity of the latter as contrasted with the great numbers of bones of domestic animals ; indicating an overwhelming preponderance of the stock-breeding over the agricultural industry. The dog was practically absent from this earlier stratum, though Knocknalappa yielded a large specimen of an unrecognized breed.

Inauguration Places

The social and political constitution of Ireland in iron-age times is a subject apart from the special purpose of the present work. Let it suffice to say that the population was subdivided into groups (*túatha*), large or small as the case might be, and ruled over by kings selected from the members of a ruling family, chosen by a peculiar and complex law of dynastic succession, which Professor MacNeill was the first to elucidate.[2] A new ruler, on his accession to power, was inaugurated with certain traditional rites, held at certain traditional places. The nature of the rites seems to have varied considerably in different communities, if we may repose any confidence in the ancient writers who have reported them to us. For example, we are told by Giraldus Cambrensis of what, if authentic, was obviously a savage totemistic rite, in the North of Ireland ; in which

[1] PRIA 47 [1942] : 1.   [2] *Celtic Ireland*, pp. 114 ff.

the Neophyte imitated the actions of a horse, and bathed in a broth of mare's flesh.[1] In almost amusing contrast, Keating tells us of a solemn function in which the chief Chronicler of the territory read before the Neophyte a book called " The Instruction of Kings " ; the Neophyte gave sureties that he would follow the precepts of the book ; and the Chronicler put into the hand of the Neophyte a wand, as a token of his authority over his future subjects, which further symbolized truth, uprightness, and equity by its whiteness, straightness and smoothness. In a separate study the present writer has endeavoured to reconstruct, from the fragmentary materials available, the inauguration rites of the Kings of Tara.[2]

In the passage of Keating's *History*, just quoted, there is a list of inauguration-places, at which such rites, whatever their nature, took place. Some of these sites can be identified and still retain traces of their earthworks and stone structures : though naturally not in sufficient measure to permit us to recover the ritual completely. Two of the most important of these sites are Carnfree (Roscommon),[3] the inauguration-place of the O'Connors of Connaught ; and Magh Adhair (Clare), the inauguration-place of the Dal gCais. At each of these sites the most conspicuous feature is a burial mound, presumably the tomb of the traditional founder of the family. Other features are standing stones, rock-cut basins and troughs, and, at Carnfree, a seat built of small stones. An inauguration-chair, that of the rulers of Clann Aedha Buidhe (" Clandeboye ", Down) is now preserved in the Museum of Belfast. It is very roughly fashioned out of a block of stone ; indeed, " fashioned " is hardly the word, for it appears to be a mere *lusus naturae*, like the " Hag's Chair " which stands beside the principal carn at Lochcrew.[4]

Of especial historical importance are the palace sites, in which the provincial and *túath* kings established themselves. Of these the most noteworthy remaining are *Cruachu* (Rathcroghan, Roscommon), *Emhain Macha* (Navan Fort, Armagh), *Uisneach* (Westmeath), and *Teamhair* (Tara, Meath).

[1] *Topographia Hiberniæ* III 25.　　　　[2] *Tara*, pp. 130 ff.
[3] Described with illustrations in JRSAI 11 [1870-1] : 250. See also a very full and well illustrated account in *Galway* 9 [1915-6] : 1, 65.
[4] There is a useful compilation by R. R. Brash, " On ancient stone chairs and stones of inauguration ", *Gentleman's Magazine*, 1865 part i, pp. 428, 548 (reprinted in " Gentleman's Magazine Library ", *Archæology* part ii, p. 27). For *Magh Adhair*, see PRIA 20 : 55, JRSAI 21 : 462. For other inauguration sites see G. E. Hamilton, " Two Ulster inauguration places ", JRSAI 42 : 64 ; H. F. Hore, " Inauguration of Irish chiefs ", *Ulster* I 5 : 216, with, as an appendix, a description with plan and sections of Tullaghog (Tyrone), the inauguration-place of Ui Néill ; PRIA 33 : 505 (description of an artificially-modified esker at Masonbrook, near Lochrea, perhaps an inauguration-mound) ; on this monument see also *Galway* 10 : 71 ; on the " Clandeboye " stone, see Frazer's paper, JRSAI 28 : 254, and compare the very similar *Cader y Frenhines* (" Queen's Chair ") at Pool Park, Ruthin, and the chair in the stone circle at Clocaenog Moor (see *Ancient Monuments Commission*, volume for Denbigh, nos. 116, 209).

Cruachu. There are here numerous mounds, most of them evidently artificial, though some seem to be merely trimmed and scarped eskers, like the Masonbrook mound mentioned in the preceding footnote. The largest of these mounds is traditionally the site of the palace of Ailill and Medb, king and queen of Connaught. Close to this is a rift in the underlying rock supposed to afford a passage to the under-world ; probably the natural feature that first called attention to the site. An artificial vestibule, constructed in the manner of a souterrain, has been erected in front of the entrance to this cave ; and two Ogham stones appear among the constructional material. In the neighbourhood is a circular enclosure which, ever since the days of Charles O'Conor, an eighteenth-century pioneer of Celtic scholarship, has been identified with *Reilig na Ríogh*, the Cemetery of the Kings (of Connaught). Excavation within the area showed, however, that this enclosure is a mere cattle-pen, not a cemetery at all. A short distance away is a mound on the summit of which stands an erect stone long identified with Nath-Í, the last pagan king of Ireland, who is recorded to have been here buried.[1] In this case, again, excavation has upset a superficial identification. The mound is not a burial-mound at all, but has been scarped out of a much larger esker. There was no trace of any burial under the pillar, and we must infer that it was an inauguration-stone, like *Lia Fáil* at Tara.

Emhain Macha, the residence of the kings of the Ulaidh, displays a gigantic mound and another of smaller size, surrounded by a large earthen enclosure.[2]

Uisneach was thoroughly excavated in the years following the publication of our first edition by the Royal Irish Academy's Archæological Exploration Committee ; and a remarkable structure on the townland of Togherstown, on the slope of the same hill, was examined shortly afterwards.[3] Foundations of protecting walls, with surrounding ditches, enclosing the foundations of single house buildings ; pits and post-holes in abundance, the latter scattered in such a random lack of arrangement that it is difficult to avoid coming to the conclusion that they were mere tree-sites ; evidence for one very large fire, and a number of smaller ones, a few insignificant artifacts in stone, bronze, and iron, but not the smallest particle of pottery ; such in brief was the result of the excavation of this important site.

There are extensive earthworks at the Hill of *Temair Breg*, now more familiar as *Tara*, the seat of the High Kings of Ireland from

---

[1] Figured JRSAI 44 : plate facing p. 28.

[2] There is a plan of this site in *Revue Celtique* 16 : 1, and another in JRSAI 16 : 409. These, however, are superseded by the fine air photograph published in *Antiquity* 4 [1930] : 456.

[3] The full reports on these excavations will be found in PRIA 38 [1928] 269, 39 [1931] : 54. For a summary of the results the reader may be referred to *Ancient Ireland*, pp. 101-9.

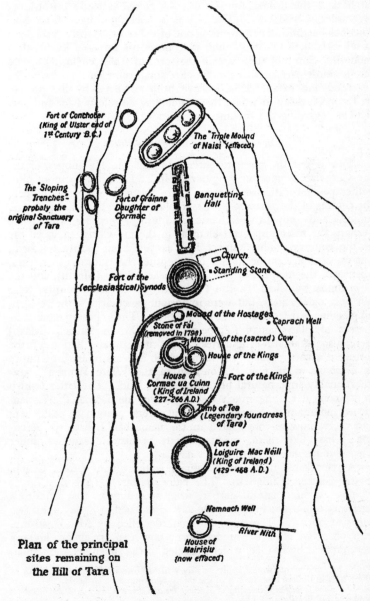

Fort of Conchobar
(King of Ulster end of
1st Century B.C.)

The "Triple Mound
of Naisi" (effaced)

The "Sloping
Trenches"-
probaly the
original Sanctuary
of Tara

Fort of Grainne
Daughter of
Cormac

Banquetting
Hall

Church

Standing Stone

Fort of the
(ecclesiastical) Synods

Mound of the Hostages

Caprach Well

Stone of Fál
(removed in 1798)

Mound of the (sacred) Cow

House of the Kings

House of
Cormac ua Cuinn
(King of Ireland
227-266 A.D.)

Fort of the Kings

Tomb of Tea
(Legendary foundress
of Tara)

Fort of
Loiguire Mac Néill
(King of Ireland)
(429-458 A.D.)

Nemnach Well

River Nith

House of
Mairisiu
(now effaced)

Plan of the principal
sites remaining on
the Hill of Tara

Fig. 36.—Plan of Tara.

the time when Cormac Mac Airt first laid the foundation of the united monarchy. For long before Cormac's time—probably as far back as the Bronze Age—it was the sacred seat of a priest-king, or, rather, a god-king. The site is a swelling ridge, of no conspicuous height, but commanding one of the most extensive prospects in all Ireland.[1] On its summit is to be seen a series of low earthen mounds. Some of these are in the form of walls, enclosing spaces for the most part circular ; others are small rounded hillocks. The recorded and extant remains have been surveyed by the present writer in an essay to which the reader may be referred for full particulars regarding the site and its traditions.[2]

Sanctuaries and Assembly-places

This is not the place to enter into the complex subject of the pre-Christian religion or religions of Ireland ; but we cannot altogether pass over the sanctuaries where the gods were worshipped, the centres of the periodical " Assemblies " for religious, legislative, judicial, and competitive (athletic and literary) purposes, which were perhaps the most important element in the pre-Christian social life of the country. This subject has, as yet, been hardly touched ; but we can have no hesitation in accepting the tradition that Tara, Uisneach, the mounds of Tlachtgha, near Athboy (Meath), and the now almost vanished Tailltiu (Telltown) in the same county, were not only palace sites, but were important sanctuaries : the resident king being regarded as a divine incarnation. The imposing mountain-masses of Slievenaman (Tipperary) and Croagh Patrick (Mayo) were also mountain-sanctuaries. The modern appellation of the former is a corruption of the name which appears in Irish literature as *Sliab na mban finn*, " Mountain of the White Women ", unquestionably supernatural beings of some kind. The latter (which in its conical outline much resembles Puy de Dôme, the ancient sacred mountain of Auvergne, and the several prominent peaks here and there, now re-consecrated in the name of Michael the Archangel) has, like them, maintained its prehistoric sanctity under Christian auspices even unto this day.

A remarkable mountain sanctuary is the hill of Crotta Cliach, in the Galtees (Limerick). The name means " Harps of Cliu " ; Cliu was a supernatural harper, who, according to that wondrous repertory of ancient folk-lore, *Dindshenchus*, used to " play upon two harps at once ". The mountain was identified by Mr. Westropp, who observed after a thunder-storm how two triangular hollows were crossed by rivulets which sparkled in the sunshine, and which,

---

[1] The same words would apply equally well to Uisneach, from the summit of which hills in no less than twenty of the thirty-two counties are visible.

[2] In *Tara, a pagan Sanctuary of Ancient Ireland* (New York 1931), superseding an earlier publication in PRIA.

against the dark background of the hill-side, had a remarkable resemblance to two harps with silver strings.[1]

This has been a long chapter, but no one can be more conscious of its inadequacy than the writer himself. No study of " dwellings and defences " could be complete without a concurrent study of the dwellers and defenders : their mode of life ; their food and dress ; their devices in the various arts that came to their hands, carpentry, agriculture, cattle-tending, and all the rest, as well as in warfare ; their kinship and community organization ; their religious and moral conventions—all these subjects, and many others, necessarily investigated not by one man but by a large body of collaborators, taking into consideration the evidence of literary texts as well as of folk-survival,[2] in addition to the purely archæological evidence to which the present study is confined, are essential to a complete picture. An expansion of such a paper as the syndicated " Conditions of Life in Prehistoric Ireland "[3] to a work at least three times as large as this, would be an approximation to what is required. When, after years of collecting and sifting of material, it finally appears, as a contribution to the series of monographs of which we dreamed in our Prefatory Essay, it will be a classic in the scientific literature of the world.

[1] T. J. Westropp, " Dun Crot and the ' Harps of Cliu ' in the Galtees, Co. Limerick ", PRIA 35 : 378. [Mr. P. J. Flynn, in *The Book of the Galtees and the Golden Vein*, has questioned the identification, but hardly on sufficient grounds.] For other sanctuary sites see the same author's " Oenach Cairbre ", PRIA 35 : 363 ; " Ancient places of assembly in the counties Limerick and Clare ", JRSAI 49 : 1.

[2] That is, for the later periods, say from A.D. 300 onwards. Our fundamental principle that literary evidence is valueless for the earlier stages is not here modified or withdrawn.

[3] *Ulster* III 3 [1940] : 5. See also the similar article on *The Celts in Archæology* in the same journal 2 [1939] : 137 ; and especially E. E. Evans's *Irish Heritage* (Dundalk 1942).

Postscript to p. 29.—Unfortunately these pages ʌere already made up at the printing office when Prof. Ó. Ríordáin's reports upon his very notable excavations at Loch Gur appeared—too late to include any adequate summary of them here. We must perforce content ourselves with a very strong recommendation to the reader to read them for himself in JRSAI 77 [1947], p. 39 and PPS N.S. 12 [1946] : 142.

CHAPTER X

THE BACKGROUND OF THE OVERLAP, OR THE TRANSITION TO CHRISTIANITY

FOR want of space, we have found it necessary to omit from the scope of this book the works of art produced under the auspices, and in the service, of Christianity. In the very few pages which it might be possible to allot to them, we could do no more than re-tread ground already trodden hard : too hard, if anything, for much of it would be none the worse for a little breaking up. What we said in our opening chapter, speaking of the earliest pre-historic remains of Ireland, we must repeat in this our closing chapter, in reference to the relics of Christianity : that they now form a subject too vast to be confined within a single volume.[1]

" Transition to Christianity " are simple words, but they involve difficult problems. " Transition " implies a starting-point, and a goal. The goal was Christianity : what was the starting-point ? Some form of what is broadly called " paganism " ; but what was its nature ? What gods were worshipped, with what ritual ? What did the worshippers expect from them ? And what was the process of the transition ? These questions we must try to answer : if the reader find our endeavour discursive, it cannot be helped— an enormous range of historical and ethnological ground has to be covered, even in a necessarily superficial study of the subject.

Popular writers conspire to persuade us that " the religion of the ancient Irish was druidism "—a proposition in which many holes could be picked, and which in any case gets us nowhere. What was " druidism " ? Was it a religion at all ? Almost certainly not. What then are we to understand by the word ? Nothing more than a vague (and entirely modern) comprehensive term, in-cluding within its scope some elementary astronomical (or, rather, astrological) notions ; a bag of miscellaneous magical tricks ; a probably conspicuous skill in hypnotism, ventriloquism, and sleight of hand ; expert familiarity with drugs, narcotics, stimulants, and poisons ; a sort of hymn-book of traditional spells and chants ; in short, all the stock manifestations of charlatanism. Were these things, and the people who dealt in them, indigenous in Ireland ? There is no reason to believe so : there is, indeed, hardly any special reason to suppose that there were druids in Ireland at all, before the first century A.D. ; literary references which would assign them to an earlier date being readily explicable as artificial backward pro-jections of later conditions.

---

[1] Happily they have received adequate special treatment in recent publications, notably those of Mlle. Françoise Henry.

But if the starting-point was not druidism (whatever that may be), what was it ? We can say no more than this : that the vague literary and folklore evidence, upon which we must perforce rely, brings before us a syncretistic jumble of odds and ends of primitive belief, in which elemental gods, animal gods, and deified men are commingled—just what we should expect to find, in a land in which refugees from Europe had been accumulating for some twenty-five centuries, each new element adding new contributions to the amalgam, and developing an atmosphere as hag-ridden with fearsome spooks, with tabu, and with other malignant forces as in any island of the South Pacific Ocean. Those who can remember the rural Ireland of a short fifty or sixty years ago, when the now moribund " fairies " had a very real power in controlling the activities of human life, can believe this without difficulty. The beings called *Túatha Dé Danann* are commonly treated by modern writers as euphemerized gods of the pagan population ; some of them actually bear names identical with the names of gods recorded in votive inscriptions left us by the Continental Celtic-speaking peoples. But the scholastic history, so far as it has any significance, displays to us the Túatha Dé Danann as foreign immigrants, like all the other " invasions " ; and it is very far from clear that they, or the gods whom they are supposed to represent, played an outstanding part in the general life of the country. If they were gods, they were the gods of the aristocratic, and essentially foreign, minority : the peasant-folk sought to propitiate the simpler, more elemental, beings of whom they had inherited the fear, and left Nuadu, Lug, and the rest of them to their masters.[1]

But were there not druids in Ireland with whom St. Patrick was obliged to contend ? So we are told, and we need not doubt the essential fact ; though the details of the story, as we find it recorded, hardly command credence. But for how long had they been established in the country before he arrived, in the fifth century A.D. ?

" Druids ", from about 1750 onward, have been so conspicuously the playthings of cranks, sciolists, and ecstatics, that it needs some boldness to introduce them to any respectable scientific society. But there certainly were such persons : in the history of the Gallic War, which Julius Cæsar has bequeathed to us, there are two chapters of inestimable value, in which he tells us something about them.[2]

---

[1] For a striking parallel we may refer to Professor Gilbert Murray's *Five Stages of Greek Religion*, chap. ii, where, after telling us that the Homeric poems " go back in ultimate origin to something like lays sung in a royal hall ", the author quoted continues in these words : " the contrast between the Homeric gods and the [Greek] gods found outside Homer is well compared by Mr. Chadwick to the difference between the gods of the Edda and the historical traces of religion outside the Edda. The gods who feast with Odin in Asgard, forming an organized community or *comitatus*, seem to be the gods of kings, distinct from the gods of the peasants, cleaner and more warlike and lordlier, though in actual religious quality much less vital."   [2] *De Bello Gallico* vi 13, 14.

This information, so far as it goes, we may take as trustworthy : it comes from an eye-witness, with a highly-developed intellect and an enquiring mind, who was on friendly terms with certain members of the druidic order, for all that he was what would now be called " an alien enemy " in their land of Gaul. If we cannot believe him, we must surely extend our disbelief to every other writer of antiquity. Taking these chapters as our primary source, and filling in details from other writers such as Cicero, Diodorus, and Pliny, we can outline a fairly satisfactory picture of the functions of these officials, as they presented themselves to the contemporary eyes of cultured foreign observers ; though their observations were inevitably super-ficial, for we may take it as granted that the druids had professional secrets which they never communicated in writing or otherwise to any outsider, and which in consequence are now lost for ever.

These authorities teach us that the druids were primarily jurists, and secondarily instructors of youth. The sacerdotal functions, popularly attributed to them, seem to have been less conspicuous in actual life ; and to have been of a mantic and magical rather than a strictly ritual nature. Like all miracle-workers among nature-folk, they must have had skill in the esoteric arts and conjuring tricks enumerated on a preceding page—such arts as are practised by the closely analogous medicine-men of Africa, wherewith they keep what we may call the ordinary lay-folk in awe.[1]

On the educational functions of the druids, Cæsar is explicit. He displays them to us, presiding over formal schools, to which great numbers of youths resorted—attracted by the exemption from military service and from taxation, which were the privileges of their *alumni*. Especially popular were the schools of Britain, where (as Cæsar was given to understand, by some to us unknown and not necessarily accurate informant) the druidic teaching had originated. He is equally definite as to their juristic functions ; they presided over courts, at which disputes of all kinds were settled.

But as the influence and authority of the Roman Empire spread over the Celtic portion of the Continent, druidism gradually faded out. Not, as was formerly believed, because it was artificially exterminated ; but, as always happens, because the lower culture could not stand before the higher.[2] In the presence of the institutions and the gods of conquering Rome, those of the " Celts " wilted away. Not much more than a century after Julius Cæsar, the druids had lost all their power and influence in the lands where, in his time, they had been regarded with awe. There was, however,

[1] Indeed, making all allowances for the different environment, we might take such an article as Van Thiel's " Le sorcier dans l'Afrique équatoriale " (*Anthropos* [1906] : 49) and reprint it here almost word for word, substituting *druide* for *sorcier*.

[2] See Fustel de Coulanges, " Comment le druidisme a disparu," *Revue Celtique* 4 [1879] : 37.

one refuge open to them—Ireland, the perennial asylum of refugees ; and into Ireland they seem to have crowded.   As we saw at page 213, there is ethnological evidence that about this very time a new tide of immigrants, most likely of Scandinavian or at least of East European origin, had been overflowing the land, endeavouring with success to establish a domination over its turbulent occupants.   To these the druids came as a godsend, in no merely metaphorical sense of the term.   With their stock-in-trade of conjuring and hypnotic tricks they sold themselves to the service of the new masters of the country ; with their judicial experience they could promulgate codes of " laws " in the name and under the sanction of the deities supposed to have given them the power to work their uncanny miracles.

These documents, rightly understood, are marvels of ingenuity.   They have a broad and easily recognized basis of primitive ethnic social custom, no doubt traditional in the country from prehistoric times ; to isolate this must be the primary goal of all future study of their content, whenever the philogists have succeeded in telling us what they mean.[1]   But all through them, from first to last, we can detect clever artificial modifications which, while not appearing to depart seriously from tradition, in fact introduce a warp, putting a litigant of inferior rank under a heavy handicap.   One barrier after another is set up to block his way : that they were designed in the interests of a dominant aristocracy, by maintaining an elaborate caste system of privileged and non-privileged classes, is obvious throughout. To mention but one out of all the possible illustrations [2] : every man has a pecuniary value, depending on his social rank or position, which is chiefly determined by the extent of his possessions in cattle or in land.   He is literally " worth so much ", be he king or vagabond.   This value affects all his relations with his environment.   It limits the amount of compensation which he can legally claim for any injury, however grave.   It excludes him from giving testimony in any case involving a sum of money which exceeds it.   And so forth : obviously such restrictions must have cruelly loaded the dice against a poor or humble respondent.   This beginning of juris- prudence in Ireland is suggestively synchronous with the downfall of druidism on the continent.

In speaking of the extant documents, we have put the word " laws " in inverted commas.   It is a mistake to apply this word to them without the reservation thus implied.   Rather are they treatises and commentaries [3] on various aspects of jurisprudence,

[1] The real importance of the " Brehon Laws " does not lie in inhuman *minutiæ* of grammatical analysis, but in their contacts with the accumulated materials and the findings of Comparative Ethnology.   Tabu, caste, and other social conventions, the doctrine of *mana*, the divinity of the king, the sanctity of the magician and almost every aspect of his art, primitive trade, customs, costume—there is no end to the wealth awaiting the workers in this mine, when the grammarians have done with it, and have given us much-needed authoritative texts and trustworthy trans- lations to work upon.

[2] Others will be found in *Ancient Ireland*, p. 93.

[3] " Commentaries " is perhaps too dignified a term to apply to them : they may be more appropriately called " lecture-notes " (whether the teachers' or the students' does not matter).   Such documents are usually nothing but aids to the memory of words spoken or to be spoken : to anyone excluded from the oral instruction of which they are mere concomitants, they are inevitably obscure and

and they can hardly be less than eight or nine centuries later than the codes which they profess to expound. The actual codes are now lost for ever, except in so far as these can be recovered by inference from the commentaries : because (like some Indian codes) they were drawn up in verse, and in this mnemonic form were committed to memory ; but were never written down, so that they perished beyond hope of recovery, with the passing of their last living repository.

Laws so oppressive could hardly have been imposed at all, unless reinforced by the divine sanction which they actually claim.[1] The extant legal literature has passed through the hands of Christians, who use Christian terminology ; but that is only what we now call a smoke-screen. Though Christianity may have modified much of their harsher precepts and procedure, they are essentially pagan, in origin and in spirit.

For the existence of a caste system in Ireland there is ample literary evidence. We have seen that the law tracts present us with elaborate details as to the shapes and sizes of the houses of members of the different castes : but more extensive exploration will be necessary before we can hope to establish a correlation between such literary details and the tangible remains. Here, as on every other road in the field of Irish Archæology, we are blocked by the lack of a complete Archæological Survey,[2] carried out with the fulness of the Geological Survey : just as every road in the field of Irish History was blocked, in a moment and for ever, by the wanton destruction

incoherent, often indeed unintelligible. A brief but highly competent and most instructive summary of the present state of knowledge concerning them will be found in a review signed J. R. in *North Munster* 1 [1936] : 42 ; and within the thirty-three pages of Professor Binchy's lecture on " The Linguistic and Historical Value of the Irish Law Tracts " (*Proceedings*, British Academy, 29 [1943]) is concentrated the fruit of a vast amount of intensive scientific research, for which we cannot be too grateful.

[1] Every ancient lawgiver, from Hammurabi downward, prefaced his code with an assertion that this god or that had dictated the laws which it contained : an obvious and easy device for securing obedience. *Senchus Mār*, the chief of the Irish legal tracts, claims (*Ancient Laws of Ireland* 1 : 14-17) that the laws upon which it is a commentary were given by inspiration of the Holy Spirit : and in almost the same breath tells us that St. Patrick was obliged to revise them ! This monstrous profanity must have been due to some well-meaning blockhead, who, without realizing the consequent implications, exceeded his duties as copyist, and officiously substituted the name of the Holy Spirit for that of some pagan deity, to whom the document, in its original form, had ascribed the authorship of the code. By this conception of an artificial code, imposed by a homogeneous college of jurists, issued in the name of a god, and ratified by terrifying magic, we can best explain the universality of the legal institutions, overlying and unifying the diversity of populations. For the fact of that universality see MacNeill, *Early Irish Laws and Institutions*, p. 90. Binchy, *op. cit.* pp. 16 ff., has shown that the passage quoted is linguistically late and historically valueless, so far as the intervention of St. Patrick is concerned. But this does not affect the explanation here given for the otherwise unintelligible invocation of the Holy Spirit.

[2] Of the Southern Counties : very considerable progress has been made in this essential work by the six Counties of the North.

of the Record Office in 1922. Until we have the volumes of such a survey, before us, and can compare plan with plan over the whole country, it will be impossible adequately to carry out an investigation on this and on many other possible lines of research.

But a faint suggestion was made to me by the perusal of A. M. Hocart's unfortunately posthumous book *Les Castes*. This scholar, in his careful study of the world-wide ramifications of the complicated subject to which his monograph is devoted, notes that in the Fiji Islands the business of the potter is on a different standing from any other, in that it has not been made a basis of caste. There is, so to speak, no potters' guild with hereditary trade secrets ; anybody may make pottery ; in consequence it appears that no one does so, except the inhabitants of a few villages who individually pursue this trade. As usual, " everybody's business is nobody's business ". If from any cause those villages should become depopulated, the trade disappears until somebody feels that it might pay to revive it, for there is no professional freemasonry to keep it permanently alive as an exclusive privilege.

Whether any such reason was operative or not, I am unable to say : but it is indisputable, that just about the time when (as it is here suggested) the La Tène culture began in Ireland, the making of pottery suddenly disappeared from the country. Surely it might be supposed that this all but indispensable and comparatively simple craft could not disappear anywhere, once it had become established : but the fact remains that in Ireland it did. Two or three large sites of that period have been thoroughly excavated from end to end. They have revealed traces of intensive occupation, including great quantities of midden material ; but nowhere over the whole area investigated was there the smallest vestige of pottery. When we remember that pottery does not decay like other human handiworks, but retains its character, practically for ever : that it is brittle, so that pots constantly break, and have to be replaced ; and that, when broken, it is useless and intrinsically worthless, so that discarded sherds are allowed to remain where they fall : we realize that if pottery has been used at all in any ancient settlement, potsherds ought to form the bulk of its archæological yield—as is in fact the case. Conversely, when no pottery at all is found, the inference is inevitable that at the time, and in the region, to which the site under examination belongs, pottery was unknown, or at least was not in use. There is no evading the conclusion ; Ireland in or about the first century B.C. had sunk to the lowest depth of uncivilization in its whole history, when even pottery-making was a lost art. And a not necessarily numerous invasion of Teutonic pirates with their iron weapons, reinforced by a concurrent invasion of Continental Celtic druids with their magic, could make of it an easy prey. It is most likely that the nebulous tales of invading and oppressive " Fomorians ", led by one Conaing (= Teutonic *koninga, konungr*, " king " [1]) are based on recollections of such an invasion.[2]

---

[1] This attractive etymological suggestion is due to Professor Eoin MacNeill.

[2] The too-energetic Micheál ó Cléirigh, who in the seventeenth century remodelled the old scholastic history called " The Book of Invasions ", has there interpolated a story to the effect that the people of Ireland, when invaded by the Fomorians, sent to Greece for " venomous beasts " to aid them in their struggle against the intruders. If we could be confident that this incident (which we seek in vain in the extant genuine recensions of the book, or in the parallel version in Keating's *History of Ireland*) is borrowed from some authentic early narrative, now lost, and is not a mere invention, it would possess an overwhelming interest. Folk-tales of animals acting as men, or of men transformed into animals, are usually to be explained as totemistic, or else as referring to men disguised in animal masks :

For the culture-history of this transitional period, enshrined in domestic utensils and in household economy, no available source of information is so full as the later lake-dwellings ; so calling them, to mark a differentiation from the few earlier lake-dwellings, such as Knocknalappa. The great development of lake-dwellings, at the time with which we are now concerned (having regard to the stupendous labour involved in constructing those most inconvenient habitations), is impressive evidence of a longing for security at any price induced by a general unrest.

A field untilled, almost fallow, awaits the systematic student of this later lake-dwelling civilization, the available literature of which is painfully amateurish and unsystematic. Only by rare exception will he have any such sensational objects as highly decorative metal ornaments or stone sculpturings to deal with. He will be burrowing in the underworld practically all the time, associating with people (whatever their rank) on the cultural level of humble labourers and peasants, and their simple, often makeshift tools, weapons, and implements. But there, better than anywhere else, will he be able to trace the gradual re-advance in civilization, consequent upon the climatic amelioration which began to set in about A.D. 400. A comparison of the contents of one lake-dwelling with another, of one occupation-layer with another, may be expected to indicate the course of such historical movements as the re-introduction of pottery, the rebirth of an æsthetic sense, the restoration of a temporarily lost technical skill, all together gradually working up to the cultural (and climatic) optimum of the ninth century A.D. Lake-dwellings possess the enormous advantage over all other ancient sites, that the antiseptic peat in which they are partly embedded has saved some of their wooden and other perishable contents from decay ; the importance of this needs no underlining.

But over this subject again, as over so many others, we must not linger. A general conspectus cannot assume specialist functions. All that can be done here is to enumerate some of the more important classes of objects which the lake-dwellings will present to the author of a scholarly study of their life and history.

Canoes. Lake-dwellings necessitated transport across the water, in boats, rafts, or canoes. Wooden framed " curachs ", covered with hides or textiles, may have been used sometimes ; the modern boats of this kind [1] have possibly a long tradition behind them,

and if only we could find means of allaying our doubts of the authenticity of the incident in question, we could legitimately see here the aboriginal sorcerers, thus forbiddingly disguised—reference to *Ancient Ireland*, p. 146, will give the reader an idea of what they would look like—pitting their gruesome appearance, and their magic spells, against the newcomers and their druids : just as the Ancient Britons painted themselves with blue woad, in the vain hope that their Roman invaders would mistake them for demons and would flee away ; and as the druids themselves impotently opposed their magic against the same ruthless and unimpressionable conquerors.

[1] On which see Jas. Hornell, *British Coracles and Irish Curraghs* (London 1938).

though there is no tangible evidence to prove this. Rafts were probably used for the transport of cattle and heavy goods along the larger rivers.[1] But the principal means of such transport, and the only one of which remains are left to us, are what are generally known as " dug-out canoes ". These are tree-trunks, split longitudinally, with the flat side hollowed, either by means of adzes, or with the aid of heated stones. Sometimes blocks were left uncut in the hollow, presumably for seats. The oars were apparently manipulated in the manner of modern canoe-paddles,[2] but may sometimes have been passed through rowlocks in the form of loops of rope, knotted through holes in the gunwale of the boat.

There are three kinds of dug-out canoes known in Ireland. The *first* is of a large size, rounded at one end or at both, sometimes with a hole for stepping a mast. and measuring anything up to 50 feet in length.

This maximum length is attained by the finest specimen yet recorded, from a bog on the townland of Lurgan, parish of Addergoole (Galway). It is now to be seen in the National Museum. The maximum breadth is 3 feet 8 inches.[3] A flat ridge runs longitudinally inside the boat, over the keel, 7 inches broad and a little under 1 inch high ; and six similar ridges cross it at intervals, from side to side. These are possibly strengthening ribs, which could also serve as seats on which the rowers might squat. There are grooves or notches in the gunwale above the first and fourth of these cross-ridges (counting from the bow) ; but they are now (whatever they might have been when the boat was intact) too shallow to give an oar any purchase, and as they are forward from the cross-ridges the latter could not have been used as seats in rowing. The crew must have faced forward, *digging*, so to speak, into the water with short-stemmed paddles, used spadewise. In addition to the grooves, there are five holes drilled through the sides of the vessel, and three others lower down. The latter must have been drain-holes, plugged when the boat was in use : the purpose of the former is not so clear. A diagonal cutting-out from the gunwale on both sides is apparently a modern mutilation.

The *second*, which is the commonest, is round or flat-bottomed, pointed at the ends and about 20 feet long and 2 feet broad. The *third* is small and portable, 8 to 12 feet in length, with handles at the ends whereby it could be carried from lake to lake. Wakeman describes a canoe of this kind.[4] We have no direct knowledge of

---

[1] A raft-dock, formed of two walls meeting at a right angle rising from the water and facing up-stream, was found in the excavation of Friars' Island in the Shannon, below Killaloe. It may well have been made for landing stones, to build the early church upon this island. A raft could be punted down-stream into it, and would there remain safe without drifting away, until its load was carried ashore : when thus lightened it could be towed up-stream, back to the quarry, for a fresh supply. See JRSAI 59 [1929] : 16, especially p. 22.

[2] For a canoe-paddle see Wilde, *Catalogue*, p. 204.

[3] T. B. Costello, " The Lurgan Canoe ", *Galway* 2 [1902] : 57.

[4] JRSAI 12 [1872] : 16. For a further study of the subject see W. G. Brooke, " Notes on an old Irish Canoe found in Lough Owel, Co. Westmeath ", PRIA 9 [1865] : 210. See also Wood-Martin, *Lake-dwellings*, p. 46 and index *s.v.* " canoe ".

pre-Iron Age boats in the country, though some such carriers must have been used by all the numerous immigrants throughout the centuries.

But we must not too readily assume that even all dug-out canoes were used for transport only. A canoe, revealed in Loch Erne by the accidental grounding of a modern steamer, which pushed her predecessor out of the mud of the shallow water wherein they had both in turn been entrapped, had nine holes drilled through the keel. Drainage holes are normal in these boats, but naturally they are always plugged with care. In the Loch Erne boat they were open. " Putting on the sea " was a form of punishment, often mentioned in the law-tracts—though it seems to have been an ordeal rather than a penalty, in that it transferred the responsibility for judicial decision to some supernatural Omniscience. The culprit was set adrift without sail or oars. If he starved or drowned no doubt he deserved it : [1] if he was cast up by the waves he became sea-jetsam, and *ipso facto* a charge upon those on whose lands he was deposited. This reminds us of the strange principle whereby a shipwrecked crew, and all their belongings, became the property of the people upon whose foreshore they happen to be cast up. It has been recorded in Borneo and New Zealand : in Fiji it appears to have been nothing short of a moral obligation for the local inhabitants to kill and eat all the survivors of a shipwreck. [2] In the Loch Erne case, the delinquent may have been set adrift in a *leaky* boat, and compelled to keep himself afloat by assiduous baling for so long as his strength lasted.

But another aspect of the case is suggested by the impressive work of Almgren, [3] who has collected a considerable body of evidence for the setting afloat and destruction by sinking or burning of a " divine ship " as part of a periodical agricultural festival. This rite he links up with the ship-figures which form such a prominent element in the Scandinavian rock-sculptures.

It should be made clear that dug-out canoes are not necessarily of high antiquity in Ireland. There is a drawing in the Pepysian Library in Magdalene College, Cambridge, made by a well-known naval architect of the latter half of the seventeenth century, Capt. Thomas Phillips, and professing to be drawn " from life ", representing a large sea-going curach, lug-rigged, towing a dug-out dinghy. This is evidence that they were in use down to about 1680. [4]

Wooden Utensils. Wooden vessels of various shapes and sizes have been found from time to time in peat-bogs, or in the sites of lake-dwellings. Drinking-cups and table-dishes, hollowed out of blocks of wood, must have been the chief utensils for food-service during the eclipse of pottery in the Iron Age : and they continued

---

[1] See M. E. Byrne, " On the Punishment of Sending Adrift ", *Ériu* 11 [1932] : 97. According to *Lestoire del Saint-Graal* (ed. Sommer, pp. 18, 19) Caiaphas was thus set adrift by Vespasian, to punish him for his conduct at the Crucifixion. This indicates familiarity with the custom outside Ireland.

[2] Lévy-Brühl, *Primitive Mentality*, pp. 233 ff.

[3] Oscar Almgren, *Nordische Felszeichnungen als religiöse Urkunden* (German translation, 1934).

[4] Reproduced JRSAI 56 [1926] : 119. For other literature on dug-out canoes, see PSA Lond. II 12 [1888] : 65 ; JRSAI 47 [1917] : 85 ; JRSAI 25 [1895] : 224.

PLATE XIV

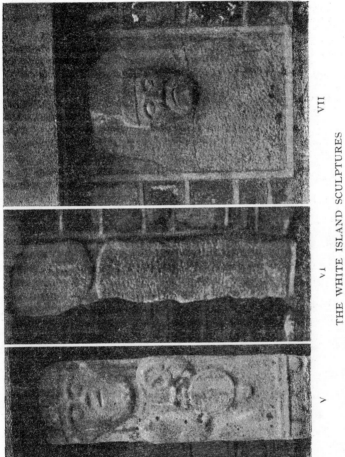

VII

VI

V

THE WHITE ISLAND SCULPTURES

in use down to still living memory. They cannot therefore be presumed to be ancient, even when found buried in bogs. Wooden receptacles containing " bog-butter " [1] are among the commonest of bog-finds ; one such vessel, in the Royal Irish Academy collection, has an eighteenth-century date scratched upon it.

On the other hand, Mr. de Vismes Kane has described a wooden bowl on five supports, found at a depth of 15 feet beneath the surface of a bog, which surely indicates a considerable antiquity ; [2] another, described by Wakeman, from a bog at Cavancarragh (Fermanagh), [3] had a simple guilloche pattern cut upon it which, while not necessarily very ancient, is certainly not modern. All these vessels, of which there is a considerable variety in shape, are hollowed out of single blocks of wood, not built up (like a modern barrel or tub) of staves. A primitive churn from Co. Derry, made in this way, has also been described. [4]

Among other wooden objects of domestic use, but of very uncertain date, may be mentioned cattle-yokes, stools, spades, hay-forks, canoe paddles, etc., all formed in the same way, out of single pieces of timber. [5] An enigmatical object in the shape of an inverted cone on a stem—like a colossal wineglass in outline, but solid, and with a solid handle at one side—was found in a bog near Killeshandra (Cavan). [6] Other objects of wood which may deserve a passing notice are a footed tray (hardly a " table ") of willow, found in a bog at Killygarvan (Tyrone)—a board, 2 feet 4½ inches, by about 1 foot 4 inches, supported on four legs 4½ inches high, all cut out of a single block ; associated with it was a dish of the same material and corresponding dimensions. [7]

Querns, for corn-milling, are naturally among the commonest of the contents of lake-dwellings, and, generally, of occupation-sites of the Overlap and Early Christian periods. The Rotary Quern now completely supersedes the Saddle-quern of earlier days (*ante*, p. 170), and its use has lasted down to our own time. It is a combination of two stones, about 1 foot 10 inches in diameter : the lower stone has a shallow cylindrical sinking in the upper surface, into which

---

[1] The practice of sinking butter in bog-holes was well known in the seventeenth century, and is referred to by the traveller Dineley, who visited Ireland about 1675 (see JRSAI 4 [1856] : 186). It was enclosed with " a sort of garlick, and buried for some time in a bog, to make a provision of an high tast (*sic*) for Lent." For further details see PRIA 6 [1856] : 360 ; JRSAI 21 [1891] : 583, 22 [1892] : 356, where analogies from such remote regions as Iceland and India are quoted. The taste of bog-butter is said to resemble that of cheese; it was probably to develop this taste, as well as for preservative purposes (and also, it would seem to enhance its nutritive qualities), that the butter was thus treated.

[2] PRIA 15 [1870] : 2.   [3] JRSAI 15 [1879] : 98.

[4] JRSAI 21 [1891] : 588. In this paper will be found further details about bog-butter, and also a figure of a wooden dish from Ballymoney (Antrim). A similar churn found at a depth of 10 feet in a bog at Ardmore (Armagh), filled with bog-butter, is described and figured by Mr. P. Keville in *Ulster* III 3 [1940] : 73. For a drinking vessel of another type see JRSAI 22 [1892] : 285.

[5] Numerous illustrations of such objects will be found in Wilde's *Catalogue*, pp. 206 ff., and scattered through Wood-Martin's *Lake-dwellings*. A rude wooden spade is figured in *Cork* 13 [107] : 118.

[6] JRSAI 55 [1925] : 136. It was possibly an unfinished bowl, never hollowed out.

[7] A fuller but slightly obscure description will be found in PRIA 3 [1844] : 21. See also Wilde's *Catalogue*, p. 211, where the " table " is figured, but not the bowl.

the upper stone, a circular slab, fits, rotating on a pivot for which a socket is provided in the middle. Another hole in the upper surface, near one side, receives a peg serving as a handle with which to keep the stone turning.[1]   The upper surface of the turning stone is frequently decorated in relief, sometimes very elaborately : a favourite basis of the decoration is the figure of a cross.[2]

Conceivably this had the semi-magical purpose of securing a blessing on the grinding, or of lightening its labour, proverbially among the most wearisome of the domestic duties.[3]   But it is only too easy to read recondite symbolism into mere rudimentary ornament : a cross of some kind is the most obvious form of decoration for a circular space ; the spokes of a rotating wheel would suggest it almost automatically, in the special case of a circular object intended to rotate.

According to the compilation called *Dindshenchas*, water-mills were first introduced into Ireland by the third-century king Cormac Mac Airt who, having become enamoured of one of his slaves, sought thus to relieve her of the heavy work of grinding with a hand-mill.[4]   This story need not be altogether dismissed as unhistorical: some three centuries later, such an installation figures in the unpleasant story of the fate of the sons of king Diarmait mac Cerrbeoil.[5] A form of mill with a horizontal wheel on a vertical axis, having turbine paddle-boards, survived down to recent times in Ireland.[6]

Deer-traps.   In various places in Ireland there have been found specimens of valved wooden traps, similar to others which have been found in Laibach Moor (Carniola), in Italy, and in Germany.[7] They differ among themselves in certain details, but have essential features common to all—a shuttle-shaped beam, about 3 feet in length, with a rectangular hole cut through the middle (indicated in the accompanying diagram by a dotted line), rebated to receive a closing door, turning on projecting pivots.   There is also provision

---

[1] This is a generalized description ; there are several varieties, for which see E. Cecil Curwen, " Querns " (*Antiquity* 11 [1937] : 133) and numerous references there.   See also H. S. Crawford, " Some types of Quern, or Hand-mill ", JRSAI 39 [1909] : 393.

[2] See for illustrations Wilde's *Catalogue*, p. 107, Wood-Martin's *Lake-dwellings*, pp. 87 ff.

[3] It was one of the privileges recorded of especially favoured saints, that when it happened to be their turn to carry out this duty in their monasteries, angels came down from heaven to relieve them of the burden : see my edition of the *Latin and Irish Lives of Ciaran*, pp. 21, 120.

[4] *The Metrical Dindshenchas*, ed. Gwynn, part i, pp. 20-3.

[5] Kuno Meyer, *Hibernica Minora*, pp. 70 ff.

[6] See R. MacAdam in *Ulster* I 4 [1856] : 6 ; J. P. O'Reilly, " Some further notes on ancient horizontal water-mills ", PRIA 24 [1902] : 55 (professedly a continuation of MacAdam's paper, with illustrations from Ireland and elsewhere in Europe) ; H. T. Knox, " Notes on gig-mills and drying kilns near Ballyhaunis, Co. Mayo ", PRIA 26 [1907] : 265.

[7] See the monograph on these objects which forms chap. vi of R. Munro, *Prehistoric Problems* (Edinburgh and London 1897) : a bibliography to the date of publication will there be found.   Also the same writer's " Some further notes on otter and beaver traps ", JRSAI 28 [1898] : 245.

for securing the ends of an elastic wooden lath, to keep the " door "
tightly secured.   In some of the Continental examples the door has
two valves, but the Irish examples have never more than one.   The
trap was set, with the " door " wedged open, in some place where

FIG. 37.—A Deer Trap and a Captured Stag.

the intended victim was likely to tread—such as the pathway to a
drinking-place.   Sooner or later it would step upon and dislodge
the wedge, and the " door ", thus released, would close upon
the unhappy creature's hoof and hold it fast.   In Larkhill Bog
(Fermanagh) a set of nine such traps was found, laid in a regular

order.[1] The species of the destined victim was long uncertain; otters and beavers [2] were named; but the shaft of a stone cross from Banagher (Offaly), now in the National Museum, appears to settle the question by showing us a stag caught in such a trap (Fig. 37 : an actual trap is drawn above, with a sectional diagram showing it as set).

This cross, when complete, must have stood at the high-water mark of the later Irish sculpture.[3] Every panel of the surviving fragment shows striking originality and mastery of technique, and is worthy of careful study. The figure of the stag, here copied, seems to have been drawn from a dead animal, like those in the Palæolithic caves.[4] This is interesting as a very rare indication of any practice of drawing from models by the Irish artists of pre-Norman Christianity. But it is hard to believe that the cross is the work of an Irish artist at all : there is a Caledonian-Pictish feeling about it, especially in its grotesque animals and the vesture and aspect of a rider displayed in another of the panels.

Whetstones are also among the commonest finds in iron-age sites, especially in crannogs. They are narrow bars of quartzite or other stones, from 3 to 5 inches in length, usually square or rectangular in section. Oval sections are also known. Often they are perforated at one end for suspension, and sometimes there is a bronze ring in the perforation. It may be that these stones were used for other purposes as well as sharpening stones, such as touchstones for testing metals.[5] At Lochpairc crannog, near Tuam, beside a number of whetstones of normal size, one no less than 17½ inches long was found.[6]

Lamps of stone have been found in various sites. Essentially these are shaped like saucers, or else like egg-cups, not very artistically cut out of blocks of moderately hard stone. The saucer-shaped vessels may be about 6 inches in diameter, and 3 inches high. The egg-cup vessels have a cylindrical stem with a bowl-shaped expansion at the top. There may or may not be an expanding foot at the lower end. Rarely is there any carved ornament upon the side of the vessel, though two saucer-shaped vessels with simple linear ornament on the sides are figured by Knowles,[7] and an " egg-cup ", from

---

[1] H. Allingham, " Wooden objects found in peat-bogs supposed to have been otter-traps ", JRSAI 26 [1896] : 379. See further in the same journal 21 [1891] : 536, 27 [1897] : 184, 28 [1898] : 235.

[2] The beaver does not appear ever to have been indigenous in Ireland, although it was the totem of the clan called *Corcu Bibuir*, the " Beaver-folk ".

[3] For an illustration of the whole cross-shaft, from a rubbing, see PSA Scot, 31 (1896-7) : 310. For the history of the monument itself see T. L. Cooke, " The Ancient Cross of Banagher, King's Co.", JRSAI 2 : 277. See also, and especially, F. Henry, *La sculpture irlandaise*, numerous references *s.v.* " Banagher " in the *répertoire bibliographique*.

[4] P. A. Leason, " A new view of the Western European Group of Quaternary Cave Art ", PPS 5 [1939] : 51. In spite of strictures passed on this article (*Antiquity* 14 [1940] : 154) I confess myself at least impressed by it.

[5] See W. J. Knowles, " Recently discovered finds in the Co. Antrim (JRSAI 22 [1892] : 46) ; Wilde, *Catalogue*, p. 87 ; Wood-Martin, *Lake-dwellings*, p. 69.

[6] Macalister, Armstrong and Praeger, " The excavation of Lochpairc crannog, near Tuam ", PRIA 32 [1914] : 147, especially p. 150 and plate xvii.

[7] In the paper quoted in the last footnote but one.

Humphreystown (Wicklow), has horizontal mouldings on the cup and the base, and a screw or rope pattern covering the stem.[1]

Wilde and others of the earlier writers supposed that these objects were chalices, which is inadmissible for both practical and liturgiological reasons ; they are too heavy and clumsy, and stone is a material forbidden for such sacred vessels. Mr. Coffey suggested to Rev. P. Power that they may have been lamps,[2] and the latter tentatively adopted this interpretation ; especially after one such cup was found with soot-stains in Newhall Cave by Mr. R. J. Ussher.[3] The subject was afterwards examined by Mr. Armstrong,[4] and finally settled by a chemical examination, which clearly revealed traces of the fatty grease that had been used as an illuminant.[5]

FIG. 38.—Stone Lamps.
(An "eggcup" lamp, a "bowl" lamp, and the hanging lamp from Cappagh.)

While these lamps are of a primitive type, it does not necessarily follow that they are of a very remote date. Mr. Moss's analysis, just quoted, revealed the presence of a relatively considerable quantity of sulphur, which he attributed to the use of sulphur matches.

A fragment of a fine lamp of stone was found in a cave near Cappagh (Waterford), and is now in the Royal Irish Academy's collection. It is in the shape of a bowl or dish, about 1 foot in diameter and 6 inches deep. There were three loop handles on the sides, by which it could be suspended ;

[1] Wilde, *Catalogue*, p. 132.
[2] Rev. P. Power, " On four or five stone chalices from early Church sites in the Decies ", *Waterford* 1906 : 143.
[3] TRIA 32 : 72.
[4] E. C. R. Armstrong, " Stone Chalices, so called ", PRIA 26 [1907] : 318.
[5] R. J. Moss, " Chemical notes on a stone lamp from Ballybetagh and other similar stone vessels in the Royal Irish Academy collection ", PRIA 28 : 162.

that suspension was contemplated is shown by the fact that the under side has a triquetra carved upon it, which would not be seen if the bowl were merely placed upon a table. A small cross, cut upon the edge of the bowl, suggests that this was an object of ecclesiastical furniture.

Other evidences of the varied life of the inhabitants of Ireland during the crannog period must be enumerated more briefly. The chase in its varied aspects is illustrated by bones and teeth of feral food animals, which are found scattered through the soil of every such site ; and by fish-hooks and iron eel-spears with numerous prongs. The domestication of animals is illustrated by the bones of all kinds of cattle, the relics of feasts : the cultivation of cereals by the querns, just described. The preparation and disposal of food leave evidence in trivets and pots of bronze and of iron, in knives and forks of metal or of bone, and in bone apple-scoops. Dress also leaves tangible traces : reference has already been made to bodies of drowned human beings, fully clothed, sometimes found mummified in the bogs ; of these some may belong to the crannog period, and may retain early traditions in their costume.[1] In addition to these garments, we possess scissors (not of the modern pivoted form, but resembling miniature sheep-clippers) ; pins of many patterns, in iron, bronze, and bone ; beads of glass and of stone ; and combs of bone. The handicrafts are illustrated by the spindle-whorls [2] and the loom-weights of the weaver, the crucibles of the metal-caster, the iron tools of the carpenter—in many cases [3] hardly distinguishable from their modern representatives—as well as knives and whetstones.

Æsthetics cannot be said to be very prominent in sites of this kind. We miss even the lumps of ochre which the bronze-age shore-dwellers used for paint, and which have been found at Whitepark Bay. On the other hand, decorative bronze brooches have occasionally been found in certain late crannogs, and a rudimentary feeling for ornament is also displayed by the numerous inlaying-slips of bone, adorned with simple engraved patterns, intended for embellishing objects made of wood.[4] Similar patterns are displayed by the bone combs, the chief toilet instruments ; of which there are two varieties, with single or double rows of teeth.[5] There are also pin-cases and other small objects in ornamental leather-work. Though not actually found in a lake-dwelling site, a sixth-century Saxon disc-brooch, unexpectedly unearthed in the Togherstown excavation, may be conveniently mentioned here. It was exceptional, for not only was it far outside the normal limits of the range of distribution of its particular type, but it was decorated with a realistic anthropomorphic design unusual in that class of ornament.[6]

[1] On this see McClintock's *Old Irish and Highland Dress*, already referred to.
[2] Wilde, *Catalogue*, p. 274.
[3] A few iron tools have escaped loss by corrosion ; Wakeman figures a flat and socketed axe-head, as well as a socketed gouge and chisel, and one or two other objects to which we may refer as illustrations for this note : JRSAI 28 [1898] : 237.
[4] Wilde, *Catalogue*, p. 342.
[5] Wood-Martin, *Pagan Ireland*, p. 535. Wilde, *Catalogue*, pp. 271-2.
[6] PRIA 39 : 80. On the type in general, see Mr. E. T. Leeds's monograph in *Archæologia* 63 [1912] : 159.

Neither Literature nor Religion makes any impression on lake-dwelling remains. There are no inscribed objects—for a so-called Ogham from Ballydooloch (Fermanagh) cannot be accepted as such—and little pendant metal crosses are almost the only evidences of Christianity in the sites. Of definite relics of paganism there are none at all. Warfare and the chase, on the other hand, are well provided for, by swords and spears of iron, and daggers of bone.[1]

Similar and no doubt contemporary objects are sometimes to be found in the midden heaps of dry-land ring-forts, though organic substances (except bones) are less likely to be there preserved.[2] Flint knives, lignite bracelets, whetstones, spindlewhorls of various kinds, pins, hones, iron knives, indistinguishable in type from the lake-dwelling material, are recorded, and will have to be discussed in detail in the encyclopædic monograph which, we hope, will at some time be written on the " unconsidered trifles " of early domestic life in Ireland.

The later lake-dwellings exhibit to us the gradual renewal of pottery-making after the La Tène eclipse. This is to be ascribed to the influence of the Roman immigrants of whom we shall hear on a subsequent page. Roman cooking-pots afford the model for the more or less globular vessels, with everted rims, made of hard, compact, well-fired ware, sometimes with loop-handles, and decorated with incised or stamped linear patterns, or with strips of pottery-material applied in the manner of encrusted decoration, and adorned with finger-prints or other impressions.[3] In texture, form, and ornament, these vessels are altogether different from anything bequeathed to us by the earlier cultural phases of the country.

With these later lake-dwelling sites we have got well into the period of Christianity, and out of the scope of this volume. Yet there is very little advance manifested in their general culture. Such a site as that of Craigy-warren [4] (Antrim), dated to about A.D. 900, gives us nothing but crude flint chips, hardly any pottery, commonplace domestic tools of wood or of iron, some leather shoes (one of them slightly decorated) none but the simplest personal ornaments, the disc of a churndash, bones showing that horses were kept as well as the food-animals ; but hardly any amenities to soften the harsh materialism of a life of struggle. In general, even the later lake-dwellers show us the people of Ireland still under the thumb of the " Fomorian " invaders and their druid auxiliaries. Helplessly, they have to submit to the bondage of the Laws, and to a religious bondage overlying their ancestral nature-worship.

This brings us back to the druids. These functionaries must necessarily have carried their educational activities into their new sphere, if only as a means of maintaining their own power and influence. Cæsar tells us that the druidic instruction took the form

[1] A bone dagger found in the bed of the Boyne near Clonard (Kildare) is figured by Wilde, *Catalogue*, p. 258.

[2] See R. J. Ussher, " A description of objects found in the kitchen middens of raths ", JRSAI 17 [1885] : 362.

[3] See a long series of fragments, illustrated JRSAI 17 : 372.

[4] PRIA 26 [1906] : 109.

of learning by heart a great number of verses, in which the teaching was enshrined. These were imparted orally, never written : and in acquiring them students sometimes spent as much as twenty years.

Cæsar conjectures that writing was prohibited, to protect the memory from being enfeebled by reliance on the written word, or else to safeguard their secrets, lest they should fall into the possession of non-initiates. But we know of analogies, hidden from Cæsar, which enable us to give a more complete explanation. The Vedas of India were preserved in memory in a like manner, for at least a thousand years : the Koran of the Muhammadans was not written down after the Prophet, himself an illiterate, had dictated it, till at least one generation had passed away—and only then, when it was discovered that individual recollections of certain sentences were gravely discrepant. For these and all similar cases one explanation holds good ; the traditional sacred literature had taken shape before the invention of writing, or, to speak more exactly, before the art of writing became current in the land of its veneration ; it was therefore accounted a profanation to confine its words within the fetters of this new-fangled device.

The Vedic analogy enables us to make one more legitimate inference. Such traditional verses would be pedantically stereotyped as to grammatical forms and pronunciation. It would be the chief concern of the instructors to see that the pupils said exactly the right words in exactly the right way.[1] Obsolete linguistic forms would thus be stubbornly preserved, in the face of the natural evolutionary changes which affect spoken speech, even within a single generation. The spoken speech, and with it the ephemeral writings of secular life, would quickly part company with the traditional sacred literature ; and it would then become necessary to study the language of the latter grammatically, like a foreign tongue, in order to understand it.

This being so, we must make the further deduction that, as in Vedic India, a study of grammar was an essential element of the druidic teaching. The alternative would be to assume, less reasonably, that the pupils spent twenty years in acquiring what would be to them as much of a meaningless jargon as a page of *Beowulf* to an average modern English schoolboy. The mysteries of those old poems *must* have been explained to pupils during their initiation : an impossibility, without some phonetic and grammatical instruction.

We learn two more facts, and draw one more inference, from Cæsar's report. The first of the facts is that the druids prohibited writing in their schools, " *although in the ordinary functions of life they make use of Greek letters* ". The inference is that as it was necessary to abstain from writing to prevent outsiders from reading the secrets, the outsiders cannot have been altogether unlettered. The second of the facts is recorded for us in another part of Cæsar's book. He had occasion, during his military operations, to send a despatch, which no doubt was in Latin : but *he wrote it in Greek letters*,[2] in order to baffle an inquisitive enemy into whose hands it might happen to fall. How so, if the Greek alphabet was the current script ?

That crucial question, strange as it may seem, contains the key to the history of one of the most singular elements in Old Irish life,

---

[1] Compare the elaborate accents and other diacritics, which complicate the printed editions of the Hebrew bible, and which were contrived with the same end in view. The vowel-points were likewise added to the consonantal script of Arabic, to secure unambiguous renderings of the sounds of the sacred texts.

[2] *De Bell. Gall.* v 48.

PLATE XV

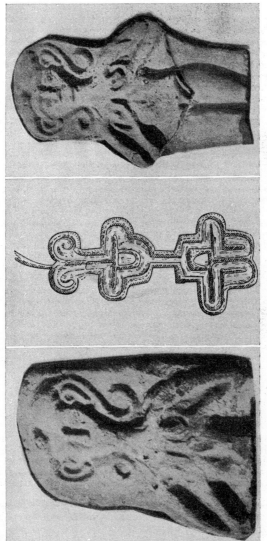

SCULPTURED FIGURE AT CORBEHAGH, CO. CLARE, COMPARED WITH TERRA-COTTA PLAQUES REPRESENTING THE SYRIAN MAGNA MATER

the chief gift from the druids to the country—the Ogham alphabet. This contains twenty-five phonetic, and one silent character, the latter

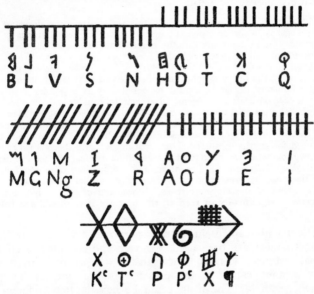

FIG. 39.—The Ogham Alphabet and its Chalcidic Prototype.

used as a stop at the beginning or end of a line of writing. The phonetic characters may be arranged in the form of a square :—

B	L	V	S	N
H	D	T	C	Q
M	G	NG	Z	R
A	O	U	E	I
X	Θ	Π	Φ	Ξ

the first four rows being classified horizontally according to the formation of the characters, and vertically according to the number of their component strokes.

This script was preserved in popular memory till at least as late as the beginning of the past century : many of the old story-tellers of the folk were familiar with it, and scribbles in which it is used are often to be found in the eighteenth and early nineteenth century MSS. which they have left behind. It is set forth formally in certain ancient codices : notably the *Book of Ballymote*, some pages of which contain a treatise upon this form of writing. And in modern times these traditions, so far as they relate to the phonetic value of the several letters, have been verified by the discovery, in Wales, of monumental stones bearing epitaphs in Ogham accompanied with translations into rustic Latin.

The principal connexion in which this script has come down to us in practical use is in the epitaphs cut upon such monumental stones. These very rarely contain anything but the name of the owner of the monument, with details of his pedigree : and that for a very good reason. The Ogham alphabet is probably the clumsiest on earth.[1] The soul-deadening monotony of the strokes, the heavy expenditure of space and time which the formation of the characters demands, would have killed it as a literary contrivance within a few days after its birth. It certainly could not have superseded the alphabet already at the inventor's disposal, whatever that may have been. That it became current and established is in the circumstances a positive *proof* that its primary purpose was other than literary.[2] It could not have been used for anything but the shortest of notes : and there is every reason to believe that when it was so used, it was with a magical or a secret intention. The *Book of Ballymote* tract, mentioned above, justifies us in assuming this to be the case, by presenting us with a large number of variations on the simple theme of the alphabet itself. These are cryptographic, contrived to increase the difficulty of reading the message if it should fall into un-authorized hands.

Though ill-adapted for literary purposes, the standard Ogham alphabet could have been used with ease and economy of effort, in manual gestures : I am convinced that it was *primarily* invented for secret communication in the presence of non-initiates by means of such gestures. The hand could be held in four different pre-arranged postures, in each of them with one-to-five fingers out-stretched, corresponding to the one-to-five component strokes of the letters. No elaborate demonstration is needed to prove that such a highly artificial code of signals, however used, is an *invention* ; not (as are most of the alphabets of the world) the climax of an evolution, beginning in primitive picture-writing. Like the closely analogous Morse code, it bears its artificial nature on the face of it. This comparison opens another line of argument. The Morse code is a device whereby two persons at a distance from one another can signal messages. The mechanism of the signals is immaterial—

---

[1] It surpasses even the complicated syllabaries of Chinese and Assyrian in cumbrousness. Taking a couple of books from my shelves, I selected at random a series of ten Chinese and ten Cuneiform characters, and wrote out their phonetic equivalents in Ogham as closely as I could. The Chinese characters were formed with 94 strokes, and in print filled 1⅝ inches : the corresponding Ogham required 115 strokes and filled 3 inches. The Assyrian required 63 strokes, the corresponding Ogham 78.

[2] It has sometimes been suggested that the reduction of the letters to strokes was contrived in order to admit of their being carved upon wood. This must be met with an absolute negative. In the first place the Runic calendars of Iceland (to say nothing of the desks of any ill-disciplined school) show that there is no impossibility in cutting ordinary alphabetical characters on wood ; in the second place—I made another test, and found that to write a quatrain of verse, containing only 79 letters, would need a line of nicks six feet four inches long. Consider the labour involved and the endless possibilities of mistakes in both reading and writing produced by the inevitably consequent mental confusion !

flags, light-flashes, a telegraphic needle, or what not. The essential point is that the letters are represented by combinations of short "dots" and long "dashes"; and, given the necessary skill, any intelligible message can be transmitted and received through its mediation. But the message must be not only intelligible, but immediately and *fluently* intelligible. A cryptical message may be sent in writing if the recipient can be allowed time to sit down and puzzle it out; but a message sent by signals, if at any moment there be the slightest hesitation in comprehending it, will pass on into its later sentences, and the recipient will be unable to catch up on it. Even a mis-spelling may involve a fatal hitch in reception. It follows that the code must be based upon a pre-existing written alphabet, in ordinary and familiar currency between the correspondents; and that the signal-code must use exactly the same selection of letters, no more and no less, to prevent orthographical deviations. *From this condition there is no escape.*

Therefore if we want to find an alphabet on which the Ogham may be supposed to have been based, we must find one with exactly the same selection of letters, no more and no less. And there is one such alphabet in the world, and no other: the Chalcidic form of the Greek alphabet, current about the fifth and sixth centuries B.C., in Northern Italy—just the place where the " Celts ", or their druids, were likely to come in contact with the Greek alphabet at the time when they were developing the literary traditions still current in the druidic schools of Cæsar's time. There, in Gallia Cisalpina, they impinged upon the peoples, Hellenic, Italian, and Etruscan, who were laying the foundations of the Classical civilizations and literatures of the Mediterranean. What is more likely than that they should endeavour to adapt for writing their own language the convenient alphabet which they found among these strangers ? [1]

The Chalcidic alphabet differs from the Greek alphabet of ordinary use, first, in the direction of writing, and secondly in the selection of letters. The writing runs from right to left, like the Semitic alphabet from which it is ultimately derived : the individual letters being correspondingly reversed, like the reflection of ordinary letters in a mirror. It contains some letters, such as Q, discarded by the Classical Greek alphabet : and it has not yet acquired others which that later alphabet possesses. These deviations are reproduced by the Ogham alphabet with sufficient closeness to establish the essential identity of the two systems. To the above table of the Ogham alphabet the corresponding Chalcidic letters have been added.

If we assume that the druids of Cisalpine Gaul, learning the Chalcidic alphabet in, let us say, the fifth century B.C., there applied it for the first time to the writing of their Celtic language, and that they carried it thence through the Continent, we have at once a complete reconciliation of Cæsar's two contradictory statements, that the Gauls used the Greek alphabet.

[1] To say nothing of the fact that the Etruscans (carriers into Europe of essentially oriental rites, customs and beliefs) are more likely than any other to have been the people from whom the druids learnt their esoteric arts.

and that he wrote his despatches in Greek letters to conceal their purport from the Gauls. Both alphabets were Greek, but they were different. The Gauls used the prehistoric right-to-left letters : Cæsar wrote his despatches in the classical left-to-right letters. To the Gauls, Cæsar's despatches would have looked like mirror-writing, which even yet is sometimes used for purposes of secrecy by rudimentary people. True, no ancient examples of Gaulish writings in the Chalcidic alphabet exist ; [1] though there are a few in Northern Italy in the closely related Etruscan alphabet. They may yet be found ; but it is most likely that such writings would have been on waxed tablets or similar perishable materials, which could not have survived to our time. Nor is there anywhere on the Continent a specimen of Ogham writing, simply because that alphabet was never intended to be written at all. The manual signs were not reproduced in writing until the very end of the time when they were in use.

It would be a mistake to assume that the Celts took over the Chalcidic alphabet, in the beginning, without some modification. Such modifications are normal when alphabets are borrowed ; as when the Greeks, taking over the Semitic alphabet, converted certain consonants which they did not require into the vowels with which the Semites failed to supply them. One superfluous sibilant ($\dagger$) was discarded. [2] Another, M, was adopted for a sound not expressed by any single Greek letter, that of NG—presumably because in external form it resembles the double *gamma* by which that sound is conventionally represented in Greek script. Two minor modifications had also taken place in the pre-Ogham period of adaptation : X, in Chalcidic = ξ, in the Celtic adaptation had its Classical sense of χ : and Ψ, in Chalcidic = χ, apparently became a mere otiose stop (not πs, which is written out thus, in separate letters, in Chalcidic inscriptions). In the form $\rightarrow$— or —$\leftarrow$ this letter sometimes marks the beginning or the end of lines of Ogham writing. It comes at the end of the alphabet, when that is set out in MS. tables ; if, as appears to be not improbable, this letter of indefinite meaning be the original form of the old Greek letter *agma*, identified by Mr. L. J. D. Richardson, [3] it would certainly afford some basis for his further suggestion of a connexion between this word and the name " Ogham ".

This reference to the *name* of a letter leads us a step further. In ancient MSS. the Ogham letters are fitted with acrophonic names of trees ; and these are transferred, in some modern grammars, to the corresponding letters in the modern Irish alphabet. This is assuredly a secondary artificiality : certain letter-names suggested vaguely the names of trees ; the branch-like form of the letters reinforced the suggestion : and mediæval pundits and pedants

---

[1] The *ordinary* Greek alphabet is used for a few Gaulish inscriptions in Southern Gaul—a region which came under Hellenic influence radiating from the Phocian colony in Massilia. That, however, is quite an independent matter. Cæsar's Greek despatches were written from the North Gaulish territory of the Nervii, far from any possible Massiliot influence. In which form of the Greek alphabet the official documents captured in the Helvetian camp (Cæsar, B.G., I 29) were written can be a mere matter of conjecture only.

[2] It disappeared early from the Chalcidic alphabet itself, as is shown by its absence from the alphabet cut upon the Marsiliana writing-tablet—the alphabet which is used as the basis of the foregoing diagram. See A. Minto, *Marsiliana d'Albegna* (Florence 1921), p. 238 : J. Whatmough, *The Foundations of Roman Italy*, p. 100.

[3] " Agma, a forgotten Greek letter " (*Hermathena* 57 [1941]).

developed the suggestion to the end. But consider the following correspondences :—

Semitic	Greek	Irish
Aleph	Alpha	Ailm
Beth	Beta	Beithe
Cheth	Eta	Edad
Yodh	Iota	Ida
Mim	Mu	Muin
Nun	Nu	Nin
'Ain	O[micron]	Onn
Pe	Pi	Pin
Resh	Rho	Ruis

This would be enough for a start : misplaced ingenuity and analogy would do the rest.[1]   Other acrophonic lists, suggested by the standard alphabet of trees, are given by the *Book of Ballymote* ; thus we have colour-ogham, food-ogham, town-ogham, and so forth.   These make us think of the alphabets in children's picture-books ; but they must not be regarded as mere puerilities : they served a very serious purpose. In a moderately literate community, two conspirators might, even *coram populo*, talk of, let us say, " bombs " in " colour-ogham " by calling them *blue-orange-madder-blue-scarlet*—a formula which, when repeated and understood with the rapidity born of practice, might pass over the bystanders uncomprehended and unobserved. The number and diversity of these acrophonic alphabets would enable the speakers to introduce variety, to the still further mystification of eavesdroppers : thus, the same forbidden word might at its next repetition be enunciated in " food-ogham " *bacon-olives-mutton-bacon-spinach*, at the next in " bird-ogham " *bittern-owl-mallard-bittern-sparrow*, and so on indefinitely.[2]

The letters of this secret alphabet are arranged in an order very different from that of the parent alphabet.   Here we see the grammarian (or, more specifically, the phonetician) at work, as we see him in the alphabet in which the Sanskrit language is usually written.   The letters there are carefully grouped into vowels and consonants, and the consonants are grouped according to the organs with which they are pronounced—labials, gutturals, dentals, etc.   Likewise, in the Ogham alphabet, the vowels are separated from the consonants, and in the grouping of letters we see an endeavour to put cognate letters side by side, either horizontally—DT : CQ : G Ng : ZR ;

[1] These correspondences convey rather more than a suggestion, whatever its significance may be, that some of the Irish names had " by-passed " the Greek intermediary in their descent from the Semitic original.   But it must be understood that we have here to deal with more or less arbitrary artificialities ; the ordinary laws of linguistic evolution have nothing to do with them.

[2] But on the whole, it is more likely that this cryptical device would be used in *writing* rather than speech.   The latter would presuppose an almost superhuman skill in improvisation, especially when the speaker had to deal with one of the Celtic dialects, in which syntax makes constant modifications in the initial consonants of words in a sentence.

or vertically—BM : SZ (refer to the table on p. 329). This cannot be mere coincidence. The palatal vowels E, I, are segregated from the non-palatal A, O, U.[1] The notion sometimes expressed, that the letters in the H-group are the initials of the first five numerals, and that, therefore, the alphabet must have originally begun with these, is a mere amateurish *Spielerei* : there is no evidence for the initial position of H ; the name for " four " begins, like that for " five ", with Q, not with C, the two letters being rigidly differentiated in the Proto-Celtic speech, current when the Ogham was devised ; and there is not the slightest trace of any numeral influence in the remaining letters or letter-names.

The twenty letters *denoted by strokes* must have been those of the Chalcidic alphabet which had been found sufficient for expressing the sounds of the Celtic language to which it was adapted. The six remaining characters were superfluous so far as that particular language was concerned ; these were X (= k'), Θ (= t'), Φ (= p'), Π (= p), ⊞ (= x) and Ψ, in which, as we have seen, the last was deflected from its Chalcidic use. These letters, however, were retained with the rest, it may be as numerals, it may be to express sounds in foreign languages ; though they were so rarely employed that no equivalents were needed for them in the digital alphabet. If ever it became necessary to signal them, they would be represented by imitating the figures of the letters, as nearly as possible, with the fingers of both hands. (A similar device is used in the deaf-mute alphabet, in the case of certain letters such as B, K, etc.). This coincidence of *shape* is another strong link between the Ogham cypher and the archaic Greek alphabet with which we are seeking to connect it.[2]

The preoccupation of the pre-Christian scholars with an archaic oral literature inevitably influenced their style. The language of the archaic verses became a literary standard, and was reproduced in their literary compositions, oral or written. The language of the Ogham inscriptions is archaic, or rather artificially archaistic. No one *said* MAQI, the commonest word in the extant inscriptions, if he wanted to express " of a son ", at the time when these inscriptions were written, round about the sixth century A.D. They may have done so five or six centuries earlier. But it was traditional and proper to *write* it, just as archaic language may even now be used on solemn occasions, *e.g.* in legal documents or in Church rituals, though it would be a mere affectation in ordinary social life.[3]

It has been objected that, as Ptolemy and other writers give us Celtic names and words in what would on this theory have been

---

[1] It is interesting to note in this connexion that Sir J. L. Myres has detected evidence of an analogous phonetic arrangement in the letters of the Greek alphabet itself. See *Man* 42 [1942] : no. 63.

[2] Note especially how the equivalent of ⊞ is represented by the crossing of *four* outstretched " fingers ", and not *three* : the former gesture being physically easier to execute. Also if the equivalent of Π be made by opposing the tips of the thumbs and stretching out the two first fingers of each hand, the slightest pressure causes the fingers involuntarily to cross, as they are represented in the Ogham character. The character X is represented in two different ways—X (two crossed forefingers) or)((bent forefingers with the knuckles opposed).

[3] On this aspect of the matter, see E. MacNeill, " Archaisms in the Ogham Inscriptions ", PRIA 39 [1931] : 33.

archaic forms, they must therefore be contemporary evidence for the persistence of such archaic forms in current speech. But there is nothing in this argument. In the first place, the writers named were more than four hundred years earlier than the date of the inscriptions, and therefore nearer to the archaic original of the later vernacular. In the second place, they were foreign writers, who picked up strange names and words with foreign ears and foreign linguistic instincts. Ptolemy and Cæsar are no more impeccable witnesses to the true form of Celtic place-names and other words—many of which they learnt at second or third hand, or by even more remote transmission—than are Diodorus and other ancient writers to the true form of Egyptian names, when they tell us of "Sesostris" and "Bocchoris". And the present argument is based, not so much upon the actual form of the names, as upon their inflections, orthography, and grammatical treatment. These are thoroughly archaic, from the standpoint of the very earliest attainable manuscript Irish, which is actually contemporary, or only just short of contemporary, with the inscriptions. The inscriptions show us the language of the sacred verses on which the druidic literature was founded, revealing it as an already antiquated form of "Goidelic" Celtic. This we might have anticipated from what appears to be the language of the Calendar of Coligny, so far as we are justified in calling upon that enigmatical document to enlighten us.

There is only one rival theory of the origin of the Ogham alphabet that deserves consideration—that of a Roman origin. I believed this myself at one time, but saw with increasing knowledge and experience that it must be abandoned. The differentiation of V (consonant) and V (vowel) in Ogham is sufficient to condemn it : a differentiation never observed in Roman inscriptions even when an accompanying Ogham might point the way.[1] A contrariwise *conflation* (a phenomenon *later* than differentiation) is suggested by the name usually given to the Ogham alphabet in Irish books—as the ordinary English alphabet is often called the "ABC", this is called "Beith-Luis-*Nin*", suggesting that BLN, not BLV, were originally the first three letters ; and that later, when Roman influence became dominant, N and V changed places, so as to represent both equivalents of the Latin V by letters of three strokes.[2] The absence of F, and the presence of G, NG, and the spirants K', T', are further barriers to the identification suggested : to say nothing of the natural hostility of druidry to Rome and all that Rome stood for, which would endure until in the end Roman influence became irresistible.

The provision of an epitaph was not so easy in those illiterate days as it would be now, when any Mr. Sapsea can within wide limits

---

[1] As in an inscription at Eglwys Cymmin, Carmarthen, where AVITORIA and CVNIGNI, in Roman letters, correspond to AVITTORIGES and CUNIGNI in the associated Ogham.

[2] I suspect that there had been a previous shift before this transposition took place, the M-group and the H-group changing places, to put the consonant groups in alphabetic order. If the first two groups had originally been BLNSV–MGNgZR, the cognate sounds B–M would have been in juxtaposition, as would also L–N, S–V, G–Ng–N, and S–Z–R. (In the dialect of Donegal especially, palatalized R has a strong Z-colour in its pronunciation.)

write what he likes about his deceased relative and commission a monumental mason to carve and set it up. Mr. Sapsea would have had to consult the local druid, who was conversant with all the literary forms. It is not to be imagined that the pundit would put his learning at the disposal of every applicant : only a limited class of people would be regarded as entitled to possess an epitaph, with all the privileges in this world and the next which such a possession conferred. If favourably disposed, and duly recompensed, the druid would prepare a form of words for the stone-cutter ; with a knife he would nick on a rod the strokes which expressed the deceased's name and parentage in the orthodox archaic linguistic forms. Mr. Sapsea would then carry the rod to the stone-cutter, who would almost certainly have no book-learning, but would copy by rote the nicks, in their prescribed groupings, upon a stone pillar.

It was no tyrannical tabu, but common prudence, which dictated this cumbersome process. Even in these illuminated days the folly of a medical or legal amateur, who attempts, professionally unaided, to cope with the specialist tasks of making a will or curing a malady is proverbial ; our hero would find himself in analogous difficulties if he tried to draw up an epitaph without specialist guidance, and would, moreover, involve *us* in reciprocal difficulties if we discovered and tried to interpret his effort.[1]

But alas, in his ignorance, Mr. Sapsea was liable to be imposed upon by charlatans and swindlers. Every profession has its camp-followers of quacks ; most of all, the professions which deal in anything that looks like magic, or at least which require special knowledge beyond the reach of Everyman. If a dishonest person realize that there is easy money to be made by cutting nicks on a piece of stone, he will do so, if he think he can, in current phrase, " get away with it " : and in fact there is in existence a number of stones, resembling Ogham pillars, and marked with Ogham-like strokes devoid of any meaning—not even capable of being grouped into letters. An example from Hawkinstown (Meath) is here illustrated (Plate IX*a*). Indeed, even the legitimate practitioner himself was not without his tricks. He was no doubt paid according to the length of the epitaph which he had to write—reckoned conveniently by the number of strokes that went to express it. Now the most remarkable feature about Ogham inscriptions is the way in which the consonants are doubled—a madness without any philological method in it whatsoever. And the consonants selected for duplication are most frequently those with the maximum number of scores— the N's, the Q's, and the R's. The monumental mason who prepared an Ogham inscription, discovered at Rathduff (Kerry) a few weeks ago, as we write, should have carved upon it the name LONOC (15 strokes). Instead he wrote LLONNOCC (26 strokes)—and presumably presented a statement of accounts to correspond.[2]

[1] For an illustration see the remarks in my *Corpus Inscriptionum Insularum Celticarum*, vol. i, p. 417, on an inscription at Llanfyrnach, Pembrokeshire, which consists of only three words, but is so full of blunders that it must have been produced by just such an amateur.

[2] I am indebted to the late Professor MacNeill for permission to quote these suggestions, which he made to me in conversation. To me they seem convincing; they are, indeed, the only reasonable explanation yet put forward of the observed and very remarkable facts.

It is to be remembered that these inscriptions were not mere epitaphs. Written in the generally unfamiliar language of an ancient religious traditional literature, and in a secret cypher based upon its ancient and obsolete alphabet, they were *primarily* magical. They were not necessarily intended to be read by everyone (or, indeed, by anyone), any more than was the Eggjum Runic stone. This stone, found hidden *inside* a grave chamber, was to be buried out of sight for ever. The inscription is extremely obscure ; in brief abstract, it seems to mean " It was drawn on a sled and sprinkled with blood. The sun shone not upon it. Who was he ? A fish on the land, a soaring bird." Here we must be reading the description of a magical funeral rite, with a tabu against sunlight ; the last sentence has been ingeniously explained as a rebus of the name of the owner of the monument. A " fish on the land " is a " serpent ", in Norse *Orm ;* a " soaring bird " is an " eagle ", in Norse *är ;* combining these words we get *Ormär*, a name known from other sources.[1] Clearly, such an inscription is not a mere commemoration. It is not addressed to the man in the street, or indeed to any man. It is addressed to whatever mystic Beings might be expected to further the welfare of the dead warrior in the new place to which he had been transferred. And although Oghams give us nothing so interesting as this, and if they did we should certainly not have the knowledge necessary to interpret them, there are tendencies which show the cryptographic mind at work. A very great deal of nonsense has been written, trying to extract a hidden meaning from quite straightforward inscriptions by postulating cryptographical devices ; and this breeds caution, if not prejudice, in approaching them from this point of view. But there is a residuum, in which we are almost compelled to take refuge in a postulate of magic and mystery. The finger-alphabet and the traditional language in which the druids communicated their inviolable secrets to one another were wrapped in an aura of secrecy and magic by their very nature : we may be sure that Ogham was never written at all until druidism was breaking down. And even when the Ogham tradition had passed, or was passing away, before advancing Christianity, the tradition that a tombstone was a frozen invocation rather than a commemoration still persisted.[2] We have several

---

[1] I follow Magnus Olsen in his masterly analysis of this heartlessly difficult inscription (*Eggjum-stenens Indskrift med de ældre Runer*, Christiania 1919) : some efforts to dethrone it have come my way, but have left me quite unmoved.

[2] It was in fact much more than this. A stone lies in an old cemetery near Dingle (Kerry) inscribed DOVETI MAQQI CATTINI (note in passing the fraudulent duplication of the Q). That means " (stone) of Dovetos, son of Cattinos ". But we must not stop there. The stone does not *commemorate* Dovetos ; it *is* Dovetos, in an embodiment through which his surviving friends could come in contact with him, and pay the honours due to, and expected by, his translated personality. The essential identity of a man with his name is a familiar commonplace of ethnology ; by writing the name on a stone, the personality is infused into the stone ; by chipping the name off, the personality is destroyed.

cases of Christian tombstones bearing a cross and the ejaculation DNE (= *Domine*), but no hint whatever at the name of the deceased. Examples are to be seen at Kilmalkedar and at Reask, both in the Dingle peninsula. (The last-named stone is now in the Museum of University College, Cork.)

Take for example the stone here figured (Plate IX*b*) from Ballyhank, in the Cork barony of Muskerry—now in the National Museum. It bears an inscription on three of its angles. Two of these present an ordinary epitaph, giving the name of a man and his father. On the third there is a short series of fantastic characters, the interpretation of which is entirely beyond our reach. Similar characters are listed in the *Book of Ballymote* tract on Oghams, which shows that many varieties of the simple Ogham alphabet were in use, for cryptographic and other purposes : and this unintelligible word on the Ballyhank stone is suggestive of a magical " word of power ", which presumably ensured some benefit to the owner of the monument. A similar, though not identical, inscription is cut on an amber bead, which was used in the town of Ennis for magico-medical purposes down to about 100 years ago, but is now in the British Museum.[1]

Now, what happened to these monuments when paganism was giving place to Christianity ?

The conquest of Christianity in this country was certainly more slow and gradual than is generally supposed ; for a considerable time there was an overlap, during which the incompatibility of the two religions was not fully realized. It is only by postulating such an overlap that we can explain the use of this script, with its essentially pagan associations, to commemorate people whose latinized names indicate them as Christian—MARIANUS for example, or SAGITTARIUS. But what I might call a spirit of Puritanism, with an implacable hostility toward the forms and monuments of Heathenism, must have ultimately come into being, especially after the Christians had felt the cruelty of the pagan Norse pirates.

As a compromise, the sign of the Cross was carved upon pagan monuments in general, which it was impossible, owing to the strength of local feeling, to abolish altogether ; transferring thus their sanctity bodily to the new religion, so that divine honours paid to them were in fact paid to the symbol of the new Faith : this practice was followed in the Oghams, for many of them have a cross cut upon them. In some late stones the cross and the inscription are contemporary. " We are using this old form of writing " these monuments seem to say to us " because our fathers did so : but let there be no mistake, we are Christians ". In such cases, betrayed by the late grammatical forms, in which the old traditional language is abandoned, the cross is where we should expect to find it, at the head of the stone. But in others it is not so—it is about four feet from the ground, on the

---

[1] For full particulars as to the contents of the inscriptions I may refer the reader to my *Corpus Inscriptionum Insularum Celticarum* recently published by the Irish MSS. Commission. This contains an account of all the known inscriptions.

side of a tall pillar : it has been cut upon a stone already erect.
And in other cases, the stone must have been thrown down, the
cross cut on the butt-end (originally left blank for thrusting in the
ground), and the stone then re-erected, upside-down.   In consequence, the inscription reads downwards in such cases, and the end
of it may be buried in the earth.   This appears to be intentional, to
hide away the name of a god-ancestor with which the epitaph closed.

But often the inscription itself is either mutilated or destroyed.
I have for some time past followed the practice of examining most
carefully the edges of standing stones which are known *not* to be
inscribed ; and I find, not infrequently, that their angles are flaked
and shattered, as though an inscription had been broken away.   If
this had not happened, I am convinced that we should probably
have had at least twice as many inscriptions as we actually possess.
Sometimes the destroyer was not so thorough ; he mutilated only
a part of the inscription ; and he always goes, not for the name of the
owner of the stone, but for the ancestor from whom he traced his
descent.   The name of this ancestor is introduced by the word
MUCOI " descendant " :   and very often—far too often to be a
mere accident—an inscription is absolutely intact, in perfect order,
till we come to this word :   and thereafter the inscribed edge is
smashed away with strokes of a sledgehammer or some equivalent
tool, which have made quite unmistakable marks upon the surface.
The destroyer had no spite against the owner of the stone ; but he
did what he could to wipe out the record of his long dead-and-gone
ancestor.

I noticed this a number of years ago, but I could not hit upon a
reasonable explanation.   This again was supplied by Professor
Eoin MacNeill.   It was to the effect that in some cases—by no
means in all [1]—the ancestor was not a man, but a god.   As in ancient
Greece there were families which traced their descent from some god,
Zeus, Poseidon, or whoever it might be, so it was in ancient Ireland.
Naturally such unashamed paganism could not be allowed by orthodox
Christians to survive once Christianity had gained the upper hand.
They had nothing but pity for the poor benighted pagan : they left
his name alone ; but against his god they must wage unrelenting
warfare.   His name they must destroy—which, in accordance with
a belief universal at a certain stage of cultural development, will be
tantamount to destroying the god himself.   Possibly these partial
mutilations were the work of Christianized members of the same

[1] Once the fashion for iconoclasm had set in, analogy would do its work,
and the MUCOI-name would be destroyed automatically, however innocent it
might be.   It should be noticed that *the formula itself* was not regarded with an-
tagonism : in the later linguistic form *maccu*, it appears freely in manuscript
genealogies of unquestioned Christian orthodoxy.   It was suspect only when
cut upon an Ogham pillar, in the obsolete spelling proper thereto, and thus tainted
with an unconcealable pagan tradition.

family, anxious to clear their kinsfolk and, incidentally, themselves, from what had by now become the stigma of paganism, but naturally tender to the memory of their own relative. Frequently the destroyer completed his task by cutting a cross on the stone, thereby altogether driving the paganism out of it.

Action produces reaction; attack produces defence. The hostility of the new creed, as it advanced in power, did not immediately suppress the Ogham tradition. But the Ogham carvers became cautious, and studied to avoid observation. Especially in the region covered by the modern county of Cork, it is remarkable how many inscriptions are cut in very minute scores—sometimes scarcely more than pin-scrapes. The bold strokes of the earlier inscriptions give place to timid little scratches, which could easily be passed over—have indeed frequently been passed over. At Temple Bryan, near Clonakilty, for example, there is a splendid tapering pillar stone about eleven feet high. A number of years ago I was taken by a friend to see it, merely as a megalithic monument, and I had the satisfaction of finding an unnoticed Ogham upon it, in tiny scratches hardly an inch in length. Clearly the writer hoped that it would escape notice : clearly it was something more than an epitaph in his eyes, and also in the eyes of adherents of the rival faith : for it would be obviously unreasonable to cut a mere *epitaph* in such a way that a passer-by will never notice it. Recently, I revisited the stone to check my reading, and although I remembered exactly the position of the inscription, it was a moment or two before I found it again, so insignificant is it in appearance. It seems quite unworthy of the great stone on which it is carved.

In other cases, the carvers resorted to what in these times we have learnt to call " camouflage ". The formula MAQI MUCOI [1] being under a tabu, they disguised it in various ways. There is one stone in Co. Cork on which this is written GAQIMU. The engraver obviously hoped that this incomprehensible combination of letters would put the destroyer off the scent. And that it was not a mere mistake, the engraver having written two scores (G) in mistake for one (M), is shown by the fact that the same device appears on another stone in Co. Waterford, where MUCOI is written GUCOI. On a stone in the North of Ireland, commemorating one BROCAGNOS, the inscription reads BROCAGNI MAQI MU-; nothing more. And there never was anything more ; the surface after the MU is quite uninjured. It is as though the writer said to his friends " We know, you and I, that he was the descendant of the divine ancestor of his family : but until this tyranny be overpast we had better not say so. We'll leave it like this, for the present at

[1] This formula appears in three varieties, A MUCOI B, A MAQI MUCOI B, A KOI MAQI MUCOI B. Conjecturally we may render these as *A, descendant of B* (i.e. the head of the family) : *A, a son of the descendant : and A, The son of the descendant*—his destined successor in the headship.

least, and supply the missing name in our minds." In some cases the inscription is completely inverted, the side-scores being interchanged; as when VEQREQ MOQOI GLUNLEGGET [1] (note the doubtless intentional mis-spelling of MUCOI) is turned into the meaningless TENREN MONOI GDUQDEGGEV: and in one remarkable monument in Co. Kildare, which is meant to read OVANOS AVI IVACATTOS CELI TURLEGETTI,[2] where CELI, " client " or "devotee ", takes the place of the ancestral formula, the harmless first three words are written out straight in Ogham, but the last two, to conceal them, have been (1) written in Ogham, (2) turned upside down, (3) transliterated into IVVEGE-DRUVIDES, and (4) cut in Roman capitals on the side of the stone in this unintelligible sequence of letters—where a fracture has added to the confusion by turning the G into a spurious R.

Of all the monuments of this *odium theologicum*, the most remarkable is the VEQREQ stone just quoted. It is one of four Ogham inscribed pillar-stones which were discovered at Monataggart (Cork) in the early seventies of the last century, built into the structure of an underground chamber—a base use to which these monuments frequently declined, as they are long stones convenient for making roof-lintels (Plate X*a*).

The history of the monument may be reconstructed as follows :—

1. At the first it was most likely a bronze-age pillar-stone ; afterwards adapted by the Ogham carvers for their own purposes. It is my belief that we must always suspect this origin for stones more than about 5 or 6 feet high, as the custom of erecting very tall pillar-stones is essentially one of the Bronze Age. The Temple Bryan stone, mentioned above, is another example. It is close to a stone circle, and may originally have been a part of the same megalithic complex. Critical inspection of the lettering will sometimes reveal evidence, in such cases, indicating that it had been cut when the stone was already upright, not conveniently prostrate in the stonemason's yard. The awkwardness of being obliged to work on after the inscription has reached an inconvenient height from the ground has sometimes had an unmistakable influence on the technique.

2. An inscription in the formula A MAQI MUCOI B (" A son of the descendant "—we may fairly say " of the earthly representative, of B.") was cut, running over two of its angles. Of this inscription nothing remains but the tips of three scores of the letter T in the first name, and of the two M's in the relationship formula.[3] Because

3. Someone split off the top of the inscribed face, carrying away the

[1] " Of Fiachra, descendant of ' Glunlegget ' "—the grotesque and quite unique second name being probably an evasive artificiality.

[2] " Of Ovan grandson of Eochaid, client of Turlegett "—the concluding name being of a suggestively similar formation.

[3] In the accompanying photograph (*a*) the surviving tips of letters are marked with chalk, and a plasticine restoration of the lower part of the fractured angle (containing the word MAQI) is added. There is not the slightest clue to the recovery of the missing name after M[UCOI]. Figs. (*b, c*) show the other side—the inverted inscription and the chi-rho symbol, with the chisel-marks effacing it. In Fig. (*e*) these marks are chalked to enable the reader to pick them out on the untouched photograph.

last three words ; but he left the name of the owner of the monument intact, as frequently happens. He further Christianized the stone by cutting, not in this case the usual cross, but a chi-rho monogram, on the smooth face opposite to that which he had mutilated.

4. Someone else, seeking a stone for a monument, determined to appropriate this fine pillar. He completed the destruction of the old inscription, by hammering away the initial name which the first destroyer had left ; then he chiselled off the sacred emblem—the chisel-marks are there for all eyes to see ; and he cut on a hitherto blank edge the new inscription —carefully disguised by mis-spelling and by inversion, as we have just noticed, to make sure it would arouse no hostility. Clearly such a disguised inscription was not meant to satisfy the curiosity of the mere " man-in-the-street ". No less clearly " a [Pagan] enemy hath done this ".

Such secondary uses of these monuments are not uncommon ; we have several stones bearing two quite independent inscriptions. These are usually mere piracies, the monument of A being stolen, as the cheapest way of commemorating B. On a recent visit that I paid to the monument " of the poet Luguttos " at Crag (Kerry) I found, what had previously escaped my notice, that the angles of the stone had all been battered and sledged away, along with whatever may have been written upon them, as a preliminary to cutting the epitaph which the stone now bears—so that even a poet was not above using a second-hand tombstone, in utter indifference to the disastrous consequences for its legitimate owner (Plate X*b*).

There are other cases, in which the secondary inscription seems to have had the purpose of counteracting the paganism of the first : there is at Ardmore (Waterford) an inscription LUGUDECCAS MAQI MUCOI NETASEGAMONAS—one of extreme interest, for not impossibly it commemorates " Lugaid descendant of Nia Segamain ", to whom the Annalists assign a reign over Ireland for the fifteen years beginning 183 B.C.[1] A certain Dolatus, who held local rank as *chorepiscopus* (which we may render " bishop suffragan "), caused his own name to be cut on one of the unoccupied angles, DOLATI BIGOESGOB. In like manner a certain presbyter, by name Ronann son of Comogann, totally defaced an ancient inscription on a stone near the summit of Brandon Mountain (Kerry) and cut his own name and occupation instead, no doubt seeking the merit of the act of purification. There is another stone, now in the Museum of University College, Cork, presenting all the attraction of a puzzle, over which I have many times pondered ineffectually ; though I got the clue on my last visit to Cork when I observed that it, too, had had an earlier inscription, totally hammered away. At the same time, the later inscription, from which I had never been able to extract any satisfactory sense, suddenly revealed itself as meaning " May the Son of God bless bishop Dinam " (the name being written inversely, MAQIL) evidently a prayer for reward for having destroyed a pagan monument. Even more interesting is a stone on the island called Inchagoill, Loch Corrib. This was undoubtedly been an Ogham stone, as is shown by the archaic grammatical forms of the inscription in Irish characters which it now presents ; the monument is absolutely unique in expressing them in the later script of Christianity. The destroyer had a spite against the pagan letters, not against the pagan dead—possibly he was a little afraid of him ! So on to a side of the stone he transcribed the old Ogham inscription in the later " Irish " letters, which Christianity had introduced, and then split off the Ogham-inscribed angles. Thereafter, to drive out completely the evil influences which had

---

[1] The date is not necessarily to be accepted as authentic ; before about A.D. 450 all dates in the early books of Annals are purely artificial.

entered in the stone, he surrounded it with crosses—two on each side except
that to the north, where he put only one. Why was this ? The reader
may think the explanation far-fetched, but it can be justified with folklore
parallels from many sources. *He left the passage to the north partly open.*
The north is the cold, Arctic side, the source of all evil and diabolism.
According to one legend, the Túatha Dé Danann demons came to Ireland
"from the Northern Islands of the World ". There is no necessity to visit
as many English mediæval churches as I have done, to see how often the
North door of a church is built up, and how rare are the interments on the
north side—essentially the devil's side. The Inchagoill stone closes the way
on three sides, but on the north side it leaves a loophole through which the
demons can escape, and go to their own place.[1]

Thus the " Laws ", and the fragments of forgotten learning
enshrined in the Ogham inscriptions, reveal to us the druids dominant, all powerful indeed, in jurisprudence and public instruction,
as Christianity begins to make its appearance. But if we critically
examine the traditions of earlier times in which druids make their
appearance, as they are rendered in the later Christian literature,
we have little difficulty in detecting a note of artificiality. The
Christian writers regard the old tales which they reproduce from the
standpoint of their own time and prepossessions. They labour to
make the druids ridiculous : performing fruitless, often ludicrous
tricks of magic : or falling off a wall " in fits and faintings and
paroxysms " when hostile chariots approach. This is obviously
burlesque ; and when we cut out the burlesque, the druids disappear.
Even Cathub, or, as he is more commonly (though less accurately)
called, Cathbad, the druid who stands by and advises the Ultonian
king Conchobar mac Nessa, is a wraith with no solidity about him.
We rise from our study with a feeling that all the druids in the early
literature have been imported into it by story-tellers who felt that
they ought to be there, and who have formed their conception of
them under the inspiration of Christian hostility. By an accident
of which the fullest advantage was taken, *drui* means " druid " and
druth means " buffoon " ; and both these classes of the community
and the superficially similar words by which they were denoted, were
intermingled without conscience. The druids of King Loiguire at
Tara knew well what the lighting of the Paschal Fire at Slane por-
tended for their order, and for their prestige.

[1] An excellent photograph of this stone will be found in *Galway* 3 [1903-4] :
146. Very much to the point is an entry in the so-called *Annals of Tigernach*,
at a date so late as 1084. " There was a great pestilence in that year, which killed
a quarter of the people of Ireland. It began in the south, and spread through the
four airts of Ireland. What caused it was that demons *came from the northern
islands of the world*, three battalions of them, with 2090 in each battalion ; as Oengus
Óc [our old friend of Dowth, whom we see here still potent] told Gilla Lughan,
who used to frequent the tumulus every Hallow e'en. He himself saw them at
Maistiu [Mullaghmast, Co. Kildare]. This is what they looked like . . . with
a fiery sword out of the throat of each of them ; every one of them as high as the
clouds of heaven. That is what caused the pestilence "—[*Revue Celtique* 17 : 416].
I do not know who the seer Gilla Lughan may have been.

The real enemy which faced incoming Christianity was not "druidry" : for in Ireland the druids were mere exotic interlopers who had not really influenced the common people—who had, indeed, allied themselves with their oppressors. It was the amalgam of primitive, unvocal, formless folk-cults of Nature, centred in lonely islands and impressive rocks and mountains, in groves, springs, noisy waterfalls, and rumbling caverns—recalling the *ensemble* which composed the awful sanctuary of Massilia, graphically depicted for us by Lucan.[1] Such scenes and sites as these had been religious *foci*, not of Ireland only, but of all Europe, from far-off ages, long before "Celticity" was born or thought of. And while the early Christian teachers were busy in the comparatively easy task of ousting and superseding the spectacular but (in Ireland) exotic and ephemeral druids, these cults, immeasurably older, and undying because rooted in the soil, slipped imperceptibly into the new Teaching and assumed therein a prominent place which they have never lost. The druids were *protégés* of the aristocracy : when these transferred their favours to the Christian teachers the druids faded away as they had done on the Continent, and the new teachers stepped into *their* vacant places, materially as well as spiritually.

When St. Senán came to Scattery Island he had to free the island of a frightful monster before he could establish himself there. St. Coemgen ("Kevin") at Glendaloch had the same experience, and was under the same necessity. When St. Ruadán came to Lorrha a terrible boar met him, but fled before him. It would not be difficult to collect other stories of the same kind from the hagiological literature. But such things do not happen : there never were such monsters in Ireland, at least since the Pleistocene period witnessed the arrival of Man in Europe. Are then these tales mere childish sillinesses ? Surely not : rather are they to be explained as based upon mis-understandings of homiletic metaphors or parables, telling, in figurative language, how the druids were expelled, and the Christians took their place. The monster was a grotesque deity in occupation of the sacred site until the Christians came. These stories are meaningless absurdities unless they indicate that wherever there was a pre-Cistercian monastery in Ireland, the site had been occupied by an antecedent druidic "lamaserai" : and I would go so far as to confess to an expectation that if extensive excavations could be carried out on such sites—which on account of the accumulation of later interments would scarcely be possible—relics of these earlier establishments would be found.[2]

The druids disappeared ; but their spiritual influence still re-

---

[1] *Pharsalia* 3 : 399.
[2] Bertrand, *La religion des Gaulois*, has an important chapter on this subject. This should not, however, be taken too absolutely, but tempered with the consider-ations set forth in Jullian's *Histoire* ii, pp. 94 ff.

PLATE XVI

IDOL AT LUSTYMORE

tained a measure of potency. There are many things recorded in the so-called " Lives of the Saints " much more appropriate to the *personnel* of the Schools described by Cæsar than to the directors of institutions founded in the name of Christianity. Plummer, in the introductions and notes to his two valuable collections of these documents, has made this clear : but let us hear the testimony of the Christian teachers themselves.

There is a singular document, wafted down to us out of the Overlap period, which bears the name *Hisperica Famina.* This is a collection of essays, or exercises, written to acquire fluency in a fantastic, barely intelligible artificial Latin, which reads more like an anticipation of the literary vagaries of the late James Joyce than anything else. The form of these compositions is obviously based upon the Psalms, rendered familiar to the writers by constant repetition ; but both in grammar and in vocabulary the language is tortured unmercifully. And it is crystal-clear that the purpose of this otherwise absurd invention is to fill the empty place of the " Ogham " language, which the druids had possessed, and in which they had been accustomed to conceal their thoughts. It is called " Hisperic ", in contrast to " Ausonic " (= ordinary Latin) ; and the two are compared —greatly to the disadvantage of the latter. We are reminded of the druids, who forbade writing lest their learning should become the possession of the common people, when we read of a countryman coming to this " Christian " teacher for enlightenment. The pundit, who rudely refers to his visitor as a " serpent " (*chelidrus*), assails him with a flood of incomprehensible " Hisperic ", congratulating himself on possessing this accomplishment— for if he had been confined to " Ausonic ", the countryman might have known enough colloquial Latin to talk him down. Is he a woodman, a builder, a goldsmith, a musician ? (*i.e.* a master of the arts which in " druidic " times conferred nobility). No, says our Chadband, he is a mere shepherd, incapable of learning. Then let him go back to his flocks, which are suffering for want of his care, and let him leave learning to his betters.

The whole book, notwithstanding its eccentricity, is worthy of careful study ;[1] for it gives us from the inside a picture, not elsewhere obtainable, of monastic life and of the monastic furniture and fittings, supplementing the invaluable record[2] which the Monastery of Tallaght has bequeathed to us. There is one section headed *Lex Diei,* " The Order of the Day ", too long to set forth here in full, but which we may present in abstract, as it describes the surroundings, and a day in the life, of a body of students. Awakening Nature is pictured, in language not without a certain illogical charm. The students rise and pursue their studies till mid-day, when they are ready for their repast. This they take, not in the refectory, but at a neighbouring farm—which must hold its land from the monastery on what was known as *daer-ráith* tenure, a form of contract obliging the tenant to supply the landlord with food up to the limit of his indebtedness. They go

[1] The Latin text was published in 1908 by the Cambridge University Press, under the editorship of F. J. H. Jenkinson. I have devoted a chapter of my book *The Secret Languages of Ireland* to a preliminary study of the documents, on which I have a fuller monograph (including an edition of the Harleian Glossary, which contains many Hisperic words) and a complete translation, almost ready for press.

[2] Gwynn and Purton, " The Monastery of Tallaght ", PRIA 29 (1911) : 115 ; Gwynn, " The Rule of Tallaght ", *Hermathena* 44 [1927], 2nd supplementary volume.

out, not without trepidation, " lest cruel murderers should torment limbs with pythonic darts "—apparently public security is not of the best. As they draw near to the farm " a doggy noise resounds amid the agreeable groves ". But here a difficulty presents itself ; they are obliged by their rules to talk Latin, and their prospective hosts know nothing but Irish : so the leader says :—

" Who shall ask of these householders to yield us honey-juicy fattening ? For an Ausonic chain trusses me.
"Wherefore I do not rattle out Irish-born excellence of speech ; but I shall strike savage blows with a stick."

However, their hosts understand what they want ; they provide water that the guests may " clean muddy soles with a glassy fluiditude ", and these " wash hands with watered soda, that laved palms may make an appearance ". Having enjoyed their repast, they bestow a blessing upon their entertainers in these words :—

" I ask of the gracious Master of the sky that the neighbours may not rush into the fiery valley of the nether regions, but may reach the highest peak of the sevenfold heaven : they who have vouchsafed the sweetness-bearing heaps of eatitudes.
" Whatsoever tax-gatherer should demand a fair she-beast : may he drink the salt waters of Lethe through ashes, may saltborn beasticles beslaver his curling coiffure."

And so the students return to the monastery, complete the duties of the day till nightfall, when " eyelids feel the pressure of sleep-bearing heaviness ". Then they prepare their beds, prudently slake the fires, lock the door, and " withdraw a drowsy warming upon their limbs ".

It is a familiar commonplace that the early literature of Ireland tells us next to nothing about pre-Christian ritual and belief—at least voluntarily : the discerning reader can detect between the lines much that the ancient scribes would gladly have suppressed. And yet, no less than other ancient literatures of Europe—in Greece, Rome, Scandinavia, Iceland—in essence it comes down to us out of the heart of a paganism ; for its archæological criteria make at least its beginnings antedate the first vague beginnings of the Christian Faith in these islands. But in strong contrast to those other literatures, it has not been permitted to transmit to us facts of ancient belief and ritual such as they yield in abundant (if not satisfying) measure. Where in Irish literature could we look for anything to set beside the priceless description of the temple of Thór on the island of Mostr, in *Eyrbyggjasaga :* to say nothing of the unveiled pagan mythology of *Volospá* or of *Völsungasaga ?* And why are these and the like treasures withheld from us ?

There is only one answer possible. It is a capital mistake to assume, subconsciously, that a certain Briton named (perhaps it would be more accurate to say " called ") Patricius (his real name was apparently " Sucat "), grandson of a British presbyter, son of a British deacon and a *decurio* of " Bannavem Taberniæ ", wherever in Roman Britain that elusive place may have been, came to a pagan Ireland in A.D. 432 after a stormy youth ; and there, to use the language of metaphor, waved a magic wand, whereupon the whole country throughout its length and breadth automatically became Christian.   Naturally, no one has ever said so : no one could venture to say so, in the face of the statement that his forerunner Palladius was sent, a year before, on a mission " to the Irish believing in Christ ",[1] so that for an unknown stretch of years before 431 there were already companies of Christians in the country.   Nevertheless, such an assumption underlies much (if not most) of the popular literature which has any bearing upon the early history of Christianity in Ireland.   There we find nothing to contradict an unexpressed thesis that before Patrick came there were no Christians in the country, and after he came there were no Pagans.

The mere formulation of such a thesis is enough to expose its absurdity.   Not even the stupendous genius, the whole-hearted devotion, of a St. Paul could have carried out missionary work so easily as that, if only because he would inevitably come into collision, almost from the very beginning of his enterprise, with a network of pettifogging but influential vested interests of all kinds, political, material, and spiritual.   " By this craft we have our wealth " said the makers of Artemis-shrines at Ephesus, when the local success of Christian propaganda threatened to reduce the number of Artemis-worshippers, with a consequent decline in trade profits : and they organized a riot.[2]   " I cannot accept a religion of Love ", an Irish king is alleged to have said, in effect, to St. Patrick, " for my father laid upon me as a charge to hate my enemies till death— and after it."[3]   In a world where instincts of the natural man such as these have to be combated, Christian ethic must inevitably make slow headway : and in criticizing our historical sources we must accord to this fact its due weight.   These have all come down to us from Christian hands : and it is necessary to take into account not only what they say, but also what they do not say.   Reports from a seat of war belittle defeats, unless these are so overwhelming that the disaster cannot be hidden ; and we shall misunderstand much of the early ecclesiastical literature of Ireland, unless we recognize that it is a succession of reports from the seat of a war, between Christianity and pagandom.

The question with which we started this discussion is here relevant. When mediæval scribes made the copies, which are now in our hands, of literary texts handed down from ancient writers in Greece, Rome, Scandinavia, the old gods of those countries were dead, mere matters of literary or antiquarian interest.   No spiritual danger was to be apprehended from preserving and studying the documents which had crystallized around their

---

[1] I am intentionally using language which presupposes current conceptions of the course of the history.   Even if these have to be modified as a result of such publications as Professor O'Rahilly's impressive brochure, *The Two Patricks*, it will make no serious difference to my present argument.
[2] Acts 19 : 21 ff.   [3] *Tripartite Life*, ed. Stokes, pp. 74, 304.

now impotent personalities. But the cults of primitive pagandom must have been still living, if not flourishing, in Ireland, not only when the associated literature was coming into birth, but actually when later scribes were copying it. Only thus can we explain the systematic suppression of literary references to pagan beliefs and practices, even in contexts where they are almost essential to an understanding of the document. This is nothing short of a positive proof of the survival of pre-Christian cults down to a date much later than is commonly supposed. Old beliefs cannot be suddenly sloughed off by a whole community : at best, a compromise is all that can be effected at first—as in Iceland, where the Althing, under the guidance of the Christian Hall á Sidho and the Pagan Thórgairr, decreed " that all men should be Christian, and that those not yet baptized should be baptized : but that the old laws should stand, in the matter of exposing children and eating horseflesh, and that those who desired to sacrifice might do so privately if they wished, under the risk of ' the lesser outlawry ' if any testified against them ".[1]

Hisperica Famina shows us the students afraid of meeting homicidal bandits, and at nightfall " fastening the square door with a tight lock, lest robbers should break in to seize hidden treasures by stealth ". The community-life afforded a mutual support and encouragement which was almost a necessity in an environment thus disordered, and still, to at least an appreciable extent, actively pagan : and it afforded a measure of peace that could be found nowhere else.[2] The almost total absence of records of martyrdom in the history of the early Irish Christianity, a fact which has been frequently observed and commented upon, is surely an indication that the Christianization of Ireland was not a matter of militant missionary evangelism, but of gradual, almost imperceptible absorption and infiltration, throughout a long period of syncretism between the old cults and the new.

Whence then came the Christianity of the pre-Patrician Christians ? By the same road as its rival, druidry—the road of the refugee. Not everyone who embraced Christianity in days of comparative peace was temperamentally fitted for enrolment among the noble army of Martyrs, whenever a hostile ruler assumed power : Eusebius lets us see many falling away when a Diocletian lit the fires of persecution : [3] and the network of Roman roads opened ways of escape for such people to the Hinterlands of the Empire. Later, when plundering Teutonic tribes in their turn were ravaging Europe, an island remote from the turmoil would seem to offer to the distracted natives of the Continent a haven of rest and safety.

In the seventeenth century, after the revocation of the Edict of Nantes, Ireland opened its doors to bodies of Huguenot refugees, fleeing from the consequent persecutions : and these made an impress upon the industry and trade of the country which has not faded away, even yet. When some thirteen centuries earlier (more or less) Ireland opened its doors to bodies of refugees from Roman or Teutonic tyranny, it profited in like wise. The newcomers made contributions to its life and culture of the first importance.

---

[1] Are, *Libellus Islandorum* (in Vigfússon and Powell, *Origines Islandicæ* i 298).
[2] This is mirrored in the picture of the monastic life attributed to Mainchín of Lemanaghan (*Ériu* i : 38)—a poem strangely anticipatory of the hedonism of Yeats's *Lake Island of Innisfree*.   [3] *Hist. Eccl.* VIII iii.

This is a new fact, only just now beginning to be revealed by such excavations as those at Garranes (Cork) [1] and Ballinderry (West-meath). [2] For in these places there have been found the relics of communities shown to be foreign immigrants by their exotic, rough, domestic pottery;   Roman or Romano-British pottery, in fact. Not the decorative *terra sigillata*, which as a "luxury commodity" might conceivably have entered by way of trade—but of which only a few fragments seem to have actually come to light in Ireland, [3] although in Britain it has been found as far north as the Orkney Islands ; but the commonplace ribbed domestic ware, sherds of which litter every Roman habitation-site wherever the Romans penetrated. This (in accordance with the principle that foreign pottery implies the presence of foreign potters) must have been made either by Roman potters, or by potters of subject communities who had learnt their craft under Roman tutelage—the absence of Roman coins inclines us to the latter alternative.   Associated with this exotic pottery, in these sites, there are other foreign arts, such as the Roman or sub-Roman technique of glass-rod mosaic (*millefiori*) which now appears in Ireland, too suddenly to have been locally developed. [4] An enclosure at Garryduff, Cork, more recently ex-cavated, tells the same tale. [5] Here, along with Roman pottery, was found a springless fibula, of a type unique in Ireland, and a minute figure of a bird, presumably intended to be attached for decoration to a garment.   It is a disc of gold, *repoussé* and ornamented with little strips of beaded gold wire, applied in spirals and other figures, and displays a curious blend of manipulative skill and artistic clumsi-ness.   Its technique carries into the country a reminiscence of the Eastern Mediterranean gold-granulation ornament ; and in its turn gives local birth to a beaded gold wire technique which, years after-wards, attained its highest perfection in the Bettystown ["Tara"] Brooch.   While we expect to find the unwarlike qualities of refugees among peaceful communities of artists, they might have been competent to instil some life into the always more or less abortive, and at the time evaporating La Tène influence in Ireland.   Among such people it would not be surprising to find the seed which, falling into that native soil, ripened in time into the Reerasta Mazer, and the now lost *Gospels of Kildare*.   And again it is in such communities, backward, untaught, unprogressive, rigidly conservative, and with a traditional horror of the tyrannies which had driven them or their fathers from their old homes, and had long exiled them from the progressive Metropolitan centres, that we might expect to find the backward, undeveloped, pre-Patrician Christianity, which out of a

---

[1] S. P. Ó Ríordáin, *Cork* 43 [1938]: 98 ; *Antiquity* 12 [1938]: 34 ; PRIA 47:77.
[2] H. O'N. Hencken, PRIA 47 [1942] : 1.
[3] At Lagore (Meath).   A bare mention in Hencken, *op. cit.* p. 49 : published by Ó Ríordáin, PRIA 51 : 67.
[4] See F. Henry, *Irish Art*, pp. 39 f.   [5] See *Antiquity*, xx [1946] : 122 ff.

misty vagueness is gradually taking shape, and may be confidently expected to crystallize into reality with further exploration of the literary and archæological sources of enlightenment. One thing is already perfectly clear : everything was there " behind the times ". A mysterious Briton, whom our ecclesiastical Latin-writing authorities teach us to call " Pelagius ", and his yet more mysterious Irish (?) coadjutor, whom for the same reason we call " Coelestius ", suddenly appear out of the void and return thereto, after producing an ecclesiastical earthquake—although their orthodoxy might possibly have passed unchallenged a century sooner.[1] The immigrants to whom we are just beginning to become introduced were like to Christians encountered by St. Paul at Ephesus, who had never so much as heard of the Holy Spirit.[2] They had no room in their polity for a bishop ; when Palladius was intruded upon them to be " the first bishop of the Scots (= Irish) believing in Christ ", in the familiar words of Prosper of Aquitaine, they expelled him, apparently with violence ; and the three churches which he is said to have founded disappeared so completely that it is only reasonable to suppose them to have been destroyed immediately.[3] Even later, synod after synod had to be convened, to screw their descendants up to disciplinary standards to which the evolution of contemporary orthodoxy had attained—but that is a story which leads us out of the limits of this book. A yet closer analogy is presented by the preexilic Hebrew colony of refugees established on the Egyptian island of Elephantine, as mirrored in the wonderful series of Aramaic documents which have survived to tell us of them—exhibiting them as being ignorant of many of the most important elements in the legislation attributed in the Pentateuch to Moses, and thus leading us to ask, in surprise, if some at least of these could not have been, in fact, later developments, due to prophetic influence.[4]

---

[1] See the full analysis of the complicated story in Harnack's *History of Dogma* (English translation) vol. v, pp. 168 ff. : see also the article on Pelagianism in the *Encyclopædia Britannica* (11th ed.).   [2] *Acts* 19 : 1-5.

[3] One of these they called, with a touch of malice, *Tech na Románach* " The House of the Romans "—thus expressing their hereditary mistrust of the once persecuting (though even then moribund) Imperialism from which their ancestors had suffered, and of which they doubtless suspected Palladius to be an agent. This is not to be identified with Tigroney (Wicklow) ; see PRIA 46 [1941] : 271. His *Domnach Arda* may be Donard in the same county ; but the old church there to be seen is an altogether later foundation ; a tomb-slab lying within it, popularly supposed to mark the grave of Palladius, is a commonplace Anglo-Norman gravestone, not older than the late twelfth or early thirteenth century. The third church, *Cell Fhine*, is absolutely blotted out, and for us is a mere empty, anchorless name. We may illustrate this conception of the reason for the failure of the mission of Palladius, *mutatis mutandis*, by the tragedy of Bishop Patteson of Melanesia, in our own time. He was murdered on one of the Santa Cruz islands by the natives, mistaking him for a " black-birding " scoundrel who had visited the island shortly before, in the guise of a missionary, and had caused havoc by there plying his nefarious trade.

[4] See A. Cowley, *Aramaic Papyri of the Fifth Century B.C.* : Oxford 1923, *passim*. For an effort to resolve such doubts, see A. Vincent, *La religion des Judéo-Araméens d'Éléphantine*, Paris 1937.

For the rest, these people, squatting within the walls of an old fort or upon an old lake-dwelling, carried on their arts while leading the simple life of fort- or lake-dwellers. Their daily round, as crystallized in their tools and other appliances, was not any less simple—not to say squalid—than that of the local population ; but they produced ornamental pins and other objects, in addition to their Roman pottery, entitling us to picture them as foreign settlers " gone native ". It seems unlikely that these sporadic fragments are relics of organized oversea trade : but the curtain is only just now being lifted, and we may surely hope for more light, later on.

How then, does St. Patrick come into the picture ? We are guided to an answer by the *Apologia* bequeathed to us, which we may accept as trustworthy with an assurance inspired by no other source of information. We must read Muirchu, and even Tírechán, with caution, not because they intentionally deceive, but because all traditions change into strange novelties within a single generation : the Broighter story (*ante*, pp. 239 ff.) illustrates this. True, the *Confessio Patricii*, the document referred to, is itself in places shrouded in obscurity, because of the writer's reticent humility, and of a difficulty in ordering and expressing his thoughts, resulting from his deficient early education. He tells his tale incoherently, jotting isolated episodes as they recur to his memory, and leaving it to his readers to arrange them in logical sequence : though these apparent defects only enhance the pathetic beauty of the tract as a whole. He candidly reveals himself as a once undisciplined youth, knowing nothing of the Lord till his fifteenth year, notwithstanding his descent from two generations of clerical forebears. In that year he was kidnapped by Irish pirates and carried into slavery. We need not repeat the well-worn tale of his adventures, which at last left him at the door of his old home. When he knocked upon it, he believed that his return thither was to be permanent ; but from this illusion he was aroused by a vivid dream, in which one Victoricus came to his bedside, as the " Man of Macedonia " had stood beside the couch of his great prototype, with an imperative summons to return for the help of the land of his servitude. Patrick was always devoutly deferential to dreams, to him, as to many another, Divine Revelations never to be disregarded ; so he arose, and obeyed the call " to the Macedonia by the Western Ocean ", as he would have expressed it himself, if only blundering copyists had permitted him.[1]

Passing over the course of his preparation for the task to which he believed himself to have been summoned, we reach the day when a friend unnamed told him that he was to be advanced to episcopal rank. The way to a consummation of the Divine Purpose seemed to be open. But by mischance, there lay upon his conscience a distressing memory of some boyhood fault— on its nature he is silent, and we cannot choose but respect his reserve— and he then, or had previously, sought relief from this burden from the self-same friend. At whatever conference the subject of Patrick's promotion came up for decision, the friend violated the confidence, revealed the secret, and thus stopped the proceedings. But Patrick was not left comfortless; in the following night he heard the voice of the Almighty, reprobating the friend's treachery, and laying upon him, through no human intermediary, a mandate to carry out the duties to which the previous vision had called him

[1] See JRSAI 62 [1932] : 19. Criticism has not led me to modify the suggestions there put forward ; or to retract to any serious extent the views regarding the Patrician mission expressed in chap. vi of *Ancient Ireland*, to which the reader is referred for further details.

—even as Amos, in one of the most sublime books in the world, tells us how, though no scion of a priestly family, no prophet or prophet's son, he had been taken from his sheepfolds by the Lord Himself, and sent to carry His message to apostate Israel. Thus was Patrick enabled to describe himself, in his *Letter to Coroticus*, as, in the most literal sense of the expression, a bishop appointed of God. In an island outside the jurisdiction of Imperial and Ecclesiastical Rome, it was possible thus to evade ecclesiastical restrictions ; in the special circumstances it was advantageous, if not necessary, to do so. Palladius had addressed himself, in accordance with his commission, to the Christians, and had tried to make them understand that from the point of view of contemporary Church discipline they were in a very irregular position ; and as such a message is always unwelcome, they gave unequivocal expression to their resentment. Patrick was wise enough to leave the Christians alone—he could do so with a clear conscience, as the mandate to deal with them had been withheld—and to bring a message of deliverance to the Pagans, king and commoners alike, weighed down as they were by the druidic tyranny. However, we cannot here attempt to extricate the true history of his labours from the mists in which they have become enfolded. Some homilist told the tale long afterwards, and figuratively expressed the facts by telling his hearers that the druids had come into the country and had spread a darkness over it, which Patrick had dispelled as with the *fiat lux* of a new Creation. It was not the preacher's fault if a childish generation, avid of marvels, took the picturesque figure with a prosaic literalness, and developed the silly story of competitive thaumaturgy with which the extant chronicles mock the saint and the common sense of their readers.

As a consequence there were for a time two Churches in Ireland ; the more or less amorphous group of pre-Palladian communities, referred to as the " Old Churches " in the Tallaght documents : [1] and the Church founded by the " laborious episcopate " of St. Patrick ; a Church naturally subjected to severe criticisms from the Orthodox within the Empire for its irregular inception—criticisms to answer which the *Confessio* was written, as internal evidence shows clearly—but reconciled to Rome in or about A.D. 441, when, as we learn from the " Annals of Ulster ", *probatus est in fide Catholica Patricius episcopus.*

In course of time the Patrician Church gained strength and absorbed the " Old Churches ", so that they dropped out and vanished from sight and memory. But let us hope that more will be found out about them, than the very little that we know as yet. For they were not to be despised. They had come out of the Christianity of, perhaps, a couple of centuries earlier than that in which St. Patrick had been nurtured, and therefore had preserved an earlier phase of religious evolution. For instance, they maintained an almost Puritan rigidity in Sabbath observance, compelling their rivals, for very shame, to follow their example in this matter ; this we learn from the Tallaght documents. The stern tradition of the Jewish Sabbath had still been strong in the persecuted community out of which they had escaped, and they carried it with them to their refuge. And who was Victoricus ? Is it too much to say that he was the real hero of the story of the conversion of Ireland ? He is the only native of the country whom Patrick condescends to mention by name ; a word, even from his phantasm seen in a dream, is enough to recall, for ever, the returned exile from his much longed-for home. He can hardly be dissociated from " Victor ", alleged by later writers to have been Patrick's " guardian angel " ; obviously such a description must have been ultimately derived from Patrick himself.

---

[1] Gwynn and Purton, *op. cit.* pp. 128, 137.

One of the MSS. of the *Annals of Tigernach* tells us that at a certain date " Patrick was loosed from captivity by an angel " and a glossator has added to this the name " Victor ". This, for what it may be worth, is at least a suggestion that Victoricus contrived his escape from the bondage into which the pirates had sold him ; that his was the voice which roused the sleeper with the glad words *Thy ship is ready* ! A resident in or near the place of his servitude, who had befriended the disconsolate and untutored waif, and who erected an edifice of Christian teaching upon whatever neglected and half-forgotten shreds and patches of instruction he had carried away from his Christian home—if Patrick laboured to bring Faith to Ireland, was it because Ireland, in the person of Victoricus, had brought Patrick to a knowledge of the Lord ?

Apart from these as yet shadowy immigrants, Ireland, culturally and politically, was left by Rome to work out her own salvation, and Roman civilization made no direct impression on the country. A provincial king invited Agricola to invade it, in order to further some interests of his own : [1] and Agricola, as Tacitus reveals to us, kept him in a show of friendship for subsequent use. It is possible that he went so far as to send a legion on what proved to be a tentative, abortive expedition ; something of the kind seems necessary to explain a passage of Juvenal. [2] But troubles arose immediately afterwards in Scotland ; and then Agricola was recalled to Rome ; so that this expedition—if it ever took place—passed, leaving no record except, perhaps, a lost coin or two ; and Ireland remained permanently outside the Roman Empire. In 1913, Professor Haverfield published a list of all the recorded discoveries of Roman objects in Ireland. [3] The list contains 25 items, to which three more had been added by the time of our first edition—a coin of Probus, found at Clones, coins of Diocletian and of Maximian at Gort, [4] and a Roman brooch found at Annesborough (Armagh) in a miscellaneous hoard of metal objects, probably destined for the melting-pot. [5] Of these twenty-eight finds, all but three were coins, singly or in hoards. The largest hoard was found at Ballinrees, near Coleraine (Londonderry) which included 1506 Roman silver coins and other relics : [6] next to it is a collection of about 550 coins of Vespasian and the following emperors, found somewhere near the Giants' Causeway. [7] To judge by the dating of the coins, these two large hoards must be approximately contemporary : in both, Sir W. Ridgeway has proposed to see loot captured by Niall of the Nine Hostages (king of Ireland, A.D. 379-405) who, with his followers, carried out piratical raids in Britain (and apparently also in Gaul),

---

[1] C. Tacitus, *De Vita et moribus Agricolæ*, xxiv.

[2] *Sat.* ii 159-60. See R. K. McElderry, " Juvenal in Ireland ? " *Classical Quarterly* 16 : 161.

[3] " Ancient Rome in Ireland ", *English Historical Review* 28 : 1.

[4] JRSAI 56 [1926] : 127.   [5] PRIA 32 [1924] : 171.

[6] See an article by R. MacAdam, *Ulster* I 2 : 182 (copied, but without the plate of illustrations) in *Numismatic Chronicle* 17 : 101. Walters, *Catalogue of Silver Plate in the British Museum*, p. 52.

[7] Haverfield, *op. cit.*, no. 4 and references there.

in one of which the boy Sucat was kidnapped.[1]   A bronze brooch from Loughey (Down) is Roman, but of a different type from the Annesborough specimen ; it was associated with a presumed Roman coin, about 152 coloured glass beads, the bowl of a spoon, and some other less important objects.[2]   An oculist's stamp from near Clonmel completes the record.[3]   A small hoard of ten copper coins (Claudius Gothicus to Constantine II) found at Cuskinny (Cork) should also be mentioned.[4]

The great find of mutilated silver vessels—now marvellously restored and displayed in Edinburgh Museum—made at Traprain Law, about twenty miles west of Edinburgh, in 1914 and subsequent years, is also a memorial of the ravages of bandits, in whose barbarous eyes these beautiful objects were merely so much bullion.[5]   One of these worthies must have come from what is now Co. Limerick, for some of his share of the loot was found recently at Foynes in that county—three fragments of ornamented vessels, and four silver ingots bearing official stamps similar to those from the Ballinrees hoard, although issued by different offices.   I must express my special indebtedness to the authorities of the Dublin National Museum for supplying me with these photographs, with permission to publish them (Plates XI and XII).   [Refer now to Ó Ríordáin's "Roman Material in Ireland", PRIA 51 [1947] : 35, published after this page was set up in type.]

In studying ancient historical records in Ireland or anywhere else, we must keep an eye of criticism—not so much of scepticism, though that also is sometimes necessary—ever fixed upon our sources of information.   Not that they deliberately deceive : but they write under unavoidable limitations of knowledge, circumstances, prepossessions, or temperament.   As when we contemplated flint implements, in beginning our study, so now, as we approach its end, and have the advantage of written documents to guide us, we must still keep ourselves constantly reminded that our evidence is equivocal.   There is a human personality in the background of even the most impersonal document, a man of like passions with ourselves ;   having a human existence, human prejudices, human limitations, and human experiences of anything up to a century in duration, of which we cannot possibly know anything ; but which

---

[1] Sir W. Ridgeway, " Niall of the Nine Hostages ", *Journal of Roman Studies* 14 : 123.
[2] Haverfield, *loc. cit.*, no. 6, and references there ; but correct the reference to the Kilkenny Society's *Journal*, which should read vol. iv (not vol. i), p. 164. Coffey, in describing the Annesborough find, mentions some other brooches in the Petrie collection ; but it is not clear that these are of Irish provenance (PRIA 32 : 174).
[3] Haverfield, *loc. cit.*, no. 17, and references there, to which add Wilde, *Catalogue*, p. 126.   [4] *Cork*, Series II vol. iv, pp. 49 ff.
[5] See A. O. Curle, *The Treasure of Traprain* (Glasgow 1923) for a full account of this hoard.

must have influenced profoundly all the media, whatever their nature, through which our hands and our minds come in contact with his. When an ancient chronicler tells us that " a horrible vision was seen in the sky " we interpret the statement in the light of astronomical or meteorological knowledge which has accrued since his time, and of which he had not the slightest conception.   When an ancient Irish chronicler tells us about the iniquities of a Scandinavian pirate, we must find out how far he was personally affected by them, before we can place full reliance upon his record.   We know from other sources that the Scandinavian sea-farers had been driven from their native homes by a complication of adverse circumstances, and were forced, in desperation, to seek elsewhere—by violence, if necessary— a habitation and a means of livelihood : and we know the gruesome trail of rapine which they left behind them.[1]   But we also know that the reliquary commonly called " The Cross of Cong ", one of the chief jewels in the crown of Ireland, is essentially a Scandinavian work of art, though an inscription tells us that its artist bore an Irish name :   and that it would never have come into existence at all, at least in the form which commands our reverent admiration, if the Scandinavian pirates had not been accompanied or followed by Scandinavian artists, who, like their predecessors from Romanized Europe, re-quickened the again moribund art-traditions of the land to which they came.   Certainly there are two sides to the story of the Scandinavians in Ireland, and we should be faithless to the obligations of scientific truth if we failed to give due importance to them both.

The gradual eclipse of paganism can be traced by comparing the presentations of the *Túatha Dé Danann* in the different mythological strata and cycles of the romantic literature.   These people must have started life as gods, as is indicated by the coincidences of some of their names with the names of deities to whom altars are dedicated in various continental sites : but in Ireland, though the war- and fertility-goddesses (Badb, Mórrígu, and the rest) still retain their divine character in the " Heroic " (the oldest) Cycle, the males of the company have already declined in prestige, and appear rather as spirits or demons.   This character they retain in the later " mythological " cycle, in which they are the primary actors ; though they are gradually being reduced from supernatural to superhuman beings, the process is not yet complete, as it is in the latest or " Finn " cycle.   Here they are merely men, but, even yet, just a little more than men.   In the very late story called *The Battle of Ventry*, which describes an invasion of Ireland, it is tacitly assumed as appropriate that the monsters among the invaders, the Catheads and the Dogheads (which of course means the magicians in their zoomorphic dance-masks) should fight with the Túatha Dé Danann among the defenders.[2]

Some incidents in the process of the Christianization of South Britain and of Gaul may be recalled as presenting analogies which will enable us to form a more reasonable conception of that of

---

[1] " Fleeing before pagans " is one of the permitted deeds on Sunday, according to *Cain Domnaig* (see *Ériu* 2 [1905] : 208).

[2] Ed. Meyer, line 284 : see also the introduction pp. xi-xiv.

Ireland. The well-known story of St. Samson of Dol is highly important ; again, not only for what it does say, but also for what it does not say. Samson, an ecclesiastic of Welsh origin, was appointed to the bishopric of Dol in Normandy about the year 521. When on his way to his new charge he travelled through Cornwall, and passed by a place, denoted in the Latin text of his biographer with the name *Tricurium* (= the modern Trigg). There he heard the sound of men engaged in pagan rites. Making a sign to his followers to stand and keep silence, he dismounted ; and, selecting two of his companions, he walked with them to the source of the sounds, and found ceremonies in progress, in front of what the biographer calls *simulacrum abominabile*—presumably a standing stone, understood to be a fertility-emblem—on the top of a mountain. Samson arrived and denounced this apostasy from the worship of the true God— though some pleaded that it was a mere stage-play with no harm in it (*malum non esse mathematicum eorum partem in ludo seruare*), some were angry, and some mocked : others, however, were more reasonable (*quibus mens erat sanior*). The biographer adds that he himself had visited the mountain, and had fingered the cross which the saint had cut upon the stone.

But what happened next ? The story goes on to tell that even as the saint was preaching, his words were confirmed by a Divine sign : a youth endeavouring to curb his unmanageable horse, was thrown and his neck was broken. Samson promised the weeping bystanders to restore him to life if they would destroy the image ; and the incident closed in accordance with this agreement.[1] This pendant to the story would not command confidence in any case : and the fortunate circumstance that the original biographer had stepped aside to tell us of his own personal knowledge of the monument brands it as a patent interpolation. Evidently Samson left the stone standing ; but before departing he hammered the sign of the cross into it, and went his way satisfied. For he had Christianized the stone : he had driven the demon out of it : henceforth, if any devotion should be paid to it, it would be paid to a Christian monument, and would automatically become a Christian devotion. There are scores of rough standing stones in Ireland bearing crosses cut upon them which beyond question started life as pagan monuments, and were similarly " converted ".[2]

If some unnecessary person should succeed in evading the vigilance of the vergers of a Cathedral so far as to cut his name upon its wall, will it make the slightest difference to the conduct of the daily services ? If an unknown stranger should suddenly interrupt an agricultural fertility-festival—for that must be what was going on ; make an unintelligible disturbance ; and cut an unintelligible mark upon the stone which had been the traditional centre of such rites from the Bronze Age ; is it reasonable to imagine that he will produce any immediate effect upon local cults and customs ? Admittedly the cross remains on the stone, and perhaps in time it will speak its message. Perhaps the impression, which in this particular case the preacher seems to have made on *some* of the participants, was permanent. But the rites will certainly be resumed, and for a time there will

---

[1] *Acta Sanctorum*, July vol. vi, p. 584.
[2] A good example at Tuberbile, Romoan (Antrim), is figured in *Ulster* II 14 [1908] : 156. Another is at Doonfeeny in N. Mayo.

be a period of syncretism, in which Christian Faith will endeavour to run its destined course in a chariot of pagan ritual.[1]

And that such a syncretism actually came into being in Gaul, and that only after a lapse of time did the local Christianity awake to its obvious dangers to Faith and to Morals, is abundantly attested by the decrees of early Church Councils. Such a superficial reconsecration of a stone, of a well, of a grove of trees, is a concession, an acceptance of the line of least resistance; sooner or later it will bring its Nemesis. Ground has been yielded at the outset; that mere fact makes its recovery difficult, if not impossible. Read the convenient summary of these decrees, and of other ecclesiastical fulminations, drawn up for us by Bertrand [2]—decrees against lighting torches and venerating trees, groves, springs, and stones; wearing amulets; consulting enchanters or sorcerers (in cases of illness); deriving omens from sneezes, bird-songs, etc.; noting the day or the age of the moon at which any work happens to begin; abstaining from work on any day but Sunday; invoking Minerva or any other " unlucky being "—and so forth. Century after century, from the year 452 till the year 1697, these and the like ceremonies and practices are denounced by Gaulish councils and by individual ecclesiastics; all of them perfectly familiar in the traditions of folk-religion, and all of them relics of a pre-Christian religious life. For 1200 years it was found impossible to eradicate them : even now, between two and three centuries later still, a modern scholar (P. Sébillot) has been able to publish a bookful of records of them, under the candid and uncompromising title *Le Paganisme Contemporain*.

In Britain, Gildas had no illusions about the "mountains, the hills, the rivers, once pernicious, but now apt for human use, upon which divine honour was aforetime heaped by a blinded people " : and in the beginning of his *Liber Querulus* he speaks of *portenta diabolica*, withering with their distorted faces inside or outside their deserted walls—which seems to imply enclosures, rather than temples, with associated statues, presumably of warped and decaying wood ; and he gives us to understand that these were still to be seen in Britain in his time. Was there anything analogous in Ireland ?

At the outset of such an enquiry we must clear out of the way one group of sculptures which, by myself and others, had been taken for survivals from some non-Christian cult. The grotesque figures in the little Romanesque church upon White Island, Loch Erne, look as non-Christian as they

---

[1] Even in the twelfth century, when the people of Clonfert wished to erect a noble Temple to the honour of " the Lord Mighty in Battle ", ancient traditions were still so strong that they did not deem it inappropriate to adorn its doorway with a pyramid of severed heads, such as used to stand before the entrance to the hall of the earthly warrior chiefs. Similar grim reminiscences are to be seen over arches in the church of Dysert O'Dea, and even Cormac's Chapel at Cashel. On this, see A. Reinach, " Les têtes coupées et les trophées en Gaule " (*Revue celtique* 34 [1913] : 38, 253). See also (and especially) Jullian's *Histoire de la Gaule*, vol. ii, pp. 200 ff.   [2] *La religion des Gaulois*, pp. 400 ff.

well can be : it is not surprising that they had been regarded as opening a window into a pre-existing paganism.   But the brilliant and entirely convincing identification of the figures, due to Rev. D. O'Driscoll, O.M.I.,[1] as symbolical personifications of the Seven Deadly Sins, withdraws them as a whole, and for ever, from the category of pagan survivals.   When the clue is given identification is easy—*lust*, appropriately typified by one of the strange figures commonly (and not inappropriately) denoted by that undignified masterpiece of verbal teratology " sheelanagig " ;   *sloth*, sitting at ease, with idle hands warming in a comfortable muff (incidentally giving us evidence, such as I do not recollect having seen elsewhere, for the use of that article of luxury in the country, at the time) ;   *gluttony* with his dinner-knife and his hand up to his mouth ;   *covetousness*, who has been raiding his neighbour's poultry-yard ;[2] *pride*, head in air, sporting a big brooch and military weapons ;   *anger*, which must have been idealized in a form so horrific that a later generation chipped away the whole surface of the figure's head and body ;   *envy*, admirably expressed by an evil face which looks furtively out of a stone slab as from a window (see Plates XIII, XIV).

Two of these figures were found about the middle of the nineteenth century by a former proprietor of the island, and were inserted into the wall of the church for their preservation.[3]   In 1928 the building, having fallen into a bad condition, was repaired by the Belfast Natural History and Philosophical Society, when the remaining figures were discovered, embedded face inward in the wall, as though the later builders were ashamed (or afraid) of them.[4]   The whole series, including the two previously known, has now been mounted in a row on the inside of the wall facing the visitor as he enters the door.

The seven deadly sins are not infrequently represented in mediæval art ;   they sometimes appear in corbels and other parts of church fabrics in England.   There is a set in a church in Bedfordshire (I have no more specific note of place) among which the representation of *luxuria* was once described to me, in a letter from a friend, as " a startling example of mediæval frankness " :   in another church, again I know not where, the corresponding figure was so very " frank " that, if I have been correctly informed, a scandalized vicar took the law into his own hands and destroyed, or at least bowdlerized it.   While the White Island series is unique, it may have had, at one time, many analogues in carven wood :   indeed, to supply an entire series *in stone* would have been beyond the powers of most of the small churches of the country—which might not all have had at their disposal an artist so skilled as the sculptor of the White Island figures.   This man, notwithstanding the crude simplicity of his technique, was beyond all cavil a real and original genius, who could instil both life and character into his grotesque creations.   There can hardly be any doubt that the " bishop of Killadeas " [5]—in its way a wonderful piece of sculpture—is another of his masterpieces ;   the word is used in all seriousness.[6]

---

[1] See JRSAI 72 [1942] : 116.

[2] True to his character, he holds *four* birds by the neck, two in each hand ; not two only, as a superficial glance might suggest.   This explains why the birds puzzled myself and others by appearing to have four legs apiece.

[3] Sketches were published by Wakeman (JRSAI 15 [1880] : 276 ff.).   There was an earlier publication by Du Noyer (*ibid.* 5 [1861] : 62) of little value.

[4] See Canon McKenna and Lady Dorothy Lowry-Corry, " White Island. Lough Erne ; its ancient church and unique sculptures " (JRSAI 60 [1930] : 23), Small but admirably clear photographs will be found illustrating an account of the repaired church in *Belfast* 1927-8 : 16.   See also *Ancient Ireland*, pp. 194-8.

[5] Figured JRSAI 65 [1935], plate facing p. 26 ; *Ancient Ireland*, Fig. 36.

[6] A carved sandstone head found in the Roman City of Venta Silurum (Cærwent) has a remarkable family resemblance to these figures : see *Archæologia* 58 i [1920] : 150.

The part may often do duty for the whole : one specimen of the ugliness of sin may for homiletic purposes be as good as seven : and it would be only natural that the most individualistic and un-mistakable member of the group should serve as a sort of compendium of the complete series.

Here at last we have a simple and obvious solution of the much-discussed problem presented by the " sheelanagigs ", so often found sculptured on the walls of churches and castles, and in modern times explained by so many weird conjectures. These figures are hideously caricatured females, summarily draped, represented in what is evidently meant to be a squatting position, and by gesture concentrating the spectator's attention upon their sex. The type is not infrequent in England ; in Ireland, except for about a dozen outlying examples, it is confined to the east of the Shannon.[1] Having regard to the general character of these figures, we might feel justified in asserting that the only ecclesiastical structure to which they would be really appropriate was Medmenham Abbey in the eighteenth century : but in fact, they are frequently displayed upon the walls of churches innocent of any such sinister associations.[2] They are also to be found on the walls of mediæval castles, and they apparently survive down at least to the fifteenth century.

We ask, why ? Surely even in the Middle Ages such figures would have seemed offensive ! This question has been answered with what are little more than guesses—that they were luck-bringers, promoters of fertility, averters of the evil eye, and so forth. It has even been suggested that they were intended to *stimulate* the im-pulses to which they give expression ; and truly a homilist, with rudimentary notions of psychology, might possibly display a didactic warning against *luxuria* so realistic that it would have an effect on the weaker members of his flock exactly contrary to that which he intended. Analogous results undoubtedly followed from mediæval

[1] See a distribution map, JRSAI 66 [1936] : 108, accompanying a fully-illus-trated list of Irish specimens (incorporating and superseding all previous lists), classified according to form and situation (*addenda* in the same vol., p. 312). See also H. C. Lawlor, " Grotesque carvings improperly called Sheela na Gigs ," INJ [1927] : 182 (but some of the figures there illustrated,while certainly grotesque, are not strictly speaking of the special type under discussion); M. A. Murray " Female Fertility Figures ", JRAI 64 [1934] : 93 ; also *Man* 31 [1931] No. 4 32 [1932] No. 49.

[2] I know of only one example of this kind of figure among the sculptures on the High Crosses. This is on the stump of a broken cross, to the north of the Cathedral of Clonmacnois. It was first noticed by Mr. J. N. A. Wallace (see JRSAI 69 [1939] : 48) ; often as I had been to the site, I never observed it, so thickly is it covered with lichen. But on my last visit, just as I was passing the monument, a sudden ray of cross-light struck it and revealed the sculpture, with an almost awe-inspiring effect ! The opposite side of the shaft is absolutely smooth, a result of the trimming away of the original surface, as the narrowing of the adjacent marginal lines of the panels on the return surfaces clearly shows. I infer that there had originally been a similar, and even more repulsive, bas-relief upon that surface, and that the local ecclesiastics had ordered its destruction.

attempts at depicting the Devil, in pictorial or dramatic art ; the lines of demarcation between the horrible, the grotesque, and the ludicrous are so indefinite, that these crude ventures had the disastrous consequence of turning the most awful enemy of God and Man into a figure of fun, a stock subject of frivolous jest. And even if the " sheelanagigs " were originally placed, for a didactic purpose of some kind, upon the walls of churches, they might appeal to the rude and unprogressive humour of castle-builders and be transferred to these secular buildings merely because of that appeal.[1]

But such a " didactic " figure is more likely to be an adaptation than an original creation. It must surely count the Epimegalithic Aphrodite in its direct line of ancestry. Mr. Hemp (*loc. cit.*) demurs to this (quoting the corroborative opinion of Professor Baldwin Brown) on account of the absence of any connecting link, in either space or time, between the British and Irish figures and those of the Eastern Mediterranean. Such a link seems, however, actually to be provided by a most remarkable rock-carving at Corbehagh (Clare), here reproduced (Plate XV), after a drawing by Westropp,[2] and placed for comparison side by side with two examples of one of the commonest yields of excavation in Palestine. These are plaques of terra-cotta, bearing crude representations of a Syrian *dea nutrix*. They were formed in wooden moulds, resembling those now used for fashioning ornamental butterpats, and were displayed in the native houses as domestic luck-bringers. The prophet Jeremiah, on two occasions, denounced the action of women of Jerusalem in maintaining or reviving a cult of Anath, the *magna mater* of the Canaanites and pre-prophetic Hebrews (who certainly for the colonists in Elephantine shared on apparently equal terms the honours paid to the supreme God of the Hebrews).[3] This worship involved making " cakes " to portray her (Jer. 7 : 18 ; 44 : 19). The word rendered " cakes " (*kavvānīm*) occurs nowhere else in the Old Testament, and was apparently unknown, or at least untranslatable, to the Septuagint, who contented themselves with transliterating it. Were it not for the fact that the first of these passages describes the cakes as made of *dough*, we might be tempted to suppose that the prophet was actually referring to these terra-cotta figures, which in his time were probably almost universal objects of domestic furniture —I confess that I jumped incautiously to the same conclusion myself when, in conducting an excavation in Palestine, I first came in contact with them. But in any case, the *kavvānīm* must have closely resembled them, and in all probability were fashioned in the same moulds.

[1] Mr. W. J. Hemp, in *Archæologia Cambrensis* 1938 : 137, has made a similar suggestion in reference to the loathsome figure set incongruously amid the glories of the church of Kilpeck (Herefordshire) ; that it is merely a manifestation of mediæval humour.

[2] PRIA 20 [1897] : 546. First published by M. Brogan, *ibid.* 10 [1860] : 440.

[3] See Cowley, *op. cit.* pp. xviii ff.

This custom, even yet, is not forgotten in its homeland. Among the peasants of modern Palestine, one of the incidents of the feast of rejoicing, which concludes the Muslim fasting-month, is the making and eating of cakes of dough stuffed with raisins, modelled in a shape reminiscent of these figures.[1] Robertson Smith refers to this as an Arabian custom also ; and he quotes a remarkable parallel from aboriginal Mexico.[2] I do not subscribe to the axiom that coincidences like this *never* happen fortuitously ; but the essential similarity of these figures is too close to be merely accidental. The identity of a man, or a god, with his name, or with an image depicting him, is familiar to all students of Comparative Religion. To eat these representations of a goddess was tantamount to assimilating the goddess herself within the eater's personality—just as Colum Cille was taught his letters by a teacher who wrote them on a cake and made him eat it.[3] Relics of such beliefs are clearly to be seen in certain aspects of sacrifice among the Semitic peoples, and in the rite of *omophagia*, the eating of the uncooked flesh (of a sacred animal), among the Greeks.[4] In a form so perishable as a cake the rite might travel far beyond its homeland and leave no relics of its passage : and a mere domestic rite of peasant women might spread over almost all Europe, unobserved, or at least unrecorded, by the supercilious literary minority upon whom we have to depend for our knowledge of folk-customs now long forgotten. A cross with the initials IHS has been cut beneath the Corbehagh figure and at least indicates that *some* sort of sanctity was locally attributed to it.[5] Thus, this strange carving reveals the possibility that Anath, whose important place in the pantheon of the Eastern Mediterranean, though long suspected by scholars, was not fully realized till the papyri of Elephantine and the tablets of Ras esh-Shamra threw a fierce and revealing light upon it—explaining why the semi-heathen Israelite women called her *M'lekheth hash-shāmayim*, which means " queen of the heavens "—that she, in the thin disguise of the *Mór-rígu*, " the great queen ", otherwise suggestively named *Ana*, and termed, by the Glossator Cormac mac Cuileannáin, *mater deorum Hibernensium*, entered Ireland in the train of the Beaker people, as one of the triplicity of war-goddesses who came in the same company.

Possibly she has left some faint footprints in her passage. There was a mysterious goddess named *Anna Perenna*, celebrated, especially by the lower ranks of society, at Rome, on the Ides of March, with

[1] See the *Quarterly Statement* of the Palestine Exploration Fund, 1908, p. 75, where a specimen of these cakes, presented to myself on one of the feast-days, is illustrated. It is an especially impressive survival, in view of the rigid tabu of orthodox Islam against representations of the human figure.
[2] *Religion of the Semites*, 2nd edn., p. 225.
[3] " Lives of Saints " from the *Book of Lismore*, line 812 ff.
[4] See Robertson Smith *op. cit.*, especially lectures VIII, IX ; H. J. Rose, *Primitive Culture in Greece*, pp. 34, 81.
[5] This modern addition is shown in a sketch in *Folklore* 33 [1911] : 52.

drunkenness and wanton rites. Ovid evidently did not know what to make of her, when he was writing his poetical Calendar of Festivals ; and everyone else who has dealt with her has been equally bewildered. There are traditions associating her with Anna, the sister of Dido of Carthage—which would give her a Semitic connexion ; others make her no less a personage than the nurse of Jupiter, which at least hints at a *dea nutrix* or *mater deorum* side to her nature. Others identify her with an old woman of the town of Bovillae in Latium, who sustained the plebs when they ensconced themselves on the Mons Sacer, after their secession from Rome in 494 B.C., with *cakes;* and in connexion with this, Warde Fowler quotes from Plutarch a reference to an Egyptian Anna, who invented moulds for bread-making. Europeans would almost inevitably lose the final spirant of the goddess's name. We may recall the Athenian feast called *Galexia* also in honour of the mother of the gods, where a mixture of spelt and honey was consumed, as well as cakes cast in moulds of specific shapes.[1]

We have nothing like the whole material before us on which to base a final decision. Behind the few stone figures which we possess there were surely wooden figures, now crumbled to dust, with all the stern truths that they could have taught us. And there are other figures, both in stone and in wood, not unlike those of White Island, and even less easy to interpret on any Christian basis. Chief among these is one, if anything yet more hideous, now in the City Museum, Belfast. It had previously been in the possession of a rector of Tanderagee (Antrim) : its history before it fell into his hands is doubtfully recorded. A statement by Professor Kingsley Porter (who first published it) [2] that it was found in a bog near Newry, is contradicted by Messrs. Paterson and Davies in a paper on " The Churches of Armagh,"[3] who tell us that it comes from Armagh Cathedral. It shows us only the upper half of the being whom it portrays. The lips are very thick, and the mouth is partly open in a sort of mirthless grin ; there is no suggestion of teeth ; [4] above the mouth, on each side of the tip of the nose, is what looks like a pair of upturned moustaches ; the nose is a straight bar, with an indication of nostrils at the lower end ; the eyes are bulbous projections, set very close to its sides ; above the eyes and the root of the nose are what at first sight appear to be eyebrows of the T-shape familiar in neolithic and bronze-age Continental art, but they form a roll worked into a corded rope-moulding, interrupted at the nose, but carried round to the back of the head, so that we are more probably to think of the furred edge of a close-fitting but peaked cap, covering the forehead and scalp ; on the temples are two knobs, which must be adornments of this cap, not stumps of horns rising from the figure's head ; a cape hangs down from the shoulders, but is disarranged by the action of the arms, which are bare ; the right hand

---

[1] See Roscher, *Ausführliches Lexikon der griechischen und römischen Mythologie*, s.v. *Anna Perenna;* Ovid, *Fasti* III 523 ff., with Frazer's notes and references ; W. Warde Fowler, *The Roman Festivals of the Period of the Republic*, pp. 50 ff. ; Lobeck, *Aglaophamus*, vol. ii, pp. 1050 ff.

[2] *Burlington Magazine* 63 [1934] : 227.   [3] *Ulster* III 3 [1940] : 82.

[4] In a note which (at the request of the R.S.A.I.) I contributed to their Journal (65 [1935] : 156) I made a statement to the contrary. At the time I had not seen the figure itself, and I was misled by some shadow effects in the photographs which had been put into my hands.

is raised to grasp the left shoulder, thus crumpling up the garment. I am indebted to Mr. Arthur Deane, till recently curator of the Museum, for the information given me in answer to an enquiry, that the figure is 2 feet 0½ inches in height, and 1 foot 2½ inches in breadth at the base.

There is another Armagh figure, which also was first published by Professor Kingsley Porter.[1] It represents an obese personage, undraped except for a pleated loin-cloth, standing in full face and pulling out horizontally what appear to be cat-like ears attached to its head. Professor Porter wished to identify this figure with Labraid Loingsech, an Irish monarch, who, we are told, was afflicted with ass-ears. But this story does not appear to be anything more than an artificial adaptation of the classical tale of Midas and his barber, and it follows an identical course ;[2] so that it cannot safely be called in evidence for any local folklore. With equal reason we might see a connexion of some sort—of *what* sort, I do not venture so much as to guess—between this figure and the statement that Cairbre Cat-head, leader of the " revolt of serfs " early in the first century A.D., was so called " because his god had the shape of a cat ". The prominent breasts, and the hairless face, suggest, however, that the Armagh figure represents a female, conceivably the local goddess Macha ; though, here again, I know nothing recorded of her that could account for the peculiar attitude and equipment. All such guesses are mere futile cloaks for ignorance ; but it is suggestive that there is another piece of sculpture, now built into the wall of a house in Armagh, likewise representing a head with cat-like ears.

These are not the only enigmatical sculptures from Armagh. Others will be found illustrated in the paper by Paterson and Davies already quoted.[3] Collectively, they engender a suspicion that the primacy of Armagh, " the Height of [the goddess] Macha ", is not merely a matter of a Christian yesterday !

After this digression to Armagh, let us return to Loch Erne for a few minutes, to visit two other of its islands, Boa Island and Lustymore (Plate XVI). On each of them we shall find a figure cut out of a slab of stone. Each of these represents a head attached to a torso, on the surface of which arms are indicated in front of the breast : there is a face on one side of the Lustymore figure, and two faces, Janus-wise, one on each side of the Boa Island figure.[4] Here again there is nothing that can by any stretch of imagination be called Christian : nor can we suppose them to be merely meaningless decorations. There can hardly be any doubt that these figures, at least, are pagan idols.

But they are something more than that : they are idols of a specific form. One hardly dares to point out what that form is ; and yet we must do so, and boldly face the overwhelming chronological and other difficulties which arise immediately. These figures,

---

[1] JRSAI 61 [1931] : pp. 89, 142.

[2] See for an opposing view the discussion of the legend in *Folklore* 22 [1911] : 183.

[3] Similar grotesque heads at Castlecaulfield, Tyrone, published *Ulster* III 1 [1928] : 96, as well as another in Armagh (*Ulster* III 3 : 68), amazingly called " The Head of St. Patrick " (though in truth it is not much worse than the modern statue of the Saint on Tara Hill) call for passing notice. Even if these and similar carvings represent Christian emblems or personages, and were produced under Christian auspices, they seem to carry on a much earlier iconographic tradition, letting us hear vague murmurs of pagan worship and ritual behind the scenes.

[4] Described by Lady Dorothy Lowry-Corry in PRIA 41 [1933] : 200.

with their pointed Iberian chins, carry down in Ireland to the seventh or eighth Christian century A.D., to which they belong, a clear tradition of the Iberian bronze-age fiddle-shaped torso idols, which are found around the Mediterranean Sea from Spain in the west, to Crete and Anatolia, in the east. The coincidence is extra-ordinary—once more, too extraordinary to be a mere coincidence. Iberian fetish-figures of the second millennium B.C. seem to have been potent in the Ireland of the first millennium A.D. !

A stone head from Corleck (Cavan) also calls for notice here. It is shaped like an Egyptian alabaster mace-head, though of the full size of a human head. It has three faces cut upon it (the figure to which it presumably belonged should not be called three-*headed*) with straight features and thin lips, of a strangely refined nature as compared with the other figures which we have had before us.[1] A head with a very similar profile is reported from Ballykerwick (Cork) ;[2] but we must know more about it before we can call upon it for evidence.

Probably many stone idol figures perished, as intolerance of pagan idol-worship gradually advanced in intensity ; but it is equally probable that such stone figures were exceptional, the normal idol figures being in wood. Only by exception could wooden figures be preserved : a few bog-finds have shown us something of what they might have been like. One such was found in the crannog of Lagore. Another from Shercock (Cavan) is in the National Museum.[3] We must bitterly regret the loss of a third, found in a bog at Aghadoey (Londonderry), which, according to an account written in 1835, some forty years after the discovery, was so hideous that a boy working with the peat-cutting labourer who uncovered it fainted in horror. It had four heads, with faces " looking opposite ways ",[4] set upon a cylindrical body : and was over all about 6 feet in length. The labourer was less sensitive than his helper : he set it up upon his garden wall, where it quickly rotted to pieces.[5]

Thus, even if we cut out the White Island figures, there remains a number of strange carvings which, though not of excessive antiquity, seem to be embodiments of primitive traditions, and even to introduce us to gods ; but to what gods ? Certainly there is nothing among them comparable with the god-figures which we see portrayed on Celtic altars from Gaul. There is only an accidental analogy between the cross-legged Cernunnos and the cross-legged sheelanagigs : none of the other well-marked character-istics of Cernunnos are reproduced in the sheelanagigs. In short, the figures introduce us to a theology, or rather a demonology, of which absolutely

[1] Illustrated PPS 3 plate xxvi. Three-faced stone figures have been found at Rheims and elsewhere in France (see Courcelle-Seneuil, *Les dieux Gaulois*, pp. 50 ff.), but not otherwise resembling this head.

[2] Illustrated *Cork* 15 [1909] : 53, with a very unsatisfying description.

[3] Illustrated *Antiquity* 4 [1930] : 487 ; *Ancient Ireland*, p. 114.

[4] This shows that the suggestion made above as to the destruction of the figure of *Iracundia* on White Island having been prompted by its gorgonian ugliness is not unreasonable. Further light on this fruitful subject may be obtained from Lebor Gabála (I.T.S. edition) part 2, pp. 257 ff.

[5] *Ulster* III 3 [1940] : 16, citing from the Ordnance Survey Letters for London-derry. Was this an effigy of " Cimme the Four-headed ", the alleged eponymus of Loch Cimme (Loch Hacket, Galway) ?

nothing is known, on which no ancient literature, Celtic or other, throws the smallest spark of light. Though comparatively late, they speak to us of a pre-druidic past—in a language which we cannot understand. Perhaps the Roman poet Lucan might have had an inkling of it, as he wrote of the sacred grove of Massilia with its " rumbling caverns ", its springs of mysterious waters, and its tree-trunks carved into grotesque images.

Let us again embark, this time on the North Sligo coast, and row across to the island called Inismurray in Sligo Bay. There we shall find a queer conglomeration of relics where, once more, Christianity and Paganism elbow, each the other, incongruously.

The island bears the name of an unidentified *Muiredach*,[1] and the traditions of an ecclesiastic named *Laisrén*, more commonly known by the hypocoristic variant " Molaise "—not the better-known Molaise of Devenish, who is said to have inspired the mission of Colum Cille, but another, who is little more to us than a name. If we land upon the island [2] the most considerable structure that we shall see is an irregular oval stone enclosure, the internal dimensions of which are given by Wakeman as 175 by 135 feet. This had already been much altered by injudicious restoration when Wakeman wrote, and its original character was thereby obscured : but there seems to be no reason to doubt that the primary purpose of the enclosure was military, and that its adaptation as a fence for a Christian *laura* was secondary. A church and a small oratory within the enclosure bear the name of Molaise ; the latter still retains its corbelled stone roof intact. Another church within the enclosure, the " House " or " Church of the Fire " (*Teach* or *Teampull na Teineadh*), though actually a later building than either of these, is involved with traditions which convey very emphatic Pagan suggestions—traditions of a supernatural fire which burned, and supplied the fire for all the hearths on the island, until it was profaned by a Scottish visitor in a way about which Wakeman preserves a delicate reticence. The fire, before departing for ever, blazed up and consumed the culprit, whose charred bones, as he (Wakeman) tells us, deposited in a niche in the gable wall of the church, were pointed out—thus branding the whole story as an ætiological myth. The hearth-stone on which the fire used to burn was afterwards, it is alleged, broken up to provide building material for the " restoration " of the enclosure already referred to. Such traditions of a perpetual fire are found elsewhere in connexion with monastic establishments of extremely early date, and add probability to Bertrand's contention that such foundations were conversions of pre-Christian establishments of some kind.[3] We find it in the Saighir of the elder Ciarán, in whose *life* we read that the sacred fire in the monastery at that place, having been wantonly extinguished by a mischievous boy, was miraculously rekindled : we find it, as everyone knows, in Kildare, under the auspices of St. Brigid, who must surely have in some way absorbed the personality of the fire-goddess, or group of goddesses, of the same name.[4] Possibly

---

[1] There is an ancient tombstone on the island bearing a macaronic inscription *or*[*oit*] *do Muredach hu Chomocain, hic dormit* (" A prayer for Muiredach grandson of Comocan, here he sleeps "). It is not likely that this is old enough to commemorate the *eponymus* of the island ; the name was fairly common and we cannot unduly stress the coincidence.

[2] Our chief source of information on the island and its remains is a monograph by Wakeman, published by the R.S.A.I. in 1893.

[3] *La religion des Gaulois*, p. 417.

[4] A legend, which has filtered into the Christian traditions of Kildare out of the memories of whatever pre-Christian establishment preceded it, and is found

the strange name popularly given to one of the Glendaloch churches, St. Kevin's *Kitchen*, may contain a vague recollection of another case of the same kind.

Passing over two beehive huts, which may be merely monastic cells and nothing else ; several memorial slabs with Christian crosses or Christian inscriptions, which do not fall within the scope of this book ; pausing for a moment to note the careful segregation of the sexes after death in two cemeteries, one for men and the other for women ; pausing for another moment at the holed-stone in the men's cemetery, which attracts the devotions of prospective mothers ; [1] bestowing a casual glance upon the Holy Wells, which doubtless are a heritage from prehistoric times ; we leave the enclosure to contemplate the " sweat-house ".

This is a structure built after the manner of a beehive cell. The building is a rudimentary " Turkish bath " : by kindling a great fire of peat or of brushwood within it the interior was superheated, and a rheumatic patient, wrapped in blankets, was introduced into the chamber and there closed up, in the expectation that the rheumatic poison would be purged out of him by the consequent excessive perspiration.

Scattered through various parts of the country, especially in the northern counties, a considerable number of such structures have been recorded. But how did the patients " get on to " this device in the first instance ? Let the following extract suggest the answer.

"The ' sweat-bath ' in use through all America, North and South, is sometimes a remedial device, sometimes a religious rite, often both at once. In the half-civilized tropical regions there are large stoves specially made for the purpose ; but among the nomadic tribes the following process is adopted. A small and very low hut is constructed, with a hollow dug in the middle. This is filled with red-hot stones upon which water is cast ; the narrow room is immediately filled with steam, so that it is almost impossible to breathe. Then one or more men creep in under the hut, and stay as long as they can in the burning, stifling atmosphere : they very soon perspire to excess, and when they come out, or rather when they are drawn out, they are almost exhausted. The sweat-bath is often an efficient remedy against certain maladies, including those which are especially baneful to a community of hunters, whose limbs must be kept supple and elastic : but the Redskin, in his ignorance of the true cause of such effects, attributes supernatural

---

in Ultan's *Vita Brigidæ* (printed in Colgan's *Trias Thaumaturga*), seems to suggest a reminiscence of the practice of the " fire-walk " at this ancient shrine of the fire-goddess. Dar-Lugdach, a pupil of St. Brigid, was seized with a great perturbation of unlawful emotions, and as an answer to prayer was directed by an angel to fill two shoes with hot coals and walk shod therewith. So the fire extinguished the fire of her ardour, and the pain conquered her pain. On the morrow Brigid commended her, promised her exemption from the fire of desire in this world and the fire of hell in the next, and blessed her feet so that the burns were healed, leaving no trace. Starting from a fragmentary recollection of a woman who walked on fire with unburnt feet, the legend would naturally take the form presented to us. If she walked on fire, it must have been for self-discipline : if her feet were unhurt, her wonder-working abbess must have healed them.

[1] Wakeman, *op. cit.* pp. 74 ff.

virtues to the sweat-bath. The cerebral congestion which it sets up in-
duces conditions of delirium and hallucinations, and to these he attributes
a religious significance, sufficient for him to see in it a religious act, well-
pleasing to the supernatural Powers ; and in the abundant perspiration,
an object of sacrifice. It represents an act of self-immolation, like the
various ceremonial mutilations inflicted on the human body. This explains
the religious efficacy of the sweat-bath, the frequency and the nature of
which have so greatly surprised travellers in both Americas : and its in-
clusion among the rites imposed upon neophytes entering one of the religious
secret societies, which are active in the New World as well as in Africa." [1]

Finally, before we leave the island, let us pause at the famous
cursing altar covered with rounded stones—some of them signed with
a cross, and thus " transitional " in spirit if not in date. Let a man
take one of these stones in his hands and walk round the altar
" widdershins ", pronouncing a curse on his enemy ; if the curse
be justified in the eye of whatever Power presides over such ungodly
ceremonies, it will strike home, if not—it will return to roost.

Imperfect and fragmentary though our material be, the list of
such survivals might be prolonged almost indefinitely ; and here,
once more, I have a vision of the last, and in many respects the
greatest of our national monographs. Let one final example serve
as a type of countless others : even though it is obviously apocryphal,
it illustrates the strange moral confusion, which it would be simple
dishonesty to gloss over, of the time of the Transition. It occurs in
one of the numerous hagiographical homilies which, as Plummer has
shown, [2] are permeated through and through with relics of the ancient
faiths. This particular document celebrates a Westmeath ecclesiastic
named Colmán mac Luacháin, [3] and it is a typical example of its
kind. Here is the story :—

" Cinaed, son of Oengus, King of Ui Failghi (' Offaly ' : the king apparently
is unrecorded in the Annals), fell in love with the wife of the King of Tara
(aliter Teltown) and came to meet her. No one but his jester was with him :
she was accompanied only by her handmaid. Then the man coupled the
two horses : Cinaed put his horse under the protection of Colmán mac
Luacháin, while the jester put his under the protection of Oengus mac in
Óc. [An interpolated " poem " describes the proceedings of Cinaed and
the woman, which are not edifying.] Then came thieves and took the horse
of the jester, while Cinaed's horse seemed to them the trunk of an alder.
The names of God and of Colmán were magnified by that miracle."

Altogether a painful story : but it is there, and we must acknowledge its existence quite as frankly as the noblest tales of devotion and

---

[1] Translated from A. Reville, Les religions des peuples non-civilisés, Paris
1883 i, p. 265. There is a considerable literature on such structures in Ireland.
See Ulster III 1 [1938] : 44 (W. McL. May, on Sweathouses in Londonderry) ;
idem 2 [1939] : 32 (P. Richardson, on similar structures in Co. Cavan), JRSAI
21 [1891] : 165, 589 ; 24 [1894] : 180. See also R. H. Lowie, Primitive Religion,
p. 23.
[2] In the introduction to his Vitæ Sanctorum Hiberniæ (Oxford 1910).
[3] The text was edited by Kuno Meyer in the Todd Lecture Series of the R.I.A.
in 1911.

unselfishness which are deservedly repeated so often that we know them off by heart. We note in it (1) the threadbare trick—frequent in this war of creeds—of writing *druth*, "jester", for *drui*, "druid" : (2) the survival of the cult of "Oengus mac in Óc" (once more, the ubiquitous personage to whom we paid homage at Dowth) down to the seventh or eighth century, the approximate though not quite certain date of the saint in question : (3) the polemic against that cult, which turns a deaf ear to the mugient fact that the alleged Christian was engaged on what by the most rudimentary standards of Christian ethic was a grossly immoral enterprise. It would be an impertinence to underline the childish silliness of the device by which the horse under Christian protection was saved from the thieves, who seized the horse under pagan protection : or what, in the circumstances alleged, is the rank blasphemy of the final comment.

In time Ireland won her way through the time of transition, so far as any country in this imperfect world can be said to have done so, even yet. For this she has to thank the fiery trial of persecution which she endured at the hands of the pagan Norsemen.

It is conventional to call Ireland " a land of saints and scholars ". So it ever was, and still is : I have enjoyed the privilege of personal friendship with many Irish saints and scholars. In fact, I have been more fortunate than the original author of the cliché seems to have been, for I have known not a few scholar-saints, who combined both functions in one personality. But some of his scholar-friends should have taught him not to commit the logical solecism of arguing from the particular to the general. If Ireland be a land of saints and scholars, so is every other country in the world, not excepting the Germany of a phase now, we hope, receding into the past ; and if we follow a similar fallacious reasoning, and choose other particular cases from which to generalize, we can maintain, with equal truth and justice, that every country in the world (Ireland included) is a land of sinners and simpletons.

Such parrot-phrases are doubly hurtful ; they induce either a mental torpor, which rests content amid dreams of an imaginary past ; or else a futile waste of energy, seeking to materialize that dreamland past amid the incongruous realities of the present—thus setting at defiance the law of Evolution, which is the Law of God, whereby the Omnipotent Creator has chosen to continue His age-long work to its final consummation. It is a truth, bitter perhaps, but inexorable, that labouring to preserve, or to restore, anything, however beautiful or pleasing—an animal or plant species, a custom, a language, or whatever it may be—doomed by that Law to pass and to yield its place to some other, can do no more than prolong its death-agony, to no ultimate profit. I learned this by hard experience. I, too, was once an enthusiast for the restoration of the Irish language. But my ardour cooled as I saw how many ridiculous situations the effort was establishing, all derogatory to the dignity of the country : when I noticed in a crowded city street an inscription over the door of a business firm of umblemished probity, libellously traducing that probity, because the company was too much engrossed in its immediate business—and who can blame it ?—to have time to spare for an irrelevant trifle of syntax : when I received an official document with certain Irish words upon it, which did *not* say " issued according to the regulations ", but which could be coaxed into meaning " for her sharp outward according to the hanging of ducks " ; when I attended a meeting convened in the interests of the Irish lan- guage, and heard from a distinguished foreign scholar an impassioned address, which rings in my ears even yet, after more than a quarter of a century ; but which was spoiled for me when the chairman—a veteran, who had won far more than a merely local reputation in science and literature—rose and called upon the assembly to give the guest " such a reception as the Túatha Dé Danann would have given him ! " This was picturesque, but injudicious ; all that we know about the reactions of the Túatha Dé Danann to such a stimulus is derived from the sad story of Ith, a chieftain from Spain, who visited Ireland in their time ; told in the *Book of Leinster*, one of the best known of the Irish manuscripts. He pronounced just such an impassioned eulogy on the country as we had been hearing ; whereupon the Túatha Dé Danann promptly slew him, lest he should incite some conqueror to come and take their land from them. Can I be censured if I saw in these—and many similar—experiences, evidences of the inhibiting work of some higher Power ?

Experience has taught me also to expect a double charge of voicing a " bias " by means of " sneers ". The first leaves me quite unmoved ; it means no more than that the critic is unable to answer my arguments, and adopts this cheapest and easiest way of evading the obligation of acknowledging his incompetence. For the second, I can but pity the simplicity which exposes so unashamedly an ignor- ance of the science of Semasiology. A " sneer " is usually a false- hood, cloaked in cynical humour. Far be it from me to treat with either cynicism or humour aspirations which lie close to the hearts of some of my dearest friends—which lay close to my own, until I realized the hopelessness of fighting against the law of Evolution ; and the observations thus foolishly characterized are not falsehoods, but facts, stern hard brutal facts, patent to all, and setting a seal on the central theme of this book—that Science, to which falsehood is abhorrent, not Sentiment, must be our sole guide in the study of Archæology, in Ireland as everywhere else.

Scholarship—I say nothing of sainthood—was far easier of at- tainment in the simple geocentric universe of twelve hundred years ago, than it is now, when the Universe is not even heliocentric, and when the aspirant must traverse a wilderness of Philosophies, then not so much as dreamed of. The Future holds no promise of a blissful *Tír na n-Óg* ; but a weary path which

> . . . winds upward all the way,
> Right to the very end . . .

leading on to the still elusive goal of a Universal Brotherhood, in which shall be absorbed and neutralized all selfish and self-centred individualisms, parochialisms, tribalisms, nationalisms, such as have been spawning war and its horrors ever since the primæval *Pithec-anthropos* and his progeny began to hinder their Creator in His divine, and as yet unfinished, task of ridding their name of its first two syllables.

INDEX OF IRISH TOPOGRAPHY

INDEX OF AUTHORITIES CITED